From the Journals of

M.F.K. FISHER

Also by M.F.K. FISHER

Among Friends

An Alphabet for Gourmets

The Art of Eating

As They Were

The Boss Dog

Consider the Oyster

A Considerable Town

A Cordiall Water

Dubious Honors

The Gastronomical Me

Here Let Us Feast

How to Cook a Wolf

Last House

Long Ago in France

Map of Another Town

Not Now But Now

The Physiology of Taste

Serve It Forth

Sister Age

Stay Me, Oh Comfort Me

To Begin Again

Two Towns in Provence

With Bold Knife and Fork

From the Journals of

M.F.K.
FISHER

Pantheon Books   New York

Contents

To Begin Again: Stories and Memoirs, 1908–1929   1

To Begin   3

1. Native Truths (1908–1952)   7

2. On Coveting (1912)   15

3. Tree Change (1912–1929)   19

4. A Few Notes About Aunt Gwen (1912–1927)   24

5. The First Kitchen (1912–1920)   31

6. An Innocence of Semantics (1912–1915)   41

7. Grandmother's Nervous Stomach (1913–1920)   50

8. I Chose Chicken à la King (1914–1920)   60

9. Mother and "Miss E." (1914–1945)   67

10. A Sweet and Timeless Shudder (1915–1953)   73

11. The Old Woman (1915–1916)   77

12. Gracie (1915–1921)   81

13. My Family's Escape Hatch: A Reminiscence
    (1915–1926)   108

14. The Broken Chain (1920)   114

15. Consider the End (1920)   120

16. Hellfire and All That (1922)   124

17. The Jackstraws (1922)   133

18. Tally (1923, 1928–1953)   138

19. Ridicklus (1924)   144

20. Mirrors and Salamanders (1927)   147

21. Figures in a Private Landscape   149

    I. Laguna, 1927: Journal   149

    II. Uncle Evans (1927)   166

    III. Examination Books: Biology 9 (1927–1928)   169

    IV. Oxy (1928–1934)   173

Stay Me, Oh Comfort Me: Journals and Stories,

    1933–1941   181

Introduction by Norah Kennedy Barr   183

1. Laguna Journal, 1933–1936   189

2. Sodom and the Potato Box   256

3. Vevey Journal, 1936–1937   262

4. Stay Me, Oh Comfort Me   291

5. Vevey Journal, 1938   321

6. Bern Journal, 1938   324

7. Two Letters to Lawrence Powell   350

8. I Don't Like This   360

9. Bareacres Journal, 1940–1941   363

10. War Story   514

11. Conclusion: Lecture to a Viewer   521

12. Epilogue: Spirits of the Valley   524

Last House: Reflections, Dreams, and Observations,

  1943–1991   537

Introduction by Norah Barr, Marsha Moran,

  Patrick Moran   539

Why Again (1965)   545

1. War (1943)   547

2. Rex—I (1950)   552

3. Rex—II (1951)   555

4. Tea with Agamemnon (1951)   560

5. Eaters (1959)   566

6. Death of a Mouse (1965)   569

7. A Few of the Men (1965)   575

8. The Blue Gun (1966)   590

9. Paris (1969)   593

10. The Green Talk (1971)   596

11. Strip Search (1972)   600

12. M. F. K. F. (1975)   606

13. Stealing (1976)   609

14. Fossils (1976)   614

15. Empty Cupboards (1977)   617

16. Thimble (1978)   620

17. Not Enough (1978)   624

18. Then (1978)   628

19. Interviews—I (1979)   629

20. Poor Food (1979)   636

21. Noëls Provençaux (1979)   639

22. One Verse of a Song (1980)   645

23. Bugs (1980)   651

24. Light Sleeper (1980)   655

25. The Hot Look of July (1980)   657

26. Interviews—II (1980)   660

27. Unsuspected (1981)   666

28. Visitation (1981)   668

29. Recovery (1981)   672

30. Rewriting (1982)   676

31. Gobbling (1983)   679

32. Kicking Old Habits (1983)   683

33. Night Thoughts (1983)   686

34. Syndrome (1983)   692

35. Les Vendangeuses (1983)   697

36. Reasons Behind the Reasons (1983)   700

37. New Year's Day (1984)   703

38. Alarm Clock (1984)   710

39. Beware (1984)   713

40. Winding Down (1984)   717

41. Journeys (1984)   719

42. Being Kind to Oneself (1984)   726

43. Games (1985) — 729

44. The Difference Between Dawdling and
Waiting (1985) — 733

45. Leftovers (1985) — 735

46. Furniture (1985) — 736

47. Jumping from Bridges (1986) — 738

48. Prisms (1986) — 743

49. White Wine Trips (1986) — 745

50. Sleep (1986) — 749

51. Vomiting (1987) — 758

52. Glory Hole (1988) — 765

53. Potato Chips (1988) — 767

54. Quotations (1988) — 769

55. Frustration—I (1988) — 771

56. Travel (1988) — 776

57. Volkening (1988) — 779

58. Ho-Hum Stuff (1988) — 784

59. Anon. (1989) — 789

60. My Grown-Up Ears (1989) — 790

61. The Best Meal I Ever Ate (1989) — 796

62. Reading Aloud (1989) — 799

63. Frustration—II (Final Scream) (1989) — 804

64. Style (1989) — 811

65. Zapping (1989) — 814

66. Query (mid-1980s)   821

67. Meditation (1991)   823

68. Notes on the Craft, Skill, Science, or Art of

    Missing (mid-1980s)   825

To Begin Again

Stories and Memoirs
1908–1929

EDITOR'S NOTE

The timespan covered by each essay is indicated by the date(s) following its title. Dates at the end of essays indicate when they were written.

To Begin

I find increasingly as I grow older that I do not consider myself a writer. A writer to me is someone who spends much of his adult life developing a certain way of using a language, and this becomes his *style*. Usually, if he is any good at it, other people will admire and imitate it.

I have not done this, even unconsciously. But by now people sometimes refer to me as a stylist, or they talk about my style, and I think this is because of my habit of putting words onto paper as much as possible as I say them in talking or telling. I have always tried to speak clearly—that is, to make what I am saying clear and logical to the listener or reader . . . and, of course, to make it interesting if the story itself is interesting. But I do not try to tell it in *my* way.

Unfortunately or not, my way, since I was aware at all of trying to catch whatever attention possible, has been both direct and as dramatic as I could make it. Since the beginning of my talking years, my family has teasingly warned me and other gullible listeners that I never spoil a story by sticking to the truth. This is a plain lie, because I do not lie. But I have never seen any reason to be dull, and since I was less than four I have enjoyed entertaining and occasionally startling anyone who may be listening.

The first time I was aware of the heady powers of creating and then holding an audience was when I was a little past three. We were staying in a rented "bungalow" on the palisades in Santa Monica, California. Father was scouting for a small newspaper to buy, since my parents had decided that they could no longer drift on the money from the sale of half of the *Albion* (Michigan) *Recorder* to his brother Walter, and I was taking my morning stroll with a maid or somebody while Mother stayed home with my baby sister Anne.

The palisades then held a long single stretch of posh winter houses for rather affluent midwesterners, so we were doubtless visiting some of Mother's relatives. Across the street from the houses and along the top of the high cliffs was a kind of park, planted with exotic palms and cactuses and generously supplied with benches for its elderly late-Victorian clientele. Sturdy fences of driftwood protected us landward from the rare carriages and even rarer automobiles on the wide street, and seaward they kept us from toppling down several hundred feet onto the rocky Pacific shoreline. This oddly dusty parkway may still be there, but more likely it is covered by high-rise condominiums for the very affluent descendants of those well-to-do midwesterners.

On this particular day in about 1911, when I was brought back from my morning stroll, I told my mother—along with other reports on things like hurting my finger on a cactus needle and falling down twice—that I had seen a man fall out of a brown box up in the sky and turn over and over, until there was the ocean.

Mother scolded me crossly, as I am sure I remember, about

making up silly stories. At lunch, though, she thought it amusing enough to repeat to my father, perhaps as proof that I was learning to speak almost too well. And he looked oddly at her and at me and then said, "She may make a good reporter. Eyewitness story." Mother looked very sad, and said, "Oh, dear! Oh, mercy," and he told her that a crazy daredevil had taken his flying machine up over the bay and suddenly jumped out, with no parachute, no nothing. The plane had gone further out to sea and then dived. "Oh, dear," Mother said, and then said something very brisk and meaningful to Father about forgetting all about it because there was no use letting little girls imagine things, was there?

And from then on, in a tacit family plot, everything that I said was taken with a grain or two of salt. If I came home from school and announced after lunch (for from the beginning we never mentioned politics, money, or trouble before dessert had been served) that I had seen a dead cat at the corner of Friends and Philadelphia, small smiles of amused disbelief would flicker around the table, and the grown-ups would settle back visibly, ready for another of my lurid reports. If I said something terse like, "Well, that's all," they would lead me on. If I said, "It was just lying there, dead," Father or even Grandmother Holbrook would ask gently, "Are you sure?" or "How did you know?" And I'd be fool enough to go on. "Well, Garland Swain and I were going to run across Philadelphia before Mr. Trueblood backed out of his barn in his Franklin, and suddenly this little kitten—"

"Black, striped, or what?" Father would interrupt.

"This little striped gray kitten scooted out from in back of the Friends' Church, and another car, not Mr. Trueblood's, appeared almost without a sound and speeded up when it saw us starting to run across the street. And *suddenly* . . ." And I was off. I wanted to please my audience while I had them caught. Sometimes I managed to hold them, and often I did not, so that I quickly grew wise about crowd reaction and attention span and all the things that people now learn in college courses about writing and acting.

But the plain truth is that I did not ever lie; I may have stretched things a tiny bit, here and there, but I never said that people were there who weren't (Garland Swain and I were going to meet Tolbert Moorhead *after* we crossed the street), and never did I embroider the real action in any drama (Mr. Trueblood's car did *not* hit either the kitten or the other automobile, which could not help giving the poor creature a glancing blow that knocked it a few feet into some bushes—and here I could have embroidered freely, but instead I began to cry because it was so shocking to see something so lively suddenly turn limp and still).

I begin to remember now about that time I saw the little cat die. I begin to wonder why I mentioned it to my family at all, for surely I knew that it was not something any of us would like to hear about after lunch. Probably I meant firmly *not* to mention it?

—*1992*

1
Native Truths
(1908–1952)

I don't know why I've always felt embarrassed when I have to admit that I'm not a native Californian. People tell me that I'm silly, and really I cannot say why I feel the way I do about this apparently delicate question of where I was born.

The truth is that I was born in Albion, Michigan, on July 3, 1908. I still know some people there and some who come from there, and all of them are good 'uns. This minute, for instance, there is a man who is the curator of an outfit called the Albion Historical Society who writes occasionally to me as if we knew each other, and I not only like but admire and respect him. In fact, everything I know about Albion is good—except perhaps that I wish I'd not been born there!

Any place over the California border would have done for me, from Oregon down through Nevada, Arizona, and on south toward Mexico, locally known as Baja. I'd have preferred to be born in Mexico (Baja), of course, because I've always hated being

pink instead of brown. That, my own mother assured me regretfully when I was about seven, was and is my fate. I am pink indeed
and forever, and what is worse, I am not a native Californian.

In Albion I was born in the upstairs bedroom of a house that
was shared with my Uncle Walter and his bride. My father Rex
and his bride Edith lived on the second floor.

This whole adventure of being born is apocryphal, of course,
and I am told that an old lady came across the street in the heat
wave that preceded and followed my birth and said firmly to my
mother, "This child won't live through the week."

"Why not?" my mother asked, probably with languor (although my birth had been an easy one), and the old woman replied
that anyone could tell that I was not long for this world because
my new little fingers lay loosely spread open on my stomach and
"healthy babies' fists are clenched." Then she questioned Mother
about why I was named Mary Frances. "It seems strange to me,"
she sniffed. "And your mother is such a Christian woman, too. I
thought you would surely name her something from the Bible."
Mother probably closed her eyes in boredom at this obvious non
sequitur.

More apocrypha: Father got his fellow volunteers from the
Albion Fire Department to spray the hot walls of the bedroom,
which meant that he would treat them later to an ice cream and
beer party. When I was five days old, I was taken for a ride with
Rex in the town's first automobile, although now it is not clear
whether it was a Willys-Knight or a Stutz. Mother consigned us
both to hell or heaven and shuddered gently when Father confessed later that we had gone forty-two miles per hour.

So . . . we did come to California by the time I was somewhat
less than three, and naturally I do not blame my poor parents for
preferring to have me in Albion, Michigan, before they headed like

helpless lemmings toward the Pacific Ocean and whatever freedom they could find there. They managed to stay in Michigan until my sister Anne was born two years after I was, and then to everyone's astonishment, including theirs, they simply pulled up stakes.

My father Rex Kennedy, a fourth-generation newspaperman, refused categorically to continue to be one. He sold his half-interest in the *Albion Recorder* to his older brother Walter. He took the boodle and literally ran westward, with two little babies and a shy, proud, asocial, snobbish woman, his wife and my mother Edith Oliver Holbrook. Rex decided he would be a geologist probably . . . possibly . . . maybe. Mother, who was literally a prairie princess, a Daisy Miller indeed, whose shy manners were always taken as aloof pride, and who was one of the most conservative people I myself ever knew, followed her husband Rex without anything but obvious pleasure. And the four of us were undoubtedly among the first beatniks of the Far West—unwittingly, of course.

Because of Mother's background we headed toward money and security, toward an island in Puget Sound then owned totally by a rich uncle, one of her father's vaguely bankerish brothers. But because of Rex himself, we rented a deserted cabin across the bay from the rich relatives' island. Rex had a rowboat, and probably when Edith needed a bath or some other touch of real elegance, he would row her over to the island. Mostly though, we lived in stately but dingy bliss in the little cabin. Every day Father rowed out into the Sound, and when there was a log of exotic wood like teak or mahogany that had cut loose or been cut from a raft of wood towed by Japanese freighters, he would tie it to the back of his rowboat and bring it back to shore. There he would either chop it into crude furniture for the cabin or sell it to a dealer in fine furniture. In other words, my father was a scavenger. And we lived on the money he made from his piracy, plus an occasional dip into the money from the sale of his half of the *Recorder,* until finally he and Edith decided that they had better try ranching instead of beachcombing.

We headed toward California then, and I was three years old in Ventura, where we lived for some five months about a hundred feet from the foggy beach. I often heard later from Edith that Anne and I barked like seals for at least the first few months we were there until finally a Mexican neighbor, probably in desperation, gave Mother her recipe for cough syrup (and here it is). Take equal parts of honey, glycerin, and fresh lemon juice, and beat them well together. Keep in a little bottle, and take a small slow swig as needed for coughs.

Ventura loomed in our after-dinner conversations as we all grew up (by "all" I mean that we were soon joined by a new sister and brother and of course by countless friends and relatives), and more often than not we sat around after dinner at the table, taking what we referred to as our White Wine Trips. These Trips may have been hard on the wine cellar, but they were always good for us. Edith sometimes withdrew to the nearest couch, convinced that nobody could discuss a thing without arguing, and she was deathly afraid of arguments. Discussions were very different, we all assured her, and we went on talking amiably for many years on the Trips.

And more often than not, at least when topics became thin or dull, we'd wonder what our lives would have been like if Rex had not turned in his option on the faltering, half-dead little orange grove he had determined to buy. The story is that a few hours before the option was going to be up, he decided to buy a shovel and dig around the roots of one of his future gold mines, because as a former farm boy he had begun to wonder why his orange trees had never grown more than an inch in some three years or so—and a few feet below the surface he hit hardpan! He ran for what was left of his option just in time, and he and Edith and their two formerly coughing brats (*and* magic cough syrup) headed for San Diego. They were dead broke by then.

Rex bowed to fate and took a job as city editor of a big daily paper. It must have been miserable for both my parents. I don't remember anything about it—although I am sure I do have one clear memory of my life on Puget Sound, when I was down at the bottom of the beached rowboat pretending to save all our lives by dipping some of the bilge water out with a little tin cup. My six-month-old sister Anne lay on her blanket. My mother always insisted that I could not possibly recall this too-early memory, but she was mistaken there. It is still clear and full to me.

Now all I have of Ventura is the Mexican recipe and a feeling of great solace that Rex did not become a multimillionaire from the oil that was discovered just under the hardpan a few weeks after we fled the place. And of San Diego I remember nothing at all! Later I was told that Rex loathed having a boss and that he and Edith were pretty miserable down there, but the real reason they left was the fleas.

In 1911 San Diego was believed to be the West Coast Port of the Future, and it was already a thriving, filthy place, a home for every wandering flea from the Far East. And Rex Kennedy, until he was about thirty-two, was chemically attractive to fleas—as he was always to men, women, and children—so that after the paper was put to bed, midafternoon, he'd stagger home, increasingly wan and thin and listless and probably proportionately cranky. Edith would brush him down on the sidewalk, and he would then run to the bathroom and jump into the empty tub, while she took all his clothes and shook them out in the backyard. And the tub would be hopping with the bugs that fell from him, and eventually he'd go flealess but sick as a dog to bed. It must have been a hell of a life in every way: they were both fastidious people. Finally a doctor said that Rex must get out of town that minute or die. (I can vouch for this whole sad story because until I was thirty-two years old I, too, carried the same chemistry and could not walk through the lobby of the St. Francis Hotel in San Francisco or even the Paris Ritz without collecting at least fourteen fleas. And the last time I lived in Mexico I, too, staggered home to California with what my horrified doctor called the worst case of flea bites he'd ever seen. There were 147 of them, and he said that if I'd had 150 I'd be dead.)

And the next thing I remember is being in Whittier watching my mother put my baby sister Anne into the top drawer of a hotel bureau. We stayed at the Pickering Hotel until my father bought the biggest available house in town from Mr. Myers, the department store owner. Of course the house was not ostentatious because it was built by and for the Quakers who made up the town. There were less than five thousand original Quaker settlers in Whittier then, and we swelled the ranks of the so-called gentiles by four, which made us almost one hundred in number. Naturally, Grandmother Holbrook financed the purchase of the big house, while Rex and Edith Kennedy filled it with more siblings for Anne and me and a steady stream of relatives. (In those days, people stayed for months instead of one night or two, and there were always a few semipermanent "visitors," all of them fascinating and half of them as batty as June bugs.)

Rex (and Grandmother Holbrook, of course) bought the *Whittier News,* a small daily of ill repute, which no decent Quaker would operate. It was tacitly understood that Father would either leave or be pushed out in one year. We were definitely gentiles, as well as genteel, to the Quaker settlers, and we were always a puzzlement because of Rex's superb training as a newspaperman and also because we were decent people despite our lack of even a faint hint of the "friendly persuasion." We stayed on for some forty-two years, and both my mother and my father were genuinely mourned after they died by every sect, including the one that had most disapproved of us at the beginning.

Although I am quite sure I remember my little sister in the bureau drawer at the Pickering Hotel, my first really keen memory of being there in Whittier, and forever and happily, too, was the day we moved into 115 North Painter Avenue. The little patch of grass in the front yard was dry and brown, as it was perforce in front of every house on our long block, and I stood looking through a scraggly privet hedge and another little girl almost as old as I stared pleasantly back at me as she masturbated. I looked curiously at her for a while, and then I went along unmoved to watch men struggle to bring Mother's piano and all the other things into the mysterious new building that was at once our home. That night Mother told me seriously that she hoped I would never do what little Ruth had been doing to herself because it would make me nervous, and I wondered what on earth she was talking about and why she thought I would try to copy anybody.

The Painter Avenue house was a fine place, indeed, and for many years. I was a completely happy person there, I think. Life rolled on and I learned constantly and eagerly. Everything was exciting to me. I never wondered whether people liked me, but I know as I look back that I had many good friends.

And in 1920 when we moved from Painter Avenue down onto a small orange ranch on what was called Painter Extension—when Mother was through producing her last batch of children and my brother David was not yet a year old—I was still a very happy child. I stayed this way, excited and enraptured by everything and especially by the new life in "the country," for at least three or four more years. But then everything crashed and I became completely adolescent and so disagreeable that Edith Kennedy, who had always been dependent upon me for my cheery usefulness to her with my siblings, wanted me out of the house and insisted that I go away to school when I was sixteen.

We always returned to the Ranch, though, as long as Father and Mother were alive, no matter how widely the whole family roamed. By now that "country" no longer exists, any more than the happy child does.

I still feel embarrassed that I was not born a native Californian because I truly think I am one. I really started to be me somewhere there between the old Pickering Hotel and 115 North Painter. My sister did sleep first in a bureau drawer until we could move, and I did indeed watch Ruthie solemnly as she played with herself, also solemnly, and I do feel "native." So pooh! to all my friends who look at me pityingly when I confess that I was not born in Santa Monica or La Jolla or Montecito but that I sprang full-blown at the age of three into a real native life here. My first sights of this new world are perhaps more vivid than they would have been to a newborn child, but I feel that I was that, and of course I don't remember my own impressions of this world when I emerged in Albion, Michigan, so perhaps I should be thankful that I was three instead of newborn as I stood there on the dry grass of our little patch of lawn in 1911.

—1989

Author's Note: We left the house forever in 1952 after Rex died. It was bulldozed and made into a park for children and old people.

2
On
Coveting
(1912)

While I don't think I am a covetous person, I do remember the first thing I ever thought that I had to have, which I suppose is a form of coveting.

There was a little shop on the Pike in Long Beach where I spent two weeks once in the spring of 1912, when I was three years old going on four. Father was trying to ready a home for us in Whittier, and through my Grandmother Holbrook, who was to live with us for the next eight years or so, we rented a little apartment in Long Beach.

My younger sister Anne and I went there with my mother, who seemed to spend most of her time in bed with what was called a Sick Headache, which was probably a form of migraine or perhaps merely shock at the prospect of continuing her life as a middle-class American woman in one more small town. Whatever the cause, we seldom saw her and instead spent long happy days with a series of faceless and probably witless missionary friends of my grandmother, who was a famous Christian woman from Iowa and one of the uncrowned queens of Long Beach, in those far days when the Iowa picnic was the social event of the year. In fact, anything from Iowa was magic in that town, or so it seemed to us, and Grandmother's name opened many doors that the old lady never suspected.

Who would think, for instance, that the name of the un-crowned queen would act like a magic wand in a little Japanese shop on the Pike? I remember that the first day we were in Long Beach the ancient missionary who was on duty to take care of Mrs. Holbrook's grandchildren led us at once to the little shop owned by Mr. Ishizawa. It was among the poorer and junkier of all the poor and junky little shops owned by Orientals on the quiet strip that was laid like a ribbon along the beach. Mr. Ishizawa bowed and smiled constantly, and his bows became even deeper when he learned that we were indeed Mrs. Holbrook's grandchildren. Probably he was told that the missionary had known his father in Japan, or some such Christianlike fable.

But whatever the charm was, it worked, and when we left that first day, and then every day thereafter for the next two weeks, we were given a little gift by Mr. Ishizawa himself. After the second or third day, the current missionary permitted us to choose our own presents, but with strict instructions for us never to choose anything beyond the ten-cent shelf. This, though, contained many mysterious and beautiful things: tiny dolls made of white plaster with cotton kimonos wrapped around them and little red mouths and slanting black eyes painted on their very white faces, and even smaller bottles of sandalwood perfume, which Mother did not care to have us open near her, and little handkerchiefs painted with kimonos and Mount Fuji, which she did allow to be laid on her pillow by her head. And there were little cakes of soap shaped like obscene pink Kewpies, which we did not like at all but which were thought to be more proper for American children to love than the Japanese dolls that we preferred.

Best of all there were sticks of joss incense. They were, of course, forbidden for us ever to light, except when Father came down from Whittier. Then Anne and I would lie in our bed that pulled down from behind the couch in the living room of the grim little apartment and listen to Mother and Father talking and laughing in the sudden warmth and beauty of the weekend, with the smell of the incense burning. And the next day we knew was the one when Father took us to the Pike alone, while Mother waited for his return and then took to her bed again.

Sunday was a great day, with everyone jostling and happy and the many sailors with their girls and the sound of rifles popping in all the shooting galleries and the steady shrieks that came from the roller coaster.

The first Sunday Mr. Ishizawa smiled at us when we passed by. The second and last Sunday, we went into his shop, and I saw the one thing that I was to covet for the rest of my life. It was not on the familiar ten-cent shelf but in another part of the small shop. I suppose I could have bought one myself later on, but it never occurred to me to do so. It seemed too bad, almost tragic, but it was plainly something of great value, especially in those first far days when it was inconceivable that I would someday have the money of my own to spend on anything I wanted. It was the Unobtainable Jewel to me then, and it still is.

This jewel was a tiny piece of carved coral, shaped like a little rose, probably the size of my thumbnail when I was almost four. It was hung on a tiny gold chain. Probably it cost something insurmountable, like fifty cents or five dollars. Anyway, it was much more than the dime I was to use as my one familiar coin for several more years. If a dime could buy a doll, or three sticks of incense, or even a tiny bottle of sandalwood perfume that my mother would not let us put on with the little silk handkerchiefs with Mount Fuji painted on them, what need was there for any other coin?

Yet I knew enough that I should not ask for the little coral rose, for Mr. Ishizawa would surely have given it to me with a small smile and bow, and that would have displeased my mother and father, and the magic spell would have been broken forever. Of course, never again could ten cents buy as much as it did then in those days when my Grandmother's name had a special charm to it. Never were there such beautiful dolls sold for a dime to any children anywhere, and never, I know, has a little piece of coral, tinted by hand in Italy to look like a tiny rose and then copied by skilled Oriental fingers to sell for one-tenth its real value, been so alluring, so forbidden.

The complexity of this small new obsession of mine was mixed with a strange Christian ethic, probably—something mysterious that flowed between our missionary companions and the little Japanese merchant on the Long Beach Pike. And the rose was an emblem of the unobtainable, and one that I could easily have asked for and perhaps got in the next seventy-five years or so.

Once, I remember, I went to a place near Naples where these roses were as common as the grains of sand along the shore. I still felt the magic of their tiny perfect little petals and knew that no matter how much they cost or how little, they were beyond any price I could pay. I see one now and know just as surely that I could ask for it and wear it myself, but I would never do that. Mr. Ishizawa would come in my dreams and take it away.

—*1990*

3
Tree Change
(1912–1929)

Sometimes the spirit of Christmas seems nothing more than a conditioned reflex, and it is hard to make it work successfully when the calendar calls it up. There must be children in it.

I am sure that my own feelings about the festival are, after many decades, still dictated by the basically Germanic ideas fed to me as a child: "O Tannenbaum" and "Silent Night"; a jolly fat man with a red nose, a wonderful uniform of scarlet to match that nose and white to match his beard; presents long planned for and worked upon—hideous pincushions stitched with yarn at school for a secret special gift to Mother and later a clay ashtray glazed in purple and mustard for our all-forgiving father.

The tree was essential, in my family, in spite of the disapproval of our austere grandmother, who felt that it was pagan nonsense. Occasionally she sat through all this un-Christian foolery, casting a firm if futile pall over it, but often she went away somewhere (where? perhaps back to Battle Creek or to a convention of Campbellites in Asbury, New Jersey), and then we indulged in rich dishes, butter cookies, candies from relatives in Pittsburgh, probably in direct proportion to the miles between our stern matriarch and ourselves.

My younger sister was usually bilious by Christmas Day and lay languidly on the couch by the fire while we brought her countless packages. She was a secret eater and used to hunt out and devour large caches of festival bakings that Mother and the cook-of-the-moment had believed to be well hidden.

I now know that her need to punish herself and all of us by this compulsive gluttony and its results was an indication of how she would die, some fifty years later. Then, though, it was simply understood beforehand that Anne would have a serious bile attack a day or so before the fiesta and be the center of all our loving attentions on the Day. In a not very funny way, it was part of our traditional trappings.

And the tree twinkled, and all our hearts were full of true happiness, even if some of our livers were in protest at the seasonal flood of delicious generous bakings and roastings, all unthought of while Grandmother was in residence. Green pastures!

The first Christmas I remember was the best one, probably because it was the most innocent one in my life. I was four, and it was our first year in Whittier. My sister Anne was two, and it was arranged that we would get into bed with Father, on the sleeping porch upstairs, while mother was at early service singing in the choir. We lay there waiting for the bugler to climb up to the steeple of the Friends' Church and play "Joy to the World! The Lord is Come." It was something special to wait for, and we were trembling with excitement because Father told us it would be beautiful.

We loved being in bed with Father, too. The sleeping porch

was like a bird's nest, high at the back of the tall house. Father was a big man, and warm, and we lay on either side of him and felt his long arms around us in the cold dark waiting for the sounds to come.

They began just as the sun rose on Christmas Day. It was still a little dark, and the sound of the trumpet came to us in a wobbling way, played by an old man, Father said. I remember feeling sharply awake, so that when the first notes of a trumpet sounded into the starry air, I cried out something like "YES," and little Anne awoke with a snap on the other side of Father's big chest, and he pulled us closer as we lay listening.

From the top of the square steeple of the Friends' Church, less than two blocks from our warm nest, a man blew the first notes bravely on his horn, sometimes trembling and flatting a little. First he played to the north. Then he blew to the east, where we lay breathless with the mysterious, triumphant beauty of the sound, and to the south, where in a few years we would move. Then he sounded his tiny blast westward, toward the great Pacific.

Father knew the words: "Joy to the world! The Lord is come." When the trumpet finally ended its announcement, he sang on softly, "And heaven and nature sing!"

Then Mother came running in, all cool-cheeked and laughing, and then we were in our Sunday dresses at a special breakfast with candles on the table and probably muffins or sausages for a treat, and *finally* we went into the living room. (I knew there was more to this day, but what?)

At the end of the long dark living room was a hole in the wall for the door to an apartment we were going to build for Grandmother, who was soon coming to live with us. The hole had been an ugly fireplace with a gas log that Mother had been very scornful about, so that very soon we were going to build another good decent fireplace on the other wall, the one to the south end of the living room. Now, in front of the hole, which was covered with a blanket to keep out the Christmas chill, there was a low table and on it were two trees, one for my little sister Anne and one for me!

They were about three feet tall. Of course, we knew that they were to go on either side of our new front steps in the next day or so. They were shaped just like Christmas trees and were some kind of pine, I suppose, set in sturdy pine tubs that had roughly braided bands of bamboo peelings around the tops and bottoms. They had been given to Mother and Father by Mr. One. He was a Chinese merchant on the plaza in Los Angeles, and he liked Mother and Father and they liked him. (F. Suey One was a tall man for a Chinese. I did not know that then, because I thought all men were tall because my father was.)

The table was a kitchen table with two fat-bellied drawers, one for sugar and one for flour—a kind of table that was common then when flour and sugar were used more than they are now. Father had found it secondhand in a junkyard and had cut off the legs, and now Anne had her own drawer for crayons and whatever she wanted in this world, and I had my own drawer, and we never thought of looking in each others'.

But the magic part of it was that on that day two little trees stood on it, one for each of us, and each one had a star on top, I remember, glistening and gleaming in the dim room. There was some tinsel, too, and there were a few presents underneath, probably crayons for us both and some coloring books or papers. And they were *our* trees!

The rest of the day I don't remember at all, but we probably ate well. There were many good things about the day for both of us, as there were about all days in those far times, but coming down to find the trees in that long dim room was one of the most innocent and loveliest things that has ever happened to me, I think.

—1978

Author's Note: I got married in September of 1929, but Christmas was always the same while Rex and Edith were alive.

4
A Few Notes About Aunt Gwen
(1912–1927)

Soon after we began to live in Whittier in 1912, when I was four, we met the Nettleships, a strange family of English medical missionaries who preferred tents to houses. Their daughter became our Aunt Gwen in a wonderful flash, and that summer my little sister Anne and I stayed in their current encampment, under a mighty row of eucalyptus trees a few hundred yards above the sea cliffs south of the village called Laguna. There was a mess tent, and a kitchen with little tents in a square around it, and even a donkey named Noisy to help carry water and supplies. We slept on folding cots, and Aunt Gwen played us songs by Harry Lauder on a little Victrola with a horn, from blue cylinders that we were not to touch.

The next summer, when we drove down from Whittier in the Model-T with a load of camp stuff for the Nettleships, we were horrified to find that someone had built a one-room cabin where our camping place had been. By then, though, Father knew a mysterious old Dutch newspaperman who published a little sheet now and then in Laguna, and from him he learned that the owner of our land wanted to sell the cabin and leave. So Father borrowed $375 and bought the shack and the row of mighty trees on their three vaguely defined township lots, and we went back there every summer for more than twenty-five years, sometimes for four or five months.

Soon after the place was ours, Father and several other Whittier heathens (that is, Episcopalians, non-Quakers) began to add rooms to it. The only one of them who knew beans about building was Uncle Mac, Peter Maclaren, who sang bass in the St. Matthias choir and was a retired Chief Mate on the India run from Glasgow and Liverpool. For about three years, Sundays in summer meant hammers and saws and a picnic, and a caravan of jalopies when we all headed for home at night. Mother usually drove home with some of the other wives and Uncle Mac, and Anne and I snoozed on the backseat of our Ford with the empty beer bottles, while Father headed the parade with a loaded shotgun on the seat beside him, in case the big wildcats in Laguna Canyon got too curious while one of us changed a tire, as often happened in those far times. We never fired the gun but sometimes saw bright eyes blazing in the bushes. Anne and I never felt frightened, but I am not sure about Mother. Gradually she stayed more in Whittier with the new babies.

The Nettleships moved their campgrounds into wilder hills after we found ourselves with a real roof over our heads . . . except for Aunt Gwen, of course, who was our mentor-goddess for the next many years, both in the big solid house in Whittier and in the thrown-together shack at the beach. We lived and ate more casually in Laguna, more carelessly, so that it did not matter that we had only cold running water in the lean-to kitchen. In fact, we felt almost too citified, after bringing water in from the one outside tap for the first couple of years, before Uncle Mac worked some magic with discarded pipe and a faucet. There was a two-burner kerosene stove on wobbly legs, with a tin box we could set over one burner for an oven, and shelves next to the stinking little stove held a few cast-off pots and cups and bowls, trash from all our friends who brought them down on Sundays instead of throwing them away. There was one big iron skillet, which Aunt Gwen used for everything from frying eggs and fish to heating the dishwater. All the china was cracked or chipped. The few kitchen and table tools were shabby and bent. Such things were taken for granted in a beach shack: rejected rocking chairs that tipped over if sat in carelessly, lumpy old quilts, thin mended sheets. It did not matter: we were hungry and healthy, snug with excitement and freedom.

Aunt Gwen, a real Nettleship born in a hammock in a jungle in New Guinea or some such place, was even happier with a campfire than a fancy kerosene stove, and we made a three-stone hearth outside the back door between the kitchen and the out-house. We heated water there, for a rare bath or for wash day, in a big empty oil can with a wire handle; it had been used so long it hardly tasted of anything but Laguna sulphur. (Water was nasty there, and we seldom drank it.) Father would always bring us old wine jugs full of Whittier tap water on weekends, or now and then we'd have the stuff we could buy for ten cents a jug at a little ranch in Laguna Canyon that also sold cucumbers and tomatoes in the summer. And we had another old oil can that we used to steam mussels in, half full of fresh seaweed over the hot coals. Now and then, for no special reason, Aunt Gwen fried our catch of rock bass out there. It seemed to taste better. . . .

The kitchen stayed the same always, one "thrown up," as Father said when he built anything. (A half-century after he and Uncle Mac and the other middle-aged hoodlums from the St. Matthias Church in Whittier had patched our summer place together, he would still say, "Let's throw up a stone wall round this corner," or "How about throwing up a little fence behind that row of bushes?" It had nothing to do with indigestion, of course, but I've always wondered how a psychiatrist would analyze his innocent phraseology.) A lean-to is never more than a lean-to, and our kitchen, tacked on to the original cabin in Laguna, leaked hopelessly in the winter rains I came to know there when I was grown up. Father never knew this, for summer was forever when he and Uncle Mac were throwing up rooms on three sides of the first house, and the kitchen was part of all the unexpected luxury we felt. It was perhaps eight feet square and had one window looking eastward past the two-holer to the beautiful bare hills and the high horizon that we called the rim of the world. On the north side were the open rickety shelves, with their sad store of rejected dishes and pans, and the two-burner stove with a wide shelf above it for matches and Aunt Gwen's ever-present can of bacon drippings. Under the window, a small wobbly table held current supplies, and dented canisters for sugar and flour, and a beat-up bread box.

On the south wall was an almost surrealistic edifice made jointly, over several summers, by Father and Uncle Mac. It was supposed to be a sink, with two hand-turned and inadequate drainboards on either side, sloping steeply so that the water would run fast off washed dishes. Father had found the little cracked sink in a junkyard, and although the two men devised a kind of outlet for it, there was no running water for several years, and we had to carry a pan or jug of it in from the faucet outside the back door. What made it astonishing, or perhaps merely quaint, was that this spiderlike creation stood almost five feet off the somewhat uneven floor of the kitchen, because Father was six foot five and a half and Mother and Aunt Gwen were both tall women. It did not seem at all strange to me to have to stand on a chair to help Aunt

Gwen with our daily "washing up," and it would never have occurred to any of us to lower it for normal human use. It stood
there for several decades, always with a couple of buckets underneath it to catch whatever might drip down from Uncle Mac's
strange drainboards, or be dropped by people trying to reach its
lofty inadequacies.

On the west wall of this odd little temple to gastronomy, the
heart of the house, THE KITCHEN, there was nothing. I remember leaning against it as I grew older, drying dishes, and probably
Aunt Gwen did, too, but there were no shelves or even graffiti or
cut-out magazine covers on it ever. It was simply the wall of the
old cabin, painted navy blue from the dregs of somebody's leftover
home-done decorating.

Aunt Gwen believed in doing as little as possible inside walls,
so our cooking when we were with her was largely of stuff to put
in our pockets for later. Mornings we ate oranges Father brought
by the crate, because he was interested in the thriving California
citrus industry in those days and got a lot of lagniappes from
ranchers and their packinghouses. There was always toast, made
two slices at a time in a funny arrangement that fitted over one of
the burners, so I thought all toast tasted of kerosene when it was
properly charred on one side and half-done on the other. When
the bread left from weekends got too stale, Aunt Gwen would
soak it in some milk and beaten eggs and fry it in bacon drippings,
and we would sprinkle brown sugar on it for a treat. It was delicious, a genuine *pain perdu.* Then she would fry some bacon, pour
most of its juices back in her can above the stove, and make fried-
egg sandwiches for us to carry greasily in our pockets on our long
treks in every direction of that wild deserted country. (Aunt
Gwen's people were all great walkers, and I remember how
Mother was astonished to learn that long before we knew them,
the Nettleships would spend three or four days carrying their sum-

mer's tents and supplies down from Whittier to the hills of Laguna on foot along the dusty roads and then on their secret trails.)

And when we got home at night, Aunt Gwen fried the fish we had caught, with perhaps some potatoes cut up in their skins and an onion if there was one, always in a good glob from her drippings tin. If there was fresh milk, we had hot cocoa for dessert.

Once I caught a big eel off the rocks near Arch Beach, and Aunt Gwen killed it fast but then made us watch it writhe until sundown, nailed to the back wall of the house. Then she showed me how to skin it and cut it up and help her make a kind of matelote, and it seems strange now that we never associated pain and dying with eating in those innocent and unfeeling days. I hated the death and slow writhings of the water snake and its blood on my hands. But the stew was delicious, the next day for dinner.

Sometimes our goddess made a kind of pone and baked it to a fine stodginess in the little oven set dangerously over one burner. Now and then, for a treat, she would throw in some sugar and raisins and nuts, if there were any.

We seldom ate meat. We walked in to the village every two or three days to get sugar or perhaps a pound of bacon at Mr. Isch's store and to check on the tide table outside the front door of the little hotel, but mostly we ate the fish we caught off the rocks. Now and then we had a big feast of mussels steamed over seaweed on the rock hearth out toward the latrine.

The mussels and the fried-egg sandwiches are what I remember most thoroughly about those first years of learning to live well gastronomically, and I have already written too much about the sandwiches in other places. I should state clearly, though, that they must be made of good honest bread. The eggs should be about three or four days old, and if possible laid by hens with roosters nearby so that the yolks stand up properly. The bacon drippings must have attained that certain noble amalgam of all decent drippings added over several weeks to a clean old coffee can. And then the warm sandwiches must be wrapped not in plastic wrap but in waxed paper, the kind that will gradually begin to sweat and drip, so that by the time the sandwich is unwrapped, some of the paper sogs off on it and tastes fine, if you are hungry enough.

The only real attraction for this recipe for Fried Egg Sandwiches is harmless as well, since I am sure that Aunt Gwen is as strong a force in life as she ever was, and what is more, she is in everyone's life in one form or another. Her own ways of nourishing each one of us are less easy to put down than the recipe I remember for the fried-egg sandwiches. They are less identifiable, and therefore this one existent recipe may well serve us for all the other unidentifiable ways she and her kind continue to feed our bodies and souls.

I am glad the kitchen in Laguna has been razed or bulldozed. By now there may even be a condominium or high rise where it once leaned against our shack. Certainly the mighty trees are gone. But the Pacific still rolls and crashes against the rocks not two blocks westward, and probably fish still lurk nearby. And surely somewhere there is another little kitchen as impossibly ugly and inconvenient, where honest food waits for hungry happy children —a fish stew, or milk toast in a bowl . . . or a fried-egg sandwich.

—*1983*

5
The First Kitchen
(1912–1920)

It is impossible for me to think of the first kitchen in my memory without connecting it with my Grandfather Holbrook. This is odd because I don't remember him at all, although I think I met him once just before his death. I must have been very young, since I was almost four when Grandmother Holbrook, his widow, came to live with us.

The first kitchen was in the big house in Whittier where we lived from my third year until I was almost twelve, and I clearly remember thinking that it was the nastiest room I had ever seen in my life and wondering how my mother and father could stand to have good things come from it. They ate very well from there always, and I myself learned to cook in its dark green shadowy depths.

The kitchen was long, narrow, and dank, and it was the ugliest room in the house. It was lit by one electric bulb hanging from the center of the ceiling directly above the kitchen table, with its two bins for flour and sugar underneath and its chipped white enamel top. The only natural light came from two high windows above the kitchen sink at one end of the room, which I never was tall enough to look out of. There was probably a view of the house next door, but I don't remember ever seeing anything except a patch of sky far above the old sink.

The sink had a counter on either side, and it was very ugly, like everything else in the room. The stove was gas and it was against the far wall from the door into the dining room. There were many cupboards and one cooler and, of course, a small icebox. There was linoleum on the floor, and between the dining room and the kitchen, there was a small mysterious sliding door that was supposed to open onto a built-in sideboard in the dining room, but it was never used. The cook-of-the-moment brought everything in through the swinging door.

In the dining room, Mother had an electric bell under her foot that summoned the help from the kitchen, but she could seldom find it and instead would ring a little silver bell. Father sat at the kitchen end of the table and Mother at the far end so that she could keep one eye on the swinging door. I never knew how it was managed so smoothly, but the service was always good. We children never addressed the hired help during the meals, nor she any of us, although we might have been jabbering happily together just before entering the room.

At the sink and window end of the kitchen, which was painted greenish brown, a door led onto the porch, also long and narrow, where there was a small toilet and a tiny stuffy little room, with one window at its end, for the current slavey. The room was without ornament of any kind, and I suppose it had the usual bed and chair and even a bureau, and the woman who occupied it was supposed to use the back toilet and do all her other personal

washing up in the kitchen sink. She was off every Thursday evening and Sunday after lunch and was considered part of the family,
but always in a subservient way.

It seems odd now that I was raised with a strange woman
always in the house, an imposition I never did like. My mother,
who was born and raised on the plains of Iowa, considered such
services as part of her life and always had someone to help with
the daily chores or, in fact, to perform all of them. Most of her
hired help had been Swedish and Norwegian people, immigrants
learning the language, and in California she had to accustom herself to live with a much more motley group of people.

Our first maid-of-all-work was a very large black woman
named Cynthia, who was without any pretensions or prejudices.
She was there the first winter we were in Whittier, and she had the
bedroom next to the bathroom upstairs. When Grandmother Holbrook came to live with us, the servant's room was added onto the
back of the house, along with a little apartment for the autocratic
old Irish lady.

Cynthia was wonderful, with warm skin, and my little sister
Anne and I loved to crawl into bed with her and softly sing hymns
and pray to her God. She sat proudly in the middle of the backseat
of the Model-T Ford on Sundays when we went for our weekly
drive, with Anne and me on either side of her and with Mother
and father sitting grandly in the front seat, dressed in their dusters
and Mother in a veil and driving hat. Cynthia seemed much gran-
der—and we were especially admired by anyone who saw the
spectacle—when she wore a high turban of blue satin with a
matching dress that she inherited from Mother. The dress was cut
very low with inserts of brown lace that did not show at all on her
skin so that she looked like a half-naked goddess.

Cynthia soon left because she was the only black woman in

Whittier, and when she went to the grocery store for Mother, nobody spoke to her; nobody had seen her at all. "I am invisible here," she said. "I must go."

Mother and my little sister Anne and I wept, and even Father was much moved, although he admitted that he had always hated to go into the bathroom for his morning shave after Cynthia had steamed up the windows with her bath.

That was my first brush with racism, and the last bath ever taken by a servant in the house, as far as I know, and nobody ever seemed to mind, although as I grew older I wondered about such privacies.

After Cynthia left, my sister Anne and I grew to accept the fact that cooks lived downstairs in their own quarters. My father was amazed to learn early on that he and Mother were considered especially kind to their help. I was always puzzled by the difference in the cook's new quarters downstairs and our own bedrooms upstairs. There must have been some signs of the various occupants of that little room, but I don't remember any of them, not even a picture of a relative or a book or magazine. Anne and I freely used the back toilet, which made us feel close to the cook. We would spend long hours in that stuffy little cubbyhole, taking turns sitting on the toilet and listening to my continued stories, most of which concerned imaginary characters connected in some way with World War I.

I remember talking seriously with Mother several times about why the servant's room was so ugly, but she would tell me that she and Father were the best employers, and she also boasted to me that her own father had felt that domestic help should form a union. Grandfather Holbrook had even proposed it several times before his death, but he was always laughed at.

The kitchen remained dank and unappetizing, although it was most enjoyable when Mother would go down to make an annual cake for my father's birthday. (It was a Lady Baltimore cake, for some reason.) And there were times when Grandmother would supervise the making of jam there in the dark room, when once a year several cousins would appear bringing fruit from their ranches, and the kitchen would be full of laughter and good smells from the pots. Mostly, though, it was a place to avoid by everybody but me, except on Sunday nights when we would have supper to make by ourselves—very simple things like oyster stew or scrambled eggs.

I soon learned that the best way to get attention was to cook something, and I easily fell into the role of the cook's helper. I loved to stand on a little stool and stir things carefully in a double boiler, so that I soon became known as the family cook on the regular cook's night out. Early on I was helping her make cake on Saturday morning for Sunday noon.

After Cynthia came Amimoto.

It was late 1912, and everybody in southern California had a Japanese houseboy: there were thousands of them, learning English and engineering and diplomacy and such, going to school and living with American families who laughed in a more or less kindly way at them and told about their funny sayings at parties.

Amimoto was not unusual and did not, like many of his fellow refugees, later become an admiral or an ambassador or a suicide pilot. He was a gentle, polite, desperately homesick boy, and my mother was one of the worst people he could possibly have worked for because she was almost paralyzed by him, by his differentness from any male she had ever seen in her life: his different color and lack of beard, the way his eyes grew in his head, his soft way of speaking and moving, which to her seemed sinister because she may have seen someone like Sessue Hayakawa in moving pictures. Amimoto disturbed her to the point of hysteria, and although she managed to tell my father now and then of his more ludicrous mistakes in English or cookery, she was basically repelled and terrified by him the whole time he was with us. She was, always, an ideal person to work for, thoughtful and considerate, but if Amimoto knew that, he must also have known that she was not happy to be mistress to his servanthood.

I see now that the way he and my sister and I, on the other hand, were completely happy together must have worried her deeply. We understood one another without words, but I have been told what I do not remember, that he used to talk and sing to us for hours in his own language and that we understood that, too, as far as anyone could tell. And we had no trouble speaking our very simple English with him: we were not looking for mistakes in either his grammar or our own, nor were we conscious of amusement or curiosity but only of our real ease with him. He would take us for walks, up the hill past the little Quaker college he went to, or to the dusty City Park, or to the Children's Basement of the Library where he was slowly reading through a series called *What Katy Did: What Katy did at School, What Katy Did Abroad,* and so on. He read parts of these exciting stories to us, and later when I was old enough to devour them as he had done, from left to right along their shelf without a perceptible pause between volumes, I could still hear his delicate voice in my mind.

We used to lie on his bed (you can see how this would disturb my mother: she had been raised when *women* tended little children, especially little female children) in the hideous "maid's room" off the back porch, the three of us crosswise like stalks of asparagus, while he worked small pieces of whittled bamboo into puzzles. They were much too complicated for our small fingers, and I don't know what he did with them all—sold them perhaps or sent them home to his brothers and sisters. There was the stuffy dark cubbyhole next to his room with a toilet in it, and when we needed to go in there he would unbutton our panties deftly with one hand and keep on arranging the bits of bamboo with his other. Or if he was fixing vegetables for dinner, which he did every afternoon when he got back from school, he would scrub and pare and somehow go right on with his homework or his fascinating letters to Japan, written on soft paper that smelled much better than any we had ever seen. We would stand as close to him as we could, our heads just by his knees as he perched on the kitchen stool, and if Mother came in she would laugh self-consciously and shoo us out of the kitchen so as not to bother him. That was *her* story; ours was, of course, never mentioned, but the three of us understood that we could not possibly bother him, for he loved us and was lonely, and we loved him and were happier with him than with anyone else in the world, temporarily at least.

That fact, which must have been incomprehensible to my mother, was why he finally left, although the story always was about the way he fixed radishes one night. My mother was a sensitive and very intelligent woman, but in a thousand years she could never have recovered from her first basic uneasiness at him, at his smallness, his brownness, his softness. He simply was not human to her. What is more, it must surely have disturbed her to see that to us he was more than human, that he was divine.

The whole thing is logical. Mother hated him because we did not . . . and she got rid of him.

Once she was to have four guests for dinner, and there were special steamings and such-like in the kitchen, with brussels sprouts, a great delicacy in those days, sent out on the Pacific Electric from Jevne's in Los Angeles. Father brought them home at noon, and my sister and I watched Amimoto peel off their tiny outer leaves.

They were the right size for fairies. That is all I remember. The rest is apocryphal. It seems that when it was time for dinner to be served, there was none, and Mother found Amimoto hunched over the sink in the kitchen, carving radishes that had been meant as a garnish into exquisite little copies of the brussels sprouts and arranging the green and the rosy-white flowers in patterns on her best silver tray. Nothing had been cooked. Nothing had even been made ready. But the radishes and the raw vegetables were, even my mother had to admit, as beautiful as jade, as coral. . . .

That, the story went, was why Amimoto left: he was undependable.

My sister and I knew better, but we were powerless to do anything but grieve in secret. Now and then a long cylinder of thin rice cakes would come for us, and my mother would shake her head half-regretfully, half in amusement, over this continued sentimentality. She would tell about the radishes again, and we could not rightly enjoy the little cakes she said had come from Amimoto.

By the time I started to go to school, they had stopped coming, and people told us he had forgotten us, but I don't think so, for we never forgot him.

After Amimoto, the best help we ever had in the kitchen were four middle-aged sisters, the McClure girls. They lived with their father far down on Painter Avenue, and we never knew which of them would be serving breakfast. Bertha was tall and thin and very nervous, so that when she served coffee or tea the cups rattled in their saucers. We were aware that Bertha had a crush on Father and watched eagerly when she would slide around his unconscious head and titter helplessly when he addressed her directly.

Our favorite of the four sisters was Margaret, of course. She was almost as small as we were, a tiny woman with a cleft palate. My sister and I used to pray with her often in her bedroom and were unaware that for a long time we were speaking just as she spoke, as if we had cleft palates, too. Grandmother and Mother finally forbade Margaret to come to the house at all, as we always spoke just as she did when she was anywhere near us. This became, in fact, a real kind of fetish with my parents, especially my mother, and we had a hard time breaking ourselves of this habit. Margaret-talk became our secret language, and finally we had only to mutter the words *sixty-four* in her strange cleft palate accent to feel safe and loving, two united against the world. This continued until my sister died when I was fifty-seven and she was fifty-five, but it was a secret between us.

Margaret was the last of the four sisters to come, and I think I began to use the kitchen more as a show-off place after she left. By the time I was ten, I was thoroughly into cooking in that dreadful room, and I knew its worst secrets and knew equally well that there was no use in protesting its many discomforts. By then I could bake a fairly decent sponge cake and had learned not to experiment with changing the proportions of spices and such in recipes. I no longer needed to stand on a little stool to stir the white sauces and less commendable messes that catered to my grandmother's austere ideas of correct eating.

We left for the country when we moved down Painter Avenue across the county road and onto Painter Extension. The kitchen there was bright and cheerful, and the servant's quarters were separate from the house. By then, I realized that Mother and Father were indeed good employers, but I always wondered how they could have subjected other human beings to such sordid conditions as were taken for granted in the first big house on Painter.

I wished fervently that I had known my grandfather, and I still do, because he sowed the seeds in me of protest against conditions that were otherwise considered normal. He probably would have enjoyed the same good food, and he might never have voiced his critical views to the people most connected with these same views. He was most certainly not an agitator, any more than they were eager to be disturbed. In other words, it would all have continued in the usual patterns, but it is a comfort to me to know that my grandfather felt strongly about the conditions of servants in America. And I don't think that by now there are any slaveys, as we took for granted. Neither Grandfather nor I did anything to change the situation, but I feel sure that Cynthia would no longer be invisible, even in Whittier, and that anyone who had to live in that little room off the back porch would see to it that a bathroom was available somewhere in the house. But Grandfather would still be an unknown stranger to me, and I would still make white sauces for Grandmother and practice the powers that lurked behind my continued interest in cooking. In other words, the more things change, the more they are the same.

—*1990*

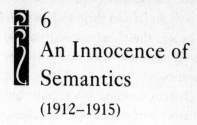

6
An Innocence of Semantics
(1912–1915)

Almost anyone who wants to can write by now of how pure the air was when he was a boy in Iowa, a child in the Bronx, how quiet the streets were, how fair the streams and gutters. Instead, most of us give a defeated shrug (or cough, or chest rattle). Yes, we have defiled our world. How could we know that it was happening? We frown with guilt and shrug again.

I can remember, though, that some forty-five years ago in Laguna Beach, clean rags and a bottle of kerosene began to be standard equipment for our all-day loiterings on the beaches, to clean our feet and our bodies of the black oil that floated down to us, several times a year, from the coastline fields. Sometimes the rims of the waves would be almost black with the stuff, and the beach would be fouled until we had a very high tide or a good storm. We shrugged in the Twenties, too: it was a small local problem—nasty, but what could one do?

By now the whales know better, and they have quickly

changed thousands of years of habit, and on their way to Mexico to breed, they avoid their ancient path between the Santa Barbara Islands and the mainland and stay far out from any possible oil slicks. Whales and seals and porpoises are smart, and so are sardines: they *git*.

Oysters, shrimps, trout, gulls, and pelicans—they have had a rougher time of it, perhaps, and already they are almost unknown in many of their old resting places and playgrounds. There is no livable water left for them. Perhaps their ways of communication are less advanced.

And for the air breathers, what is there?

My father worked with the first committees formed to study air pollution in southern California in about 1925. As a small-time citrus grower, he could already see what was threatening the orange and lemon groves; as a small-town editor, he could hear what some keen doctors were muttering: chest rattles in unborn babies, old men dying slowly from lack of oxygen in the streets. The second nearest I ever saw him to weeping in public was after a meeting one night in Monrovia or Glendora, made up of concerned people trying to talk with the unconcerned, the cupidinous. He was in a state of near-hysteria from frustration. There he was, a newspaper editor, by ethics a *voice*. But the big manufacturers, the oil refiners, the producers of patently noxious goods and gases would never hear him. They were deaf to everything the committee tried to tell them. He felt defeated, which is painful to the soul. He rose to fight again and often, of course, but from that night on there was a shrug, no matter how concealed, in his editorial stance.

Still, when we were first in Whittier, the air was good, and we used it as our rightful element, having been born in it. It blew gently to us and then up the mild slopes of the hills from the flatlands between Whittier and the sea, where some dairy cattle grazed and where there was cultivation of the less soggy ground:

potatoes, wheat. Then there was the ocean. Probably the air that reached us was blown for thousands of miles across waves and flowery islands. While I was a child, oil wells were sunk at Huntington Beach, but we never smelled them or thought of them in Whittier, and only occasionally did we in Laguna when the beaches were fouled and then washed clean again.

Many growing things cleansed the air for us and kept it sweet. The Spaniards and Mexicans had been great ones for planting, and olive trees flourished in long avenues and hilly groves around the town. There were fine stands of eucalyptus trees, which had been brought from Australia by adventurers who dreamed vainly of selling them to the government for telephone poles. They grew generously in the new land, and their seeds rolled here and there and took hold. The leaves sent out a steady subtle odor, almost dusty when the air was hot and still and as exciting as a new young wine when the trees were in bloom and the jade-gray horny buds produced their astonishing fragility of little honey-colored hairs.

Then the bees worked, high in the gangly trees and low on the ground, where sweet alyssum seemed to thrive in the soil that many gardeners felt had been forever contaminated by the oil in the eucalyptus leaves. (We had good honey in Whittier, before easterners came to demand nothing but that vapid syrup from the orange blossoms.) For twenty-five years of my life I listened to bees, high above me as I lay against a big fallen branch, and then watched them as they stopped, half-drunk, for a few sips of the tiny white weeds all about me. And when I was little my sister and I used to rub the tender new leaves roughly on our forearms and sniff ourselves: how clean and fine!

Another thing that made the air in Whittier special, to my inner nose anyway, were the great fields of wild mustard that almost surrounded us. It grew on the hills, of course. But between us and Los Angeles were long stretches of open meadows, and in the spring they were dazzling, like pale yellow gold. They sent up a wild sweet blast of perfume, an invitation almost, hinting of strange pleasures not yet understood. As we tooled sedately on a Sunday, in our open Model-T, toward Los Angeles or perhaps the Busch Gardens in Pasadena and got past Pio Pico's crumbling White House and over the Rio Hondo Bridge, the fields opened out on either side of us and rolled as far as we could see. There was the little village of Montebello, and from then on to the out-skirts of Los Angeles, with its peculiar Chinese and Greek ceme-teries, its huge brick Catholic orphanage, there was nothing but gold. On a still day, the air was so little moved by our cutting slowly through it that the honeyed heavy perfume almost drugged us.

And orange groves were being planted fast, to the south and east and even the hilly northwest of our town. Which was more profitable was the question: to raise the subtropical trees for their blossoms, to be shipped by canny Los Angeles florists to the east-ern wedding markets, or to raise the fruit and risk having it freeze on the trees? Many people gambled on the second choice, like my father, and few of them made very much money, but they kept the air perfumed for us!

By the time I was nearing my teens, I felt that orange trees were the dullest bloblike growths on the planet, tidy and stupid in shape and crawling with several kinds of lice. I hated oranges because of years of surfeit and can still forgo them easily, except perhaps in a good marmalade or tart. But the word *ineffable* was made for the perfume an orange tree in full bloom will give forth, especially in the moonlight—and especially if it is near a lime or lemon, when the blend with oxygen is dizzying.

There were other things in Whittier to make our air better than almost any other I have breathed. Many of the old ladies, ancient widows or withered daughters of the First Settlers, cultivated bushes that had grown from the slips brought by Mrs. Aguilla Pickering and all her fellow Quaker ladies from their eastern and midwestern gardens; rose geraniums, lemon verbena, night-blooming jasmine grew everywhere around their houses.

The hills rose right above the town to the east and north, and they were still almost virgin, blanketed at the right times with poppies and blue lupine and a dozen other less obvious blossoms, all of them with their own subtleties of smell.

And there were no factories, few cars, and still plenty of animals, like horses and cows, to add their healthy blotters of good dung to the ecological balance.

The soil was young, as earth goes on the planet. It needed help, if it was going to be plowed and used. Cover crops were planted generously; it was found that the topsoil would not support the native weeds, once it had been turned over. When I first walked through a new orange orchard in what is now called La Puente, I was five or so, and poppies grew tall enough to brush my face and make the tiny fruit trees look foolish. Within a few years, though, the bright orange satiny blossoms grew only in roadside ditches, where their sensitive seeds could still take hold without risk, and ranchers planted controlled mixtures of weeds to add strength to the soil's minerals. They were murderous to walk through with bare legs, seeming to lean heavily on the nettle family.

By the time gases from the diesel trucks, the cars, and the factories started to stunt and kill the orange trees, all the fertilizers were prefabricated, so much simpler to spread, and anyway, where was there still for hire a worker who knew how to use a plow and disk? Then, for every tree that died, a new settler arrived and needed living space, and the oranges and lemons and walnuts were pulled out to make room for subdivisions, laid like cookies from a stucco pastry tube over the broken roots. By now there are no orchards, and most of the hills have been bulldozed and leveled into unrecognizable shapes, to offer dubious support for upper-bracket "ranch-type" or "Mediterranean" homes, and there are not any ditches left. They have been burned out with weed killers, as fire hazards, and the poppies are gone.

As for the water, I cannot imagine what the rivers are like now. When I was little, I knew the Rio Hondo best, because we crossed it often, and of course we used to get watercress from its upper banks.

Soon after we landed in Whittier, in 1912, there was a cloud-burst and flood. The bridge between us and Los Angeles washed out and on down to the Pacific. My father, going against Mother's protests, took me out to the edge of what was left of the county road, and I sat in the back of the Ford while he photographed things like the pulley that had been rigged to get mail across the boiling yellow flood. A tree raced along in the middle of it, and in its bare branches a big gopher snake was looped intricately, its jaw set in a frantic impotent hiss as its strange craft whirled toward the sea.

I do not think that I would ever want to find out what has become of the little rivers that once ran down from the foothills of our part of southern California. They used to be laughed at by visitors from the East, who knew the Hudson and the Mississippi, for most of the time they were invisible or just little trickles into an occasional shallow pool. Their beds were wide and sandy, with willows always growing along them to make the air smell like witch hazel. There were three or four places where gypsies encamped. They were a dark and aloof people, up from Mexico to pick the walnut crops or to rest before another long move, but they never went near the Rio Hondo or any other "California river" in a season when a flash storm could stretch the banks in a few minutes with its crazy roar of racing water. I suspect that by now such potential danger has been piped underground to be used to carry effluent out to sea and that the wide white sands of the riverbeds have been paved for roads or covered with houses in straight lines.

My sister and I perfected one act of mimicry that at first amused Father and Mother in the front seat of the car, on our Sunday afternoon drives, and finally got on their nerves to the point where Mother said sharply, "Oh, please *stop* that!" and he said, "Yes, *do,* and *pronto.* Enough is enough." We understood that our vocal fun was over, but forever we would say silently, as we crossed the bridges in our home county, what for a short riotous season we had chanted in unison, in fluty shrill shrieks of exaggerated refinement, no doubt in mockery of some visiting relative: "Oh, *LOOK* at all the *PEEple, swimming* in the *RIvah!*" This would send us into whoops of delight and amusement every single time. What wit, we felt, what delicious sarcasm! There was no water in the river; there were no people to not-swim—oh, *hilarious!*

I can see how this proved boring to adults, but it lent a fine satirical sparkle to many a routine promenade for Anne and me. The backseat of a car driving slowly over familiar roads, Sunday after Sunday, can grow a little dull. . . .

Norman Mailer has written somewhere that the need of a city is to accelerate its growth, while the pride of the small town is to retard it. In California there can be no such pride, as thousands of people a month move across its blandly welcoming borders and elbow a place for themselves. Whittier's population is now over one hundred thousand. The soft hills have been cut into recklessly, to make holes and cliffs for houses, and native plants like poppies and lupine and holly and sage have been shaved away forever. Houses and stores sprawl clear to the continent's edge, half hidden by mustard-brown smog. Except for an occasional road sign, it is impossible to know when one has driven past the city limits of the "Queen of the Foothills," as the little Quaker settlement was called hopefully in its earlier days. When has one entered Montebello, if it still exists, or Norwalk or even Yorba Linda?

There used to be a good little co-operated orange packinghouse on the edge of that last small settlement, and in another place nearer to us, La Habra, there was a weekly newspaper in a shabby little store building on the main street. After Father's own daily was safely off the presses, he would sometimes pile Anne and me into the car and take us spinning along the country road, through miles of orange orchards on the sloping land, past an occasional fine planting of walnuts. We would go into the big shadowy packinghouse, unless picking was in swing, when my sister and I would wait in the car. There was a bitter smell of discarded fruit, almost good to inhale, like medicine. Father would exchange views with anyone still hanging around the plant: Mexican pickers were much handier with the fruit than whites, but undependable; a new kind of smudge pot was being developed; young fellows from Whittier College should not be allowed on the nighttime crews of fumigators: they were too eager, and one whiff of that cyanide . . .

A little further back toward home, in La Habra, while Father went in to gab with his colleague, we sat in the car, decorously watching the housewives walk along the one sidewalk in the village, so different from our own comparative metropolis of almost five thousand people. Boys did tricks for us on their bicycles right on the main street, soft with dust. That would never have been permitted in Whittier, where Greenleaf and Philadelphia crossed to form the hub of business, traffic, *life*.

On the way home, toward the slanting sun, the orange trees looked taller, darker. As we turned up Painter, fine magnolias and sycamores and deodars that the first Quakers had planted sent great shadows across our street. It had been a nice jaunt, as always, in the lightly perfumed air. We were innocents, unaware of all the words that would someday change our minds. *Smog, pollution, effluence, ecology* itself were still part of an unsuspected semantics. We felt fine and hungry.

—1957

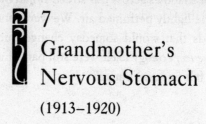

7
Grandmother's Nervous Stomach

(1913–1920)

One of the fine feelings in this world is to have a long-held theory confirmed. It adds a smug glow to life in general.

When I was about five, I began to suspect that eating something good with good people is highly important. By the time I was ten I not only knew, for myself, that this theory was right but I had added to it the companion idea that if children are given a chance to practice it, they will stand an even better chance of being keen adults.

In my own case I was propelled somewhat precociously, perhaps, into such theorizing by what was always referred to in the family as Grandmother's Nervous Stomach, an ultimately fortunate condition that forced her to force us to eat tasteless white overcooked things like rice and steamed soda crackers in milk.

Now and then either Grandmother's stomach or her conscience drove her to a religious convention safely removed from us, and during her pious absences we indulged in a voluptuous riot of things like marshmallows in hot chocolate, thin pastry under the Tuesday hash, rare roast beef on Sunday instead of boiled hen. Mother ate all she wanted of cream of fresh mushroom soup; Father served a local wine, red-ink he called it, with the steak; we ate grilled sweetbreads and skewered kidneys with a daring dash of sherry on them. Best of all, we talked, laughed, sang, kissed, and in general exposed ourselves to a great many sensations forbidden when the matriarchal stomach rumbled among us. And I formed my own firm opinions of where gastronomy should and indeed must operate in any happy person's pattern.

A great many seemingly unrelated things can be blamed on a nervous stomach, as ladies of the middle and late years of Queen Victoria's reign well knew.

Here I am, for instance, at least ninety-five years after my maternal grandmother first abandoned herself to the relatively voluptuous fastings and lavages of a treatment for the fashionable disorder, blaming or crediting it for the fact that I have written several books about gastronomy, a subject that my ancestor would have saluted, if at all, with a refined but deep down belch of gastric protest. That I have gone further and dared link the pleasures of the table with our other basic hungers for love and shelter would outrage far more than the air around her, to be sure: kisses and comfort were suspect to such a pillar as she. They were part and parcel of the pagan connotations of "a cold bottle and a warm bird" or vice versa—wanton and therefore nonexistent.

The Nervous Stomach was to Grandmother and to her "sisters" in the art of being loyal wives and mothers of plump beardy men a heaven-sent escape.

The pattern was one they followed like the resolute ladies they were: a period of dogged reproduction, eight or twelve and occasionally sixteen offspring, so that at least half would survive the nineteenth-century hazards of colics and congestions; a period of complete instead of partial devotion to the church, usually represented in the Indian Territory where my grandmother lived by a series of gawky earnest missionaries who plainly needed fattening; and at last the blissful flight from all these domestic and extra-curricular demands into the sterile muted corridors of a spa. It did not matter if the place reeked discreetly of sulphur from the baths and singed bran from the diet trays: it was a haven and a reward.

In my own grandam's gradual but sure ascent to the throne of marital freedom, she bore nine children and raised several of her sisters', loaned from the comparative sophistication of Pittsburgh for a rough winter or two in what was to be Iowa. It is not reported by any of the native or transplanted youngsters that she gave them love, but she did her duty by them and saw that the Swedish and Irish cooks fed them well and that they fell on their knees at the right moments. She raised a good half of them to prosperous if somewhat precarious maturity.

As the children left the nest, she leaned more and more in one direction as her dutiful husband leaned in another, toward long rapt sessions with the Lord. Fortunately for the social life of a village such as she reigned in, His disciples were hungry, young, and at times even attractive, on their ways to China or Mbano-Mbang.

In a Christian way things hummed during the protracted visits of these earnest boys, and everyone lived high, even my grandfather who took to retreating more and more lengthily into his library with a bottle of port and a bowl of hickory nuts.

As inevitably as in the life cycle of a female mosquito, however, my grandmother passed through the stage of replenishing the vessels of the Lord, as she had already done through ministering to the carnal demands of her mate, and she turned to the care of her own spirit, as represented by her worn but still extremely vital body. She developed protective symptoms, as almost all women of her age and station did.

There were hushed conferences, and children were summoned from distant schools and colleges for a last faint word from her. She went on a "tour" with her husband to Ireland and the Lake Country, but for some reason it seemed to do him more good than it did her, and while he pranced off the ship in New York wearing a new Inverness cape, she left it retching and tottery.

At last she achieved what she had spent almost a lifetime practicing for, and she was sent *alone,* with no man or child to question her, to some great health resort like Battle Creek.

There the delicious routine laved her in its warm if sometimes nauseous security. Duties both connubial and maternal were shadows in her farthest heart, and even her morning prayers could be postponed if a nurse stood waiting with a bowl of strained rice water or a lavage tube.

One difference from our present substitute for this escape, the psychiatrist's low couch, is that today's refugees face few gastronomical challenges, unless perhaps the modish low-sodium-low-cholesterol diet can be counted as such. My grandmother found many such challenges in her years of flitting with her own spare crampish pleasure from one spa to another. Certainly what she could and would and did eat played a vigorous part in my own life, and most probably provided an excuse for my deciding to prove a few theories about the pleasures of the table in relation to certain other necessary functional expressions.

Grandmother did not believe in any form of seasoning, and in a period when all food was boiled for hours, whatever it was boiled in was thrown out as being either too rich (meats) or trashy (vegetables). We ate turnips and potatoes a lot, since Grandmother had lived in Iowa long before it became a state. We seldom ate cabbage: it did not agree with her, and small wonder, since it was always cooked according to her mid-Victorian recipes and would have made an elephant heave and hiccup. We ate carrots, always in a "white sauce" in little dishes by our plates, and as soon as my grandmother died I headed for the raw ones and chewed at them after school and even in the dark of night while I was growing. But the flatter a thing tasted, the better it was for you, Grandmother believed. And the better it was for you, she believed, the more you should suffer to eat it, thus proving your innate worth as a Christian, a martyr to the flesh but a courageous one.

All Christians were perforce martyrs to her, and therefore courageous, and therefore all good Christians who had been no matter how indirectly the result of Grandmother's union with Grandfather had to eat the way she learned to eat at such temples as Battle Creek.

They could eat her way, that is, or die. Several did die, and a few more simply resigned from the family, the way one does from a club, after the cook had served Grandmother's own version of white sauce once too often.

By the time she came to live with us—a custom most aging ladies followed then after their quiet withdrawn husbands, helped by gout and loneliness, had withdrawn quietly and completely— my sister and I had already been corrupted by the insidious experience of good cooking. Thanks to an occasional and very accidental stay in our big crowded house of a cook who actually cared whether the pastry was light or not, we had discovered the caloric pleasures of desserts. And thanks to an open house and heart to the south of us, where we could stay for dinner now and then while Mother was "resting," we had found that not all salad dressing need be "boiled" and not all fried things need be anathema. The mayonnaise: it was a dream, not a pallid loose something made of flour and oil and eggy water. The pineapple fritters dusted with white sugar: they were dreams, too, tiny hot sweet clouds snatched at by healthy children.

We soon learned, however, that to Grandmother's way of thinking, any nod to the flesh was a denial of her Christian duty, even to the point of putting a little butter on a soft-boiled egg, but although her own spirits as well as her guts may have benefited from the innocuous regime, ours did not.

Fortunately at least one of my grandmother's phases of development impinged upon another, so that when she felt herself hemmed in by ancestral demands, she would at one and the same time, in her late years, develop an extraordinary belch and discover that a conference was being held in a town at least thirty miles away, one in which there was a preponderance of well-heeled as well as devout dyspeptics. She would be gone a week or so, to anywhere from nearby Oceanside to a legendary religious beachhead somewhat south of Atlantic City. She picked conventions where she could drink a glass of lukewarm seawater morning and night for her innards, and it made slight difference to her whether the water was of Pacific or Atlantic vintage. It can never be known how coincidental were these secular accidents, but they were twice blessed for her and at least thrice for the rest of us: she could escape from children and grandchildren into a comfortable austere hotel, and we . . .

We? Ah! What freedom! What quiet unembarrassed silences, except for the chewings and munchings of a hundred things Grandmother would not eat!

No more rice water, opaque and unseasoned, in the guise of soup. No more boiled dressing in the guise of mayonnaise. No more of whatever it was that was pale and tasteless enough to please that autocratic digestive system.

She would start off, laced into her most rigid best, her Jane pinned firmly under the white spout of her noted pompadour. We would wave and smile, and as the Maxwell disappeared down past the college, with Father tall and dustered at the wheel, we would edge avidly toward the kitchen.

Mother would laugh only a little ashamedly, and then we'd make something like divinity fudge, a delicious memory from her boarding school days. Or if it was the cook's day off my sister would set the table crazily—ah, *la vie bohème*—with cut out magazine covers scattered over the cloth to make it crazier, and I would stand on a footstool to reach the gas burners and create.

Of course there were accidents, too revolting to detail here. But it was fine to feel the gaiety in our family, a kind of mischievous mirth, and at the same time all of us, even the small ones, sensed a real sadness that we could not share it with the short, stiff, dutiful old woman, eructating righteously over a dish of boiled carrots in a vegetarian cafeteria near her churchful of "sisters" and even "brothers."

It was magic always then to see the change in Father's and Mother's behavior at the table when Grandmother was gone. They were relaxed and easy, and they slumped in their chairs as the meal progressed. Mother would lean one elbow on the table and let her hand fall toward Father, and he would lean back in his chair and smile. And if by chance my sister or I said something, they both listened to us. In other words, we were a happy family, bathed in a rare warmth around the table.

It was then, I am sure, that I began to think of the spiritual communion of the act of peaceful eating—breaking bread. It is in every religion, including the unwritten ones of the animals, and in more ways than one, all of them basically solemn and ritual, it signifies much more than the mere nourishment of the body. When this act is most healthy, most healing to the soul, it obeys some of the basic laws: enemies do not break bread and eat salt together; one communes with others in *peace*.

And so we did, now and then when I was young. We met as if drawn together for a necessary communion as a family. The fact that we were refugees from the dietary strictures as well as the gastric rumblings of a spoiled stern matriarch added a feeling of adventure and amusement to those stolen little parties. We sipped and we dawdled, and I can still remember that occasionally we would *all* put our elbows on the table after dinner and Mother would sing, or she and Father would leave and let us stay on to indulge in the ultimate delight, in our pre-teen years, of putting a cupcake into our dessert bowls and covering it with sugar and cream. What ease, what peace, what voluptuous relaxation!

At home without Grandmother, we gobbled and laughed, and more and more I began to wonder about the meaning of happiness and why and how it seemed to be connected with the open enjoyment of even a badly prepared dish that could be tasted without censure of the tasting.

I was puzzled, of course, for I could not see why anything that made all of us so gay and contented could be forbidden by God. I did not know then, nor do I care to recognize now, the connection between self-appointed moral judging and the personal hair shirt of physical subjection, as my grandmother must have known it when she had to bear one more child and yet one more child because it was her Christian duty.

Now that I am much older, probably as old as she was when she first began to escape from her female lot by feeling dreadful pains throughout her Nervous Stomach, I can understand more of the why, but I still regret it. We escape differently now, of course, and today Grandmother would consult a couple of specialists, and perhaps stretch out on an analyst's couch, and then become a dynamic real estate broker or an airline executive or perhaps even a powerful churchwoman, which she was anyway. But she would have more fun doing it, of that I feel sure.

Of course, there was a slight element of sin, or at least of guilt, in the delightful meals we indulged in when Grandmother was not there, and as always, that added a little fillip to our enjoyment. I suppose my parents felt somewhat guilty to be doing things that Grandmother frowned on, like drinking wine or saying openly, "This is delicious!" My sister and I had not yet reached the age of remorse: we simply leaned back and sighed with bliss, like little fat kittens, unconscious of betrayal.

I think that I have been unfair to my grandmother. I realize now that what I've written about her has made many people think of her as hard and severe. She was neither. She was never a stranger in our house, and she taught me how to read and write, and I accepted her presence in my life as if she were a great protective tree. This went on until she died when I was twelve years old. I felt no sorrow for her leaving, but I missed her, and all my life I have felt some of her self-discipline and strength when I needed it.

Increasingly I saw, felt, understood the importance, especially between people who love and trust one another, of a full sharing of one of our three main hungers, which are for food, for love, and for shelter. We must satisfy them in order to survive as creatures. It is our duty, having been created.

So why not, I asked myself at what may have been a somewhat early age, why not *enjoy* it all? Since we must eat to live, why not make the best of it and see that it is a pleasure, something more than a mere routine necessity like breathing?

And if Grandmother had not been the small stout autocrat, forbidding the use of alcohol, spices, fats, tobacco, and the five senses in our household, I might never have discovered that I myself could detail their uses to my own delight. If my grand-mother had not been blessed with her Nervous Stomach, I might never have realized that breaking bread together can be nourishing to more than the body, that people who can sit down together in peace and harmony will rise from the meal with renewed strength for the struggle to survive. My grandmother, who was stern and cold and disapproving of all earthly pleasure, because that was the way she had been raised to think a Christian and a lady should be, would never understand how she taught me otherwise. I revolted against her interpretations of the way to live a good life, but I honestly believe that I have come to understand as much as she of the will of God, perhaps, as Saint Teresa said, "among the pots and pipkins."

And like my grandmother, I am apparently touched with the missionary zeal, the need to "spread the word"! At least, I *suppose* that is why I began to write books about one of our three basic hungers, to please and amuse and titillate people I liked, rather as I used to invent new dishes to amuse my family. I had a feeling it might make life gayer and more fun. A Nervous Stomach can be a fine thing in a family tree, in its own way and at least twice re-moved.

—1971

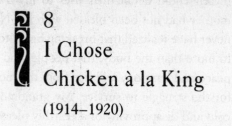

8
I Chose
Chicken à la King
(1914–1920)

Everyone, no matter how much he likes the life he is leading, has an escape hatch. Often he is unaware of it as such. More often he recognizes it, or even invents it, to save his inner balance, commonly called his reason.

My parents, living in a pattern circumscribed and dictated by their backgrounds and their ambitions, occasionally fled Whittier in a vaguely nervous way, as if a dog were nipping at their heels. Inside the invisible walls of our good Quaker compound, there was of course no alcohol, just as there was no riotous living. People who believed in "plain living and high thinking" ate simple food in their own quiet homes, and two or three dismal cafés took care of transients, except for respectable drummers who could put up at—and with—the Pickering Hotel. My father had to stay there when he was dickering for the *News*. It was grim, I understand, at least in its provender. It was not a place where a man would want to take his lady for a gastronomical frolic.

So Rex and Edith Kennedy would take off in the Ford now and then for "dinner in town." That meant Marcel's, I think, and the Victor Hugo, and a couple of other places either downtown in Los Angeles or on the sportier outskirts. Occasionally Mother brought us back a tissue paper hat or a rolled whistle that would shoot out when blown, with a pink feather at the end perhaps. We would discuss the menu at length, slowly and sensually. By the time I was six, I knew several names of procurable California wines, and I can remember Cresta Blanca for its beautiful sound, although I have never tasted this brand. (Only a few years ago, when we dug out part of the abandoned cellar of the house I now live in, a half-bottle with the Cresta Blanca label on it rolled to the top of the rubble, and I brushed it off respectfully and then gave it to a collection of local artifacts.)

When my parents went to the Scarlet Dens then available and pleasing to them, they ate and drank as they could not do at home—things like mushrooms under glass bells and sometimes two wines, matter-of-factly, not the one bottle sipped occasionally for a family festival. A white wine and then a red! It sounded almost too beautiful, as did the way things were served by the waiters to each person, instead of being put in front of Father and then carried around by Bertha or Margaret or whoever was holding down the kitchen at the moment. Through my mother's long happy descriptions of her rare sorties, I grew to feel almost familiar with *la vie mondaine* as she lived it, and when the time came for me to visit my first restaurant, I was ready.

I was about six, I think. The D'Oyly Carte troupe was playing at the Mason Opera House. I am sure there was a lot of planning done, with overt disapproval from Grandmother for such extravagant tomfoolery, unfitting to our years, and it was decided that Mother and Anne and I would take the Electric to Los Angeles,

have lunch at the Victor Hugo, and then go to the matinée of
H.M.S. Pinafore and take the Electric home.

It is a wonder that I did not break my string like a balloon
and float off before the day, so excited was I. I am glad I did not,
for the restaurant was exactly as I had known it would be: white
tablecloths gleamed more brightly than ever at home, and the
silver twinkled more opulently, if without our Irish hallmark, and
on each little table in the hushed room were several roses in a tall
vase that made my little sister and me look up at them somewhat
as we did to the star on the Christmas trees that had so far dignified our only debauchery. And kind waiters pulled out our chairs,
which had already been discreetly heightened for us, although I do
not know how: perhaps a couple of middle-sized baking pans
covered with towels? Napkins were whisked open in the air, like
stiff clouds, and then laid across our especially scrubbed knees.
Mother was given a menu.

It was then that I tried my first deliberate step into the sea of
public gastronomy. I asked firmly a question I had been practicing
for a couple of days. It was based on everything I had learned from
Mother's recountings of her flights from the family board. I said,
"May we eat chicken à la king?"

It is quite possible that this caused a little ripple of interest if
not hilarity among the staff, but all I remember is that we seemed
to have a covey of black-coated men bending attentively over us
for the next two hours, cutting all kinds of capers with the enormous silver chafing dish, the large glittering spoons, the general air
of excited well-being. Mother probably sat back happily and
watched the game. I took double enjoyment from seeing and
tasting a dish she had often described to me as one of her
favorite things in the whole world (I doubt this . . .). Anne very
probably started, that noontime, her lifelong inability to do more
than nibble at food in public places: forever she would ask

for something special and then seem to sneer at it or push it away, so that it became family legend that her eyes were bigger than her stomach, or something like that. As I recall it now, I ate heartily, observed everything, and had enormous fun. The flame burning under the dish interested me. The hot plates interested me, and the simple but subtle flavors. The waiters interested me.

When we had to leave, after some kind of dessert I cannot remember, my sister folded her napkin with unusual nicety and then asked the headwaiter, "Do these poor men have to wash all those dishes? May we help?" We swept out on this tag line, and as always, she had timed it perfectly to win every heart.

The rest of the day went well. I still remember Buttercup, who was indeed very plump and jolly. The best part was during the intermission, when Mother let me stand up on my seat to watch some of the audience go outside, and a tall Hindu wearing a large pale turban and a silky beard walked past our row. *"Jesus,"* I cried out excitedly to my parent and the rest of the theater. "Look! It's Jesus, all right!" This should have pleased my grandmother: one Christian impulse in an otherwise pagan fiesta. I am not sure that it did. My thoughts dwelt on other possibilities. I had tasted "sin and iniquity," and I wondered with impatience when I would next be able to eat chicken à la king with a flame under it, and perhaps someday much later order one or two wines to twinkle and shine on the impeccable linen of a Scarlet Den.

As far as I can remember, we kept our orgies well removed from Whittier during my childhood and forever beyond it. Except for almost secret temples like the Elks Club and the Parish House for seasonal routs, and our own home for quiet little gastronomical celebrations when Grandmother was away and we could indulge in such foreign stuff as French dressing, there seemed nowhere to go in the town.

And Prohibition cut heavily through the lists of good places farther afield.

As local editor, Father was wise enough not to be seen drinking in some of the dimly lighted ex-French restaurants in the region, although he continued to leave the sherry and port decanters on the sideboard and buy pinch-bottle Scotch from runners stationed off San Pedro. Marcel's was hard hit, and I think it closed, after a shady decline as an "inn," which in those drab days was synonymous with "roadhouse" and therefore with "speakeasy." A place I never went to until I was in my forties, the Goodfellows Grotto, managed somehow to stay open and relatively unshattered, thanks largely to its loyal newspapermen and lawyers. The Victor Hugo, which I believe used to be down on Spring Street, moved uptown to Olive between Fifth and Sixth or something like that, and in a mysterious and obviously well-backed way it stayed elegant throughout the dismaying cultural crisis brought on the nation by doughty ladies like my grandmother, who had fled alcoholic Northern Ireland only to land in the sodden Saturday nights of the midwestern prairie villages.

The "new" Victor Hugo was upstairs—shades of the Elks Club! The carpeting was soft and thick. Of course the linen and the mock silver gleamed and twinkled. The waiters, some of whom remembered us, or at least my little sister and her ladylike concern for them, seemed to scud along on invisible roller skates to whisk things before our noses. There was, within my memory, a lengthy prix fixe dinner that began God knows how but ended with a Nesselrode pudding, and my mother would always say faintly, "Oh, no," as I firmly settled for it, while she and Rex sipped cognac from their demitasses, in proper Prohibition style.

Once when we ate something under glass bells, one bell sealed itself hermetically to the plate, under which braised sweetbreads slowly died in their artful sauce, and the waiters puffed and groaned, and finally my father suggested that we continue with our meal and that a double-grilled lamb chop be brought to him, *rare.* Another time I went to luncheon with a contingent from home. I do not remember any of them, because Miss Hope was there, and in my heart and eyes she was the most beautiful fairy princess of them all, a tall slender woman with a soft rich voice and enormous eyes, perhaps gray.

The noon buffet of salads and hot things over flames was always exciting to me, but that day I ate shrimps in honor of my lady.

We never ate shrimps at home. Most probably it had not occurred to Mother to see if she could even buy any. In Iowa they were undoubtedly alive in the good fishing streams, but if anyone ate them it was the Indians. (Only a few hours ago, when Mr. Villa the fish man blew his horn along the street for us St. Helena ladies, I got some tiny defrosted bay shrimp from him for a Solari salad, and the elderly neighbor from across the street watched me with strange coyness and then squealed a little as she said, "Oo, I've always wondered about those things! Of course, I'm from Wisconsin." I told her they were delicious but that of course she had millions of them in the streams at home, the freshwater kind. She looked as shocked as if I had proposed eating a slice of her grandmother, and said, "Oh, we never eat anything but trout from our brooks in Wisconsin." Mr. Villa and I smiled invisibly at each other.) I had never, heretofore, put a succulent shrimp in my mouth, fresh or tinned. They looked in a distant way rather like curled snails, and I did not like anything that slid silently along, in water or on dry land. But Miss Hope was there, and in a gesture of which I am sure she was quite unconscious, I served myself generously from the great pile of them in the silver bowl, let the waiter help me add mayonnaise, and walked to our table in front of the tall open French window.

Below us the gentle sound of Los Angeles traffic circa 1920 purred past. Somewhere nearby Miss Hope sat, speaking melodiously to the other older people at our table, her great eyes haunted and her long nose twitching in a way that later seemed quite familiar to me when I fell in love aesthetically with Virginia Woolf. The first shrimp was a test of courage and honor for me, because of my conditional aversion to its general shape, but once I tackled it my whole life changed, and I knew that I would never feel anything but pure enjoyment again on contemplating in any and all forms the subtle water beast, the scavenger. No ugly tale could turn me from enjoying it, nor ever has.

I like to think that Miss Hope missed sipping a glass of good white wine with her lunch that magical day. I know that she was used to a less austere life than we all led in those strange times of the national disrepute of an age-old panacea. In Whittier I am sure she drank an occasional glass of wine with her family, the Lewises, when they all lived in our old house on Painter, and I know they drank a little sherry or whiskey at the Ranch. But that day in the twinkling sunlight at the Victor Hugo, when I really broke through a possible dietetic prejudice in order to prove my love, should have been graced with an important vintage. And perhaps it was.

—1971

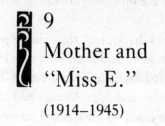

9
Mother and "Miss E."
(1914–1945)

Edith, my mother, really understood dried-up hometown librarians better than anyone I know. She had a pet one always on hand when we were in Whittier and was in cahoots with her about things like my bringing home eight books once, when I was perhaps six, from the children's basement in the public library. The young (but already dried-up) librarian, of course, called Mother and told her that I had lied through my teeth, since I knew that only two books were allowed to be taken out at night by children. Mother was properly chilly and embarrassed.

Then the young dried-up librarian said she wondered how old Mrs. Holbrook was getting along. My mother replied that her mother was doing very well indeed and had not been ill for some thirty years, and then it came out that I had told the librarian my poor old Irish grandmother was on her deathbed and that she needed me to read to her . . . all night long, every night. Of course, this blatant fantasy was nipped in the bud, and from then on I was allowed to take only four books out at night, instead of the usual two.

As I look back on it, the episode proved Edith's power over the whole system, and I am glad that I was to benefit from it all my life, or at least until after she died. It was then that I realized *why* (and *when* and *how*) Mother had always been, in her bizarre treatment of dried-up librarians. I learned at last that Miss E., who for some twenty years had been the object of our extreme disaffection as well as mockery, had loved Mother dearly and loyally. This was partly because once a year, at Christmas, Edith always sent her a flamboyantly sexy and extravagant nightgown.

Of course, as we matured, we knew of these strange gifts, and Mother herself even discussed them and now and then showed us her yearly purchases with what was almost a titter from her and a universal snicker from us, her children. She'd spread out the beautiful gauzy flimsy whimsies over her bed, and we would make cruel, stupid, and often funny remarks about them, and about the person whose skinny old body they would soon hang on.

Of course, we envied Miss E., or her temporary equivalents, for we were young and spoiled and at times even given to moments of beauty, and Mother never bothered to shower us, her offspring, with any such extravagant dainties. This was a yearly custom, one of many in our household, but one we all puzzled over with obviously latent jealousy. We were convinced that Miss E. never really knew what to do with these exotic offerings.

Then, after Edith died, the dried-up librarian wrote to me from her desert "retirement home" such loving and even adoring letters as I hoped never to see again. They were amazing to me, and I knew that Edith had been right and that she had not bought the servitude of the strange remote disagreeable "old maids" for all those years in Whittier but that she had instead understood and appreciated something that was beyond our own caring or understanding.

To us, the children, Miss E. was a kind of ridiculous public dictator of our tastes and needs. We hated her for refusing ever to give us anything from the Closed Shelves, even when Mother would telephone to request that these sacrosanct supplies of local pornography and filth be opened to us. Miss E. stayed adamant, even in the face of Mother's yearly Christmas sensuality; she refused to heed the doctors, the local priests, and the pastors when they suggested that some troubled soul might find in her library a book that would instruct them better than their professional ethics could.

Once, when I came home from boarding school in a real puzzlement about the lesbian pleasures that were suddenly too much for me to understand and Mother asked Miss E. to let me take some books from the Closed Shelves, there was a firm *no!* Briberies, Christmas or otherwise, apparently meant nothing to this strange arbiter of our local morals. Mother ordered copies of most of Freud, Jung, Adler, and Krafft-Ebing, carefully and through "our" doctor Horace Wilson, and after she and I read them, she presented them to the library, as she had almost all the other good-dirty-sad books that were on the Closed Shelves there.

I remember that while we were waiting for the currently undesirable psychological exposés to arrive, Mother saw to it that I read *The Well of Loneliness* by Radcliffe Hall before she presented it to the Closed Shelves. Miss E. never acknowledged the presence of any of these books, just as she never thanked Mother with anything but a short impersonal note at Christmastime for her sexy nightwear.

Edith was Miss E.'s despair in many ways. She asked for and got any book that she did not care to invest in herself, and her deplorable taste in detective stories was locally known by anyone who visited the library, since Miss E. religiously let her read them first, before they went on the public shelves. Thanks to Mother's cryptic and avid habits, we had complete runs of every English writer of mysteries, from Agatha Christie on up and down, and our collections of Dorothy Sayers and her ilk were the best and the newest always, in California or even in America. Of course, our own shelves were always full of new books as well as old ones, but Mother was not about to invest in everyday literature when Miss E. was so amenable to her suggestions, and I feel sure that the Whittier Public Library circulated more current British and even American fiction than any other small Carnegie in the country.

Of course, Mother loved anything *English,* but her taste was good. We read *The Forsyte Saga,* but we also knew all about Vanessa Bell and the Bloomsbury gang almost as soon as they did themselves, and Leonard Woolf and his wife were as familiar to us as were the Churchills and even their American counterparts, the Roosevelts of both Republican and Democratic leanings. The Hogarth Press worked hard to provide us with Anglophilic trash as well as the "good" stuff. We read *The Spectator,* along with the *Times* and the lesser London kitsch, and all the American periodicals that were then in the mails.

This last important part of our literary upbringing was due less to Edith than to my father Rex, who subscribed to every periodical in print in America, whether or not it was free to him. He himself read probably ten magazines a week, and we all had a running undeclared war with him about remembering the plots of each continued story in every one of them. We prided ourselves on never reading the weekly résumés, and it was a game that was played with great success for more years than I can now remember.

Father, of course, read the magazines first, but as soon as he laid down an issue, it would be snatched up by one of us children and read as fast as possible.

Colliers and *The Saturday Evening Post* had perhaps the best serials, but there were also real dillies in magazines like *The Ladies' Home Journal* and *The Woman's Home Companion* and *Redbook* and *Cosmopolitan*. And then of course there was *The American Boy*. And Grandmother Holbrook saw to it that we always got—and *read*—*The Youth's Companion*.

And then there were all the magazines like *Motion Picture,* and there was something about automobiles always, and there were several farm journals and then house organs of clubs and organizations: Elks, 4-H'ers, and later Rotarians and Lions and the Kiwanis Club, and *The Iowa Morticians' Quarterly.* And then there were the literary digests—*The Atlantic Monthly* and *Scribner's,* wonderful things by Aldous Huxley about LSD or mescal buttons, and a long story by Scott Fitzgerald once, and always Upton Sinclair somewhere around—and Bernard McFadden's several different monthlies, all about diet and physical culture and how to conceive boy babies instead of girls, and so on. And there was *The Masses,* which I read hungrily when I was thirteen or so.

And all the time, as a kind of background to Mother's Anglomania and Father's Chicago-to-Whittier newspaper life, there were the reminders of Miss E.'s disapproval of our concerted and wildeyed literary spree, which continued uninterrupted from about my fourth year in Whittier to the final bulldozing of the Ranch house when I was nearing fifty. By now I think of Miss E. as a sort of goddess, unwitting certainly and willy-nilly, floating austerely above our unconscious heads, wearing a very sexy nightgown over her presumably chaste body. She's rather like the airborne fellow who plays the fiddle in many of Marc Chagall's pictures: omnipresent and unexplained. She's much clearer now than when she was trying so desperately to curb our hungers and to keep them under proper local control.

In actuality, she was a tall, thin woman with faded colorless hair and skin, and she dressed properly in clothes that would fit her position as head librarian, which is to say in a way that made her almost invisible. At least, that is how I remember her in the name of my grandmother and my parents and my siblings. But by now, and in my mind anyway, and from her letters to me when my mother died, she has turned into a really loving woman, gracious and adoring, dressed always in those sheer, alluring, glamorous, and completely unfitting nightgowns that my mother gave her for so many years, in spite of our derisive mockery. And I wonder who actually got the most pleasure from them. Certainly my mother did not need to buy her way through the Closed Shelves, any more than Miss E. needed to be so unfailingly severe and disapproving.

—1988

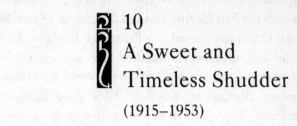

10
A Sweet and
Timeless Shudder
(1915–1953)

This is a footnote on either the general study of gastronomical atavism or on the disappearing profession of candy selling in
front of movie houses and theaters. As far as I know, the old white-
dressed men with trays of nougat and suchlike hung over their
shoulders are gone, at least from downtown Los Angeles. But I
know, too, that when I watched my two girls on the Quai des
Belges in the old port of Marseille eat some of the same powdery
candy that I first ate from one of those trays, it put me back to
when I was six or seven.

The memory came to me as I was doling out some incredibly
sticky powdery little slabs of what is called something-or-other
Loukhoum in Marseille and what was called Turkish Delight in
Los Angeles in 1915 and may still be: my two children shuddered
and puffed with pleasure over its inimitable sweetness. Ah, they
sighed, blowing out little gusts of powder. Oh, how good.

And poignantly I remembered doing that so long ago, when

my mother got three press passes and boarded my sister Anne and me onto the Red Electric into Los Angeles on a Saturday afternoon to the Orpheum Theatre, on Broadway, I believe. All I can recall of the first of perhaps a hundred such performances in the next ten years are some trained white dogs and then the way the big numbers changed at each side of the stage for the next act of vaudeville. There was an orchestra. (Other times there was Nora Bayes, a music hall singer, loud and tricky, whom my father considered worth driving in for, in the Maxwell or the Hupmobile or whatever he was driving or could borrow, when she played within driving distance.)

Inside the Orpheum, all was pulsating excitement and the throb of drums to such young ears as ours, so uncalloused by the artful assaults of radio and TV. Outside, there was the still-timid tinny sound of what was beginning to be called traffic. A great many rich easterners were flocking to neighboring towns such as Pasadena, and while the electrics driven by their wives never got as far into Los Angeles as the Orpheum, the gentlemen and even their offspring occasionally ventured there in high black-and-tan motorcars with basketwork on the outside of the doors and American Beauty roses nodding in crystal bud vases inside.

There were, of course, a few grim-jawed Bohemians like my father who got their wives into veils and dusters and their children under wraps and set out a good hour before curtain time in their open cabriolets, and on nights when they could get away without the kids they stopped usually at Marcel's for a good French dinner, wine included. All this giddy brouhaha of street sounds went on then, but the thing outside the Orpheum for my sister Anne and me was the candy man.

He was very dignified and withdrawn, with thick white eyebrows and a white mustache and small hands in thick white cotton gloves behind a kind of glass bulge over the tray on his stomach, a transparent screen that would seem normal to modern children accustomed to such things but to us was immeasurably mysterious, unaccustomed as we were to the fact that rubber and even glass could be made to curve that way and be seen through.

He had a little hammer, which he tapped remotely on pieces of marble, as white as his hair and hands. Our mother said it was nougat. This meant nothing to us, and I had to go to France years later to find out what nougat was—probably because many of Mother's teeth were not very strong at her age and she was afraid to buy a bag of it.

Then deeper on the tray, in a kind of mud or dust or embedment of confectioners' sugar, were oblong pieces of Turkish Delight. Ah, thank God my mother's teeth could handle that! She bought some the first day we ever went to the Orpheum.

We sat in a kind of trance with the orchestra of real-live people pounding on drums for the clown's pratfalls and sawing on violins for the love duet, and the clever little fluffy dogs, and perhaps even Nora Bayes, and as we watched we reached happily, blindly, for the candy, so that by the time we came out, still happy and even blinder, into the bright bald Los Angeles sunlight, we were covered from chin to hem and up both navy-blue serge arms with powdered sugar.

Mother flapped maternally at us as we staggered toward the Pacific Electric Depot, and we managed to get clear back to Whittier, some fourteen miles away, without feeling motion sick. It was a triumph of music over mind, perhaps, or the mystery of that old man with the transparent bubble on his belly and his little white hands inside it, doling out the powdery candy, the hard stuff and the insidious sweet Delight.

We often bought more from him, after that first day, and many years later I would go by and feel guilty about not stopping to see him, smaller but always white and dignified, beside the empty, dirty, near-deserted old theater. I could still taste the voluptuous stickiness of that candy, and then when my two girls shuddered happily at it on the Quai in Marseille, I was back in the Orpheum in Los Angeles, with its black velvet curtain covered with diamonds, the curtain that parted after the fire curtain with its wonderful paid advertisements was raised, while the men in the orchestra pit threw themselves wearily into the West Coast eleven-man version of Wagner's *Overture to Tannhäuser*. That curtain, that music, that two-hour dribble of powdered sugar! Is it a kind of atavism that made my children shudder the same way, so many years later, at the same gummy taste and texture of a candy? Or is it only my own memory that made me want to think they did?

—1957

11
The Old Woman
(1915–1916)

When I was halfway through the first grade, the private kindergarten that met every day in the Sunday school rooms of the Friends' Church went the way of most such ventures in a small and democratic town, and Anne came to Penn Street School.

I felt aged and responsible. For a while I held her little fat hand all the way from our house to the door of the girls' basement, which had been painted white and yellow and decorated with paper animals to make it look more like a kindergarten than a barren toilet.

As soon as she knew the way, she was impatient to be independent of my rather oppressive guardianship. But I made her walk close beside me when we crossed the two deserted streets between our house and school, and on the playground I sometimes quelled her into taking my hand.

There I liked to have the other girls see me leading her. I was the only one in the first grade who had a younger sister in Penn, and I felt that I should make the most of it.

How I should have hated to be my classmate Evelyn Wolf, who came every morning and afternoon in the tow of her big sister Emma, who was in the third grade! If Emma had been in the fourth, which was the highest in the school, there would have been something almost envious about being seen near her or even touching her, but in our minds the third was much less awesome. In the fourth you learned Long Division, whatever that was. Sometimes we heard the girls talking about it, and it sounded magical, like Aunt Gwen's songs from New Zealand.

But Emma Wolf was without much distinction, and poor Evelyn was uninteresting. Perhaps Evelyn felt the disgrace of being led around by such a plain thing.

I knew that Anne felt differently. She thought I was much older than an ordinary first-grader, if she thought at all. That was almost enough. And of course I had nice hair, not two little dust-covered twigs with dirty pink ribbons braided into them, like the Wolfs'.

I would make her hold my hand as long as I could. And I knew that if anything went wrong, she would take it instinctively. I almost hoped for trouble—not real trouble, but something that would be easy for me and hard for my sister.

On the way to school, I liked to walk past the house with the high fence around it, because sometimes a dog came bouncing toward us. He was small, and the fence was high. But his bark sounded vast, and Anne's hand always clutched mine desperately.

If I hadn't had her there to impress and show my bravery, I would have been half a block down the street before the end of the first bark, or perhaps I wouldn't even have walked on that side of the street at all.

With her there, though, I went slowly, holding her hand

firmly and sneering toward the furious little dog. It was a great moment, and one that seemed never to fail me.

Other things were less certain. There was a visiting dog, once, in a house farther up the street. He gave me a bad moment, which was all the more delicious for its first terror when I had made sure that he was on a chain.

And sometimes automobiles appeared unexpectedly far down the streets as we crossed them. Then I would seize Anne's hand and run madly for the opposite side of the curb, a full five minutes before it was necessary. But that happened rarely on the quiet streets of Whittier, so long ago.

By Eastertime my moments of lordly protection had narrowed down to the little dog, and even that was wearing away. I noticed that his most horrible barks had less and less effect on my sister. My power was slipping.

On the school grounds interest in the new little fat girl had died away, and it was more trouble than it was worth to make Anne take my hand and keep it to the door of the kindergarten room. And now the dog, too, was becoming almost friendly, and her fear of him less real.

It was then that I invented the Old Woman Without a Face.

She lived in a dark green house on the corner opposite the little dog's place, the one with the blinds always down. We had never noticed it before, Anne said. That was true, but only because I didn't want to scare her. Now, though, I must tell her: the Old Woman Without a Face lived in it!

She was a witch of the most terrible sort—no face, no children, no furniture. She lived on grass, which she crept out to pick at midnight, and on old shoes stolen at the same horrid hour from rag bins.

She was little, with long black hands.

But the worst part was her face, because it wasn't a face at all.

What was it? Just—a place. Yes, just a place where a face should be.

My poor little sister turned gray with fright and cowered beside me. I looked at the terrible blank green house. I, too, was scared. What if the Old Woman Without a Face should—Horror!

I grabbed Anne's clammy fingers and we ran for our lives, clear to Penn Street School and the welcoming busyness of the playground.

And for the rest of that year and even into part of the next one, I was the firm protectress of my sister Anne. We grew to know almost the whole history of the Old Woman, but I always stopped talking about her when I felt my flesh begin to crawl with terror. It took just a small dose to restore any of Anne's waning need for my presence.

The Old Woman was a dreadful creature, but when I wasn't near her dark green house, I almost liked her.

—1957

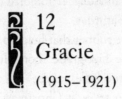

12
Gracie
(1915–1921)

I

It was a sunny day, with soft warm air in all the cracks. I could feel the softness and the warmth between the back of my neck and my hair where it hung in heavy pieces, and in my ears air seemed to move with a new freshness.

The windows of the schoolroom were open even during classes. Usually Miss Newby put them down at the end of recess or at most left them open three inches from the top, like the picture in the third-grade hygiene book. But today was different.

It was almost spring, Mother had said. If this weather kept up, Anne and I could change into cotton underwear!

Anne was so little she had forgotten the wonder of that annual shedding of woolen shirt and panties, but I remembered two times when I had taken them off before an afternoon bath and felt almost naked in the thin cotton things I had put on afterwards in place of them.

Today was Thursday. If tomorrow was like this, perhaps we could change on Saturday.

I snapped the rubber that held up my panties and looked out the windows. The first-grade room didn't have curtains. It was because we were too little, maybe. But we made flowers and birds and pointed green trees at Christmastime, and Miss Newby put them on the glass while we were home. Then in the morning we would see them as a surprise, sharp against the sharp clearness of the windowpanes and not at all as if they were meant to be there.

This month we had a row of red and yellow tulips springing starkly from the brown wood of the frames. It was pretty, I thought, when the windows were closed. But now it made me smile: paper tulips looked better close to the floor and not stretched tightly across the air up near the top of the room.

Gracie Meller, across the aisle from me, saw me peering at them and glanced up quickly, too.

She hoped to see something exciting. It was Gracie who always told us about accidents and houses that burned down and babies that fell into laundry tubs. She seemed to be everywhere just at the fatal moment and had a fine memory for details, especially ones of gore and shriekings and the crack of bones. But this time she saw nothing much.

She looked loweringly at me from under her thick black Mexican eyebrows. I watched her expectantly, my ludicrous tulips forgotten.

She moved her jaws deliberately, her eyes fixed on mine and daring me to look away. Then she slowly pursed her wide mouth into a tiny purple knot like the middle of a starfish.

It trembled. I watched it, without breathing. It seemed hours, but I knew Gracie would finish things somehow. It would be worth waiting for.

The purple knot settled into a firmer pucker. And suddenly a bright green worm shot out from the middle of that place. My mouth fell open. Back darted the worm. Gracie looked impassively at me, so I knew it wasn't over.

The next time the worm came out a little farther. It was clear and shining and not very long, and it seemed to have no head. I leaned closer to see it. It darted back, with a little pop as if it had closed the door after it. Gracie winked at me.

I sat motionless. I was glad my hair was getting long, because when I bent my head that way I couldn't see Miss Newby. And of course that made it impossible for her to see me.

I watched Gracie reach slowly into her desk. For another worm? Was it loose in there? I hoped not; it might fall into the aisle and be stepped on. That would be nasty, certainly.

Gracie worked at snail speed, as if she were opening a secret door. Her hand hardly moved, and I envied her skill but wished she would be less mysterious.

Miss Newby was writing at the big desk in the front of the room. I could hear her pen swerving steadily across the paper. There was no danger, but Gracie worked her fat brown hand into the desk with infinite caution. I began to feel very excited, like Jack in the sleeping giant's room.

The hand came slowly out of the desk, holding a small sack of gray paper with faint lines of blue and red on it.

The corner store! Gracie must have stolen some more money. Gracie was a bad girl, I thought. Mother had said so. But I liked her because she was so surprising and so courageously rude to people I had to be polite to.

She opened the sack neatly with one hand. The paper was soft and hardly made a sound. But Miss Newby stopped writing. I kept my head down, and Gracie's shiny black eyes shifted quickly from my face to her primer.

I felt a hideous need to giggle or sneeze or call out. But it would be a pity to miss the secret of the bright green worm. I thought as hard as I could about the paper bag still held lightly in Gracie's hot hand, and her purple mouth, and the way the worm had popped into the middle of it, so quickly I hadn't seen any of it before it was all there.

Muffled scratching started again at the big desk, and Gracie's eyes swung without expression from her book to me.

Her fingers began to work at the rolled top of the dingy bag. It opened finally, like a flower, and she tipped it slowly down into the sag of skirt between her legs. There was a small sliding noise.

Her hand put the bag delicately on one knee, and felt into the sagging gingham, and then came very deliberately out into the aisle and toward me.

Mine went as slowly toward it. They met, moistly. And I was left with something that I had expected to wiggle but that instead lay motionless in my folded palm. Of course it wasn't a worm; even Mexicans don't eat worms. I should have known.

It was small and duller than Gracie's, half-clear like the glycerin soap that company had once left in our bathroom, and it was shaped like a tiny cucumber pickle. On one side, that is. On the smooth side were raised letters spelling HEINZ.

I looked at Gracie. She stared at me as if I were a stranger and put a little pickle into her mouth. I did the same with mine.

First it tasted like sweat and dirt, the way my hands tasted before lunch on Saturdays when I'd been playing all morning. Then it tasted smooth. That was all. I could feel the letters on it and the cucumber lumps.

Now was the time to pop it out. I began to move my mouth around. But Gracie was frowning at me. She meant, Wait. I could see that she was sucking on hers. Oh, yes. That was to get the lumps off, so it would slide more easily. I sucked hard, until my cheeks went in between my teeth and my tongue got prickles on it.

The green cucumber was growing smaller, turning into a slick worm. I looked expectantly at Gracie. She sucked once or twice more, and then her mouth began that queer process of shriveling into a purple knot.

Mine felt less round somehow. I wished that I could see it. When I went home I'd practice in the bathroom mirror.

The purple knot began to tremble. Out shot the little worm. In it went, then out, then in again, without a sound.

Gracie looked impassively at me, waiting for my turn.

I sucked once more, nervously. My mouth felt loose and soft, not at all efficient. Gracie frowned slightly. Her worm made a flashing appearance. Now she looked impatient.

The room was silent as a cat. I made my mouth tight, felt the green worm slippery behind my lips—and shot it forth. It hit the primer of John B., The Teacher's Pet, three seats away, and then fell to his desk. I saw the wet marks on his book.

A loud slippery laugh, like a worm but not a green one, suddenly shot out of Gracie's mouth, and in the second before I looked at Miss Newby I saw that the sky was graying so that it would surely be cold on Saturday.

II

After the trouble about the worm and getting John B.'s book dirty, Gracie had to move her seat. She was scolded more than I, too, because she was the worst girl in the first grade and probably in the whole school, and I was so nice.

She cared much less than I did about all the talk and had already been sent out of the room for two other offenses.

Now she had a terrible cold. Ever since the day of the worm, rain had fallen and the wind had blown, and now Gracie coughed like an old and rattling steamroller.

She never stayed out of school, as the rest of us did when we had colds or stomachaches. We all rather enjoyed those too-transient ills. The next day other children would ask us what was the matter, and if we'd been really sick, our mothers would write notes to Miss Newby about letting us eat oranges at recess or making us wear sweaters.

But Gracie won even more attention by spending every day of the year at school. Her mother had too many other children around the house as it was, without any ailing ones.

And of course Gracie was never really sick, as far as we knew, not sick enough for bed and a thermometer as we had all been at least one thrilling time. She only had colds.

Once in a while she put her head on her desk, with great daring, and when Miss Newby asked her rather coldly if she felt tired, she would deny it with brave weariness on every curve of her mocking dark face. We felt that she was sophisticated.

And once she had thrown up on the floor. That was exciting but disagreeable. I felt sorry for the janitor.

Now, however, it was only a cold. But I had never heard one like it, nor have I since.

She was small and rather fat, with square shoulders and a round head covered with straight navy-blue hair with pink cloth woven into the braids, but when she coughed I felt as if she had changed into six baying hound dogs and a big brass horn being blown with rain in it, all at once.

There was something of cracking wood, too, like branches being torn away from a tree, or Father breaking sticks over his knee.

And there was something of the booming of high tide in the hollow cliffs near Woods Point in Laguna.

When Gracie coughed, everything in the room stopped. Miss Newby, if she was reading or talking to us, stopped. If we were singing or reciting or spelling in chorus, we stopped. We stopped even when we weren't doing anything.

Sometimes we looked at Gracie, but as we grew more accustomed to it, we looked away. She was not pretty. She struggled terribly. Her dark face turned darker, and her shiny eyes stuck out with the whites turning red with pressure. She shook.

For a week or two Miss Newby felt sorry for her. She was very nice to a girl who gave her so much trouble, a "bad girl." Everybody said so. She patted her on the back and let her go out for a drink. We'd hear Gracie whooping and booming down in the girls' basement, underneath our room. The sound came up hollow and like a threat of something.

Sometimes she would stay down there too long after she had stopped coughing, and Miss Newby would be ready to go for her, but always as she walked toward the door the noise would start again.

Yes, Miss Newby was very patient. But now we could see that the whole business was getting on her nerves. She jumped as if a door had banged when the cough started, and when it lasted too long she frowned—slightly but unmistakably. Finally she told Gracie that she wanted her to do something about it.

Next day Gracie coughed more than ever. Miss Newby began to look wrinkled and gray, like the time her mother died. She asked Gracie to bring some cough drops to school the next day or else to stay home until her cough was better.

But Gracie came, and her cough was like a truckload of empty oil cans on a bumpy road. Miss Newby pressed her hands to her temples. And then she opened her locked drawer and gave Gracie a nickel for some cough drops.

We all watched silently as Gracie clutched the money and walked toward the door. Going out like that in the middle of the morning was unheard of. We were tight with envy and interest.

She reached the door, turned to Miss Newby, coughed once loudly, and disappeared.

When she came back, at least half an hour later—although we all knew that she had only gone half a block from school to the corner store—she had two boxes of black candy, with two bearded men on the cover of each box. It was pretty good candy.

She gave one piece to me and one to Bertha Wolf, the girl who had fits, and ate the rest. But her cough grew worse.

About half a week later Miss Newby, gray as mold, gave her another nickel. Gracie winked slightly at me as she coughed her way out the door. This time there was only one box, but the candy was better, with a taste of mentholatum.

A week later Gracie was bowed over her desk, her face dark brown and swelling, her fists clenched.

Miss Newby walked to her. I wondered what kind of cough drops Bertha and I would eat at recess. But Miss Newby led her from the room. In a minute we heard a yell from the basement.

Gracie told us at recess that Miss Newby had painted her throat with iodine, but it had taken three teachers to hold her. And true, when she spat, it was a little brown. That was iodine, she said.

III

Gracie was a figure of romance.

For one thing, she was so dirty—not with bad dirt but simply with a different dirt from any I was used to. To see her and smell her made me feel ordinary. I felt ashamed of my dull self. She had a warm rich smell, like manure, while I never smelled anything but clean, except maybe on hot Saturdays before my bath.

But too close to Gracie the smell was less agreeable than manure; it was an odor that made me catch my breath. Now I recognize it as digested garlic, but then I just thought it was Gracie. And even that added to her fascination.

And of course she was brown. Everybody else I knew in the first grade, except Lucille and Alice Lunt, was white or pink, and from what Mother had said I knew that even Lucille and Alice would be like me if they didn't drink coffee. That seemed to tint them.

Gracie wasn't coffee-colored, though. She reminded me more of the living-room floor with fresh polish on it.

Then she had navy-blue hair like so many of the Indian Mexicans. That alone made her romantic.

We talked about her sometimes, although many of the girls were almost embarrassed to. Ardine and Eileen, who loved each other and whose fathers were a mayor and a professor, never said anything about Gracie but only about the girls who did talk of her and to her. They looked at me with some condescension but were nice to me because my father was editor of the town paper.

Jacqueline, the banker's daughter, hated me because I had told her I liked Gracie better than I liked her. She would have liked to be my best friend, but Gracie spoiled it. So she hated me and loved Hazel Montague instead.

Another thing about Gracie was that she was hard, not soft and yielding as we all were in varying degrees. In any of the accidents that happened during recess, the falls and bumps and slivers and skinned knees, I never saw Gracie shiver or squeal or turn faint. Only once did she cry, either, and I made her do that.

It is easy to make children cry, even the strong ones, by singing at them one of those diabolical songs that rise and fall on playgrounds, those songs usually two lines long, sung on two or three notes over and over.

Gracie Meller's name was too fortunate to let pass. Often the song about it would start, in recess or at noon, for no reason except that the children wanted to hop up and down in rhythm, their lungs open. It would grow softly, venomously, like fire in an old house, until the whole playground rocked:

> *Gra-cie Mel-ler*
> *Had-da fel-ler*
> *Gra-cie Mel-ler*
> *Had-da fel-ler—*

At first Gracie pretended not to hear. Her eyes grew watchful and her back straighter, but she seemed to hear nothing.

If it kept up, and it usually did, she ran to the squeakiest swing and pumped high into the air, her skirts flying shockingly above her round, half-naked buttocks.

Sometimes that worked. Gracie was the best girl in school for pumping up, and we watched her always with the horrified feeling that one day she would swing clear over the bar, like a circus performer. But more often the dreadful song rose with her into the air and into her ears with the rushing wind. And she would let the swing die down, her face set.

Still she never cried, as any of us would have done, until the day I made up the variation on our song.

Everybody knew that Mexicans liked red and yellow together, a color combination that froze us with exaggerated disgust. We had a song for it:

> *Red-and yel-ler*
> *Kiss-your fel-ler—*

So, I concluded logically, people who kissed their fellows, a process that was mysteriously vulgar to all of us, must thus be Mexicans.

And one day, when all the girls I knew were singing gently and insidiously in a nasty circle around Gracie, I whispered to Ardine and Eileen,

> *Red-and yel-ler*
> *Gra-cie Mel-ler*
> *Kissed-her fel-ler*
> *Red-and yel-ler*
> *Gra-cie Mel-ler—*

The little girls squealed with joy, and up rose my song like a pagan hymn, over and over.

Finally, Gracie's face, like stone usually, began to pucker and move. Her shiny eyes dropped. I felt terribly uncomfortable and wondered desperately if I was going to begin to cry in front of the other girls. But Gracie did instead.

She broke roughly through the circle of swaying, delighted children and ran toward the girls' basement. I could hear her sobbing angrily, with hard noises.

The girls stopped singing, and Jacqueline muttered something about a crybaby, and then they wandered away. They had already forgotten that I was the poet of the most delightful song of the week, of the year even, but I was miserable for a long time.

Another of the many reasons for Gracie's romance was her mother. Sometimes we would whisper together, four or five of us, about her. Gracie's mother was hard to see. Often we walked past the shack that held so many people (we knew Gracie had at least a dozen brothers and sisters), but we never saw her.

I would tell the little girls about the one time I had walked home with Gracie, and her mother had come to the window.

She was a woman black as a Negro and wide as five white women. Jacqueline, who hated me, asked if she was as wide as my mother, always having babies, too, and the girls gasped. I decided I hated Jacqueline too much to speak to her and went on talking. She was embarrassed.

Gracie's mother had worn her hair, which was black with blue places in it, in a braid, and the braid was in a flat knot on top of her head. The knot was as big as a pie.

Her ears hung down to her shoulders with gold in them, so Gracie must be rich. And her eyes were like Gracie's but no bigger than a parrot's.

She hadn't said a word, just leaned there in the window and looked at me. Gracie had run into the shack without telling me good-bye, either, and I had gone home full of regrets and wonderings about other families.

I did not yet see how any of them could be different from my own and still be called a family. It was hard to realize that my friends all had families when I knew that mine was the only one. There was something imitated about their families—like the paper tulips stuck row after row on the glass of the first-grade windows. I felt irritated at them all, and jealous.

It was some comfort, though, that none of them had a little fat sister named Anne. Gracie, of course, had several fatter ones, but they were less like sisters than round puppies, barking and nipping and rolling in the pressed-down dirt in front of their shack. They urinated against the side of the house like dogs, too.

And their noses ran. Gracie's did even more than theirs. I

thought perhaps it was because she was older—something to do with Mexicans.

The other girls at school had handkerchiefs, which they used with delicacy, like Ardine and Eileen, or with ostentation, like the slightly coarser Hazel Montague. But Gracie sniffed—occasionally.

She never combed her hair, the girls said, shaking their sleek bobbed heads. But I defended her. Every Friday, I reminded them, she came with new braids or at least with water plastering down the front of her cap of thick blue-blackness. Of course it got rather fuzzy in back, where she slept, but Japanese ladies did that, too.

The girls were silent with respect. I had told them a lie about Mother's having lived in Japan for countless years, so I was a recognized authority on things oriental.

But Gracie's hands! Ardine shuddered, and she and Eileen looked proudly at her long pallid fingers. We all knew that her mother took special care of them because Ardine was going to play the piano.

I liked Gracie's short dirty fingers much better. They had a certain pudgy strength in them, and they reminded me of Anne's —a gentle stillness, like the Kewpies' hands in *Good Housekeeping*.

Suddenly I felt very bored by all those little girls in their clean dresses and went off to look for Gracie. She had never said anything about the song I made up, and I knew that although she would not forget it, she still liked me.

She would be scratching faces on the walls of the girls' basement. Or maybe looking through the wire fence by the boys' drinking fountain. Both things were forbidden, and as I went to join her, I wanted to do them, too, yet I still couldn't help praying that Miss Newby would not see me from her window. I loved Gracie and I loved being a nice girl too.

IV

In the second grade and, as I remember, well into the third, we were swept by waves of being pictures.

Today little girls probably have attacks, singly and in groups, of being Shirley Temple, but when Ardine and Eileen and Jacqueline the banker's daughter and her less genteel shadow Hazel Montague and I were in the throes of such periods, we were all of us drawings by Jessie Wilcox Smith.

By that time we were seven or eight years old and not only able to read but capable of cutting out pictures by ourselves. We made scrapbooks of our heroines, "Galleries of Beauty," in which each picture represented our own selves in one guise or another.

We were those roundheaded children with pointed chins and rabbit eyes, those quaint peasant girls and princesses, those merry blank-faced moppets with unreal accoutrements and prissy rosebud mouths.

Fortunately for us, the magazines were well larded with Miss Smith's works, and at least once a month there was a cover by her, a mistily beautiful cover that told such a simple story that even our budding brains could invent elaborations on it.

If two children, the daughters surely of nobility, stood twined with apple blossoms and each other's arms on the cover of *Good Housekeeping,* they were Ardine and Eileen, no others.

Even Gracie Meller, who usually scorned our pictures as silly (Jacqueline whispered spitefully that it was because Gracie had no magazines anyway), even Gracie would look stonily at the picture and then with recognition at the two dainty smirking little white girls who loved each other.

Then she would laugh her strange jeering laugh and go off alone.

Ardine and Eileen, their faces flushed, looked pityingly after her—poor Gracie was *so* common. Their eyes met, understanding and passion burning gently in them. Each sighed rapturously, recognizing herself in the other's prettiness.

They walked off, an aura of apple blossoms and ancestral gems about them, their soft-colored dresses even more mistily lovely than those on the magazine cover.

Jacqueline and Hazel Montague and I were less easily identifiable; still, we managed to fit ourselves, at least to our own satisfaction, into most of the Smith pictures.

We were chubby peasant children sometimes, and I remember how patiently my mother allowed me to dribble milk all over myself, simply because the Smith peasants on the cover drank theirs from round bowls instead of cups.

Or we were especially misty dream children looking for magic birds. That was more difficult, since it was solely a matter of imagination, with not even the comforting prop of a milk bowl.

My little sister Anne was enviously recognized by my friends as the exact counterpart of all the Smith babies: she was round, charming, obviously childlike.

I was proud to have them envy her, but I was already beginning to know that Anne was far from the simple babe she looked. She was emerging in my mind as rather mysterious. I blandly let my friends use her as Jessie Wilcox Smith's silly infant in their pictures, but to myself I identified her firmly with any or all of Rose O'Neill's more uproarious Kewpies. I knew her better than the other girls did.

It was harder to place people like Emma and Evelyn Wolf. (Bertha, who had fits, was never, of course, depicted in Miss Smith's pretty pictures.) The Wolfs were nice children, so quiet, so clean, so unmistakably damned.

They would do anything we wanted, even Emma, who was in the fourth grade and should have had more dignity. It was always she, or our classmate Evelyn, who played the starved kitchen slave or the hungry beggar child or any such picture part that was not too glamorous.

(In the case of Sarah Crewe or a Little Match Girl, though, I always had first place. I seemed to have a feeling for starvation, for pressing my cold nose against the window separating me from the rich children's Christmas tree, that even a thin, cowed Evelyn Wolf could never imitate.)

Once both the Wolfs were in the same picture, to our intense jealousy. There they crouched, as real as life, two little pinched dreary figures with snow swirling around them. Even their funny twiglike braids of mousy hair were there.

We covered our envy as best we could: by teasing them. But it wasn't until Jacqueline started singing,

> *Holes* in your *shoes*
> *Holes* in your *shoes*
> *Holes* in your *shoes*

that they cried.

Soon after that the Wolfs' scrapbook began to be much better than ours. They had pictures we had only seen in books from the library, sometimes duplicated even, which we eagerly bargained for.

The two little girls fairly blossomed in the warmth of our attention: they looked almost happy. Finally they whispered that Gracie Meller had given them all the pictures, and please not to tell.

(Of course someone did, but it was not until three years later, when we had all left Penn Street School, that the city library found it was Gracie who had stripped all the Jessie Wilcox Smith illustrations from its books. She was suspended, for that and several other reasons, from the public schools.)

Except for one pang I felt, to think that Gracie would give pictures to the Wolfs when she might have offered them to me, I almost forgot her for a while. My whole life was a series of Smith pictures, and Gracie, so blunt, so—yes, I must agree for once with Ardine and Eileen—so *common,* was hardly a picture person.

Filled as we all were with visions of ourselves as glamorously dark-eyed or fairylike heroines, Gracie's square strong body and her coarse hair were distasteful to us. And her manners went ill with our dreamy floatings about the school yard. She became less real to us than the pictures we lived.

One night, however, I reached the peak of this fatuous existence and have never been able to resume any part of it since (as far as I know).

The last cover of *Good Housekeeping* had shown a lovely Smith child saying her prayers. She knelt, her body dimly outlined under the quaint white nightgown, before an open window. Two little pink feet peeked from the ripples of white, two little hands folded piously, and the lovely misty head, candle lighted, was bent and yet somehow managed to lift two deep blue eyes to the starry blackness of the night.

It was a warm night. I knelt before the open window. My nightie was striped and rather short, but from the street my feet might well be imagined as peeking, pink and tiny, from folds of white.

And of course there was no candlelight behind me. I had arranged the door, though, to let in a glow from the upstairs hall.

I raised my eyes to the dark sky. I had never prayed and certainly never on my knees with my hands clasped, but that night I asked God fervently to send someone along the street, someone who would look up and say to himself, "Oh, how exquisite—a lovely child at prayer, just like the cover of the last *Good House-keeping!*"

Suddenly I leapt up and into bed and far under the covers. I was shaken with horror and embarrassment. What, *what* if Gracie Meller should see me! What would Gracie, so simple, so straight, think of me? My ears rang with her hard laughter.

The next day I tried to give my scrapbook of fair princesses and dreamy peasant children to Anne, and when she wouldn't take it, I threw it away.

V

In the first grade, when we sang "Red and yellow, kiss your fellow," it meant final damnation. The color combination was considered thoroughly bad, and for that reason, perhaps, kissing your fellow was, too. We never thought much about it, one way or the other, although we knew that when we grew up, probably in the third grade, we would have fellows. Maybe we would kiss them, but—sufficient unto the day was the evil thereof.

When Ardine and Eileen and Jacqueline and her toady Hazel Montague and Gracie Meller and I were in the second grade, though, we were rudely thrown into a drama of passion, long before our time. It was because of my little sister Anne.

Anne was in the first grade by then, and that was one of the worst things about the whole exciting business. At Penn Street School nobody *ever* had a fellow before she was in the third grade, and there Anne was, madly in love and hardly out of kindergarten.

When I first heard about it, I was shocked.

> *Anne*'s got a *fel*-low,
> *Anne*'s got a *fel*-low,
> *Anne*'s got a *fel*-low,

Jacqueline sang it gleefully at me, and her friend Hazel giggled rather apprehensively.

"Who? *My* Anne? She—has—*not!*" I was furious, as if someone had made a lewd remark about her, which indeed it almost was, then.

But it was hard to deny the truth in Jacqueline's malicious song much longer. The whole school soon knew about Anne and Thomas.

I never mentioned it to my sister. She suddenly seemed much older than I, and I did not feel hurt or reproachful but only moved, as I do now at the little I can remember of the affair.

The teachers did, too. At first they were amused, and then they were touched and strangely upset, and fortunately the whole thing died before they could feel alarm or irritation.

Anne and Thomas were drawn together like two rare animals or insects who, alone of their kind in a great forest, find each other for love. They looked alike, small fat merry things with dark eyes and fine dark hair. They both had four dimples on the back of each hand.

As soon as recess began, they would meet at the wire fence that separated the boys from the girls and stand close to each other. Sometimes they would kiss, delicately, on cheek or mouth. Usually they embraced by pressing their small dimpled hands palm to palm. They spoke little and looked at each other without smiling.

It was strange and mysterious to see my sister so quiet. I was not surprised, though. I wanted to protect her, not possessively for once, but almost religiously.

Of course, everyone could see her at recess, standing brazenly with Thomas, and sometimes at the beginning of the affair the older girls would draw into a group near them.

Then I would lure my friends away by starting a game of tag

or daring one or another to pump up in the swings. Gracie Meller seemed to know what I was doing, and between us we usually managed to keep a clear space around the lovers.

(It wouldn't have mattered about an audience, probably. I doubt if anything could have shattered their intensity. They were drowned in each other.)

When the girls teased me about Anne, I could only beat them at their own game, because although they didn't have fellows, I knew enough about almost every girl to be able to flick her private scars.

We none of us had felt love yet, and Anne disturbed us. She and her lover soon parted, as easily and unknowingly as they had come together, and she seemed the same as before. The rest of us, though—and probably the teachers, too—were changed.

We could never say "fellow" again with the same fine first-grade scorn. We could never again be quite oblivious to boys; from now on, willy-nilly, we must wonder if every one we met could be our own fellow.

In the third grade we found out. I forget about the other girls —they probably had fellows, too—but I know I fell in love with Red Somerville.

I can't remember much about Red, except that he was tall and rakish, one of the "bad boys" and one I had never noticed in the two years I sat next to him. The beginning and the end are gone from my mind, but I know I really loved him for a time, and he me.

My affair was not as pure as my little sister's, because it was more worldly. I was older, and for a few months Red and I were the darlings of the sophisticated element of Penn Street.

We were more daring on roller skates, we could run faster on our long legs, we could spit drinking water further than any other boy and girl. Separated, we were perhaps a little above average; together we were breathtaking. And I loved my glamorous new life almost as much as I did Red, which was a great deal.

I never touched him. Our whole affair was taciturn, like a modern comedy. Once I kissed my hand to him, behind his back, but only because Jacqueline dared me to in such an insulting way that I had to do it or kill her.

He used to give me presents, though.

He started with the gold stars from his spelling and arithmetic papers (he was a good student and earned lots of them).

Then, as he grew to know my tastes better, he managed somehow to buy me things that were forbidden at home: jawbreakers, licorice whips, ghastly little marshmallow bananas that I was sure must be delicious because Mother had told me they were made of unmentionable stuff.

Red and I reached one of our highest moments as Penn Street's most popular couple when he gave me, in public this time instead of nonchalantly leaving it on my desk as he usually did, the first five-cent candy bar that any of us had ever seen.

It was called a Cherry Flip, I think, and was a large lump of pink cream around a red cherry, with thick knobbed chocolate on the outside.

The thought that Red had spent a whole nickel on me was almost more than I could stand. I insisted that he take half of the candy, but even then I felt rather awed. I knew he loved me, perhaps more than I did him.

I gave a decent-sized bite of the Cherry Flip to Gracie. She had always been generous with me, the few times she had cough drops or a stick of gum or some fruit. I felt sorry for her. There we all were, lapped in love, and Gracie was out of it because she was a Mexican. If there had been any dark-skinned boys at Penn, she would probably have had a flirtation; even sturdy Gracie could not have withstood the lovesickness that hit us in the third grade. But as it was, she walked alone.

After the Christmas holidays, there must have been some cooling in my feelings for Red, because when a new boy came to school I was very conscious of him.

His name was Luke Bartholomew. It was such a beautiful name that I felt sure he would fall in love with me. (Now I can't follow that reasoning, but then it seemed obvious.)

Luke, though, fell in love with nobody. He may have loved God or Jesus—he had a faraway look always, as if he were listening to a voiceless song, and he often smiled at friends who were invisible.

He had few visible ones, certainly. He was too far away from us. On the playground there was always a space around him. He was taller than most of the boys, and when he walked to the school door or the toilets, he seemed to glide a little above the ground.

He had large eyes with rings under them, a dead white skin, and cinnamon-colored hair, which he wore longer than the other boys', in soft curls all over his head.

We were much interested in him, and I at least would have renounced all my exciting races and my Cherry Flips for his attentions.

It was a long time before I realized that Gracie Meller felt that way, too. She said nothing, of course, and probably it never occurred to any of the others. To them, Gracie was Mexican; that automatically canceled any normal "white" reactions to Luke's strange beauty.

I noticed that Gracie had stopped playing with us. She often played alone anyway, because Ardine and Eileen and some of the others were nice to her only when they felt like it. Now none of them missed her.

But it seemed queer to me that she always did the same thing, instead of pumping up one recess and hurling herself around the Giant Stride another as she used to. Now she went straight to the camphor tree by the fence and climbed it quickly to the most hidden branch, because we were forbidden to go into the trees. From there she watched Luke Bartholomew, standing alone on the boys' side. That was all. She did it every recess from New Year's, when he drifted into our school, until he drifted away from us again.

That was on Valentine's Day. I remember because we always had a box, gaudy with red hearts and ruffles of crepe paper, into which we put valentines for friends and which we opened on the afternoon of February 14.

The teacher usually gave us each a little sugar heart, and the day was quite gay in spite of the sadness of children who got only one valentine and the mock surprise of favorites who got piles of them.

"It is too bad," the third-grade teacher said, "that Luke Bartholomew could not be here one more day for our party. He has gone away."

I looked quickly at Gracie, but she was imperturbable. Perhaps I had imagined that she loved him?

That afternoon the valentines were distributed, we thanked our teacher for her candies, and then we counted what we had been given.

As always, the children who were socially and physically strong got most of the cards, and little forlorn girls like Evelyn Wolf were grateful for one or two of the cheapest ones.

Any discomfort I felt at their pitiable gratitude was almost wiped out, that year, by my getting more than anybody else, even Jacqueline. I think now that Red Somerville saw to that, disguising his handwriting several times on the envelopes.

The only one he admitted putting into the box for me, though, was the first and last one I ever got that had several layers. Each layer was on paper springs, so that when I unbent them a little, the whole beautiful lacy thing was inches deep.

It was a ten-minute marvel. Everybody gathered around my desk, where it lay, and I glowed with gratitude to Red for it and for my popularity.

Even at that age, though, I knew I should at least pretend to be interested in other people. Before the wonder of Red's valentine had waned, I went to look at the other girls' displays, especially generous with my admiration since I had received more than any of them.

I looked at Gracie's last. Most of my friends were tired by then, and only Jacqueline and I were at her desk.

She showed us her sparse collection, and we guessed who each one was from.

"Who sent that one?" Jacqueline asked scornfully of the last card. It was unusually flimsy, with writing on the back.

When Gracie didn't answer, Jacqueline picked it up and then exclaimed, "Luke Bartholomew! Why, he didn't send any to the rest of us!"

Gracie laughed jeeringly and said, "Oh, he's crazy!"

As soon as we went away, I saw her put her head down on the desk, and I knew that the way she loved Luke Bartholomew was much different from Red Somerville and me, or even Thomas and my little sister Anne.

VI

It seems strange to me that anyone as important as Gracie could be lost so soon from my life. I never saw her again after I was maybe fourteen, and only twice more after I was nine.

I remember once she came to the house when I was nine or ten, and my mother did not like her. She was probably a little jealous of her because I had once asked her why I could not have beautiful brown skin like Gracie, and she had replied crossly that nobody nice had brown skin. And she had held me close to her, and I could feel her heart beating through her great white breasts, and she had said sadly to me that I would always be pink and white and that I should thank God for it. I didn't ask her why, but I felt very protective of her for the first time in my life, and I felt sorry for her, too.

Soon after that Gracie came to our house, along with Ardine and Eileen and two other nice white girls, and we ate bowlsful of cornflakes and milk and sugar, kneeling on the floor around the piano bench. Gracie was very messy, and I could tell that Mother was cross with all of us but especially Gracie, and we never did it again.

Then once about a year later, the first of two embarrassing moments happened when I found myself standing in front of our house on North Painter Avenue with Gracie and four or five friends. We all boasted that we had fathers who made more money than Gracie's father. Gracie became very ashamed and did not deny it, and we were laughing at her and I began to feel bad. Then Gracie said that she had no father, and all the other girls laughed at her. I laughed, too, and said that my father made more money than any of them. Jacqueline, the banker's daughter, argued with me a little, and my voice got very loud and I said that my father earned at least fifteen dollars a day, and we all broke up and Gracie went away without saying another word.

I felt ashamed about this, and as far as I know we never mentioned money again.

We soon moved to the country, and my years were very happy there. But when I was fourteen, I went to school in Whittier again, because I was the editor's daughter and I had to try anything new, which in this case was the intermediate school between grammar and high school called John Muir. It was for the seventh and eighth grades. I was in the eighth grade and suddenly I was supposed to be grown-up.

The first day I went to school it had been going on for about six weeks, and I felt out of place and shy. I had a grown-up dress on, made of a nubby ratiné cloth that was stylish then. It was a hand-me-down from a rich cousin in Pittsburgh, and I had looked forward to wearing it. It was bright orange with black binding around the neck and sleeves, and it had a wide black belt of silk down around my hips. I was a tall skinny girl, slab-sided and shapeless, and when I put the dress on, I knew at once it was unbecoming.

I hated everything about having to go to school in town again, and I went alone to the playground for recess. There, suddenly, was Gracie. We greeted each other like old friends, and we went together to a far corner and started talking almost hungrily. She told me of her two older brothers who were in the pen together at San Quentin and that she was leaving that night forever, to live near them. It all sounded very exciting to me, and I longed to go with her. Instead, I said that I might go to South America with my uncle, or I might go back to Ann Arbor, Michigan, to live with my aunt. I added that my mother did not approve of my aunt because she thought that I might turn into a social butterfly.

"What is a social butterfly?" Gracie asked rudely, and she glared at me and then laughed harshly and walked away.

I watched her straight blue-black hair hanging down, and I knew that I would never see her again. I knew that I was damned forever to be pink and white, as my mother had told me several years before, and I felt like crying. I still do now and then when I think of Gracie, and I wish that I had never told her that my father made more money then her father ever could, and that we lived in a bigger house, and all that nonsense about social butterflies. And I wonder what ever happened to her. I hope that if she is alive she does not remember me.

—1957, 1991

13
My Family's Escape Hatch: A Reminiscence

(1915–1926)

San Francisco has been my family's escape hatch for at least sixty-five years, our favorite prescription for everything from blues to blahs to plain animal bliss, and in spite of some current suspicions that the city may be trying to imitate the overcrowded evil confusion of many other great spiritual watering holes, it continues to be our help in times of uneasiness.

I first learned of San Francisco's magic in 1915 when I was going on six and my father and mother went on a wild spree northward from Whittier, California, to visit the Panama Pacific Exposition. They arranged to meet their favorite friend there, Mother's brother Evans, a young law professor fairly fresh out of Stanford. He had been sent there to get him as far as possible from the East Coast and the Midwest, where he had been firmly expelled from three universities for merrymaking.

The three of them had what was called, in our family lingo, "a fine old time," which means that they felt completely carefree and rather silly and slightly tipsy for at least the week they were there. Plainly, they forgot small children and duties and classes and getting the *Whittier News* out on time, and frolicked giddily from one beautiful thing to another in what many people have said was one of the most enchanting fairs seen by man.

When Mother and Father came home, they brought my younger sister Anne and me two little cardboard suitcases covered —as was then the fashion—with imitation hotel stickers from all over the world.

They were easy to open, just like what were called satchels or "grips" in those days. And they were filled to their tops with souvenirs, always one for each of us, from almost every display in the great fair. There were swizzle sticks and matchboxes, tiny Japanese fans and theater programs. There were even two sugar cubes from the Garden Court of the Palace Hotel, hand-wrapped in thin Chinese paper, and cable-car passes and postcards.

After Anne and I had laid out every exotic mystery and been told its what and why, we packed them away again neatly and set out to show all the neighbors on our side of the block on North Painter where our parents had been. I don't know if Mother telephoned ahead, but everyone seemed delighted to see us and invited us in to show them the contents of our little satchels. And nobody asked us for even a wee bar of Ghirardelli chocolate.

Mr. Fay, five houses up, pretended that we were selling something. He almost closed the door on us, very grumpily, until he seemed to recognize us. This was somewhat unsettling, but we pulled ourselves together and let him choose a postcard of an open taxicab rolling decorously through Golden Gate Park between banks of bright pink flowers, with two ladies carrying open parasols to match. Mr. Fay said that all women in San Francisco were equally beautiful and stylish. We were sure he was right, because he was from Boston.

By the time Anne and I, in a week or so, had nibbled our way through everything in our treasure bags, we knew a surprising lot about the wondrous city, filled with palaces and opium dens and lying like a seductive arm along the edge of the world, with the wild Pacific on one side and the wide quiet bay on the other. We even knew what opium was. We learned about rex sole—obviously named, in some way, for our father, Rex Kennedy—and about sand dabs. Father said the latter were the most delicate fish in the world, especially as served at Sam's, but Mother stood up for rex sole meunière, because of her husband's name and because Uncle Evans had found it at Jack's to be even better than the pompano at Antoine's in New Orleans, wherever that was.

When we were not much older, we learned to look for the big billboard of an enormous bright parrot with a moving head, just before the red Pacific Electric cars brought us into downtown Los Angeles on our occasional shopping sprees for things still unknown in Whittier. The bird was telling us, "Say Gear-ar-dell-y," but we would feel very sophisticated because we already knew that from our tiny samples. (We also knew how to pronounce Dröste, from another delicious little sample our thoughtful parents had gathered for us, but we were too courteous or naive to say, then anyway, which we preferred.)

A few years later we went for a birthday or some other family fiesta to the Victor Hugo in Los Angeles, and Father found sand dabs on the menu. After learning that they had come down that morning on the Lark from San Francisco, he ordered them for all of us. Mother found them delicious, but not as good as the rex sole at Jack's, and it was several more years before Anne and I could judge them for ourselves.

In 1924 we were sent up to Palo Alto to boarding school, and when I was a senior my sister and I were allowed to go several times to the city without a chaperon. We felt like gypsy queens. The first thing we always did was to stop at the flower stand just off Geary by Union Square for blossoms for our left shoulders. The old man pretended to know us and had a magical trick of folding out the petals of a fresh tulip to make it seem as big as a butter plate. We felt infinitely stylish and carefree and silly and even tipsy. Although we did not yet know fully what that meant, we knew exactly where we were, because we had been there before —through those little satchels of souvenirs of the exposition, almost our whole lives before.

Of course, Anne and I never went to restaurants on our wicked little Saturdays; we preferred the Golden Pheasant or some long-forgotten tearoom. The theaters, though, seemed familiar to us when, with a chosen few other students (thoroughly chaperoned, of course), we saw people like John Drew and Jane Cowl and Pavlova at the Geary and the Curran and the even dustier old place on Powell. We'd really been there before, with Father and Mother and Uncle Evans; now we always saved our own theater programs to give to our own still-undreamed-of children.

When either of our parents came up from Whittier to see us for a weekend, which they found a surprising number of excuses to do, we stayed at one of the small hotels where Rex as an editor had a due bill, but we knew exactly what the elegant Palace Hotel would look like, from our old postcards, and felt immediately at home in its airy grandeur. And when Mother escaped from southern California now and then, with her two poor homesick starving daughters as a fairly feeble excuse, we always lunched at least once in the Garden Court. We knew its vast atrium by heart, from the first days when fine carriages pranced into it until that very noon. There were no more hand-wrapped sugar cubes, but we always ate a legendary salad whose name I forget (*not* a Green Goddess, although that was good, too); it was a kind of pyramid of tiny crisp shrimps and finely cut pale tender lettuce, set on a monumental artichoke heart as wide as a baseball.

Mother said that the melba toast there was the best she had ever eaten, the thinnest and most intelligent—which from her was a rare accolade. Once we were taken down into the kitchens to smile and bow at an ancient Chinese who sat at a special little table cutting long loaves of bread by hand for the toast. He was very small and did not smile or miss a stroke of his long knife. Some twenty years later, when I was in San Francisco alone, writing about all the young soldiers heading from there to the South Pacific, I went down again to the cellars. The white-tiled walls remained, but the cooks stood on raised wooden gratings to avoid the kind of mess of spillings we had tried to ignore the first time. The ancient man still sat there slicing bread. He looked even smaller and did not smile, but his knife went up and down in the same careful rhythm.

In the twenties, Prohibition was firmly in sway around Los Angeles, but in San Francisco there always seemed to be whatever one wanted to drink, and my parents obviously did not suffer when they both came up to share the escape hatch with us. When Mother came alone, of course she would not dream of drinking either privately or in public with two young ladies, but with her husband alongside we drank wines in good restaurants. They were often served from tall, dark green soda-water bottles and poured into dark glasses. Anne and I were not interested, past the first polite sip. A few times the older people sat after a long lunch over liqueurs brought to the table in demitasse cups, and my sister and I were excused and went off to prowl, innocent and unbothered, around Union Square's side streets.

In my senior year, Uncle Evans spent his sabbatical from the University of Michigan at Stanford, and he had once introduced us to old Mr. Gump, so we felt all right about snooping from top to bottom of his store, of course with permission. Mother knew a few shops in Chinatown where we could pass easily from the front to the secret back and look with awe at the beautiful things behind all the shoddy junk put out for tourists. And Union Square itself was a place of bright windy spaces and ever-changing miracles of flowers and trees, with fine sweeps of lawn and sedate old men sitting on benches. I don't remember any signs saying "KEEP OFF," but nobody ever lay down on the green grass or threw litter there or fell down and threw up. It, too, was innocent, like us.

Marriages and divorces and deaths and births happened in our family, of course, but San Francisco stayed firmly in our credo as the cure, the salve and balm, the escape hatch. We fled there singly, or in twos and threes when sadness or ennui threatened us. Now and then we even lived there, but every minute seemed always a kind of *event*—to breathe deeply of the clean cool air, to look at a long perspective up to a known hill, to feel the four o'clock fog sweep eastward from beyond the Cliff House.

And when I lived about two hours northward with my young girls and had to go down often with them for long painful sessions with their orthodontist, it was still an adventure. It still made us feel carefree and silly and slightly tipsy, just as our parents and Uncle Evans had felt in 1915 when they brought back to us two little mysterious magic kits, all printed over with hotel stickers from Florence and Paris and London and Heidelberg and a dozen other far fair cities we would seek out later for ourselves. But first, and I honestly think, forever, the little satchels brought us San Francisco, the fairest and most magical of them all—and the most healing.

—*1983*

14
The Broken Chain
(1920)

There has been more talk than usual lately about the abuse and angry beating of helpless people, mostly children and many women. I think about it. I have never been beaten, so empathy is my only weapon against the ugliness I know vicariously. On the radio someone talks about a chain of violence. When is it broken? he asks. How?

When I was growing up, I was occasionally spanked and always by my father. I often had to go upstairs with him when he came home from the *News* for lunch, and pull down my panties and lay myself obediently across his long bony knees, and then steel my emotions against the ritualistic whack of five or eight or even ten sharp taps from a wooden hairbrush. They were counted by my age, and by nine or ten he began to use his hand, in an expert upward slap that stung more than the hairbrush. I often cried a little, to prove that I had learned my lesson.

I knew that Rex disliked this duty very much, but that it was part of being Father. Mother could not or would not punish us. Instead, she always said, by agreement with him and only when she felt that things were serious enough to drag him into it, that she would have to speak with him about the ugly matter when he came home at noon.

This always left me a cooling-off period of thought and regret and conditioned dread, even though I knew that I had been the cause, through my own stupidity, of involving both my parents in the plot.

Maybe it was a good idea. I always felt terrible that it was dragged out. I wished that Mother would whack me or something and get it over with. And as I grew older I resented having to take several undeserved blows because I was the older child and was solemnly expected to be a model to my younger sister, Anne. She was a comparatively sickly child, and spoiled and much cleverer than I, and often made it bitterly clear to me that I was an utter fool to take punishment for her own small jaunty misdoings. I continued to do this, far past the fatherly spankings and other parental punishments, because I loved her and agreed that I was not as clever as she.

Once Rex hit me. I deserved it, because I had vented stupid petulance on my helpless little brother David. He was perhaps a year old, and I was twelve. We'd all left the lunch table for the living room and had left him sitting alone in his high chair, and Father spotted him through the big doors and asked me to get him down. I felt sulky about something, and angered, and I stamped back to the table and pulled up the wooden tray that held the baby in his chair, and dumped him out insolently on the floor. David did not even cry out, but Rex saw it and in a flash leapt across the living room toward the dining table and the empty high chair and gave me a slap across the side of my head that sent me halfway across the room against the big old sideboard. He picked up David and stood staring at me. Mother ran in. A couple of cousins came, looking flustered and embarrassed at the sudden ugliness.

I picked myself up from the floor by the sideboard, really raging with insulted anger, and looked disdainfully around me and then went silently up the stairs that rose from the dining room to all our sleeping quarters. Behind me I could hear Mother crying, and then a lot of talk.

I sat waiting for my father to come up to the bedroom that Anne and I always shared, from her birth until I was twenty, in our two family homes in Whittier, and in Laguna in the summers, and then when we went away to three different schools. I knew I was going to be punished.

Finally Father came upstairs, looking very tired. "Daughter," he said, "your mother wants you to be spanked. You have been bad. Pull down your panties and lie across my knees."

I was growing very fast and was almost as tall as I am now, with small growing breasts. I looked straight at him, not crying, and got into the old position, all long skinny arms and legs, with my bottom bared to him. I felt insulted and full of fury. He gave me twelve expert upward stinging whacks. I did not even breathe fast, on purpose. Then I stood up insolently, pulled up my sensible Munsingwear panties, and stared down at him as he sat on the edge of my bed.

"That's the last time," he said.

"Yes," I said. "And you hit me."

"I apologize for that," he said, and stood up slowly, so that once again I had to look up into his face as I had always done. He went out of the room and downstairs, and I stayed alone in the little room under the eaves of the Ranch house, feeling my insult and anger drain slowly out and away forever. I knew that a great deal had happened, and I felt ashamed of behaving so carelessly toward my helpless little brother and amazed at the way I had simply blown across the room and into the sideboard under my own father's wild stinging blow across my cheek. I wished that I would be maimed, so that he would feel shame every time he looked at my poor face. I tried to forget how silly I'd felt, baring my pubescent bottom to his heavy dutiful slaps across it. I was full of scowling puzzlements.

My mother came into the room, perhaps half an hour later, and wrapped her arms around me with a tenderness I had never felt from her before, although she had always been quietly free with her love and her embraces. She had been crying but was very calm with me, as she told me that Father had gone back to the *News* and that the cousins were playing with the younger children. I wanted to stay haughty and abused with her, but sat there on the bed quietly, while she told me about Father.

She said that he had been beaten when he was a child and then as a growing boy, my age, younger, older. His father beat him, almost every Saturday, with a long leather belt. He beat all four of his boys until they were big enough to tell him that it was the last time. They were all of them tall strong people, and Mother said without any quivering in her voice that they were all about sixteen before they could make it clear that if it ever happened again, they would beat their father worse than he had ever done it to them.

He did it, she said, because he believed that he was ridding them of the devil, of sin. Grandfather, she said quietly, was not a brute or a beast, not sinful, not a devil. But he lived in the wild prairies and raised strong sons to survive, as he had, the untold dangers of frontier life. When he was starting his family, as a wandering newspaperman and printer of political broadsides, he got religion. He was born again. He repented of all his early wildness and tried to keep his four sons from "sinning," as he came to call what he had done before he accepted God as his master.

I sat close to Mother as she explained to me how horrible it had been only a few minutes or hours before in my own short life, when Rex had broken a long vow and struck his own child in unthinking anger. She told me that before they married, he had told her that he had vowed when he was sixteen to break the chain of violence and that never would he strike anyone in anger. She must help him. They promised each other that they would break the chain. And then today he had, for the first time in his whole life, struck out, and he had struck his oldest child.

I could feel my mother trembling. I was almost overwhelmed by pity for the two people whom I had betrayed into this by my stupidity. "Then why did he hit me?" I almost yelled suddenly. She said that he hardly remembered doing it, because he was so shocked by my dumping the helpless baby out onto the floor. "Your father does not remember," she repeated. "He simply had to stop you, stop the unthinking way you acted toward a helpless baby. He was . . . He suddenly acted violently. And it is dreadful for him now to see that, after so long, he can be a raging animal. He thought it would never happen. That is why he has never struck any living thing in anger. Until today."

We talked for a long time. It was a day of spiritual purging, obviously. I have never been the same—still stupid but never unthinking, because of the invisible chains that can be forged in all of us, without our knowing it. Rex knew of the chain of violence that was forged in him by his father's whippings, brutal no matter how mistakenly committed in the name of God. I learned of what violence could mean as I sat beside my mother, that day when I was twelve, and felt her tremble as she put her arm over my skinny shoulders and pulled me toward her in an embrace that she was actually giving to her husband.

It is almost certain that I stayed aloof and surly, often, in the next years with my parents. But I was never spanked again. And I know as surely as I do my given name that Rex no longer feared the chain of violence that had bound him when he was a boy. Perhaps it is as well that he hit me, the one time he found that it had not been broken for him.

—1983

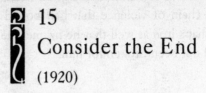

15
Consider the End
(1920)

In Scotland once, mid snow and ice,
A youth did bear this strong devise:
Avise la fin!

It was a clan call, albeit in Norman French, and the youth was one of my father's ancestors, and the devise said with blunt Scotch economy, Consider the end!

That is what my father did, gastronomically as well as in several other ways, for his offspring. He wanted us to taste life in the round, with all of our senses as well as our wits to work for us. He considered the art of eating a basic part of the plan. He was ably abetted by my mother, a voluptuous woman who had a fine teaching hand with pastry and custards when she cared to and who managed to be assisted, for all I know of her life, by a series of devoted sluggards who may have forgotten to dust beneath the beds but who could produce a dramatic cheese puff for Saturday lunch or a prune tart worthy of any bishop, with children helping and learning under their feet. My father sat back, well nourished and watching, and his clan had little idea that he was considering at least one more end of human fulfillment.

It was sometimes hard, however, to consider the end of our purely gastronomic development when I was little, because of Grandmother's dietetic and emotional strictures, but soon after she died, Father hired a spare little virago he called Anita-Patita. The chef of King Alfonso of Spain had taught her a great deal, she told us, simpering. She spent five days at a time making one meal of enchiladas. She spent three days making a flan, a kind of caramel custard. This casual dismissal of clock and calendar fascinated us children. Nothing must interrupt Anita-Patita's creative concentration. Mother could sit tapping her foot for a few dry diapers for the last batch of babies or waiting to hear the piano under our heavy hands; Father could stop everything but the presses of his newspaper to dash over to North Spring Street in Los Angeles for some correct tortillas and an ounce of the right chili powder: Anita-Patita would move like an imperturbable cricket about the kitchen, reliving other giddier days, no doubt, while my sister and I watched, listened, sliced a tomato or beat an egg, and measured one trembly tablespoon of this or that.

Anita-Patita served her enchiladas with inestimable flourish and pride. She usually neglected to prepare anything else, in her creative flush, but all of us—even Mother, who was suspicious of all exotic flavors as well as domestic melodrama—ate them with both relish and respect. We were indulging in a kind of rebellion from Grandmother's digestive Puritanism, and we permitted ourselves indecorous enthusiasm, at least enough to send the little lonesome scornful Spanish woman back to the kitchen, cackling happily.

There was nothing on the table, besides what plates and silver my sister and I had hastily laid there, but the great steaming platter of delicately rolled tortillas (*we* had helped roll them), with fine chicken in them (which *we* had helped boil and slice), and the big bowl of salsa (our *own* salsa). Father, the boy from Iowa whose ancestors had once cried savagely in the Scotch crags, "Consider the end!," picked up with unexpected skill the fist rolled pancake of fine cornmeal and showed us how to be deft about the dipping and biting and so on. He was preparing us.

Mother forgot that for many hours the usual duties had been ignored and that the table did not look as "set" as she had been trained to see it and that there seemed to be not even a salad. She forgot to tell us to sit up and keep our elbows down.

And then Anita-Patita glided into the room with clean plates and a beautiful flan, so bland and perfect after the hot salsa, and a pot of coffee "black as hell, hot as love, strong as death." And we brought down one of the babies who was chirping, and my sister steeled herself to sing a song about "I saw a little dewdrop," and everything was really fine.

The Spaniard went on her way, as good cooks mostly do. But Father had broken at least a part of the web of cautiousness that Grandmother had spun with her gastronomic asceticism, and from then on we had a series of cooks who did everything from receiving an excessive number of male callers to relieving us of the family silver for worthy causes but who managed, drunk or sober, to tolerate the watching children in the kitchen and to slap amazing victuals on the table whenever the occasion arose, once or twice daily.

All the time my father observed our epicurean education. Consider the end, his face and shoulders said. Dozens of young ones in addition to his own ate their way past him, the big man always at "his" end of the table, always The Carver, always savoring and listening. He shaped us—and, through us, our own children—into a pattern of deliberate and discerning enjoyment.

I know that I still put tortillas over a hot grill or griddle the way I watched Anita-Patita do so long ago. And I know that I would never use cheap oil for the beginnings of a salsa like hers, or an elaborate French sauce, or even for a plain old sauce like Aunt Emma's "receipt" for giblet gravy. And I know, by now, that my own children will never accept haste or suspicion or adulteration in their own ways of sustaining the breath within them. This is because they have seen how not to. They have eaten, as well as cooked, with intelligence since they could hold a spoon, and they have absorbed much more than food over a bowl of good soup.

It is very hard, for more of us than seems possible, to keep some sort of steady serenity in our present noisy mechanized way of life. But I know what strengths I have drawn on, from things like my parents' acceptance of Anita-Patita's slaphappy creations, and I have tried to pass some of it along.

—1958

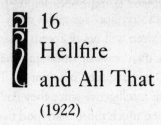

16
Hellfire
and All That
(1922)

It is not clear that I really saw Billy Sunday, the evangelist, standing up in the bandstand in Bailey Street Park and shouting insults for all of us against the God-defying Huns. That would have been in about 1918. Perhaps it was one of his many mimics, who toured the far hinterlands of America in his wake, copying his forceful noisy style. I seem to remember the real "him" though: a strong, wide man, with fists like hams that clenched in the air and trembled with wrath or pounded the Bible as he roared jointly about hellfire and brimstone, and Liberty bonds.

It is strange that my dignified grandmother listened to such crass ranting, but she felt it was "in a good cause," no doubt, and it got me out from underfoot at home to go with her into the green shade of the park and listen, sitting beside her on a bench, while the Billy Sunday brother gave us a good free Christian show.

That was in Whittier, California, when we lived on Painter

Avenue. Life was exciting and rich for me then. Everybody I knew seemed to love me, and that was all I needed. Things were even more interesting after we moved down to the Ranch, out on what was called Painter Extension because it was in the country and not the town. It was like living in Whittier, but across all moats, over all bridges, so that we knew about the town but were no longer of it. We were out of bounds. It made everything more intense. And it was there that I became aware that people love other people, not only as parents and children, but otherwise as well.

Then Grandmother died. I was sorry when one day I found my mother weeping on the living-room couch while the old woman lay in her bedroom with a nurse beside her, softly breathing off and away. But I was puzzled, too. Why weep? I had the detached lack of curiosity of any normal young animal about tears and departures, and it was fine not to have the old lady anymore at the dining-room table.

Grandmother would never have tolerated Rose as our maid-of-all-work, so it was well that she died when she did, a few months before Rose came. Rose stayed at the Ranch for several years, partly because she liked Mother but mostly because her friend Billy could come to the Ranch on Sundays and not be alone in Los Angeles.

Rose was a very tough person, one of the toughest I have ever known, and the first. She had been a hardworking hustler since she was sold to a lumber camp as kitchen help when she was thirteen. Her language was simple and foul. She was complex and ferociously clean. She worked like a horse, keeping us well fed and the shabby old Ranch house sparkling. She was close-mouthed about her past life, but once, when Mother told her she was sorry to add to Rose's chores by inviting two cousins to stay with us for a few weeks, Rose said firmly, "Listen, Miz Kennedy! Get this straight! Bein' here with you and the Mister and your goddamn kids is the best life I ever had. How'd *you* like to work thirty tricks a night and then clean toilets all day! How'd *you*—"

"Yes, Rose. Yes . . ."

The two women got along well. They both had dark eyes and hair. Mother was tall and had once been willowy, a perfect Gibson girl, although by the time I first really looked at her she was hung with an indolent heaviness. Rose was short and square, built close to the ground, as tight as a saddle that is broadening with wear. They respected each other. Once when Anne and I told Mother that Rose had been cross with us in the kitchen, she said that we must always be nice to our cook because she had never been happy. And another time, Rose added a line that still lives in our family collection of favorite quotations, when Mother told her that next week she would have to take down all the curtains and wash them. Rose stood like stone for a minute, her eyes snapping. Then she said flatly, "Now get this, Miz Kennedy, and get it straight. There is only one goddamn thing in this world that Rose *has* to do, and that's die." She stamped out of the room: nothing was ever said about her dictum, and from then on my mother minded her tongue.

She did tell Rose, early on, not to use a few of her saltier words in front of Anne and me, and I am sure the other woman expurgated a lot of them and toned down her basic dialect. Sometimes, though, when my sister and I would come panting in the back door from a long dusty game of Run Sheep Run through the orange orchards that lay between us and our neighbors, Rose would give us each a cup of water from the kitchen sink. "Let me do it, kids. You keep your crappy hands off my clean tap, you hear!" she'd say. And then she would snarl at us to stop that puking noise we bastards always made when we were thirsty. No doubt Mother knew about this lingo, but nobody bothered one way or another, and we learned to gulp politely, not like slurping little puppies.

Rose grew heavier as she stayed with us, and now and then Mother sent away to a mail-order house in New York that made extra-large dresses to buy what Anne and I thought were sumptuously giddy clothes for her. (Just as Mother herself grew fatter and perhaps longed to wear the kind of clothes she gave her servant, so she may have felt an unconscious envy for Rose's wild ugly past, so different from her own sheltered education in living.) The box would come by parcel post, and my sister and I would hurry out to the cabin under our big walnut tree, and Rose would try on the new dresses for us. It was a secret, warm moment. Anne and I would groan disapproval, or say yes, yes, *yes.* She would smooth the cloth over her firm, round body and look almost beautiful; then she would strip it off and fold it carefully back into its tissue paper for Billy to see on Sunday.

I don't remember if she ever actually wore any of the New York clothes. But neither do I remember how she looked with nothing on but her underpinnings: she dressed and undressed in front of Anne and me as casually as if we were her own children, or perhaps Billy. Once, Mother, who doubtless knew of our quasi-secret fashion shows in Rose's cabin, asked us if the blue silk fitted. We said, "Oh, yes—she's saving it for Billy to see," and Mother smiled a little.

Billy's gentling effect on Rose was one reason Sundays at the Ranch were special. Another was that, soon after we moved down Painter from the town and almost immediately after Grandmother died, Anne and I wrote a manifesto to our parents. In it we outlined our reasons for not wanting to attend Sunday school at St. Matthias. As potentially deft young politicians, we argued that Father should not have to interrupt his Sunday ranch jobs to drive us up to Whittier and then go again to bring us home and that Mother should not have to supervise getting us properly into our Sunday clothes and then out of them again, while Rose was occupied with Sunday noon dinner. We also touched on how much more useful we would be to everyone on the Ranch, doing countless small chores instead of learning for the *n*th time about Moses in the bulrushes.

We printed the manifesto, got Rose and the handyman, Little Ears, to sign as witnesses on two carefully dotted lines, and won our case with dispatch and to general rejoicing. As far as I ever knew, my parents felt serenely guiltless about depriving us of our weekly spiritual guidance, and Sundays were *free!* They were days of tranquillity and general bliss. Perhaps we slept later on rainy winter Sundays, but usually we got up early and eagerly. Breakfast was special, with waffles now and then, and no school, and no piano practice. We talked and laughed. The new batch of babies (Mother would have presented us with a fresh couple of siblings every eight years or so, if nature had permitted) splashed cereal and spilled milk happily, and Rose mopped up the table without scowling at them and hummed in the kitchen. Father would come to the breakfast table in his coverall instead of his usual office clothes (three-piece navy-blue serge, stiff white shirt, Sulka tie). The coverall was a huge, shapeless khaki jumpsuit that a garage mechanic had given him. Many years later, prime ministers and paratroopers made it stylish, but in about 1919 it was unlike anything we had ever seen—a mysteriously Sundayish garment that summed up our loose-limbed holiday enjoyment. He did not even button it at the throat, but Mother smiled at him as she dreamily untied the smallest baby's bib and pushed back the high chair.

Father puttered over the Ranch all morning, from his cramped little toolroom in the back of the barn. We tagged after him, never intruding on his Sunday reveries, awed by his concentration as he checked on when he had last mated his sole buck rabbit with one of the does, and how many eggs his pigeons were hatching into doomed squabs, and what his six hives of bees were doing with the three new queens he had bought. Sometimes he would put on his bee hat, oddly glamorous with its thick green veil, and pull on his special bee gloves, and climb up to the hives on the roof of the tractor shed. Anne and I would watch silently from under an avocado tree, but he seemed unaware of any of us as Rose called out to Mother, "There goes the Mister, up on that shaky old roof," and the other woman would stand silently in an upstairs window of the Ranch house. It was dramatic and tense. It was part of the special magic of Sundays. Now and then, angry bees would hum around Father when he lifted the lids of their hives, but he never was stung—more magic!

Sunday noon dinner was something we all thought about as soon as our voluptuous Sunday breakfast was over and Mother had stood up from the table. We dressed nicely for it, but not in churchgoing gear. Father wore a white shirt and a tie, but in summer no jacket. Mother now and then stuck into her topknot a flower Anne and I had picked for her, and we, too, had extra-clean fingernails and smooth hair. And the meal would be delicious, well served by strong, violent Rose. Mother always looked fine at her end of the table, serving the vegetables while Father stood to carve the roasted fowl or meat. Then there was a Sunday dessert—something special. We ate in contentment, politely and with controlled voracity.

We knew that we must sit down precisely at half past noon, because at twelve-fifteen Billy got off the bus at the corner of Painter and Whittier Boulevard, and since he and the bus were always on time, he was already in the backyard waiting for Rose to be free. Once he appeared, Rose leapt into action as if she had been lagging all week, ever since he last caught the night bus back to Los Angeles. She always did everything fiercely, but on Sundays she was almost ferocious, in an inspired and genuinely contented way, and she served us the good meal she had cooked with a special dexterity. We did not dawdle, but we ate with quick enjoyment, knowing that Billy waited outside while she did her dance around us and in and out the swinging door. We all felt happy. Oh, strawberries and little cupcakes; oh, fried rabbit! Fresh peas!

Father had hung a legless bench from the big walnut tree by Rose's cabin and had painted the old thing white. Sitting in it was a nice way to move back and forth in the dry air, and Anne and I loved it. We never climbed up onto the seat on Sundays, though, because it was Billy's then. Rose said to us, a few days after she came to the Ranch, "When Billy's here, you kids just leave him be. He's got things on his mind. He needs his rest." We would wave to him from the back porch as he sat in the swing, his short legs dangling just as ours did. He smiled at us, timidly, and once he brought a bag of hard toffee and gave it to us when Rose was not around; but he plainly liked to be by himself on the old bench swing until Rose was free for him—free from all of us.

Billy was a slender, shadowy man, with thin, graying hair and a remote face. It surprised Anne and me, as we peeked at him on Sunday mornings, that he could climb up into the swing so nimbly and keep it moving without touching the ground with his short legs. He was a pimp, I learned much later, but was planning to retire. He had been in the pen twice for something or other.

Billy loved waiting for Rose, swinging slowly back and forth until she signaled to him and he came silently into the kitchen to sit beside her, in the little corner called the breakfast nook, and eat her good food. Then they deftly and swiftly prepared the room for our Sunday night family foray, and they disappeared. They went out to her shabby quarters—slipshod housing that was considered fitting for hired help in those days, but at least it was private—and they spent the rest of the day together, making love and probably talking. They sent out a feeling, to Mother and Father and to us children, that they loved each other.

Sunday night supper was fun, with Rose not there to glare at us if we guzzled or slouched. Mother sometimes made oyster stew. At breakfast on Monday, with school starting again and Father deaf behind his morning papers, Rose would be scowling her fierce black scowl at us—but somewhat more gently than later in the week.

Then for a couple of Sundays in a row Billy did not come down from the bus stop, and Mondays were rough for us. Mother was cranky and withdrawn. Rose seemed to grow even heavier and thicker and snarled more foully in the kitchen. After we had sweated our way home from East Whittier School through the dusty orange and walnut groves, we steered clear of her and drank from the dogs' faucet in the backyard.

Rose asked for an extra day off, and went to Los Angeles, and never came back. She telephoned to Mother: Billy had been killed —knifed to death. She was already back in her old job on the street. Mother must send her stuff from the cabin to the Salvation Army.

It seemed impossible to Anne and me. Billy, kindly quiet shadow, would not come again on Sundays, to wait patiently in the old swing until Rose had taken care of us and then to love her alone in the little shack. We felt baffled. We missed Billy more intensely than we did her—for a while, anyway—and certainly more than we ever had our grandmother after her quiet disappearance.

Mother cried and ordered two new dresses from the New York catalogue and sent them to the address Rose had given her.

I doubt if they ever got to her, or if they were suitable to a way of life that my mother could only imagine but that she perhaps accepted for Rose in lieu of herself. And perhaps this was what the other Billy Sunday was shouting and pounding the Good Book about when Grandmother and I sat together in Bailey Street Park —hellfire and damnation, and all that.

—1982

17
The Jackstraws
(1922)

Every thinking man is prone, particularly as he grows older, to feel waves large or small of a kind of cosmic regret for what he let go past him. He wonders helplessly—knowing how futile it would be to feel any active passion—how he could have behaved as he did or let something or other happen without acknowledging it.

The only salve to this occasional wound, basically open until death, no matter how small and hidden—is to admit that there is potential strength in it: not only in recognizing it as such but in accepting the long far ripples of understanding and love that most probably spread out from its beginning.

A good time for me to contemplate such personal solutions, or whatever they may be, is when day slides into night. In almost all weather I can sit for a few minutes or an hour or so on my veranda, looking west-southwest and letting a visceral realization flow quietly through me of what other people have given me that I can only now understand.

A clear one, tonight, was of the jackstraws my Grandfather Kennedy whittled for my siblings and me in perhaps 1922 or before. It was never pointed out to me, as I now think it should have been, that an old man had spent long hours making something to please us. I blame my mother for this: she was constitutionally opposed to in-laws, and her whole attitude was that they must perforce be equally antagonistic toward her as the bride who robbed their roost of a fine cock and as a person of higher social station. This was unfortunate for all of us, and my mother lost the most by it and realized it much too late.

Meanwhile, whatever Grandfather Kennedy did was put into limbo in a subtly mocking way, and as far as I can remember we laughed a little at the clumsy set of jackstraws and pushed them into the back of the game closet, tempted by glossier packaged things like a new set of Parcheesi and even the baby stuff Tiddly-winks.

I still have a couple of the jackstraws. They are made of fine dry hardwood, and I think that some at the first had been stained faintly with green and red—dyes Grandmother may have brewed for her dotty husband, grinning sardonically as she prophesied in silence about the obvious end to the caper. One of the straws (were there a hundred in each set, with one hook to be passed around among the players?) is shaped like a crude mace. There were others like arrows, daggers. . . . Each one, according to its shape and then its color, was worth a certain number of points.

I cannot find the rules anywhere in my otherwise somewhat gamey shelves, but I know that the person chosen to be "first" held all the jackstraws firmly in his one or two fists, depending on his age and the length of his fingers, with the hook or perhaps the king straw in the middle, and then twisted them while everybody held his breath around the table. Then the hand or little fists let go, and the pile fell into a contrived heap on the table. And then —yes, the hook was kept out, apart, in order to start the trembling battle, and it *was* the king straw we'd left in the middle!—then we took turns and delicately plucked out one straw, then another if we had not jiggled anything, no straw at all if we had, always aiming for the main glorious one so deftly buried under the little heap. The hook was passed around. Whoever got out the prize won the game, and unless it was time for bed we had another game, drunk with the taste of deliberate skill and *kill:* after all, if you have dug down to that king straw and tweaked it out smilingly, you are yourself king—no matter what your sex—for at least twenty-three seconds!

This sounds competitive, a boring word to me. It is: competitive and therefore boring and probably to be frowned upon by now. But it is a game that was played very quietly, over and over, by men like my midwestern grandfather no matter what his age, and he handed it on to us. It was a silent game, except for occasional shudderings and little groans from the younger ones, quickly snubbed as weak. Grandfather sat like a giant prophet behind his silvery beard, which we knew in a completely disinterested way (at that age!) had been grown to hide his beauty from a horde of young ladyloves, and with an enormous bony brown hand he plucked one jackstraw and then, when his turn came around again, another from the wicked pile. We watched him like hypnotized chickens and tried to do likewise. If one of us missed, there may have been a quiet moan from the others but never a chuckle: we were taught not to *gloat* in public.

Outside the quiet house there was, as far as I remember, no sound, except toward morning an occasional coyote. Of course, there were wild rabbits and moles and mice, but we paid them no heed. Inside, the game was as intense as in any elegant casino, although that connection would have outraged Grandfather: he did not believe in gambling, yet he practiced it every night of his life with jackstraws, Parcheesi, and later crossword puzzles that he transposed into Latin. He would never say "bet," but he would say "wager"; he never said, "My little mare is twice as good as yours," but rather "She is better, I believe." His differences were semantic as well as religious.

So we picked delicately and passionately at the pile of whittled sticks, with their faint colorings, when we played in Grandfather's house. It was *quiet* there on his ranch near La Puente, in southern California. At ours, the game fell flat. He was not there. I see now that such was the reason, although then I thought, if I thought at all, that it was a silly *kid* thing, to be played patiently and politely with an old man. And as I now remember it, I barely thanked my grandfather for the set he had so carefully whittled for us. I had grown past all that. I was in another environment, another age in my own rapid transit from here to there. He was, in a way, stopped at what I hope was the enjoyment of sitting at a table in soft light and watching young people fix their eyes and lick their upper lips and control their fingers to pluck one nicely carved stick from underneath another, in order to edge toward the king itself.

I wish that I had told my grandfather then, in all the hurly-burly of Christmas when he presented the little box of jackstraws to us after such lengthy whittlings and colorings, that I realized what he had done. But I did not. I had no actual physical conception, much less a spiritual one, of what his gift meant. He was an old person and I was a young one. I knew nothing of patience, pain, all that. He could not possibly have tried to tell me about it. So he made a set of jackstraws, and here and now I wish to state that I finally know how to accept them. (At least, I *think* I do.)

It is too bad that my mother waited so long to slough off her conditioned reactions to being related by marriage to people who, in spite of everything she did, were better educated than her own parents but not as affluent. She held us away, willy-nilly, from much warmth, and knowledge, and all that. I don't blame her now. I simply regret it, as I do the fact that I cannot tell Grandfather Kennedy how much I love the two faded pieces of the jackstraw set that he made, and that we casually pushed aside, and that I still have.

—1987

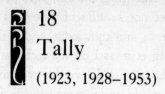

18
Tally
(1923, 1928–1953)

No doubt there is a rich lode of written information about the invisible companions who sometimes walk beside us, or warm our chilly hearts, or wait timelessly to take our groping hands. Sometimes they have been called guardian angels and sung about and painted and made into statues and music. Probably students of the human mind and heart have made charts and lists and even diagrams of their appearance, of when and why they manifest themselves and to which human beings. Probably I should try to find out about all this, since surely records have been kept for our scientific if not spiritual edification. For I feel muddled, as I try to think about the reason why I slept for about twenty-five years with my hand hanging over the edge of any bed I lay in.

Until this night, perhaps a couple of hours ago, it had never occurred to me to wonder why I did this with such a warm feeling of trust and confidence, such an unquestioning surety that if ever the moment was right, my hand would be held in a strong warm other hand.

It is not a usual thing for a child to live with an invisible companion, but neither is it considered very rare, as far as I know. My brother David, who was eleven years younger than I, had a friend none of us ever saw, named Tally, and we seemed to take it for granted that although Tally was not visible to us, he was closer to David than any of us and was therefore our important friend. David and his sister Norah, two years older, were deeply attached to each other, more like twins than plain siblings, but I don't think Norah ever played with Tally, and I am not aware that she ever felt any jealousy. It is part of our general family acceptance, probably, that I have never thought to ask her.

When my next-younger sister Anne and I would come home from school and ask where were the kids, the little ones, Mother would say, "David's upstairs reading with Norah," or "Oh, he's been out all afternoon in the walnut tree with Tally." And on Sundays, when Father did not publish the *News* and we sat longer at table, he would ask David, "How's Tally these days?" David would say, "He's fine, I think. He cut his finger, though. It's all right." Then we would talk about other things, but not deliberately changing the subject. It was all very simple.

When David was perhaps eight, though, Father asked him one day at lunch how Tally was, and David said in a clear flat voice, not looking at any of us, "Tally has gone away." We did not speak for a minute, which may have been filled with shock or even horror. Mother made a little sound, finally, a kind of muffled *oh,* and Father said something like "That's too bad!" and we never mentioned Tally again, at least not to David and indeed almost never otherwise. It would have been rude or something like that.

As I think about all this, for the first time in perhaps half a century or even a thousand years, it seems improbable, but certainly the general acceptance of my little brother's companion was as real as everything else was then—as real as all our voices, and the smell of the old walnut tree, and the long dusty walks home from school, and the Sunday lunches. Now I wonder: Tally was invisible to us, but did David see him, as they played together for long fine hours? I remember that David read and talked aloud a lot to him and that he answered many questions that we never heard. It seems strange, now, that although Norah must have known more about Tally than any of us did, we never felt indiscreet enough to ask her what we knew we must not ask David.

And now I am trying to put into satisfactory words a description of another such visitor as Tally: the nameless, faceless, shapeless spirit who for about twenty-five years stayed under my bed, nearest to me while I slept.

Today a friend, whose left foot must feel wooden for a few months after a hardened artery was repaired, wrote that she was letting her leg dangle over the edge of the bed at midnight. It felt naked and silly, she said. And suddenly I was remembering about my companion, the ancient man who stayed so long nearby in case I needed reassurance. (Of course, I often did, but never enough to ask him for it, like putting off taking two aspirins in case you may need them more later than you do now.)

The person under my bed was a man, all right, and it seems strange that I never questioned or bothered about that nor about the fact that he was indeed somebody. I knew all this without any wondering at all, as a small child may understand without words or worry that someone loves and will care for him. The old man must have been tiny, because it did not matter if I slept on a real bed or on a pallet on bare boards: I simply let my left hand stay trustingly over the edge of whatever I lay on, even if I lay close to a dear lover or a sweet little child. And it did not matter if my hand hung sweaty in the tropics, or carefully escaping from heavy warmth in a snowland, or even from a high sterile hospital bed: I knew that when I most needed it, the old man there, tiny as a pea or big as a skinny child perhaps, would reach out and clasp it confidently in his own strong clean hand.

This comforter or friend or whatever he might be called was never named, at least by me, and indeed I seldom gave him a thought, consciously anyway. If anyone had asked me what he might look like, so faithful there beneath wherever I slept, I would have said something vague about tiny-bones-long-nose-wise-eyes-white-beard, perhaps. Mostly, I am sure, I would have got rid of the whole intrusiveness with a shrug and dismissing smile. I don't think I have ever told any human being about him, which as I write this now seems very odd. Certainly I was not embarrassed. It was simply that it seemed unnecessary, the way it was unnecessary to ask about what Tally did when he was with young David.

And now that I think about it, the strangest thing is that I do not remember when I stopped needing to put my left hand down over whatever I lay on, knowing that he would hold it if need be. (Once, I remember, I was lying on a bed of wild garlic in a Swiss forest!)

Certainly I need help now—or at least the assumption of its availability—as much as I ever did and perhaps more. But all I can do, at this stage in my life game, is feel very thankful that for a long time I knew that I was not alone. As I try to remember the hows and whys of this strange certainty, I feel truly puzzled about the whole silly business. All I know is that the tiny old man was there, if ever I needed anything more than my unspoken and largely unfelt belief that indeed he was. And I like to think that such presences, the kind that come and go without question or

mockery or indeed even recognition, will stay near all of us. Tally
was much more a part of my little brother David's life than my old
man was of mine. He had a name, and perhaps, for David anyway,
a recognizable image. My own guardian was nameless, unseen. But
I knew that the firm grip of his hand would be there if ever I called
silently for it, or even if *he* knew that it was time to take the hand
I left out for him.

Sometimes now when I am between sleep and wakefulness, I
wish that he were still down there, underneath the bed or the
blades of grass between me and the earth. Once in a hospital I felt
actively hurt, or at least baffled, that he was gone. Why had he
left? I wondered irritably, half-amused at my childishness.

Well, it is plain that he is needed more somewhere else. I
suppose David knew that about Tally, too, philosophically. And
clinically, I doubt that my leaving my left hand free for a warm
reassuring grasp from an invisible and nameless and formless presence was at all like spending long agreeable hours with a friend, as
my brother did. My old man, who could be either bent into a
bundle two feet tall under a real bedstead or tiny as a pea in the
grass—but whose hand was always ready to hold mine—may not
even have been one of the "invisible playmates" that child psychi-
atrists write books about. For one thing, I was too old: I think that
I was about twenty when I first knew that he was there, all right.
(That was in Dijon, under a high ancient French bed where I slept
with my first husband. Need for any other comfort was not in my
conscious mind, certainly, and yet that is when the little old man
first took up his watch-and-wait station.)

As for his leaving me, I was not aware of it until a long time
later (I've said twenty-five years, but it may have been much more)
when I realized that I no longer put my hand outside the covers
and down over the edge to tell him that I was there.

When did I stop? Speaking dispassionately, I would say that

I need his warm strong hand in mine more now than ever, but he is not there. My hand, left out, would grow cold and awkward. He is gone. But he and Tally are somewhere, of course, and that is good to know.

—1985

19
Ridicklus
(1924)

I am thinking about the word *ridicklus*, not *ridiculous*. It's one of my private words, because of its ridiculosity, its complete silliness.

I think I began to use it when I was seventeen and in boarding school, first about Mrs. Brownley, our housemother. She was a dainty, extremely ladylike person, and she was ridicklus only because her first job at being a housemother was such a nasty tough one, for her at least: she had to spy on and then break up a ring of hard-core pornographic activity that went on for about two weeks, every night and often most of every night, after school started in the fall.

My younger sister Anne was one of the willing girls in a kind of cult or guild that had me a little worried about her, but never enough to tell her so. Of course, I knew all about it, but I was never a part of it. From what I remember of those toplofty years, I may have considered myself above it in some strange way, although all the people concerned with it trusted me and told me everything that went on. This may have been because I was so stupid or naive, but I really do believe that they trusted me because I would never have dreamed of telling on them.

The leader was a girl named Ivy, or Ina perhaps. She left the school in about a month and nobody ever missed her, although she was in complete control of the ring while she lived in the next room to ours. She was overtly in a change in her life when she became completely masculine. Of course, we were all like oysters at that age, so that we could go either way according to the tides and so on. My sister, for instance, was always very female and was disturbed by the maleness of Ivy/Ina, whereas I recognized the male-girl immediately and never thought any more about it. This recognition was tacit. No words were ever spoken between us, but Ivy/Ina knew that I did not worry about her, or myself, or even her partners in the hard-core porn cult and that my small worry about my sister was of no importance to anyone. I knew that Anne would survive it, and she did.

Ina/Ivy's roommate was a very feminine, exquisite little kid, very sexually aware and alert. It was said that she had been secretly married and had been separated from her lover by her irate and very rich parents and hidden in our prim and private boarding school. She was young, but only I knew about it all apparently, because she escaped one night through our bathroom window to her husband or lover and was never mentioned again.

While she and Ina/Ivy were together, they gave a little show late every night on how men and women made love, with Ina/Ivy always on top. I suspect that it was very primitive and simple "missionary" stuff. The girls, though, were even simpler, all of them, so this was an education in a way, and it could have been worse for them.

The night they were raided, I knew it was all arranged, and

by then I felt very sorry for Mrs. Brownley, and part of me wanted to warn her about it, but of course I did not. I did not warn the girls either. It went very quickly and discreetly, of course, and there was no talk at all on the surface, and the next night the little girl disappeared with her lover and then two weeks later Ina/Ivy went away, too, and my sister Anne went on in her own ways and Mrs. Brownley and I did, too, and I don't know who was left feeling the most ridicklus. To me, it was Mrs. Brownley herself, so impossibly ladylike was she and so ridicklusly impregnable was I. Or were we?

—1989

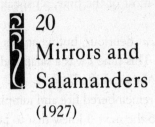

20
Mirrors and
Salamanders
(1927)

The fact that this visible, tangible world is only a hard and brittle reflection of the real existence in dreams has always seemed very clear to me. My sister Anne, too, knows that it is true and understands things that to many people seem unintelligible, preposterous, false. We both believe that to dream is to live—fully, completely. People say, "But when you dream you sit useless and staring, or lie like a corpse." It is true that when one dreams, one's body is useless, uninhabited—but how small a part of life is that weird machine called Body!

Several years ago I had the measles, and when I had recovered I told Anne and my friend Margie of my experiences. Among other things, I mentioned quite casually that one day I was a salamander. Margie snorted. I was silly, she thought, to say such things, because they were nothing but lies that might be heard by grown-up people. Why tell stories when I knew perfectly well that I had been lying in bed most of the time, all speckled? I was delirious, probably.

Yes, I *was* delirious, but what was that but an easy way to be —anything? This time I was a salamander. I could remember.

What? Margie sniffed.

Well, I remembered fire and jumping on my tiptoes from one flame crest to the next. I knew that to fall into the hollow between the flames would make me rather faint, because I was a very young salamander. I was very small and lithe and beautiful in body, and my hair was little bug wings. My eyes were pale green and flickering. Sometimes I ran across great stretches of ice.

That was a dream! vowed Margie. Of course, but I was the dreamer, so why wasn't I the little salamander?

Well, how could I be one, when I was lying on the bed right in plain sight? Anne demanded scornfully if Margie thought my body was the only part of me, and I added that just because I showed myself in a body to common people (meaning human beings, I now suppose), it was no sign that I was chained to it and obliged to wear it all the time.

Rather involved, you think, for small children to discuss? But no! We were only putting into words what almost every child knows, and what a few grown-up people remember and thank God for: existence is not beef and steel, but beef and steel are reflections in a crooked glass held before existence by—Adam and Eve?

—*Essay written at Miss Harker's School, Palo Alto,*
May 6, 1927

21
Figures in a Private Landscape

June 7

Several exciting things happened today.

Sis and Charles and I walked past Goff Island and back. We carried a lunch, laughed, shouted, leapt—three young fools. I love to spend a day like that—and end it hot from sunburn, tired as a dog, and very happy. A dog followed me all day: a lovely brown spaniel. Nothing flatters me more.

At about 4:00, E. Gilman came rushing in, sobbing that Dave had been gone since nine o'clock last night. Mother went right to their house. I was so worried—for D., but mostly for dear Mrs. Gilman. I could see him at the bottom of a cliff, kidnapped, arrested—but not running away, because he adores his mother. In an hour, she and Mother drove in—she white, haggard, but happy. He—the damned little brat—had driven up to Los Angeles to a show with two other young smart alecks and had spent the night at one of their houses! Oh, I could beat him. He just said, "Ah, what the heck! Don't you think I'm old enough to take care of myself? What the heck!" Mrs. Gilman told me that she had passed her high mark of worrying over Dave—if he is gone for a week or a month, she will never worry again as she did last night. He should be spanked—perhaps.

I notice in the paper that George Griffith is leaving next week for Liverpool, where he will live "on his own." I am so glad. He is probably going in order to study ships—and I think his parents are unusually gifted to see that he is made for that and nothing else. He will be doing what he is intended to do, thank God. It is reassuring to see something like that. He is young, not through high school, but very resourceful—a man of thirty in steadiness of purpose and dogged fineness. I like George.

Tonight I read *The Insidious Dr. Fu-Manchu*. I unconsciously see a red scorpion, an exploding fungus, under every cushion, and a yellow hand swaying the curtain. What a book! And isn't it queer that one part of me can be having the creepy horrors while most of the others are sane, quiet, amused?

My nose is red, Mother and Sis say. I asked Charles, and he remarked in a rather embarrassed way, "Well, it's not exactly flaming!" But I don't care—the trip down the beach was worth it, even if we didn't do what we set out for—explore the reef. Another time, that.

Mother mumbles, "Go to bed, Dotey." I will. It will be pure enjoyment.

July 2

One of the things Noni took to camp yesterday was her "line-a-day" book. She's been writing in it ever since May 30—most unusual in a child her age. I don't think I ever wrote for more than a month after January in all my attempts at keeping one. And how loathsome it is to read what I put down! I must have been a *very* objectionable child—especially during my first year in high school —so serious, so sad and drudging in my pursuit after things. I can still see myself, trying to look down my nose at popularity, and sex, and cheating—all in the same category, then. Now I realize that I *can't* look down my nose—perhaps because it turns up at the end. How I've grown!

But seriously, one reason I'm keeping this diary, as Mother insists on calling it, is because I *have* grown, in so many ways besides inches and vocabulary. I'd like to see if I have the mentality to write what I *want* to write—what I think. I doubt it. Damn it —what's my idea in forever playing to an invisible audience? Or not an audience so much as an observer? Sometimes, in those rare seconds of companionship that flicker between people I meet and me, I almost say what I want to, and then as I say the words in my mind, something utterly different comes out of my mouth and is twisted into a meaning I don't recognize—hate—sneer at. Well, I shall see—maybe—and this book will be amusing, even if it doesn't say what it's supposed to—maybe.

I felt as if a cannonball had plowed through me—painlessly, but leaving a clean, empty place—when Dave and Noni capered off with Mr. Downes. They were so excited. When we were driving down from home, Dave said, "There's a kind of half-laughing, half-crying feeling running up and down my back when I think of camp." I hope it stops at that. Noni looked beautiful—lovely clear mouth, chin, nose, and shimmering brown eyes. She's all the looks in the family, though Dave gets more comment. He's a male and has the same kind of body I have—not built for close inspection, especially from the shoulders up.

Last night Mother and I talked for hours, turning over and over in those uncomfortable beds, relics of our 1917 extra-poverty. We talked of marriage and men—her beaux; her family; mine;

marriage and other relations with Jews. This morning I dreamed I was engaged to a horrid little Jew—funny-paper type—and had to get his immigrant mother off the boat. I recognized her—a beautiful woman like Jo Isenstein's mother—and went up to her as she sat on a bench. I forgot my fiancé's name! I said, "Oh, you're Morrie's mother, aren't you?" and she said, "Not Morrie's." "Then you're Izzy's." "No, not Izzy's." "Sidney's, Levi's, Ben's?"

It was terrible because she was so calm, so dignified and benign, and I felt as if each horrid name I threw at her was an insult to her beautiful eyes. I don't know how it ended.

Mother has been heating a little water, and when I asked her what for, she said it was to wash some towels. Now I find her mopping the kitchen floor! Now why did she lie? I think it was because she knows I would offer to help her, and she wants to do that job—to pull, and moan, and flop onto the daybed with a long dying note like that of a balloon with a beautiful whistle—if there is such a thing. Tomorrow when Father and Sis and Helen and Norris and the kids and N. and I are all in one room, she will say, in that high, gay voice that sometimes is forced, "Well, I got down on my hands and knees and simply *scrubbed* the kitchen yesterday!" We will say, "Heavens!—*Why!*—Damn fool thing to do! —How terrible!" Then she will look at us in that seemingly deprecating way of hers: "Well, I *know* I shouldn't have done it, but it was perfectly *filthy*—*rotten* filthy—and it gnawed at me until I felt just as dirty! I finally decided there was nothing to do but clean it. Now look at me—stiff as a board—but it was worth it. 'S nothing I despise worse than a dirty kitchen!" We'll all grin inwardly—with her—and outwardly send out waves of appreciation of her love of cleanliness.

We may drive to the Gilmans' this afternoon. It will be nice to see Mrs. G. and the girls—it will be bothersome and sad to see

Dave. He is building his wall of henpecked shyness so fast that I simply haven't the energy to climb over, much as he wants me to. Poor boy.

Last night Mother and I went to the new café, Las Ondas, and I saw Don Brown with his family and a nice girl whose wool-covered ear he whispered into. He looked at me, long and seri-ously, from his sad eyes. I looked at him, ruminatively, I think. Then we both looked away and studied each other covertly until Mother and I left. Now why? Why do a stupid, lazy thing like that? Oh, hell, this is going to be a mixed-up summer, unless my feelings are all crooked. I wish Tony were here—he was so restful.

Yesterday, M. and I went to Van Altman's, and I picked out two presents which the kids will give me tomorrow, much to my surprise and delight. Darlings! I also bought a kind of yoke of Chinese embroidery—colors enchanting and outlines very arty. I may use it—probably not—but it is so satisfying!

July 12

I've just finished my sixth—or seventh—cup of coffee. Mother is in Whittier, putting up apricots, and Sis is at Dana Point with Carlos, so I seized the chance. I *love* coffee, and it gives a very delightful sensation to gulp down one more cup than I really want, knowing that M. and Sis would say, "Now, *Dotey!*" if they were here. I'm so full of coffee that if I jumped up and down I could feel it make little waves in me. That's amusing, in a way.

I feel very sad today. My eyes ache, my foot aches, my heart aches. Sis always reduces, or raises, relations with my friends to a sex basis. Perhaps she does it unconsciously—what does it matter? —but it simply spoils things for me. Last summer she broke up my perfect triumvirate, and now she has completely spoiled my feeling toward Carlos. She flatters him, teases him, irritates him, presses his hand—things I do, but in a very different way. He is bewildered—he knows that she has suddenly become interesting, in a new way. Damn it—I wish she'd leave him alone. He's just a little boy and, until she started, was my young brother. Until last night I have never needed to powder my nose—of course I have done it, but not to please him. Now he announces that he likes Anne's nose—probably the first time he's ever noticed a girl's feature in a masculine way. Oh, well—I've always known he'd grow up, but I'd looked forward to one more summer of companionship.

Saturday afternoon Sis and C. and I walked down to see the children and I suggested that he and I climb the big rock. The tide was high, and the only way to get to the top, on the waveside, was half-covered, but I knew we could do it, helping each other. I went first, because I've done it so often before, with Carlos right behind me. I was halfway up and with my fingers and toes well placed, when a rather large wave washed up the rock. I had a good grip and was wondering if C. was safe, while the wave was still on me, when I realized that the spray was spoiling things. It rained on me and pulled my scarf up and then down over my mouth and eyes. I seemed to be wrapped in horrible wet silk, clinging to my eyes, pulling them shut, filling my mouth and nostrils. I shook my head frantically and let go of the rock with one hand to pull the damned thing from my face. Before I could do it, I heard the second wave coming and swung my arm back to the rock. I couldn't find a crack or hole to fit my fingers into, and called out as well as I could to Carlos. The water poured over me—a bigger, heavier wave—as I swung around. My fingers slipped and slipped, until I could not feel the rough rock under them. I pressed with my shoulders, my knees, the soles of my feet, against the rock. Then the wave receded and casually, carelessly flipped the scarf from my face as it did so. I slid down the rock and dropped on all fours on the wet sand, numb with pressure on the rock, and fear, and sick with anxiety about Carlos. Why hadn't he answered me? I couldn't see him in the water. Oh, God, I thought, what shall I do? I raced around the dry end of the rock and saw him there, giggling at Sis's efforts to throw his knife in a straight line. They laughed when they saw me come dripping up the sand—my scarf slapping against my arms, my eyes full of salty water, and my freckles standing out. I was furious—furious! To think that I had risked my life —almost drowned—for some silly fun with this cackling little brat! I wanted to fly at him—spank him—ridicule him. Instead I let him wrap his towel around my foot and tried to get it just as bloody as I could. The hole was deep and I succeeded in making it look awful—like Caesar's toga. Carlos and Sis were really awfully sorry I'd hurt myself—and so was I.

Do I sound like a jealous, disappointed baby? God knows I'm disappointed—and in a purely selfish way, I think—but I don't believe I'm jealous.

July 14

I simply *must* find something to do! It is wicked to waste these perfect months—three of them—I, young, strong, brave, and the world rolling round and round. But what can I do? If I get a job, it means that Mother and Sis are tied to the house. I feel, too, that there would be a silent (or not silent) reproach continually dogging me—"How can you leave this comfort, and love, and thoughtfulness, to go out in the world? Is this gratitude? Here we have planned a wonderful summer for you, and you throw it in our faces!" I see the point. It's up to me.

I'm praying to God, or Something, that I will be able to

sidestep this college business. But only two more months! God, you'd better work fast. If I only had some definite purpose in starting out, for Italy, or Uruguay! I'm just a mumbler in life, as far as I can see. I do everything poorly—much worse than not doing it at all. The only thing I do well is see—mistakes, blunders —the why and wherefore—and my own clearest of all. Is that unusual in a nineteen-year-old?

July 23

A great deal has happened—in a way. Dave has been ill, quite ill at times and at other times almost well. He came down from camp a week ago, cross as the devil and swathed with wet, soppy compresses. Mrs. Downes, the headmistress, brought him and I hated her. As mother said, she looked and talked like a woman who loathes children.

Dave grew worse—turnings, and tossings, and a temperature at times very alarming. Dr. Day, a consumptive, pale-eyed Bostonian whom both Father and Mother liked immediately, finally decided that D. *didn't* have intestinal flu. He was afraid a little briar scratch on the back of his neck had become infected on the inside and was poisoning his system. He advised us to take Dave home to our own doctor, as we no doubt realized that he himself was not strong enough to undertake the treatment of any possible complications. He thought the child was physically strong and doubted that we would have any trouble, but—home was the best place. Here the sanitary conditions and—uh—well, good-bye, and please let me know how the dear child gets along.

That night, Monday, I telephoned to Helen, and the next morning she and Mother and Dave sailed off to Whittier, he leaning back, grinning quite sheepishly.

Sis and I followed, into awful heat. I felt quite ill and wondered if one could possibly have a sunstroke through an auto top. At home, we found Dave without fever and still cross. Dr. Wilson, confident that the gland under the scratch was infected, had him firmly and wetly bound with compresses. Poor Dave! He longed for some fit mode of expression.

I perspired and squeezed orange juice. The next day Sis and I drove back and had fun wandering all over this end of two counties. Mother always keeps us on the beaten track, even in the way of eating places, so we exercised our comparative freeness by eating ham sandwiches at some little dump by the roadside. I went so far as to try to drink a bottle of near beer (why can't it be neer beer, or near bear?). I found that the teaspoonsful I stole from Father's glass were more enticing.

It was late when we reached the cottage, and the change from Whittier heat to Laguna coldness made us shiver, so we had a cocoa orgy. In the middle of it Mrs. Gilman came in, with a distraught look in her queer eyes. We lied beautifully about having finished our supper, and after the usual preliminary remarks, we found that she was very worried about Dave. He was picking peaches in Ontario—it was 107 degrees there—he was so careless about shaving every day—he always had nosebleeds when it was hot—he would forget to wear clean trousers—he was a careless driver—would one of us (of course she meant me) drive up with her to see if he was all right? But our plans were dependent on what Mother said over the phone the next morning—we might have to go up and get her and our Dave. Yes, that was so. Had we noticed the movie set on Goff Island?

The next morning she came at nine o'clock, and I naked. She *must* go to Ontario. I put on some clothes, phoned Mother and found Dave was worse, and started out with the poor woman.

The heat!—it was horrible to come out of this cool clearness into such pressing, choking heat! The perspiration ran down my arms into my hands, down my temples into my ears, down my cheeks. Mrs. Gilman talked about sun worshipers, love, Dave, and at Santa Ana stopped to buy a volume of Edna St. Vincent Millay. She couldn't find one. We ate a salad and an ice at some place where the seat was so hot it made me feel like a Japanese housewife or a South Sea priest. We went on like a fast wind to Ontario. I sat in a wicker chair under an apricot tree. Oh, my head! It was an ache that reminded me of my last week at Bishop's. I watched the sunlight in the poplars and looked at a big book of Thévenet's drawings. It slowly drew cooler. Dave came home, bellowing songs —loud and crude and abrupt as ever but tantalizing me with that ever-present hint of something better. I am always on the edge of something with him, and was never nearer than that night on the rickety pier—last summer. I think he hates his face and loves mine —and that night was very dark.

We came home that night, and the next morning when I phoned Mamacita, I told her that Dave went to sleep at the wheel and I drove. She said very calmly, "The hound!" She hates him for that awful day he didn't come home.

Our Dave had ear trouble. *That* was it! I felt like shouting, Hurrah! Hurrah! At last we knew. My darling little brother—my poor little brother—no more compresses for him! Of course, ears are worse, especially when they must be lanced, as his were, but to know! Aha! And he is much better, or was when I last talked with M. Tomorrow, if they—M., Dave, and Father—are not here by noon—that will mean he is worse! I can't think of it.

Yesterday I saw Noni—for the first time in almost a week. She is so beautiful. I love her. She was simply vibrating with ecstasy over a letter Father sent her. She had asked him for an accordion, but told me with shining eyes that she would rather have that letter than even *fifty* of the best accordions in the world. I know what she means and feels.

Bill, the lifeguard at the camp, has finally dared to talk to me, after three weeks of admiring and rather appraising glances. I am afraid he is something of a scrub—in more ways than in being shorter than I. I imagine that with a little encouragement—but shall I give it? Who knows—who cares? I hate his mustache.

Thinking of the other kind—Bob Cowling may come down with "Cholly" Greene tonight. I wonder if he'll even see me this time. I don't believe he's the type that will be embarrassed by last year's innocent interlude. Of course, I can't tell, because I don't know him. He's very apparent, however.

Just for the amusement, I hope I attract him again. This thing of swearing off the company of both kinds of the species has its dull side. And I want to dance tonight.

The Chinese blue-green bowl is full of shining plums, and some have rolled onto the maize linen napkin. It is unattempted and delightful, but the combination is disturbing, too.

Aunt Maggie has inspected the suggested room and finds it unpleasant. She wants Mother and me to go to Los Angeles with her and look at other living places. Oh, *who* has seduced my fairy godmother? I'm sure I have one, someplace. Only she and Circumstance can keep me from college, for a definite stand on my part —really the only solution—would hurt Father and Mother to their hearts' cores. No, it's college for me.

August 27

And how very disgusting that I'm too lazy to keep a promise— even one made to myself! I swore that I'd write in this stupid book at least once a week—even under difficulties. I have had those. Right this minute I can hardly write: I am sitting on the very edge of a couch which is at least two feet farther from the desk than it should be. I think that I'll slide off in a minute. I am in Mr. Altman's shop now. I've been working for him, in the afternoons, for about three weeks, and he has just left for San Francisco, leaving me in complete charge. Sis is helping me make change and so forth. Thank God he's put the dripping fountain and the green vase and the coats in the bank. I'd be worried about them. I like to work here, and besides earning $2.00 a day, I have learned more than I thought possible about Chinese art, and customs, and beliefs. It has been worthwhile in other ways, too: I've learned more about people, myself, my feet. I have more sympathy for salesgirls who have to stand up all day. Of course, I don't, but it sometimes seems so.

Astounding! I am going to Illinois College—have escaped the Ranch! Hurrah! Half an hour after Uncle Walter arrived with the announcement that Nan is going there this winter, we decided, telegraphed, arranged, talked, and carefully avoided the fact that I will be gone nine months—and for Christmas! It will be the first of many times, I suppose.

From what I can gather, the college is small—five hundred—coeducational Presbyterian, cold, old, famous for debates and sports, and loads of fun if you can avoid the YWCA and like splendid groups. I will.

Mother and Father have bought me a gorgeous fur coat—pony and beaver—and of course I have a lot of lovely new clothes, so I feel very well dressed.

I'm going east with Uncle Evans, which will be much more fun than by myself. I'll probably spend most of Christmas vacation with him, and the rest with Uncle Walter's family. Easter vacation I'll go to Aunt Ab's—I *hope*. I'm really scared to see her, because

I'm afraid my eight years' old memory of her will spoil the reality —or vice versa.

Yes, this year will be amusing, and *much* better than nine months in a boardinghouse. *Every*one congratulates me on not going to the Ranch—everyone except Ernesta Lopez. She's disappointed, sincerely, which is a true compliment.

For Saturday, the shop is very dull. I wish people would flock here while Alty's gone, so he could congratulate me when he comes back.

Yesterday Sis and I went to see Margaret Leslie, who is working for Florence Barnes. People say that her family is furious at her for working as a "common" maid, but we admire her immensely. As she says, she'll need money at Mills this year (she's won a scholarship there), and she does nothing but waste her time at home. More power to her! She's a very charming girl. I hope she and Sis see each other this winter. I told her about Betty Hull, who's going there, too—both nice girls, well meaning, subtle as brickbats, and good students.

Just finished reading a letter from Eda. She annoys me intensely, stirs me a little—too much for comfort—and fills me with rather amused pity. She asks me to go to the University of London with her, in 1928. It would be a glorious adventure—with almost anyone else—Sis, perhaps.

I hope Sis never knows how much I love her. This year rings like a knell in my soul—when I let it. I feel as if I'll never be with her again. Last night she said that we'd have to have separate Christmas cards this year. True—but my heart turned on its side. Our trips to Samoa, to Somalia, to France—our bicycle tour through Ireland—where will they be in ten years? With other dreams dreamed well?

Grandmother and Grandfather came down yesterday, laden with zinnias, and eggs, and peaches. They look . . .

. . . I suppose I was going to say—They look very fragile. But why not? They've lived long, and strenuously, and hard. I'm fond of them both, but I think I really love him the most—she's irritating.

The summer's over—done—finished. I feel filled with tears, and longings, and very vain regrets. How criminal it is to waste three months—but were they wasted? Assuredly, I did nothing I had planned to do, but I did other things—worked for Alty, made six hats and a negligee, thought a little, talked a great deal—and so on.

I don't think I made any friends—in fact, I may have lost some. I grew to like Hannah much more, and Elizabeth less, and they me in the same order. Louis has liked me, judging from his letters, more and more, and I him, but not in a heart way at all—on my part, that is. I was lazy this summer—didn't go out for men and therefore not with them either. I can say, as can almost any girl, no matter how ugly or how good-looking, that I didn't have the usual men around me simply because it was boring to attract them. That is sincere.

But for the sake of the gaiety of nations, I hope that this winter I won't be so damn lazy and particular. I hope the Illinois men are more interesting than this summer's crop of Lagunatics—and better looking. And while I'm damning, I'll damn Tony Lowett. He completely ruined the mental and physical appearance of any man I've ever met since. Of course, he couldn't help it—poor dear.

I have on a very attractive new black crepe de chine and my new black patent-leather oxfords from Paris. I feel very swagger—even with no one to look at me.

Sis and I've been taking roll after roll of pictures. I hope one of her and each of the kids is good enough to enlarge for my new pigskin frame. A horrible, sick fullness is always behind me, ready to slip into me whenever I dare think of going away. This is the fourth summer's end. I've felt it, but never so strongly. To leave Sis for nine months! And the family!

The house is charming—new paper on the walls—shiny floors—bright paint. Mother delights in it.

Last night Noni and Sis and I drove up in the closed car, and Dave came with Pete. Oh, it was so blissful to take a hot bath! Next summer, thank God, we're going to have a tub and a heater at Laguna.

September 6

A rather eventful day—Father went to a luncheon of the cast of *Gentlemen Prefer Blondes* and sat with Charlotte Treadway, the leading lady. She wrote a message to me on his menu—Mary Frances, Just oceans of health, happiness, and success—Charlotte Treadway. Aha! She almost sent word that she'd be glad to hear from me. We're all going to the opening night of the play, as a last windup, and I may meet her.

A very fervent letter from Louis—special delivery—announces that he is coming to say good-bye. He asks for several dates—in my last week at home! He'll be down Thursday, I think. We'll take him to *Gentlemen*. I'll be very glad to see him—but I do wish he could have come earlier. However, he's a dear boy—very dear.

Bob Ridgeway called tonight and, after talking for what seemed hours, asked me to go to the show tomorrow night. He's a pathetic person. I think I like him—and I'm afraid he's a little off about me. It won't hurt him—but I hate to have him spend his hard-earned salary on a person who cares so little for him.

Today I got two very kind letters—one from the head of the YWCA at I.C. and the other from my "big sister," who says she is "almost five feet tall." Oh, dear, oh, dear.

Joy and Carlos are coming over for luncheon tomorrow. Oh, dear. They are darlings.

September 8

Carlos was terribly shy and bored—held my hand a long time when he said good-bye and kissed his hand to me. Poor kid! Joy is as nice as ever.

Bob Ridgeway took me to see a very amusing comedy at the Playhouse, and then we went to Coffee Dan's. It's an interesting hole—supposed to be in a sewer, of course. The crowd was largely Jewish—pugilists and vaudeville actors—and the host is a very entertaining young Jew who introduces everyone to anyone and sings and so forth. We had to leave too early. I wished that I was with someone else. Bob is so awfully serious.

This has been a quiet day. This morning Sis had her gland removed. Poor kid—it wasn't pleasant, but she's very brave. I tried to make a hat this afternoon, and narrowly escaped apoplexy.

Tonight we went to the Ranch to bring the children, who've been spending two days there, back to home and Mother. It meant saying good-bye to Grandfather and Grandmother—perhaps forever. She said, "Good-bye, my dear. We'll try to be right here when you get back." Oh, hell.

Louis just called up from Pasadena. The same soft, slow voice and amusing laugh—but idioto! Why doesn't he come before tomorrow night? He hasn't so much time to diddle-daddle. He's so damned ponderous—but I do like him.

I'm *cross*. I'd better stop.

I am at Illinois College, in Jacksonville, Illinois. Several interesting things have happened since I left home, ten days ago, but I'm too cold to write about them—and until day before yesterday I was too hot.

Uncle Evans and I had a very quiet trip—so hot the last two days that we panted. Bernard met us in Chicago, and we did all kinds of things solely for my amusement. (I was too hot to appreciate them, however, until later.) We rode on a bus top out to the lakefront, went to the top of the Tribune Building, ate in the Grillroom of the Bismarck, and went to the stock exchange. I saw a horse faint, which impressed me a great deal. Chicago seems dirty. The women don't wear as much makeup as those in Los Angeles do, and their skirts are shorter. I didn't notice the men, except in the stock exchange, where they looked hard, keen, and very nervous, for the most part.

The trip down was awful—long and hot and sooty—and my first impression of Academy Hall worse. I can't describe it, now, anyway.

I must stop.

This thing is mostly starts and stops—but then, what isn't?

Things grow better. My frame of mind is very queer; I can't analyze it. I am lonesome, uncomfortable, full of longing for my family and decent climate and surroundings—and yet so interested in these people, their looks, conversation, habits, everything, that I would hate to leave. That may be my ultimate degree of contentment—who knows? I feel, too, that to admit defeat this third time would simply prove to Father and Mother that I am a coward for life.

Aunt Tim sent my curtains yesterday, and they make my room look twice as nice as it did. They are printed linen—orange and black and green and so forth in a very "modern" design. My floor lamp is orange. I hope Mother sends my India bedspread. I want to put it on the wall. Then with one or two more pictures and my Chinese pieces, it won't be a bad alcove.

Tonight is a wet, cool one. The streets look like patent leather.

This afternoon Nan and Rachel, her roommate, and I walked downtown and bought a lot of little things—pins, thread, grapes, and so on. It was fun, in a kind of detached way. That is how everything seems and has seemed ever since last spring. I feel as if I were swinging between two groups of existence—as if I needed some awful shock to bring me into reality again. I dread that, but this living without realizing it is futile, it seems to me. I *want* to do things intensively.

Nan is an awfully sweet little thing, and I'm very glad I've come here, for I'd never have known her in any other way. I hope she gets into Stanford next year, but I'm afraid she's definitely decided on Chicago. And I've definitely decided on Cal—though I *can't* think of cheering a team against Stanford. But I *must* be near Sis next year—maybe, if she's at the Good Samaritan, I'll go to the Ranch! How amusing.

—1927

II   Uncle Evans

(1927)

Uncle Evans was my mother's favorite brother and perhaps my father's favorite man friend, and he was my favorite relative because he was worthy of all this family worship. He liked us, too, and spent many of his sabbaticals near us, writing unread law books. When I was eighteen he suggested, to my astonishment, that we travel together from California to Chicago, where he would go on eastward to his university post and I would go south to a small college. I now believe that he did this on purpose, to help me into new worlds.

It was my first train trip of more than three hours. I was dazed at escaping the family nest. My clothes were correctly navy-blue *crepe de chine* (because of the soot), and I slept in the upper berth because I was younger than my uncle. I spent most of my time on the observation platform or in the ladies' room washing my hands. We met for lunch and dinner.

Uncle Evans was a seasoned commuter between West and East from the turn of the century until about 1940. He even had special clothes made for those gritty but delicious "trips," as they were always called: odd-looking three-piece suits made of "dirt-proof" alpaca or something. (Only white shirts, of course, with starched collars: he was a *professor*.) The trains were good. He knew them. He knew the conductors and porters and dining stewards. He even knew the engineer.

In those days (1927 for my maiden voyage), the trains stopped often, and there were still a few Harvey Houses along the line. ("The only test of a good breakfast place is its baked apple," Uncle Evans said mildly. "The Harvey girls never fail me.") One time Uncle Evans walked me up to the engine at a desolate stop, and we stayed too long and were hauled up bodily into the cab until the next slowdown. It was exciting. And there were still prairie-dog huts along the track and conelike ovens in the westward country, in silent ugly Americanized villages that still dared not tell the Indians what kind of bread to bake.

As an old hand, Uncle Evans knew where to ask the dining-car steward to put on things like live trout, venison, fresh corn, melons. They were served to him at our twinkling, snowy little table in the restaurant car, at noon and at night, and I paddled along happily in the small sensual spree my uncle always made of his routine travelings. I probably heard and felt and tasted more than either of us could be aware of.

One time when he looked at me over his menu and asked me whether I would like something like a fresh mushroom omelet or one with wild asparagus, and I mumbled in my shy ignorance that I really did not care, he put down the big information sheet and for one of the few times in my life with him, he spoke a little sharply. He said, "You should never say that again, dear girl. It is stupid, which you are not. It implies that the attentions of your host are basically wasted on you. So make up your mind, before you open your mouth. Let him believe, even if it is a lie, that you would infinitely prefer the exotic wild asparagus to the banal mushrooms, or vice versa. Let him feel that it matters to you . . . and even that *he* does!

"All this," my uncle added gently, "may someday teach you about the art of seduction, as well as the more important art of knowing yourself." Then he turned to the waiter and ordered two wild asparagus omelets. I wanted for a minute, I still remember, to leave the dining car and weep a little in the sooty ladies' room, but instead I stayed there and suddenly felt more secure and much wiser—always a heady experience but especially so at nineteen. And I don't believe that since then I have ever said, "I don't care," when I am offered a choice of any kind of food and drink. As Uncle Evans pointed out to me, I either care or I'm a dolt, and dolts should not consort with caring people.

—1945

III   Examination Books:
Biology 9

(1927–1928)

I

To state and define the characteristics of protoplasm is a thing I should know how to do. Once I did know how—two or three months ago, perhaps. Now, in the final examination, I do not know—and I do not care. I am losing five hours of credit. Too bad, isn't it?

I broke the promise I made to myself, to let my so-called diary go for a year without reading it, and read it yesterday. I found it most interesting. I think it would bore and perhaps disgust anyone else—but it isn't meant for anyone else. It lacks unity, but so do I, at times. That sounds silly, because I suppose it's impossible.

II

This year has been an amazing adventure in many ways. I've been interested, but thank God I'm ending this part of it tomorrow. My train leaves for dear old California at noon—and I'm going to do nothing but read, and eat, and sleep, and look at the country. It seems to me that that's what I've been doing for five months. I've been lazy, scholastically. There's been no incentive to learn—and I've missed so much that it was impossible to make up botany—impossible if I wanted to pass my other subjects, which I did. I think that I'll emerge with about ten and a half of the sixteen hours I've been working for.

I feel sometimes as if I'd spent most of my time either on the train or in the hospital. Of course, that's exaggerated—only four trips across the country and two weeks at Passavant—but it's too much.

I hate like hell to leave Nan—but it's a good thing, I think. The newness of our very true friendship toward each other is wearing off, of course, and I'd rather say good-bye before we irritate ourselves. She's a fascinating person—I love to look at her —her Brenda-like face, her youngly voluptuous lines. She is very intelligent.

Rachel I hate to leave, too. She is comforting—like a great warm woman who smells cinnamony and feels soft—like a tender-eyed bitch. She gets on my nerves, though—just occasionally. I hope I see her again sometime.

We three have had a lot of fun this year. I've spent most of my time in their room—mine was so hideously colored and so empty of humanity. (The dainty, proper librarian had it last year and seemed to leave no feel of occupation, as most people do. And I don't think of the girls who have lived in it before—they were probably like the girls who go to Illinois College now, unalterably boring.)

III

We've been poor, and rich, and just moderately both—and have spent all our money on silly things: movies, and hot chocolate, and *food*. Ye gods! We must have bought twenty-five packages of cream cheese, quarts of ginger ale, hundreds of crackers, a whole garden of lettuce, barrelsful of jam. It was fun to eat the pale green leaves, and the richly colored jam, and the suave cheese, and drink the exciting ginger ale—on a candlelit table, with the Victrola moaning blues in the corner of the room. Sometimes Rachel and Nancy sang, and I lay on the bed, watching the light on their hair and their soft young throats. Sometimes we went to a movie, and sat in the balcony, with all the little boys, and laughed and clapped uproariously with almost no excuse.

Sometimes we went to the College Boys' Café, where we ate

waffles and vegetable soup and more waffles, and drank coffee, and once ate an awful apple dumpling. Usually Nan and I went together. We laughed at nothing—and Rachel isn't much good at that, tho' she's learned to do it more easily than she did in September.

IV

Once I gave a party. We all went to the C.B.C. and ate a ghastly meal with great gusto and then went to *Seventh Heaven,* presented by a very poor stock company. Funny things happened to us—I smile now when I think of them, and I shouldn't, because the botany assistant might notice it and come to see how I'm getting along with my examination. That would be embarrassing.

I've met some interesting people this year—Nan, Rachel, Mr. Anderson, Mr. Smith, Miss Elly, Miss Moore, and Miss McCune —these are the most interesting. Of course, I like the Rammel-kamps, and some of the boys I've had dates with, and Sally Carter —and maybe I won't forget them as soon as I think.

It's queer about Mr. Smith and Miss Elly. I've seen him often —every time I've gone to history—but I've spoken to him perhaps four times. He's fascinating—not as a man to me, but as the epitome of brave looking in the face of awful odds, as the spirit of careless adventure. His lectures are thrilling. He has a dramatic instinct or urge—and when he tells how Marie Antoinette teetered into the Estates-General, how old Uecker drove through his report, how flaming Mirabeau pulled at the emotions of the representatives—I feel faint with excitement. I think I shall read much history.

As for the poor Miss Elly—I met her one night eating her thin little sandwiches wrapped in lace napkins and drinking her peptonized milk from a silver thermos bottle—sitting in the huge, dark, gaunt dining room that she once laughed and flirted in. Once she had lived there, in that shadowy house that the Art Institute has got and is using—and now, when her companion is "taking her day out," Miss Elly brings her supper and sits all alone at the long black table in the dining room. The electric bulbs, naked and dusty, send awful glaring light down on her mottled, diamond-heavy hands and on her thin silver hairs. The only sound is that of her chewing, or perhaps rats skittering through the great dim rooms upstairs.

That night she talked to us almost constantly. At first we were secretly cross—our nice picnic with Miss Moore and Miss Mc-Cune spoiled by a garrulous old lady. Then we realized her proud loveliness, her need to tell us of this room, this house, fifty years ago—of the mistress with her stiff brown side-curls, the carriages, the traveling farmhands, the butler house with its cold twinkling stream—on and on, in a fascinating stream of sometimes almost incoherent chatter. When we said good-bye, she said, "I want you girls to come see me. I'd *like* to have you call on me. You'll come? Now, young Harry Capps—he's a nice boy—lives right next to me. Ha—*that*'ll bring you!"

I wish I could write about Miss Elly—poor little Miss Elly.

Miss Moore and Miss McCune and their beautiful old house and their delicious things to eat, I shall never forget. I must write to them, because I feel much affection for their gentle charm, and I think they are fond of me.

I've really done lots of exciting things this year—the weekend in Chicago with Tim and Walter and Nan—my trips with Uncle Evans, the weekend with the Ridgestones, my trip to Bloomington with Ed Cleary—oh, many things. I know that when I go home I won't do as many things and won't have as many dates, but other things will make up for it. I'll have my lovely room, and my own bathroom, and good food, and clean air and warmth, and no more

pains in my chest—and books and concerts and plays, God willing. And Dave and Noni! I love them, love them.

Such things as checking trunks and so on bother me, but I
know that God protects fools. Tonight will be amusing, as I'll have
to sleep under a pile of coats—perhaps under a rug—all my blankets will be packed. Nancy goes at eight o'clock, so Rachel and I
will hold the fort. She goes tomorrow night. I think she'll come
back—she's conscientious. I think she should, too, but not to that
awful hall.

Thank God this will be my last day of skidding on icy walks
and looking at mangy, sooty snow—for years, I hope. If I leave
California to live, I want to go in other directions from this country
—to the South Seas, maybe, or perhaps Alaska, because there the
snow is entire and white.

How queer to think that I am going—going as unexpectedly
and with as little cause as I came, leaving a few marks of myself
which will soon rub out or remain faint smudges—taking a few
permanent lines on my own—what should I say? blackboard? I
took much more of Jacksonville than I gave or than it took from
me. That is as it should be, perhaps.

Now what am I going into? I am glad that I do not know.
Whatever it is, it will be interesting—to me, at least.

—*Illinois College, Jacksonville, Ill.,*
January 30, 1928

IV Oxy

(1928–1934)

When it was first suggested that I try to write something for *The
Occidental*, I was scared. My mind was full of things I often say to
myself about my two short but deep experiences in the college,

but it seemed impossible to me to sort them into the neat little sections that such an imposing assignment should have. How could anyone possibly care about a sophomore in 1928 who tried so hard to get a Gertrude Lawrence tan that she almost knocked herself out several times on the hot bright roof of Erdman Hall? And why would it matter to anyone but perhaps a few ghosts that several years later the same foolish female found herself a faculty wife, chaperoning dances and trying to look at least twice twenty-five years old?

I even asked a couple of current college celebrities about my fumbling need to put nostalgia into focus and to find one salient thing to write about instead of several dozen, and they both murmured comforting advice that flowed past me with futile speed. One told me soothingly to close my eyes and let images come and go. Another asked me, much like a kindly priest or doctor, what I felt as a ripe old graduate about being able to remember landmarks (like Oxy, of course!) in most of my seventy-eight years hereabouts.

I felt impatient but did as they suggested. My theory is that when outside help has been asked for, one should either put up or shut up, and as the free-flow images surged past me and the landmarks grew and then shrunk and grew again, I doggedly sorted and agreed and rejected. It was fun, especially since I learned more about my two advisers than they would ever guess and met my own self on a few new planes. Finally, without author qualms, I decided to try to state why I feel strangely proud and fine about belonging willy-nilly to the Fifty-Year Club of Occidental College.

Now and then I recognize almost frantically that I was a lazy bum, which is always uncomfortable while it lasts. I knew that I was waiting for something to happen, and meanwhile I consented with innate dignity to live in a delightful little apartment in Erdman with my younger sister Anne Kennedy and even to join a sorority and, of course, go dancing as often as possible. And I worked hard on my tan. . . .

Dr. Ben Stelter was my best teacher. I admired him in a shy awed way and still do. He was the only one I really worked for. I was not brilliant, but I was fairly bright, and because I had gone to a couple of very tough prep schools, I did not have to turn more than a hair now and then to breeze through exams. I drew well and helped two or three people cheat on their papers in botany, without any qualms that I remember. I worked on the newspaper, second semester.

Anne and I had plenty of people to make our lives interesting. Her best girlfriend was Fay Shoemaker. I was less inclined to have one special person in my smug self-centered life, but probably enjoyed Helen Betts the most of the several attractive young females available. And I probably saw more of Count Jones than of any of the other men, because he was such a good dancer. I was not really interested in "dating" because I had an off-campus romance well into gear with Alfred Fisher, whom I married as soon as possible (in September 1929).

Larry Powell, a senior then, was the campus hero as far as I can remember: an irresistible little fellow, always in hot water but magically immune from open disgrace, who played politics and the piano with equal irreligious wizardry. Of course, I was too much in awe of him to do more than smile timidly when he began to date Fay Shoemaker (a freshman!), but soon after I left college, he joined my husband Al Fisher and me in France, and we all began a lifelong friendship, which included Ward Richie and Jim the Dutchman Gruenewegen and Gordon Newell, graduates from Occidental just before I went there.

Remsen and Helen Bird were in the president's house when I was first at Oxy and then about six years later, when he actually invented a job for Al Fisher as assistant to Dr. Stelter in the English

Department. Of course, I was in correctly respectful fear and trembling of the Birds when I was an undergraduate, but gradually as I peeked at Helen Bird sitting circumspectly in the curve of the piano at faculty wives' meetings, I permitted myself to feel a presumptuous fondness growing in me for both of them. Later we got over all the student–faculty-wife thing and became friends and even wrote letters, and they were as kind and amusing and subtle as any people I have ever known. The last time I saw them, they were walking down Geary Street in San Francisco, hatless and gloveless and laughing, and my two young daughters and I were walking up Geary, hatless, gloveless, laughing, and we hurried together just across from the two big theaters and embraced happily.

I wish that could have happened with Dr. Cleland. He was a warm fine person, too, but when I was a student I was much too shy to do more than tremble politely in his presence, and later I knew him only through other less mute admirers and, of course, what I read about him and by him. And there was a young bright man named Coones who carried on Dr. Cleland's work and whose wife I liked (still mutely) at our genteel afternoon meetings around Helen Bird's piano.

(The gray knitting that Helen always worked on in the crook of the big instrument was a trick, she told me later: she never had to say much, because she always seemed to be counting stitches. She would look up with a puzzled faraway smile if anyone asked her a direct question, and smile graciously again as one of her prestigious husband's henchmen's spouses would apologize for disturbing her, and then go back demurely to the gray pile in her lap. And after each meeting she would pull out whatever she had done that afternoon, so that several years later I spotted the same old knitting spilling out of its big straw bag by her bedroom door, waiting for another appearance with the president's wife! At least she never said it was for the missionary box, which I had been taught to do when I first picked up my knitting needles at the age of six or so and started to work on a gray woolen scarf for the poor freezing Alaskans—or was it for the poor naked Zulus?)

When Remsen Bird finally created a little job for Al Fisher, after we had got him safely into his *Docteur és Lettres* robes in Dijon and had spent the next three years sitting out the Depression on $45 a month in Laguna Beach, it was fun to swing into the mad social life at Occidental!

Al and I were almost suspiciously popular as chaperons, and the older professors encouraged us for obviously logical reasons connected with complete boredom. Of course, I loved getting a chance to whirl around the dance floor now and then with a senior or even a middle-aged teacher, after several years as the devoted wife of a nondancer. And it was fun to have to wear old-but-still-good clothes and even a hat now and then to a very respectable club or restaurant. And once, in the college gym, Count Jones himself turned up, and for a few minutes I was about nineteen again (in Scott Fitzgerald's first novel, written when he was about that age, he spoke very seriously of someone who was "a faded but still lovely woman of twenty-seven," which was about where I was, chronologically!), and the tall big-nosed fellow forgot that he was embittered by failing to pass his medical exams as his pal Bob Freeman had done so easily, and we pranced with incredible grace around the old gym. We were Ginger and Fred, Scott and Zelda . . . until I caught my dear husband's cold astonished glare.

And what was it about these separate and strange years that make me glad now that I am a member of the Fifty-Year Club? Can anyone really tell me? Was I learning how to be a thinking adult while I acted like a blandly unthinking child? Why did I not take classes and people and even *things* more seriously?

Actually, I believe that I am basically a serious person, and by now, more than fifty years later, I feel ashamed of a careless *acceptance* of all the easy good things, as if I had earned the right to them! I concentrated on tanning my lazy young body, and dancing, and clothes and cars. I assumed that I was intelligent, because I had learned how to bluff. Intellectually I was a lazy zero, even though I had been reading everything from Thomas à Kempis to *The Oz Books* since I was not quite five. I never worried about whether I was good-looking or a decent dancer or an easy learner but simply took all that for granted. (And here I must smile, because my sister Anne and Fay Shoemaker, roommates at Oxy in 1929–30, once almost parted forever because Anne said "for granted" and Fay said "for granite." They argued with fury for long weeks and then did not speak for several more. Who won? Anne died a long time ago, but if I remember I'll ask Fay Shoemaker Powell.) Yes, I took it all for granted/granite!

And as soon as I could escape the trap, whatever it was, I fled family and friends and security like a suddenly freed pigeon, or mole, or wildcat. I probably thought that at last I was MYSELF! And just as probably I would have faltered and even returned with new docility to my cozy cage if I had known how long it would take to start real questioning.

Today, this minute, much more than half a century since I went to Occidental, I begin to understand what I was really learning when I boasted blandly in Dr. Stelter's class about how many books I read each week. Who cared? And when I smugly helped people cheat by doing all their biology drawings for them: what I was really doing was to cheat myself, as I now see it. What about taking for granted that I would get straight A's? I can never be that arrogant again, because now I know how hard many of my peers worked and studied while I played grasshopper. And I know about skin cancers that come from too much sun, and I know about arthritis that stops the heedless endless nights of dancing of both dolts and dukes (or even Counts).

And how about the long process of living with and without people as well as for them, instead of the ignorant pattern of acceptance that for so wasteful a time I believed was the only one for me? Did I start changing all that because I went to Occidental exactly when I did, instead of someplace else some other time? Why do I feel that for undefined reasons I began to look about me there in 1928, instead of in 1924 at the Bishop's School or in 1932 at the University of Dijon?

Who will answer? But I know that it is true, now that I can take the long view.

—1985

Stay Me, Oh Comfort Me

Journals and Stories,
1933–1941

Introduction

NORAH KENNEDY BARR

In these journals, letters, and short stories, Mary Frances Kennedy Fisher tells her story of the death of her marriage to Alfred Fisher and the beginning and tragic end of her "fifteen minutes of marriage" to Dillwyn Parrish. Mary Frances put this manuscript together before her death in June 1992, because she wished her life to be read as it really happened to her and as she felt it at the time, not as interpreted later by a biographer or even by her older self.

After their marriage in September 1929, Mary Frances and Al Fisher spent two idyllic years in Dijon. While Al worked on his doctorate at the university and on an epic poem, "The Ghost of the Underblows," the world of the senses opened up to Mary Frances. Al already knew that he was a poet; Mary Frances was alive with creative energy but undecided about the direction it would take. Her strong family feelings brought her back to the Ranch in Whittier, California, for a vacation at the end of the second year of her marriage, and then our mother Edith persuaded her to take me, her youngest sister, back to Dijon with her.

Journals are fascinating in part because of what they do not say. Mary Frances was hurt at the easy way in which Al had agreed to a separation of three months, but she faced this only seven years later in an unsent letter to their close friend, Lawrence Powell. She may even have unconsciously welcomed the presence of a fourteen-year-old sister in their third year of marriage as a shield against her feelings of betrayal.

After Al earned his doctorate, we three spent the winter months in Strasbourg, then went to Provence, where we were joined by Lawrence Powell. He had spent the previous year studying for his doctorate at Dijon, and he returned there for a second year after Al, Mary Frances, and I boarded an Italian freighter in Marseilles for the long trip home to California.

The Kennedy family to whom the young Fishers returned consisted of our mother Edith, our father Rex, our sister Anne (Sis), caught in an unhappy marriage to Ted Kelly, and our thirteen-year-old brother David. During the years covered by these journals, Edith began having bouts of pain that culminated in a severe heart attack in 1939.

Nothing in France had prepared Mary Frances and Al for the Great Depression. They had been insulated from its devastation by three years as poor students on a fixed stipend. Our father Rex, as editor and publisher of the town paper, knew its full extent, although it touched our family only indirectly. As a community leader, Rex tried to muster some sort of work and food for the hundreds who had lost their homes and who were wandering the roads, subsisting on free oranges from the surrounding groves. By 1932, when we returned from France, the great experiments of the New Deal had just begun. The overpowering uncertainty and feeling that the entire country was close to revolution was strong, as Mary Frances's journals reflect.

Al immediately began to look for a university teaching job, but two long years went by before he was offered one as an English instructor at Occidental College in Los Angeles. Those two years were spent at the Kennedy family Ranch in Whittier or at the summer cottage in Laguna Beach.

The Laguna cottage was built before World War I by my father and willing friends. It stood under six enormous eucalyptus trees, next to a deep arroyo and a short block from the ocean. Once the Coast Highway had been built through Laguna in the 1920s, our block filled in with other cottages, but ocean and trees were always within sound and smell. Each summer in our childhood we made the hour-long expedition from Whittier with a two-burner stove, discarded quilts, and bent pots and pans for three glorious months of freedom. Mary Frances loved Laguna, as did we all. It was not, however, an ideal place for Mary Frances and Al to begin their new life in the United States.

Al faced the death of his father in August 1934. This, and perhaps life in Laguna, had a disastrous effect on his creative life as a poet. To me, he was always remote, kind, beautiful—a man I was confident would eventually be acknowledged as a new Keats or Andrew Marvell.

Friends were important to both Mary Frances and Al during their two years in Laguna, and some mentioned in these pages remained close to Mary Frances for the next sixty years of her life. Most important of these was Lawrence Powell, who found a place near Laguna Beach in 1934 for himself and his bride Fay. After an apprenticeship at Jake Zeitlin's famous bookstore, Larry became an authoritative writer on Southwest literature, a critic, and a novelist, as well as chief librarian at the University of California, Los

Angeles. The journals also talk of Mary Frances's warm friendship with Gloria Stuart Sheekman, a beautiful and generous movie actress, who has become both an artist and fine-book designer.

The central event of these two years in Laguna was her meeting with Dillwyn Parrish and Dillwyn's very young and beautiful wife Gigi. Dillwyn, who was fourteen years older than Mary Frances, had met Gigi while working as a tutor to relatives who were wealthy expatriates, raising their large family in Europe. Earlier, at Harvard, Dillwyn (Timmy) had joined the Volunteer Ambulance Corps and had been sent to France. There he was under repeated gas attacks—a possible cause of the circulatory illness that later cost him his leg and finally his life. Tim's deft and insouciant handling of depressed times, his worldliness, deep sensitivity, and compassion, sparked his correspondence with Mary Frances during 1935, when the Fishers were at Occidental College. I am confident that it was Timmy who helped Mary Frances begin to focus on her gift for writing.

Timmy invited Mary Frances to accompany him and his mother on a voyage to France and Switzerland during the summer of 1934. Gigi had decided to concentrate on a career that held much promise as a movie actress, and she was deflected from this only by meeting her future husband, John Weld. As Timmy's marriage ended, he returned to Europe with his sister Anne and bought a crumbling house, Le Pâquis, in a vineyard above Vevey. Al and Mary Frances joined him there in a wildly ingenuous idea that somehow they could succeed in communal living. Al escaped this situation a year later by accepting a position at Smith College, and at the end of 1937 Mary Frances made the trip back to Whittier to announce her intention to divorce Al and marry Dillwyn.

One year of life (1937–38) together was allowed Mary Frances and Timmy before he lost his leg. In the summer of 1938, not only Mary Frances's brother David and I but also Timmy's sister Anne and a good friend came to Le Pâquis. We were together on a weekend jaunt to Bern when an embolism struck Timmy and, in its progress up his leg, destroyed it, so that soon after a first operation, a second one was needed to amputate. He was never without pain again.

After Bern and Adelboden, Mary Frances did not write again in her journals until she and Timmy bought their house, Bareacres, in 1940. This remote, barren, but beautiful ranch near Hemet, California, was to be her home and base of operations for many productive years.

The year between the Parrishes' return and their purchase of Bareacres was spent undergoing two more operations in Wilmington, Delaware, and making a frantic trip back to France to procure the drug Analgeticum, which was essential to relieve Tim's pain.

Timmy's sister Anne proposed a trip to the Mayo Clinic in 1940, which is described in the Bareacres journal. There Timmy and Mary Frances learned that there was no hope of recovery or even of relief from the progression of Buerger's disease.

Timmy, during the painful years before he shot himself in the summer of 1941, worked every day at painting. His paintings are a treasure that Mary Frances guarded until her death, but she was generous in giving them to friends who wished to have them.

Mary Frances, of course, had to live on, day by day, after the loss of her love. Although she always considered herself a "ghost" after Timmy's death, she was very much a person who continued to love and be loved during her long productive life.

1
Laguna Journal,
1933–36

In the last three days, the currents have changed as many times. I feel them shifting all around me. It makes the thickness of a blue rug and the hard beauty of zinnias in a bowl seem more than ever things to feel and see.

Tonight Father and Al and the children [David, thirteen, Norah, fifteen] are playing poker. They started out with Father facetious and Al quiet and the children bickering, while Mother laughed with pleasure at Dave's dullest sayings. By now they are leveled out, all quietly chattering and amiable and good to listen to. It is good to see Father's face lighter. When he is low, he seems to be thick and rather gross; his table manners are unpleasant; he speaks little and then in a rudely taciturn way. He has been so for two days. Today both the kids asked me, Noni in the car and Dave while we were oiling tools in the barn, about the family finances. Dave said, What's this about our getting poorer?

I forget what Noni said. She is a little sour about it—feels, I think, that Sis and I had an unfair chance at boarding school and clothes and so on. Really, she is not rancorous, but occasionally she is a little sour.

When Al and I went away and drove through all the little villages with our faces like insects' behind dark glasses and my arms burned scarlet, everything that had piled up in two days seemed not to exist. I don't think we thought. It was hot, so we took off almost all our clothes. Our tongues were dry, and we stopped and ate a watermelon so propitiously that we were bathed in a sensual rapture by its color, its icy crisp flesh, its delicate faded taste. Or we stopped for beer, which I have never enjoyed, though Al says he has tasted one brew that is as good as the good beer of Strasbourg. It all has a fake taste to me. Perhaps it is because it is served mostly in hideous roadside eating places.

We ate, slept, bathed, loved each other. I thought of starting a vague diary, an attempt to tell of the fourth year of our life together in this fourth year since the Crash. Fifth, I mean. It was our fourth anniversary, September 5. Yes, it seemed quite clear— in San Jacinto. Now I feel bewildered, set upon by my unruly wants. And there are all the complications of my love for the family, my interest in our friends. The main thing, though, the only thing, really, in the whole disturbed scheme, is Al's and my private life. That I will fight for. It is important and should live through more than a mere world revolution.

12. ix. 33

We went to Laguna with the children and that night, Saturday, took a basket of food and piles of old coats to the cove north of Emerald Bay, where there is a deserted camp. Cliffward from a beached log, we made a little pit, and Dave threw down jagged stones for Al to line it with. Later, one stone exploded three times, showing its scar very white in the coals and blackness. Noni and I picked up wood, which lay untidily against the rocks under the point of land near our log and our fire. When we had deep coals, we broiled steak and put it into buttered round buns. I liked mine better in my fingers, hot and dripping and tasting delicately of wood and smoke as only broiled beef can. Just before the steaks were done, there was that still moment of no color, when all the things and the sky and all the hills seem to exist in some other way than the one we suppose. Then we saw Venus, and then two others —stars they were, though—and I thought that I would watch to see if Venus made a path where she neared the water. But later, when I looked, she had gone. We were very warm after the good meat and in our many old clothes. Dave and Noni had dug little hollows up the sloping sand of the cliff bottom and lay with their feet to the fire, not talking. Al and I sat under a rug, our backs to them and the fire. Occasionally he kissed the top of my head gently. It was very dark and cold. Then we all drew together and began to talk and sing, and in a minute were telling a long silly story. Finally we went home.

Yesterday was the first day of school, and both the children, Noni especially, were very tired and depressed about Latin. Al helped them, and they were cheered. We played poker and I broke even. I usually do that or even get a little ahead, but I make astonishing blunders. Four times now I have blandly passed on a straight flush. It makes us all laugh. Today Mother is pickling figs, and the house is filled with a tangy smell from the spices and the vinegar and brown sugar. Occasionally I think it would be very pleasant to be an old hausfrau of means in the last century, and have a great cellar and pantries filled with things in crocks and jars and kegs, and a reputation through the countryside for my special pickles and mincemeats. Or it would be as good, or better, to have a spice trade in the late eighteenth century, with a little redolent office and ships buying from the far countries. Just for the names —and the smells.

And that reminds me that for this Christmas I am going to make a lot of that fruitcake Sis and the kids like, from Mother's old book, and give nubbins of it to people. It will be nice to give, and nicer to receive than anything I could buy.

Larry is back. We saw him first at Ritchie's. He was very nervous, and then when Ritchie and Gordon came, he began to show off with vigor and bombast. He had an accent, a slurring of inner r's, rather Scotch. Going home, Al condemned him until I told him that when we first knew each other, he himself at times used an English accent or an Eastern one. I think that months in England and relatives and a *petite amie* with the typical English repugnance for our flat sounds had made Larry self-conscious. And three days later, when we saw him Sunday night at Bieler's, it was almost gone, and he was calmer. At Ritchie's, with us all there watching him and looking for changes after his long absence, he was on the spot. And he knew it. Sexually he is even more sure of himself than before, after a year of good hunting. He has a new trick of looking long into women's (my) eyes, with his own very deep and blue. For the first time, I found myself wanting to touch him. I would have been glad to lie with my arms around him or my hands in his. I was not moved sexually at all but was glad to have him back, to see him by me. Here when I use *I,* I mean Al and me, because I have never been able to think of Larry without feeling that I was Al, too. Perhaps I am mistaken.

Larry and Al and I were going today to Laguna for a few days, but L. phoned that he couldn't leave until Thursday, as he is looking into a job. When Al told Mother, he said instead that Larry was seeing about his book. He didn't want Mother to think, Well, Larry's getting a job and Al isn't.

Today I wrote to Grandmother Holbrook's friend Wilhelmina Loos about her date ranch down in the Imperial Valley. It is warm there and isolated and perhaps cheap, and Al and I thought we might go there or to Mecca, three miles from her place. I'm afraid Murray Brush* will decide that he can afford us, and then we'll have to go there. And if we go there, we'll do all the dirty jobs for the whole faculty. But it would be interesting, too, and would only last nine months.

I really wouldn't care much. I'd feel awfully silly playing hymns for all the little boys in morning chapel. But we'd get at least our room and food, and now that is quite a lot. Maybe we'd be paid a little, too. That would be good, because our money is going fast enough. I think we might be able to do our own work, too, in spite of our "duties." I'd like to get some work with French —tutoring or something—or I'll forget what I know.

13. ix. 33

Al, talking with Rex and Denny† (Joanne's husband, here for a night), is telling of J.B.'s communistic turnings. Denny says communism is growing. Al tells of the increasing number of intellectuals who swing to the Left. Rex sits with his face redder, his eyes half-interested, half-scornful. Al and Denny say that if their families hungered, they would grow rabid. What do you mean, rabid? asks Rex. Denny says, Smash, steal, kill! What good would that do? from Rex. We'd join with others and overthrow the government! And who'd control, the hoodlums? No, Al says, the other men like

---

* Headmaster of Thatcher Preparatory School in the Ojai Valley near Santa Barbara.
† Harvey Denham, married to Joanne Holbrook, M.F.K.F.'s first cousin.

Denny, like B. Well, Rex says, there are several hundred men on
starvation wages or alms here in Whittier. Now why don't they
band together and storm a grocery store? Why, they are afraid!
And it is amazing what people will take, what they will endure.
They are afraid. Mother puts down her book and tells of Ethel's
brother-in-law who works for the county at what the county, formerly for fifteen days a month at about $3.50, now pays for nine
days at less than $3. He is supposed to live on that and raise the
new generation. And so on. A little talk of the strikes in Iowa and
so on. Then talk of Rex's manorial system, with the children on
the farms, all a self-supporting community. We would even knit
our clothes, says Al, and Denny, knowing I knit, says, Rather hard
on Dote! Yes, Mother says, we'd have to be nudists, but that
wouldn't shock anybody in this family!

Now they're talking of Russia, and Denny says to Rex what I
often say and think, that he shouldn't read only the memoirs of the
ex-grand-dukes. Rex's reading on Russia is guided by a business
partner, who never having visited the country nor known a Russian
gives lectures to service clubs about the evils of the five-year plans
and communism in general. In the middle of the talk, Denny leaves
to wash his hands and *faire pipi* before taking the tram back to Los
Angeles.

A letter from M. Brush says that he can't let us know about
being at the school until the day it opens. I doubt if he can have
us there. If there are no emergencies, our money will last at least
six more months or maybe longer. Then what? We'll have to live
off my family, as Al's, after thirty-five years of serving the Lord, is
almost destitute. I have an allowance of $300 a year from Mom,
which I expect her to be unable to continue much longer, and
about $20 a year in dividends. Al has nothing and an insurance
premium of about $60 a year to meet. If his Aunt Helen would
die, we *might* get $5,000, of which we owe $1,000. Last night I was

thinking that there are only two ways to live with any promise of bread through the next few years: (1) tie in with some power— France, Japan, Russia, États Unis—as secret agent or as official correspondent or as propagandist, perhaps, and live in the centers —always, of course, a target, but good while you last, a good life; (2) go far into the land, there to dig for water and plant and spin, there to live the life of a slave but with, certainly, times for looking at things and for love. But being a professor, being a good novelist —I doubt them, for the next years.

Tonight Father and Denny talked at each other for an hour or so, sometimes one at a time, sometimes together and trying to drown out each other. From the talk I gather that they both think the N.R.A. [National Recovery Act] doomed, Denny a Democrat and Rex Republican. D. says it is too complex. Rex, scornful of a handful of economists controlling a nation's industries, thinks immediate war the only alternative to chaos and revolution, and one that Roosevelt will choose rather than see his plan a too-obvious failure. He says the national press is primed now to such an extent that war with Japan (or, second choice, Latin America) will be accepted as natural and inevitable by the people whenever it is declared. Men long unemployed will welcome enlistment and drafting and will be sent over after the first shock has been taken by the C.C.C. [Civilian Conservation Corps] forces, now beginning to be toughened and strengthened for warfare. Rex gives it—this state of present peace!—a year or eight more months. Then war, to save our face. And so on. Talk talk talk.

Why, Rex says, are we killing a hundred thousand hogs to raise the price of pork while ten million people are hungry? And why are we plowing under every fifth row of cotton when so many children are naked?

Today Mother and I drove to Los Angeles for various reasons and stopped on the way home at Lucca's pastry shop café, bulging with NRA and affluence—the latter due to the fact that they give people too many little cakes for dessert and then invite them to take them away free—in a box that they provide for five cents. Accordingly, many hundreds flock to pay seventy-five cents for a dinner in order to take away those free cakes. Mother bought two dozen of them and just now has come to turn on the radio for the ten o'clock news, with two in her hand. Those cakes certainly aren't much good, she says as she licks a little piece of chocolate from her finger. They have no taste, just a mouth of fuzz. While she waits for the news, a woman with a clipped voice tells against a background of Chinese music about the Hotel Blahblah in colorful San Francisco. A man says something about Standard Oil. Then the news.

Today at lunch I remembered, as I watched an imitation Russian waiter (we ate at the Russian Eagle in Hollywood)—can't write while the radio talks— When I saw the waiter bend his knees slightly as he poured beer from a bottle into a glass and slowly straighten as the glass filled, I remembered seeing Al do that last night with ginger ale and then seemed to see dim hundreds of bent knees grow straight as wine, and porto-cassis, and Dubonnet filled glasses. I must watch. I think I remember all those knees.

One of the reasons I am glad to go to Laguna tomorrow with Larry is that then it will be easy to eat simply, of milk and lettuce and yeast and vegetables. Tonight my side caught as I crouched on the fender to warm myself. That was because for about ten days I have eaten what was served, both here and in restaurants, from politeness and laziness and a certain pleasure in the knowledge that sooner or later I would be sorry. Now I am sorry. If I don't go to Laguna but stay here and continue to eat potatoes and rice pudding and cakes, I shall be even sorrier. Because rather than make an effort, and not even a great effort, I shall continue to eat what Mother orders for her cuisine. I eat it knowing it will hurt me, but God knows I hate to see Dave and Noni eating it.

Just now I went into the desk for more ink and when I came back here and sat down, I thought, Did Al come in and touch me on the arm and shoulder? I am quite sure he did not, as he sits calmly by the fire some thirty feet from the desk. I do not ask him, for I am quite sure. But still I can feel where he touched me. I can still feel on my arm and shoulder the loving touch of his—hands or what, I don't remember. But I thought without thinking, I *felt* him on my body.

I do not read any of what I write in this book, once it is written. Much of it I certainly would not say again, if I remembered it, nor if I thought much would I *ever* say some of it. But I think that for myself later, perhaps even for others much later, but certainly for myself now, it is a good thing to put down some of what seems to me now a disturbed life. Tonight Denny said, What about forty, fifty years from now? And Rex said, Oh, we'll be riding along. Whether we will or not, now I am alive, and I see that there is movement, a new troubled aching everywhere.

Tonight I ate a passion fruit, a rather new fruit here, from Australia, I think. It is small and dark and hard, very uncompromising. It needs a knife, a sharp one, to cut the shell. And inside is a viscid yellowish mess, all filled with olive-green hollowish seeds growing neatly from three sides of the shell and filling it as if it were a little bowl. To be sucked out or eaten with a spoon. The mouth is pleasant long after. It is a delightful fruit. The man we bought them from puts boxes under the vines one day and picks them up the next day filled. They do the work, he said, and grinned rather sheepishly with his wide thick mouth and his blue pig eyes. A big sign over the road stand said his name was Slim Craddock.

It has been some time—a week or so. I find that I am lazy—lazier, that is, than I had planned to be. And I am often in a frame of mind that might be too monotonous. When I write letters now, they all veer away from chitchat to stewings and sputterings about "conditions." I don't know what good it does to talk—but always it comes round to that. Of course, I think about things. The day A. interviewed a pompous man with more conceit than tact, I was quite disgusted. It sickened me to think that a man as fine and intelligent as A. should be forced to have *anything* to do with such a person. And there he was asking him for work as a ditchdigger! A man with A.'s mind! God, I was sick. And there's still a chance that he may get the job. I am afraid when the phone rings. There is so shallow a well, for all we take from it, and what Al uses heaving dirt all day will be just so much lost. It's not right, in his case, to talk of "interesting experience" and all that. He's done it before, and worked in the oil fields, and hauled potatoes in sacks. Now is his time for writing. And he must exhaust himself to feed us. I wish I could do something. I've thought of everything, but there are a hundred people for every job. My only chance, I think, is radio work—maybe. But that means going to town again—and so on. I can carve rather nice little toys—but they can be bought at the five-and-ten for less than I could make them.

We've seen Larry several times—at Gloria's one night, two days he spent with us at Laguna, last night at his place. Next week we go to a dinner given in his honor by the arriviste president of the college that was so embarrassed, at the time, by L.'s presence. Now he has a doctorate—now he is somebody! A pox on them.

All our plans to go away, get away from the twenty-four-hour attention, always loving and generous and thoughtful, have gone by the boards. The only sensible and decent thing we can do is to go to Laguna for the winter. In many ways we are glad—the water, the quiet, the room for Al and me to work in, and the piano, and the bathtub, and on and on. But I did want to go *away*. I do these people no good—open a few car doors for Mother, run errands, be present for talk and this and that. But they get along as well, sometimes better, without me. And when I'm here, I worry and scheme and stir up and smooth down, and when I'm away—away too far to telephone or summon—I am all in one piece. That is what I want, to be whole. It's Al and our life that count for me. These people, my family—they all have to go their own way, with no help. I am no use to them. I've chosen my way. I want to go. But now things are hard to buck. For years we went as we should, and now we are tangled up in the intimate living of between six and ten people. For some people, others, that is all right. But I suffer when I hear Dave sniffle. I think of crying, and what I can do, and go from that to Mother's apathy (between earaches) and from that to doctors and then back to M.'s discipline and swing to Noni. I think of her laziness or worry about her clumsy, pained walk or her embarrassing bursts of tears. I suffer. I sound very silly and like a tender lily wringing its sensitive emotions like a wet handkerchief. But it is true. And when I am away I don't hear that sniffle from Dave. He may do it. But I can do nothing about it, and there is no reason for being here to listen and fume and fuss and use up energy I want to save or spend on A.

Today A. saw a ragged little boy sitting on the curb, his feet in the gutter. In his lap he held a dead cat, very stiff. He was picking the fleas from it.

24. ix. 33

Laguna—at night on a tuffet by the fire. Edwin Fisher [Al's younger brother] is playing—mostly Bach. He looks very funny, so tall and awkward and not yet of a piece, with his hands going as fast and delicately as mice. He plays well and, when not well, with a constant love of playing. It is good to hear him. When he said last night that he really wished to be a concert pianist, I said, Well, it's not too late. But I wonder if it is. He has no money, no prospect of anything better than the salary of a classics professor!

I remember writing that Larry's eyes were blue. They are the gray that is greenish or tawny—not blue. However, I felt that they were very blue.

I think it will be good to live here at Laguna again. This time there will be no baby coming,* no trip east for Mother to call us up to the Ranch as happened last year. Of course, there are other things to interrupt, but in the meantime—my housewifely instincts are out in full armor, and I look at each old piece of furniture and long to make it new. I shift everything in a room, as some people strip the clothes from a desirable body, without moving more than the eyeballs. But this house is familiar, every crack in its floor and stain on its ugly walls, and I can do little but imagine how charming it might be. The best thing would be to raze it and build again.

Last night we took Edwin to dinner, from the aunties' in Pasadena, where he had driven them the day before from Palo Alto. It was Sunday, so we inserted a few equivocal remarks about dinner with friends, invitation, and so on. Both Edwin and Al are good at that kind of lying—long training in a Christian minister's family. Before we got away, we heard at great and round-the-mulberry-bush length about the aunties' trip to Sitka—about the

* Shaun, Anne and Ted Kelly's son, was born in San Francisco in 1932.

salmon fishing, and the glaciers, and on. We looked at many post-cards. The aunties are remarkable chiefly for their enthusiasm. They will be seventy soon. Their spirits are about as old as their minds—seven or eight. It is very tiring to be with them, for aside from the fact that I must avoid religion, drink, etc., as conversation and be careful of my goddamns, my attention must be theirs constantly and without wavering. They dart and rush from one subject to another, and when one is breathless from inane chatter about nothing, the other dashes in, her eyes snapping with enjoyment. It is with guilt and embarrassment that you realize a second's lapse of attention. You feel that your eyes have glazed, that your mouth has sagged open like a dolt's, and you snap up in your seat and listen visibly and nod and beam. I was very glad when we left. We went to a Japanese place for sukiyaki, which E. did not really like, and sake, which he did.

It seems that things are bad with the Fishers—he lumping up in the lymphatic glands with what is said *not* to be cancer, she insomniac. Al will probably go up there when Edwin goes back, at the end of this week. I am very sorry. I think that one of the foulest things about the way a human life is arranged now is the last part of it. For the human rats, there is really little difference between old age and the rest of it, but for fine people who have spent many years of labor and struggle, the living decay of their bodies is even more horrible than the slowing down of their brains. They should be able to die decently—no bad odors, no ignominy. It might be fairer to start out at puberty in a state of general decrepitude, and for several decades grow stronger and more beautiful than any youth ever could be, and die as clean as young corn in the fields.

31. ix. 33

The last night of the month. In October I am going to eat more as I should, less as *la cuisine de ma mère me dicte. C'est difficile, mais nous allons à la plage dans une semaine. Au moins, espèrons-le.*

Al est parti à 7 h. ce matin pour Palo Alto. Son père est malade —mourant peut-être. On ne le dit pas, mais—

Hier soir, sa derrière nuit, nous avons peu dormi, et ce matin, debout à 6 h. moins le quart—et maintenant je dors yeux ouverts. Je n'aime pas ce lit froid, morne. J'ai mis des petites fleurs pourpres sur la table près du miroir. Je les vois. Mais je suis trop seule, trop seule. Encore une semaine. Ce matin je lui ai dit, Reste donc à Palo Alto—tu vas aider tes parents, les réjouir un peu. Reste donc—deux, trois semaines. Mais j'ai menti quand j'ai dit que j'en serais heureuse, de le savoir loin de moi.

Je vois que le français m'échappe. Et je l'aime tant.

Dix fois par jour je vois une chose, ou je le sens, ou le touche, ou le goûte, et j'en pense pour ce cornet. Mais ça passe si vite, les choses venues. Et maintenant ma vie n'est pas à moi. Je suis compagnon de dame.

Encore dix jours—une semaine même—et nous vivrons à deux —à un. J'ai sommeil. *

---

* . . . my mother's cooking dictates. It is hard, but we are going to the beach [Laguna] in one week. At least, we hope so.

Al left at 7:00 this morning for Palo Alto. His father is ill—perhaps dying. No one says so, but—

Yesterday evening, his last night, we did not sleep much, and this morning, up at 5:45—and now I am sleeping with my eyes open. I do not like this cold, mournful bed. I put little scarlet flowers on the table near the mirror. I see them. But I am too alone, too alone. Still one week. This morning I said to him, Stay in Palo Alto—you're going to help your parents, cheer them up a little. Stay—two or three weeks. But I lied when I said that I would be happy, knowing he is far from me.

I see that French is escaping me. And I love it so.

1.x.33

When I think of Al's father and then of his mother and then Rex and Edith, I wonder that after so many thousand years of training we continue to be surprised when our friends die. We are well hardened to the fact that more will be born.

2.x.33

In 1930 I read *Opium*, by Jean Cocteau, and its pain and some of its ideas impressed me. Tonight I reread some of it, and I find that I am still impressed, certainly in a different way because of the time between then and now, but still glad to read it. One thing I remember well: *"Il y a chez l'homme une sorte de fixatif, c'est-à-dire de sentiment absurde et plus forte que la raison, qui lui laisse entendre que ces enfants qui jouent sont une race de nains, au lieu d'être des 'ôte-toi de là que je m'y mette.'*

"Vivre est une chute horizontale.

"Sans ce fixatif une vie parfaitement et continuellement consciente de sa vitesse deviendrait intolérable. Il permet au condamné à mort de dormir.

"Ce fixatif me manque. C'est, je suppose, une glande malade. La médicine prende cette infirmité pour un excès de conscience, pour un avantage intellectuel.

"Tout me prouve chez les autres le fonctionement de ce fixatif ridicule, aussi indispensable que l'habitude qui nois dissimule,

---

Ten times a day I see something, or smell it, or touch it, or taste it, and I think about it for this journal. But things sensed pass so quickly. And now my life is not truly my own. I am a lady's companion.

Still ten days—perhaps a week—and we will live two together—like one. I am sleepy.

*chaque jour l'épouvante d'avoir à se lever, à se raser, à s'habiller, à manger. Ne serait-ce que l'*album de photographies, *un des instincts les plus cocasses de faire d'une dégringolade une suite de monuments solennels. L'opium m'apportait ce fixatif. Sans l'opium, les projets: mariages, voyages, me paraissent aussi fous qui si quelqu'un qui tombe par la fenêtre souhaitait se lier avec les occupants des chambres devant lesquelles il passe."*

3.x.33

I have just finished a good novel, written this year by Josephine Herbst. It is strong and robust. I met a man last summer, and when by some chance one of us mentioned J. H. and I said that she had published *Pity Is Not Enough* and had many good notices,

---

* "There is in man a sort of fixative, that is to say, a sort of absurd feeling stronger than reason which allows him to think that the children who play are a race of dwarves instead of being a bunch of 'get out there and leave room for me.'

"Living is a horizontal fall.

"Without this fixative any life perfectly and continually conscious of its speed would become intolerable. It enables the condemned man to sleep.

"I lack this fixative. It is, I suppose, a diseased gland. Medicine takes this infirmity for an excess of conscience, for an intellectual advantage.

"Everything convinces me of the functioning, in others, of this absurd fixative, as indispensable as habit, which conceals from us each day the horror of having to get up, shave, dress, and eat. Even if it were only the photograph album, one of the most comical ways of turning a helter-skelter into a succession of solemn monuments.

"Opium gave me this fixative. Without opium, plans, marriages, and journeys appear to me just as foolish as if someone falling out of a window were to hope to make friends with the occupants of the room before which he passes."

(An excerpt from Cocteau's Opium, *translated by Margaret Crosland [London: Peter Owen Publishers])*

he was delighted. He had known her when she was a husky, silent woman who cooked for many talkative and intellectual menfolk. He was glad of her book, because he used to look at her as she went about her work so stolidly and think that she could say more than all the rest of them, if she wanted to. Now she has written this good novel, and it and her first one have made her an important woman.

I haven't heard yet from Al. Mother had notes from C. Y. F. and Edwin today, but of course nothing was said about H. H. F.'s health. I'd be very happy if Al telephoned tonight that he had died. I am afraid of a long and harrowing end for him.

Today was very hot. It reminded me a little of the days off Guatemala last year, when my bones felt gone from the flesh, leaving a limp yawning emptiness. But today I felt sleepy, and all afternoon fought against drowsing by changing my position often and violently as I lay on the chaise longue.

Yesterday Douglas Kennedy* was here on his way to Stanford from Buenos Aires. He is a pleasant young chap and is amusing because of his scatterbrains, but more than a day of him is too much.

It is night, and Mother on the couch has dropped into a little nap. She breathes in short, abrupt puffs. Suddenly one of them changes to an awareness, and I know that she has dreamed that she is asleep. For a minute I cannot hear her. Her breaths start again to make audible puffings, and then she clears her throat and moves briskly and picks up her book again. I do not look at her, but if her eye met mine she would smile with embarrassment and perhaps say, Well, I almost dropped off!

Upstairs I can hear Dave taking a shower. He is growing used to football practice again. For two weeks or so after it started, he

* M.F.K.F.'s first cousin from Buenos Aires, Argentina.

was so tired that he was far from civil—and he still expresses disapproval or grouchiness by a discarding of all politeness. He is a fine boy and a charming one, but when he is sullen there are few humans more unattractive.

The other day I bought new oxygen-grass and cleaned out Father's fishbowl and put in new fish. Since then I have felt much more interest in the bowl, which has been there on the music cabinet for several years without more than casual looks from anyone but Father. He sits watching it from the chair by the radio, or from his chair in the living room sees through the dining room into the side porch and through one side of the bowl, with the fish glinting slowly among the green weeds. That is what I like, too, to look up from my book and see the two fish moving counter to their reflections, slow and easy and very lovely in the many-colored water.

A letter from Dillwyn P. to A. says that there is a slight chance of selling the scenario they wrote. I hope it comes off—for many reasons.

All the time I eat and talk and live here I am full of the consciousness of A. He is all through me, like a virus, and I doubt if I will ever get over him.

28. xii. 33

I think that many people want to write, but of them few have the will to. I write more than half the things I do or say or think. I can see the words on the sheet of paper and see the pen writing them. And in my head a voice, a kind of silent reading voice, reads them not from but to the paper. Often what is read is good. There is a quick sureness about some phrases. At times they come too patly, with a smart-aleck tone. But I *don't* write. I write a few letters, which grow less interesting as I age. But that is all. It is because I am lazy, and that is true of most of the people who think in prose. Laziness and a vague fear.

I sit here, sleepy on top and thinking of the long steaming shower I shall take in a few minutes, but my mind is buzzing with many things to say. Christmas is over, a good one with us all in gay humor, weather cold for a fire in the morning by the tree and warm and sunny for walking after the dinner, which was not too big. The next day we all felt gay, too. Gordon Newell* gets $26 a week under the P.W.A. [Public Works Administration] for carving two panels of the Spirit of America. They are to go in a new school. H. W. R.† gets the same for hand-setting copies of the Declaration of Independence. Same destination. I have suggested that Al's penchant for writing lusty ballads might be turned into a flow of patriotic hymns for eighth-grade glee clubs. A fine chance for equivocal punning. Larry goes to work in Zeitlin's bookstore next week. He and Gordon sup with us tomorrow night, Rex and Mother being on their way to Carmel and New Year's with the Kelly ménage. Saturday Al and D. and N. and I go to Prado, where A. and I went just when I started this book. It is a gathering of bowed-down Mexicans and a few hard Italians who sell their pottery. The Mexicans work hard, using the soil they live on. They live in great poverty. They seem sweet and dull. The pottery, too, is very simple, with a few lewdly painted jars for the imitation balconies of suburban "Mediterranean" houses. Once in a while there is a little joke—a pig bank turned quietly into a monstrous elephant by some clayey fingers or a squatting dog bank with a crude human head.

* Gordon Newell, sculptor, lifelong friend of M.F.K.F. and Larry Powell.
† Harry Ward Ritchie, book designer and fine printer, another lifelong friend.

There is too much noise in this life. At Laguna it is better. But still there is too much. I listen with disgust and with my ears sickened to the radio now, telling news.

30. xii. 33

When I put pine branches in the rooms, we said, How they will smell nice when we take them down. But now, standing by the fire warming my knees, I pulled a little branch from behind a candlestick on the mantle and squatted down to hold it against the flame. The needles spat and burned up. When it grew too hot, I dropped it, but the room is scented almost disagreeably. Perhaps we were remembering a myth about the perfume of burning pine. This is rather *écoeurant* [stifling].

It is raining now. It seems as if I know about the grass reaching up and how green the leaves feel when newly washed. One sensation I've long desired—a California hill, dry after summer, being rained upon.

New Year's Eve, 1933

The radio mumbles a "cross-country dancing party," with bad bands and throngs saying, Whoopee, and Oh, boy, into the microphone. A minute ago we switched to another station just in time to hear a farmer announce by telephone that he could not leave his place, cut off by flood. It has been raining steadily for about thirty hours now, but we hadn't thought of flood. It is a likely thing, however. So many hills are stripped bare by fire. The rain scoots down their black sides.

It is 11:30. In a few minutes I'll make a hot punch and Noni and Dave and A. and I will drink. Mom and Rex are in Carmel with Sis, stormbound. I feel slightly moved, rather sentimental, though not much about the New Year, I think. For me, the years begin September 5. As for resolutions, I have always wondered at my impatience with them. I used to think something was wrong with me that I could not resolve to do certain things on a certain date. Now I do not mind.

The radio grows louder and more maudlin. Here the fire burns bright. A. and I have just taken showers, and our hair is damp around the edges. Noni in a burning-colored dress looks cool. She is reading, and I see that her face is flushed. She and Dave were excited by the snatch of flood news. He sits by the radio. I think he is rather sleepy. He has black paint on his fingers from a drawing he made and burned, of a tree blowing and a little shepherd sitting under it in the falling leaves.

Now I will make the eggnog. I can't find a recipe. I'll heat milk, beat the eggs and sugar, add them, and stir in port and a little brandy. It may turn out—a kind of thin zabaglione, I suppose. I hope we'll sleep untormented into 1934.

11.i.34

My pen is broken, and I have not written because of that, putting it off each day with a feeling of disappointment and relief. This old pen of A.'s makes a startling difference. If I wrote long, I should be cramped.

I smell the shellac from a plaster mask Hal Bieler made of A., which he gave us for Christmas. I can't put it on the wall. There is something unpleasant about a known face breaking abruptly from a flat surface. With a grotesque or even a thing like Beethoven's mask it is different, but I couldn't stand this green, dull look of A.

It is a good mask. I am glad to have it, too, but I think I'll put it away.

Tonight we have supper with Ann and Bud Leland at the Hinchmans'. Mr. H. is to be cook. He is a stubborn, shabby man, always a bit dirty but very unperturbed and comfortable. Ann says he looks like a tipsy plumber. He is cheerful in a brusque way and at times speaks a surprising jargon of very "advanced" art. His wife is quiet, with a withdrawn, fine, melancholy face, like an Italian painting.

12. i. 34

The supper chez Hinchman was one of the worst meals I've ever eaten, but the people were good. There was a great tub of spaghetti cooked with cheap oil and hamburger meat and no imagination, a salad so badly mixed that the salt and the oil and the garlic came in gobs, and, most god-awful, saucers of pink gelatin. I was almost too depressed to be revived, but the people were quite interesting. One, an old sailor who held himself in because of the "ladies present," had the hearty, knee-whacking mannerisms of a professional "salty sea dog," but was genuine for all of that. When we took him home and he wanted us to slow down in front of his house, he said, Slack away there, slack away!

Just now when I went to the bathroom I thought of how good it was to live intimately and freely with someone so that the sounds of washing teeth and urinating and so on were not something annoying, to be hushed and ignored. I like privacy and am quite modest, too, but without any talking or exhibitionism, we never make a fuss over functions of the toilet. I haven't said quite what I mean.

I must make some tooth powder. It is something we started

this winter. We like it and save quite a sum of money. We use about three parts each of powdered magnesia and baking soda, and one of table salt, with one drop per teaspoonful of essence of peppermint and wintergreen. Mix well and bottle. Our teeth look all right. So far.

Larry may come down tomorrow or Monday for a few days. He sold an article to *Touring Topics* for $50. I'll give him the little panel I made of the Lawrence phoenix emblem. I don't think it's very good, though the coat of hot oil and wax improved it some. I wish I could have made something really beautiful and give it to A.

Letters from France today, in answer to my Christmas notes. Miss Lyse wrote a long incoherent letter on Christmas Eve, sitting alone in her little attic room. She spent some of the $3 we sent her on some flowers, some English holly. She said her friends lamented that the birds, this hard winter, had eaten the berries from it, but she told them it was right. The birds were made to eat berries, even English holly berries. So she tied red ribbons on the twigs. It is hard not to become very sentimental about Miss Lyse. She is highly pathetic—the kind of little old lady who would delight the hearts of imitators of K. Mansfield—but she's a fine little old lady, too.

13.i.34

With my pen back from hospital, I should write often!

Today the family came and went in a jolly mood. I think they like to come. We eat, and have a highball before lunch, and afterward Mother and I sit by the fire and chat while the others take a little walk. Then they go, and Al and I do the dishes and feel warm and hospitable and glad they're gone. We're usually restless and not able to work any. Tonight, par exemple, we'll probably go to a show even though we don't want to.

I am reading *The Way of All Flesh*. It is a fine book. I'd like to have, someday, a style one *n*th as simple and direct.

Last night we had supper with Bronson Barber and stayed late. The air was heavy with counterromances and alcohol-inspired plottings. I hate gin and can't drink it without several days of malaise, so I was very sober. But most of the others were tipsy. It was rather tiresome, and I was saddened by some of the emotions I felt around me. People thought I was or should be piqued at Al because he talked for a long time in the kitchen with two women while I sat by the living room fire—but we came away feeling that we were the only ones there who really knew what they were doing. All the others were uneasily living, suspecting and fearing and not knowing what everything was about. There is too much suspicion and fear between men and women.

On the mantle are some Chinese lilies from the Ranch. The warm room makes their perfume breathe out quickly. I suppose they will die sooner because of that, but it is nice now. Dave polished the little man I carved on a block of oak—not very well carved on not very good wood, but he liked it. I was going to give it to him but was afraid to because I had nothing for Noni. So this week I'll make a little thing for her, before Friday if I can. We're going up then while Rex is in Santa Barbara.

Al came in very wet from a walk to the village in a cold and milky fog. Now he is dozing on the couch. I wonder at the things that work constantly in his brain. I know that when he sits looking at his pipe or talking so nicely to any person, his head is working hard on some mad paragraph. And when he suddenly needs a little nap, I am for some reason as proud of him as if he had climbed a high mountain, because I imagine what has tired him.

Last night he was the best person at Bronson's party, because he talked with two queer girls who sat unnoticed except for him, while other people laughed and whispered meanness about them and pitied him. He was nicer than I. One of the two women I disliked very much, a boringly affected little thing about thirty-five with a flat yellow face and the blue hair and puffed lids of a Eurasian. She and the other women were closeted for a long time in the kitchen with Al. Finally she came near me by the fire and with many silly and attemptedly "deep" remarks tried to comfort me for being neglected. I parried all her thrusts in the same affected, semisubtle style but more cleverly. And finally she grew quite excited by me, and forgot Al, and would have leapt at any advances. I could have had her under the sheets. But I hated her. I am too curious, I think, and quite detached. If she had been attractive to me, I'd have led her on farther to see how she'd act. But this woman was odious to me. I was prejudiced before I knew her personally, first irritated indirectly because she and her friend were causing talk about Al and me, then definitely annoyed by her lavish commiseration of my "neglect," finally revolted by her oozy interest in me.

There is something very coarse about the attitude people have about married couples—like mother-in-law jokes in the funny papers. If Al and I had sat holding hands all evening, it would have been stupid and stupefying. But because he learned what he could from other people and so did I, there was almost universal conviction that he was philandering, that I was neglected, that I was secretly raging, that he longed to be unfaithful. And when we finally left, I saw glances between the two kitchen women, saying, She's dragging him home by the ear! And all this came without the slightest hint from either of us but simply out of the minds of all those people who saw us as they were themselves and from habit and repetition interpreted us as a conventional "married" joke in the Sunday comic supplement.

Eucalyptus leaves half-float in the dim fog, and more than ever before I can imagine myself living in the sea.

27.i.34

I meant not to answer it [a letter from Sis], but I did. I love her very much indeed. The thought of her boredom, so young and intelligent and fine to look at, is almost intolerable to me. But now she is not being intelligent. Of course, that is very easy for me to say.

I feel an increasing triviality about what I put in this journal. I'd like, for instance, to tell something that has happened, perhaps a whole incident. But I think, In fifteen minutes I must put on the cabbage, or go to bed with A., or do something else. It is very disgusting to me. I really want to write, and I can write—but I'm not driven by a fire intense enough to make me say to hell with A.'s supper. I make beds and clean and wash and manicure my nails because I *want* to be clean for him and make him comfortable. If I really were an artist, his comfort and even his opinion of me would be secondary things. And so would my own. I'd work and, if I did not starve first, perhaps do something very fine. As it is now, all this sincere but ineffective piddling with chisels and journals is to keep me limber. I won't be all stiff and dulled when my time comes. If it does.

Al is fumbling through a book of German songs. Sometimes he plays softly and sweetly, although he is very uncertain, but tonight he hits each note hard. It hurts my head a little. The piano is rather off-key, too.

I notice many similarities between Balter and Gide, at least in their sentiments about the family.

I can't continue. The noise A. makes is really hideous.

19. ii. 34

Tonight there is a gentle rain, with sound all around us from the eaves and, outside that, the noise of water in the waves. They are rolling in fast and heavily, with much foam all along the shores and some lifted into the air.

Today I told the head of the little tutoring school that I could not continue my two hours daily of watching the children and teaching music and reading. For several days I talked back and forth to myself. I was uneasy at the thought of not finishing what I had started. I was afraid I'd lose some self-respect. And I thought I was a fool to turn down $10 a month for work I really could do. But in the end I did tell Miss Johnson. I think she was relieved, because now she has a chance to get a real teacher, one who has studied child psychology and pedagogy and schoolroom ethics. I am relieved, too. Little children are lovely. I like their fresh smooth bodies and their slender necks and many of their speeches. But in a classroom I hate their smells and their dirty noses and their bitten fingernails and their flat blank innocent eyes and the way they pout their red mouths. I hate their guts, in other words. But I still feel uneasy about the $10. I have a feeling that I can make it up, though. I'll make five or so on the stool I'm doing for Mother to give to Betty Benson, and I have made two little boxes I may perhaps be able to sell. They are very well done and ought to sell. I'll have photographs made of them and the bench, and send them to Hammold and anyone else I can think of who might have some jobs. We'll see.

I like the rain. I remember one time lying most of a day in bed in the Ranch guest house, listening while rain fell all around me. I could hear it on four sides of the little house, and it made a shell over me.

The sweet alyssum is growing wild now on the vacant lots. I have three bowls of it in the house. The first day the dusty, cloying smell was everywhere, but now there is none. And the eucalyptus trees are more than ever in flower. Last night we drove under the trees in front of the house and looked up at them. The sky was high and dull, and the flowers glimmering like stars in fog above us. In the daytime bees are busy at them, and all together make a continuous hum.

Sunday I heard Toscanini conduct Beethoven's Ninth with the New York Philharmonic and the Schola Cantorum. There were 270 voices singing. At the end of the last movement I was swept up by them, and tears welled out the corners of my eyes, but I was not weeping. It is celestial music, and there is a movement in it like the swift unearthly lines in some of Blake's drawings. Or Dante.

I can hear a frog, quietly enjoying the rain, like me.

In three days we start to drive to San Francisco with Dillwyn and Gigi Parrish. We are excited. We like them. And it will be fine to be in S. F. together.

T. had an abortion performed Saturday. I am glad it was all done decently by H. B.—no scuttling, no drunken doctor. She stayed in the clinic. Last time she went home and worked and then was sickly for months. She deliberately misuses her body, in a kind of complicated masochism and as a silent reproach. Many women are that way. They will iron longer than they need to so that the backache they acquire, even though they never tell anyone they have it, can be used as a little incentive for the recrimination they never utter: While you sit reading, I work, my back breaking. It is very complicated. Long after, they think with pleasure of their years of silent sufferings, especially if they are dying of cancer or heart trouble. Then sometimes they tell of their slow martyrdom and bask in their families' abject abasement. It is a kind of revenge, but how many know for what?

King Albert of Belgium fell down a mountainside and died, and last week, after a short revolution in Paris against the corruption uncovered in l'affaire Stavisky, Austrian socialists fought for four days. For a time that looked like the spark Europe waits for, but now things have quieted. On the surface.

We finished *Les Faux-Monnayeurs* last night, one of the most artfully arranged books I have ever read. It is very mature—a contrast to Wilde's precocious sophomoric style. The last sentence was bad for me—the first semblance of a leer. The rest of the book I found very pure and real.

The other day I wrote one page of a letter to Gloria S., and when I decided not to send it after all, I put it in this book to copy. But tonight when I read it over, it sounded so damned noble and frank and disgusting that I threw it in the fire. That is, I threw it around the gas grate we burn for lack of wood, and it hit the edge of the hearth and rolled under the piano. But I am thinking of how words change on the page. It is very disturbing. How do we know what we write? There were the letters I put down, my mind aggravated by G.'s suspicions and small grievances and my heart somewhat hurt at the numbing of a pleasant friendship. But my God, how hollow and how nobly frank they read tonight—not what I said at all. Words shift and reform themselves in the mind, folding onto themselves and begetting new connotations like colored glass in a kaleidoscope or cells in a plant. What did Mr. W. S. really say when he said, To be . . . Whether to take arms against a sea of troubles?

The rain is quiet now. A heavy drop falls here or there from the eaves, and the waves are slower and stiller.

In S. F. I want to ride on the ferry at night and listen to the music in the Chinese Theater and take baths in the hotel. I also want to buy Gigi a corsage from a corner flower stand near the Palace and take Al to hear the bird whistle at Gump's. That is one of the funniest sounds I have ever heard, so breathless and embarrassed and ending with a few bars of "Over There." Now I begin to think of many more things I want to do. But those are the main ones.

Later

I just realized that the uncomfortable need to write in this and the constant realization that what I write has no significance are almost what I feel about carving. I have to do it. All the time I despise the work I do, but I go on simply to be ready. I don't know what I need be ready for, but there is evidently something. How strange if I lived all my life doing things almost without wanting to, always feeling that they were just a substitute for what I was really meant to do and never finding what that was.

1. iii. 34

We didn't go to S. F. Gigi got a job on a Barrymore picture— and the weather was bad, anyway.

Now Al is giving his weekly lecture. In an hour I'll get him, and we'll go to see a picture called *Thunder over Mexico*. Tomorrow he will earn $3.50 by sweeping and cleaning a house that has been empty so long that the windows are broken.

We came back down after a night at the Ranch, I very discouraged. The Kellys were there, biting and jibing at each other. Shaun [their baby] was there, with tension between Sis and the maid over open safety pins and so on. Noni was in bed with a bad cold. Dave was impudent and thoughtful by turns. Father was low as a snake because he'd had a cold and rheumatism in his chest for ten days and, in spite of many pills and light treatments, was no better. Mother was in the hospital with a cold, demanding constant attention, alternately wheezing out coughs straight from her toes and snoring violently. And so on. I thought, Hell, what a family—all at cross-purposes, muddling along! I fled with my tail between my legs, leaving Sis fuming and griping at how they imposed on her and how indispensable she was. I used to feel that way, but now I know it's not true. They'll get along just as well or better without me, and I'll spare myself a scarred heart if I can only remember that. A scarred heart and many a gray hair. It's hard, though, to be impersonal. But I'm beginning to realize that it's as important for me to inoculate myself against my family as it is for hay-fever victims to stay away from goldenrod and mimosa.

I dread tomorrow because I *have* to sharpen tools. I can put it off no longer. I have an idea to read a few books on photography, borrow Father's good camera, and learn all I can by myself—so that I can present a project to some foundation: a thesis, illustrated, on Scandinavian folk carvings in wood. Of course, learning the languages would be another thing, but I could handle that. God, if I could only swing it, I *know* I could make a good piece of work. Of course, I have no American college degree and only a minor French one and have never gone to an art school. But I think the idea might do, especially if I could publish one illustrated article first in an architectural journal or some such thing. Of course, photography is a field in itself—but I have a fairly good eye for light and shade and pattern and ought to be able to learn how to develop and print. Well—I've had so many big ideas—but *I want to pull out*. It is necessary for Al and me. We're sinking now, slowly.

11. iii. 34

Late Saturday night. I have just pushed Al away from here to dance down in the village. He wanted to go and felt he should not. He has been waiting on me all week, bringing grapefruit juice and listening to me blow a cold away. Tonight he was twitching to be off. I urged and coaxed and commanded him to go, and I really didn't want him to at all. I hate being here alone tonight, I am lonesome for him—and *I* told him to go, for heaven's sake. I don't want to go to bed and I don't want to stay up and every car that passes I hope may be his returning, and I urged him to go and stay a long time and go on to parties if he could. I don't know what I'll do. It would be awful if I seemed sad or grouchy when he came back, yet I am so sad that I could easily be that and grouchy at once. I am probably sad because I still have a cold in my throat, enough to give me a dull senseless monotonous cough, and I am three days late with the curse and have abortion-$75-curettage-abortion in a corner of my mind. And my nails need manicuring and my hair shampooing so that I am not well groomed, and that always disturbs me slightly. And today Sis and Ted drove the children down and for a few hours I was in the thick of an atmosphere of veiled bickering, affectation, strain. I am so sorry for Sis because she loves me, and Ted does not and doesn't want her to, and she is torn and is as yet incapable of any balance between two such diverse loves. She is bewildered and pained and sulky. The children are puzzled by two couples before their eyes, Sis and Ted and A. and me. They wonder at us and no doubt try to make us the proof of many theories.

Gloria came down, as usual laden with exotic jars and bottles, South African gooseberry jam, and Stilton cheese in port wine, and Russian cake. She stayed four days. Although no one even hinted at her long silence, the first three days never quite reached the open-eyed friendliness of last summer. But the fourth day had the old easiness.

Gordon was here two days and sharpened all my tools really sharp.

The day G. and G. left, Fay and Larry came with the baby. Everything happened to make it a bad visit, but if nothing had happened, I still would have wished them nevermore with me. I knew the minute I saw their car at the curb that I should not see them, for our common happiness. I reached the saturation point during their visit here, and now if I heard them coming, I think I would run up into the hills. The second morning they were here, I woke up and told Al that I couldn't see them. I was staying in bed with a cold, and I thought it would be easy, but all day they were with me. I was desperate. I don't know just why it is. I am very fond of Larry and occasionally I almost love him, and although I am not fond of Fay and never have been, I do not actively dislike her. At times I feel very friendly toward her. I wish A. would come back.

Tonight I put the designs on the legs of the bench for Betty Benson. I hope Mother will like the design. I am almost through with the third and last box. I hope I can sell them. I wish I had something made for Mother's birthday, but it is the twenty-seventh, and here it is the eleventh, and we may go to S. F. with the Parrishes next week. I might be able to. Begin anyway, show it to her.

A. bought me some Transvaal daisies, different shades of

coral. I look up at them on the piano from my tuffet; half-wilted and drooping, they are like fireworks, stars shooting out from long green stems. Very delicate. I love them and the tulips he gave me in Dijon that came every morning fresh from Holland, some of them black. The brodiaea are out now on the hills and every vacant lot. Gloria called them water-nuts when she was little, because of the little bulb at the bottom. She ate that. I will eat one this week. I have seen some lupine and a few poppies. I remember when Father bought the orange orchard in Puente, poppies were solid gold between the trees. We didn't pick them, but in three or four years they had disappeared, as everywhere. I think the cultivating buried the seeds too deep.

I sit quite stolidly, but I feel that at each window are faces peering. And when leather creaks on a chair seat, I jump inside, or when a eucalyptus bud hops down the roof, I wish Al would come. I think I'll go to bed. But I'm not at all sleepy.

6. iv. 34

What I mean to do and want to do is write something every day. Many small interesting things come to us, like letters and people for lunch and perhaps an idea. But I am lazy and I put off, and also I am often tired by late night. Now, for instance, it is about 11:00. Al, who cleaned a vacant house today for Tom Harper and for $3, has just hobbled to bed. I want to go soon, before he is asleep. I am rather tired. I didn't get up until 9:30. The morning was dark gray. By noon I had done a lot of dishes, taken a bath and breakfast, made the beds and done the usual bedroom straightening, and cleaned most of the house quite thoroughly. Then I got lunch and, after we'd eaten it, washed the dishes. I went to the beach for an hour and read *Ulysses,* into which, past my first wild gallop, I've settled at a steady pace of about fifteen pages at a time. I'm at the spree between the lying-in home and the brothel now. While I read it, I turned myself neatly to brown on both sides in the sun, which had come out beaming. Various reports of the resultant horrors of the suntan craze had almost decided me against any brown, but the sun is so warm and the sand so soft and lying flat out in the heat so delightful. And I am so nice looking when I'm brown. So now I have a judiciously done three-day coat of tender pink.

Between 2:30 and 6:00 I carved, made a chocolate cake that stuck to the pan but looks all right frosted, went shopping, and got a very good dinner. Of course, Al cooked the steak, and we bought a piece of coconut cake at the Kooky Krock—but I assembled it all and timed things to be done at 6:15. And that is something. We had yams and bananas and artichokes and steak and cake and coffee—rather heavy but very good. And before dinner we found some bourbon of R.'s we had thought all drunk and made a little old-fashioned with it and with some bitters that Larry found in his garage and gave us. Then we went to a movie—and from its end until I began this, I carved. I finished a leg of the Benson bench. It is all right.

9.iv.34

Yesterday, another sunny day, Mom and the kids to lunch, with Father on a stag party, and, of course, I had a steady flow of talk from Edith. Every Sunday is the same. Off she bundles the family, to start to talk to me with eyes ashine. Sometimes I give her nods, or even tell her something new, or perhaps I just say, Ah and Yes and Oh, no. Almost always now she discusses the Kellys. God, how tired I am of them. I love Sis. I love Mother. I am not jealous.

But oh, God above, how sick I am of hearing about the Kellys. I don't like Ted; I think a divorce is the only good end and that soon. I am sad that Sis is unhappy—but why in God's name so much talk? Over and over the same ground, over and over he said and I said and I think and I just told him and what do you don't you I really I'm just.

Anne was here for a night. She and I talked until early morning in the stuffy room. She asked me what I thought and what I'd do and so on, and at first I kept clear. But in the end I told her. I told her I'd go to S. F. with the baby, borrow money if necessary, and live alone for a time and try to find work. She said little, but next morning told me she'd decided to do that. She was bitter at the family's discussions of her most intimate problems, and without saying that the best way to stop that would be to keep quiet herself, I suggested that she say nothing of this venture until it was well started one way or another. She agreed. It would be easy, since Mother already knew she was hunting for an apartment and would not think to ask for how many people. But Sunday I found that Anne hadn't been able to resist, telling just enough—that she was looking for an apartment for S. and herself—to throw Mom into a wild state. Any suggestion of actions not fully predisclosed to her puts her into a frenzy. Anne says that when she has nothing else to fret about, she'll begin on Al and me—how do we live, what is to become of us, why doesn't Al find work—and it all boils down to a fuming anger at her own ignorance of our "plans." It is inconceivable to Mother that we might have none. She feels that we are living independently, secretly almost, and her impotence makes her rage.

Last night we went to a cocktail party in Timmy and Gigi's canyon house. It seemed dull and messy without them. Everyone was drunk. After my second or third glass of the gin punch, I felt very careless, but with the next one I became sober and saw everything with a too-clear eye. The women looked ghastly, their faces gray, their lipstick half gone and discolored. The men looked very silly. The host has the pop-eyed foolish face of a gutter terrier in permanent erection.

We left at 10:00 and hurried down the coast to Larry's house, for we'd told them we might come. But the windows were dark. We felt badly—it's annoying to wait or half-wait for people. And this morning when I found they'd had a bottle of wine for us, I felt worse.

We had a picnic at Emerald Bay with them. Bart barked a lot, and the baby gnawed at a soggy sand-coated zwieback, and I had the curse, but it was all right. I'm at one of my off times with L., when everything he says is either dull or annoying, and all his actions bore me or disgust me. Sometimes I like him so much. He and Fay seem quite happy. I think they ought to get some kind of radio—it would help Larry a bit.

12. iv. 34

A day in bed, long awaited. It is most weak and selfish of me to continue to eat chocolate and cake and things I know so well will lay me low. Al is miserable when I am not well. And I can avoid being so.

To a stupid party chez Harper this week, and yesterday to the Ranch.

I go to night school almost every night, on the Emergency Educational Program. Al makes $7 weekly for two two-hour lectures—we are living on that and my allowance and an occasional dollar he makes cleaning houses for Tom Harper.

Today a letter from Stelter at Occidental asking if we'd consider a part-time job for next semester. We answered yes and suggested that the bigger the salary, the more we'd have to eat. By that time our money will be kaput. I'd like to live on the hill between Broadway and the library in Los Angeles. Last night at dinner with Painter the Old Sea Dog, he told of an immaculate room he gets there for $2.50 a week. What I'd like to do would be to rent two or three rooms unfurnished and borrow enough stuff to live with. The family would squirm at our living in such a quarter.

16. iv. 34

I know that three years from now I'll look back with a certain longing at this time of careless living. Even now I feel it—a nostalgia for the present! But I'll be glad of change, any change. I want life, want to feel, to realize it with all of my being. And it's only now, bit by bit, little by little, that I am becoming conscious. Gradually I see myself shaping up, forming. For years I've been fetal, in the egg shape. I've known it all along. Now I begin to hear, to smell and feel, still through the shell, but I do hear and feel and search. Always before, I've known that I might. I've been uneasy and half-conscious of life outside of me. Other people suffered and were joyous. I was, too, but in an unfilled way. I was living as the reflection in a mirror lives. Now it begins to be me.

Well, no doubt I've written incoherencies. There are times when I feel very acutely my own tiny forming. This is one of them. Often after I've had the curse I seem more acute. That is more than a physical purge, certainly. It has its value. If it weren't so futile, I could easily rage and rebel at its demands. It is so damnably inevitable. Affairs most important, an absolute need for beauty or action or nerve—and no matter, it comes. I am dull. I suffer. I am helpless. I feel a pariah. It is hell. What a god-awful waste of time.

A month or so each year of actual pain, a year or so each decade. God, how mean, how very mean and ignominious a treatment! But, yes, it has its value. If I could live simply and healthfully enough to reduce it to its bare demand of a day or two of annoyance, I'd be months ahead. I could get more done.

That is the joke, of course. Get what done?

Last night we started *Moby Dick*. I think we'll like it.

Today I began to write a quasi-serious article about Laguna: to be or not to be an "artist colony." I want very much to sell it. I'll try to finish it before Thursday. Then when we come back from two or three days at the Ranch (to have the roadster doctored), I'll peer at it again. I do want it to be good enough to sell. I'd like to make a few drawings for it. It would be wonderful to make a little money to give Al, so he wouldn't worry. I'd give him a little present first. Maybe we would take a little trip—to Catalina for a night,. perhaps, or Caliente. Well—counting my chickens.

The children were here for the weekend. When Mother came down for lunch on Sunday, she was twittering with excitement and kept saying, Come, Dote, I want to talk to you—I want you to do something for me—Come, I have something to ask you. I thought, Oh, Lord, she's going East and wants us to take care of the kids or something. She dragged me into the bedroom and closed the door. I kept thinking, Oh, hell, what now. Dotey, she said, and her eyes were very bright, I want you to trade me your old black dinner dress for this. And she had a lovely dress, long and slim, with full sleeves and a funny round collar and jabot of sequins. I was very happy. I tried it on to show to Father. He sat by the fire and said, Now *I tell you*, those lines are—now those lines—turn around, let's see the back—well, *I tell you*, those lines are *good*. I found I was a bit fat, especially my buttocks. I've been eating too many avocados.

Tonight I went to Hinchman's class on modern art and got in

a half hour of typing at each end of it. I want to improve my typing: maybe I could get a job if we were in a city next year.

Last night Fay and Larry came for supper. For a time Larry will be moons away from me. Marriage is making him see many new things about women, and he hates them and feels victimized, so he'll hate me as a woman who has been close to him. He'll suspect me. Perhaps *she* has tricked me, he'll think. It is interesting to watch him change and turn and grow new corners and new colors. Soon he'll begin to rebel. Already he is ready to imagine every kind of wifely imposition. If Fay asks him to lift a heavy pail, Henpecked! he thinks to himself.

When I wonder what Dürer's mother looked upon, I am filled with amazement and with fear, too. I am helpless. She looked into another world, beyond us, and she looked, at the same time, back and in upon her own past and the lives of all her loves and hates and the lives of every person she served in her own life. She looks and looks. There is a kind of expectant immobility, her soul like a pointing dog waiting to leap away from her.

17. iv. 34

Finished an article on Laguna that Al likes. Also did a fairly good sketch of bust and shoulders of a woman, a life class. The clothes are a bother.

26. iv. 34

Beautiful days at Laguna after a short week in Whittier. I went into the water this afternoon. The beach is hot and good. I do little work, other than dishes. Night classes continue in spite of several more contradictory letters to the contrary from various boards and committees.

16. v. 34

It is late, with A. long in bed. Tonight people for supper caused me to drink coffee, so I'm not sleepy. I usually write in this late at night. When A.'s up, I don't want to.

Tomorrow night, after A.'s class, we'll go to Whittier for the weekend.

Today I finished a charcoal drawing for a bookplate for Dave's birthday. I am not much pleased by it. I must do one for Noni before tomorrow night.

5. vi. 34

I sit in a low chair by a good fire. I wear soft black velvet pajamas with green on the neck and sleeves, and my nails are stained green from painting this house. It is the Parrishes' beach house, and we are cleaning it and earning $30. Today we painted hard until late afternoon. Then a rainstorm blew in on it all and floated the paint right off the railings. It was very depressing, but it was fine to be so near the ocean and be rained upon. Now the waves are rather sullen and make a steady peevish noise that sounds all around us instead of just on their side.

Gloria came down with her usual load of strange victuals and a bottle of fine cognac. So I have drunk a little of it here tonight by the warm fire.

Since I last wrote in this book, a great many things have happened. But I think that they really are not very important. Or else they are so complex as to be beyond my writing. If I followed the several separate plots of my own life or anyone's, with all their developments and with all the people who never touch out of their own tales, I'd write all day and perhaps all night. And soon I'd never see any people, and the stories would kill themselves.

I seem to have made a grand big blob of a blot.

My toenails are very long, because I forget to bring scissors from our house every time I go there. It makes me remember reading about a man who was almost overcome by a fearful disgust at the thought of all the whiskers growing in the world on millions of chins, growing and growing and being shaved off and growing more ferociously.

Al's father is dying of Hodgkin's disease. According to some medicos, this is a tubercular infection of the lymph glands. Others call it cancer, glandular cancer. Honky and Bieler call it thus. They say it is cruel and foolish to try to dispel the lumps by rays—the treatment H. H. F.* is following. They say it tortures the victim and leaves his family in debt. H. H. F. writes that for three weeks after a roentgen-ray treatment he lies in bed in great pain (kidneys, spleen, and so on). And I know the Fishers have borrowed money.

This week Father and Mother and the children start for Victoria. I think their trip will grow very wonderful long after it is over, but really while it happens it will be scratched up with many bad moments. They are, all four of them, very selfish people in different ways. The children are most so, of course, because they have never yet realized the existence of any other real people in this world. And Mother, in spite of her pose, justified often, of a self-forgetful and self-sacrificial mother of four fine children, is a most demanding and pettish woman. And Father, half as his "just due"

* Herbert Fisher, Al's father.

and half in self-protection, simply takes, or does, or says—if he wants to belch, he belches, by God.

So they'll all hate each other and sulk and perhaps cry a little bit and feel very much abused or misunderstood. But it will end, in a few years, rosily.

I try not to think of finishing the painting and cleaning the cupboards and washing the windows and waxing the floors and seeing the curtains are back from the laundry by June 14. I hate things like this. And having the sink mended and calling the electrician. Hell, I say.

The ocean still rushes and snaps all around me, and the fire and the cognac cool. My feet look quite far in front of me on the rug, and very thin and elegant in black pumps, because now I am almost always soft-shod in espadrilles. If I wear shoes for a long time, it is reversed, with occasional espadrilles making me feel quite naive and sophisticatedly rustic, like a drawing of the Duchess of Dalrymple Sunning Her Dogs on the Plage.

Jobs look vague. Occidental dwindles, and what looked mildly encouraging at Stanford now seems hopeless. A tentative chance to ship as scab steward and -ess to New York, thanks to strikes, can't be decided for some few weeks. A letter to a friend of Aunt Bess about a job in a Detroit prep school is probably a wasted stamp. And so on. Our money will last a month more, anyway. Then it means debt. I wish Aunt Helen would die. But we still love each other, so I am content.

27. vi. 34

Several months ago I began to write in this book because I thought that what was happening to us was interesting. Or rather,

I thought that the effects of today upon two young people in love would be of value on paper. But it's not the Depression that is happening to us. It is almost unrelated inner things that I cannot or shall not write about. I am sincere when I say that this book is not for anybody. It is perhaps for myself—to read in ten or twenty years and wonder about. But when I think of writing about the real things, I am outraged at the thought of their ever risking others' eyes. They are bitter and tragic and damning and very beautiful, too, and hopeless with the hopelessness of all human passion, and they must stay locked in our own silent hearts.

Al is in Palo Alto, after a week of trying to find work in San Francisco. He tried newspapers and boats, mostly—all with no luck. A bad strike is on among the longshoremen. He was in danger. But what really disheartened him was the first night in town, when he fled at 1:30 from a crawling bed. He suffers so about little bugs. (I remember how I had to wash the lettuce, in France, seven or eight times, with a trip to the faucet in the hall each time. And there'd always be bugs left, when we ate it.) So he was miserable and probably imagined itches all the time he was in S. F. And his pocket was picked. So finally he gave up and went to Palo Alto.

He has written several letters from there, with never a word about his father. Perhaps he's better, but probably worse. A. meant to come back yesterday but instead will come tomorrow, because Herbert [Al's older brother] arrived from China this afternoon. He is invalided home with Chinese dysentery, supposedly—but I sense a scrape. We'll see.

The way we feel now, we'll borrow enough money from Father to go north and will settle in a shack somewhere on the Peninsula. We'd go now, if I hadn't agreed to care for the children until their school starts. We both feel that we must get away from

Laguna. Al's work has come to a standstill, and I don't think he'll be able to start again here.

A good letter from Dave today, in Victoria. He writes tersely but well, of fishing trips and shopping tours and the funny English hotel with its murmuring tea-sippers who so delighted Mother's pussy heart. He wrote, "fished at the mouth of a creek, just where the swift green current met with the blue of the lake." When Sis read that, she looked very disgusted and said, "Well, little Davie's going arty on us! Can't you just see him getting an A in composition for that?" All of which is partly true, but it explains a lot about the scarcity of good letters in our days. People are shamed out of saying anything more polished than "Dear Mamma, We're having a swell trip. Wish you were here. Rained this morning. Love to all." I remember how I guarded against stepping out of that formula all the time I was at school. As I grew older I became a little freer, but I have never written a line to Mother without watching my words to save her embarrassment. For it does embarrass people to read good letters, except in books. I don't mean by that that mine were good—but they would have been much better if I had written more as I wanted to.

14. vii. 34

I am working hard. Dave and Noni are here, and although they are very helpful, there is much to do. I carve as much as I can, though I seem to go at snail speed. I am still paring away at the mahogany bench legs—which are *not* for B. Benson, I suppose, since her engagement is indefinitely postponed. I can probably sell them, or keep them.

The night A. came home from the North, Ben Stelter arrived,

very sheepish, with a job for A. at Occidental—part-time instructor of English at $750 a year. So now we're trying to find a house, and I'm scouting for a job. I want to work anyway, but for money, too, this time. We'll need it. If we possibly can, I want to pay a little of Mr. Bright's $1,000.

I sold the Laguna article to *Westways* and may sell three or four drawings. Don't know yet how much I'm making. I hope it's a fat check. I'll take the kids and the Kellys and Rex and Noni on little parties, and the rest will make me feel easier about buying what we'll need for a house. Yesterday I went to town with Noni and bought two beds (box springs with legs, and hair mattresses) for $42.00. They were repossessed.

The longshoremen's strike in S. F. is very ugly now, with a general strike declared and the town in siege state. It's a hideous mess. This Labor-Capitalism business will be our death in the end. I think it may be necessary, before the country is in revolution, to avert such a seeming catastrophe by declaring war on another nation. But that will just put off for another twenty years an inevitable thing.

*J'ai une élève—une jeune fille de dix-huit ans, de Kalamazoo. Elle hait le français, et elle ne le parle jamais. Chaque leçon est une supplice pour tous les deux—elle s'ennuie horriblement et moi je souffre de son manque total d'intérêt.** Oh, well—fifty cents an hour.

---

* I have a student—a young eighteen-year-old girl, from Kalamazoo. She hates French, and she never speaks it. Every lesson is a punishment for both of us. She is horribly bored and I suffer from her total lack of interest.

25.vii.34

The air jerks and flutters with news of the murder of Dollfuss. After the Nazi "blood purge" of June 30, people sit uneasily. Trouble fills all our brains.

This week I made many quarts of chili sauce and Baltimore relish, for some reason. The reason, I suppose, is my weakness for old odorous recipes. They were given to Mother by a fine cook, one who kept slaves in old Illinois and had a Preserves Pantry. I feel like a cloud of vinegar fumes. My hair, my hands—

I keep thinking about this assassination. The San Francisco strike has almost sputtered out—longshoremen and train drivers still on strike, but the siege over. It seems almost entirely futile. It did throw a little scare into la bourgeoisie, as Comrade Harry Carlisle dates himself by calling it.

Once a young woman walked every afternoon along a stretch of beach. She was tall, with a slender tanned body, and her bathing suit was very short and tight and of a soft gay green yarn.

Every afternoon as she crossed the warm sand to the steps up the cliff, she passed close by a rug, on which sat two people. She was conscious that they both noticed her and waited for her. Especially she knew that the man watched her. She walked very straight and stuck out her two small round breasts a little.

It surprised her that the man and woman were together. He was a tall rather soft man, a few years away from being very handsome. He wore bathing trunks and was busy tanning his skin. The woman rubbed oil on him, and even with her strong hands rubbing him, he watched the young girl pass by. His eyes were spoiled and laughing, the slightly moist brown eyes of an attractive middle-aged man.

That was what surprised the girl, his blatant charm and the woman he was with. There were so many lone lovely women to be with him, but he was always with the plain, gray, strong woman who never spoke but sat watching over him and rubbing his skin when he wanted it rubbed.

The girl thought they were probably the same age. But the man was still boyish and his eyes roved, and the woman was a stocky middle-aged person, blunt looking and never dressed in anything but a white apronlike dress and a coarse misshapen sweater of dull gray.

Every day the girl grew more conscious of the man. She knew he waited for her to pass. She could feel him watching the rise and fall of her little round buttocks, and she was glad that her legs were straight and firm. She stuck her breasts out proudly and wondered about his staying always with an old stubby woman.

One day she walked past them. The man half-lay against the woman's shoulder, and she was humped strongly like a rock to support him. His hand dropped lax beyond a raised knee.

He watched the girl. The woman seemed not to. The girl was very conscious. Just before she got to the steps, she turned and for the first time looked at the two people. Her head was up, very triumphant, because she knew she would catch the man finally with his bright roving look and hold him.

He smiled confidently into her eyes. Then the woman leaned slowly around, and with her white clean teeth she caught hold of the soft sidepiece of the man's hand, the piece from the base of the little finger to the wrist, and she bit it. Probably she did not bite very hard, but it was a stern, an authoritative bite. And it told the girl suddenly of a deep real passion she had not known yet nor even thought about.

The woman looked at the girl. Her eyes were clear and impersonal and swung from the young face out to the ocean. The girl turned and walked quickly away, and for a long time felt very young and humiliated.

26. vii. 34

On the beach—my first picnic in a long time.

Much is being made of the coincidence of the Dollfuss murder with that of the archduke in Sarajevo, which happened exactly twenty years ago, almost to the hour.

The saddest thing, I think, is that such a devout little man was denied the last sacrament or even any religious comfort at all. That would be agony for him.

I thought I had much to say, but I have not. I might put down here something about the house. Perhaps later.

4. viii. 34

While my French pupil scratches her small soft head over an easy examination, I sit very uncomfortably on a wooden chair. It makes me wonder why something bad doesn't happen to the flesh on the human bottom that is so often pinched and ground between bones and seat. It might so logically mildew or turn to leather warts.

One of the things I wanted to put in this book, one of the interesting things, was the trip we made to San Pedro during the strike. Or did I? I never look back in this book—too dull and plain disgusting.

We had a rendezvous with Del Mouran, whose friend, chief steward on a big boat, might get us a job because of the strike. We made wild plans of shipping round the world as steward and stewardess. It turned out to be nothing, all the way. But what was exciting was the atmosphere on Terminal Island. We were very neat and white-collar looking, deliberately: we had debated going in old clothes, in rags, and so on. The streets of working-people's shacks were very quiet. When we crossed the loading tracks and swung onto the wide street that runs along by the docks, we were suddenly in the midst of a strike. Men stood very quietly along the near side of the road, moving slowly up and down with their hands in their pockets and never forming groups. They talked a little but mostly just drifted sullenly along the road. On the other side, the dock side, hundreds of special police, in plain clothes, bustled officiously in cars and in and out of the huge buildings. They were big ugly men mostly, all armed very ostentatiously and all wearing large billies, which they swung from their wrists. They seemed to be delighted by making sudden fierce gestures with them, rapping truck tires and then guffawing and saying, That's what I'd do to 'em. They always had their eyes turned sideways across the road, but they never really looked at the strikers.

The air was hot and gray and horrible with hatred. I was moved. I had never seen men carrying clubs before, and it seemed very awful. The ones with the clubs were so viciously pleased, practicing delightful head-smashers, and the ones without clubs were so ominously and silently hateful.

All my sympathy, my human sympathy, was for the strikers. Of course, if they had ceased their sullen pacing and attacked, I'd have been one of the filthy bitches of the bourgeoisie soon smashed. I may be smashed anyway, before I die another way, by the mad workers. It won't be my fault or theirs.

Hindenburg died, Hitler declared himself supreme ruler for life, the Austrian civil war is curbed for the moment, and stock markets shudder slightly while we all wait to see what will happen.

This week I went to town and for the first time in several years tried on many beautiful dresses and finally bought one. I was crazy to do it—I can't bear to think of all the bills we'll have to pay somehow, the next three months—things like garden hose and window screens and clothesline and dishpans. But I bought it and I'm glad I did. It is a long thin dress with a short jacket, made of a soft silk patterned rather gaudily in clear bright colors. Sis says I look like the cover of a seed catalog in it, and I do. I like it.

Our house shapes itself in our minds. In three weeks we'll go to the Ranch and from there go every day to Eagle Rock. This next week we'll go up to look for a carpenter and a plumber. There are many puttery things to do, like moving shelves and putting on faucets. When we get through, we'll have a jolly little place. We are going to spend about $150 on it, instead of paying rent.

As it is now, the house is made into small stuffy rooms, except for a fine big enclosed porch. We'll knock out the partition and make one big room, with French doors across the front. We'll move the johnny from the back porch to the bathroom and have a little dining room on the porch. The big porch I'll use as a workroom at one end, and at the other our beds will be dressed like couches in the daytime. Al's study will be our main expense, and we plan to use old lumber for it and do all we can ourselves.

The location of the house is wonderful. It is on the saddle between two very high hills. On one side we see down past and over the campus and all its tall trees to the far hills. And on the other we look into the face of the mountains, blue and close. At our feet on that side is a playground. We see only green grass and trees, but shoutings from children come up to us.

18.*viii.*34

Sunday we leave early to go to a cocktail party chez Gloria Stuart and her new husband Sheekman. He is nice—hypersensitive with a too-fine face and sad large brown eyes. Gloria is completely gaga —introduces him as her "honey baby." He is very good to her. His attentions seem thousandfold after Gordon's* slapdash manners. They want us to stay all night, but we want to start on the house Monday morning. But perhaps we'll have drunk too much. I think not, though. I'm gradually working out my own system of intoxication—a pleasant long glow with no bad waking up.

I hope the Parrishes are there.

Leaving Laguna is strange. I am sad and very much relieved. It is exciting to change. It is funny to go from one awful old shack to a worse one, but the new place will be ours, and all the things in it. That will build over us like the sky an inviolable armor. Here we felt helpless, like hermit crabs without shells to back into. But chez nous it will be good.

I have been and still am making a skirt and dress of the blue cotton Herbert Fisher sent from China. It was very stiff and hard blue, so I sent the whole forty yards to a laundry, with instructions to treat it roughly. It came back in a great squishy roll, soft as old linen and of a clear high blue. I can see that it will fade unevenly to gray colors. I am glad. The scarlet and the moon-colored silks still lie in a box. I am stumped by their narrow width—too hard to make a dress—and a pity to use anything so lovely for such quick passing. I'll think of something.

Just then, as I looked out the window, all the light changed very suddenly; the fog had given way to sun. It made me wonder a little, with the slight feeling of awe and skulduggery afoot that you

---

* Gloria Stuart was first married to Gordon Newell.

have when the one window at which you look in a dark building suddenly squares with light—or when a leaf, the one you are watching, trembles on a still tree. It is a coincidence that stirs and soothes us by its promise of strange things meant only for *us*, for a certain person. Our ego puffs itself. Astronomy is successful with a like system.

I was just paid $20. With it I shall pay a seamstress $9.50 for making over one of Mother's dresses and a coat for me, and this afternoon I shall startle my girl by taking her to tea when she thinks she is to have a verb lesson. Then I shall buy Al a good pair of shoes. And with what is left I'll pay a little on our milk or ice bill.

I had a good time with the $35 I got from *Westways*. I bought four dollar books—*Crime and Punishment* for Al, a mystery omnibus for Dave, Shaw's *Intelligent Woman's Guide to Socialism and Capitalism* for Noni, and *The Well of Loneliness* for myself. I paid Mother $10 of the large sum I owe her for beds and stoves and so on. Then this week I took her and Rex and Al to Hollywood. We went first to Don the Beachcomber's for a cocktail. Then we went to Sardi's, where we had a good table, good waiter, good dinner, good wine and coffee, and a very amiable time. Then we went back to Don's where Rex bought fine cognac for us. We tried to call the Parrishes, but when we couldn't get them, drove slowly home in the warm dark night, all very comfortable and pleasant.

The rest of my money I used for food. This summer has been very agreeable. Dave and Noni have been nice all the time, with never any fussing and always ready to help. They have been well and seem very happy—for people their age.

Muscat grapes begin to be raisins already. That is the only good result of a dry year. Papers and radio news say, The worst drought in America's life. Occasionally ghastly newsreels are shown of cattle falling over on dry naked plains or bellowing with cracked voices in stockyards, with their hipbones almost through their hides. And people sitting listlessly at their bare blazing door-steps, while their fields show sharp rows of twelve-inch corn, which turns to dust in the fat hands of the cameraman's assistant. Not many such pictures are shown. They disturb people. And people must not be disturbed.

In the Middle West farmers are beginning to say that the drought is God's punishment for Roosevelt's plan of plowing under every fifth row and killing surplus hogs—all to raise prices last year. Now there is too little instead of too much, and good pious farmers mutter of God's wrath. It may be Roosevelt's doom song. It is ominous, Rex says, when religion mixes with politics.

21. viii. 34

At the Ranch. We came up Sunday, piled to the gills with an incredible amount of what seemed junk at the time. I still do not understand the human faculty for collecting social increment. We took eight or nine large boxes of books, papers, letters from the house, and yet it didn't look much emptier. And then all our clothes, and linen, and blankets and knives and forks. The relentless piling frightens me. We've fought it ever since we married.

Sunday evening we went to a cocktail party given by the Sheekmans. It was very restrained—many too-cultured voices and silver-fox capes, with everyone there for business. Except us and Dillwyn. I can see that he may be of value to Gloria—but why us? Everything seemed very shoddy and pretentious and terribly and dreadfully dull. A strange difference from G.'s parties of a year or so ago, so noisy and alcoholic and littered with interesting tramps. This was alcoholic enough—but badly "refined" by large incomes and Hollywood architecture. We left early.

Monday morning we spent looking at French doors donated

to our house by two of Father's friends. In the afternoon we took old Trueblood the Quaker carpenter to Eagle Rock and spent two hours or so going over the house. It emerged a very amusing little place, as we had expected. Then the proprietor appeared. He hummed and muttered for almost an hour to tell us what we guessed at his first sentence—the property had to be sold, and the house was to be wrecked immediately!

I was really much disappointed. So was Al. We hurried home silently and had a drink of whiskey. After dinner we went to a fight with Rex. We sat in ringside seats, and for a few minutes I was a bit overwhelmed by the thudding and gasping of two bodies so close to me and the occasional whiff of sweat. But soon I forgot. The fights were mediocre, except for two lightweight Negroes. I liked looking through and across the white ring to the steep wall of people watching. At the beginning of the late rounds, the air was full of bright drops where the boys struck, because they'd been doused to make them springier.

This morning we started out to look for another house. We drove toward Eagle Rock, going up and down streets that looked as if they might have shacks on them. It was tiring. But we have a fine six-room house on a wooded slope of hill, almost invisible to other houses and in need only of a little plumbing and a lot of paint. We are delighted. It is roomy and full of light and air from many windows. The living room and bedroom are large, and Al will have a workroom and I a screened porch for my carving table. The bathroom is bad—small and dark—but more than we had in France, ever.

Now I am in our house. We have lived in it ten days and nights, and we are very happy in it. It is a good peaceful little house. We grew tired before we finished painting, even with much help from the Parrishes. And after the Sunday we moved—on a truck from the *News* office, with Harrison's help—we were quite numb and incoherent. For several nights we slept like stones in our new beds. Now we are wide awake again.

There are many windows still to be scraped and washed and other little things to do. But the country lies flat with heat, and here in the house I move languidly and do only the basic things like dishwashing and the making of beds.

Al is well set into the routine that seems so necessary to him. He has classes in the morning, and in the afternoon he works in the library after he has eaten his bread and cheese and fruit and drunk a little bottle of milk. At night we eat a simple but rather large dinner slowly by candlelight. The dining room is white and cool, with the silly yellow organdy curtains with big white polka dots on them moving across the sill silently in the air. Then Al goes to his study and I read or write or bathe. Then we read—now *Crime and Punishment*—and go to bed.

Two days ago Anne had her stomach split, an ovary removed, her uterus shifted about, and several ligaments tied tighter. All that was caused probably by careless haste after Shaun's birth. The repair of such damage is very important. It may rescue a woman from frigidity and ill health and neurasthenia. Anne needs rescuing. She insisted on a spinal anesthetic and watched the operation with interest that dwindled to faintness by the end of the forty minutes. She felt very miserable for two days, but today was better. She had been stimulated by an intravenous injection of glucose, and her voice was very dreamy and lilting. I took her some rock sugar on three little strings, wrapped primly. She was reminded of other times—not special ones, but just times—as I was when I first spotted the dusty jar of crystals in our corner drugstore. They are scarce now.

23. ix. 34

Our house is very nice. It is a Sunday afternoon after a soft rainy night. The air is cool and clean and thinly lighted. Ashes crack metallically on the hearth of our square, ugly, yellow rock fireplace, which was so hideous until we put bookcases on each side of it. Tonight we are going to supper with the Powells, because we'll have to sooner or later and might as well get it over with. It's horrible to feel that way about people who may be our best friends. I like Gigi and Dillwyn very much indeed and think they like us especially well until I see them being just as nice to dozens of other people. They are right to be so withdrawn in their intimacies—we are the same—but still it is sometimes disturbing. But the Powells bore me completely—and I think it is mutual.

When I was putting some papers away, I looked at several diaries I have kept during the last ten or fifteen years. I am struck by their dull sameness. It is far from interesting and utterly unimportant to record that on June 11, 1927, I felt very bored and wondered what I was meant for and wished I could work or do or create. That went on and on. I think that it is better to write of food or people or sleep, after all. I've always disapproved of "Line-a-day books" that say, Rain today—twelve quarts of milk, three dozen eggs—J.'s earache. But now I think they're better than pages and years of incoherent dissatisfaction. Perhaps from a genius such mutterings would be valuable—significant, anyway. But God, how dull from me.

Yesterday I read about sixty freshman English papers. Al assigned an autobiographical sketch. Most of the girls became very introspective. Their papers sounded as if they were saying, "See how frank, how self-understanding, how subtle I am! And how complex, how unusual! How misunderstood—but what a sense of humor!" I retched to recognize myself. And the glib ones, too: there I was, the facile, occasionally clever and very self-conscious student who came to college with straight A's in high school English. How plodding and forced was my would-be sparkling irony. And how very wide-eyed was my wonder at my own depth.

But I really couldn't help it, nor can they. They do stand above the average high school writer. Their teachers, numbed by years of misused English and grateful for even a faint glimmer of enthusiasm for the language, flatter them and accept their most idiotic papers as a kind of manna. They become very self-satisfied and glib. And then the hell of it is that when they get to college, there is rarely anyone to help them. If some older, keener person had only shown me how crude, how cheap my papers were, how makeshift my work, I'd have been forever in his debt. I know I was recognized, just as I recognize these children. But nobody bothered. Perhaps they thought it labor lost.

I believe that I began to write today with the firm belief that only incident matters in a diary, that people and objects are much more interesting than my own badly expressed beliefs and dissatisfactions. Belief on the brain. So I have covered several pages with belief.

Last night Gigi and I went to see Mrs. Leslie Carter in *The Circle*. Ten years ago Mother and Father saw her and Drew in it, and since then I have thought of it as a very lively comedy that made them laugh for many days. But last night it sagged horribly. Not one line was funny. The cast was ill at ease. The only good parts in it were very poignant and almost melodramatic. Mrs. Carter was an oddly misshapen monster with enough of her old fire to shift the audience from a dismayed gasp at her first entrance to a politely enthusiastic series of final curtains. Her buttocks were pulled up into the small of her back by bad corseting, and her heavy shoulders and breasts made her old-woman arms and legs look like brittle sticks. She was very bad until the last act. Then she revived and was almost grand. The curtain came down on a fine, sparkling old actress—and suddenly her third or fourth curtain showed a little witch, collapsed and death-tired, clutching at a chair in the middle of the empty stage.

24. ix. 34

Above the tub in our small white bathroom is a square window that once opened into the yard. Right there a room was added to the house. Now it is Al's study, and when I go into the bathroom quietly and try not to make too much noise on the johnny (the obsolete kind with a resounding well of water into which a tinkle hurls itself like Niagara), I peer on tiptoe over the tub into the lighted room. Al taps on the typewriter or writes minute tracks on little scraps of paper. He smokes a pipe with a kind of absent-minded sensuality, or holds a cigarette gingerly in his fingers. His hands have the arrested movement, the unreality, of great carving. He frowns slightly.

Last night at the Powells'—an evening that started rather dully with us feeling rather de trop, and ended smoothly and amicably at nine o'clock after a bad dinner and going out into a cold hard night that you could feel go in and out your nose—last night Fay gave me a strange red and black garment. It looks Tibetan, of thick crisp wool like a good blanket. The neck, V-shaped, and the pudgy sleeves with uneven mouths halfway between wrist and elbow are edged with black silk tape. A black stripe, about four inches wide, runs from the right front to the bottom, and on the back it is on the left. The robe has four openings, the neck, the sleeves, the bottom: there are no buttons. It falls straight down, in thick clumsy lines, from my shoulders past my knees. There is a fading smell of camphor about it. I wear it tonight, in this rather cold room, and I feel that I shall wear it for a long time. I like Fay for giving it to me. The color is not an ordinary red but a high clear pungent color, like a perfect young tomato or an English horn.

In this robe and fur slippers, I could work well in a very cold room, except for my hands. I really love this robe.

25.ix.34
Faculty Women's Club Meeting

I go at 2:30 in spite of my resolve to be an hour late. Even so early, I am the last to arrive. The house, new and waxed and with the carefully planned discomfort of synthetic "genuine pieces" and catalog Orientals, bulges snugly with women. It is horrendously refined.

My hostess, new president of the club, is a singer, wife of the music department manager. She is tall and very vital, with crisp gray hair that grows at right angles to her scalp rather than parallel to it. Her dark eyes flash professionally, and her tall stout body seems always ready to breast an aria.

Women rise up at me, curiosity hard on the heels of their warm cordial words. I make smiles and hide behind the part of Our New Member Young Dr. Fisher's Wife She Is Really a Member of Our Family. Yes, '27, or was it '29? I find myself kissing Mother's old music teacher, who gives piano lessons out here and watches her diet because of neuritis in her hands. Finally I sit down.

The large careful room is ringed with women. They are not distinguished. A few have kind faces. Some are dressed with clumsy consciousness of La Mode as exposed by advertisements in the *Times.* One or two are very strange looking. The secretary, sitting with a black notebook of minutes, her hands trembling a little, has a round pale face that looks quite normal from the front. But when she is in three-quarter profile, I see that her eyes are set in her head sideways, like a rabbit's. Another woman with small meek shoulders wears round glasses with lenses ground to so many different strengths that her eyes appear to be at the far ends of two long gleaming tubes. Her clothes are a caricature of the frowsy faculty wife. Where are such hats made, where sat upon? Her shoes are improbable.

The meeting is called to order by my hostess, and for an hour and almost another, there is much parliamentarian formality, much Madam Presidenting and seconding of idiotic motions. The president holds her little black book below her bosom with that gesture peculiar to divas. I feel that she really is peering discreetly at it to remember the second line of "Tes Yeux, Tes Jolis Yeux."

The secretary takes trembling notes, after reading last year's leavings. She speaks English softly and well and occasionally lifts her strange eyes obliquely. The treasurer, a compact, efficient woman who reminds me of a business school director I once knew, reads a report of money lent to girl students, of a large bank account, and of eighty cents for postage stamps.

There is talk of how to make more money, all woven through with All those in favor signify—and I move that the motion be— and so on.

I look around the room, behind my mask of the New Member. A hairpin keeps slipping down, and I wonder if I have on too much lipstick. I smooth at my upper lip with one finger. The president's wife suddenly looks out at me from behind a far sofa.

Her large flat blue eyes flicker with comprehension. I feel better. She bends her chic head down and knits at a blue skirt. She is the only one who is occupied.

A lean bright-eyed young woman plays rather well on the cello. Then the wife of the dean of men tells of last year spent in China. At times she is quite interesting. Her pronunciation is good, without affectation, but her English is involved and most of her sentences get away from her. She is dressed rather well except for very vulgar kid gloves with colored appliqués on them, but her figure is inexcusably ugly. She is evidently unconscious of it, for her clothes, bought with some care and pleasure, accentuate by their cut her loose belly, her swayback and sagging breasts, and the rolls of fat above her hips. She is distasteful to look at. Her face, too, is one of those pudgy, heavy white faces with dark eyes and rather thick peevish mouths—the face of a passionate woman with a sallow disposition.

As she talks, a man's voice mumbles in the hall, and I know it is four o'clock and teatime. It is the biology professor who comes first and tiptoes straight to the dining room. It is college legend that frightened coeds at sorority banquets can and do put themselves and him at ease by talking voluptuously of food. He is most sparkling about the heavier dishes like German fried potatoes and pancakes with sour cream. Then his little round eyes peer most jovially over the tops of his spectacles, and the coeds feel very worldly and able to make conversation.

Now he heads a straggle of men. The president looks anxiously at the wife of the dean of men, who continues talking for several more minutes, her mouth secretly peevish. Finally she invites people to look at a satchel of her little boy's Chinese clothes and some little dolls, and the women flock politely toward the dining room. The biology professor stands by a large tray of little sandwiches. He has put down his teacup to have two hands for eating.

The noise is frightful after the cultured elocution of the hostess and the gurgling murmur that welled swiftly up from all the women like one big bubble after any of her mild waggishness. Now the men's deeper mumble holds it only one notch below monkey-house pitch. The tea makes a fine decent smell in the air. I finally get a cup and drink it. People pluck at me, and I listen beamingly to many almost soundless shoutings.

Finally I go. I am exhausted. My face is stiff and my head rings. As I go out the front door, I remember taking ether and how the voices go in and out, *boom* sway away *close* boom away. And I see the controlled nervous face of the president's wife, flushed and smooth and like one hideously wrenched underneath, as a tall stringy woman crashes down two steps to the floor. She is the wife of the head of Religion. People rush politely to pick her up. The president's wife goes on knitting, and the sudden red in her face fades slowly until she is very pale.

10. i. 36

I sit close to the basket of coal fire, alone in our sweet neat dear little house. A. has gone to see his mother, somewhat alarmingly depressed, last night at least, with a cold and the realization of a year now past since her husband died. On my knees, crooked over the pillow on the walnut love seat, is an elaborate pattern made of *War and Peace,* Toby the kitten, and this unwieldy copybook.

It is maybe a year since I last wrote here. I haven't looked. My mind steams with words. I am on the point of beginning a novel, and may God help us. I have good material—the founding of the Quaker town of Whittier. I have no experience, except for the book I wrote last winter. It is a strange and satisfying thing to finish a book. I'll finish this, and it should be good. I suppose all writers think that.

This vacation—Christmas—Noni, home from Wells, and I took an afternoon's ride into the country between home and Prado and back, a slow circuit over empty back roads. I remember saying, as we drove into the old finished town of Orange, that if I should sell a book it would be queer, because then I'd be called the "writer" of the family, and really I have no more talent than any of the others. Noni laughed in agreement. Then today, as I hoed ferociously in the side yard, preparing a bed like a big grave for seeds when this rain comes, I thought, That's right but not right, because I shall have *written*. They'll not. Comparisons are not possible.

I know, after correcting several thousand themes from every kind of class, Junior League to freshman, that there are countless, yes, countless people who *could* write. They could write much better than I. But they don't. I do. I don't know why. I seem to have no special interest, *no* interest really, in selling things and seeing them printed. I believe there are too many books, too many people writing, above all too many women writing. But I write, without really wanting to. I write probably ten hours a day, mostly in my mind. Now I am writing while I garden, mulling over and over, almost like the daydreams that flow with somnolific music, the actions in this damned, this goddamned novel about Whittier.

On the radio a Handel program trips and bounces smoothly. The fire putters flatly, like butterflies.

Tonight at the dinner table A. and I talked prosaically—my God, is there such a word?—of having a child next fall by our own work or by the courts. Is he sterile? Am I? Are we fools to get a child? Will we breed a fiend or adopt an idiot? Would it be better to grow old alone, unbothered, dry, inverted? Or shall we oil our joints with the troublous juices of children all about us? I see the heart tearings, the million small anguishments of a parent. But I grow to believe them better than the sapless life of old lone beings. Our years in England, in Russia, in Italy, and dear France I see swing irrevocably into dimness, and in their places are the illnesses, the lies, the cruelties of new humans—we in their power and forever relegated to second rank. But I choose it so. Six years alone with A. have given me a fortitude that I know will withstand any torture. Children, much as they will cost us, cannot but bring joy, too. At a puppy or a kitten we laugh and exchange quick sweet glances. How much more at a child, our own by flesh or law? And I feel this might be better for it, too—to feel free from us from the beginning.

My garden gradually smooths itself down into an ordered chaos. I pull leaves off iris plants now and wait for rain, although I know the soil is bulging with wild barley seeds that will grow madly at the first moist encouragement.

I look forward to a summer here, although I feel that next June will find us going somewhere again. Our courtyard is most pleasant, and if we were going to be here all summer, I should feel justified in buying a few big canvas chairs and a lantern or two. As it is—I shall once more plant it with yellow flowers and hope to be able to care for them.

For seven months now I've written to Timmy instead, really, of writing in a journal. I think that by this time he has started on his travels, and my correspondence with him has ended, at least for a time. It has been good, in many ways. He is, both unconsciously and by intent, a master at drawing people out of their commonplace shells into the full glare of introversion, self-appreciation, and neuroticism. That is very valuable, and for that and many other reasons I value my friendship with him, and my true love and affection.

I feel foreboding and a weight of ominous sorrow about C. Y. F., as always when someone I love is even partly ill. I remember how I went to see Mother a few hours after she went to the hospital with influenza. She lay, gray and enormous, under the light covering on the bed. Her chest rose and fell quickly under the uncouth wrappings of a pneumonia jacket. I tried to talk to her, but she answered perfunctorily, as if breathing and even living were much more important at that moment. I left, and as soon as I had got out the front door and down into the high bushes that lined the walk to the parking space, I was contorted, inside and out, with bitter sobs of suffering and anxiety. I felt that Edith was surely near death. My little mother, so young, so old with suffering, so annoying, so endearing, was near death. And I was helpless. What could I do? I suffered, trying not to cry aloud, there in front of the implacably noncommittal building that hid her preoccupied breathing.

The next day when I went to see her, full of dread and resigned to that awful moment, she was gay and quick, her skin its usual creamy brown and her brown eyes bright. I felt strangely cheated, even in my elation.

I notice that same feeling now that A.'s Aunt Mary draws hesitantly near what she calls Home. Her death will be double for Aunt Evvie, bound to her by the mysterious veins of an identical twin. We call each day to see if Mary has died. We are prepared for it. But if, after all this, she recovers, we shall feel that shameful disappointment known to all men whose dear friends have almost but not quite died. I think it is because we really hate life. When a man dies, we feel that at least he—we, vicariously?—has escaped. Then if he comes back, we are irritated. So nearly to have put off all the trivia! And how painful, how wearisome, again to resume them! We suffer for him, and for him take up once more the grim burden of brushing teeth, excreting waste, buying gasoline. Why the hell didn't he get out of it when he had the chance?

I have a fine new dress, purple in daylight and a silver-grayish purple at night, with a low décolletage and a full-skirted soft-flowing coat. I think it should have been made of some stiff material to be as dashing as its picture. But in this soft crepe it has a certain dignity, rather too mature for my taste. (The first sign of maturity, to resent that?) I shall wear it tomorrow night to a fraternity dance, with silver combs in my hair and silver slippers, a judiciously heavy makeup, and an air of preferring to be with the fraternity rather than anywhere else.

A. is home, with a sack of chocolate peppermints and the news that his mother, in bed and looking like a girl with all her wrinkles smoothed out, is better and much happier.

I hear, between recordings of a Mozart quartet, that rain is predicted for tomorrow. Well, I had planned to finish peeling the iris leaves in the lower meadow. But it is better. I should clean the house. Rex and Edith come for supper next day, and she, like most rather lazy housekeepers, is very conscious of other women's dust. Then Monday I drive to the Ranch for a rabbit to jug* for Wednesday and, I hope, on to town to get a decent pair of shoes for A. Tuesday we should go to Occidental for a lecture. Wednesday Guy Nunn and his girl come to supper. Friday we go to the theater with a couple whose male half A. has met at the Huntington. Saturday there's another dance. Sunday—and so on. But this is a good life, I think. I have a fairly good body, an active if insignificant mind, a charming house to live in, and most important, all-important, my dear love by my side and all about me.

---

* Rex Kennedy raised rabbits (as well as pigeons and chickens).

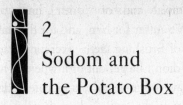

2
Sodom and
the Potato Box

Sodom looked once more into the dark depths of the half-covered potato box. It was hard to see in there. Down in the canyon behind the sloping eucalyptus wood, Sodom squatted among the dark, wet leaves, his head bent half-fearfully over the old box. It was a serious task he had set himself, this burying of his soul, and he wished that he had never heard the troublesome word. He'd have to go through with it, though, or else be tormented for the rest of his life by a feeling of self-apology. Once before he had been nagged by that itching emotion, when he had delayed for weeks the simple and easily told end of a story for his father, and he knew too well the unpleasant fatigue of such weak procrastination.

He frowned and peered resolutely through the crack in the top of the box. It was growing dark, and the cool earth of the little canyon sent up damp odors from among the tree roots. He must hurry.

A moldy mass of sodden papers, pages of print and pictures torn from journals, and with them three pale silken strands of ribbon, stained and faded, showed in the blue light. He shook the box gently and felt the bottle bump against the side and then roll into view—an old green bottle, its unmistakable color glowing dimly, glassily, through a mist of innumerable scratches. Beside it lay the skull of a rabbit, tiny and finite and sharply white in the deep shadow, but connected with the darkness by a string of beads that curved through the eye holes and away into the black corners. Sodom rattled the box once more and squinted anxiously into the crack in the top as if he were rather afraid that something else would slide into view. He heard the bottle thump heavily into the lowest corner, and the beads rattle quickly after, but nothing more. A look of quiet satisfaction crept over his face. All was ready, then, and he was about to dispose in the most gentlemanly way of his encumbering soul. He sat for a minute in the dim little canyon, his hands resting lightly on the box and his eyes half-closed.

It was queer that he had found out so easily about his soul and had known so clearly what to do with it. He remembered that day very well. He was in the window of his father's study, sitting on a pile of books behind the long red curtain. Outside slow drops of autumn rain slipped down the pane of glass; and he could see the eucalyptus trees twist and bend through the tiny wet paths. He was almost asleep.

Suddenly he heard his father, with a voice that jerked him awake as if his dreams had been cut short by a shriek, a groan, anything but this dull soft sound, say an interesting thing.

"You are a creature without a soul, Lydia." Sodom heard his mother walk toward the door, and he peered quickly around the fuzzy edge of the curtain to see what she would answer to this puzzling observation that seemed to hurt his father's throat. Lydia stood with one hand on the dark wood of the open door, as if she were thinking. With a quick movement she threw back her head and laughed silently, then closed the door sharply behind her.

Sodom pulled back his shoulders so there would be no chance of his being seen and sat waiting for his father to leave the room.

His mind was jumping with excitement. He realized keenly that the ever-present sound of his father's pen had stopped, leaving a kind of buzzing shadow of itself in the dead silence of the room. Not even a breath came from the still figure of the man seated at the cluttered table, and Sodom himself had forgotten that his own breath came and his heart still beat. What was the thing his mother lacked, the thing his father spoke about as if it were a curse, a magic spell? Here was something more to know, something so important that the mention of it could make his mother move from her accustomed pattern of gestures and toss her head with a laugh almost audible. As the little boy realized that he had finally seen his mother smile, he felt a shock, a thrust of horror that made him dizzy. What was her soul? He wondered eagerly if he had one, being a man instead of a woman like Lydia, and then hoped passionately that he had not.

He felt as if he must know, but how to do it? There was only his father to tell him, and Sodom knew that something had made the subject unpleasant to him. He turned the situation over and over in his teeming brain, feeling that if he could not find out about this new thing he would die.

Then the luncheon bell rang, and Sodom kept himself from leaping to his feet until his father had walked slowly out of the room. The dining room was silent except for the restrained chewing of the three people at the table. The man and woman sat stiffly in their places and ate in a politely businesslike way. Sodom, between them on his lonely side of the table, looked from under his eyelids at them. How could he ask them a question that they themselves had planted violently in his mind a half-hour before, when now they looked as if nothing had ever happened to disturb their usual deliberate behavior? He felt as if he were going to explode—or be very sick.

The meal dragged on. Finally he saw in a kind of agony that his mother had wiped her lips and then put the napkin beside her plate of nutshells and desolate-looking grape skins. He must say something before she pushed back her chair.

"Father," he heard his voice squeak in a high, defiant tone, "what do you call the soul?"

The room seemed suddenly full to the brim with startled and rather disapproving attention. Sodom felt that his mother had stopped breathing, but from the corner of his eye he could see that her fingers still played casually with the edge of her folded napkin. His father looked at him seriously, as if he were some interesting but slightly distasteful animal. The boy thought for a minute that he was not going to be answered. Then the gray man's lips opened slowly, and from them fell slow words.

"The soul, Sodom, is a collection of emotions that is deified by weak men into an intangible idol upon which he turns his own punishments from God," he said with a sly look into the blank eyes of his son. Then he glanced quickly up at his wife, who sat across from him stiff with attention.

"The soul," he continued in a quiet voice that chilled Sodom with remembrance of the one he had heard that morning in the study, "is the result of emotion. It can be hidden, but it is immortal because it grows from love, sentimentality. Hate has no soul. Sodom, if you ever have a soul, hide it. It is precious junk . . ."

For several seconds the man and the woman looked at each other, as if they were discussing things long ago dismissed from their common conversation. Then Lydia lowered her white eyelids, and as at a signal her husband stood up and walked deliberately from the oppressive silence of the room.

Sodom knew for the first time that his mother hated his father. That is why she had no soul.

He went quickly on to the next problem, having solved that one so neatly. His father advised him to hide his own soul, if he had one, and since he was quite without hatred, he realized that there must be one belonging to him. He was puzzled. He looked quickly at his mother to see if she would remind him of anything and found that she was staring at him as if she saw him for the first time. When she saw that he looked at her, too, she started and then smiled into his bewildered young eyes with the ghost, more tender, of her morning's quick laugh. In a flash she went away from the table, as if she'd had enough of such nonsense.

Sodom left the room in a fog of thought. He felt sure that he had a soul. What was it his father had said—"a collection of emotions . . . hide them . . . precious junk"? Yes, precious junk. That was it.

The boy was filled with relief, his bewilderment dissolved by the words of his father, which still sounded in his ears with a kind of rhythm. He walked rapidly to his room and pulled his old wooden box, once made for potatoes, from under the bed. That had been almost three weeks ago, and now he was ready at last to hide his soul. Here it was, in the box beneath his hands, its various parts rolling and rattling to his slightest touch. He wondered idly if it would mind being so thoroughly dismissed from the warm, secret life of his room, where it had lived so long with him. And he hoped he had chosen the right parts from the collection of precious things that he had been making all these years. It had been rather hard to know what was really his soul and what just things, but he had finally decided on the oldest and most valued of his clutter of junk.

It was almost dark. He rose stiffly to his feet and picked up a little garden trowel that he had brought with him. He worked fiercely in the thick dusk, digging with rapid thrusts into the wet mold of the canyon's side. Roots of the trees that whispered distantly above him twisted through the earth and out into the calm air of the ditchlike little gully and made it easy for him to hollow between their bendings a tiny cave. He worked furiously for several minutes, and then, panting and sweaty with effort and an almost unbearable excitement, he thrust his short arm into the black hole. Yes, it seemed big enough. He picked up the box, holding it on a level so that the green bottle would not roll about, and tried it. He laughed. The hole was really too big, too high.

He suddenly had the idea to turn the box on its side; then the dirt would not fall down through the crack in the top. He did this gleefully, then shoved with all his might against the end of the box until he could feel it pushing bluntly against the spongy earth at the back of the cave. His arms ached with tiredness, and he wished that he had dug the cave lower down instead of on a level with his face. However, it was done now, and a fairly good job he had made of it, he decided.

The visible end of the box was a faint yellowish blur in the canyon side, about a handbreadth in from the face of the ditch. He pushed a few fists of sticky loam against it, pulled a vine down over it from the bank, and then stepped back to view the resting place of his most precious junk, his soul. It was hidden now even from him. He and the dusk and the wet earth had worked well together.

He walked home, stumbling a little in the cool dark and feeling rather lonesome. He began to hum a song he had thought of several days before, and slapped the trowel against his trouser leg to make still another sound in the hushed evening air.

—*Laguna Beach, California, 1936*

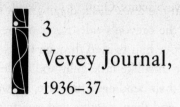

3
Vevey Journal,
1936–37

31. x. 36
Vevey

A week ago last night we were together for the first time. Al
and I came at noon, inwardly very nervous: would T. be here,
would he still like us, would he want us to live with him when he
saw us? Outwardly we were quite calm, remembering the gargan-
tuan omelet we had tried to eat the night before in Bâle and the
pocketsful of monies we had juggled on the wagon-restaurant from
Holland, drinking coffee in Lausanne, looking for Le Pâquis as we
raced along the lakeshore toward Vevey. And then T. was not here.

But Otto Trettman met us, tinier than ever, shaking and
flushed, with tears of nervousness and perhaps emotion rolling
slowly in the corners of his sharp fierce eyes. As always, he took
care of everything and came with us to the pension where we are
now. (It is the usual excellent Swiss establishment, clean, chaste,
filled with ancient dames and damsels and a few grumpy men in
toupees, all of whom totter slightly as they walk through the ugly
dining room to their tables ranged with tonic bottles and tin boxes

of laxative biscuits. Oppressive—we feel like rowdies if our voices rise above a low hiss.)

Here were chrysanthemums, gold ones growing and ragged lavender ones in a bowl, and sherry, and brandy, and cigarettes. "At Mr. Parrish's orders," Otto explained, but we thanked him, too. We drank together, two tears rolled for every one before from his eyes, we toasted each other and T., and he left.

When T. came on the 6:10 train, we had a little advantage over him because we had bathed and settled our bodies if not our souls, but all three of us were jittering for many more reasons than could be written. Otto disappeared discreetly toward the baggage while we kissed and touched each other and tried to see months in a few seconds. T. looked well, strong, handsome. Al was almost knocked down to see the change in him, from the broken man so old and wounded who had cried as they had gone to the station eighteen months ago in Hollywood, to this young man with the calm eyes. And not only physically, Al saw, had he changed. I was glad that Al felt that, too.

We nibbled politely at dinner and talked too fast, interrupting almost every sentence and laughing at nothing. Later we went to a café, two cafés, and drank rather a lot of vin de Vevey but not too much.

The next day, a Saturday, we took a car through Chardonne to Chexbres and ate soup and salad and cheese in the café of the Lion d'Or. Then we started slowly down the road toward Le Pâquis. It was a clear cool day, with the thin sunlight of October on all the yellowing leaves of the vineyards. Windows were open; we could hear women singing and stirring things in bowls. Cats and children sat on the doorsteps. A black dog barked from a balcony.

Al saw Le Pâquis first. The rusted iron door was off its hinges, but we lifted it back and walked in again to feel really there. Leaves still hang on the trees, and the grass is short and green, with still some purple clover and an occasional snapdragon or harebell in it. The little source trickles peacefully, as if forever, clear and very cold, and the brooklet is very busy and tiny, like Otto.

We went into the house. I was surprised at its size and good condition. There is the skeleton of a fine little stair in granite. The two rooms are airy. There is a funny little toilet, a privy, with one seat for people and another, much lower, for children.

The whole place was unbelievable. Since the first day I saw it, last March (the last day it was, too), I've been warning myself that nowhere would there be anything as lovely as it was that day in the first of spring, with the burgeons reddening and swelling and violets thick in the grass. And I was right. It is even more beautiful. The lake far below, the mountains, the curve of the land, and the strong fine smell of the air are more than seem fair for one spot on the world. But there they are, all. I saw them again, felt the trees growing and the earth beneath me, walked through the sturdy cottage, drank from the source and ate mint beside the brooklet. It exists, and so do we.

We were very happy.

The next days are important because we did so much and with such amazing ease—thanks, of course, to Otto. We drew many plans, one night in the Buffet de la Gare, over beer, then supper, then coffee, and finally a bottle of champagne, and the next morning met with Otto and an architect. He was a tall, taciturn man, competent looking, who reported the house in good condition and put our plans into his portfolio.

That was the day we started early, with Nicolas conducting, first to Le Pâquis and then across the road to meet our neighbor the head vigneron of the *faverges,* the vineyards of Fribourg. We went to his cellar, the old site of a convent, with a fine vaulted ceiling. The wine was in fermentation, and the air full of heady decay. We closed the great door to keep the temperature right and in the light from one bulb drank several bottles of *faverges* 1934—the architect, Otto, Nicolas the chauffeur, T., Al and I, and the vigneron. He is a strong, heavy man near sixty, shrewd and probably violent in anger, inquisitive but impersonal—a good peasant, and a good neighbor or a bad one following our own behavior. I think all will be good.

We visited the *pressoir,* descended to the cellars for more wine, talked interminably of crops and rival vineyards. Finally we left, with the germ in T.'s and Al's heads to make Al winemaster of Le Pâquis. (By now the idea has matured, and Al plans to study the art and perhaps practice it—and perhaps, with his training and intellect and some acquired experience, contribute to the Swiss industry. Why not?)

On to Otto's for a drink of wine and an introduction to his wife, a round, soft-voiced woman from Czechoslovakia. The daughter Anna was there, too, round and soft and pretty, speaking better French than her parents, pale and spoiled. And a white cat, Zizi, who has already caused fourteen kittens, Anna told me, although he has not that many months.

Lunch with Otto and the architect, who is not much socially —very shy, I think. Then to Lausanne in Nicolas's car, and visits to various garages for a car. Finally we bought one—a *voiture de luxe* in appearance (old de Soto with special sport-cabriolet body) and very inexpensive: $500. Nicolas gave it a fiendish test ride and enviously reported that it was a *belle occasion.* I hope so. It's very handsome and comfortable, anyway.

We were exhausted, but the day was far from finished. At 8:30 that night Otto appeared and led us to his house. There we spent a strange evening. At first we tried to put some limits on our drinking and our hours, but we soon saw that any such plans were useless and commended our souls to our hard-drinking Irish ancestors. The result was interesting and pleasant, although not to any of our tastes its procural. We started with coffee and liqueurs —one liqueur first, kirsch, until we started discussing distillation and Otto had to introduce us as well to his *pruneau,* cassis, and some other white liquid. Then we got down to business and, as T. said later, had a wine dinner without the dinner—white wine of the country, an excellent Côtes de Beaune rouge, much champagne (for which Otto couldn't resist letting on he paid only 3.40 francs a bottle), and finally (I never thought I'd see myself drinking this!) Türchenblut. We ate very good sandwiches of ham and pâté and smoked a great deal.

By the time we reached the Turk's Blood, Otto was weaving and shrinking by the minute, and when we left, perhaps just in time before he disappeared completely, he was curled up like a little child or a goblin, frowning fiercely and very gaily, waving his tiny chapped hands and trying to imitate an American millionaire with many strange sounds.

At the beginning of the evening, his wife tried to squash him, afraid perhaps that we would laugh at him if he lost his dignity. But soon she realized that he was safe with us and went docilely whenever he said, "Another bottle, Anna." She chattered softly to me of her child's delicate stomach, of preserving pears, of the cost of servants in Switzerland. I listened and nodded and smiled, trying at the same time not to miss too much of Otto's increasingly vague mumblings of the menace of Freemasonry in Suisse and of his secret society of rationalists, most of the members hotelmen who can control the visiting tourists—out with bad Jews, encouragement of good Jews, and so on. And of the franc, down again in six months, and of the pound, down, too, with the dollar alone a good investment. I wonder.

Coming home we laughed a lot but walked quite straight. The next morning I felt well, except in stuffy rooms.

And then we have looked at apartments, and rented one, and

bought an electric stove and lights and percolators and so on. And we've signed many contracts—everything takes a contract, even a stove. And furniture, secondhand—a beautiful round tip-top table, three or four chairs, two fat little armchairs with slipcovers, a desk, a kitchen table, a bureau.

And on and on. Now we wait for our furniture, which is on its way and should arrive Monday. I hope very much that it does. It will be good for all of us to live more quietly, more regularly, than is possible in a pension where one's main impulse is to stay away. Staying away means cafés and cafés mean drinking, and even such fine nectarial water as the white wine can be hard on unaccustomed systems. We ate well, but not natural.

Last night T., tired from a week of bustling and emotional strain, grew very fidgety in the theater where we were listening to a poor play. We got him out just in time; he collapsed on the stairs —not a vertigo faint but what Hal would probably call a nerve- bile crisis. He was unconscious for perhaps fifty seconds, very stiff for thirty with a gray face and his eyes rolled up. He made a few snoring sounds. Then he relaxed, and we bent his head over his knees. Immediately he flushed and broke into a cold sweat. He became conscious and mumbled like a child for us to go back to the play. We sat for a few minutes more and then walked quickly home and to bed. (I was collected at the time, but in the night lost my nerve and existed through a kind of half-waking nightmare until morning. Today he looks tired but all right.)

It is snowing now in the Savoys. Each morning more white has filled the ravines and the meadows. The air is colder today but clear. Women hurry toward the churches with pots of white chrysanthemums for All Saints' Day.

This morning the architect came with four projects, all bad as far as we were concerned. He, so far at least, has missed completely our desire to build a house "of the country," not new and garish and "chalet" like the Villa Rose-Baloy that went up near Le Pâquis this summer. His plans are for suburban villas, and it is, of course, incomprehensible to him that we *want* the old house left as a kind of germ, or nucleus, for the new. "It's not worth fifty francs," he says in bewilderment. But I think we can wear him down and away from his fixed ideas and get something out of him—with T. doing most of his work and letting him sign the papers for law's sake.

Another thing that puzzles and secretly shocks him, and Otto, and Mme. Doellanbach, and so on is that we're not planning to have a *homme*. They look at us crosswise and try not to smile when I say that I like to cook and prefer to have a charwoman occasionally.

While T. went up to Le Pâquis to make some sketches, Al and I inspected the apartment with the agent, noting nail holes and so on against the day of wrath six months from now. We looked down at the market, in full swing, most of the flowers white for Le Toussant, under the white snow air and the whitening mountains. And as we crossed the marketplace, later, I spotted a little walnut chair like the one I bought last week (this week? time is out of joint), and we bought it for four francs and put it on Al's shoulder and took it back to the apartment. People smiled at us.

Then we went to Mme. Doellanbach's for a market-day *petit salé* and a glass of wine and a little angling (successful) to see if she knew of a charwoman. To the pension to find T. in a cloud of smoke, his eyes blurred and his smile vacant as a thousand house plans surged in his head. He had drawn a picture of the facade just as we want it to be. Now to get an architect to make it possible!

After lunch, he drew, Al took one of his ever-surprising cat-naps under the afghan, and I wrote. They're gone now, to buy toothpaste and breathe fresh air.

Oh, I will be glad to settle, even for six months. Too long on the wing.

I am tired from nightmares, and the day is cold. Perhaps a bath and the chaise longue and supper here in my room? I want to write to Anne,* though, to tell her why I like *Golden Wedding*. I've never written before to an author to say that. Perhaps it is better not to. But if I ever wrote a book, I should be glad to know what some people thought of it.

2. xi. 36

This morning we went to the apartment, where a mildly friendly little man was making ready for the advent of our stove tomorrow and putting in light bulbs. All was clean and fresh. We felt even more anxious to be there—chez nous. I never thought I'd feel that way about a rented apartment, but I do.

Then while Al saw the agent about a stall for the car, Tim and I went to a brush shop and bought many brushes—scrubbing, dusting, bath. And a doormat. And coat hangers.

The coat hangers are a little demonstration of the only rub, so far, in our domestic relations—a very small rub, but I note it because it may be interesting later to remember. It has many developments, all contradictory—the thin life Al and I led when T. knew us in Laguna, the same life he led on Fuller Street in Hollywood, our mutually careful but more decent existences in 1934–35. Then came last spring in Europe, when I traveled with T. and his mother, always first class and reveling in it after so long second and third, all of us spending money rashly and unthinkingly in a mixture of rank sensual enjoyment and desire to keep Mrs. P. comfortable. Then came this summer, when Timmy with Anne bought bicycles and rode them five days and then gave them to

* Dillwyn's sister, a novelist in the 1930s and 1940s.

agreeable hotel servants, furnished their private sitting room with lamps and left them because they were too hard to pack.

The result, showing daily in small and so far very safe ways, is that Timmy is afraid of my sybaritic tendencies, and occasionally, when I talk of liking linen sheets (for instance) enough to make a tentative list for the next fifty years for Le Pâquis and of giving it to Otto who could get us a 15 percent discount, he tightens his face almost like his mother and gives a vague speech about disliking to borrow money, Anne's generosity and our probable abuse of it, the need to live simply and fittingly as peasants in the peasant Le Pâquis.

I, on the other hand, when he and Al suggest staying at the Compote or the Gare for dinner, think resentfully of the meal already paid for here at the pension and almost unconsciously add up the five-franc pieces that we would be spending on linen sheets instead of cotton. Or if T. goes into a shop, heads straight for a rack of coat hangers marked "1–4 francs," and gathers together two dozen of the most expensive, I automatically say, "How about these at 2.50?," and when he as automatically answers, "Very nice, but I want the four-franc ones," I feel a faint sure prick of resentment that he can imply my extravagance without noticing his own.

As a matter of fact, we are all three of us fairly sensible people about money, and I feel confident and safe in thinking that such puny contretemps are without menace to our peace. Each has some whim or foible, far from serious and easily passed over. *Ça ira.*

Last night T. read us some of his Cornwall journal. It made this very poor stuff. However, I shan't try to "write," simply because he has succeeded in doing so without any apparent effort. What I'm putting into this book is meant, basically at least, to tell us later a few of the early occurrences. I doubt if even that simple purpose will be fulfilled. I'm afraid, really, of the personal. And how to write of three people with complete impersonality? The result will be a stiff chronicle of vegetables bought, charwomen paid, meals consumed. Or it will be a pseudo-personal gossiping, skirting with timid words the truly important relations and instead relaying small "bright sayings" and amusing anecdotes. T. has a happy touch with flowers, with a priest picking clover, with seagulls. I feel heavy and obvious in such company—now, at least. Perhaps that is because I am in a state of inward puzzlement. When I can answer my own questions, I shall be able more clearly to ask them of others, and more firmly, too.

3. xi. 36

Nine o'clock of a sunny market morning, and I sit in the window of what will probably be our salon, waiting for goods to arrive from the station, where Al and T. and Otto are identifying them.

The electrician just blew a fuse, and I heard him clear his throat quickly as it popped, very much as a man does who inadvertently belches or breaks wind in church or at a dinner table.

It will be good to cook again. This morning I felt eager to begin, as I walked along the edge of the market. The flowers were crisp and beautiful, and the cabbages and salads and all the leeks and leaves and colored things were like the flowers. The bread in piles, onions woven into necklaces, the potatoes, the rumps of all the patient standing horses were warm and gleaming and clean. The people looked sturdy and quietly spirited.

12. xi. 36

Some days later, and I am sorry to see what a poor bluff I am at keeping a journal, even while I say sincerely that it might be better to cease trying. We have been installed for a week now. The apartment, large, light, filled with chrysanthemums in pots and vases, is very impersonal and pleasant. We continue to acquire pots for the new electric stove, lights for our bedsides, chairs to sit upon. We consider a fine Valaisanne table, inlaid and carved. Tradesmen's faces emerge from their first anonymous fog, and the unctuous clerk at the Bel-Bâle gives me presents of chocolate. We have thirty bottles of wine in our cellar, bought in a mixture of diplomacy and enthusiasm after Al and T. had tasted it with the vintner-mayor of our *commune de St. Saphorin.*

A wind has blown down most of the wide coarse leaves from the plane trees and several times has sent the swans scuttling into their haven at the edge of the market. The gulls have tossed themselves valiantly into every slightest breeze.

One day the mountains, the water, the houses in the town looked as tiny as a Christmas tree ornament and at the same time very fierce and as if chipped from cold pewter.

It is cold today. The mountains are near and high.

Otto came. I wish I could write his remarks about weeds and plants. He says I must have an herb garden, with "all the best cures for all troubles of all the interior, automatically." Of them I remember that three days of drinking an infusion of dried chervil stems cleans the whole body, "just like the espiragasses [asparagus]." Peppermint tea after dinner helps digestion. The brewed roots of nettles, mixed with alcohol and "two to three drops perfume," form a fine hair tonic.

Also he says to pick a few onions, dandelions, cabbage leaves, any meadow grasses, and nettles and brown them in a little butter and make a fine soup. "If they did not *pique* [sting], all those nettles in the world would by now be *détruit* [destroyed], on cause they are so good for curing sick animals which would automatically *mange* [eat] them all."

It grows dark. In the kitchen T. cuts little pears from Le Pâquis into a saucepan. Al is out, buying a brioche for his breakfast. I lie lazily on the couch, feeling well now but still scared from a mildly unpleasant bout with what I think was my forgotten enemy the appendix. All goes well now, and I am puzzled as to what caused this morning's trouble. Certainly my life could not be called debauched. My only excesses are mental, if they exist at all.

We have bought the beautiful table. I am glad. It will be good in the grand salon.

Our plans for the house are almost decided on, and Jeanneret now makes the detailed drawing. Then it must be exposed for two weeks in *la maire de St. Saphorin,* that our neighbors may see what we plan to do and say if they do not approve. Then we can begin. We hope for good weather.

We have rented a radio, which crackles constantly and painfully. Where are the fine programs of Europe that are discussed so nostalgically in America? So far, whatever we have been able to hear between crackles has been mediocre "safe" music, the kind that makes old women in respectable pensions say, "Ah, Beethoven! Ah, Brahms!"

15. xi. 36

The night of the day I thought for a few hours of appendectomies, I had eaten nothing. Al mixed a very good martini before supper. We ate well of vegetables and milk and then went to see the latest movie version of *Michel Strogoff.* We had a small beer in the entr'acte. The movie was mildly entertaining, as familiar as *Uncle Tom's Cabin,* with Michel's mother as obscenely objectionable as are all cinema mothers—even worse than most actual ones.

When we came out the door, wind blew violently against us, rain flicked us, and we all tried to suppress the instinctive hysterical laughter of humans when a girl's hat blew off and rolled madly down the street, with her scuttling after in a mixture of embarrassment and anxiety.

By our door the overhead lights from the *place* were wagging wild shadows. It was too exciting to go home. We clung together and pushed on down the *place* to the Lion d'Or. Four people played cards there. When we asked for grogs, they smiled delightedly and scuttled in four directions, the game waiting with the hands laid out like fans. Rain ran across the floor from the two doors, and we felt warm and falsely safe from the violence outside.

The grogs were simple and crude but hot. We drank them slowly and watched the white flick of cards at the reassembled game table.

"This is the night for a fondue! We've never tasted one! Oh, they are delicious! Yes, this is the night! Too late? Never too late for a fondue!"

We all felt very gay as we whirled up the *place* toward Mme. Doellanbach's. Al had a few misgivings about the lateness, but I felt very careless and happy and pretended to ignore them, and he really didn't care much, I think.

Le Vieux Vevey was crowded and smoky. Four boys I have seen in every café were playing cards. One of them has been trying to flirt with me—dark, gaunt, with sunken hot eyes and the stretched smile of a corpse—and all evening I was afraid Al would ask them to have fondue with us. They had almost no money, and we wouldn't finish the fondue—but I didn't want that cheeky boy at our table.

It was fun, dipping the bread into kirsch, into the thick pungent cream, up into our mouths. We drank a little white wine. We chattered. I felt very gay, pleasantly drunken although I had drunk little.

On the way home, the rain seemed wilder. We went quite silently to bed, where T. worried some at my foolishness in eating and drinking in such silly ways after a bad cramp, where Al tossed miserably and for the hundredth time swore never again to eat cheese at night, and where I, unjustly perhaps, lay in a pleasant Gruyère-flavored wakefulness, puzzled still but conscious of well-being, warm and listening to the wind.

The next day, free for some reason from appointments, we drove up the Rhône valley. At first I was timid in the car but soon grew used to it. It is a good car, I think—smooth, easy to handle, powerful, and very comfortable. We all drove. We ate dried beef and a large sausage with bread and *fendant du Valais,** and bought a rocklike chunk of the beef to eat before dinners with aperitifs. We drove up a narrow coiling road to Leukenbad, where we drank bottled beer and were watched by two pretty little girls, and then we looked at the beautiful pine pews in the church. It was there, too, that we looked down a narrow steep street at a flock of white sheep with black muzzles, and suddenly between us and the mounting beasts appeared first a twig broom, then a ladder, and then a chimney sweep carrying the broom and the ladder, and all of them of the softest, heaviest, most profound black that we had ever seen. We had walked on past the mouth of the little street before we realized how black, how odd, the sweep and the troop of beasts had been. Then we began to talk and laugh excitedly,

* A slightly effervescent white wine from the Valais.

feeling that we had seen something witchlike at least, and perhaps not even so. All of the pitched village of Leukenbad immediately swung into unreality in our minds.

We passed another fairy story—two steep peaks, close as two fingers of a hand, with a high chapel on one, a crenellated castle ruin on the other. St. Maurice was nice, and Sion, and one little town had a square lined off with plane trees that reminded me of Tarascon.

Yesterday we went to the Bel-Bâle and down into its cellar, where we tasted discreetly of several things and bought twenty liters of Châteauneuf du Pape '29, two liters of twelve-year fine champagne, three liters of Malaga, and five liters of old Jamaican rum. Next week we go to try sherry.

The young manager, who tasted with us, took one sip or perhaps two and then tossed the rest of his glassful back over his shoulder against the wall. It was plain that he enjoyed this gesture, although he looked nothing but nonchalant. Once, too, he insisted on showing us how strong an uncut rum was by filling his mouth with it and then blowing it into the air over a lighted match. It made a great tongue of fire, but even that did not bring any apparent happiness to him. He had a good time, I know.

Our table has come. It has been a week since T. and I first saw it, dusty and covered with other furniture, in the dark shop of a Jew. We told Al. He and T. looked again. Al chatted with Ebenezer (M. L'Ebèniste), and then after much visiting and parleying with Otto, finally he and Otto bought it, for 250 francs instead of the 300 the owner demanded and the 600 to 800 everyone declared it was worth. And at that Otto was somewhat hurt that Al hadn't let him haggle the price down to 230. Now business is done, and we have a beautiful table. It is long, high, narrow, of dark walnut, very crude. The ends are simply carved, chisel work. The two sides are more elaborate, with a queer running border of acanthus, grape, stipple—a mélange but pleasant. The top is fine—inlaid crudely with the letters, numbers, and a religious symbol cut in. I am very pleased by it. I like to think of Le Pâquis with this table in it.

Last night we talked to Jeanneret (with Otto, of course) for the last time. The plans are good. Main change is that I now have the upstairs room in the old house, Al the middle room in the new, and Anne the end room with a little fireplace. Their rooms have the balcony, mine the fountain, theirs the bath, mine the old stairs. I hope they'll be as content as I.

It is midafternoon of a Saturday, and I am newly amazed to see that the *place* is clean and bare again after the morning's ordered beautiful bustle of market and after the scattered cabbage leaves and straw of noon. The little men who creep under the horses' tails with buckets and brushes have gone with their rich gleanings, and all the wine has been washed into the lake, and not a single forgotten carrot top shows where three hours ago the whole countryside's hunger was given its weekend's satisfaction.

A letter from Sis says she is troubled about Christmas. I knew that would come. Mother *demands* that she come home, with all the pathetic horrible maternal demands: pathos, trembling, all. Anne feels desperate. I know why. I think she should not go, but I think that in her place I would submit as she probably will, and in a vain essay try to make Mother feel strong, important, protective again. That's what Edith is searching for and clinging to—any sign that she may still be the young vital woman who led, who taught, who directed the four loving children. Things like Christmas trees may, she still hopes, give her back some of that dissolved importance. And how hard I've worked, and all of us, to give to Christmas even an atom of its old festivity. Every year, as we all grow older, less needful of Mother as she longs for us to need her, more desirous of our own kinds of living, we drink more and more to keep up the bluff. Doesn't she see that? Perhaps she will not. Now she is using Shaun as a wedge—we must give Shaun the real family Christmas. Can't she see him, the shy quiet child, tired from travel and crushed with attention and too many presents, the only young one in a circle of bored, half-drunken old people? No, I think she can't. I hope Anne stays in San Francisco. It will be hard for Edith and Rex. Many things are harder, though.

16. xi. 36

A good day today. We rose late, after a few dances at the Trois Rois to a poor but interesting orchestra, and after coffee strolled to the park of La Coupole, where we drank sherry and changed a bill. Then we went by funicular to Mont Pélèron.

The funny music machine was still there in the little slanting station, with the same many-pockmarked disk of le Beau Danube. We played it. It is very off-key and so silly and nostalgically gay— we'd like to buy it.

We walked along the ridge of the hills to Chexbres. The curves of the land seemed very sweet, and we wondered at them, near as they are to the cruel upsweep of the Alps. Little brooks ran swiftly through them, little boys raced over them on a vague paper chase. On the road all the Sunday walkers greeted us politely.

We were hungry by the time we got to Chexbres and ate cheese, local ham, and bread with the wine. Le Lion d'Or was full —a rather noisy but pleasant reunion of young men with lavender chrysanthemums in their lapels, several families, a few old men. One small-faced old one with good blue eyes sat by us and talked pleasantly with Al. He knew our neighbor at *faverges,* but not very well, since he had only been in this district forty years! He missed his dead wife. I heard him say, "Oh, my son is far away in Geneva

—but, of course, I still have several more left!" When we went, he shook hands and wished us luck, health, a welcome to Le Pâquis. We went down the hill.

Le Pâquis was beautiful. With all the leaves fallen, it was easier to see the curve of the earth and to imagine the bulk of our house. It is a good spot, and its life is worth any personal ennuis that may occur, I think.

Some day I should like to own, or even rent, the ridiculous little hut and the dwarfed dignity of La Roche Ronde, with its ten-by-twenty vineyard and its little balcony. I should like to work there, by myself. I could even live there—cook and sleep and work in the two rooms, bathe and live otherwise at a hotel in Vevey. It's a silly idea—but such a complete fine little place seems very desirable, for a few weeks or months of the year anyway. But Le Pâquis, too, is good. I am anxious to be there.

6.i.37

Late in the afternoon I walked with Timmy along the esplanade. Gulls whirled and coasted like black ashes in the pewter sky. The snowfields in the great crease of the Grammont were warm and radiant, but all the other snow was as repellent as frozen flesh. Air moved freshly across the smooth surface of the lake and blew in sweet rainy puffs against my face. I felt very happy. We looked down into the water, in the little port, at the flashing minnies nibbling around a chain. They were like live stars, mostly invisible.

Otto told T. that homosexuality is alarmingly on the increase in Switzerland. He says it is because there is so much unemployment, with all its slackness and dissatisfaction, and also because so many depraved, ill, and wealthy foreigners stay in this country and influence the Swiss. I had thought of the first reason but not the second. They both seem reasonable. Certainly most of the Englishmen I see here, especially the younger ones, are a sad set of tubercular alcoholics.

On the fourth of this month, we started to dig into Le Pâquis, to build our house. It was a cold bright day. We drove up there early in the afternoon and found several men at work. They wore soft blue clothes and dug and wheeled earth with the slow thoroughness that seems characteristic of all labor here. They spoke politely to us. A round man with a sheaf of blueprints seemed to be completely bewildered and looked quite overcome when he found we were none of us the architect. Schyrr *fils,* round, too, but much larger, a sturdy pleasant man, was directing the disposal of the dirt. He showed us the outlines of the terrace, which will be large and beautiful.

I liked the way the men were cutting the turf very neatly and piling it to be used again, instead of mutilating it heedlessly as they probably would have at home. I was glad, too, to see that the primroses have started to bloom in the grass.

That night the long clear spell broke, and rain started—the first of much, I am afraid. I hope it won't slow the work too much.

The next day, or the day after, we trimmed the willows along the wall and the brook and cleaned our side of the brook. It was fun. We felt very happy then, too—got quite scratched and, of course, were stiff the next day, especially Al who had chopped some of the great pile of fruit-tree wood.

2. iii. 37

I had not been to Le Pâquis for several days, and they told me that at last the snowdrops and crocuses were in bloom, the ones we planted last autumn. Mine, down in the open space beyond the garden, were in a wide ring, very gay, and Tim's were thick along the brook slope. Yesterday we went to see them, but all were gone. Some lay broken on the grass, and a few of the bulbs, hacked across with a sharp knife, lay like white mushrooms. But most of them were quite disappeared. It was sickening. Timmy and Al thought it was vandalism—some resentment from a neighbor or a peevish child. Otto spoke soothingly of the dandelion hunters. My explanation was best, I think: I remembered the countless pots of meadow flowers for sale that morning in the market and was sure that a hurried thoughtless vagabond, sure of selling a few francs' worth, had spotted our flowers and roughly pried them loose, discarding any hurt ones. It is too bad. We'll put up a sign asking people not to pick the flowers.

There were (and are) still primroses thick as stars, and many daffodils and daisies, and a few violets. The tulips have not yet come—perhaps they won't. By two years from now I want to have many more daisies and daffodils.

The walls are going up. Unlike Al, who seems capable of standing for hours watching the snail-pace of the work, I cannot enjoy it. It is ugly. I know it will be thoroughly done, since it is Swiss. There is no aid I can lend. So I prefer not to see it in its present cluttered hideous form. I think I seem unsympathetic to Al. I am sorry.

There is so much wood that we are going to have Jules, the vigneron, help us cut and pile it.

We saw old man Schyrr this week and have pretty well settled the garden for this year. I think we can handle it. He will plant strawberries, *asperges* [asparagus], tomatoes, and eggplant for us. We'll sow the rest. I am very glad that we decided against the hothouse this year—it would have been too luxurious. We'll get along very well, and as soon as we're settled will lay one or two *cloches** up near the road wall.

Every time we go up there we bring back a plate of primroses, with one or two daisies and a little clump of violets in them. They are lovely, especially when we put them on low stools and can look down on them as if they were still growing in the meadow.

If I continue this journal, it will be almost wholly about Le Pâquis. I can see that. Other things, in spite of what I'm afraid seems my lack of interest in the building, are unimportant. I eat, sleep, dress, bustle about paying bills. I live my several lives. They are evanescent.

3. iii. 37

Today is a beautiful blue day, with white glitter in the air near the mountains. It is cold outdoors but warm here in the sunny bedroom. I drink slowly at a bottle of beer. On my windowsill, to catch the rare sun, is my little garden—two pansies, a deep blue cineraria, two pots of spindling morning-glory sprouts I hope to raise. In the courtyard of the École Préparatoire, across the street, some twenty children hop to the clapped hands of their exercise teacher. Timmy writes at the dining room table. Al is at Le Pâquis chopping wood and then going to Chexbres to eat soup.

* Bell-shaped covers for plants.

At the moment I find it difficult to write. I have some things to get out of my head, but I wait to hear from Mr. Saxton about my next move: will he like what I sent, does he think I should try for a Guggenheim, and so on? I cannot settle down to anything. I am, as often, tempted to start a personal book, *mais à quoi bon?* I think my present life is a strange, complicated, interesting one. But my deep distrust—or is it timidity, cowardice even?—of such self-revelations will, perhaps, always prevent me from thus relieving myself. I don't know, though. As I grow older and farther away from the first effortful amenities, I feel myself, nevertheless, more dispassionate, more able to see myself with all the other bacteria squirming on a culture slide. So instead of writing or of loosening my self-censorship, I'll put down what I know of Mme. Chapuis, my cleaning woman.

She was recommended to me by Mme. Doellanbach, who owns Le Café Vieux Vevey and knew Timmy ten years ago. Mme. D. did not know Chapuis but had been told by a client who employed her that she was good and needed work. I left my address at the Vieux Vevey and learned that she would come to see me at a set time and day.

I was a little nervous—I had never before interviewed a servant. When I saw her, I was surprised at her slender, tall body—I had thought that all cleaning women were short and stubby creatures. She sat on the edge of a chair, fussing nervously with her purse. She was dressed neatly in a half coat, a black hat, a knitted scarf. I was anxious to get the thing over with. I tried to speak good French. Her voice was rather high and nasal. When I said, in a terse, scowling way, that I wanted only two things, to have absolute cleanliness in the bathroom and kitchen and to pay her one franc an hour instead of the usual eighty centimes, her voice wavered in a singsong effort to keep from crying. I felt even gruffer and much moved in a petty way.

I ended the interview. She went to the door and stood fumbling in her purse for two or three envelopes. "You see, Madame," she said, pulling papers from them and spreading them before me, "I have very good, *excellent* references. I am not used to work. But everyone has been satisfied with me."

"Good, good. I am sure . . ." and so on I muttered. I realized that I had made a blunder in not asking for her references before.

I set a date for her to start. The door was almost closed after her. Then she turned to me and said rapidly, "I should tell Madame that I am divorcing my husband." I could see she was being very frank, that she expected me to say I didn't want her to come.

"Good, good! Come tomorrow at 2:00, Madame. Good-bye."

The next day she came and literally tore through the apartment, not breaking anything but cleaning with a kind of frenzy. She told me her husband had been taken from her after eighteen years by another woman, that she had a son nineteen who was with the father and who had not even visited her for three years, that her sixteen-year-old daughter was with her and was a naughty girl. But mostly she worked, and very well.

I went through a period of figuring many kinds of fantastic schemes for employing servants. In them I pretended I was deaf and so on. The best one was to hire through an intermediary, who would say that I was harmlessly insane and wished to hear absolutely no details of any life but the one the servant led as a duster and cleaner in my house. *Why,* I thought, *why* must I always know the cavernous agonies of the cook's mother, the travail of a café waiter's wife or sister, the flat feet, the divorces, the earaches of everyone who is near? Why can't the functions of society be performed without interrelation?

But I did nothing. Occasionally I ask Chapuis how she is or something like that, because I am human and humane. I hate to hear. I want to do all I can to help her, but I do not want to hear about it. She was sick for two weeks: I visited her, I helped her financially, I sympathized. Now she is working again, and I do not want her in any way to overtire herself, to do what she should not, but I do not want to hear about her.

She is given to female details. I discourage them. I told her when I hired her that I did not want her ever to do too much during her periods. I should have added that neither did I care to hear about them. (I ask myself if my extreme distaste for any mention of female disorders is a small sign of homosexuality. I am almost sickened by any talk of such things and care nothing for details of pregnancies and confinements and less than nothing for talk of other women's sexual experiences. Once I thought it was because I am childless, but I notice that other childless women are quite avid for such conversation.)

Chapuis says she has a vaginal catarrh and is going weekly to a doctor in Montreux, for three months, to be "cauterized." She probably has gonorrhea. I feel very sorry and am horrified at her being so treated and so duped into an expensive torture. But I do not wish to hear about it.

She talks (it sounds as if she jabbered constantly, and as a matter of fact she has learned from my noncommittal replies and my long silences to say almost nothing) . . . She talks some of her daughter and asks me for advice, which I never give. The girl is finishing high school. She is well developed and highly sexed. Chapuis, who likes her bit of fun, refuses to let the girl go out, and when she herself is out at night, she locks her daughter into the rooms. She seems hurt and surprised that the girl resents this. At Christmas the girl went to her father and stayed without warning her mother until time to commence school again. The mother was cross and more so later when she found that the father had deducted two francs a day from the alimony for the girl's keep.

Chapuis is thirty-eight. She is, as I said, taller than I and quite slender. She has a low brow over small close-set eyes, and a rather loose mouth badly colored with lipstick. Her hair is beginning to turn gray. She goes every Saturday to have it washed and waved. Her clothes are always neat and simple. Her rooms, which she earns by being concierge of a building near here, were very clean and fresh when I visited her during her illness. She is polite, deft, quiet in her housework, and seems quite intelligent.

For some reason I do not like her.

8. iv. 37

Tonight, while Al and Timmy play Camelot, drinking beer, muttering now and then, or breathing heavily, and while I sit on the couch feeling agreeably tired after a day of curtain making, I'll write a few things about the house.

Last Saturday we gave our "bouquet"* for the men who up till now have worked there. We had waited far too long for the signal, a little fir tree nailed to the new rooftree by the carpenters. Finally it was there, a lopsided tree aflutter with what Otto calls "robbins" of colored paper—streamers of red and white, large bright magenta roses, and Italian colors on the tip, intentionally or not. The men pretended not to watch us as we first looked at the tree, but I could see them beaming.

---

* A celebration that occurs when the tree, or bouquet, is attached to the rooftree.

We had planned things fairly thoroughly already, but there was still some bustling to do. Otto was very useful, the epitome of bustlers. We bought forty-five little glasses, mustard, colored paper, and twelve kilos of sliced ham and meats at Uniprix (after some argument, for I disapprove of those chain bazaars. Their high quality and their undeniable cheapness won. I continue to feel unfair to small tradesmen, though). We had a pound of bread for each man, and three little cheesecakes, ordered from the corner bakery. We commanded sixty bottles of 1934 *faverge* from our neighbor Rogévue. And Friday afternoon, after the workmen had gone, we decorated the upstairs, still one big room, with red and white for Switzerland and blue and yellow for Vevey.

Saturday was cold and mizzly, after several blue days. We were sorry. It was not anyone's fault. We put on several layers of clothes, and at 11:00 Al and I went up to Le Pâquis to cover the tables with white paper and arrange things a little while T. collected Otto, little Anna, and the cheese pies.

We had wondered if anyone had warned Jules, the vigneron, to be there, but he had felt it in the air. When we said hello, that we were glad he was there, he looked rather embarrassed and said that he was just happening to stop in to see how the building was going. "But you'll stay for the party, won't you?" He pretended great surprise, and said, Why—why, yes, I'd be very glad—thank you! And he went lumbering across the road to help carry the wine, with a pleased grin on his face.

The foreman, a deep-voiced handsome blond man who never looks upset, even when we discover that he has left out an essential wall or put in an impossible one, was laying planks for two long tables. Soon we had them covered with white paper. Then Anna, T., and Otto arrived, with the cheese pies steaming on a great tray wrapped in lap robes, and a big basket of bread. We put bottles, glasses, mustard pots, bread, piles of ham and sausage in a line down the middle of each table. The cheesecakes fumed. Otto and Al pulled corks. We all bristled.

I went out for a minute onto the windy balcony. It was noon. I looked down by the fountain, and there were all the men washing themselves, wetting their hair, even tying fresh handkerchiefs around their throats. They were quiet.

They came upstairs in several groups. The young ones walked right in and sat down. The older ones stood shyly for a minute before they went less surely to the tables. As soon as we could, we filled our glasses, said, Santé, drank, and went upstairs, where we had taken some of the food and wine.

We could hear everything and see a little through the hole where the stairs will be up to T.'s room. Things were rather quiet at first. Men drifted in—excavators who had hurried from other jobs and so on. There were about thirty-six, I think. They ate and drank earnestly.

They were quiet partly because Schyrr *fils* was there. He should not have been, because he is a contractor. I am pretty sure he was sent there by his father to keep an eye on his men, who alone of all the workers had to go on with their jobs. I saw old Schyrr the day before, and when I mentioned the party, he acted quite surprised, although he knew about it from Otto, and then he told me, in a grudging grumpy way, not to give his men too much to drink. I said that that was something the men would have to tend to but that I didn't think there would be any orgy. He looked very disapproving. (Rogévue told us that old Schyrr had a few words with him while the Schyrr laborers were working on the excavation—accused Rogévue of enticing the men into his cellars just to make them drunk, and so on.) Anyway, there was young Schyrr where he shouldn't have been, and I am sure his presence kept the men quiet, although they like him.

It was cold. We ate the delicious hot cheesecakes and some bread and meat, and drank the white wine, and kept moving to keep warm. Otto jumped around like a little flea, and so did Anna, who was helpful and for so young a girl very efficient. (I think she and Jules had the most fun at the party. He was the only one who showed any signs of being drunk. He had a beatific beam on his ugly good face all during the meal. I could see him discussing politics with the whole table, a piece of bread stuck on the end of his knife, two slices of ham dangling from the hand that held his glass. By the end of the party, when I gave him a package of meat, a bottle of wine, and some bread for his wife, he was a bit glassy-eyed and could only open his mouth especially wide for a thank-you.)

We saw Baublebottom, the private fool, the jolly idiot of a workman who always gets the dullest simplest jobs and always does them wrong. The man who casually causes all the accidents by doing things like tipping a barrel load of rocks into a cellar full of workers—we saw him pick up the tray of cheese pies and spill the whole thing onto the dusty floor. The men roared. He grinned nonchalantly, shoveled the pies back onto the tray, blew some of the cement off them, and carried them to the tables.

Suddenly all the men began to sing, and sing as Swiss all can, sweetly, truly, rather sadly: "Sur la haute montagne était un vieux châlet." We kept very still. Timmy's face got very red and crumpled, and he cried slightly, looking so much like his mother for a minute that I was startled. Al smiled and looked up toward the mountains. Otto and Anna and I all looked quiet, probably.

At the end we clapped. The men sang some more, not so well but pleasantly. When Anna and I went down with tobacco for them, they started a song about "Lift your lovely blue eyes"—but Schyrr shushed them at his own table. It was nice of them.

One young man came upstairs, thanked us very politely, and

excused himself to go to the practice of his *sapeurs-pompiers*. A few others left. Finally Schyrr went. (I know one reason he came was to drive his men up in the truck—otherwise, they could never have walked and got back to work. But he was sent by his puritanical father as well.)

Things grew noisier, but because of the cold, the wine had less effect than I had expected. Of course, I didn't predict any riots, but I thought there would be more singing and shouting. About three o'clock we went down and told the men to take what bread was left to their families. They were pleased. Soon after, they had gone. The tables looked strange, because almost every man had cut a half-circle of the paper in front of him to wrap up what he didn't eat.

Little Anna washed the glasses in the fountain, while we talked stiffly to Jeanneret, who had wandered in with his shy silent wife and her little niece, who looked like a child's drawing: round eyes, stiff bobbed hair, a wide mouth, colored with blue, yellow, red Crayolas and utterly blank.

Now Al and Timmy have finished their games and their beer. I have finished my white wine and soda. It is about midnight. Tomorrow I must sew hard, and I want to go up to Le Pâquis, where this week we have done a lot of work in the garden. Perhaps it will rain, though. Well, that will be good for the seeds we have put in—peas, carrots, lettuce, onions, and flowers.

In the meadow now are violets and buttercups. The crocuses are gone. Daisies and primulas are almost gone as well. On one slope the double daffodils are in full flower, and some yellow vetch shows.

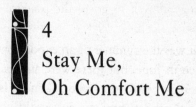

4
Stay Me,
Oh Comfort Me

There is an urgency, an insistent beauty, about words written while they are hot in the mind, soon after something has happened to make them burn there. I wrote that way the morning after my last meal with Rina. I sat in the gentle sunlight, just inside the great open window of a *brasserie* on the Champs Elysées, and the words flowed onto the letter paper like melted stone, swirling in strange shapes and mysterious shadowy meanings that I can never find again. I kept the sheets of paper for a long time, without reading them. I knew that what I had written could not yet be talked about or even looked at. And now that I feel it is all right, the paper is gone. I shall have to tell this from recollection, and it is a kind of consolation to admit to myself that I can do it in tranquillity, the way the poet said it might be.

That was the summer of an exposition in Paris. It was supposed to open in June, but there were strikes. At least, that is what the reactionary newspapers said . . . and it is true that when you went on the riverboats past the autoworks on the little island, the men leaned from the windows and yelled and raised their hands in the clenched worker's salute.

Some of the exhibits were ready to open, incredibly neat and even beautiful behind the rubble in the half-finished pathways, and the cafés were full of foreigners come to Paris to work in the fair or to see it. They sat gaily in the June sun, drinking their native drinks, or *citron pressé,* or even champagne, waiting for things to begin.

I was in Paris because my father and mother were coming from California. I was excited about that, but I had used them as an excuse to be by myself. Nobody knew this but me, and I was not ashamed of it. I had to be by myself for a few hours, so I lied a little, where I lived in Vevey, and came a day earlier than the boat was to arrive.

I do not think I knew, on the way to Paris, that I was going to see Rina, but as soon as everything was in order at the hotel, I called her.

The next morning, as I sat in the sun and wrote about it, I still felt sickish. It was almost like a hangover, but I knew I had not drunk much the night before.

When the waiter first came, and I asked for paper and a pen, I told him I would order later. I felt a little strange, alone in the big place. There were only a few people at that hour, and although the tiny tables and the trim wicker chairs on the sidewalk were in twenty neatly impenetrable rows, the back part of the *brasserie* was still dark and smelled dankly of Javelle water from its late scrubbings.

There were a lot of places like that then, high priced and badly served, along the Elysées: big tawdry rooms, usually with balconies at the back and windows that slid away so that the wide *trottoir* and the interior of the café could be one establishment on any sunny day or warm lovely night. There was always either a "gypsy" orchestra or a "ladies'" orchestra. Sometimes it was called *"orchestre de dames tsiganes,"* to be thorough. They were usually pretty good, too, in spite of the contortions of Romany abandon that their contracts apparently called for. The leader, always a violinist, was the prettiest, and winked and wiggled her way through night after night of Liszt and Enesco without ever quite forgetting that she had almost been first at the conservatory in Lyon or Clermont or maybe even Paris.

And there were the beautiful German girls that summer. There had been a few for three or four years, but that summer they were in full strength. I had noticed it at Easter time, when I went to Paris to decide a few things, but now that the fair was to begin, it was even plainer.

I sat at my table, writing fast and then resting, watching people, and as the chairs on the terrace filled, I thought that I had never seen so many beautiful German girls. I knew, without much surprise, that they were there for a reason—to show all the hungry, thirsty, excited tourists that they were the most beautiful in the world and the happiest, being the most German.

It seemed like a dirty trick to play. I remembered the fat girls from little Prussian villages, and their dowdy muckle-dun suits, and the way their eyes squinted and their hair smelled, in the classrooms when I was going to the university in Dijon. Those girls had won scholarships and worked like slaves at their lessons. After

1933 you didn't see them anymore. And now Hitler's machine was sending these lovelies . . .

They were tall, slender with the lithe flatness of youth. Their skin was firm and beautifully gilded—not burned brown enough to look un-Aryan but gilded to show what you knew anyway, that they could sail and ski and dance. They all had rather shaggy hair, bleached a little in streaks so that you were to be sure the sun had done it. It was startling and lovely, after the neat tourist hairdos and the elaborate whorls of the French women, and the girls would stand hatless, tall and young, beside the tables of their acquaintances and shake back their hair softly against their shoulders, like sensual colts. And they all wore beautifully tailored gray flannel suits, casual but as artfully revealing as any Hollywood extra's, and white shirtwaists open at the throat.

They never worked together, but there was at least one at every big café in Paris that summer. They would stand up and call out to people they knew or stride from table to table—anything to make people see them and know by their accents that they were German. They all used that seemingly childlike, voluptuous soft way of speaking that is supposed to be Viennese, so that the French would not possibly think of them as Boches.

An Alsatian *brasserie* was just across the street. I knew it was supposed to be a Nazi hangout. I saw two or three of the girls come out of it and then head for their next jobs, up and down the boulevard. I felt very bitter suddenly, and when my waiter came slapping and scowling toward me, I asked him to bring me a double porto-flip. He looked sourly at me and probably was about to tell me that the barman was not yet on duty, but I said very firmly, "Double, please, with two egg yolks . . . and the best red port."

I loathed port, and raw eggs, too. But I had left the hotel without breakfast, and I knew that it would be silly to drink an aperitif and then feel even stranger than I did already. Soon my dear parents would be in Paris. . . . I must meet their train and be young and happy and untouched by evil.

After I drank resolutely at the sweetish, creamy eggnog, I felt steadier in spite of my resentment of it and began to write as fast and as impersonally as I could about the night before. I wish I had not lost those papers. This would be much easier. . . .

It doesn't matter whether I meant to see Rina or not when I went to Paris early: I did see her. I kept saying to myself, or rather my mind kept saying, the way a mind does when a person is trying to ignore too many facts at once, Flagons and apples, flagons and apples. My mind would also say things like, Involution, convolution, trivo-intro-spinolution.

But as I sat in the hotel bedroom and knew that flowers were in vases and mineral water was ordered and English novels were on the bedside tables for my parents and that all was in order at least a day too soon, my mind was saying, Flagons and apples . . . oh, stay me with flagons, stay me with flagons and comfort me with apples, for I am tired of love.

Was that it? It was in the Bible. Did it say tired or sick? I was tired. I wanted love, but I was tired of it, wearied by its involutions, convolutions, its complex intraplexities. I had fled from it, leaving there in Vevey the husk and the bud, the empty and the refilled, renewed, revived, recrucified. . . .

When I tried to write a letter to tell my husband that I was well and happy, I knew that running away had not helped us at all. I loved him too much to lie, although not enough to live with him . . . and it was the same thing again: Stay me with flagons, for I am tired, sick, tired, tired of love.

It was then that I decided to call Rina. She was the answer.

She would be like cool water, I knew it. I felt younger and suddenly freed from all the wordy anguish of the last weeks. Rina knew everything about love. She knew so much and for so long that she had left it all behind. I felt sure of that, convinced of it.

Rina had known every kind of love in the world, and by now she must have left it all behind, she must have. By now she must be a woman beyond purchase, dispassionate at last because she had known all passion, cool at last after all the fires. I wanted terribly to be with her for a while, to rest my weary self with her. I knew now why I had come so resolutely, so slyly, a day early.

It was five years since I had last seen her, perhaps, but everywhere she went she sent me her new address, as if I would be likely to find myself, or her either, in Berlin, or Minorca, or a Baltic fishing town. Now I even had her telephone number in Paris.

My heart was beating hard, partly from the nervousness that telephoning always brings to me and partly from a strange physical reaction, the way it might if I had been lost in a dark cave and had suddenly found the exit.

A maid answered, and then I was talking with Rina. Her voice sounded low one moment and then high and foolish the next, and I realized quickly that she was saying things to me, the usual things two women say after a long separation, but that through me she was talking to someone in the room with her. She was trying to impress someone.

It annoyed me. She must know that after so many years she could not impress me, but doing it to another person was important enough to her to risk my scorn before two minutes had passed. I listened to her voice, lush with affectation and little laughs and murmurs, and wished that I had stayed in Vevey.

There was some nonsense going on about a Packard. "What do *you* think of them?" she demanded lightly, and then before I could answer, she said, "But that's exactly what I say! You've never driven anything else! That long gray roadster . . ."

There was a lot more like that, and I kept thinking, Oh, to hell with it! I've never had a Packard in my life. Long gray roadster!

Rina's accent grew more and more British, and I felt cold and bored. She . . . they . . . just leaving for the Riviera . . . she must see me . . .

I looked around the sterile little room and thought of eating alone: any table in Paris would be one at which my husband or my own true love and I had sat . . .

"I'm leaving, myself, early tomorrow," I said politely. "But I'd so like to see you. Can you have supper with me tonight?" I heard my voice, almost as silly and affected as hers. There was more chatter: I was to come first for a cocktail. . . . I said yes and hung up, bone weary, almost empty of the fine hopes that had leapt in me.

It was a charming afternoon, though, light and limpid, the way Paris can be. There was a big chestnut tree in the courtyard, and a few of its white candles, nearly burned out by now, moved in the pure trembling light against my balcony. The walls looked silvery, not gray, and the dingy mustard plush curtains were golden. I took a long bath and lay on my bed drinking slowly at some brandy and water, and when I finally got up, I dressed almost as carefully as if I were meeting a man I loved very much, instead of a woman who by now should be past such things.

I remembered that I had always dressed with extra care for Rina. She wore very conventional clothes herself, like a rather horsey Junior Leaguer from Pasadena or Milwaukee, but she always made other people want to be extraordinary, to tie a scarf as it had never been tied before or wear one pink glove and one black one. I was satisfied with myself, Rina or not: my dress, the color of a green almond, was like a good dressmaker's idea of what human skin should be, with all the tucks and gores just so instead of as God put them. That was two or three years before women began to wear veils, and I had a big green net that held on my black priest's hat and tied under my chin.

I gazed at myself coolly for a few minutes with great pleasure, as I put on my black gloves in the sweetly dying light. I was slender, chic, with a face as smooth and almost as meaningless as a doll's, and my mind felt quiet again. The bath and the brandy and then this agreeable vision of myself made me put far out of my mind the weariness after my talk with Rina.

By the time I was in the taxi I was excited again, thinking that perhaps she would be as I wanted her to be, wise and rich and dispassionate. I needed someone like that, someone far past sexual wonderings, like a mountain, like a true priest. I needed to withdraw from the lists, to stand for a few minutes away from the battle.

Rina's name was printed on a card for the sixth floor. The apartment house was quietly swanky, somewhere off the Étoile, and I went up in a tiny elevator. A middle-aged maid with a mean face opened the door, and then I was standing in a big room at the top of the building, meant for a studio. Light still glared hotly in through the huge tilted window so that I was dazzled. Rina always liked darkness, I thought. She must hate this.

There was a pleasant fragrance in the air, like full-blown roses.

It seemed as if I waited several minutes. I stood motionless near the door, noticing and thinking several things at once, like any animal in a new place. I still heard the maid saying, "The young lady will be here soon." That sounded queerly insolent when I repeated it to myself; she should have said Rina's name, she should have asked me to sit down. Something rang false as hell.

The room was attractive, surely, in a way that had been made banal by French decorators: white plastered walls, several good pieces of peasant furniture, hand-blocked heavy cloth on the low couches and the chairs. The floor was darkened to look "provincial," and there were good rugs. It is queer . . . I don't believe there were any pictures at all—the walls must have been quite blank.

But it was a pleasant place, except for the loud glare of light —and, except for that, completely characterless. I felt surprised; Rina always took possession of wherever she lived, and I could see nothing of her here. I began to feel very curious about her, in a detached way—what she would be like, after so long.

I took off my gloves and then started slowly to put them on again, knowing without caring that she was going to make an entrance. That at least would be in the right tradition, I thought, not maliciously but almost with relief to find something still left.

The last time I saw her, what did she look like? It was in the rain, in the station at Dijon. I was catching the midnight train for Paris, to go back to California for a few weeks. She stood with her arm through my husband's, and I thought he would probably fall in love with her. Men always did, helplessly. She would do him good, I thought.

I stood in the train window, watching the wet lamplight on their faces turned mutely up to me, and probably I felt a little noble to be so fatalistic. Rina was beautiful, so thin from China and fevers and Leningrad that the bones showed everywhere in her, yet she still looked strong. Yes, it would do them good, I thought, looking down at them as if I were already a thousand miles at sea.

(But he did not fall in love with her. Instead, she gave a disease to our best friend, and when she found out about it, two years later in Berlin when she was having an abortion, she wanted to kill herself. She wrote to me, but by then there was not much I could say.)

I thought of all these things and probably more, and when Rina finally came through a door at the other end of the room, down near the big glaring window, I stood without speaking for a moment.

She put her hands behind her, in a strange childish gesture, and said, "Don't look at me that way. Don't, don't!"

Now, I was not looking at her in any way at all, unless maybe past her, and her low violent pleading was planned. It was a deliberate command to look at her and to be shocked and speechless. I know that my face, which can be very stolid, showed nothing. That was to reprove her for trying to make me gasp or turn away, as she wanted me to do so that she could suffer more.

I sat down on a couch and took off my gloves again without touching her. "Hello, Rina," I said, and she began to talk in a high affected voice, twitching all over the room, moving ashtrays and pillows and such, asking questions too fast and too silly to be answered: how was I, how was the trip up from Vevey, did I like Gitanes or Gold Flakes?

She seemed much shorter, probably because she was so fat and because she wore beautifully cobbled brogues. Her stockings were exquisite, and she still had fine legs, and her tailored suit and shirt and necktie were fine, too, as I had known they would be. But it is true that I never would have known her.

I had met several women who looked almost exactly as she did now, in Hollywood mostly, but it had never occurred to me that Rina would ever resemble them. I suppose it is a glandular condition. She was fat in a certain way, with compact hips and very heavy, almost bull-like shoulders. Her head stuck forward, making her neck look shorter still, and there was a roll at the back, like a caricature of a German burgher, so that the close-cropped hair made unattractive bristles. It was thin at the temples, like a middle-aging man's.

Her face was the strangest, yet I knew it well . . . on other women. It was dead white, with the close-pored vaguely dirty whiteness of an alcoholic's. Her eyes had grown very small, it seemed, and were timid now, instead of large and deep blue and gravely intelligent. She had no eyebrows left at all but only a thin silly penciled line above each puffy socket. And her mouth was small and carefully made up. It looked like a baby's, covered with lipstick, meaningless and nasty.

Perhaps I was less stolid than I thought, for Rina suddenly stopped fussing at the books on the big oak table and came over and took my gloves away.

"Don't put them on again," she said quietly. "You're nervous, too, aren't you? Let's have a drink." Her voice was natural, the low almost harsh voice I remembered. I could smell a heavy scent —she had always liked them.

She pushed an electric button in an elaborate little cloisonné thing on the table in front of my couch, and because neither of us had anything to say, we waited silently. She rang it again. She ran her fingers back over her thinning hair. "It's because *I'm* ringing it," she muttered, not looking at me. "She knows I'm ringing it. She hates me." Then she pushed crankily at the little bell several times and said in the affected English voice, "Servants are so difficult, what with the Exposition . . . I'll simply have to do it myself."

She laughed like something in a drawing room comedy. "A sidecar. You do want a sidecar, don't you?"

"No, thank you, Rina. May I have some brandy and water, please?"

"Oh, but I make such heavenly sidecars . . . Well . . ." She put her hand on my shoulder, the first time we touched, and said, still in that foolish voice, "Just like a little boarding school girl: please . . . thank you, no; thank you, yes . . ."

Then she went hurriedly out of the room. I could hear her heavy flat footsteps go down a long hall.

I was shaking a little all over. I didn't know why, then, but now I think it was the same way a cat shakes after she gives birth to a kitten. I had got rid of something, some burden inside me, and it was a physical shock. For fifteen years I had known Rina and, without words, had believed that she sometime would be my comfort, my very present help in time of trouble. I had lied for her and condoned her eccentricities, her cruelties to people who loved her, without ever loving her myself but because I believed that someday she would save me. And now I knew that she never would. I pushed all that trust away from me, and it was like relieving myself of a great burden, like a birthing of something I had thought was dependence and was really my own freedom. That is why I trembled, but I did not know it then. I just wondered a little.

She came back soon with two tall lovely glasses, the kind that should have flowers in them and are too heavy full of drink. My highball was thin but good. Rina was drinking barley water.

She sat down at the other end of my couch and began to talk rapidly, as if she wanted to tell me everything before it was too late. I listened without speaking, very coolly, as to a tactless stranger.

There was almost nothing I recognized: she was still a snob, but her old small references to social position had become crude boasting about titles and hunting lodges; she was still conscious of money, but her old mannerism of pretending that it was too base, too vulgar to talk about, had turned into a long financial whine.

She seemed to feel misunderstood now and persecuted: Tanya the Polish cook sneered at her, her uncles had cut down her share of her rightful inheritance from a sixth to a thirty-sixth of the estate, Moira always rented places with studio windows when she knew what torture the light was, she went to doctor after doctor and they deliberately hoaxed her into taking medicines that did no good, Moira was wonderful but wouldn't let her help in any way so that she simply felt *kept.* . . .

"Who is Moira?" I asked politely, knowing that she must be Rina's mistress.

She looked oddly embarrassed, as if I were too young to be told. I grinned to myself, thinking of when we were in boarding school together and in college and of all the girls who had hated me or tried to hurt me or wept in my arms because Rina was cruel to them and loved me better. "Do you love her?" I asked as if it didn't matter, which was true.

Rina frowned peevishly. "We . . . I live with her, if that's what you mean," she said in a stiff way. "Her name is Moira Bentley-Wivers, *Lady* Bentley-Wivers. She is an exquisite Irishwoman. She will be here soon."

And then she was off again on her monologue: Moira's dog was more important in the ménage than she, the doctors took her money and laughed at her behind her back, Tanya did, too, and told Moira lies about her. . . .

Rina got up two or three times to get more barley water for herself, and when she came back, she smelled more strongly of the heavy perfume, so I guessed that she was drinking brandy or whiskey and trying to hide it. She asked me each time if I wouldn't change and let her make a wonderful sidecar, but I said no and nursed my glass. I did not feel like drinking anything at all, or even breathing.

"I fixed those flowers for you," she said, interrupting herself as if she could no longer stand the sound of the high silly voice. She sounded like my old friend again but pleading, not proud. "Do you like them? They remind me of you."

I saw that behind me, almost hidden in the angle the couch made with the wall, was a copper kettle filled with pink peonies, the pale bruised gray-pink color that only peonies can have. It was their subtle roselike fragrance I had first smelled. Now it was lost in Rina's crude perfume.

"They are lovely," I said politely. They were, but I felt bored and mean.

"I fixed them for you . . . that color against the copper . . . I knew you would like it . . ."

"I think pewter would be better," I said, and as if my small cruelty had broken open a wound, she cried out harshly, "Oh!"

And she called me a name that only my husbands and my family have ever called me. It is a short ugly little name, but nobody else has ever dared call me by it because it is completely private. Rina had heard my sisters say it, of course, and my brother, too. Now it was more shocking than I can say to hear her use it. It was past impertinence, past importunity, like seeing a father show his idiot son for money, and it was sad in the same ignoble way.

"Oh!" Rina cried again, again calling me by that name, and she was like someone in hell, praying to the last god on the list, beating on the last closed door.

I put down my glass on the low table and thought as coldly as I could, This is probably a game she has often played, often rehearsed. It is the usual masochistic whine of a once proud, once strong and beautiful human seeing herself, whimpering in self-pity for her perversities.

But when I looked at her, I saw in her blinking pale little eyes that she was there, the old intelligent Rina, perhaps for a few seconds but truly, and I had to answer.

"What can I do, Rina?"

"You are the same. You haven't changed." She turned her

head away as if she could not stand to have me look at her eyes and said, very low, "Take off your hat. Take the pins out of your hair. Let it down so that it will be the way it used to be just once."

I had to, I felt so full of pity for her. I put my handsome little hat and the fine green veil beside me on the couch and took out the pins so that my hair fell softly down my back.

Rina looked at me without smiling, but I could see that she felt better. She leaned a little toward me, and I tried not to smell the heavy perfume on her breath.

"Oh," she said, using my private name again, "is there anyone who can help me? Do you know anyone? Look at my hands!" She held them in front of her as if they stank: pale, puffy, trembling, with bitten nails. "You know how I used to be! Is there anyone to help me?"

I remembered her firm strong body, and the way she could always do anything, *anything* at school better than we could, and how she was more exciting and brilliant than any student had ever been so that the professors feared her and girls wept for her and men stopped breathing for wanting her. All that grace and wit, all that strange electricity had been mine for the taking. But I had taken nothing. I had waited too long, and now I felt a deepening remorse in me. Perhaps if I had been more generous . . . it was too late now to tell anything but the truth.

"Rina," I said, beginning to shake again a little, "there is a man in California, an endocrinologist. It might kill you, though. You're rotten. There'd be no liquor, no love . . . no drugs. . . . I don't know whether you have the guts."

But she did not hear me. The little elevator was humming. The doorbell sounded, and then Moira and her dog were in the room, and me with my hair down and my fine hat on the couch. Tanya half-followed Moira, her hard sly face full of pleasure, and then pulled back like a snail when she saw my disarray.

Rina stood up and began fussing at ashtrays and books as she had when I first came, but I sat still, not knowing what else to do, while the tiny dog sniffed circumspectly at me and Moira stood in the middle of the room, as I had stood, slowly drawing off her gloves. I liked her, and she liked me, but we were wary. We recognized a mutual knowledge of what time could do and of our fleeting unimportance to each other.

She was a tall woman, about our age or perhaps a little older. Her torso was solid and mature, and she had lovely legs and a small head rather like mine. She wore very high heels and a subtle hat, and although her suit was tailored like Rina's, it looked female, not male. And she did not wear a shirt and cravat, but a soft silk blouse with a cairngorm shawl pin at the throat. Her hair was short, too, but not like Rina's. It was tawny, and all her clothes were the soft colors of toasted bread, warm and clear.

I cannot remember anything about her face except that it was all right—good bones, noncommittal—and that the corners of her wide mouth were as pointed as an adder's tongue and as sensitive.

All this time Rina was fidgeting. I left my hair the way it was, and I knew Moira was looking coldly at my hat and veil there on the couch. Rina had introduced us in her incredibly affected voice, and then she said, "Oh, darling . . . the embassy has been calling frantically . . . and there are flowers for you from the *vicomte* in the kitchen. Tanya wouldn't let me open them. And did you get the Packard, Moira, darling?" Like that, on and on.

Moira pulled her hat off and threw it with her gloves on the big table. "Let's have a drink, shall we?"

She smiled at me and began to talk politely about the weather and what a pity it was that the Exposition was late and weren't the peonies exquisite this year. I felt back in school again, taking a deportment lesson and saying, Yes, Miss Moira, No, Miss Moira, with my ankles crossed. And yet, as I say, we liked each other.

Rina came back in a few minutes with a shaker and three glasses, and the perfume in a cloud about her.

Moira said, "But, Rina . . . I always drink whiskey."

Rina laughed shrilly, as if Moira had made a great joke. "Darling! But it's all gone . . . I hate to say this, but Tanya looks . . . Oh, well, for once, Moira, drink one of my sidecars. You *know* how good they are . . . and we love them, don't we?"

She leered archly at me from under her crazy penciled eyebrows. She was a stranger, and an unpleasant one. I took one of the cocktails. I never tasted it, but I knew Moira did not care, any more than she cared when Rina clinked glasses elaborately with both of us and said, "First drink today! I've been a good girl today, Moira . . . nothing but barley water. Of course, Tanya would love to tell you another tale!"

"How did you two get along today, dear?" Moira spoke dutifully, like a nice husband home from the office.

Rina laughed again, like a parrot. "Beautifully," she cried. Then she turned to me. "As Tanya so aptly puts it, Moira got all three of us the same week. We all get our pay, too. Tanya cooks for her, and the Pekingese amuses her, and I ———— her."

And she used a word that I have never been able to say. I had never in my life heard Rina say anything like it. In school, she had never even goshed and helled and gollied, like the rest of us.

Moira went on sipping at her drink, and I started to put the pins back in my hair.

"M'ing!" Rina called. The little dog raised his head. He looked like a Chinese carving, there in his basket under the table. He stared for a cold second at her and then closed his eyes.

She laughed again and said gaily to me, "Do you remember

those wonderful hunting dogs your father used to have? I've told Moira about them."

Of course, my father never had any hunting dogs . . . just one old broken-down hound that wandered to the Ranch and stayed there until he died. But I murmured yes to that and some other equally outrageous things that Rina knew I knew for lies, and then said I must put on my hat. I stood up.

Moira said quickly, warmly, "Oh, but we're having supper together, aren't we? You *must* have supper with us!"

I was surprised at her urgency. And I had forgotten my invitation. I wanted more than anything in the world to go back to my hotel: I felt sleepy, the way you do when you go up a high mountain and then come down again all in one day, or one hour.

"Oh," I said, "I had hoped that you and Rina would have supper with me. We could go to Michaud's or Daniel's—they're nice—"

I saw Moira look strangely at me. "No, no," she said. She sounded almost cross. "No, we insist, don't we, Rina? You *must* have supper with us. We have a favorite little place . . . so quiet . . . and tonight is Tanya's free night or we'd all stay here . . . but I know you'll love this little place. It's very near here." It was queer to have Moira suddenly so eager. The room was almost dark, but I could see her looking at me, insisting with her whole body that I stay, that I be their guest.

"Thank you . . . I should love to." There was nothing else I felt able to say. After all, it was my own fault. I would leave early. . . .

"Rina!" Moira's voice was sharp, and Rina spilled some of her drink as she stood up heavily, clumsily, from the chair she had finally settled in. "Rina, I must call the ambassador—no, I'll write him a note, and we can post it on our way out. Will you please show Mrs. Fisher our room? She wants to rearrange her hair, I'm sure."

She's a smooth one, I thought admiringly, as Moira sat down at the desk and switched on a light beside her, and Rina went ahead of me into the shadows under the big window.

I fixed myself in the bathroom and then went into the bedroom, where Rina stood quietly by an enormous mirror. It was like the window in the other room, except that now the light on it was very delicate and somber. Rina turned her back to me, and we stood looking at each other in that glass for a long moment, not really saying anything but feeling the only peace we were ever to feel again together.

Then she laughed shrilly, and turned back, and said like a boastful little girl, "This is *my* dressing table."

It was covered with large bottles of very expensive perfume, and there were boxes of powder and several lipsticks, more like a movie star's than this pathetic woman's.

"And this is my armoire. See?" She pulled open the doors, and there were more beautifully cut suits and piles of fine silk and linen. It was like a finicky man's wardrobe, and yet not like it. "And there," we turned about-face, "are Moira's dressing table and armoire. And there is our bed."

How narrow it was, I thought. It seemed impossible that two such large people could sleep together in it, night after night, every night.

The room was like a big setting, like a sardonic Ziegfeld parody of a boarding school bedroom: matching furniture stage right and stage left, bed upstage center . . . and then the great mirror where the audience would be. Perhaps there were chairs and such . . . oh, certainly there were . . . but I really remember only that ridiculous little bed and the mirror.

We went back into the studio. Moira was writing busily under the light at the far end. Rina and I stood for a minute looking out into the soft beautiful Paris night. The horizon behind the chimney pots was like Venetian glass, lemon clear, but stars showed, and underneath there were lights, more and more.

Rina was talking, not too loud but loud enough for Moira to hear if she wished. "Now I can live. It is dark now. This window hurts me, kills me. She knows it. Everywhere we go we live in a glare like this. It tortures me . . ."

"Oh," I cried, and at my voice Rina stopped breathing, just as I had, to see flaming against the dark glassy sky a kind of torch. It was gold, and it glowed but was solid, too. Suddenly it had leapt into the night there, perhaps a half mile away from us across the roofs, and it stayed, instead of flickering away again as such strange things should rightly do.

"Rina! What is it?"

"What does it look like?" Her voice was low, impatient. "It's the statue at the Soviet pavilion—a man and a woman on a pillar."

"A man and a woman!" I laughed. "But it looks like a seal from here, with a ball on his nose. Yes, I can see it better now. It's a seal with a ball on his nose." I felt silly and almost happy, like a child. The golden thing there in the sky was magical.

Rina said something very distinctly about balls. She said it the way an old man will murmur a rhyme to a little boy, watching him to see how many of the words he knows.

"You don't think that's funny, do you?" she asked softly.

I could see by the way she swayed that she was abruptly drunk. I have watched that happen to other people who drink the way Rina did: they stay coldly, deliberately steady for almost any length of time they want to. Then, perhaps because they cannot fight their own secret demons any longer, or because they are bored, or because it is dusk or high noon or they hear someone singing in the street, they are drunk. They are drunk in the middle of a sentence. This is how it was with Rina. She was all right, in a pinched hard way, and then, standing there beside me watching the golden torch, she was suddenly very drunk.

"You don't think that's funny, do you?" she said again, loudly.

"No."

Moira came quickly to us and put her arm through Rina's. For the first time she sounded Irish when she spoke, soft and cajoling.

"Supper! Forgive me, both of you! I've kept you, and it's time for supper, surely now."

She led Rina into the bedroom. In a minute they came out, Rina in an awful hat not quite a man's but never meant for a woman, Moira smooth and cool looking, with only a finger or two on Rina's elbow to guide her.

When we got to the elevator and held open the door, it looked too small for even one of us. I said, "Please let me walk down. I hate elevators." I wasn't being polite; it was the truth.

Rina lurched away from us. "No," she said violently. *"I* hate elevators. *I'*ll walk down."

Moira tried to seize her arm. "No, Rina," she cried, and her voice was full of anguish. It was the only time I heard her talk with any love. "Rina, please! It will be bad for you. You aren't well . . . your heart . . ."

I thought what a pity it was that this fine tender woman, so full of compassion, should not have her own children.

Rina laughed sneeringly, like a man who is mean drunk. She pushed Moira hard into the tiny elevator and then, without touching me, started down the first flight of curving stairs.

I got in as quickly as I could, closed the door, and pushed the button. Moira stood leaning away from me, all drooping, like the leaves on a broken branch in the hot sun. She said, "Oh, God," quietly.

"Are you unhappy?" I asked it without thought and then knew that I had been wrong: she raised her head, and her eyes were cold and the fine thin corners of her mouth trembled like adders' tongues.

"Why should I be?"

"Is she . . . are you used to this then?" I felt impertinent, like a brash child, and glad that there was no more time to be rebuffed, for we were down already.

The elevator door rolled open. Rina stood there, trying not to pant. Her face was an ugly red. She must have run all the way. It made me shudder to think of it.

"Rina! That's wonderful," Moira said warmly, and Rina's face lit up. She laughed and pulled off her horrible hat, and we went out and got into a taxi, and Moira gave an address.

Rina sat next to me. I thought for a few minutes that she had stopped being drunk, but when Moira got out to post her letter, I could tell that she was perhaps worse. She leaned against me a little, needlessly, and breathed in an excited way. It was mechanical, like a prostitute pretending, or an old man.

It was as if Rina did it because all women that close to her expected her to, but I was not all women—I was me, her longtime friend, who knew her too well ever to love her.

I made no sign of anything, and when Moira came back and saw Rina so close to me, she looked sharply at me, but I still made no sign of anything. You should go along the Elysées, I thought furiously, and get yourself one of the German girls. Yes, go along the Elysées, with some of Moira's money. Go anywhere. But *I* am *me*—

The restaurant was small, the kind that is a café during the day, with a little bar beside the cash desk and wavy mirrors behind the marble-topped tables around the walls. It was like the Roy Gourmet, if you remember that, except that it was just one room instead of two, and it was mediocre instead of good. There were waitresses, big taciturn girls. The patrons were big, too, perhaps young lawyers and functionaries and store people, with their wives and a few middle-class whores. When we came in past the row of tables under the open widows on the sidewalk, everybody stopped eating and talking and looked at us.

Now, every woman who holds her head up and looks as if she has known good love has at times made a room quiet when she has walked into it. There is something silencing, even for a few seconds, about her. It is not because of beauty or her vestments or the people with her; it is a kind of invisible music, or perfume, or color that surrounds her and makes people stop their usual thoughts and motions. When they pick up their forks, they may not even know why they put them down and may never think of the woman again, but for a time she has touched their lives, usually without meaning to.

This had often happened to me, of course, because of my bony structure and the fortunes of my years, but I had never been made either comfortable or uncomfortable by it. I had probably taken it as part of being human.

When we walked into the little restaurant, though, and all the heavy people in their black office clothes looked at us, I felt as if my skin were being pulled off. I saw their eyes slide with amazement over us: Moira so cool and disdainful, with her mouth thin and tight and her mature body tight, too, under her beautiful clothes; Rina all puffed and bullish, like a monstrous caricature of a creature neither man nor woman; and I so obviously not a partner to either, I like a slim and modish cuckoo in this ex-normal nest. They looked most at me, wondering about my green dress and my green veil probably, trying to place me in their vocabularies of behavior.

Moira and I sat against the wall at the last small table, with Rina facing us. A waitress brought us the usual blurred menus and then with a smirk took Rina's hat and hung it on the rack by the cash desk with all the other heavy dark fedoras and straws.

I was ravenously hungry—I had only eaten some cold chicken and salad that day on the early train from Vevey—and besides being empty, I felt a sort of hectic need in me, as if I had rid myself of something enormous, and all my bones were now crying for new nourishment. I wanted a meal to satisfy me, a real meal chosen with thought, a long good meal with the right wine or two.

The menu looked fairly promising. But Moira was already ordering for the three of us. She spoke French correctly but with a rather scornful flatness, as if it were a language not worth sounding out, which reminded me more of an English than an Irish person. The waitress stood looking down at us, her face blank and her eyes wearily entertained.

"The day's specialty . . . that sounds all right," Moira said. "It's too hot for anything first, of course . . . or would you like something first, Mrs. Fisher?"

I felt annoyed that such a seemingly well-bred person could be so careless, and I was disappointed, too: I had thought Moira would be more intelligent. So I said, "Yes, I would, thank you. I am awfully hungry. I'd like some pâté . . . it says *pâté d'été* here . . . that will taste good."

"Madame will take the *pâté d'été*," Moira said to the waitress in her flat insensitive French. "We will have the entrée at once and . . . and a bottle of the restaurant's *champagne nature*."

"No salad, no vegetable for the young ladies?" the waitress's voice was subtly insolent, the way Tanya's had been when she told me Rina would come in a minute.

"No. And hurry, please."

I looked at Moira, and suddenly I realized that she was terribly anxious about Rina. She wanted to get food into her as soon as possible; Rina was swaying in her chair, and her poor pale eyes were glassy. I felt ashamed of myself for changing her orders, for interrupting the quick functional flow of food into belly that this meal must be. How stupid of me to think that with a person like Rina at the table a meal could have any grace or ease or pleasure in it. It must be a feeding, that was all—a sort of sponge for extra alcohol, which was to be swallowed as quickly as possible.

Why do people like this ever eat in public? I wondered. They should take food as they take physics, in the privacy of their bathrooms.

I looked at the menu: the specialty of the day was *coq au Chambertin*. It would be ghastly with *champagne nature*. It would not be made with Chambertin either. I could tell by the looks of the place. The pâté might be all right . . . probably veal and spices with a little cubed ham discreetly through it, but cold and savory.

"Rina, some bread? Here, split it with me." I held out a big piece to her. She pushed it away.

"Rina hates bread," Moira said, "Don't you, darling?" But Rina did not answer.

Moira sat stiffly against the cheap cloth seat, and I felt that she was forcing Rina with every muscle in her body to stay conscious, to sit up, not to fall over or be sick. Her face was almost as expressionless as mine.

The waitress brought the unlabeled bottle of wine. It was very crude, but we all drank it thirstily. It seemed strange to me not to click glasses, no matter how perfunctorily, the way we always did in Vevey. It was very sour with the bread, but I felt starved.

The people, except for an occasional shrug and almost surreptitious look at us, had gone back to their own problems. Rina sat without speaking. She held her glass in both hands and drank in small rapid sips, as if the wine were hot consommé. Moira was talking to me about her house on the Riviera. She and Rina were joining her parents there, she said politely, as if either of us could be interested. There would be other people there. Did I love to swim?

"Tell her about Raoul," Rina said suddenly. Her words were almost impossible to separate one from another.

Moira looked upset for a second. "Oh, Mrs. Fisher doesn't know Raoul," she said. Then as she saw Rina open her mouth again and scowl, she went on, "Raoul is our dearest friend, our . . . father confessor, really."

"Show her his picture," Rina commanded brusquely.

Moira shrugged and without saying anything took a little leather folder from her purse. There was an old-fashioned photograph of a man in it, a slender delicate face, the hair long, the eyes rolled up, one finger of his bony hand pressed against his temple. It looked like a cruel parody of an 1890 aesthete. There was nothing to say about it, except perhaps "Oh," which I did.

"We are very fond of Raoul," Moira stated flatly. "He spends a great deal of his time with us."

"Moira keeps him. Moira keeps Tanya and M'ing and Rina and Raoul. Moira is kind, isn't she?" Rina muttered.

I could feel Moira praying desperately for the day's specialty to come. I looked at the picture facing Raoul's. One of the women was Moira, in a bathing suit. Her figure was beautiful. The other woman, sitting at her feet on a beach, was in slacks and had a heavy long mop of bright blonde hair, and for a minute I did not see that it was Rina. She looked very beautiful, too, the way I remembered her except for the hair.

"Let me see," Rina said, and pulled the folder out of my hand. She shut it after a quick look. "That's me. That was last summer. I dyed my hair. I thought it would change things." She pushed the folder back toward Moira, and I sat wondering how any human could be so different within so few months. I didn't look anywhere but ate little pieces of bread and drank my wine.

Then the waitress came with our plates piled up her arm. "Messieurs-'dames," she said insolently, and put down a casserole, and then my pâté, and the serving spoons in front of Moira. "Or does Madame prefer me to serve?" she asked. Moira picked up the spoons quickly.

"What's that?" Rina asked loudly, and looked up at the girl.

"*Coq au Chambertin,* as ordered."

"Coq?" And very distinctly, without smiling at all, Rina said something completely obscene about a cock in clear and perfect French. The waitress drew back, frightened, I think, and then flushing, and people around us stopped everything, the words heavy in their ears.

"Thank you, Mademoiselle . . . I can serve," Moira said, and there was something so dignified and suppliant about her voice that the girl hurried away, instead of screaming or striking Rina as she might have.

Moira put quite a lot of the chicken stew, for that is what it was, on a plate for Rina and filled her glass again. She began to eat, too, watching Rina all the time.

Rina ate a little, but she was dreadfully clumsy and kept getting bits onto her fork and then watching them fall slowly off again, the way I had seen old drunks do in hash houses on skid row in Los Angeles. There were already several smears of the dark sauce on her suit. She looked as if swallowing hurt her.

I was still very hungry, in a detached way, but I couldn't eat. The pâté, as I had thought, was far from disreputable. It was simple and savory, just what I had wanted. But now I couldn't. I tried to eat the chicken. It was fairly well made but too heavy for such a summery night. I wanted a salad—but I knew that if I had one it would not go down my throat. I drank some more wine.

Moira was talking, and perhaps I was, too, when Rina suddenly stood up. Her chair squealed against the floor, and people looked at us again, a kind of alarm now on their faces.

"Shall I come with you?" Moira asked softly.

Rina shook her head without speaking and walked unsteadily out the door and past the sidewalk babies.

We all watched her—all of us, even the waitress. The men shrugged, and the women leaned over the tables toward them to whisper strangely excited little questions, and I kept seeing long after she had disappeared down the dark street the heavy shoulders, the thin black hair on her temples, the neat hips and slender legs.

But more clearly I saw the other Rina, the proud sure one, the reckless handsome woman who had gone like a flash of lightning through so many hearts and bodies.

"The water closet is down the street," Moira said casually. "It is really too hot to eat anyway, isn't it? We should have stayed home and raided Tanya's kitchen. But sometimes Rina thinks Tanya is trying to poison her."

"And I leave so early in the morning," I lied. "I should really go back to my hotel and pack."

It seemed silly to keep up that kind of bluff, but we both did it. Rina came back. She looked a little soberer and ate some of the cold sauce on her plate with a piece of bread. She drained her glass and then said, "Pay the bill, Moira."

"I wish you'd let me," I said. "You know I asked you this afternoon, Rina . . ."

"No. Moira always pays the bill, don't you, Moira?" And Rina laughed shrilly, like a parrot again, without looking at either of us.

In the taxi we sat without talking, after I had told the driver my address. It was as if we were too tired to say anything. Moira sat up straight, but Rina was bent and sagging, like an old person. We had to stop often: the crossings were crowded with people strolling slowly, the way they always used to in Paris on warm summer nights. I felt an almost violent impatience to hurry, to end all this.

Moira shook my hand in a polite, detached way when I finally got out. "Mrs. Fisher is going now," she said to Rina.

Rina roused herself. "Good-bye," she said, and she used the name that nobody ever uses but my family and my husbands. This time it did not sound importunate or brash but only final, so that I could not resent her.

"Good-bye," I said, and went into the hotel without thanking them.

I took another bath and went to bed as fast as I could. It was as if I had a rendezvous with something in my sleep. I rushed to meet it.

And this is where I regret the lost pages I wrote the next morning in the *brasserie,* because I wrote mostly about the dream. It was a long dream, one of the most vivid I had ever had, and I woke from it panting and shaking with a kind of abysmal horror such as I had never felt before.

This is all I can remember now: I was on a high wall, watching a long stretch of beach where little blue waves edged with white curled symmetrically, as in a Chinese embroidery. And down the beach raced a great roan horse with a golden mane. He reared back at the wall, and then, time after agonizing time, he hurled himself at it in an orgy of self-destruction. It was terrible. Time after time he leapt straight at the wall with all his strength, and there was a sound of breaking sinews and flesh, and everywhere there was his blood, bright imperial yellow blood, while the little waves rolled silently, symmetrically. . . .

I awoke, and it was as if I were drowning in horror. Then I went to the bathroom and was sick, and put cold water on my face and brushed my hair very hard. I went to sleep again, and everything was all right, as if I were a little child.

In the morning, as I have said, I felt strange. It was as if I had been poisoned and then violently washed clean of the poison. The porto-flip finished the job and made me feel warmed and fed again. I drank it dutifully, not liking it but knowing its reason, and paid my bill and put all the sheets of paper in my purse and walked out into the sunlight, past the filled noontime tables on the sidewalk.

People looked casually at me as I went by, as I would have done in their places, and suddenly, because of last night and the stares and shrugs there in the little restaurant, I felt as shy and ill at ease as a young girl. The thought of going alone to lunch, *anywhere,* was impossible.

But my father and mother would not be in Paris until late afternoon. . . .

I walked slowly toward the Tuileries, gradually getting used to humanity again, like a soul sent back to earth. I stood in the sun for a long time by one of the round fountains with the fat glass pigeons.

In the gardens under the plane trees I bought a ham sandwich and sat on a chair eating it and watching some little boys sail their boats across the pond.

By the time I had to go back to the hotel I was young, untouched by evil. I was ready to be with my dear parents, and I was ready to meet love alone again, not asking for another person's comfort, nevermore to thirst for any flagon but my own.

—*Paris, 1937*

5

Vevey Journal,
1938

The purpose of any diary I might keep in this book, when I started it over a year ago, was to tell what was happening with the building of Le Pâquis. It was soon plain to me, however, that any such chronicle was beyond my talent as a writer and that even a poor compromise between the house and its builders would be impossible. Things went too fast and inevitably toward an undreamed conclusion. The house was built, and much we had built or hoped to see grow in it was forever broken. What grew in its place, in our several hearts, it is too early to identify.

For a long time it was better to write nothing than the stiff comments I permitted myself. Now I feel easier, but I admit that today I write this simply because I want to write and am too lazy, too mazy, to work on something that needs more thinking. Here I can write some, at least, of the thoughts that drift in and out of my brain. A story or an article would need construction.

I am in a high-tide pool just now, waiting for the cold impetus to send me working again. I have sent off some stories to London, to the woman I finally decided to have for my agent for a trial of six months. Until I hear from her, which will probably be after she returns to New York, I feel do-less. That is one way of trying to vindicate my laziness.

I have several new books for research and a fat envelope of notes, but I have an aversion to doing anything but vague mental nibbling at the Quaker story for a while yet. Laziness again, partly.

I have been back from America for sixteen days now and have done no work except a short introduction for Jake Zeitlin. My whole existence has become more completely physical than ever before in my life: I eat, sleep, listen, even cook and read with an intensity and a fullness that I have never felt until now. I am completely absorbed in myself—but myself as seen through Timmy. It is a strange life, and one that cannot last long probably. I am abandoned to it now—and probably this need to write in a journal is one sign that it is almost over. I know it can never end completely. It must shift and change, though. I know enough to know that, at least.

After the monotonous dry perfection of the climate at the Ranch, this weather is as stimulating and exciting as a new symphony or a play. I stand at the windows or lie in my bed, watching and wondering about it: what does that round brown cloudlet mean? Will it be clear tomorrow, or in half an hour? Where do the feathers of snow go after they drift down so surely? They go on through the earth's surface—and then where?—like ghosts through a closed door. Do I see burgeons swelling the lilac twigs? No. Yes.

At night my ears hear the fountain as easily and constantly as a mother hears the blood-beat of her child still to be born. I awake to its changed rhythm and know in the second before I sleep again that one of our winter lettuces, bought days ago and kept fresh in the cold water, had drifted under the stream spouting from the short bronze spigot. Or perhaps the extra beat I hear is Lou-Lou from across the road, slaking a midnight thirst with thick slaps of his tongue. Or even a quiet wanderer is there. I am not alarmed, as long as the rhythm is resumed.

The days are growing longer. I like the long days of summer, but I feel cheated, resentful almost, that this winter I missed all the short ones. Last summer when we were working so constantly on the garden, I'd think, When winter comes, there'll be no long lighted evenings so good for watering and picking, and I'll go into my warm dark hole like an animal and write and think and listen to music.

But this winter I was in America, more occupied with time-bound things than I have ever been, and now it is almost time to start digging and planting again. I have another excuse for not writing, and feel relieved and disappointed and ashamed.

Occasionally a car goes by too fast. I hear it coming up or down the hill, and almost before I can look up, it is far past the window. Horses are different, slower and easier to hear. They still wear their winter bells. (I wonder why not bells in summer?) Sometimes two men are on one cart, and then I hear the rough low voices. In another month, they will be singing.

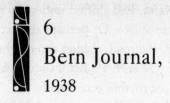

6
Bern Journal,
1938

1. viii. 38

Oₙₑ thing about writing is that it takes time. This last month I have thought of perhaps a thousand things, to estimate conservatively, that for some perverse reason I should like to write about —sights or smells or sounds, or occasionally ideas. This last month—

It is 9:14 at night, a queerly noisy night, with at least two radios blaring from somewhere over the Kornhaus Bridge, and many people walking past the hospital, and trains racketing with extra fervor from the stop by the theater across the Aare to the Kursaal. I can look out and see the lights slide along the wet black bridge and the dull shapes of two floodlit towers push up into the sky.

I finish a glass of brandy, and want to write about this month, and know that I am too sleepy. And then I wonder why I do want to write about it, because I despise talk, and the people who talk, who tell others about themselves, and the dreadful necessity that pushes them to such confessions. They must talk. They must expose themselves. It helps them, and more horribly, it helps others.

That is what bothers me. I hate this need. I've never done much of it, and I despise it in others. But I know that I am more articulate than some, and I think, Well . . . my God in heaven! If what I've learned about pain or food or the excreta of the sea snail can help even one poor human, I am a rat not to write. Then I know I am wrong.

And now, at 9:23, I am writing, for the first time in more than a month. My eyes are sanded with sleep, and my back is numb against the two limp Swiss pillows.

I look up at the mirror above my washstand to see if there is light reflected from Timmy's room. We tried two pills tonight, which did no good, and then gave the old faithful shot of Analgeticum at 8:00. He is asleep, heavily, with his mouth dropped askew. I am fairly sure that by 12:00 he will call me. Then it will be Pantopon.

I can't understand so much noise from town, but, of course, people are still celebrating that there's no war. It would have been today. Yesterday Switzerland would have had general mobilization. Of course, we are all glad. I am, and so is Timmy. I don't like the idea of those bombs the Germans tried on Barcelona, which are made of aluminum filled with liquid air. I wouldn't mind being killed outright by one, but I am sure that the people who were a quarter mile away and were stunned by them had dreadful headaches.

I hear the cathedral clock strike 9:30. It always rings first. I have tried to listen to one certain hour to see if all the clocks ever make the same pattern, but even at 3:00 in the morning they never strike the same way twice. Sometimes they make a beautiful sound. I heard that Shostakovich regretted using so many themes in his first symphony, because he had so few left. He should come here, to the Viktoria Hospital—the night bells across the dark Aare would tell him many new ones.

2.x.38

After three days of rain it is really hot in the sun. I sit on Timmy's balcony in a green skirt, a white sweater, and his gray coat, which I'll soon take off. Through the crooked glass I see him, distorted as one of his own drawings of pain, being bathed by Sister Irma.

Yes, I must take off the coat. As I wriggle out of it, I smell a faint musky hot smell that almost reminds me of something, about something, we once did together. Was it walking up a hill? Or was it something about a sea pool, with us bending over? No, I cannot say. I feel as if some sound or smell had almost recalled a dream. There for a second was the dream. But what dream? It is too late. Perhaps again sometime it will almost be clear again.

I smell rather rummy, too. I am sure that I've read of people who put wine in their pipes to burn out the varnish or some such thing. So with the awful-looking pipe I bought yesterday, because Timmy has decided that now is a good time to learn to smoke one. Sister Irma and I have been playing with it for the last half hour. It wouldn't light at all at first, and the nasty pinkish rum kept dropping out of the mouthpiece, and finally it sputtered a few times. Now I stink worse than the pipe well, I know, in spite of its being a cheap shiny one. I wish I could remember how Al liked his—he did it so well and lovingly.

Anne left this book, which is hard to write in. It's the one she meant to keep a journal in. She told me that this was the first summer for twenty-five years that had passed without her filling several notebooks with diary. A good thing, I think. This time last Sunday, or perhaps a little later, she and Timmy and I were listening, by his open door, to the earnest singing of ten Swiss. They came, dressed in their church clothes, to sing to a member of their club who is ill here. Their voices were strong and sweet, and a yodel came up like bells through the hideous hospital corridors. We were truly thrilled, and Tim's face looked quiet. So I put twenty francs in an envelope and wrote on it that someone wished the singers to drink to the world's health. Irma took it down, protesting that such a thing had never been done and beaming with excitement. And then there was a great scuffling and stamping of thick shoes and a whispering, and there was the *Sängerbund* outside the door. They sang and sang, with that rather forced lugubrious hymning that creeps into all Swiss songs but with a yodel that never missed the tone, like a true bell. We were pleased by that, and I at last was bored by the chapelish verses, and then to our surprise all the singers shuffled in and shook hands with Timmy, Anne, Irma, and me. They got in a great tangle of crossed arms and embarrassment, and I, too, felt quite self-conscious, saying, *"Merci, danke schön! Merci bien,"* to ten stiff young men.

I was sorry David and Noni weren't here to listen—they'd have been excited and amused, and Dave jealous of the yodeling. It was my fault that they had not come early. When they left the night before for Die Pension Schmultz, Noni had said, "When shall we see you—9:00, 10:00, 10:30?" And I'd said, "Oh, tomorrow's Sunday—let's all sleep." They had looked a little disappointed, I thought. And then how sorry I was, in the morning, that I'd said that!

But still I dreaded to see them. At 8:00 in the morning, Dr. Nigst came in while I was drinking tea, and when I asked him how things were going with Hitler, he lifted his arms and let them flop against his sides, and said, "I really don't know. I cannot feel war near, but—yes, it looks bad." That was the first time he had said that. And then in about ten minutes came a cable: "Arrange children sailing have written Edith." I read it to Tim and for a minute almost cried, thinking of their disappointment and how much more excited Noni was about the accordion lessons than the German ones. But I knew Edith and Rex wouldn't ask them to change all their plans for a hasty thoughtless reason. So I began to gird myself to tell the children they must leave Europe and us and go back to American schools again. I watched for them to come across the bridge and rehearsed how I'd tell them. When I saw them striding along, with the rather shambling deliberate steps of all tall people, I felt sad and nervous.

They were quiet, of course. Noni cried a little, not with sobs but with silent tears that ran down her cheeks and made her blow her nose. Then I told them to . . .

3. x. 38

A cold hard night, the first really cold one. It is only 8:30, but I am tired and in bed. Tim sleeps motionless as a tiger. These nightly bouts of pain are dreadful. I don't know how many more of them either of us can stand. He had Analgeticum at 8:00. Last night Nigst tried a mixture of Pantopon and scopolamine that made him cry out and weep and babble in the few hours of sleep it gave him. His nerve is finally breaking. He shakes and cries when he feels one of these bouts coming. I am weary and so often frightened. And what must he be?

There is a fair in one of the squares across the Aare. Its melodeon annoys me, faintly, like a gnat. It reminds me of the fair in Vevey.

But I'll write about that another time. My brain teems with memory, but my eyes are heavy. They always are now. I know things will change soon. They *must*. Almost five weeks of ceaseless agony—

5.x.38

This morning the handsome tall postulant came to make my bed, and I went into Tim's room. In a minute there was a small crash. I wondered what—perhaps a vase, or the blown-glass chicken filled with curaçao that Anne and the children had brought me. In a minute more, I went in to get a handkerchief. The postulant was whiter than ever, and the brown circles under her eyes were almost black, but it wasn't until tonight that I noticed that the bedside lamp with its glass shade was gone. Now I have an unbelievably old-fashioned thing in a discreet wired skirt of faded cretonne, which throbs with misdirected electricity when I come within two inches of it and gives, with the mellow generosity of a drunken miser, not quite enough light to write by. It was so silly, like a Rube Goldberg invention, that Tim had to stop his strange yelps of pain to laugh at it when I took it into his room.

I am drinking what is left of a bottle of bad champagne, now slightly warm, from a toothbrush tumbler. I like it.

When I opened the windows tonight, Bern looked like the more than beautiful backdrop in a heavenly Orpheum Music Hall, with bogus lights on all the towers—cathedral, clock tower, market, parliament—and lights pricked fakily all along the Aare and then up the funicular beyond the town to the high hotel.

I can think of a lot of things to write about. Almost any sentence starts a long string of—not thoughts—of reminiscences, impressions. For instance: today an enormous box of really exquisite pale powdery gold chrysanthemums, on long stems with intense dark leaves, came from those inane pale stupid people, the

Beutlers. Immediately we thought of how she had been so ill and we had not even asked what hospital she was in. Of course, we hardly knew them then—but still— And then I remembered her truly warm sincere note, after Tim came here—the schoolgirl language, so banal, and how nicely and thoughtfully and dully they had entertained us in their new house. I remembered the good bad paintings and the Third Symphony that nobody really heard but was still played from a something-or-other kind of cabinet that had been copied from one in the Palace at Avignon by Freddie's cabinetmaker. And then the queer people—the pudgy misunderstood genius of a bank clerk who dribbled his way egotistically from Chopin through Brahms and on to Grieg, with none of us daring to break the rapturous spell of Real Music.

The little fair across the river bellows out its silly gramophone records. It makes the sight of Bern at night even more theatrical—and sometimes I can hear the measured racket of a coaster machine, and the occasional scream of an excited girl, or a man's hoarse shout.

I had tea yesterday at the Nigsts'. It's a queer apartment, with a dressing table all laid out with silver-backed toilet things in the hall so that the patients can tidy themselves before or after they see the doctor. A shy little maid stood by helplessly while I wrestled with my rubber boots. Then I went into the salon, which has very bad, very modern paintings on mulberry damask wallpaper, and an elaborate, shiny-as-only-Swiss-furniture-can-be-shiny set of furniture upholstered in "rich" blue damask, and a table with some flowers on it and the kind of Japanese china tiger—scarlet—that could only be won in a shooting gallery at home.

Tea was strong enough to trot a mouse on, served from the kitchen already poured in after-dinner coffee cups, and a huge basket of delicious hot stuffed croissants (we each took one), and then a huge tray of rich cakes (we each—three of us—took one), and then dry vermouth for the doctor and me, and cigarettes for us all.

Coming home, the doctor got around for the third time to his vacation and how he'd be alone and dining out, and finally said (I felt like the innocent girl being asked to come up to see some etchings), "But do you never go out anymore for meals, now that your brother and sisters are gone?" Hell, I thought to myself. "No," I said sadly. "But why not, Miss Parrish?" We swerved wildly down the street. Well, he's asked for it, I thought. "Because I really don't like to eat alone," I said with a brave, sad, resigned look—I think. "But"—and we swerved a double swerve—"may I ask you to dine once with us? We have—we eat—I mean to say—" "Oh—but how nice of you, Dr. Nigst! Of course, as you know, if my husband does not go well—" "Oh, but Miss Parrish, I *promise* you that all will be most successful and content!"

I have a half-inch of flat mock champagne still to finish. The mock music grinds flatly on. I think with sharp poignancy of my poor Rex, Edith, torn by the first doubts of old age and their own impotence, of Anne ground between the wheels of self-knowledge and self-dramatization, of David and Norah all too quiet and too knowing. I think of Tim, lying rocked in the dark opiate arms of Analgeticum, lulled by the weariness of a shot of Pantopon. I think, vaguely and not too close, for safety's sake, of myself here, there, drugged or alive or dreaming or hysterical—

Schwester Irma left a vase for the Beutlers' chrysanthemums in front of a pot of small white garden blossoms. From my bed I cannot see that the flowers are not springing, cut off and lovely, from water in the vase. But I know that it is empty and that they are growing in the earth, behind it.

It is reluctantly that I write, and truly I don't know why I bother. Shall I write in that book tonight, I have asked myself several times today, or shall I have a whole day without a duty letter or a letter home or even a scrap of bread cast upon my own literary waters, even a note thrown to my own future?

Now it is 20:20, and I am in bed, and I have a more than moderately amusing detective story, in a green and white paper cover, called *Obelisk at Sea,* and a brandy and soda. And Timmy seems quiet, with the *piqûre* earlier so that Irma could go have her heels straightened before the shoemaker closed shop.

But I am tired—and dull. Last night I slept a long, disturbed, wretched sleep, filled with half-waking dreams of puzzlement and stress. Tim only called three times, and I slept until 8:00 this morning—but God, I am tired. I look well. I *am* well. But sometimes I feel weary, weary, weary.

This morning I woke stuffily, heavily, to realize that the winds of the night had probably blown, too, for Anne and the children, a few hours out of Liverpool. I thought of them with love and pain, pain for them all but especially for Noni. And I was thankful they were gone, at least by distance, from my immediate life.

I hurried to wash and put on a little lipstick, Vaseline on my eyelids, two faint lines of brown eyebrow pencil, two swipes of blue eye shadow to match the blue stars on my scarf and my blue flannel bathrobe, and then a little powder. I brushed my hair and put a ribbon around my head—a blue ribbon, of course.

Then I fixed Tim's coffee. He was dreamily cheerful, after the best and the longest (six hours) sleep for over five weeks. (It's five weeks today since he had the second operation, and I lay here wishing he would die.)

Then I came back to bed and drank my pale tea and ate an

unusually tasteless bun, with butter and synthetic apricot jam. I had a faint nagging ache in my belly.

For a change, I got up before Tim's bath, and dressed, and then held him by his beautiful blue-white hair while he bobbed helplessly about the tub of saltwater. Sometimes he is really very funny. I cackle—I can't help it—and so does Irma—and then we sound so funny that he laughs, too, even in great pain. I couldn't possibly say what is funny, but I find myself really *cackling*—and then when he begins his careful, high, cautious half-laugh, I am helpless. I know he has to do it, so he won't budge his side—but it is funny still.

Then there were massages and so on, with Nigst coming in in the middle, moving very carefully with what I suspect was a hangover from his wife's leaving last night, and then Irma and Schwester Agnes Ina almost driving Tim crazy trying to clean his leg with benzine. They dabbed balsam juice of some kind on the two places in his leg that look bad.

Then he had a raw egg, and we each drank a little brandy highball while I read a story by G. B. Stern, an obvious, facile, and very entertaining one in a book called *Pelican Walking,* I think.

Tim dressed for lunch, and we ate in my room—always his wretched bouillon with a bromide tablet in it, sweetbreads with aubergine (not enough), a roasted pigeon with rice, a glass of St. Emilion 1929, some strange vegetable-marrowish-looking vegetable we didn't taste, a bite of the watery Bernois salad, and some surprisingly good plum tart.

Afterward we put on a few more scarves (the hospital is still far from well heated) and walked across the Kornhaus Bridge. We stopped at the bodega, the Café Zu Den Pyrameau, and drank a sherry. It was a bad sherry, but it is a sympathetic little bodega, and the waiter and the pudgy proprietor are nice—so quietly thoughtful, without drawing attention to us.

We hopped on down the cold street, with people looking nicely at us or not at all, and Tim doing things with his usual meticulous grace. I have a horror of his putting one crutch into a grating, but I don't think he ever will. He is so well balanced that the vision of his ever crashing over fills me with a nightmare terror. But he won't.

We went to the Café du Théâtre, where the chasseur and the waitress were nice and brought us English journals full of diagrams on how to build a bomb-proof shelter or where to run in Hyde Park, and two café-cognacs—with free cookies! We wondered if anybody but us remembered the fine meal that Timmy ordered there, a few minutes before he felt the strange cramp in his leg more than five weeks ago. We'd often cogitated about going to the Théâtre, and then when we finally decided to, Timmy couldn't until today.

We walked to the taxi stand by the casino, and a kind ratlike man drove us slowly to the Viktoria. Timmy managed the getting in and out beautifully.

For almost half an hour after he got into bed again, it looked as if he'd fool them this time. But then, after one swallow of hot tea, he was almost out of his head, with the teacup rattling on his chest and his eyes wild. It was a bad siege. He whispered craftily to me, for the hundredth, the thousandth time, that *now* was the time to help him die. Then he yelped and chattered, like a hyena.

Irma, her eyes red—that, too, for the hundredth time—gave him two Pyramidons with a solemn impersonal face. And somehow, with radio and Rachel Field's new book and me and so on, we lulled him on until 6:00. I lay down for a while, weary and feeling a little sick. But supper, except for his fretting, tapping fingers and an occasional strange look in his wide eyes, was fun. And then soon after, he washed himself and undressed, and we gave him the little glass of heart drops, and the swig of Niyol, and the tea with a Urotopin tablet in it, and finally the shot of Analgeticum.

And now he is quiet, and I am tired, and I think I'll read a few pages of my green and white book and then sleep. My brain is almost bursting—Noni, tomorrow, Adelboden, La Tour—but I know that before midnight Tim will need me—

17. x. 38

"D'you know something about my leg?

"It's that, from where it was cut on down, I can't remember *one goddamn* distinguishing feature!

"It was just a leg.

"It had an ingrowing nail on the big toe—on the inside. I *think*. But I'm not sure.

"Isn't it queer? Simply another leg."

Probably there is in all intelligent people, of whom I consider myself one (perhaps mistakenly, I add without any apparent coyness), a constant warfare between innate delicacy and reserve, and the desire to talk, to Tell All. I am often conscious of it, and oftener than not I refuse to indulge in my natural itch to write because of an overfastidious fear of what may be scratched into being, into the light of paper. Often, at night, I don't want to go to sleep when I come into my bedroom from the last business of tea and injection and pillow smoothing with Timmy. I say, Now I can write in my book! Then I add, What? Then quicker than is decent, I add, But what? What can I, what *should* I say? Why in hell, why in the name of Edith, Rex, and all the host *should* I write *any*thing? Why should anyone write anything? And so the old hackneyed twice-cursed thrice-monotonous wheel turns once again.

Next week we go to Adelboden. Already I eye the eight weeks' collection of books on my bureau and my table and count the number of cakes of soap we may need. Of course, there'll be an adequate and probably, during the ski season, a highly sophisticated pharmacy up there, but my pioneer instincts are still adamant, in spite of some thirty thwarted years. The hearts of all my white chrysanthemums are turning brown. I was thinking I'd give them to the little scullery maid with pale hair and hectic cheeks, who came shyly to play the guitar. But they are no longer lovely.

Tonight we went to Doetwylers', and unfortunately it was mediocre. Going up the stairs I spoke, without turning or loosening my grip on Timmy's arm, to the shopwoman, and Tim very neatly fell back a whole step. It upset him, and me, and the shopwoman, and the busboy who leapt up and practically carried . . .

A little whimper—

"What's the matter, darling?"

"Those goddamn mice!" in a deep voice, like Chaliapin.

. . . carried him to our table. None of us raised an eyebrow. Later Timmy said that his leg suddenly seemed to grow six feet long and to search frenziedly all about for a step, like the gigantic proboscis of a moth feeling for nourishment at night.

23.x.38

Today, after almost three weeks of fine blue autumn days, it is cold and darkly gray. I am listless, moonstruck. Timmy is in greater pain than usual, feverishly ill at ease. We go out, and after peering into several steamy cafés, whose floors, cluttered with dogs and cigar butts and spittle and a few children, spell disaster to crutches, we go to the Schweizerhof for beer and a gin-vermouth for me.

Home in a taxi, and while I watch Irma massage the smooth white curve of his hip, I am quietly horrified to see a purplish blotch above the bandage. It seems slightly smoother. Is it a bruise from trying on the temporary peg, day before yesterday? I am appalled and go away without speaking.

24. x. 38

The first four hours in Adelboden. Yesterday was bad, because of weather, and what is probably a bruise from Timmy's trying on a prosthesis, and so on. But last night was fairly good. This morning Irma was like a little excited brown badger, and I became amazingly vague, wandering between the two rooms with my hair down and pieces of packing in my hands. Finally she got us all into boxes and sacks and bundles, like refugees. Tim and I fled to the Café du Théâtre for lunch. We had each planned secretly to order caviar or perhaps oysters and champagne, and we both ordered grilled steaks with *pommes* chips and a good old *bourgogne*.

I drove up to Adelboden. Nigst's friend, the Colonel Garagiste, who may be buying our car, sent us a monkeylike little chauffeur in very good livery, who worked hard and well to get all Irma's bundles arranged and then wedged himself into and under and over them beside her on the backseat. She permitted herself her sole ribaldry by saying, "Oh, Madame, there is not even a package between us, and I doubt if there is any danger—but one never knows!"

I drove up, under, and through, and then suddenly above a

milky October fog, and occasionally saw in the mirror the wan simian face of the chauffeur. He leaned his head with complete relaxation against my gray coat, which was wrapped around the dreadful *prosthèse provisionneur* [temporary prosthesis], a thing heavy and rigid with plaster and black wood for a peg and wretched canvas straps. Now and then he dragged languidly at a cigarette from one packet Timmy had given him and looked with slow mischievous eyes at Irma.

Up here all was ready, even to a gay bunch of blue and yellow flowers in the sitting room. We bustled. Timmy and I drank, between suitcases, a flat brandy and water. We kept looking at the mountains, the nearest and most beautiful I have even seen. Near their tops they are like the mesas in the West, hard and sculptured against an infinite blue sky.

Now, after a good supper, Tim sleeps precariously from Analgeticum, and I sit in my narrow bed, under the strange high feather puff. I hear the slowed autumnal rush of water far below, and even past my balcony light I see the hard prick of the stars. My cheeks burn; my eyes, too. I am excited and yet half-asleep, eager to wake early to watch from my window the sun upon the mountains.

27. x. 38
13:40

In a few minutes I go down through thick milky mist to the pharmacy, along the straight sleeping street lined with closed shops and pensions. It is cold. When I look out the window, here in the warm room filled with the staid strains of Handel's Concerto Grosso, I might be on a ship, fogbound to the sound of invisible cowbells from below, or in an airship, as well as in this snug Swiss hotel.

I cannot permit myself the doubtful luxury of thought. I am too close to frenzy, to a wild anxiety.

The first day was not bad. The second day, after only Timmy slept well, thanks to Analgeticum and Pantopon, was exciting. The Nigsts came. We had drinks on the terrace and then went down for lunch, with Nigst clucking like a hen over Timmy's agility on the stairs. Timmy overate, to please him. Later the local doctor, von Derschwanden, came for café on the terrace. At first he reminded me of a wretched sordid little snob I once knew from Manchester—not so much his manner, which was brisk behind his English pipe, but his mussed and pudgy English slacks and brown tweed coat. (Now I like him, even more than Nigst, I think. His hands are sensitive and investigatory, and he thinks of everything.)

That night was not bad. Yesterday was wretched, with fever for the first time above 37.5 degrees, and the right leg very painful. Last night was all right—injections, of course.

This morning the doctor came. I could see he was worried—congestion in the main artery of the right leg, general low condition.

Timmy lies for hours with an open book or journal before him. Occasionally he turns a page, but he has read nothing. Slow tears slip down his cheeks, and now and then he shakes violently and clutches me and sobs.

I must go down to the pharmacy.

I stay in the sitting room because I think I upset him a little when I sit in his room. I keep thinking, He may die—other people do—and then I will be sick at the thought of the times I spent here when I could be there. I'll try to begin a book today.

Whenever I start to write, I seem to think of nothing but sadness. Perhaps it is because I never talk of it. Tonight I am almost intolerably depressed. I don't know quite why. I'm not one to be downed by weather that is usually thought to be mournful. But all seems wrong. Of course, the main thing is that Timmy is not so well. I try to tell myself—and him, when I have to—about the effects of altitude and so on. But I cannot convince myself that all those things could make such a difference in him—fever 37.8 ½ degrees now again, and surely higher at 8:00, and pain in the *other* leg, and this general withdrawal from me and life. He looks at me and seldom sees me. Everything he must save, all his various strengths, to fight the weariness, to hold at bay the bouts of pain, to keep himself on the right side of hysteria. I can see it all.

I stay near but away, where he can see me but not have to look at me. Often I keep the radio going. (It plays now, and it almost drives me frantic.) I tried to write, this afternoon, but I couldn't—Irma, a nap, talk, Tim calls me, so on.

I try to play the phonograph. That, at least, I have thought all along, will be wonderful, this wonderful. But it has something wrong, a grinding sound that creeps above everything but jazz. I tried to play "Es ist Vollbracht." It was terrible. And even with that grinding, it made things seem too sad. Then, when I said, "Do you like that, Timmy?" he answered, "What?"

I found that my favorite album is not here, the Sibelius concerto, and I paid for sending them all from Le Pâquis only today. Others are missing—and now it is too late to reclaim them.

And the man called about the car, to sell it at 2,700 francs. I said yes, probably unwisely. But it will be one less thing to worry about.

Of course, we have often been low before. Occasionally things seemed so bad, at the Viktoria, that I wondered if we could stand it. We never spoke about it. And then in the morning all would be well—a decent night, a blue sky, a good letter—

The strange faculty I developed, during my last years with Al, of shutting myself off has stood me in good faithful stead lately. It is only occasionally, as now, that it *almost* doesn't work. Usually I can shut parts of my realization, of my intelligence, off, rather as a ship's engineer shuts off various parts of a sinking ship. I can almost feel doors close—then—then. It is good, for the moment at least. I think it may have turned me into a duller person than I was—but at least I'm safer from myself.

There is much I can never write about. All this is superficial.

1. xi. 38
Hotel Bärem Adelboden, Switzerland

Dearest Rex and Edith—

Night before last things looked very bad, so I asked von Derschwanden to call Prof. de Quenain in Bern. (He is the famous surgeon and diagnostician who did the first two operations and has been away for six weeks. I think he is much better than Nigst, who is really just a surgeon, although a very good one. Nigst is in Paris now and will be absolutely sick to find what has happened. Everything looked so well in Bern.) De Quenain told the doctor to call him again in the morning, after a urinalysis. He came up about noon. After a long consultation, the two men decided that a very bad case of phlebitis had developed, concentrating in the right groin and lower abdomen. They are completely mystified, not only as to what caused it but as to why it formed in the veins this time, instead of the artery. I asked them if it was a condition of the blood, and they said perhaps—but perhaps also it could be a paralysis of the walls of the veins. When I asked what caused *that,* they simply raised their hands. They have never seen anything like it, especially in a man of Tim's age.

It means from six weeks to three months of absolute motionlessness, and then all the walking to begin over, if he can. I asked them if it would mean the right leg would always be dangerous, and they said no. But I think they are lying.

You can imagine what this new development has done to Tim, who was already beginning to be dreadfully worn down by the constant pain from the amputation. He has no desire to live, and I feel the same way often. I don't know what will happen—he has that terrible strong heart of the Parrishes, which has already pulled him, against his wishes, through two things that should have killed him. He looks like a ghost and has lost all of that spirit which even in the worst days made him do very funny things with a perfectly straight face. He lies absolutely still, of course, with his leg raised on pillows, and seldom talks or even looks at Irma or me. He holds a book in front of him and turns a page every hour or so. His one interest is to get the first shot, about 8:30 at night, but he doesn't even mention that anymore—just looks at the clock.

There are constantly things to be done—compress, drops, injections, on and on. Irma is staying indefinitely—has given up her case in Lugano.

Both doctors said that even if Tim could be moved, they'd advise our staying here. I feel rather uncomfortable, because no matter how nice the *Huldis* [hotel managers] are, a trained nurse and all the hot-water bottles and so on *do* make a difference in a small hotel. But there's nothing to do about it.

It's beautiful now—the snow is melting after two clear blue days, and I can sit on the terrace for lunch.

Tim is still quite nauseated—de Quenain said it was because

the vein to the stomach is almost closed, which causes congestion —and has eaten only a little bouillon and cooked fruit for a week now. He's very thin.

We've ordered a hospital bed from Bern, or Lutenaken maybe, and as soon as his fever goes down, he can be out on the terrace.

All this is rotten luck, and I hate to tell you about it because I know how sad you'll be for both of us. It's really terrible to me to see Timmy without any spirit, because that has never yet deserted him. I feel confident, though, that if he lives through it at all, he'll get back his old life.

Thank God we have money enough to last for several more months. That would be the last straw, to have to be separated, with T. in a charity ward and me at the Y.W.C.A. or some such place. We're very comfortable here—and I sold the car for $575, which will help.

I must stop. Do write often, and tell me the news about everybody. Don't worry about me. This is no fun, but I'm taking very good care of myself—

2. xi. 38

I just posted, after much deliberation, an order for 115 Tanchnitz and Albatross and Penguin books. Aside from their costing about $80 and so becoming one of the most extravagant actions of my whole life, I felt from the first that they were an admittance of weakness in my nature. It is easy enough for me to justify wanting them, as Timmy said today that it was easy for any woman to defend her inability to eat less than she wanted. But the truth is that it is and will be much pleasanter for me to read book after book of silly "mysteries" than to make myself work. Of course, if

I were a real writer, predestined, dedicated, I'd work in the face of everything. (And even without that fate, I write constantly in my head—stories, paragraphs, phrases, sometimes the skeletons of novels.) But as it is now, I feel almost hysterical at the thought of concentrating on one thing. I am never left without interruption (here are the self-justifications!) for more than fifteen or twenty minutes, and when I am in another room from Timmy's, his door is always open so that I can hear what he does or says and be ready to interpret Irma's talk or help her. I've never held one way or the other with some creative souls' demand for absolute privacy, although Woolf's theory of 100 pounds and a room of one's own seems attractive personally—but I truly don't feel keen enough at this time to be able to put aside all thought of the present while it is moving and moaning ten feet to the left of me.

I notice two things about this life, since the first night at the Bärem: my increased fastidiousness and my equally increased *gourmandise*. Since I can remember, I've been very clean, but now I spend long serious minutes, after my bath, drying each toenail; I wash my navel or my ears as if they were Belleek china teacups; a tiny hangnail sends me hurrying for scissors, oil, all the minutiae of a complete manicure. And I have become almost piggish . . . not in my manners, for I eat slowly and daintily . . . but I eat too much. The food here is good, especially after the tasteless monotony of the hospital. But there is too much of it. Today at noon there was a rich clear consommé with egg cooked in it, ravioli with tomato sauce and cheese, roast chicken with puree of potatoes, brussels sprouts, and a chocolate cream with wafers. So rich! I eat in the little sitting room. First I have a small glass of vermouth with T., while Marta is setting the table. Then I take him a cup of the soup and the crust of a slice of bread broken into bites. Then I sit down, with a book—today, *High Wind in Jamaica*. I ate all the raviolis, with a glass of wine. Then I took T. a little chicken cut into morsels and a little applesauce. I ate the brussels sprouts, and drank an-other glass of wine, and then some chocolate pudding and three wafers. Then I ordered a cup of coffee and drank a small glass of cognac with it. Usually I eat a lot of salad, on which I put a spoonful of meat juice with a strange voluptuous solemnity. I am interested in this slowness and this solemnity. I suppose it is a desire to escape, to forget time and the demands of suffering.

Another thing is the way I dress: I've always been rather finicky about colors and so on, but now I find myself looking at my reflection in any mirror with a smug satisfaction, noting complacently the way my sweater, my socks, the ribbon in my hair are the same blue as the shadow on my eyelids, and how the black of my slacks and my sandals makes all the blues more beautiful. It is queer, and slightly boring, but I suppose it won't get any worse.

After a day part cloudy and part sunlit, light from behind the western mountains beams suddenly across the valley and brings my mountains close enough to lean against. The snow of seven nights ago melts fast, and cliffs I never dreamed of stand out with abrupt starkness from the white slopes, their rock sides cozy in the unexpected light. Lower down, the pine trees are oily green-black, clustered like plant lice in diminishing dots up the mountain. At the bottom, the foamy, dirt-white ice water rushes, with a steady hissing, to the warm valleys.

6. xi. 38

Before the light of the sun had quite faded from the mountains, the moon rose over them and cast downward its flat shadows, to make everything look like cheap scenery but beautiful, as such backdrops would look to a wise child.

I stood on the balcony and listened to the lazy melody of a

man's call in the far slopes, and the sharp excited bark of a child or a young dog in the village, and beyond all of it the quiet rushing of the river, full from thaw. As I walked toward the rooms, I saw Irma sitting beside Tim's white smooth rump, rubbing rhythmically, and the stiff ruffled curtains framing her in her white cap and pinafore, and then I saw my shadow, faint and clear in the afterglow of the full moon on the door.

7. xi. 38

This afternoon, after a half-night of wakefulness, I began to write a book. It will be impossible to show it to anyone but Tim . . . if I ever get it that far along . . . because it is about this last summer. Of course, all of us, and above all myself, are changed, muted one moment and caricatured the next, by my own licentious mind. If a person could ever be seen truly, it would be by himself. But that seldom happens. Or perhaps, is that rare inward vision of oneself what explains the look of rapturous amusement on a dying person's face, which is always interpreted by good Christians as the first peer at heaven?

A letter to T. from his mother, fairly spitting and steaming from the envelope with rage that Anne, who had been two weeks home, had not yet come to Claymont, whereas *she* had defied nurses, doctors, and hospital to get home to welcome her errant darling . . . ten days too soon. I can understand her chagrin.

A quiet and prolonged scene with Schwester Irma today, solved finally by petting, cajoling, babying, playfully teasing her into a good humor. God, these complicated middle-aged nitwits who feed on attention! Am I headed for it, too?

After two years of having experts try to fix a gradual crescendo of whir and squeak in our extremely expensive and completely pleasing gramophone, the fumbling, puzzle-witted local radioman came in this afternoon and arranged it as it should be. Of course, I don't know how long it will last, but I enjoy it meanwhile. This afternoon I played a few things, and then the Brahms Second Concerto. The third (?) movement of it, I thought . . . my favorite piece of gentle music . . . it will soothe us, it will solace us. But I almost didn't hear it at all, so busy was I trying to keep T. from looking at the clock and crying wildly at the filthiness of a life that is only endurable with *piqûres*.

It is 10:00 at night. I'll try to stay awake until T. calls, about 12:30 to 1:30, to give him his shot. Irma has fussed so about how badly she feels that I'm bitch enough to want to fool her and do the night work myself for once. It's a shot-and-a-half, and I hate the idea of it, but I'm sick to death of her nobly stifled yawns in the mornings. I hope I can work it. *Piqûres* make me sick still, but not actively, as they used to.

It is satisfying, in a queer way, to have written the bones of a book today. I'm puzzled by it and feel quite doubtful that I can do it as well as I want to—but at least I'm working. As I told T. today, I've been proving with so much conversation that I'm through with the lost cause of literature that at least I can go to work now with the courage of my convictions.

8. xi. 38

It's become almost impossible for Timmy and me to talk anymore, except now and then when he is almost human after an injection and I'm not too sleepy. I find myself, after almost eleven weeks of encouragements and quiet words of good sense or jaunty or plain goddamn cheerfulness, so sick of myself that I can't help feeling that he is, too. Perhaps I'm hypersensitive. I know that I'm growing a little nervy: the last few days have found me several times cold with exasperation at Irma or even at the fact that no matter how Tim feels (always badly, but in degrees) or what he says, it is pessimistic. God knows I can't blame him, but lately I find myself wishing that when I ask him if he has slept, he will simply say, Yes, instead of Yes, but very badly, or Yes, but it was a queer muddled sleep. I know it could be nothing else . . . but I wish for once he'd leave it at that. And that shows that I am growing cranky. I feel very low today, partly because the few minutes I have had each day with Tim, since this started, have gradually become a listening to his crying and moaning and a fierce battle with myself not to break loose and tell him for God's sake to buck up, when I know that he has no strength left to do it with, and partly because Irma grows daily more cavalier in her behavior toward us, and such treatment always depresses me and makes me feel self-scorn at my weakness in putting up with it. But at the moment I simply can't have any more trouble. If T. were better I'd tell her to go. She's been very good, but she is haunted by the fact that she is in her fifties, and she is of a moody type that thrives on "hot emotional baths" and I can't supply her with them. She would love me (as would not how many other women in my life!) if I'd only weep upon her breast, or scream with rage, or sulk. But I can do none of these things with my inferiors. So *she* sulks and sobs in my place. Now she feels unwell, and I hear every detail of her malaise and heap coals of fire on her wordless resentment of the whole situation by seeing that she has extra fruit, extra rest, by not calling her even once at night, and all *impersonally*. That impersonality is what outrages her preconceptions of being human, of being warm and sympathetic. I regret it, as I often have before. I recognize it, as I should, after so many years of frightening people, of making them feel cheated by my lack of confidences.

13.xi.38

For several days I've not had time to write, although I have thought a good deal about the book I'm working on. I think I made a mistake to talk with T. about it. Now that he knows, there may be less incentive to work on it.

I read to T. a lot every day and every night. The sciatica, which is being treated with an unguent made of bee venom that spreads a delightful warm incense in the air, has diminished a lot, and the phlebitis, although still increased in spite of ichthiol salve, is no longer painful. Temperature and pulse are normal, for the first time since September 1. But the theoretical foot is pure hell, reducing T. to a twitching hysterical wreck unless he can stay mildly doped. Today we gave him ½ cc. of Analgeticum, instead of the whole ampule, and although he was still in pain, he was somewhat soothed. He has been exposing his wound for five- to ten-minute periods to the sun, and that seems to aggravate the pain. The doctor is really deeply concerned and says that as soon as the one open place is closed, he can try injections of vitamin B-1 to nourish the cut nerves and so on . . . and that T.'s being able to move about will help. But in the meantime there is nothing he knows of, except injections. Last night T. told me he would infinitely prefer another amputation to this pain, if it would be able to retie the muscles or something. It's really terrible.

The weather is beautiful now. We eat lunch on the terrace every day.

I am stupid. I dozed along, half-dreaming, listening to Irma and T. whispering for my sake, until almost 11:00—the first time I've stayed in bed since early last summer. I've lost my skill at it, evidently!

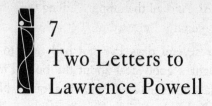

7
Two Letters to Lawrence Powell

2. xii. 38
Hotel Huldi
Adelboden, Switzerland

Unsent letter to Larry Powell

And Al . . . the "man almost crazy with grief" when I went home . . . did anyone ever ask how *I* felt? Did anyone wonder what my own grief was, when I waited and waited for Al to show, *in any way,* that he wanted me to stay with him when my mother suggested I come back to America for a summer? I was naive, of course, and unskilled, but I used every wile I was capable of to get Al to show, no matter how, that he would rather have me stay than go. I said to myself that he was proud . . . and this and that. Finally I went away, watching until the train left Paris for some sign that he would rather spend the summer with me than with you and Liger and Pierre Simonet and the waiters at the Café de Paris. If you'll look again, Ghuce,* you'll see bitter tears for the summer I

---

* Name used by Mary Frances in all her correspondence with Lawrence Powell. As a joke, he had inserted a footnote in his doctoral thesis attributed to "H. Ghuce, Docteur ès Lettres."

left Al. And all that about "killing the Ghost"—I've had it bitten into me until I'm tired of it. If a thing has life in it, it will live. The pain of absence, if it is a real pain and not an excuse for something else, will nurture beauty and poetry and music. That summer, it never occurred to me that Al could stand my leaving him, because the idea was absolutely insupportable to me. Then . . . and with what beaming relief! . . . he said, A wonderful idea! The two and more months I was away were the worst of my life, up to then. And when I came back to Dijon, Al looked better than ever and had made friends he was most unwilling for me to know, and in a kind of jubilant relief had stopped working on the Ghost. The first time I heard him imply, with that delicacy of which he is such a master, that because I'd left him a great poem had died, I was so shocked that I went home and vomited, for the first time in years. I felt as if my heart were being torn out, because I was still completely in love with Al, and I realized that in spite of his too-eager protestations, to everybody who would listen except me, that he loved me more than life itself, he did not. He loved what he wanted me to be . . . and more and more I wasn't that: the ideal he'd built in the East Adams Presbyterian Church of a girl who was well bred but who did everything he had been taught was not so: smoked, drank, wore lipstick, read T. S. Eliot, liked Picasso. Oh, what a sad mess, with such faults on both sides of the canvas! I regret it bitterly. But I am tired of being told that I "killed the Ghost." I . . . time . . . lassitude—who can say this or that thing was the culprit? And who ever wonders about what killed that part of me that may have *made* the Ghost?

Well, Ghuce . . . I meant to swallow all this . . . or at worst leave it until we met. Perhaps I should have.

As for the "haunting talks . . . when he told me hesitantly of the triangle of Le Pâquis"—oh, Larry, how many people have reproached me for that! How many women, drowned in the poignancy of it, and how many men, full of wrath at my cruelty, have written to me of those haunting talks! Go back to him, they beg. He has told me all! He has confided in me! You are his world, even if you *have* cut off his genius in its prime. He swears he won't hold it against you, because he *loves* you. Other people may blame you, because you are an adulteress and a nymphomaniac, but he promises to forgive you . . . and on and on. What does it all add up to, Larry! Certainly I am not "unconscious" of it all as you say. I wish to God I could meet Al as one human adult with another— but he has hidden himself behind a ghastly bulwark of The Woman He Loved and Married, an ideal formed when he was very young and Christian. I am not that woman. I never was. But when I was young and he was fresh from college, he thought he saw in me a proof to his omnipotent father and family that a woman could make up and read "daring" books and still be a lady.

Gradually he began to tire of that and want roast beef and mashed potatoes and chocolate cake for Sunday noon dinner, as he'd been raised to feel was concomitant with Marital Happiness. Gone were Proust and the grilled lamb chop and green salad. Gone were the nights when a few of us sat with some wine perhaps and talked and read and sang. Instead, Al and I went almost every night to a double-feature movie, and ate chocolate bars and came home drugged with bad air and drivel, and were too tired to "talk" —a thing he dreaded like poison, perhaps because his mother had tried to make him do so when he was young. . . .

Well . . . I think a great deal about it, because Al will always be one of the finest things in my life. And I will always have a feeling of unfulfillment about our life together . . . a feeling that his past came too soon too strongly between me and what I knew was there in him. I don't know how other women have fared with him. I hope that *something* I gave him (because I gave him everything I had) has held over, to make him easier to know and help and love

... and to make him easier with himself. All this may sound queer —I don't know because I shan't read it—but you are the only one I can say it to. You know Al better than anyone except me, and you and I are so much alike, in our male and female ways, that we know him pretty much in the same way.

2. xii. 38
Hotel Huldi
Adelboden

Letter sent to Larry Powell

Dearest Larry—

Before I forget it, this check is for a copy of *The Ghost* for me. Will you please keep it until I come? And if there's anything left of the check, I want you and Fay to have a little party or something you want: if you're not on the wagon, drink to me, and if you are, you can do it just as well in water. It's my last cut of the royalty from *Serve It Forth,* I think. (I was hoping that book would have a small steady Christmas sale, but apparently Harper's has already stopped issuing it—several people have written to ask where they could get copies, but of course I have none. Oh, well—)

I can't tell you how glad I am that *The Ghost* is finally to see light—and especially that you three are going to do it. I think you're doing it in exactly the right way, too. Of course, Al is convinced that he has no interest in the project, but you mustn't take that too literally. Unless he is an *entirely* different person now, he is really pleased and excited by it. I don't need to tell you how strange it makes me feel to have something so intimately a part of my life now going on as it should, with me no longer having anything to do with it—except to stand helplessly on the sidelines and ask to buy a copy. That's a bad sentence, but you know what I mean. Anyway—I'm sad but I'm not jealous, and I'm glad you're doing it.

Thank you for writing me such an interesting and good letter. (Timmy thanks you, too, and says he knows he's lucky to have me here, as you said. I hope you're both right!) I was truly fascinated by what you told me of Al's visit with you and the things you had heard about him. (Incidentally, it was a fine piece of direct narrative writing—wrong of me to notice in a description of Al's conduct probably, but I couldn't help being moved and impressed.)

I should like very much, sometime, to know "the whole story, from Al's viewpoint." As I told you, such astonishing tidbits have come back to me, from various sources, that the only decent thing I can believe is that Al, a born romancer, must occasionally have got carried away. Certainly he is reported to have told things about us, and especially me—in strictest confidence, of course!—that no person who had ever met me could possibly believe. Probably if he heard them, he'd never believe that he himself had said them. If he did. Of course, Al has always been thoroughly convinced that he is the most secretive and noncommunicative of souls, whereas a matter of fact he is a friendly and almost garrulous person, willing to talk intimately to practically anyone. That is one reason why he's an almost inspired lecturer, especially to young people.

I'm sorry, in a way, that he knows I told you of his sexual impotence toward me. It's not a thing that any man likes to have told, and although only you, my father, and Tim know about it, Al must wonder how many others there are.

Of course, nobody saw more clearly than I how difficult it would be for Al and me to go to Switzerland with Tim, and in letters and in countless conversations I did all I could to convince him. But he loathed Occidental and his profession—or thought he did—and he remembered how happy he'd been in Dijon, young, in love, free. Tim and I, too, felt that it was terrible for a man as fine as Al to be so miserable as he felt he was, at Occidental. So— We all went to Switzerland, and before we'd been there five hours Al knew that even my exaggerated tales of how difficult it would be were not wild enough. He was stuck in a prim, stuffy little commercial town, no longer young, no longer passionate, isolated from any erudite colleagues. You know Al really believes that he is the lonely philosopher, who needs only his pipe, his books, and an occasional evening of Bach or a solitary roam over the hills. But have you ever known him to do much more than talk about such an existence? He is an extremely social, gregarious person—he *loves* people, and life, and movement—parties, gossip. I don't say this at all bitterly—but I do regret terribly that I didn't realize it before. You remember the constant moviegoing we did in Dijon? We were *never* settled down—it was always with some good excuse: our accents or something—but we were always restless. And then in Laguna, I really think Al almost went crazy with boredom. We had absolutely no money, so we couldn't entertain—but he'd roam off down to the public beach, or visit people, preferably alone—and every spare nickel we got went for movies. By that time I knew his real need for more variety and movement than I could provide (especially on the $32.50 a month that we managed to live on), so I was glad when Stelter gave him a job.

You know how Al protested, constantly and bitterly, his loathing for that job, and indeed for teaching in general. I wonder if he always will? I really believe he loves it—he loves the attention of adoring students, the intrigue and conniving among the faculty— even the occasional weighty research and the occasional publication of an erudite little book on some obscure Greek epigrammatist. But I doubt if he'll ever admit that. He is one of the most thoroughly self-fooled people I've ever known.

You ask if I really thought I could live in the house with two men who were in love with me. (I seem to be going in for Confessional—don't let it bore you, and please realize that it's not my general habit.) It probably seems as strange to you as it does to me, now. But for so long I had throttled all my sexual needs (it took me a long time to get used to living side by side with a man whom I still loved passionately and who was almost actively sickened at the thought of being with me) that I was pretty sure they were well in control. And I had proved that I could be with Tim without setting off any bonfires. So, as far as that part of life went, I truly hadn't a qualm. It was certainty that Al would be bored that worried me—but when I talked about it, he would always assure me that the only thing he really wanted in the world was complete solitude, time to *think*.

As for my leaving Al for Tim, it is quite untrue. I have told Al that, and I think he knows it, but no man likes to admit that a woman has left him for any other reason than another man. If I had been going to leave him, though, it would have been some six years ago (for Tim, or any other man). It is true that I am with Tim now and will be as long as he lives or wants me—but I would never have left Al for him. I am sorry that Al won't admit that.

Yes, I've gone ahead with the divorce. It will be granted some time in January, probably. It is very unpleasant to me to be the theoretical wife of a man who has not even seen me for over a year —it's distasteful and dishonest to me at least, and I should think would be to Al, too. I can't understand his wanting things to stay that way—except that being legally married is a kind of protection to him, perhaps.

And that leads me to what you tell me of all Al's talk of needing a large measure of ripe flesh. It is rather difficult to talk about. I wish I could tell you how deeply I wish that Al really would *take* some ripe flesh. He *does* need it, and *want* it. But I am fairly sure that he has little of it. Of course, he pinches and pokes and leers and strokes—and above all he *talks*. Al is a master of implication. He can (and does) imply the thousand affairs of a rather pedagogic Don Juan.

But what are they? They are wish-dreams, almost all of them. Al was twenty-six or twenty-seven when he married me, and still a virgin. He was, and still is, frightened and repelled by the actual physical act of love. Even at his freest and happiest, he had to condone it and make it acceptable by quoting what Plato, and Bertrand Russell, and Marie Stopes said about it. And it was disappointing—partly because he was inexperienced—and frightened by years of churchly training from Y.M.C.A. leaders and a father who after thirty-five years of parochial life could still talk solemnly and sentimentally of "the sweet mystery of love and life"—that is to say, sexual intercourse.

Al was, and still is, horribly frightened by the thought of venereal disease, which has made him take out his urges in the more or less safe forms of pinching and writing schoolboy notes. God—I hate to admit all this, even to myself. I'm proud of Al and want him to be a full, happy *man*. Of course, it was hard on my female pride, for a while, to realize that I had failed to make him one. Then I hoped desperately that his getting away from me would help him. But I don't think it has. Teaching in a girls' school, always having to be circumspect and cautious, certainly doesn't help—but there *are* men who can do that and still live vigorously and wholly. And now I hear, not only from you, that this damnable half-life of flirting and giggling and tickling is still going on, stronger than ever. I am sad.

You are right about Al's letters—they are not the best side of him, inclined to be sententious and humorless. That's not a new development, although I think it is exaggerated at this time by what you rightly call the "spiritual chip on his shoulder." I hope, and very very much, that some day he will allow himself to be loose and easy and free with me. I rather doubt it, though—it will take the warmth and completeness of a life with a real woman to bring that about, and Al is stubborn and self-torturing enough to prevent himself from ever enjoying life. He is capable of living forever now on pinching-and-telling and the idealized vision of his life with me. (Even before he left, he was almost sleeping with a picture of me when I was sixteen which he'd found at the Ranch. He so hated actuality that he had made a dream of what I was then some five years before he even met me! It was a kinder, sweeter, weaker Child Bride he loved—one he'd never owned.)

Well, dearest Larry—I remember the first time I ever met you, at a dance at Orr Hall, I said that you had something of the father-confessor in you. Certainly I've proved it today—and for the first time, as far as all this goes. I was too unhappy and sad to talk to *anyone* when I was home. And, of course, I am quite alone with Timmy, who knows most of this from having been so close to both Al and me. Let it stay in the confessional, and think no ill of any of us.

I am so glad about the Newell boy. Please tell them.

Jean Matruchot could never say that what I'm writing now is *"charmant, délicieux."* It is so terrible that I reread one chapter and was almost sick. I doubt if I will ever try to publish it—no point in rubbing people's noses in their own filth. It's good for me, though, and hard work—different from anything I've ever tried. If I finish it, I'll probably ask you to read it.

The change to high altitude that was supposed to help Timmy recuperate almost killed him, and for about three weeks it looked bad. Fortunately I had a good nurse. I am convinced that he should be at a lower level, and as soon as he can be moved, I want to go down to Vevey, for a few weeks at least. Then he must get used to walking again, and then we'll probably go back to America. He is almost recovered from the phlebitis that occurred when he came up here, but the theoretical foot and leg cause him such agony that he has to be kept doped most of the time. It's no life for a man, and at times he's hard put to it not to despair. So am I. But we'll see what going down does. Of course, it may be even worse than staying here, but we're willing to risk it—*some*thing must be done, and we've tried almost everything (including injections of cobra venom! They almost sent him off his head, among other reactions. It's terrible to be so trapped: I *know* what blundering dolts most doctors are, and yet when one suggests something that may help this agony I see before me, I can only say, Yes, yes, anything!).

Please write, and to *30 rue du Château, La Tour-de-Peilz, Vaud, Switzerland.* If I don't write before Christmas, this sends you and Fay and the beasties my loving good wishes for then and all the New Year. Tim, too. I hope we'll see you before the year ends. Please don't be afraid at my sudden burst of confidence—

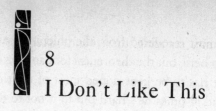

8
I Don't Like This

Tonight I looked at the cover of a current issue of a weekly magazine all about peace and war. The picture was of an angry mother in Texas or Israel or Beirut with her two hot-eyed sad children clinging to her proud heavy body, and I said firmly, I do not like this.

Then I was thinking about the word *like,* and I remembered one time when I was looking down at the poor anguished body of my love, while a group of young doctors and nurse nuns stood about the famous doctor who was using him as an object lesson of some kind. Tim lay in the cold Swiss light. There was a thick ring of faces above him, around the bed, trying to be dispassionate but still sad for him. His one leg lay firm and beautiful and naked, and the stump beside it twitched helplessly now and then and was open and angry, with yellow in the middle of the gaping open end. The doctor was speaking stolidly, elegantly, and the younger nurses hummed little sounds as he paused. He looked sternly at me, standing there, and asked, "And what does the lady think?"

I said in French against his German, "I do not like it."

There was a long pause, filled with shock and an almost physical disapproval. The ring of sympathetic cooing little nuns drew back, and behind them the young doctors stood like sentinels, alert and ready. The doctor looked straight at me, and then shrugged and smiled and said to the circle. "Madame does not like something, eh?"

He laughed shortly, and they all twittered in obedience and waited. I stood there and did not look down at Tim, who lay like a drugged beast—a small neat beast, like a fox perhaps, but still drugged and unknowing. The doctor laughed again, looking full into my open face. "Madame does not like this," he murmured as if to himself, and he bent over the open bone end of what had once been a fine leg and rubbed at it with a long swab. Every face drew closer, and I pulled away, forever outside of that or any other circle.

Tonight I do not like the faces of those three people who have no home. But what can I do for them? What could I do that time for Tim? We had no home, either. Still, I think these sad angry-eyed children may survive, just as their mother has, and perhaps as I have, too.

I am warm and I have, temporarily anyway, a place to call my home, and they do not. But the mother knows that there will be something more, I suppose, if she thinks about it at all. Perhaps she does not. I did not think any way at all when I said flatly to the great doctor, "I do not like this." The mother does not like what she sees now. But there is no arguing about it, except to make it clear that it is not right.

That is what I keep trying to do. I doubt that anyone listens, but I keep on saying it. I do not *like* this. It stinks. It is hideous. It is a filthy trick. It is a cruel trick. It will lead to intolerable suffering. It is ugly and twisting.

That day in Bern I stood while the doctor mocked me, and neither I nor the man drugged on the high white bed blinked an eye when all the little nurse nuns and the student doctors gave out a kind of exhalation of amused consent as the doctor bent over the stump and twisted expertly at some gauze, reverting into German as he continued, "And although she does not *like* it, she will have to see that the inflammation increases as the general state of vascular deterioration . . ."

Yes. Yes. Where can we sleep tonight? Will there be any food? Where will it come from? Will we live or die?

We do not ask. We say, if asked, that we do not like it—war or hopelessness or hate or love or or . . . .

—*Glen Ellen, California, 1991*

9
Bareacres Journal,
1940–41

18. *iii*. 40

I am beginning some two months late to keep a kind of record, diary, journal, about Bareacres. I have meant to do it ever since the first day we saw the place, because the few times I have found parts of such records they have been really interesting to me and to Timmy. This one will be written for the two of us, quite frankly, with the idea that some time far from now it will interest us again. Of course, such a record is often dull and almost as often embarrassing, but surely by now we are old enough to be tolerant. I can remember finding, some ten years later, a diary I kept when I was fourteen and being so sickened by my adolescent priggishness that I felt actively nauseated. Then I decided that I should keep those few pages, as a kind of token that change is right, for I was sure that even with my faults at twenty-four, I was better than I had been at fourteen. I run across them occasionally, and although I never read them—that would be too difficult—the sight of those ruled pages stiffens me a little and makes me hope to God that another ten years will change me again. I remember how uncomfortable Al was about his diaries. He hated the thought that I had read them, the ones he kept in high school, and once I made a great mistake, when he said something about always having been unusually tolerant, in quoting something or other from one of them. He never forgave me, and soon after the diaries disappeared. I don't think he destroyed them, since he wanted to keep things like that for his biographers—but he made sure that no contemporary eyes would fall on them. It was too humiliating. I know a little bit what he felt . . . but I believe that he should have been proud to admit how he had matured and how he could still change.

This is not about Bareacres, directly at least.

Mrs. D. moves from there sometime before this Friday, which is Good Friday. Yesterday we were there, and I tried with blatant "goodwill," the kind that made me smile too much and be too gracious and then feel ashamed when she responded so hungrily to my false food . . . when I tried graciously and smilingly to find out when she planned to leave, she could not tell me. Tim and I both felt annoyed, but there was nothing to be done about it. At first we were afraid, some two months ago, that she might refuse to leave . . . have the old man go to bed or some such common trick. She was very unfriendly. But now we are pretty sure she will get out on the twenty-second when she is supposed to. Once we were sitting up under the eucalyptus tree, and we heard her say to Dad, the old man, "Well, we'll only have one more week here now." We could not tell by her flat, high voice whether she was glad or sorry. Another time we went up there, and she was putting small boxes of stuff in the back of her nephew's car. So I think she'll go sometime this week.

I feel rather ashamed of pretending to be so friendly toward her, since I find her very unpleasant. I am friendly simply because I don't want to antagonize her in any way. Tim and I are almost desperately anxious to move up there. We go over often now when we should be working here, and sit on the hill looking around us.

Yesterday we took the little radio over, and sat in the bushes against a rock, and listened to the *Emperor* Concerto and a funny Mozart concerto for clarinet, from New York. The sky was milky, and occasionally a cool wind would make us pull coats around us. Then it would suddenly be too warm for them. There were several kinds of wildflowers around us, and the ground was covered with tiny white forget-me-nots. We were comfortable. I gave T. a good shot, so that he looked better, and we drank some beer (I drank vermouth, because I am trying to lose eight pounds before summer) and ate celery and radishes and I an artichoke and he some peanut-butter sandwiches that I willfully ignored. Then after the concert we read some Bulldog Drummond, which we have decided is a model for thrillers. But the main thing was being up there in the sweet air and looking around at the wild rock slopes and down toward the little house. Bareacres was ours.

While we were there, Arnold Elliott drove up to look at the spring and stopped to talk to us for a minute. It was surprising that we were so well hidden in the sage bushes—he had difficulty finding us, although we could see him clearly and were waving and calling to him.

He told us that he had opened up the other spring and connected it to the main pipe—"all the same job." That was a good surprise, although we are a little puzzled as to why he is suddenly being so altruistic. He also told us that looking after the two springs went with the job, which we hadn't counted on, and that if anything went wrong with the exit pipe from the tank, he would replace it himself, and that he would keep his eye on the leaks, if any, and patch them free of charge. As I say, we are puzzled but grateful. Probably the reason for his sudden and almost protective interest in us is that he feels that he is much better as a workman than Miller, who graded the road for us last week and, according to both Elliott and Timmy, did a pretty poor job. I think that might make Elliott feel superior and therefore generous.

He asked us if we wanted him to make some dining room chairs and a table. I don't think we do, but we were amused to hear about them. Some time ago, when we stopped at the pub in San Jacinto for a drink, Sherm Lewis, the proprietor, told us with what we thought at the time was not very commendable glee that he got Arnold Elliott to make his chairs for $2 apiece, when the wood itself must have cost almost that much. We looked at the chairs, which were good sturdy pine chairs, really handsome, and then we thought of Elliott and three children to feed and a wife, and then we looked at Sherm Lewis and thought that he should be ashamed. But yesterday Elliott told us, with the same amusement and a kind of proud self-ridicule, that he made the chairs for $2 and that the wood itself cost him $1.10. He seemed really amused at his own foolishness. We couldn't help laughing. They are good chairs, and we might get some later or give some to somebody.

What we need now is some more comfortable furniture for the porch and eventually the patio. We bought two chairs from Mrs. D., mainly to grease her skids, but I don't think they are especially suitable for the porch, even if we paint them. We got a rather nice little footstool from her, too. I'll probably scrape the varnish off it. And a low fat bureau, which Tim insists will be good-looking when we paint it. We do need more drawer space, especially in the kitchen . . . and although I think the bureau is hideous, I have great confidence in anything he says about furniture and furnishings. (As well as everything else except maybe me, and, of course, he is very prejudiced about that.)

We have to go to the Ranch tonight and will bring back some hammers and saws and so on. We ought to be able to take them over to Bareacres and start puttering by the end of this week. The thought of it makes me feel quite trembly.

I never thought I would ever be that way again. To tell the truth, I always had reservations about Le Pâquis, in spite of thinking it the most beautiful place in the world . . . but we put so much of our lifeblood and our inner love and misery and strength into it that I felt sure I would never again be able to do it about any other place. And now, some three years later, I am even happier about Bareacres, because I truly have no reservations about it.

It is a little like marrying for the second time. I could not understand how Gigi, who was living with John, was so positive that she would never marry him after she got her divorce from Tim. She did, after a year or so. And then when I was divorced from Al, I was the same, even though I was deeply in love with Tim. I felt an active aversion toward marriage with him or with anyone. No, no, I thought, it is better to stay clear. You hurt people when you marry them. I'll never marry again. And now I am married and would not have it any other way.

We have to go to Hal Bieler's* tonight. It will be extremely dull and uncomfortable. I used to like to go there and listen to records and eat some good vegetables. But now he serves only muffins and milk and plays the piano instead of the gramophone, demanding constant praise and worshipful attention . . . and, of course, Tim is antipathetic to him (is that the word? I mean that Hal makes Tim's hackles rise) and cannot smoke. So I hate to waste an evening there. However, we have an appointment at his office at 5:15, and he has asked us to go home with him afterward.

I want to talk to him strongly, but I don't know if I will. The

---

* Doctor and friend to both M.F.K.F. and Larry Powell. His approach to medicine through nutrition had a strong influence on Mary Frances.

last two weeks have been harder than usual for Tim. It may be spring. Anyway, he's had two really terrible bouts of pain and nausea, and I have had, most unwillingly, to increase the shots of Analgeticum. I hate to do that because it shows retrogression on his part and because we have not yet heard whether the last order has been able to get through from Switzerland. If I don't have to increase the dosage any more and if there is no accident to our supply, I have enough to last for about fourteen months. And then, Tim says, if he still needs it, the jig will pretty well be up anyway. (And that is where I am counting on Bareacres to give him strength and more courage and will to live.)

We have lived pretty much as Hal prescribed for about nine months now, and he says that he sees great improvement—weight, urinanalysis, and so on. I see some, certainly . . . but this constant fight against pain is unfair. After all, it has been over a year since the last amputation. Eighteen months of what Tim has had are more than any one man should have to face.

Of course, I haven't a leg to stand on, really, in my criticism of Hal of Tim's condition, because we have not followed his diet to the letter. We drink a little whiskey and beer, and Tim smokes, and occasionally we have coffee, and we eat pepper. So I can't complain to him, of all people. It is mainly my fault that we have slipped in our rigorous following of Hal's directions. But I know him pretty well and have watched many people under his care, and I know that it is inevitable that all but the most sheeplike of his patients end by adapting his advice to their own natures. Probably they are wrong . . . but it is inevitable. And I know Tim, and since he does not have some actively painful condition like a cancer of the stomach, which would have an immediate reaction to food, I cannot help feeling that for him the monotony of Hal's diet would do more harm than an occasional divergence from it. I hope I'm not too wrong . . . because if I insisted, Tim would do his best to live by the law.

I must manicure my nails before lunch. We start soon after. Tomorrow I have an appointment with Dr. Kelsey. I have always been a little coquettish about him and take more care than usual to look and smell nice when I see him. He is attractive, in a clean, dry way. He has also been very good to me, although he is very dull about everything but teeth and mouths. As usual, I am nervous about what he will decide to do. If it is, at last, time to renovate the work he did some twelve years ago, I shall be really discouraged. It will take a week of time that I could spend working at Bareacres, and a lot of money that we need.

22. iii. 40

In a few minutes we go to Bareacres, and I am really nervous. The woman is supposed to be either gone or on her way today, and if she is still lingering there, I feel that I'll perhaps cry or be sick or something. I know Tim is nervous, too. We haven't been over this week, as I remember.

As we drove toward Pasadena and Hal's, we began to get so hungry the other day that our stomachs growled and we "saw dark spots in the shape of hamburgers floating before our eyes." We thought of his ascetic meals of bran muffins and milk . . . nothing else to eat, nothing else to drink, no smoking. The nearer we got, the more we were haunted by an almost physical need for strong drink, food Hal would think vile, and cigarettes. Every time we passed a roadside stand, Tim's head snapped around dangerously to stare back at it. And finally we weakened and risked being late, and I forgot my dieting, and we went to a very swanky Carpenters' just outside the racetrack at San Marino and ordered beer and hamburgers. I gave Tim a nice shot, and we took a swig of whiskey from the flask and gobbled mediocre hamburgers with complete delight. Then we dashed on to Pasadena, only a few minutes late.

Later

It is about ten o'clock. I have just got out Tim's Speechless House-boy, as Mother calls the small rack called by the department store a Silent Houseboy.* (I rub his shoulder just behind the bone and wonder how much he notices that sometimes I have drunk too much or am preoccupied with cramps or an idea. Generally, the main idea is to give him a shot and give it to him quickly—to rub his skin hard with the wad of alcohol and cotton and to stick in the needle sharply. I think deliberately, always, of how to pick up the delicate little ampules most expertly so that they will not tip or spill. But sometimes I know that for one reason or another, volun-tary, like drinking too much, or involuntary, like the twentieth of the month, I am clumsy, and I wonder how much Tim notices or if all he minds is how quick relief comes.)

Yes, I have just got out the Houseboy and sped through the little cold end room to pluck the three hot-water bottles from the end of the tub and the pee bottle from the top of the hot-water heater. I have filled a glass with water, and taken it and the pee bottle to the front porch, and put them on the blue-painted lug box beside Tim's bed. I have turned down the beds, and then sped back and filled the hot-water bottles and fixed one-half cake of yeast in each of two large teacups with hot water, to be drunk later

* A wooden rack to hold a man's jacket and trousers.

by us. Then, after writing a few words ostentatiously on this machine and wondering what Tim would think of me to start tapping suddenly after so long a silence, I have given him the first of the night's shots (I don't count the one at 7:00), and have told him as he went through the door that I would go to bed soon.

I am tired in a pleasant way, not like the night I came back from Los Angeles, when I was too tired even to get into bed and stood for a long time in the bathroom, not able to get undressed or even look at myself, feeling sick. Tonight I am very happy.

We went up to Bareacres about one o'clock. All the way we had been saying very casually that probably Mrs. D. would be there or probably she would not be there. Finally, as we jogged over the road, which is getting a little worse every day, I said, or maybe it was Tim, "Well, if there are still curtains in the windows, Mrs. D. will still be there tonight." (Because she is convinced that every night people stare into her window, and she keeps every one covered with curtains pinned together in the middle.) As we went 'round the final curve before we came to the gate, I saw that the windows were naked. I felt elated, so happy that I cried out. Mrs. D. was gone.

There was a gleaming nobbin above the edge of the terrace, either a vase that she had left or a man's head. Could it be her old charge Dad, the mild old man with senile dementia?

It was Septimus.* We were furious. He told us wheezily that he had been ill again for five days, that the new doctor thought it was probably ulcers, that the medicine seemed to be helping him. We smiled and condoled, and all the time we were seething with annoyance that here, now, the first time the house was really ours,

* Husband of Elsa Purdy, who later spent many years working for Mary Frances as nursemaid and friend.

we should be bothered by this ghastly old hypochondriac. We soon left, to eat our lunch farther up the hill. "You folks go right ahead," Septimus said graciously.

Later Mrs. Purdy came up to tell us that two friends and the children of one of them were there, too, having a picnic on our porch. We could do nothing but were somewhat gratified that she seemed a little apologetic. Finally, after we had gone down to the town, they left, and we had the house to ourselves.

We wandered through it, feeling suddenly tired and empty. It was not until, after taking many measurements, that we began to think on the way home. By now many things are clear, and Timmy has a fine plan for saving about $300 or $400 for a studio: lengthening the present dining room, thereby shortening the too-long porch as well. It looks fine on paper. Now we must talk to the carpenter, a gunsmith named Martin Lausen, a thin tall man with pink eyes whose even taller wife moves like an awkwardly graceful adolescent and talks with the slight accent that should belong to her husband.

We go over again in the morning to see the plumber, Louis Aden, the electrician, and Lausen.

This morning Tim took pictures of several of his canvases, while I filled flowerpots with earth and peat moss.

27. iii. 40

Sunday, Easter, we went early to Bareacres. The Purdys came, to our intense annoyance, and sat and sat. Finally we both had to excuse ourselves, since Ankum the electrician was asking questions, and then the carpenter came. Sometime later they left, after asking us if we wouldn't come down for a little meal and some beer. Neither of us wanted to, and in a rather shilly-shallying way

I said we'd love to, but since Timmy had to be back here for medicines soon after 6:00, we couldn't stay long. "But you'll eat a bite, won't you?" Mrs. P. asked in her soft voice, looking more than ever like a bright-eyed squirrel. "Oh, of *course,*" I said heartily, knowing that we were both of us (T. and I) too exasperated at them. Then I was sorry, remembering her life with poor rachitic, asthmatic, ulcerous, perhaps cancerous old Septimus.

Martin Lausen the carpenter is a tall lean man with red eyes, but quite handsome. At first he seems slow, but then you realize that he is thinking. And what he thinks, about carpentering at least, is solid and often ingenious. He is garrulous, but where Mr. Purdy's windy conversations set your teeth on edge, his are rather nice—quiet and sometimes funny. He told us of an accident when his knees got knocked backward so that his legs bent both ways and of various experiences with snakes (he is an amateur taxidermist). He and his brother have invented a machine run by perpetual motion! The brother plans to take it to Washington as soon as he raises enough money—which probably means as soon as we pay Mr. Lausen. (The tentative estimates for work on the house are $400 top for Lausen, $65 top for electricity, and $45, including a new toilet bowl, for Aden the plumber. Then the electric line has cost $48.)

We ate lunch rather late (I ate part of a green pepper, four stalks of celery, four large radishes, and part of a dill pickle) and sat around until time to go to the Purdys'. On the way down we decided to stay only a few minutes, and Tim was determined to be *"very distant*—by God, I don't *like* them at Bareacres all the time!" But a table was set by the fireplace in the little Indian house, and a special Easter supper of baked rabbit and baked potatoes and spinach and an egg salad—and beer, of course—and we were very nice and even enjoyed ourselves and did not leave until almost 7:00. As we left, Mrs. Purdy said very softly to Tim, "Ralph and I just think it was wonderful, kind of a good omen, that we could've spent this Easter with you folks!" Of course, we felt like rats.

About halfway home my stomach started to ache, and by the time we were here it had gone down to my guts. I drank some hot water and soda, but it did no good. Pretty soon I tried to take a small enema, but by that time it was almost too painful to move. I was frightened and discouraged, because I had all the symptoms of my bout at Sis's in November '37 and at Adelboden in December '38: distended belly, extreme pain, fever. I got to bed. By 1:30 my fever had risen to 102 degrees, and the pain in my abdomen was worse than it had ever been before, like white-hot metal filling my bowels.

Tim called Hal, who said to give me soapy enemas every two hours, even if I passed out, and (to our amusement) a shot of whiskey after them. It was a sleepless and very unpleasant night—pain, Tim's anxiety and hard work, no bedpan but a kitchen pot, no enema bag but a glass jar. But by morning I felt a little better, although I was still in the worst pain I have known. We called Hal, who said as soon as my fever went down I must be brought up to a nursing home. At that I cried—I could *not* leave Timmy, who has to be given six or seven shots a day and helped and who needs me, but hardly more than I need him. So Hal said he'd risk treating me by telephone if I improved. I was to take enemas of one part milk to two of water every two hours—nothing by mouth except cracked ice or a little whiskey—hot Epsom-salt packs or hot-water bottles on my belly. I ruled out the packs—Tim had too much to do already, even with Mrs. King's help mornings and at six o'clock each night.

(She is a well-made woman with a flat ordinary face, a hideous high rasping voice, and a really *good* nature, who comes from the next ranch to do what Mrs. Purdy did until she moved to Hemet. Mrs. King works harder than anyone I know—five hundred chickens, a cow to milk, pigs, corn to plant, a house to care for, two children in high school, a husband who works hard, too, for the Hendricks ranches. Maybe that is why she has such pretty legs and hips. But I doubt it.)

She took Tim into Riverside for his second of twelve roentgen-ray treatments, which so far have done no apparent good and have perhaps made his pain a little worse, and then yesterday to Hemet to get Mr. Lausen's estimate. It was more than we had counted on, but we decided to go on with it even if we have to borrow a hundred or so from the family or Uncle Boney. The five pairs of French windows and the large window in Timmy's workroom are the most costly things—about $75—but that idea of his is wonderful, since he will have a good, well-lit, well-heated studio right in the house, instead of building one in a year or so to which he would have to climb up or down. One hundred dollars now will save us five or six later.

Yesterday Hal cut the enemas to every four hours, with a quarter cake of yeast in half a glass of hot water every hour. (I give these details because I think his treatments are interesting.) By this time my temperature was subnormal, and the pain was less severe, although my abdomen was still swollen and extremely uncomfortable. I could lie on my side, though.

Today he ordered two ounces of pineapple juice in four of water every hour, and to cut out the yeast—and only two enemas daily, thank God. He said I could eat some green beans or zucchini for supper if I wanted, and start tomorrow eating lightly of cooked vegetables (only the ones he approves, of course). I may not eat any tonight, if my fever goes up, which it shows signs of doing for the first time since night before last.

Timmy does too much for me and looks tired, but he takes pretty good care of himself. Today for lunch he had a large cold artichoke, some potato chips, and a bottle of beer. Last night he made himself some beautiful scrambled eggs and toast. In a way I suppose it is good for him not always to be on the receiving end of everyday bustlings.

I feel much better today and ate two artichokes for lunch, slowly, delightfully. I am still in bed, and tomorrow will get up for a little while. My abdomen is still somewhat tender. I have lost ten pounds, which pleases me, although I do not recommend the method.

Tim and Mrs. King went to Bareacres at 2:00, he to see what is happening there. (It is maddening to have to be in bed at this time.) Mrs. King had a long list of food to get.

Soon after they went out, the Purdys arrived. My heart sank —I wanted to work on a catalog I am doing of some of Timmy's paintings, to send to Anne. They stayed two hours, which was stupid of them, but were nice and solicitous. I had to listen to much talk of diet, hemorrhoids, ulcers, doctors, and so on from Septimus, while Elsie filled the back of their car with vases, boxes, and such for Bareacres. It was kind and helpful, and I was very glad to see them go.

I hope I feel like driving by next Tuesday—I want to see Hal, and I have an appointment with Kelsey, who found that everything was in good shape except my gums and wanted me to come back after I had used a certain dentifrice for two weeks. Tim and I were so relieved at his news that he made me buy a new hat. It is of fine black straw, shaped like a tiny curé's hat, with two black taffeta ribbons that tie in a rather large bow over my chignon. I think it is chic, and becoming, too.

This morning, lying in bed, we talked about politics and decided that we might vote for Roosevelt if nothing better turned up. We think Cordell Hull is good, in spite of the present campaign to turn him into another Lincoln—he is a trained statesman and believes in reciprocal trade agreements between nations. Timmy thinks an isolationist president would do terrible harm at the moment, and I think a man like Dewey would be bad, mainly because he is totally ignorant of statesmanship. A bad fault in America has always been our inclination to put a man successful in, say, journalism into a high political or diplomatic position and expect him to be equally successful. I remember talking with Paul Mourset, who was then attaché to Maréchal Lyautey, about the American ambassador in Paris at that time. He said the other diplomats scorned him for an arrogant bounder. He was a millionaire, of course (apparently that's necessary in such a position), and spoke no French nor any other language, and did countless things like referring to Frenchmen as frogs in the presence of other Frenchmen or announcing publicly that French apples weren't fit to eat and sending ostentatiously to Oregon for large shipments of American apples. It was sickening. Bullitt, in Paris now, is much better and even something of a trained diplomat—unusual in the American foreign service.

I seem to feel quite strongly on the subject of international relations. My first reaction is always to try to make people tolerant and understanding of "foreigners." I really think that America, in spite of her heritage of mixed bloods and nationalities, is even more insular and pigheaded than Great Britain in that way.

We turned down an invitation from the Moreno Valley Community Club about Switzerland. To our own surprise, we were sorry to, in one way: we both felt that it might be a way to make these few people a little less sneering and scornful of "them Yurru-

peens"—a little less smug about being American and at the same
time prouder and more thankful than they are.

8. iv. 40

Last night when we came back from Bareacres, the house was
almost empty. When we turned on the lights, the sound of the
switch was hollow. We were tired, and I had one of the few really
bad, really terrible headaches of my life. And on the mantel was a
pickle jar filled with deep red anemones and box leaves. It was so
beautiful and so comforting and satisfying to find in this somewhat
desolate place that we lay in our beds and looked up at it and felt
that Mrs. King was one of the kindest people we had ever known
to put it there. She is a contained person, without the beguil-
ing sympathetic softness, the almost blurred gentleness, of Mrs.
Purdy. She is not, apparently, sentimental. But she must be sensitive, because she knew how tired and how bleak we would feel,
coming back last night to the nakedness of these rooms. And the
flowers were beautiful. They are now.

I finally paid bills that have been collecting and read Mme.
R.'s letter about the deaths of Papa Zi and Plume. We opened the
letter on the hill behind Bareacres several days ago, and I was
reading it aloud, and suddenly I felt too sad, so that my throat was
full and my voice vanished. I had been thinking of Plume, of *le
petit singe* [the little monkey]—and now he was dead. It was a
shock, and yet right. His mother's letter was almost melodramatic
and yet sincere. I was relieved for him to be dead, and yet terribly
sad.

We move in three days. Yesterday T. got tired of the boon-
doggling of Lausen and his half-wit brother-in-law helper and is-
sued an ultimatum or two. Today work was better. We may be

able to close a few doors at least by the next weekend. It is exasperating to see men spend six hours fitting a piece of wood into a little hole in the floor that they and you know will be covered by linoleum.

5. v. 40

I think it's some time since I wrote—I don't look, fearing embarrassment or boredom.

It is 1:30, Sunday afternoon, of a fine May day with blue sky and clouds. Behind me to the west I hear cars climbing and honking already toward the Bowl where the year's last performance of *Ramona* starts in an hour. A man sings in one of the cars. On the stone wall of the porch, Butch sniffs abruptly. A hummingbird whirls and chirps in the rangy tobacco bush outside the porch. It sounds idyllic and is—even the telephone that now and then shrills twice for the Bowl, asking probably for our tickets, and the afternoon breeze that already has started to pick up leaves and the magazine by my side and will probably carry off the actors' lines as soon as they are said, this afternoon over the hill.

I am alone, somewhat against my better judgment as a hostess and more so as myself. Anne Kelly and T. and Larry Bachman have driven in Larry's discreetly opulent Buick to Idyllwild, some twenty miles from here, to look at a summer camp for Shaun—T. because he had to move or go jittery with the pain in his leg, and Sis because she has to have constant if meaningless movement about her, and Larry—I don't know him very well, but I imagine from his thinness that he is in love and from his preoccupation that he has family troubles. I alone, in what Gloria Stuart furiously calls my "phlegmatic way," can sit by myself and assuage my own inward pangs by a sandwich of cheese and salami left from yesterday and a balloon of gin and vermouth, which makes me feel somewhat pontifical.

My excuse for staying here, besides the obvious one that three people are much more comfortable than four in a two-passenger car, is that I must, I *must* write to Aunt Grace* and my Cousin Harry. So I sit here, with my legs in the air in a deck chair on the porch, and I look occasionally at Butch on the stone railing and think how his eyes are like those of Albrecht Dürer's mother's, withdrawn and remote and impersonal, and I sigh and look down at my feet in their green socks and their striped cotton shoes with rubber soles, red, green, blue, yellow, and I think many things, including that the few men who have the energy to write whatever comes into their heads are very stupid.

7.*v*.40

While T. takes a shower, I write some words. Apparently yesterday I was in a nasty mood. I remember it, but vaguely. I remember disliking myself. Today I feel much less preoccupied and am able to paint and eat and do smaller things like filing my nails without accompanying each with a silent running commentary of bilious and even masochistic self-deprecation.

We just finished painting the patio—cream walls with the lower fourth terra-cotta, and soft green on the doors and windows. We both think it looks extremely well, but, of course, we think everything about Bareacres is right, good, proper, and completely satisfying. It is fun to be so complacent about anything. It is true, though, that I have never lived in such an agreeable house. When people tell us about Captain Hoffman's unfortunately messy sui-

---

* An old school friend of Edith, dear to all the family.

cide, here in this room I know now as my office, I can only pity them for any hopes they may have to dismay us. If that poor clown's ghost ever waxed enough to come back this far, it would be too pleased to bother us. I think I have probably entertained other better ghosts and would truly not fear this one.

One reason yesterday was a bad day for me was that my secret worry about T. crept up on me. Today I feel stronger than it . . . but still I must admit it and recognize that behind all my pleasure and well-being about Bareacres is the miserable reality of his pain. What can I do? At times I am near despair, and how much more so he must often be. But what can I do? I see the supply of Analgeticum grow smaller, in spite of our fight not to use more than the absolute necessity, and I know that if the war goes on, it is most likely to be all we shall get of it. I read over in my mind the letters I have had from doctors, and I hear all the conversations we have had with them, and then I know that I could never blame T. for whatever he might feel that he must do to settle this problem that no one else seems able to settle for him. I am deadened by the very thought of it. And yet I must think of it with the same routine thoughtfulness that it takes to recognize hunger or peeing.

12. v. 40

I finally got completely fed up with this life T. leads (and I, too) and wrote Hal a sort of ultimatum, and as I knew he would, he answered at once. It is action at least. We go up Monday, first to an X-ray specialist who will take "soft" pictures, whatever they may be, to see if there are any swollen nerve bulbs in the leg. Then we go to an orthopedic man. Hal talked with him and tells me he is good. So many times we've thought that *this* time we'd get something done, and always the experiments have been useless or even harmful . . . but this time I really do feel that we'll do some good. It may mean hospitals and even another operation, but we don't care. Life must be sweeter than it is for Timmy to endure it much longer, even though we are so happy here together.

The weekend was hectic, in a queer controlled way. The Powells were here, with meals and so on, of course. Then, the night before they came (they wrote they'd be here for lunch and drove in casually at about 4:00 in the afternoon), Pizzi, out on the hill, let out an agonized wail, and there were heavy feet thudding, and she was gone. She was heavy with kittens, and I suppose easy pickings for a coyote or wildcat. Timmy felt badly . . . worse than I . . . but I felt badly, too. About 1:30 Saturday night, then, Butch went out into the patio to take a whizz or something and began to scream and moan, more like a person than a little dog. I ran out. I was scared, because I thought he would be fighting with a rattlesnake, and . . . I was scared. He was cowering by the old trunk, and when he saw me he dragged himself into the middle of the patio, still crying terribly. I picked him up, and Tim and I looked all over, but there was no sign of bites. His left front leg seemed stiff, but he was not biting at it. He hid his head under Timmy's arm. Finally we got him quiet and went back to bed. But in half an hour he let out another yelp, this time in the kitchen. We thought he was dying. We got him quiet again and pulled on some clothes and started for West Riverside and Dr. Walkerdine. The ride seemed terribly long. I took along what was left of a bottle of whiskey, but neither of us wanted any. Walkerdine got up, sleepy but nice, in pale blue flannel pajamas, and he couldn't see anything wrong with Butch, except that he was suffering from shock. He gave him a stimulant, and we stood in the little operating room looking down at him. "Poor little dog," I said. "His nose is pale." "Not only that," Walkerdine said, in his queer Scotch-Cockney accent, "but the little chap has an exprrrression of grrrreat anxiety." I left Butch there, and we drove back here, another forty-odd miles that seemed shorter than the way over. We slept for about two hours. Then I got up, hearing a queer sound that was more in my dream than in the air, and found Tawny just finishing having her sixth and final kitten in my typewriter stand. I was sorry I had not come sooner, as I've never seen anything being born, unless you can count an egg I once saw pop out of a hen. Things were quite messy. I helped her clean up and spent the rest of the day, it seemed to me, moving her and the litter about the house, looking for cool air. It was a stifling day, and I really think they almost died. She was too hot and weak to clean herself, and felt badly about it. Today is hot but better, and she's almost all clean except a little stiffness around her tail, and the six kittens are very much alive. In a little while T. is going to drown the three yellow and white ones, and we'll keep the three gray ones. I said I'd do it, and I would, too . . . but I was relieved when he insisted that he'd do it. He doesn't want to either.

The Powells stayed until 5:00 or so, although they had written they'd leave about noon . . . I sound terribly ungracious . . . and by the time they left I was in an interior dither of heat and messiness. I felt that the house and everything in it, especially me, was disgustingly dusty and grimy. So I gave T. a whopping shot and then spent quite a long time taking a shower. Then I felt very nice, and we had a good supper on the porch. T. ate two soft-boiled eggs and some Swedish rye crisp, and . . .

13 or 14.v.40

Yesterday before we went to West Riverside to get Butch, who seems quite well after his scare, T. killed the kittens. Tawny tried to stop me when I picked them up and put them in a basket, but I think that was her only feeling then or now that anything was wrong. I dug a hole while T. killed them. He chopped each one twice, across the throat and across the skull. I climbed up the slope to take them from him where he stood holding them in a little bunch by their tails. "Poor little rats," he said. "What?" "I said, 'Little rats,'" he mumbled. He was not pale, but he did not look at me. He laid them on my shovel, and I went down to the hole. I slid them into the ground, and as they touched the cool earth at the bottom, they all three made one movement, the same they made when they nuzzled against Tawny looking for her dugs. I stood looking, although I knew they must be dead. T. called down, "Don't look. They're dead all right." I covered them up and put three stones over the loosened earth. As I climbed up again, I said, "I'm sorry you had to do that." T. didn't answer, and I saw him hurrying into the house. He went to the bathroom, and I thought maybe he was going to be sick, but he was crying instead. He took a long shower, and we have only mentioned them twice, when I said that Tawny looked much more comfortable and when he said that drowning was worse than being chopped.

Underneath everything we do or think, now, is the incredible knowledge that Europe, the part we knew of it, is forever gone. The actual invasions and bombings are less final than what is dying in the people. They will go on, naturally, and will build a life that will soon seem natural to their children and to them. But a part of their spirit, and a part of ours, too, is dead. It makes all of us zombies, if we are what we have been. I can smell my own decay. It has grown stronger since last September. I can smell it, my own and other people's, and feel it unsuspected in the air about young children and the most thoughtless ninnies, who do not know what is happening to the world and to themselves.

T. has just finished making another beautiful little cat door, this time in my workroom so that Tawny can go out at night while

Butch is shut into the kitchen where the other door is. This one is too small for Butch, much to his disgust. He can get only his head through. It has a little zinc panel that slides down and closes it against drafts in winter, and a curtain of fringed brown leather to keep out flies.

These boondogglings are good because they keep T. so busy, and he does them all so nicely. We'll be glad when they're over, though, and he can get to work again. He made himself a fine strong easel and has the studio pretty much as he wants it . . . but now we'll have to be gone for some days next week, and there's little point in getting into the swing of painting before then.

It is still hot. Occasionally an almost violent breeze sweeps through the house, blowing the curtains about and closing a door now and then.

17.v.40

The news that the Germans are within seventy miles of Paris sent Timmy, crumpled and terribly old, weeping away. I could not follow him. I felt that anything as actual as arms and kisses and tenderness would be obscene. I sat for a time and then played Tchaikovsky's concerto, that rather bangy silly piano thing, on the gramophone, and in a while he came in and I finished the album without looking at him and then went into the bathroom and found when I put on new lipstick that my mouth had gone all crooked and sideways, apparently forever.

Many times lately I have had the time, and even the wish, to put something down in this book. But some of those times I have felt almost morbidly slack and in a way resentful of the way T. feels—resentful that this is happening to *him*. I don't want it to happen to anyone, of course, but especially not to him. And then other times have found me all at odds with myself so that I could hardly think in phrases, much less sentences, because of the things happening in Europe and even in this country. It is queer what a hopelessness has crept into all my thoughts. It is almost a slackness. Why be so economical? Why be generous? Why have children or plant trees? This time next year or next month or tomorrow—who knows what irrevocable change will have been made in all our values? Will we have soap to wash with, or a blanket, or even any spiritual honor? Then I am ashamed, as well as startled, and I know that I am dauntless, just as humans all over the world are dauntless. Pain and disaster and grim dreary poverty can never kill me and my inner self.

All this probably seems exasperated and neurotic. It is true, though, that at this moment the whole pace of existence, here at Bareacres as well as in fallen Brussels and in London awaiting its annihilation, has been sped up past reality into a state bordering on nightmare. We live fairly calmly here on the hill and have even sickened somewhat to listening to the radio news . . . but within us is the same dumb watchfulness, the same feeling of helpless inevitability, that soldiers and pregnant animals everywhere know too well.

The doctors could do nothing for T. The day was an exhausting one, and we were sick and dismayed when we saw that there was nothing. We had even welcomed the idea of more hospitals, operations . . . anything to change this half-life of pain for T.

One of the orthopedic specialists leapt agilely from his own field into psychiatry, with unbecoming haste, and talked behind closed doors of night dreams, fear of impotence, brooding . . . practically said that all T.'s pain was a foolish idea and no more. Hal prescribed rest, more B-1 pills, another visit to Pasadena in three weeks. Zubzubzub.

Bill and Jane Evans came down this last weekend and brought and planted a great many trees, vines, shrubs. It will be beautiful if they grow . . . and two days later they look very happy, thanks to good planting and fairly cool weather. Bill embarrassed me by not letting me pay him anything for them. So we gave them our album of Tahitian chants, and I'll find a nice plate for the plate rail in their new house. They are apparently quite absorbed in plans for that and hope to move in another month. The plans we saw seemed quite dull and usual, but then they are, too—dull, usual, and very nice. I think, after many years, that B. is a much better person than J. She is growing more and more like her mother, who is one of the two women in the world who completely shock and frighten me with their active repulsiveness. I was startled to find that J., who has in the past attracted me with her soft sweet ways, this time seemed merely affectedly "cuddlesome" and that her little body had grown stringy and old. *Tout passe* . . . and soon I, too, will be older than I am this minute, but I hope that I can remain nicer, to myself at least, than I think Jane is becoming. Of course, she may have no faintest inkling that she is anything that she was not ten years ago. Perhaps that would be better. But on the other hand, I would prefer not to have her wear such cut-down shorts and halters that I have to see her flat leathery puckered little belly and her hollow sharpened flanks. From my point of view, it would be pleasanter to have her realize the changes of time enough to cover up some of her body a little more discreetly. I don't know how old she is. To believe Gloria, who has always hated her guts, she is about forty. She may be thirty-five. Anyway . . . it is boring to have to avert my eyes, inwardly at least, from something that once gave me pleasure. And perhaps she feels so about me.

Time, whether good or bad, passes too quickly for me, and I am almost resentful that it is Thursday of this week and not Monday or even Wednesday.

We bought a rather pretty little sable bitch this week to be a companion for Butch. He was mooning toward the valley and growing capricious about his meals, and we thought it was loneliness as much as lovesickness. So now he is at the Rose of Sharon Kennels, being wormed and becoming used to his wife. I miss him. They'll be back in a day. I must learn more about coping with bitches in heat and all that; we don't want her to have puppies for about ten more months. Butch looks very funny and sweet now, with all his fur cut off. That horrifies Peke fanciers, but he was wretchedly hot. She (I don't know what we'll call her—she already knows "Brownie") has a much lighter coat.

The three kittens are beginning to play now and have their eyes open, like little shiny blueberries. When I bring them in by Tim's couch at night, Tawny makes a special show of being maternal. She is a good mother, as a matter of fact.

I start work today revising a book Tim wrote some twenty years ago. I may be wasting my time . . . don't know yet. I don't mean that it isn't good—parts of it are fine—but it may not benefit any from my effort, and I should be writing something more my own and sending it to Mrs. Pritchett while she still feels stirred up about "What Happened to Miss Browning." However . . .

30. v. 40

Memorial—or is it Decoration?—Day brings out a special flood of emotional crap in the radio serials, which we listen to almost every day with a kind of ghoulish nauseated interest. Some of them are well acted and sometimes well written. Once when I was ill, I listened deliberately for several hours, and at the end I felt stranger than I have from any other drug . . . light-headed and terribly depressed, in an almost numb way.

I got to work yesterday on [Timmy's] *Daniel Among the Women*. I need to see a few popular magazines of about 1911. The local library has found me some old *Theatres,* which I'll look at tomorrow.

Tomorrow we go to get the two dogs. I'll be glad to have them here. We had the kittens on the porch during lunch today, and they were very diverting.

Last night T. asked me to hide the .22 bullets. I do not mention this from any martyr complex . . . Pity me, oh pity me . . . but because I think I had better. It is strange about suicide. I have always felt strongly on the subject. I remember arguing and then growing angry with Rex, years ago, when an old friend of his who was penniless found he was dying slowly and expensively of a terrible cancer and jumped out of the hospital window after arranging for some kind of pension for his helpless sister. "I never knew the judge was yellow," Rex kept saying. It was a terrible blow to him, to his idea of honor and strength. I argued with him that it took courage. I said that shooting yourself for exhibitionism or because you failed your exams or lost your job or your love was cowardly, usually . . . but not what the judge had done. But Rex kept shaking his head and saying, "I never knew the judge was yellow." Now I find that I have been living with the constant thought of suicide in my mind ever since September 1, 1938. That

is a long time. I often think I am used to it. And then T. says
something like his request last night, and although I answer quietly
and do what he asks, I realize that in spite of all my thought, the
actuality of killing oneself is hard to accept. Once in Bern I knew
that if I left T.'s bed near the balcony edge, he would jump. He
had talked of it often, begged me to help him, to carry him there,
and I had argued calmly with him and asked him to give me one
more day, one more week, three hours. But this time I knew,
without any reserve, that he would do it. I wanted him to, with
almost all of my love. I looked at him, and he averted his eyes and
started to smile a strange crafty smile. I turned away, to leave him
to what he so desired . . . and then I turned back, and pulled his
bed away from the edge, and could not look at him for knowing
that I had condemned him to more torture. And that sort of thing
has happened several times. Once I found a razor in the night-
table drawer at Adelboden, slipped cunningly under the paper
lining. I took it silently and crept from the room covered with
shame. But I could not leave it there. In spite of my love for T.,
my horrible primitive instinct to prevent suicide was stronger. I
remember talking and talking about suicide with him and making
bargains: wait seven days, wait six weeks, and when it is worse, I
swear by Christ crucified that I will help you. We talked of ways.
No drugs, although I had them under my hand, because it would
make trouble for Soeur Irma. Not slashing wrists—so messy and
so scandalous for the kind hotel owners. What, then . . . what?
That sort of thing went on and on. And now when I hear a strange
noise or when I hear too long a silence, I think, This is the time: it
has happened, and I make myself call out in a quiet way or walk
slowly, unhurriedly, heavily, to what I may find. The strange thing
is that oftener than not I have a quick wild hope that perhaps this
is the time. "Let us accustom ourselves to desolation," I find that
I have scrawled on a scrap of paper, thinking about this war and

how news that a month ago would make me weep now goes in my mind and out again as if I were rock. But I know that such a thing is not possible, any more than it is possible completely to accustom oneself to the acceptance of murder. I know how to kill T. and to do it easily and probably so that I would never have to be accused of it . . . but I know that I never will. But even after so long, I don't know that *he* never will.

I think maybe I am wrong to write about this.

I went to tea at Miss van Benschoten's yesterday. Three of the local gentry were there. It was pleasant enough, as such things go, but I came away terribly ashamed of myself for having managed to let them all know, in a charming gracious way, that Mrs. Purdy was my cleaning woman and not my intimate. God. Why did I do that? I wonder, feeling sickish. What the hell difference does it make? How could I lower myself to such peewee behavior and insult not only myself but my hostess? Well . . . I feel ashamed.

The first picture T. did when he started to work again last week, after so much time of carpentering and such, was fine; it is a portrait of four Mexican dolls, called *Les Fiançailles* [The Engagement Party]—very virile. Others have been good, but less good. He is working now but without wanting to. It is too hot to do any more of the siding that we started this morning. That will be wonderful—redwood, wide, already making the house look solid and much lower to the ground. It will cover all the cracks between the pine boards, too. We'll go out as soon as the sun is less hot. I must work on *Daniel* at least a few minutes before then.

5.vi.40

I sit down, feeling I must say something that for one instant seems important, at least to my own scheme. And all I can think of is the soft trusting relaxation of the little dog, who lies put along the crease between the couch pillows, his legs bent whitely at the wrists, his belly bare to our whims.

My mind is filled with the enormity of people. It is two days now since our parochial visit, and I am still immeasurably disturbed by it.

Mr. H. is a tall man, with the face, at first glance, of a matinee idol like one of the Barrymores. He had a languid air, and he pops his pale eyes at times to help this illusion, probably—possibly— unwittingly. Now and then, *hie und da,* as the pathological analysis of Timmy's amputations says (I typed it this afternoon for a doctor who believes T. is stalling and fabricating pain because of a fear of impotence)—*hie und da* his finely modeled lips curve in an almost subtly quizzical smile as he speaks.

He speaks seldom. When he does, it is about the great number of books he owns, the "artist colonies" he has known, the people like Emma Goldman and Earl Browder he has heard . . . trying to show us that he is worldly and broad-minded.

Most of the time it is the woman who talks.

She is a coarse-faced woman, wearing thick-lensed glasses that accentuate her small mean eyes. Her coloring is crude. As I remember, she wears sensible navy-blue dresses and shoes with what look like built-in arches. She left a wretched printed silk scarf, black and white, and I think she did it deliberately so that either she or I must respond courteously.

Her conversation is typically that of a village minister's wife, with that ghastly tinge of whimsical baby talk that means that years of guild members have laughed at even the most inane remarks. She almost talks baby talk, and she has the same habit that Mrs. Lewis and one or two minister's wives show, of saying things with an air of irrefutable certainty. "Why on earth, my dear," meaning you poor ninny, "did you ever pay $16 a cord for oak?" and then it turns out that that is a very decent price and that she was thinking of olive and that it is really impolite not to have let her in on the bargain. But the first reaction is one of positive and noisy disapproval.

6. vi. 40

I'll write a little more about the H.'s because they made a strong and almost shocking impression on both of us, so that we found ourselves thinking many hours later of this or that about them.

They were very curious about the house, and I showed it to them room by room. His reaction was to hasten to tell us, in his vague dead manner, that he, too, was an artist, that he, too, had books and many more than we did. She chattered constantly and with her own strange ministerial impertinence, and fingered the curtains and estimated the number of pewter trays we had.

I made tea for them because I could see that they wanted it. All the time she talked and talked and told some anecdotes about Indians and so on that did not seem shocking until much later, when we suddenly realized that she had been boasting about fooling them and about being suspicious and stingy.

"What do you think about Leopold? How could he have done such a miserable cowardly low thing? Tell me exactly what you think," she commanded with what I'm sure she has been told is charming imperiousness. But she did not want to hear; she wanted to tell *us*. She did, at great length, and seemed to enjoy berating the king. Tim tried to say that it was hard to judge a man in Leopold's position, and I tried to say that one man alone might choose death rather than dishonor where he could not possibly do it for his whole family or his nation. But she did not hear us. In her chattering half-laughing way, she said some violent and cruel things.

Finally, after some other talk, she asked me, "Doesn't it make you simply furious to see ships of Red Cross supplies going to Germany?" "No," I answered, feeling suddenly sick. That actually stopped her for a minute. Her jaw dropped, and before she could start talking again and really before I had time to think and to realize how little good it would do, I said, "Germans bleed. They are humans, too. The Red Cross is for all suffering men." She looked surprised and perhaps even chagrined, but only for a second. Then she laughed gaily and said, "Well, perhaps you're right. Of course, of course. But all I say is, I wish they'd bleed a little more."

Her husband sat without talking, as usual, his pale eyes fixed on something above our heads, his pale hands posed before him, his pale lips twisted into a subtle smile.

She got up to go. As so often happens, I said good-bye and thanked them for their visit with more warmth than I could possibly show to anyone I liked. I was terribly disturbed by them and still am. I know that a priest is but the instrument of God, but it would be impossible for me ever to take communion from Hill. How could any decent man, and especially a man of God, let people talk as he lets his own wife talk? It is horrible.

I meant to tell about the little bitch we bought for Butch, but other things came into my head. She was a sweet-faced delicate little creature and clung to us, but when she walked her feet splayed out in such a weak rickety fashion that after only a few hours we knew that we couldn't stand to have her around. She had very bad table manners, too. So we took her back and refused to ask for any money back, so that our twenty-four hours with her cost us $12.50. We charged it to experience. She reminded me unpleasantly of a very good charwoman I had in Vevey . . . weak physically and spiritually, with a pretty face and a loose-moraled prudery about her.

Yesterday I was all ready to sit down and say that the French were holding the Germans and that T. seemed to be better. He does, still. I have been able to cut down a little on his injections without letting him know, of course. But the French are not quite holding the Germans, who are supposed to be about fifty-five miles from Paris now. They are going slowly, though, and even that is better than the blitzkrieg tactics of the war so far. The French are trying to exhaust them. I think they will succeed.

Here the term *fifth-column activities* is already so overworked as to be nauseating, and the air is full of spy scares and rumors of armed invasions. This noon we hear over the radio that the veterans of the last war are trying to raise a volunteer army of 100,000 men in Southern California to combat foreigners. It is sickening.

Two new air schools are to be started in the valley, it seems, to turn out a hundred pilots every ninety days. That seems a terribly short course to me, but I suppose it's not much harder to handle a plane than an automobile, and I'm pretty sure I could learn the mechanics of a car in less than ninety days.

The siding is almost up, and the house looks fine and solid, although much yellower than we'd thought. It will darken with time. I hope we're here to see it when it's chocolate black.

We heard this noon that Paris has surrendered to the Germans. My blood stops at the thought of what this must mean to the millions of people like Jean Matruchot and Connes and Jeanne Bonamour. But there was nothing else to do.

Tim is putting boiled linseed oil on the redwood and turning it a soft intense red color. It is beautiful. The porch now, with the dark red walls and the floor painted a soft green and the gay furniture, is one of the loveliest rooms I have ever seen.

I brought portulacas and zinnias back yesterday from our trip to the Ranch and planted them around the front door and in the patio. T. hates to see me get anything more to care for, and I really will stop now. Today the plants look droopy, of course, but I think tonight's watering will revive them. The plants that Bill thought would need watering only once a week need it at least three times as often, so I find myself carrying about thirty buckets a day to them. It worries T., and I am sorry about it, but I can't let them all die.

We are to increase T.'s doses of thyroid one capsule a day each week until he begins to have heart flutterings and headaches and then let Hal know. I think I see some improvement these last six or seven days . . . at least no bad cramps.

The worst thing about the relationships in my family now is the way Mother and Sis are about each other. They are malicious, sarcastic, and truly bitchy and seem to make no effort to be charitable or tolerant of the other's mistakes. The situation upsets me, but I do not know what to do about it. I hate to see Mother lose any of her dignity and find myself feeling slightly sick to hear her say some of the things she does about her daughter. I know, too, that she talks to other people about Sis more or less as she talks to me. It is bad. And Sis is the same way . . . or no. I don't think she talks about Mother much to other people. But she makes absolutely no effort to understand or help Mother and goes nonchalantly on using Mother's money and getting into debt and taking it for granted that the parents are damned lucky to have the privilege of supporting not only her child but herself. The weekends usually end either with a row between Sis and Father about money or tears and sarcasm between Sis and Mother about the discipline of Shaun. It is an unpleasant situation to find in a family that for so many years has seemed such a nice one to belong to.

Of course, the thing that has made both the parents lose their faith in us children as a group is the complete disappointment they feel in David. That is disagreeable for Tim and me, since without us it would probably never have happened that he would leave college and decide to become a painter or whatever it is he is. Their whole attitude has changed this last year. They are quietly bitter and in a strange way insouciant, as if it did not matter whether we stayed decent or even alive. I know it is not true, underneath their new callousness. I can understand them, too. But I regret it.

We are calling a halt on the work on the house, although we can still think of many things we want to do, like paving the patio and building a barbecue and so on. Timmy is painting again, and tomorrow I start work in earnest on *Daniel,* which I meant to do today. But this morning I went downtown. This afternoon I cleaned up my desk, and just as I started to pull the various piles of notes and papers together, the liquor man came with a case of beer and two or three bottles of whiskey to try, and then the garage man arrived with the Bantam, which was in the shop getting a new muffler and a generator repair.

We are trying to live economically, but today I have spent a lot of money. I went to the grocery store and bought a lot of canned things: a case of milk for the cats, a case of Pard for Butch, some salmon, soups, beans, and so on—$30. Then I went to a furniture store and ordered two beds for the guest room—about $60. Then I bought $30 worth of whiskey and beer. And the car cost $18.95. It is frightening when I put it into a paragraph. The liquor and the beds we could do without, of course. And, of course, they are nice, especially the beds, which Tim and I will use this winter, but which will be much nicer for guests than the cots I have had to make up in the guest room from the studio couch. The couch we'll put on the porch. And, of course, I'll have to get some kind of bedspreads. Oh, dear.

It is hot now, but we like it when we can live at our own speed. There is almost always air moving up here on the hill. It is delightful . . . the most beautiful place in the world, to me at least.

Later

I meant to get to work on the book, and then I thought about one or two things that I want to put here. One is that a group of women in Whittier is trying to witch-hunt Miss Ellis, the librarian. They say that in 1935 she personally frowned on a book that one of the group presented to the library . . . a wild book that attracted some attention, most of it jeering, called *The Red Menace* or something like that. It was endorsed by the D.A.R. and a few like organizations, and Miss Ellis accepted it for circulation but followed her customary good and often amusing habit of pasting a review or two in the back of the book. This hurt the donor's feeling, since one of the reviews was full of ridicule. She withdrew the book, with a scene during which she says Miss Ellis said that she was glad to have it out of the library. The woman seethed and went to some expense to have photostatic copies of the review made. Now, in 1940, with all this talk of fifth columns and spies and Communists, the group of women comes to Rex with a long story that Miss Ellis is a Communist and a menace and a subversive and that she should be hounded from her position. Miss Ellis, a prissy yearning virgin nearing sixty, is one of the least dangerous people I have ever met. She is boring and affected, God knows. She has worked hard and conscientiously for most of her life and supports an invalid crotchety old mother, and I am pretty sure her only sins are ones like feeling a slight flutter in what she innocently thinks is her heart when Alfred Lunt gets as far as Los Angeles in his current drama, and perhaps even suffering an occasional mental orgasm at some especially well-written bit of English prose. But the pack is after her now for being a dangerous agent of a foreign power and so on.

The other thing I want to note now, and I don't know why unless it is because I am in a rather soured state about humanity, is something Mrs. Purdy said the other day. She has a funny mannerism of laughing a little when she repeats anything or when she tells me something, some anecdote. She almost whinnies, very softly. She seldom gossips, since we have few common friends and I am not exactly encouraging anyway, and when she does she always laughs softly and says, "Oh I have some *goss*-ip for you." One morning, after she had been to a picnic given by the Moreno Community Club, she laughed that way and said that. "Oh?" I said. "Yes," she went on, still laughing softly, with her eyes twinkling, "the new tenant of your house in Moreno tried to kill herself the other night." "Oh, the poor woman," I said, remembering the strange distinguished girl, tall and faded, with her four children and her beautiful clothes and her queer dopey way of talking to me. I can't remember her name, but I always think of her as Mrs. Scatterbrain. "Poor Mrs. Scatterbrain," I said. "She must have been very unhappy." Mrs. Purdy stopped laughing for a second or two, and she looked almost startled, and then she began to laugh softly again. "Yes, she drank Lysol or something like that," she chuckled. "Maybe she had those children too close together, or maybe she has husband trouble," I said. "Well, I never thought of that. I suppose we shouldn't judge, should we? But still . . ." and Mrs. Purdy turned away, laughing again, "still, that's no excuse to act that way. Mr. Canterbury kicked her out of his place at 11:00 one night, and she was so drunk she didn't get home until after 3:00 . . ." I didn't say anything, because there was nothing to say —but I felt terribly sad to know that a woman as gentle as Mrs. Purdy, a woman who has lived a cruel hard life, could be so cruel and hard. I should think she would be understanding and full of compassion. T. says I am really naive, and I suppose this is a proof of it.

16. vi. 40

I know what I must do with a rather confused chapter of *Daniel,* and indeed I have looked through it and even put the paper in the typewriter. But I do not feel like working on it.

Last night we broiled a steak on the temporary barbecue in the patio. I did it according to the *Sunset Barbecue Book,* and basted it with strong French dressing, and did not prick it with the fork, and we had made a fine bed of oak coals, and the result was good. The steak was truly delicious and made us realize that meat, a primitive hunger, is a primitive thing and best cooked as the cavemen did it, minus French dressing and some other refinements, of course.

We sat in the cooling dark courtyard, and Butch gnawed quietly at the T-bone, and now and then a lizard slipped clumsily through the dry leaves of the cottonwood trees. The moon, half full, was high in the sky. In my office the three kittens clawed occasionally at the screen door, and Tawny scolded at them.

The night, for me, was troubled with a steady dreaming of the war, as always now. This time I took care of Czechoslovakia, Poland, Finland, Estonia . . . I evacuated them, I reorganized the cabinets, I supervised the Red Cross.

At 2:00 I gave T. an especially good shot, knowing that he had not yet slept and that perhaps if I did so he would not need one at dawn. I did not tell him, hoping to surprise him with relief. But at dawn I opened one eye from my dreams and saw him looking at me. I turned over quickly and thought that if I showed no intelligence he would think, Poor girl, I'll not waken her, and then go to sleep again. But in a few minutes he was still looking at me. I pretended not to have seen him. Soon I heard him getting up, terribly cautiously. I knew that he wanted a shot but that he was trying not to ask for one. So I said nothing and went to sleep again, to settle, this time, the evacuation of Paris.

When I finally got up, about 9:00, we found that poor Butch had been hit by diarrhea and had made three shameful places. T. cleaned them up. Then, in the hallway to my workroom, there was a neat little pile of gut, probably from a gopher. I cleaned it. "There is a dead baby rabbit in your bookcase," T. warned me. But by the time I got to it there were two. They were sad little carcasses. I suppose Tawny brings them in to accustom the kittens to warm meat. They looked fairly neat, lying against the suitbox full of letters on the bottom shelf, but when I lifted them up by the ears and put them into the wastebasket, I saw that they were quite mussy. I cleaned up as much as I could of the blood from the new wood. There was a loathsome gray little thing, which T. said was a tick. It is hard to find burying ground for all these dead creatures in the hard ground. I put the two little rabbits under the irrigating ditch of the cottonwoods near the arroyo. The kittens had licked at their fur, and they looked terribly little.

T. had been painting and walking about the place. It was about 10:00 before we got through cleaning up the messes and the little bodies, and I got the animals fed. Butch would eat nothing and looked up at us like some sad sea monster. T. had already got himself a nip of whiskey, in the coldness of a dripping early-morning fog. So he had another nip and a prairie oyster . . . with seven capsules of Hal's thyroid mixture and a small *goût* of Epsom juice. I drank a pink gin and bottle of beer, and after T. went back to his painting, I sat in a strange alcoholic Sunday stupor and read an old copy of the *New Yorker*. I knew that I should work and that Paris was in the hands of the Germans, and still I sat there in the little bar, feeling the sun through the curtains and not even remembering what time it was.

Now it is after lunch. We ate chili con carne in a continuation of our matinal decadence. At 1:30 T. thought that it must be at least 3:30, and finally he broke down and asked for a shot. Now he is sitting on the porch, waiting for relief. He feels discouraged because he has not been able to paint anything good until maybe this morning, when he did a disturbing, chaotic thing about Creation, full of snakes and beasts and three or four men, full of pinks and greens and trouble.

Two of the kittens play languidly on the shelf spotted with rabbit blood, and one lies beside its mother but not too close. Tawny, about twice a day now, is teaching them to jump, to pounce, and bite the neck of their prey. They all practice on one another.

18.vi.40

I remember that I wrote a few days ago about suicide, so I think that I shall put down what happened this morning. I find myself disturbed by it.

Last night was a hard one for T., and he said once that he wanted to know where I had hidden the bullets. I told him I would tell him this morning. Finally he went to sleep.

This morning we both woke rather early to a beautiful hot bright morning. We lay in bed for a few minutes, I stretching and he reading a magazine. Finally he said, "I suppose it's because I'm curious, but I would like to see Anne and see what the new house at Quantness is like, and I'd like to see Mother, so I think when the next check comes we'd better get an Oldsmobile and drive east and maybe show you the Grand Canyon and use all the Analgeticum I need to be really comfortable, and then come back and finish it up, after a really good time." He was very serious about it. For some reason I began to tease him. "Yes, it does sound awful," he admitted, half-laughing. " 'Dear Mother, if you want to make my last days pleasant how about sending me a nice check for a trip to see you?' " There wouldn't be enough money anyway, I told him . . . we'd be lucky to get a thousand dollars, and that wouldn't even buy the car. I was laughing at him. Suddenly he muttered, not rudely but almost laughing, too, "Oh, shut up, shut up!" And then I saw that his eyes were more than full of tears.

I felt *awful*. I hated to think that I had mocked him, and suddenly, talking so positively about killing himself in the morning, not during the night, made me sick. It almost seemed real. I still feel dreadfully upset. There is nothing to do. While I was dressing he came into the room, and I told him how very sorry I was to have laughed at him, and I could see that he, too, was upset.

It's like the surrender of France or T.'s having his leg cut off. I *know* those things have happened, but I don't *realize* it. This morning, for just a minute, I realized about T.'s possible escape from this business.

30. vi. 40

It is almost 6:00, and I am just now beginning to feel like work, so that I know that I should arrange my days differently. I should work in the morning, here in my room, I mean, and do things that take no thought, like dishes and beds and sweeping, in the afternoons. Because now, just when I begin to feel awake, T. is through for the day and will need a shot as soon as he gets out of the shower, and then, on most days about this time, there are the plants to water, and supper.

Tonight I'll get the wood together for supper in the patio. The patio is dusty, and the plants are still very small, of course, and the barbecue is makeshift, but it is already a lovely place. Several times we've had supper out there and sat quietly in the dark. It has been fine. Tonight I'll broil sandwiches of eggplant and sausages and make a salad. We'll drink some beer.

The most surprising thing about our life is our new interest in swimming. I have said very sincerely for many years that I'd be perfectly happy never to go in the ocean again, and as for public pools, I couldn't be bribed to put a toe in one. But the other day while the parents were visiting us, we decided to drive over to Soboba Hot Springs, and there in that startling cool green oasis under the bleak mountains of San Jacinto we found a lovely mountain pool that T. had seen once years ago and still talked about without remembering where it was.

It is big, irregularly shaped, with a stream pouring in at one end and out the other. There may be one person in it or nobody, and the cottonwood trees that shade it drop their leaves on the brownish water.

Father and T. and I went in. I had to rent a suit, and the only one I could get was an old-fashioned man's suit of gray wool that kept slipping off my breasts. I must have looked funny as well as immodest, but we were alone. It was fun. I wish I could swim beautifully, like a fish maybe. I am so clumsy in the water.

Then we had massages, and we all felt so nice and T. slept so much better than usual that night that it was easy to convince ourselves that we should and could afford to go often.

So I bought a cheap but pretty suit of white Lastex with red dots ($2.95 at Penney's), a white cap, some white sandals, and a pair of gabardine shorts for T., and we got out the red bath towels and the suntan oil and hurried back to Soboba the next day, and found the pool being cleaned. It was too bad. But we're going again tomorrow. I am really excited. I look very nice in my suit, which would have shocked me a few years ago, but I wish that I weighed about five or ten pounds less. The trouble with me is that I eat and drink more than I need to.

About this time every year a small idea nags at my mind about how wonderful it would be to cut off most of my hair. It creeps into my other thoughts, and I find myself speculating willy-nilly on how it would look, feel, be. I always decide, because I know it to be true, that I had better leave well enough alone, and that I would regret it, and that it would be even more bother than my long hair. And so on. But still I can't help wishing that I had nerve enough to cut it all off. I think that it might look quite nice. The trouble is that short hair would accentuate my baby face, and although that might have been very attractive ten years ago, I have no longer the flat-hipped look that goes with boyish coiffures. I don't know, though . . . I may weaken yet. My hair grows fast, and I could wear an artificial chignon on the rare occasions when I put on "city clothes."

A letter from Anne suggests that we go to the Mayo Clinic and says that her finances are in a strange state, war or no war, and that she might soon be unable to help us. We answered that we wanted to try more of Hal's treatment plus the new promise of the baths at Soboba. I can't help worrying a little about our money. It is all so indefinite. I am terribly and deeply grateful to Anne for all she has done and is doing for us, but I wish she would understand how difficult it is for both Tim and me to be living on an uncertain amount of generosity. We never know what she will send us. Sometimes she forgets, and we have to ask. She has made definite annuities for the servants, but with T. she has done nothing so that we are always in doubt and always feeling a worried gratitude that at times cannot help being almost grudging. There is nothing we can do, though. I could not get work here without leaving T. and paying a housekeeper for him, and he could not get work, unless it might be as an illustrator. Anne is a fine sensitive intelligent woman, but this is one thing I think would be impossible to explain to her—that if she is going to give us money to live on, we would infinitely prefer a small sum sent coldly at set times from a bank, to her erratic checks, which may be much bigger.

It is beautiful now, with a golden haze in the air. In the patio the two great yellow ceremonial lanterns, which Mrs. Edith Kelly once gave to Mother and which we now use for the first time since they came from Japan some twenty-five years ago, tap now and then against the thin steel wire that supports them. In a minute, I'll take out two chairs and get the wood, and while T. builds the fire I'll put the supper things on a tray. I can hear Cinnamon and Smokey mewing for their supper. Tawny has almost cut off their milk and is already flaunting her tail at Butch. I'm going to try putting some sex repellent on it. It is for bitches, but I think it would have the same effect on Butch whether it was on a dog or a cat. Tawny is as thin as a razor, and not only do I not want her getting him all hot but I don't want her having another batch of babies so soon. The little ones are seven weeks old today.

We gave one to Mrs. Purdy a week ago. It was the one that T. had picked out as his favorite. And it got crushed behind a sofa the night she took it.

She has been sick—a kind of "summer complaint," I think, although she is too discreet to go into details. (I find myself enjoying the housework and doing many jobs like cleaning the icebox with the firm if conceited feeling that nobody else is quite as thorough as M. F. K. P.). I took her some turkey soup and a little cold meat last night and found Septimus stretched out on the porch swing, with bed pillows propping him up instead of the many ordinary porch pillows. "How is your invalid?" I asked, noticing that Mrs. P. was not in bed. "Oh, we're better," he said. He tottered to his feet and called, Sweetie-pie. She came weaving in, like a somewhat pasty ghost, with her eyes off-focus. She really looked ill. "How are you, Mrs. Purdy?" But before she could answer, the old man stuck his face between us and told me all about how *he* felt. I was hot with a little flash of exasperation: poor Sweetie-pie couldn't even have a little dizzy spell to herself, without having him steal all the fun. I felt like saying, "Mr. Purdy, I am quite used to hearing all about your feelings and your symptoms and your gas pains. But *tonight,* odd as it may seem, I am asking about your wife's feelings. Move aside. I am not interested in you—*ever*—and now even less than that." But, of course, I only waited until he was through and then rather pointedly continued talking to her about taking things easily and not working too hard and so on. She was quite fluttery and grateful, and I escaped as soon as possible and left her cooking the old boy's dinner.

T. has done a whole series of beautiful pictures of vegetables and fruits, very sure and rich.

3. vii. 40

I am thirty-two today, which is a rather murky steamy day. I am dressed in my best white silk playsuit, which I bought last year at Palm Springs, and white socks, and blue and white canvas shoes. My hair is done up on top of my head, for coolness. In a little while, Tim and I will go over to Soboba to swim and have a massage and then maybe a couple of martinis and lunch. I'll wear my new bathing suit, which he gave me and Mother bought for him in Laguna. It is black silk jersey and very soft and light and becoming, although I am still surprised to find myself wearing anything ruffled in bathing. (The white and red suit from Penney's is pretty much of a flop, because it is very stiff and cold, so yesterday I wore a seersucker playsuit and was much more comfortable, although perhaps somewhat too naked for a beach censor.)

I don't know quite how I feel about being thirty-two instead of thirty or twenty, except that I much prefer being as I am now. I have a much larger capacity for everything. I see a lot more and care a lot less about things like people and whether they like me. Physically I am in much better condition than I was ten years ago, although I am now a little overweight. Mentally I think I am better off, too. Of course, I was going to school then, and now I might find it harder to follow lectures and so on. I doubt it. I should certainly find more lectures not worth following . . . which may, of course, be a form of mental deterioration. I doubt that, too. I am much less eager, in that way young people have of being eager. I find myself unable or unwilling to give anything of *myself,* that is. When I was younger, I poured some of my own élan vital into all my contacts with the rest of the world, unthinkingly. Now I am perhaps more cordial, suaver, in my relations with people, even with people I like or love, but I realize with a feeling almost of shock that I am cold and selfish about that pouring out of my élan. I hold it back, saving it perhaps for T. and myself. Now and then, after a weekend with old friends, I realize that in spite of my niceness and my ability as a hostess, I have let them come and go without giving them one spark from my own self, and I feel a kind of disappointment and wonder if they do, too, if they are asking themselves what has changed me. Sometimes I wonder if, instead of not *wanting* to give away any of my élan, I have none left to give. That is an ugly thought. Usually I do not think it, because I know that my relations with T. are warm and complete as ever. But they aren't with anyone else in the world. I have withdrawn, willy-nilly. I have been that way ever since the night in Bern, as if I were concentrating every part of my inner spirit on myself and T. It is wrong, I think. I wonder if other people are that way, too. I imagine a great many are.

We may offer to take one or two refugee children. I had been thinking rather hazily about it, and so had T. without saying anything, and today a letter from Anne about her doing the same thing made us both speak. Of course, it is a terrible gamble . . . but any children would be . . . and I can't bear not to help in some way. We could feed and clothe them better than some and send them to the public schools. It would mean more caution with our money and, of course, would change our peculiar and delightful way of living. I don't know how to go about it. Of course, every autumn I go through a kind of heat for children anyway. We can't have any ourselves. And adopting them has become complicated now that it would be impossible for two divorcés ever to get permission to do so. Which seems too bad. Certainly Tim and I, in spite of our former marriages, are a lot better qualified to raise children than many people. Well . . . I often wish we could. I think there have been several times when Sis would have let me take Shaun, but that would have been a mess because of family complications, to say nothing of Sis's bland ability to give me (or Mother, as the case is now) every responsibility and then feel quite free to criticize Shaun's manner, clothes, and everything else.

Mrs. Purdy came back today, somewhat tottery. I was hoping she would stay away longer, since I enjoy coping with the house myself. I may have to cut her down a bit, especially if we take a child or two.

I'll try to finish *Daniel* this month. That may bring us in a little money.

15. vii. 40

I finished the book three days ago and am started on the typing. It is a pleasant book, in a quiet, unimportant way, and I do hope we at least get some advance royalties on it, as we need the money.

It is steadily hot now, with delightful nights. We eat in the patio quite a lot.

The country, or our hills rather, are turning a soft coppery brown, very beautiful. In the valley the apricot pickers are living in tents under the trees.

24. vii. 40

We have decided to go back to Rochester to the Mayo Clinic. When Anne suggested it, we talked about it and decided not to (I don't remember whether I wrote all this or not). But a letter from T.'s mother makes us feel that Anne is rather hurt about our refusal, so we are going. I know that she understands our hesitation, and I am sure that she hopes, as God knows we do, too, that there may be a chance of help.

We leave Monday noon, the twenty-ninth. There will be many interesting things about it—we both like trains and, of course, the strange uncomfortable excitement of being in a new town and a new bedroom and a new toilet—but now and then I am almost sickened by a quick realization that perhaps we are in for another time of waiting rooms, of pompous puzzled doctors, of the smell of antiseptics and hospital food. I think that I cannot stand it, and then I know what T. must be feeling, remembering the poke of fingers and needles and the looking up from an operating table into the mirror of the light reflectors, and a thousand things that I cannot guess. The whole thing is wretched, and I'll be glad to get it over with. It is hard to say how I really feel about any cure except time's for Timmy's pain. I feel quiescent, I suppose you could say. Perhaps I am a defeatist. I read about fighters like Helen Hunt Jackson, and I am shamed, recognizing my own inertia.

26. vii. 40

Everything is pretty much in order for our trip . . . money came from Anne, tickets are paid for, and so on and so on. It seems strange to be packing again, after so many months here in California.

I feel sad and worried all the time, underneath my natural actions, for several people, and especially for Georges Connes. He is most probably in a concentration camp, in spite of his German decoration and so on from the last war . . . allied with Communists, Jewish name, and so on. I am afraid to write to him, for fear of causing more trouble. We would be glad to help him with the children if we could. I cannot feel that he would want them ever to leave France . . . but strange things are happening. Pierre is the most charming little boy I have ever met. I don't know Marie-Claire . . . but her parents are good.

I got hungry, so I put some cold peas in a dish and put a little soy sauce on them. The combination was terrible.

It seems queer that David never mentions anything about war and conscription and so on. I know he did feel very strongly against all that . . . but he, too, may have changed. Two summers ago, at Le Pâquis, I bet him $50 he'd be in an army, voluntarily, before he was thirty. He'll lose his bet, I think.

30. vii. 40
Raton Pass, Colorado

Dearest Rex:

Edith gave us this nice supply of airplane stamps and so forth, and I'm not even sending her the first letter. All of which shows the power of a $5 bill, I guess! We do thank you for it. It was a complete surprise, and I'm hoarding it—probably for a nice lunch and a drink of German beer at the Muehlebach tomorrow.

The train is so comfortable that we hate to think of leaving it. We had to get two "roomettes," which looked pretty cramped when we got on—but the porter rolled back the whole wall between the rooms, and now we have the most spacious room I've ever seen on a train. The toilets are super-double-deluxe—you turn a little crank, and they swing out from under the beds, complete in every detail!

It seems queer that we're within a couple of hours of Dave. I do hope we can see him on our way back.

The servants and the food are excellent on this train. There is a very nice little headwaiter, and today when we were the last people (as usual!) in the dining car, Timmy asked him if he was Swiss. He whispered that he always said so now but that he was really a German. He looked scared to death, and we left, much embarrassed.

I think we all sort of kind of jumped on you, the other night at dinner, when you confessed that when Noni said she liked journalism more than anything in the world, you couldn't see why she went into training. I can see how you would be puzzled. I imagine she is, too. But I can't help thinking she's making a good choice. You spent quite a lot of effort, when I was in my late teens and early twenties, convincing me that journalism is really no game for a woman, that it toughens and hardens her. And, of course, being a nurse won't stop Noni from writing, if that's her real talent. Look at Mary Roberts Rinehart, and Mignon Eberhart, and a lot of others. And she *will* have a sure and honorable profession behind her, in case of war or her own need of a job.

Give her and Mother my love—and tell Edie I'll write from K. C.—and much love to you from us both—

31. vii. 40
Hotel Muehlebach
Kansas City, Missouri

Dearest Edie:

I got my nice airmail equipment out and then decided to treat you to a sheet of Muehlebach's best stationery.

The hotel is odd, to say practically nothing—1923 elegance plus 1903 cracked lavatories plus 1939 cocktail bars. We had a very nice martini in the Rendezvous, but decided it was too full of schoolgirls and went to the Grill, which was even fuller of women trying to be schoolgirls. There was a very loud band in powder-blue suits—somebody or other and his Sugar Blues Boys. We ate cold roast beef and drank Muehlebach *brau* (which is much better than the hotel), and although we had a lot of fun we felt as if we were escaping from the inside of a large and very sweet cream puff when we "hopped out," as Shaun says.

The trip was easy and fun, in spite of what the altitudes did to poor Tim. We stayed in our room most of the time. And when I say room, I mean *room.* If you ever go east again, try to get a double bedroom. They cost about between a compartment and a drawing room—and I've never seen such a spacious setup. We had a very nice porter—the whole train was nice, in fact. There were a few Hollywood people and a couple of loud-mouthed politicians going back to D.C. to tell the boys what to do. I took you and Sis at your words, and wore my blue silk slacks to lunch, and felt rather queer and extremely comfortable. Boiled mushrooms and bacon on toast made me feel even more so.

We came to the hotel at 7:30, and after baths and whatnot I went to sleep for three hours! I was surprised, too.

I'll write tomorrow from You Know Where. If we have too uncomfortable a night, we may do as we did today, and take baths and so on, and then take a gander at Cousin Kate's line of five hundred people in the afternoon and go back the next morning. I imagine it will be mostly schoolteachers with colitis at the moment.

Give my love to Noni, Rex, Sis, and Wee Edie—Tim's, too—

1. *viii.* 40

Dearest Edie—

We got here about 8:00 this morning—only some ten hours ago, which seems incredible.

The trip from Kansas City was one of the two bumpiest I ever took. Timmy had to sleep in the upper berth, since it was impossible for him to keep from bouncing out of the lower! You can imagine what fun it was to climb up and shoot him. I longed, and not for the first time, for a sturdy tail—or at least a couple more arms.

The hotel is very nice, in the typical chain-hotel way—a pincushion with two threaded needles on the bureau, lots of little signs under the glass tops telling us how passionately the management yearns to be our friends. The wallpaper is fresh, though, and the beds are good, and there's plenty of hot water. The coffee shop is only open when the Elizabethan Grill isn't, so we had to eat lunch (for the first and last time) in the latter. It's a ghastly place, very refined and oak-paneled. As you leave, the well-upholstered hostess gives you a smile and two little mints in a cellophane envelope.

The town is odd. I don't yet know what makes it so. The people don't look any sicker than people you see on the streets anywhere. There are a lot of very poor-looking people—farmers, I'd say—and, of course, a lot of nurses, most of them young and slender. There are a few very unattractive bars and an amazing lot of restaurants and candy stores—and drugstores, naturally. You see and hear many foreigners—Spaniards, Hindus, Chinese. There are a lot of Jews, American and not.

We went over to the clinic about 2:00. It is just like all the stories—impressive marble and bronze and wonderful direction. We were sent here and there, and after a two-hour examination by a famous young neurologist who acted very dyspeptic, Tim emerged with a sheaf of appointment cards. He is now in bed, full of castor oil, and can't eat or drink anything but tea, and has to take an enema at 6:00 tomorrow morning and be at the X-ray place at 7:00! What a life! Then, after a morning being blood-tested, he is free maybe until the next day, when he sees doctors again. These boys are thorough, at least.

I feel silly to ask it, but will you save these letters? I meant to keep a diary, but have a feeling that a letter home will be about my limit, literary or otherwise—and I'd like some notes.

Much love to you all—and thank you for the grand letter we got today. I do hope Rex didn't catch cold at the Norconian. How is the place where I gouged him? I agree with you that we are extravagant—but only now and then, and in between bursts we lead a spotlessly economical life. Much love—

2. viii. 40

Dearest Edie—

This note will really be one, as I am too sleepy and hot to write a letter. We got up at 5:30, after a very bad night for Tim, thanks to an ounce of castor oil which might better have been nitroglycerin, and by 7:00 were well along the path—Desk D-3, third floor—Desk N-7, seventh floor, and so on. He was X-rayed, blood-tested, etc., etc.—and now we'll see what's next when the doctors take him over at 8:00 tomorrow.

We got through at 11:00, and after some breakfast hired a taxi and drove to Winona through beautiful rolling country and fields of corn and clover. We crossed the Mississippi twice.

Tonight we had a very poor dinner in our room and then

went for a walk and decided we'd rather be hung than live anyplace but the Kahler, which is at least impersonal. It's very sticky and hot, and the worst part is that it's impossible to wash any gloves or stockings, because they take days to dry.

I'll write more tomorrow, after we've been to the clinic. Love—

3. viii. 40

Dearest family—

The first two days I spent in the waiting rooms I was interested in the people, but now suddenly I have looked at them all I want to—or perhaps more than that. The thing that impresses me most about them is a rather pessimistic feeling of their lack of dignity. Most of them are middle-aged or old and look as if they should have lived and suffered long enough to acquire that clear outline, that repose—that whatever it is that is supposed to show the Dignity of Man. Of course, many of them do look nice, or kindly, or funny, or something. But that isn't what I mean. They are *not* clear but smudged in their outlines, like a bad photograph which could show their spirits as well as their bodies. They are incoherent, bewildered, petty—and make me wonder what use there is in spending a life without really learning anything. Well—

Of course, practically every person here is completely absorbed within himself—and that is understandable, because it is hard not to be if you have a gut ache or any pain. All your thoughts and actions focus on it—and here that is true of everyone you see, except an occasional companion like me who is equally preoccupied by the pain of another person. The only way you can make any contact with others is to ask them about their experiences with suffering, either real or imagined, and since we are not interested in anyone's but T.'s and don't care to discuss it, we live in a kind of vacuum.

The waiting rooms are impressive marble rooms, very cool and spacious. There are rows of comfortable chairs, and a soft buzz of exchanged weights, temperatures, and other more clinical confidences fills the air as people wait for their names or numbers to be called from one of the two desks. Then they hobble or mince or waddle or bound or totter into one of the rows of little consultation rooms, where young and solemn doctors talk to them. Many of them are ill at ease as they go out of the big room and grin and blush and pull at their clothes and look more like self-conscious children than people going to learn about their lives and deaths.

Last night there was a mighty thunderstorm as violent as the ones in Switzerland but much longer. It made the air better.

There is a carillon on top of the clinic, which is silent at night but rings out a pretty off-key bar or two of a hymn every hour during the day. But yesterday about five o'clock it suddenly broke loose with several Schubert songs, Rachmaninoff's Prelude in-whatever-key-it-is, "Flow Gently Sweet Afton" played like a Bach fugue, part of Dvořák's *New World* Symphony, and a few other such things—and it was actually beautiful, in key and with chords of many bells at once and as many modulations as a fine organ. I looked out the window, and people down in the streets were stopped, puzzled and excited. I think it must have been some famous carilloneur, maybe from Belgium, who is here to get his gizzard fixed and simply broke loose for a while. Whatever it was, it was certainly swinging those bells around. It is the only time that I have wished you were here.

Our drive yesterday was pleasant. We went up to Winona, across the river, and back—had lunch at a fairly nice little place called Ye Hot Fish Shop, where we ate walleyed pike fixed in butter and drank a watery local beer called Bub's. The country seems like a park, with many woods and neat irregular fields of wheat, corn, barley, and pink clover, and the cows and horses are very handsome. The farmhouses are not beautiful like the ones in Pennsylvania, but the silos and the red barns with curved roofs are very handsome and look Russian.

Our driver was a pleasant young man who talked occasionally and drove very well. "From here on it's nothing but bluffs, bluffs, bluffs," he said. "All they eat in Wye-nona is fish, fish, fish." "Most of my work is emergency calls, emergency calls, emergency calls." He was not especially bright.

There are a few children here. They all yell when they get stuck for blood tests, because everybody babies them so.

The hardest thing for most people about the routine tests is having to go without breakfast until 11:00 or so. In a way it's good, because it diverts their minds so that even people who are obviously in great trouble can think of nothing but how hungry they are and for once can discuss that first cup of coffee instead of their metabolism.

Last night it was too hot to sleep, before the storm, so we got dressed and walked around the town. Looking into the sitting rooms and lobbies of all the lodging places was horrible, but we couldn't help it. Apparently the men go to bed, but the women stay up and collect in little circles and talk, talk, talk, as our driver would say.

The shopping district of Rochester looks like that of a much smaller town (it's about 28,000)—mostly candy stores, cafés, flower shops, and uniform shops. There are a couple of movies and a few very dingy-looking bars, which we seem to have no interest in, although the Kahler serves only beer, and that with compressed lips.

Later

After four hours of consultations I brought what was left of Timmy back to the hotel (he tried to escape once to the toilet for a cigarette and got called before he had even lit it), and then we had lunch and went looking for a possible place for me to stay. (Meals have sunk to a mean average of liverwurst on rye and beer, but don't think we're starving). I looked at several hotels and will probably spend $2 more and stay right here.

Tim goes to St. Mary's (Catholic) Hospital at 10:00 tomorrow for experiments on his spine. The biggest man in the clinic (for nerves, etc.) said that he could guarantee absolutely nothing and that nobody knows why men with "good" amputations keep on suffering, one time out of a thousand, when they aren't supposed to. There are two things to do—open the whole leg and trace every nerve for nodules, etc., or block the leg nerves from the spine. They'll do the latter first, and just with novocaine. If that works, they'll cut the nerve, which will mean complete paralysis of that leg and no more chance of an artificial one. It may also do no good, because all the trouble may be coming from some trouble between the spine (or along the spine) and the brain, caused by shock, disease, what have you. In that case, they say there is absolutely nothing to do but live partially doped until you die.

Tim is in pretty good shape, mentally and otherwise, and is more than willing to gamble on getting some help.

I'll write tomorrow, probably. Love from us both—

Dearest family—

It's about 8:30, Sunday evening, and I have finished my first day at St. Mary's. I must confess it was a long one—and, of course, it's still going on for Tim. I hate to leave him, but he got quite worried about my supper, because the Kahler kitchens close at 8:00. I could have gone to a diner or something, but after ten hours at the hospital in my Sunday clothes I felt too hot and sticky. So I came back here and ate some broiled sweetbreads and a vegetable salad, both of which tasted of absolutely nothing but certainly not of sweetbreads and vegetables.

I am horrified about our expenses, in a helpless way. Of course, it's Anne* who'll pay, but still— This hotel is expensive, and the food is not only dull but prohibitive, and although I can and will hop buses, I know I'll also fall into taxis now and then. Tim and I looked at several hotels yesterday, and the only nice one is even farther from St. Mary's than this. But there's one right across from the hospital, very small and noisy but clean, where I could get a bath and room for $2.50. I think if T. has to stay long I'll go there, although he's opposed to it because the bed really did look like a soggy pancake. In the meantime, write here—and often!

I should be doing a few little jobs like getting laundry together, repainting my toenails, bathing—but all I can do is sit.

Tim goes for a trial anesthesia of his spine early tomorrow. If it works, he'll have the real one in a day or two, and it will mean the end of much trouble. If not, they may try a brain operation, or nothing.

Last night we went out about 8:00, after resting from quite a day at chez Mayo, and had two martinis at a very chromium-plated

* Anne Parrish Corliss, Timmy's sister.

little place called the Palace Garden because of three aspidistras in the window, and then went to dinner, where two very strange men who met in a circus twenty-two years ago and have cooked together ever since put on a terrific act for us, and spun full cups of coffee through the air, and cooked us the first decent food we've had here —a ham and green pepper and mushroom omelet made exactly as Tim says the famous omeletteers used to make them at Mont St. Michel, in little black slippery skillets with round bottoms. It was quite astonishing, and we left with an invitation to drive out to Lake Winnetatashahawa or some such place, to meet-the-wife and have some *real* food, and some beer, which is not served there— at the diner. I asked them why, and they said it interfered with the eating! I may go back, if I get hungry enough, but I'm rather leery of being a privileged character—if any.

We then went to a movie, since it was too hot to think of bed (only 80 degrees, but we both longed for an honest-to-God 109 degrees at Bareacres), and saw the first picture we'd ever seen but often heard about made by Republic or Monogram for the sticks. It was acted very bouncily but enthusiastically by farmish people and was about a farm boy whose uncle beat him but loved him after he rescued the uncle's $200 from a hobo, and the little city girl who realized that the country life, represented by many good shots of apple blossoms and pigs, was the best life—and I tell you, it had them in the aisles. The audience laughed and wept and muttered and nudged total strangers (us) at the hot love scenes when the hero took the girl's hand in his, and it was very interesting —especially since we already knew from Hemet that cowboys are only interested in cowboy pictures. And farmers, now, in farm pictures. So I wonder what about gangster pictures?

I hope these letters don't bore you. I'm terribly anxious to hear more about Noni—et al.—

Love from us—

5. viii. 40
St. Mary's Hospital
Rochester, Minnesota

It is perhaps a good thing to write about sitting here waiting for T. to come down from surgery, because if I put on paper the number of times and all that, it seems less immediately terrible—like talking of how many miles the stars are from the earth or how many pennies are in a great fortune. There were three times in Bern, the two operations and then the amputation. In Wilmington there were the two. Now here we begin again. Today is a trial anesthesia of the spine. If it works, the nerves of the leg will be killed in another few days, and as it seems to me now, we will be in paradise. But the doctors are very doubtful that it will work.

Mother asked me to write to her every day—the first time she has ever done that, and I resented it mildly. It seems—it *is*—a selfish demand. But I know why she did it. So far I have been good and have killed two birds with the one stone by making a few notes about Rochester versus Lord and Lady Bareacres at the same time. I felt foolish to ask her to keep my letters, but did so. I should guess that they have been more interesting than if I were keeping a diary, too, since I have written more about everything than I would if I were also putting it here—but I doubt if Mother has enjoyed them as much as she would more routine letters. She is always irked by what she calls "literarian" touches and likes straightforward writing about the weather, how we feel, and what we do. I think most mothers are that way. Of course, in spite of being more discursive in my letters home, because they were at the same time my diary, there are many things I've not said. Perhaps they are better, then, than a more intimate, less controlled report would be—one I did not expect to be read. Perhaps a diary should be written, not as this one, but as letters to one's family. I can see that it is probably just as well that I do not say that Dr. K. has bad breath or that I am so lonely that I have the toothache all over me, at night, missing T. I don't say things like that, feeling them better unsaid to anyone except myself and perhaps someday T. if he ever reads this. So why say them at all, then?

Across from the hospital is a short row of drugstores and little cafés. I can't eat here, so I have started at one end and will eat to the other, unless we leave earlier than I think we will. Yesterday I had lunch at Stirters, a place with a new chromium and black-glass front. It was wretched food. This morning I had coffee and a cinnamon bun in a little bakeshop, so now I feel rather sick, as always after coffee, but at least it makes me go to the toilet if I only drink a little once in a while. It's a queer reaction, I think—and can be one of the most unpleasant, like protracted airsickness.

The nurses here are nice—all graduates and much easier and less pompous than the student nurses at the Delaware. I have never been to such a big hospital—about seven hundred beds, and a new wing building. I wish I could see one of their new operating rooms. A nurse told me that they use a kind of blue light, which is dark toward the floor and then grows lighter toward the ceiling.

Yesterday T. and I decided, more or less, to try to earn our own living if he gets better. If he stays the same, we'll continue to take all the money we can get, from Anne and anyone else who will give it to us. But if he loses his plantar foot, even partially, we are going to leave Bareacres—perhaps rent it, or preferably keep it for our own vacations—and try to support ourselves for a time. We would have to go to a city, where T. would try to get some jobs doing drawings or paintings for advertising, and maybe try to have some shows, and use all the "pull" he could, and I would try to write articles or get a column job or free-lance or anything I could. It would be awful to leave Bareacres, and live in a wretched apartment, and have to pull wires and do a lot of the things we both hate. But we seem to feel that it would be a good thing. If we could we would continue to take Anne's pension and put it in a savings bank—and then maybe we would make enough money to be able to send it back in a year or give it to somebody or something.

I feel upset about Noni's going into training at the Good Samaritan in Los Angeles. It is not a particularly good hospital anymore, but the real reason I am against her being there is that she will be in Los Angeles. She doesn't like it as a city, and the climate is not at all stimulating to her, and for three years she would be expected to check in, every five weekends, at the Ranch or with us or with Sis. Her dates, her clothes, her manners—everything would be inspected, judged. Families can't help that, naturally. But I think it is wrong for a girl of Noni's age and temperament to be quite so close to her home. She'll be expected to go to Aunt Maggie's* for dinner—all her new friends will be suspect (What does his father do?)—if she wears her hair a new way it will be criticized. We can't help it. I have kept quiet to her —but perhaps I am wrong. I often interfere and never know whether it is right or wrong—but this time I'm too far away, and if she has already decided, there is no use in upsetting her. And, of course, N. is clearheaded and probably has thought about all the sides of living in Southern California anyway.

I wonder what T. will be like when he comes back—pale, sick, flushed, silent—I know he has to lie flat. He may be nauseated.

---

* Edith's relative, living in Los Angeles with her daughter Mary.

5. viii. 40

Dearest family—

I spent from 7:00 this morning until 10:30 tonight at the hospital and have to be there at 7:00 tomorrow, so this will not be a letter.

The trial operation was a failure and proves that further surgery is useless and that the trouble is located somewhere along the spine and is therefore impossible to find. They say time may help a little but probably will not, and the only thing to do is keep Tim as comfortable as possible. They say he is in wonderful condition "considering" and should continue to do as Hal says. They are working to find some substitute for Analgeticum.

The disappointment was hard for Tim but hasn't downed him. He is very shaky from the experience this morning—if I hadn't seen his bathrobe on the stretcher I would never have recognized him when they brought him back from the theater—but ought to be able to leave by the end of the week. Tomorrow, unless he has a shock collapse, he has to have some more X-rays —although it seems silly to go on when the doctors all agree there's nothing to do.

I'm upset about Noni. Why is she determined to stay in California? Why not cross the border? Surely there must be an accredited school in Arizona or some such place. I think we all could probably scrape together her fare there if she wanted to go badly enough. Probably the answer to that is that it's none of my business.

How does Rex enjoy being a political martyr? It's really a privilege to be fired from Olsen's regime, I'd say.

Much love—

6. viii. 40

Dearest family—

Tim left the hospital at 8:00 this morning, much against the nurses' and my better judgment—but in Rochester it's kill or win, and Tim says he can see how many a man comes in on roller skates and goes out on a stretcher or whatever the phrase is backwards. He could hardly walk, but we waited for an hour in the clinic and then had a two-and-a-half-hour consultation with five doctors—this with no breakfast but castor oil, to prepare for an intravenous urological examination at 1:30, after no lunch. That lasted for one and a half more hours, which he passed strapped to a steel table on his back, which is black and blue from yesterday. So you can imagine that he is somewhat shattered, as Mary Powers would say.

I don't feel very chatty, but I suppose I might as well tell you, and then we can close the subject permanently, that all the discoveries are very bad and that Tim is in great danger of losing his other leg or, if he is lucky, of dying relatively quickly. He may also get much better and live to a ripe old age, which according to the doctors would be miraculous. By living in a kind of Venetian glass box he might evade another thrombosis—no cigarettes, no excitement, no movement, no painting. Or he could live as normally as possible, as we've been doing at Bareacres, and take the quicker chance. I think I know which way he'll choose.

He has one more consultation tomorrow—the men are trying to find some substitutes for Analgeticum—and then we'll flee, if Tim is well enough. Our one idea is to escape.

Anyway, I'm getting to the end of my airmail stamps!

Love—

7.viii.40
Clinic

This is probably the last consultation, to discuss substitutes for Analgeticum and learn how to care for Tim's one leg. We are in a passively frantic state to leave and, if we were here on our own will and money, would have gone away yesterday. The ninety minutes in the anesthesia room were the second worst T. has ever spent, he says. I do not care to write about it, but think I should. He was given novocaine in the spine, locally, and then 80 cc. of ether. Then he was given an injection in the hand, probably adrenaline, and whenever he got too far away from the doctors in his mind, he had to breathe oxygen. He can't talk about it very coherently, but says that his whole body grew yellowish and numb, except his head, shoulders, and amputated leg. (The ether was given through a rubber sheet into the middle of the back.) His fingers twisted into strange shapes. He lost all sense of space and was now like a pea, now like a great echoing deserted warehouse filled with strange winds and blue brilliant lights and terrible noises. The doctors poked everywhere with a kind of cobbler's awl, asking him if he felt it and if it was dull, sharp, hot, cold, so that now his body is covered with small red spots.

When the stretcher came in, he was making strange soft noises, quite insane. He seemed to have shrunken and lay in a kind of boneless way, crying out for me. It took about three hours to quiet him and to get him warm. He was violently sick once, about an hour after he came down, but in three hours drank some vile coffee through a tube as if it were nectar. He ate a little lunch and later drank a small glass of beer—able to lift his head about noon. His back ached badly, and his little leg was terribly painful. I gave him a shot about 3:00. The big doctor came in and said the operation was a failure and that it proved further surgery was useless, and then went out abruptly.

The next morning T. was very shaky still and inclined to cry for no reason, much to his embarrassment. He had some coffee and castor oil, and then we came to the clinic, where after an hour's wait he had another two-and-a-half-hour consultation with doctors, who told him that he has Buerger's disease (a kind of chronic phlebitis), and that he must choose between cigarettes and losing his other leg, and that really there is no way to prevent another Bern episode, a quicker death, or, for that matter, a long life. At 1:30, after an enema and no lunch, he spent one and a half hours strapped to a metal table having an intravenous urological test—an injection of 100 cc. of something that caused bad neural pain for a few minutes and then a tingling all over that lasted several hours. When he finished, he was completely exhausted.

He rested, with a good shot, and then asked to go to the one pub we know, where he had beer and a sandwich, and then had a haircut. He was sick again when he got back. We went out to dinner, and he ate a little rare steak and some sliced tomatoes, which he managed to keep from losing. He slept very well and today looks better, although his hand still shakes and he feels tearful and "whuddery inside."

I don't feel like talking about this. We regret bitterly that we came back here—but, of course, the result might have been different, and we agreed to take the chance. The life the doctors yesterday said T. should lead—no cigarettes, no action, no excitement, no painting—would be less than life. If we had not come here, we'd have gone on at Bareacres as we were, living easily and compromising with the pain. And I imagine that is what we will continue to do, although T. knows that I am willing to do whatever he decides.

The man next to us has a strange, bad smell. On the other side of us, two plump women compare visits to the clinic. I am going down now to try to find out something from Information about finances, which so far have been veiled in a heavy and discreet silence.

It seems that everything is in code, which can only be read at the conclusion of the treatment. Ho-hum.

One thing we noticed in Kansas City and here when we first came, but do not anymore, was the pallor of all the faces. Of course, there are a few brown farmers, but most of the people are very pale. A great many of the women, even very well-dressed women and girls, chew gum all the time and everyplace. Many people use toothpicks.

It seems to me that if we could go back to Bareacres and see *no* one, not Mrs. Purdy, nor Arnold, nor the grocer, nor any of the family, for a few days, we could get rid of all this—get rid of having been poked and pushed and talked to and fed and smelled by all these people, the doctors and all the people in the waiting rooms and the cafés and the streets, those we have seen and those others hidden from us in their rooms everywhere.

7. viii. 40

Dearest Edie—

We leave here tomorrow evening and will spend the next day in Kansas City and arrive the next morning at 10:15 in Colorado Springs, where we will spend a day or two at the Antlers' Hotel with Dave if he is not off for the weekend and with some of T.'s old more-or-less friends if he is.

We slept until 9:00 this morning for the first time in months, and it did us both good. Tim was worn to a string. We were all afternoon at the clinic, and then after a rest we took a taxi out to a little bend in the Zumbio River and had an awful meal that tasted almost delicious.

Today I've been sorry I sent you such a bald statement of our present situation, but that is the way it is. Tim, one out of several hundred thousand in the world, has Buerger's disease, and thanks to a strong heart and Hal's treatment and the quiet life of Bareacres is in pretty good condition in spite of it. We have pages of written instructions and hours of oral ones, all of which are reduced to the facts that he must keep certain niggling care of his foot (remaining), and keep absolutely quiet, and not smoke (nicotine very dangerous). I think he is working out his own little plan for life, and God knows any man of his age and brains should have that privilege.

It will be fine to see Dave.

I'll telegraph from Colorado Springs when we'll be home. We'll get off at San Bernardino and telephone from Bareacres or drive over or something—it will be wonderful to be home again—

Much love to you all from us both—

28. viii. 40
Bareacres

At this moment my chief feeling is one of a kind of triumph that I have got T. to consider starting a journal. He writes naturally and clearly and from long since, and I think has often felt the need of it. So now he has the book half of my diary, with some sheets in it that I will add to tomorrow, and a pencil . . . and I hope for many reasons that he will begin to write.

We've been reading the journal he kept in Cornwall, and it is good because of the watercolors on almost every page, because of the minutiae of a life that can never be repeated because of war and age and other accidents, and because it shows sides of T. that he strives hard to keep covered. It also shows pompous, whimsical, wordy sides now and then, which in the reading make him squirm . . . but the main thing is good. Of course, to me as his wife it is more than that. It appeals in some ways to the Peeping Tom side of me—I feel that I am snatching peeks at a man usually well hidden, and therefore I am victorious. But there are better parts. Some of his thoughtful phrases, set down almost apologetically, move and stir me. And I am ashamed of my own sporadic and egocentric efforts at journal keeping. I realize more than ever how completely monotonous I make this fairly unrestrained chronicle . . . it is I, my thoughts, what happens to me, what I do. God, it is dull. There again the idea is probably to write as T. did, knowingly for an audience of at least one, Anne, and hopefully for perhaps me and Al and one or two others. This idea of mine is not much more than a kind of mental masturbation, which I have to admit relieves me now and then of things in my mind—still egocentric— that are bothering me and that must not be said aloud. That may be all right as a kind of medicine but as anything worth reading to another human it fails completely. Of course, I have not read any of this . . . but when I think of opening it four years from now, as T. let me do with his Cornwall journals, and reading it aloud to him and perhaps Norah, I am embarrassed not only by some of the disgusting or defamatory things that would appear but also by its inescapable dullness. How much better to write of the animals, the weeds, the changes of weather, than of my internal woes!

Perhaps I shall try to. But really I have no idea of risking such a reading as Noni and Tim and I gave his journal last week. I shall get rid of this book. And in the meantime, at least now and then, in spite of my efforts to talk of cats when my heart is full of terror, I shall occasionally if not altogether ignore the cats.

I sent off the uncorrected typed ms. of *Daniel Among the Women* today. I tried it out on Norah, who was noncommittal except for saying that she found the sisters more interesting than Daniel and that he was an annoyingly dull young man. That, of course, was what we meant him to be . . . so perhaps our one guinea pig proves the novel a great success. I wish Pritchett could sell it to a slickie and make us some money . . . but the chances are slim. It is not an especially exciting novel. And she is not a very good agent. And the times are bad, to put it obscenely.

T. has decided to detoxicate himself from the use of Analgeticum beginning October 1, when the weather will be better and the visits from various relatives fewer. We will do it under Hal's direction, of course. Hal and the doctors at the Mayo say it will not be too difficult, since T. is not a true narcotic. I do not look forward to it, and yet found myself last night delivering a stiff little lecture to T. about the danger of romanticizing the whole thing into another *Journal d'une Désintoxication,* complete with Cocteau's drawings and phrases like howl-like-a-dog and between-iced-blankets and so on.

To tell the truth to myself, I don't see how T. can go through with it. He has been much worse since his trip to Rochester, with an almost constant backache, probably from the spinal anesthetic, and a really frightening weakness. He paints little, although what he does is very good in a strange exaggerated way. The lines and the colors are violent and twisted. At times he is hardly rational. I have more than doubled the shots in strength, feeling that he should rest as much as possible before October and that there was no use saving something for nothing. But they don't seem to do much good. He is in almost constant pain. The last three days he has drunk more whiskey than before. He says it makes his little leg feel warmer . . . and I can't see any other effect on him. But it makes me remember sitting in the Restaurant Français du Casino

in Bern with David, just before T.'s amputation, and telling him
that if T. lived through it, I was afraid he might become an alcoholic. That is silly, probably.

Nevertheless, I have been filled, for several weeks now, with
a terrible silent inward depression. When T. goes to bed in the
middle of the day and lies there quietly without even reading, I
think, He'll never get up again. And when he is nauseated from a
meal, which happens quite often, I think, He'll never eat again.
And so on. It is ridiculous. I don't seem to brood and mope—
I sleep fairly well and eat too much and drink more even than I
want and talk a lot about too many things—but underneath it all
is this terrible empty resignation. I hate it. It follows me like my
own shadow, and I wonder for how long. Perhaps October will
decide it.

We had Arnold Elliott build a fine kennel for us between the
sleeping porch and the dry brook where someday we hope to have
a little swimming pool. It is about twenty-by-thirty feet, with a
three-section roomy house at one end, with a top that lifts up for
cleaning and airing, and at the upper end a hydrant so that I can
keep fresh water there without too much bother. Saturday Arnold
will cut out some steps down to the gate so that it won't be so hard
for Tim, and me, too, to get down there. Now all we need is a dog
for it. We are afraid to put Butch in it alone because of wildcats.
T. wants a dachshund. Myself, I would like a large mixed-breed
dog with a heavy yet easy frame and loving brown eyes. Perhaps
we can get both, which really would not be much more trouble
than one. Of course, two, especially if one were large, would be
more expensive to feed. . . .

While Noni was here, last week, Arnold came up with a box
of very pretty little pins and buttons and so on that he had made
from tiny pinecones. T. gave Noni a pair of becoming waxy brown-
green earrings, and I got some sweater buttons for Sis. Arnold is

ingenious, but like so many such people, he will soon lose enthusiasm for this new pastime and drop it just when he had promised to fill many orders for his buttons and such. I have a lovely cluster of pepper berries that I picked Sunday at Soboba, and I think perhaps he could take such clusters while they are still juicy, and dip them in a kind of shellac he uses on everything so that they would not shed and crumble, and make very pretty boutonnieres and hair ornaments of them. I must remember to speak to him on Saturday. But by then he probably will be heart and soul in some scheme to change the drinking fountains at Ramona Bowl or to become governor of a western state, which last he confessed to Tim was his great ambition.

Norah's week here was a pleasant one. I think she and Georges Connes are the two best people to have around . . . best in that they are both easy and stimulating. I noticed that although T. and I led an almost uninterrupted life while she was here—not so easy for two people and a guest in five rooms—we at the same time made an enjoyable effort to be more entertaining, more interesting, more amusing. That is a good sign now and then, I think. Some guests make existence itself seem a bloody chore, no matter how fond you are of them as people, people unassociated with the private life you must lead no matter how many extra meals there are, and clean towels, and beds, and tender feelings. Rex and Edith, for instance, exhaust me almost painfully after only a few hours, and it is not only the many extra things I must do for them —things that they take for granted that are quite foreign to T.'s and my usual life, like breakfast with eggs-toast-marmalade-coffee-morning-paper—but it is their constant *presence*. They are always on my mind. No matter how well I know them nor how accustomed to their manners and their lives, I am spiritually unable to accept them easily. I must constantly *think* of them . . . of the chairs they are sitting in, and the look on their faces, and the way they slept last night, and the cigarettes near their hands to be smoked or not, and what I shall next say to them and they to me. That all makes for fatigue. I think it is stupid and try very hard to combat it. But the fact remains that I cannot live easily with them, as I can with a few people like T., Norah, Connes, sometimes David, in the past Larry Powell, and now and then Eda.

The last weekend was miserable. At first, until a few hours ago in fact, I was much upset by it, but now I see that the best thing is to think of it as something long since past, instead of writing letters in my head about it to Sis, Noni, myself.

When Sis arrived with Dave she looked exhausted. Her hair was untidy, and her face was gaunt and sallow, with swollen eyes. We sat for a time and had a drink, and then at my suggestion she went in and took a shower and changed into some of my play clothes and came out, looking fresh and happier. Supper was pleasant, and afterward we went in and built a fire with the windows open, which is always especially nice.

We played some records . . . I began to play certain ones for certain people, I must admit with some amount of flattery and cajoling in my mind, for I have known for a long time that the best way to have a pleasant time when Sis is around is to flatter and soothe her in every possible way with her favorite foods, colors, sounds, and all.

Then, for some reason, we began to talk, and before we knew it we were having a pretty emotional argument about modern cemeteries and how despicable the whole system of graveyard hypocrisy has become. Sis likes her job, as we all know, and we all said we were glad she did and that she had it and was making a decent salary, but in our own ways we all told her that she should not let the crap she has to hand out from 8:00 to 5:00 each day ever creep into her relations to her family. I talked, inevitably, of the strange experience Al and I had getting his father buried in Forest Lawn, where she works, and Sis said quite plainly that I was so prejudiced by one experience, which she intimated broadly was pure imagination, that I had influenced the whole family against the place. At that Dave, who was fairly silent, said that it was wrong to think that I had given Mother and Rex ideas that they had held strongly ever since he could remember. Tim kept saying things very calmly. We all talked without any shouting. I remember that Sis looked very pretty, sitting on the couch, and that Noni was upset. None of us had had much to drink, but once I found myself almost crying at the thought of Sis's being swept away by the vulgarity of the things she was saying—all about how people needed F. L. and how happy it made them to be cared for in their sad moments by trained grave psychologists, and so on—and I left the room for a minute. Then I came back, and it was still going on. There were some more sharp criticisms of the system as *we* hated it, not as the public, and then Sis said something like, "Why, those fine people out there are *glad* to do anything in their power to assure the poorest man in the country perpetual care for his loved ones," or some such phrase that was obviously part of a sales talk, and I said, "Yes, at 25 percent." Sis looked at me, not pretty anymore, and said very calmly, "Dote, that's the dirtiest, most low-down, sneakingest thing you have ever said to me."

I was simply floored. I truly had no idea what she was talking about. I kept thinking, Well, here it is. Here it is. She had always hated me, and now it's out. Now here it is. We can never be easy and nice together again. At last she's come out with it.

Then I began to think of Mother, and of the awfulness of family quarrels, and of how Sis and I have always hated sisters who fuss in public, like Constance Lewis and Mrs. Hall. I knew it could not go on from there and that if I did not do something that very moment, it would be impossible ever to stop the tide of malice and suspicion that had opened there between us. So I said that I was very sorry that I had said anything to make her feel that way and that I hoped she would forgive me. It was one of the most difficult things I have ever done, especially there in front of the children.

She did not accept my apology, nor did she offer to apologize to me for saying such a hateful thing. Soon after that we all went to bed.

The next morning she was fairly nice but never once looked at me. I felt wretched, as I had all night, even in my dreams— wretched that such a bad thing had happened at all and that it had happened for the first time in either of our lives and in front of T. and the children. I had talked about it to T. when I went to bed, and he said very quietly what I should have known all along, that, of course, Sis was planning to sell lots or some kind of funeral business at Forest Lawn and that my remark about percentages caught her unaware on a spot of uneasy conscience. I think he is right. It is a bad business.

We were all to go to Soboba to swim that morning, but David asked to stay home to draw. He was polite but obviously upset. We went swimming and had a nice quiet time. Sis and I walked to the Lonesome Pepper and talked casually of Shaun and the weather and such. T. and Noni talked a little, waiting for us, and Noni said that Anne was almost speechless with rage, not only at me but at all of us—that she felt we had deliberately ganged against her.

Driving home she made some of her unpleasantly sneering remarks about Mother's friendship for and dependence on what Sis calls her "inferiors"—Mrs. Svensen, Lera, and so on. Of course, I don't like either woman, but I made a few platitudinous remarks about nobody's ever liking anyone else's friends and so on, because Noni is currently pleased by Svensen, and I thought that any chance the poor child has to have a little fun and go to concerts and so on should not be hindered, stuck as she is there at the Ranch. But Sis said that it was very queer how I had changed, since I always used to agree with her about Lera and Svensen and Mother's other stooges. To her it was another proof that I was siding with the children against her. But how could I go into it in front of Noni? I just had to say something about not being too harsh on other people's friends. We finished the drive in uncomfortable silence.

Then at lunch David descended from his tower of silence, and we all began to talk about influences in art, and I made some very silly and really rather funny remarks about Rouault, and we were all laughing, and then Sis began to talk about me—about how much less dictatorial I used to be, and so on. I found myself trying to hide her ill temper from the children, wondering at myself as I did so. It was a kind of vanity, I suppose . . . not wanting them to see how she, and therefore I, as her contemporary, could be small. But it did not work. Their faces grew stony, and we all tried to talk of other things.

She did not look at me as she left but spoke politely, as did I. I had ashes in my heart, truly, and longed to say, No, no, don't let this bad weekend stay so, don't let all this go on. But there seemed nothing more to do. I planned to write to her at once. I talked to T., very troubled. Then I waited for the Monday mail, thinking perhaps she would write and accept my apology and tell me that she had not meant those cold mean words. But no. Tuesday a postcard came, asking me to send up her bathing suit and coat, which she had left, and thanking us for a grand weekend. There is nothing to do, I suppose, but I am upset and sad even now. I wish that I could write to Sis, because I have a long and deep horror of family trouble. But there is nothing to say, I suppose. I think if I did write, she would laugh and pretend at least to have forgotten it. Perhaps she has. Perhaps it was all in my head. But sometimes since Sunday I have thought that she is basically a bad-tempered woman and that as she grows older she is making less and less effort to act any way but exactly as she feels at the moment. It is one thing in novels about tempestuous and beautiful nitwits but another when one must adapt not only one's own life but the lives of one's guests to an undisciplined person such as Sis is becoming. As I said, the only way to have a good time with her . . . and she can be a lot of fun if she wants to . . . is to direct all attention of every kind—food, light, drink, conversation, color—to please her. As it was, for that hateful weekend, I debated a long time over the menus, knowing that Sis would not eat melons, that onion made her ill, that she hated beer and white wine and red wine, that she would not eat in the patio because of insects, that she liked her bed made with the blanket around her face . . . and so on. It is ridiculous, I kept telling myself . . . because she does little to please other people, unless it is to her advantage in either a physical or a material way.

Well, it was hateful. I shall not mention it again. This weekend will please her, since she is to drive to Laguna with David and a friend from Princeton and spend the weekend down there with them and Noni. She will feel beautiful and attractive and dominating, and she is all of those, especially when she is far from me. And that, of course, is what the whole thing is about.

But I shall never feel the same for hearing her say those calm hateful words to me.

30. viii. 40

This morning, after a wretched night during which I prickled here and there constantly as if little fleas were nibbling me, and once felt very put out with T., and then went into a little nap and dreamed that I was really making to him the icy speech that I had only thought about . . . this morning about 6:30 I got up to give T. the sixth shot he had asked for and got since 10:00 last night. I gave it to him—they were all double strength, too—and then said very calmly and noncommittally that the last two days had proved how impossible it would be ever to live with narcotics available without strict discipline, since he had been asking for more shots every day and had had as little help from them as if he only took one or two. In fact, yesterday was an almost impossible day . . . in spite of the fact that he had five and a half ampules instead of the usual one and a half. He said that the days had been unusually bad, and I said that perhaps that was because he knew that he could have as much help as he asked for. Then I pretended to go to sleep again. I had not been at all cranky and had said what I had to say very simply.

He dozed a little, and then I began to read and the new kitten Blackberry climbed up the screen and began to cry, and T. woke up and we listened to the 7:45 news . . . which seems a little better lately, especially since French Central Africa had pledged to support de Gaulle and the Allies. Tim looked at me with his face quite flushed and a strange embarrassed look and said, "Now for a good breakfast of cereal." I said, "Fine," and then realized that he wanted me to say, "Why?" So I did. "Well, I've gone on the dope wagon . . . bang . . . like that." I said, "Oh, that's good," or something like that, and we decided to let Dave come down Tuesday as planned, and live every other day on watermelon as Hal said, and keep ourselves mildly occupied. It was all quiet and easy. But inside I was in a tremble and still am. It means more to both our lives than almost anything that could happen, and now that it's finally here I am not at all scared, as I have been increasingly as I waited for October 1 to come. I think T. is brave and good and that he has been infinitely wise to decide abruptly this way, both for himself and for me. I have been miserable and frightened and have noticed it in my sleep and all the time . . . a kind of nervy bravado about thinking and talking and even eating. Now we can do what there is to do and then perhaps start all over again, in a few days or few weeks.

After breakfast I put away the Analgeticum and the alcohol and the distilled water and the syringe, and as I did it I found myself cold and a little sick with a really live disgust, especially for the syringe. I hated it and could hardly bear to treat it with care and gentleness. Of course, I must . . . there may be times when I will need it, to give T. a shot of Pantopon if he ever has any more of those mysterious cramps of the rectum. Perhaps he never will . . . or not for months, anyway. In the meantime, I feel as if I had been freed from a noisome enslavement to that horrible little metal box. All the horror it used to give me, to see even a needle or a photograph of an injection, all the struggle I had over my own nerves and stomach before I could even watch the doctors shoot Tim in Bern, all the times I practiced in Adelboden and then hurried into my room to drink water with ammonia in it . . . all that came over me this morning as I put the things delicately away, and I was nearly sick.

Now I feel strange and light and a little silly. I hope it lasts. I am keenly interested in the various stages of poor T.'s next days and will write what I remember of them . . . perhaps.

We are both of us disturbed and worried by what we hear and infer about Anne and Jo and Quantness. Of course, Mrs. Parrish, who has been writing often lately in a passing rush of loneliness and ill health, is still bitter about Anne's marriage. In fact, I think she is more so than ever, since she sees that after two years Anne still prefers Jo's company to hers. She pretends that she is only happy at Anne's happiness and says all her reiterated things about Jo's deceitfulness, snobbishness, weakness, on and on, as quotations from Uncle Boney and Doctor Springer and the McCartneys and so on.

Anne, who has only seen her mother twice since she married almost two years ago, although she has lived within from two to four hours of her, writes voluble letters about how terribly busy she is, and how "frighteningly ill" Jo is, and how desperately tired she is, so that it is impossible to go to Claymont. In the meantime, she entertains a constant stream of Jo's friends and, in an effort to amuse her mother, paints lively pictures of their various oddities. She also invites Mrs. P. to come to Quantness, at the same time telling of her rushed fatigue, and has twice committed the unpardonable sin of entertaining the McCartneys. It is all miserable . . . mainly because Mrs. P. is very old, is ill, and through years of adoring and generous treatment from A. has been turned into a spoiled child, so that now at Anne's apparent heartlessness she is bewildered and hurt.

T. and I have always felt that Anne was foolish to let Jo's friends build Quantness and to run it for him and them in an almost hysterically generous way, and now we are almost disgusted with her for the way she is talking about Anthony Hope, the refugee they have taken in. It was all a mistake, as well as a silly mix-up, due, according to Anne's first written admission that some of Jo's friends are not only foolish but definitely crooked, to Auriol Lee's promising to get them eight-year-old girl twins and then telling them casually that a fifteen-year-old boy was on the way. So Anne, frightened and dismayed, has made no bones about being disappointed and writes with her usual entertaining garrulity about its unfortunate heredity and worse environment and what in God's name shall she do with it. And T. and I think that is a wretched preparation for any child, no matter how bad he may be. It fills the air with prejudice and discomfort. Worse, it seems to indicate to us the whole unhealthy atmosphere of Anne's home, which more than most should be clear and good.

It is wrong for us to criticize her, I suppose. But we both know her pretty well and like and love her . . . and it is impossible not to wonder about her. The fact that she sent us a present of $500 after Rochester does not make it any easier to dismiss things she does that worry us.

We decided to spend some of the money on a kennel, which we would then fill with Butch and one or two other dogs, preferably a dainty little dachshund and a nice big sheepdog. But yesterday morning I telephoned Walkerdine and the Humane Society and talked to a lot of other people . . . and no dogs. It was something of a letdown. Today we may go to Juniper Flats or some such place, where we have heard of a man who raises coon dogs, the only kind that are known to kill wildcats. In the meantime, Arnold is making some unusually nice steps down the embankment to the kennel, which he insists on dyeing with a bright brown cement paint he invented himself and is proud of. I hated it . . . but perhaps it will fade, and the outline of the steps is good.

I am somewhat at loose ends, but only temporarily. I do puttery jobs about the house and yesterday read a book about some Anglo-Catholic nuns in India that made me wish that I had written it, because I would have done it better, I think. But I didn't write it . . . and what is more, I probably could not.

31. viii. 40

It seems strange to eat the half of a melon with precision, pushing the spoon meticulously into its side for each bite, and listening to the radio play some goddamned silly *Variations on a Theme* by Elgar, and feeling jubilant that T. has gone into the bathroom to wash his teeth but anxious, when he coughs, that he may have gone in there to be sick again.

He started at noon yesterday, some six hours after his last shot, to be violently sick at about two-hour intervals and to cry ceaselessly into Kleenex tissues without wanting to. He cried until about 3:00 this morning, but from then on he cries only occasionally and, to his surprise and distaste, when I touch him—because the time before he liked it—or when Butch brings a little rubber chewing doll into the room. He is somewhat sickish still but without vomiting. I rubbed his back and buttocks about every one and a half hours during the night and today, and it seems to relieve him for the time and to divert him. He is not so much jittery, although he is that, as in great pain. As he says, he has no special craving for Analgeticum as such but simply a great suffering. I can see that he is better even than he was yesterday or four hours ago, but, of course, I would not tell him so. He perspires freely and naturally, and in spite of absolutely no sleep, his eyes are quite clear.

I called Hal at 8:00, feeling that he might be away for the Labor Day weekend, and almost in spite of myself my heart was warmed to hear his enthusiasm, his thankfulness almost, that Tim had decided to do this. He said it wouldn't last more than two or three days, and that the vomiting was a good sign, and that T. would never right it. He said no food or yeast for two days, but frequent glasses of hot water with a small pinch of baking soda.

I think T.'s washing his teeth is a very good sign. Last night I slept on the porch, while he was in the bedroom. He drew a few horrible pictures of monstrous tortured faces, and had at several magazines, and kept the radio on at some scratchy all-night station. I was in a state of subacute horror, I think. I made my ears stop hearing his cries and the sounds of the worn-out records—almost —and my mind stop thinking—almost—and slept in many

patches to dream unusually agreeable dreams, mainly about the
duke and duchess of Windsor, who came to see us and precipitated
a terrible war in Hemet between us and all the social matrons led
by Oliver P. Dusley's worthy if uncomfortably pompous woman.

Those were the *Enigma Variations*. I think Elgar often tried
to add a little depth and interest to his musical piddlings by such
titles or by saying they were portraits of his friends—guess who—
Quite possibly I malign him, but fortunately or not, it doesn't
matter.

A nice letter from Noni, thoroughly swept on by the familiar
family-tide of Take-Shaunie-to-the-dentist, doctor-it's-time-to-go-
uptown-let's-go-to-a-movie, so that she has not even one word
done on the two stories she thought to send us this week. I know
all that too well. Tim, too.

Thunder behind Tahquite makes me look up at the mountains
in spite of myself and see in their dark heavings the strange flat
slopes to the Grammont and a storm rolling from the Savoie, oily
and portentous. San Jacinto is farther and bigger and finer, as
mountains go, and I have a better feeling about it, but sometimes
I try hard not to look at it because of something there that brings
the Grammont into my mind's view with a sad feeling of right and
pain and homesickness. I never felt "put" there, as I do here. But
it is true, in spite of my fairly skittish feeling that such a phrase is
hackneyed and literary, that I left much of my spirit at Le Pâquis.
When we drove past it, a year ago, I could not bear to look.
Someday I shall go back. Of course, I looked at the house. I saw
that it was sweet and well cared for—not now, all sandbagged and
alone—but I did not really see it, for fear of seeing us there, in the
garden and under the federal wall and pollarding the willows and
sitting at some silly picnic with Mary Powers and David and Noni
and Anne in the forest of Arlburg.

Louise Elliott, Arnold's oldest, a fourteen-year-old with a wise pointed face and a tiny body, is singing a song that reminds me of one I used to hear from an unseen Majorcan woman in the place on the Rue Monge in Dijon. She is stringing wire into the fence of the new kennel. Lena, Arnold's wife, is talking as always in her harsh flat voice, and Arnold answers her abstractly. The thunder grows nearer. "Gee, don't it seem, don't it seem, honey, as if it ain't no time from Christmas to pageant, once Christmas is here?" Her voice rasps amicably into the crisp air. "Arnold, this morning I was walking down to the spring and *Honey* and this crazy old man says—and I says—and—" she laughs. Arnold laughs and slops a little cement onto the rock steps. Lena bores him to distraction with her gabble, but there is a nice feeling between the two of them, and I can see how she is a good wife, generous, severe, with a trim waist and full firm breasts, attractive in spite of her cockatoo voice and her strange stringy Egyptian hair.

It has begun to rain, large drops but sparsely, so that the hot air has that dusty but cooking smell that I have almost always liked. Little Louise, wrinkling her thin face, laughs and prances between the drops delightedly, looking at me without shyness as I stand on the front terrace watching Arnold get an old tarpaulin from the Bantam to protect the steps.

A few minutes ago I heard Louise call to her mother to come watch Arnold take off the leaf. I watched, too, from the porch, as he peeled the big castor-bean leaf from the puddled cement on the bottom step. It was thundering nearer, and Lena was shrieking amicably with her hair in curlers for Saturday night, and Louise was talking excitedly about some black granite that her father had once shown her near Pala, I think. I could hear T., at the other end of the house, retching violently in the bathroom, for the first time since 6:00 this morning.

The shower is over, but the air is still heavy and gray. I have paid Arnold ($19.50 for labor for kennel and steps, with a bill for about $30 yet to come from the lumberyard), and we are alone here on the hill. I made T. a little drink of cold water and whiskey, but doubt if it does him any good. He feels very sick, but it is the pain in his phantom foot that is torturing him. Still—he is much quieter than yesterday at this time, partly from fatigue and partly because he is accustoming himself, I think.

I am sticky and shiny. It is no use bathing yet, though. I remember a day like this in Laurel Canyon, when John and Gigi and Al went swimming and I was afraid to write to T., so I started a long letter to Al about our six or seven anniversaries. I typed it and bound it together, months later, with his beloved stapler, and gave it to him. As far as I know, he never read it. Finally, in La Tour when I was going through the books last year, I tore it up. It was interesting because it showed how very much I wanted him to love me instead of some misty picture he worshiped called My Wife and because it spoke of the first time I ever saw this valley, on our fourth anniversary [1933]. I loved it and wanted to live here, and we talked to Bev Grow in San Jacinto about renting an old mill or garage, but we knew that we had no money to live anywhere but in the family's home in Laguna and that Al would really loathe it anyway. I remember writing about San Jacinto village, and the hot sweet night as we walked back to the Vosburg from the movie, and a big rich car full of haughty careless young people with dark eyes and hair, who swept down from the hills and through the village as if they had owned it since God. They were beautiful, in a wild ugly way.

N.B. Soeur Irma—I have always had a certain precision about my actions, but it was from her that I came to crystallize my need to formalize, to "tidy." Now, when T. goes into the bathroom, I straighten the bottles of alcohol and Dorothy Gray Hot-Weather Cologne, the Mennen's Antiseptic Oil, and the Squibb's Baby Powder into one line. I wipe off the top of the little radio case and the table with a piece of Kleenex. I empty and wipe out the ashtray. I put all the magazines in a neat graduated pile and tighten the bottom sheet of the bed and plump the pillows. I do all this and more as I would wash my teeth to avoid feeling fuzz on them, because I know the hopeless fuzzy feeling, especially in a "sick-room," of a place without order. And I remember that big room at the corner of the third floor of the Viktoria Hospital, with the round parlor table and its completely unused complement of two armchairs and two straight chairs. The table was covered with a cut-velvet "throw" of green or red or mustard—God knows—and over it a clean white cloth edged with wide crochet. On it was the formidable array of bottles, ranged thoughtfully according to their usage and all toeing an invisible line some inches back from the blotting pad and the inkwell for the clinic sheet. A chair waited for Dr. Nigst's handsome, outwardly confident behind, and the pen was wet for him, and the bottles were in their recommended order for his daily ballet of injections—and behind all this Soeur Irma moved quietly, automatically, just as I move now to put the four-inch powder can carefully in front of the five-inch oil bottle and the two-inch cologne bottle. Nobody cares but me—and Soeur Irma—but to us it makes, perhaps, the difference between reason and delirium, the inch of order that justifies a mile or so of agony and sweat and chaos.

This may sound foolish. Truth to tell, I do not care.

Adelaide Arnold just called to ask us to a tea tomorrow when the illustrator of her next book would be able to chat with us of mutual acquaintances—probably Dorothy Lathrop and the children's librarian of the N. Y. Public Library. I asked about her book. She spoke wearily, deprecatingly. She asked about mine. I spoke nonchalantly. Then she said that "old friends from the Smithsonian" were going north with her. I spoke of the lovely weather in San Francisco now, and while she said knowingly that it would be cold later and I murmured, "Yes, yes," inconsequentially, I thought, They would be old—from the Smithsonian—like my little dressmaker, always little.

1. ix. 40

Today, at about five o'clock, it is dark and almost cool, the first straight gray day we have had since we came here. The rusty bloody slopes of wild buckwheat glow in the impersonal light, and all around the valley there are occasional shots from the heights, as there were this morning, for the opening of dove season.

Last night we went into a complicated soothe-Timmy routine, as he said, and gave enemas, warm drinks, massages, this and that. Then I went to bed and immediately to sleep, about 11:00. After about two hours of concentrated fidgeting, including several trips to the toilet to get rid of the aftermaths of the enema and a violent bout of sickness, not to mention a severe coughing spell and so on, Tim, who according to himself was twitching like an old mule with hives, set himself foggedly to sit out the night, complete with rugs, water, cigarettes, and radio. He dimly remembers throwing himself on the bed for a minute, and he woke up some four hours later. I gave him a rub then, and he slept for another hour.

Today, although he is obviously in great discomfort, is nothing like yesterday. He looks worse, probably, with pouchy eyes and a swollen lower lip, and his wrists are swollen, too. But he is able to sit still for half an hour at a time, and has laughed several times, and told me that although he felt god-awful in his poor little leg, it was wonderful not to feel the dreadful time sense that he felt when he knew that six o'clock or two o'clock meant a shot to help him. He feels freer now, and that is good.

Contrary to Hal's council, he has eaten a little today . . . some

vegetable broth and for lunch a broiled peach and a slice of bacon
. . . probably foolish, but I can't help believing that the psychical
effect of a somewhat exotic dish offsets the harm it might do,
whereas a plate of unsalted zucchini might send T. into a little tizzy
of depression. I would not feel the same way about a child, probably . . . but a man forty-six years old cannot be built or rebuilt in
one day or year.

I feel tired and will write no more.

I have been invited to a lunch at Freda van Benschoten's on
Tuesday and am going. I like her a little more than I dislike her,
probably. She is harmless, I think, until I see her in my mind's eye
the frightening heroine of a strange story full of well-bred murder,
arson, rape, and mayhem, always discreet and always speaking like
a lady.

Later

Gastronomically I have in me the makings of one of those fat old
women who before this war lived in expensive hotels in Europe,
mainly because of the cuisine, which was heavy for the rich old
German women, solid for the English "ladies," complex and rich
for the old French women, and thoroughly delightful for the Italians and everyone else.

Or, on the other hand, I have in me the makings of the old
Czech peasant woman, Otto Truttmann's mother-in-law, who
came once a year from her little farm to rich, beautiful, wonderful
Switzerland and tried so hard to eat enough goodness for the next
eleven months that she had several *crises de bile* and made poor
stingy Otto call out the doctor more than once at night, which cost
double a day call.

In other words, I see in myself signs of a strange piggishness, which might be called with more nicety but no more precision *gourmandise.* It usually crops up during times of undoubted strain, such as now, when I am almost shocked to find myself sneaking a bite of potato chips (stale at that, in the kitchen when I am really not hungry, and after a weekend of unusual boredom, when I usually crave pâté and champagne for breakfasts and, that being impossible, eat leftover chops or bacon and a glass of beer).

This is a strange sign of unrest . . . or rather one of its aftersigns.

2. ix. 40

Now and then I think my heart will break, listening to T.'s low weeping under the sound of the radio or watching him try two or three times to get up from a chair. He slept about an hour last night and is quite weak now and depressed. There is nothing I can do, nothing—except rub him, which I do every two hours or so.

We talked last night of my writing a fair, lively (if possible) journal of my own experiences in American restaurants. It might be a good idea. Many people thought I was biased and unfair to our native gastronomy in *Serve It Forth,* which annoyed me, because it was a hasty criticism. I can never say that all apple pie is delicious simply because apple pie is a great American dish. Nor would I ever damn all apple pies for the same reason. I have never made the usual gastronomical pilgrimages, of course, to places like the restaurant in New Orleans's old quarter for Huîtres Rockefeller, etc., etc. But I have traveled an average amount here at home and had to go to average places—with perhaps a more-than-average amount of interest. So—I am milling it over in my mind. The book would be controversial, naturally—and in order to write naturally I would have to do it straight, which would necessitate a lot of name-changing if it ever saw light.

Today is a fresh gusty day, with moving clouds and an occasional slamming door. The air is good.

About 6:30 P.M. I just had an unusual experience, brought on partly by fatigue and anguish, partly by a diet of watermelon to keep T. company, and partly by a generous lot of wine I drank at noon. I felt, after a half-hour massage for T. at 5:30, so tired that although I knew the air was beautiful and the plants were thirsty, I could only look out the windows as I walked languidly past. I lay on my bed, watching the golden shimmering of the cottonwood leaves, and my mind seethed with words—the lush reptilian blue-green of the tobacco leaves, and so on and so on—while I broke into a weak steamy sweat. I went to the kitchen to get more watermelon and tried not to stagger, wondering if I were unconsciously dramatizing my own position as the timeless loving wracked automaton. I got the watermelon and ate it calmly, and I began to feel better. But I cannot describe, ever, the feeling of almost-complete foolish trembling that came over me. I still feel queer and have about decided that if I want to get through what might be a difficult night, I had perhaps better eat some eggs and toast than try to live on melon.

For the moment T. looks quieter, but I have put in a call for Hal to say that he is weak and has only slept five hours in four nights and can I not do something to relieve the constant pain in his poor leg? I have little hope of help, except Hal's warm voice and another assurance that it will soon be over. But will it?

I don't yet know whether we'll have David down tomorrow or not.

The air in the Ramada at the Soboba Hot Springs is cool and gray and full of the soft sounds of falling water from sprays tended at twilight by the gnomish gardener. Below me on a rustic seat a young man talks with apparent charm to a girl whose hair is pulled into a soft dark knot on her nape. She is more at ease than he, but both of them laugh too soon and twist their hands unknowingly.

David left Bareacres a while ago, with Shaun down the hill from camp. I thought it would be best not to have him come out and indeed decided strongly not to, but then I said all right, and it turned out to be a very good thing. Having him in the house made it necessitous for quiet, so that sometimes when if we had been alone T. would have cried out, he was quiet—and that was probably better. Dave took us on drives, and talked when spoken to, and was easy and friendly.

This is the ninth day since T. started to stop, and I can see that this far at least there is great improvement. He feels discouraged, because the pain in his leg is there constantly, but I know from his physical shape, his reactions to things, that the pain is less now—or else that he is more able to combat it. He seldom cries and is able to sit for sometimes an hour at a time without twitching about. Occasionally his conversation is rather flighty.

The night of the last day I wrote in this—when was that? three days? four?—was the worst. I rubbed him and gave him milk and so on—did I say that Hal said to give him milk or raw meat every two hours?—but toward morning he broke down more completely than I have ever seen him do. He had slept only six or five hours in as many days and was wracked, literally, with the pain and with nausea. He quite lost control. I had been expecting it, but to my intense surprise and chagrin it was a terrible shock to me, and I was immediately and almost overwhelmingly sickened, so that I swayed with nausea. I did what I could for T., with arguments and scoldings and massages and so on, and then drank some ammonia in hot water and sagged into my bed, where I lay for perhaps an hour in a kind of passive physical revolt against things I could not even name. My guts heaved and my heart flapped in my chest, and I was an uneasy soul from stem to stern. Finally I went to sleep, and poor Tim slept.

The next morning I decided that Hal or no Hal, a few sleeping tablets would be a good moral companion, if nothing else, so I telephoned Edith and explained to her that I did *not* want an opiate of any kind. She sent some out that night from her doctor (I tried unsuccessfully first to get them from Ginager, the local druggist—it would have meant prescriptions and on and on)— Dave brought them—and the first night T. took two, and the last three nights he has taken one and has slept about six hours every night. So I think the harm of the soporific is offset by the benefit, and perhaps I am criminally wrong.

It is queer, or perhaps not, that when I hear of what must have been a very nice easy weekend with Sis and the children and a college friend of Dave's, I am in a minor way jealous. But I am, because I want the children to see Sis and me together in a nice way. But when they see us, Sis is very conscious of sides: are they on Her side or on My side? And the only way to avoid that is to have a man for her when I am around (with them, at least): she is very conscious, I think, of being thirty and unattached, and there I am with T., and she hates every move of courtesy David or Rex or even T. makes toward me. And unfortunately for our sisterly harmony, T. and David have been the only men when she was around, so there has been not only the siding of me versus her for the children's favor but her unwanted while I was wanted. Oh, dear. Anyway, I wish sometime I could invite the children and Sis and some completely pushover man for her, so that she would have a really nice weekend and would be happy and fun and the children would see that she and I could be together and still agreeable. As it is (I may imagine the whole thing), I feel jealous to hear of how gay and easy weekends are away from us, and wish desperately to be able to show David and Noni that Sis and I are not always queer and ill-tempered with each other. God knows I don't feel so—and God knows that several times this winter Sis has had a really good time at Bareacres. But when Noni came it was changed—and when Dave came it grew impossible. Dave's being male precipitated the whole business.

Two days ago T. and I paid $200 for the beginning of a gray, green-leather-lined, convertible, six-cylinder, hydromatic-drive, cabriolet Oldsmobile, 1941 model, which is to be delivered, we hope, on October 1. I feel rather awful about buying anything like that and wonder if we'll ever pay for it—but T.'s intense pleasure at being able to drive the demonstration car (there is no clutch) is worth even bankruptcy, I think. Now we are trying to figure how to build a garage for $25.

10. ix. 40

I am continually irked, as if by a dormant eczema, by the knowledge that I not only should but want to start work on a book about American gastronomy. But I find myself unable to, partly from procrastination and partly because of things like the constant attention I must pay to T.'s food and how much he sleeps and whether he goes to the toilet. I do not need to tell myself, even in print, how much more important such things are to me than the partial accomplishments of a chapter finished or a story brought to its end. Such pip-squeak reassurances of my own intelligence are unnecessary. But when these sad tasks are over, when my poor

Timmy no longer counts sleep as a perfumer would his drops of attar . . . that seems a queer thing to write, but it is what I thought . . . then I will get to work and write what I think about American gastronomy. And in the meantime, as I said, the knowledge that I should be doing it and that I could earn money by it irks me. Does that negate my whole paragraph?

It is still a gray day. There is a storm somewhere. David is here, presumably to help us build the garage we have found would cost too much, and sits on the wall of the front terrace, sketching the black clouds or perhaps the blacker mountains. T. is painting in the studio. I, after putting the kitchen to rights, am in my little honey-colored workroom, all open to the occasional air, thinking that my mouth tastes too much of the cold cauliflower we ate in the salad for lunch. Perhaps in a minute I'll make myself a drink of vermouth à l'eau or even whisky.

I have never remembered how to spell whiskey. Perhaps it is because I am basically afraid of it. But on the other hand, I have never remembered how to spell parsley, and certainly I have no fear of that fine strong upstanding herb.

T. and I have been reading aloud rather a lot lately, and twice I have been haunted by such strong memories of things that I cannot even now remember completely that I have been almost unable to go on. Once we were reading . . . well, the last one we read was so good that I cannot possibly remember the one before it . . . but a book. And suddenly, in a passage that had nothing to do with hotels, I thought so deeply and thoroughly and intensely about hotels, and walking along the impersonal corridors, smelling of wax in Switzerland, whether it was the Trois Couronnes or the Bärem in Interlaken, and of cigar smoke in America, and of opening the door in the long row of doors and suddenly finding myself in a room that even in five minutes had mysteriously assumed the character positive or negative of the person stopping there, and then of what that character might be and whether or not I liked it, and even of other people walking down hotel corridors not even in my memory and what the rooms meant, warmly, passionately, horribly well, when they opened the impersonal doors—I thought of all this and much more while we read aloud some passage that had nothing to do with hotel corridors, and could hardly go on reading.

In the same way, while Tim and I were reading an unusually well-written book called *Verdict of Twelve,* by an Englishman, which is much too good a novel to be billed merely as a "murder mystery," I was almost silenced, somewhere with complete irrelevance, by a memory so intense that it was tactual, sensual, of the mosquitoes that beat slowly up and down the cold white tile paneling of the bathroom at Le Pâquis. I remembered that small room, stuffy as soon as it was warm, and intolerably cold if it was not stuffy, which the architect put in grouchily as a concession to our foolish exaggerations of sanitation. It was irregular in shape, not from whimsy but because it had to be sandwiched in over the pipes and between the clothes closets. It was a room that was conceived and built grudgingly, and from the beginning that was plain. It was too high for its size, and the walls, which we tried despairingly to soften with a tile more on the creamy side than the blank white or the poisonous turquoise that were suggested, rose hardly and stiffly to about eye level and then whuddered into plaster of a deeper, more indeterminate yellow. There was one window, a miserable affair that canton law made us fill with opaque glass, the kind of window that was so hopeless that I never even bothered to hide it with a curtain of chintz or voile. The toilet, offset in a half alcove, flushed directly into the ceiling of the living room below, with a loud sucking Swiss enthusiasm, and continued to do so in spite of consultations and wavings of contracts to the contrary. There was no washbowl, since Timmy in a moment of Continental enthusiasm

. . . also Swiss, largely . . . had decided that the idea of having a lavatory in each bedroom was really the best in every way except perhaps the aesthetic. The tub was ample, although, of course, not up to the 1890 standards of the Three Crowns. There was a fine soap dish . . . built into the tile wall.

I remember several things about that bathroom, besides how stuffy it got. Several times boys, and even girls, would swing down the road from Chexbres, which ran outside in a fine curve at almost roof level, and they would yodel, inexpertly but with that same Swiss enthusiasm as they pelted along. I would be lying in the tub, which was filled with Le Pâquis luxury to its brim with the hottest water this side of hell, and I would hear the clear youthful voices, tremulous but exuberant, come toward the horrid opaque window and then shoot by it full and fine, as unworried as apples.

But the thing I remembered about the bathroom . . . I remembered other things as I suddenly thought on it, the other night while I went on reading about the terrible murder trial in *Verdict of Twelve* . . . I remembered how hot and perfumed it smelled after Anne Parrish would bathe in it and how she never washed out the tub, and I remembered finding little splashes of blood when Mary Powers was there and thinking that she had left them there on the toilet seat deliberately to frighten Anne and us into thinking she was desperately ill, and I remembered feeling ill one night and how T. fixed a tub for me and undressed me and brought me a little glass of brandy warmed in his hands . . . but most of all I remembered how the several large mosquitoes put their noses against the tiles, always cool, and buzzed up and down, up and down.

They made a strange noise and seemed quite absorbed in what they did. They seldom bit, and then only absentmindedly, as if it were their unfortunate duty. Their bites were strangely virulent and raised big white welts edged with angry red, but I never hated the mosquitoes, as I would have had they not been so driven. Up and down they went, their sensitive proboscises pressed painfully against the hard white tiles. Up and down. Through steam and stink and the fine Swiss odor of Pine Bath Essence, they filed away at the white tiles, never making anything but perhaps a tiny track on the mist, which soon vanished. They buzzed like little serpents and bit with violence at the smooth blankness of the solid, sturdy, ugly, practical white Swiss bathroom tiles.

And that was what I remembered, only much more, as I read aloud something that had nothing to do with it.

I should very much like to get myself a little drink. The day is dull, I feel dull, I feel depressed. There is something to drink and make me feel less mindful of everything. But I know that I am inclined, at least at this period in my life, to drink too much. Not much too much, but a little. So I shall try to combat it. Because I think any person, or even any beast, who is not quite in focus is not only pitiable but despicable.

My typing is bad. I could make it better. Or even worse, if I tried. But the thing is that I do not try to make it better. This is the place for a well-pointed moral.

I think instead I shall go and take an enema and a shower and perhaps manicure my toenails and my fingernails.

T. and David are painting now in the studio, and Butch tick-tocks.

. . . T. just came in and said, among other things, "I can't remember what it feels like to have two legs. Sometimes I look at people in amazement and think, 'How can they go along on only two sticks, when I have three?' It must be very queer to be that way. It's funny." I said, "Not very funny." I wasn't grim . . . but it simply didn't seem funny to me. He said, "No . . . perhaps not funny. But it seems very queer. Only two legs."

There is rain, now and then, on the roof. It sounds beautiful, dripdripdrip, and strange in this dry land.

The new dog Wheeler whimpers and scratches at the door, trying to get Butch out into the brush. He leads the little dog miles away, and we call and call, and finally they come back, Butch too tired even to greet us. So we have Butch locked in, and Wheeler the foxhound whimpers, foxed for fair.

15. ix. 40

The air is changing fast so that it is cooler and filled with a fresh golden color and a different smell. I am quietly excited to think of winter here.

Timmy is better, I think, although the nights are bad. Sometimes he takes only one of the yellow capsules I got Mother to order through her doctor, but more often it is two. I hate to have him take them, and I hate to trick Hal this way, but I couldn't endure the nights any longer . . . not for my own sleeplessness but for what they were doing to T. Today he seems to feel better than yesterday, and I find myself able to look forward to things like winter.

Winter means some work, too. It is only about 5:30, but already I can hardly see to write. I'll have to get some kind of good working lamp in here. And the same thing must be done in the bar, where we will perhaps eat suppers more than we do now that we can stay on the porch, and for the studio. Then some shelves and so on must be put in the front bedroom if we are to sleep there. And worst of all, as far as expenses go, we must soon see about buying an oil heater for the house. It means about a hundred dollars. The check from Mr. Sheppard has not yet come—I dread having to go through the humiliating business of telling Anne again that it is late and that we need it. I wish to God she would do what she planned to and settle some sort of annuity on Tim, even if it were half what she sends him now. We are in an almost constant state of worry and embarrassment.

Arnold may come for supper tonight. He was here about 6:00 last night and talked with many sighs about how dull it was to eat in cafés while Lena was staying with her mother, but I did not ask him to stay for supper, partly because that kind of obvious hinting always annoys me and mainly because we already had Merle Armitage here.

He came down within two days after I had thanked him for a note and told him that T. had been very ill but that we hoped to see him sometime later. I was really cross when his letter came Friday saying that he would be down Saturday for the afternoon and dinner. It seemed callous and pushing, but, of course, he is an unusually callous and pushing man. It is partly his boundless vitality and partly his thirty years of being an impresario, which probably left him feeling that all people are to be treated with the same naive protective boldness that he used on Chaliapin and Mary Garden and Stokowski. He is something of a glandular phenomenon, I think—looking nearer forty than fifty and with an enthusiasm and vigor and curiosity that are not only tiring but frightening.

He is tall and fattish and wears affected clothes: last night, a well-cut loose suit of blue cotton with a navy-blue shirt and a red cotton bandanna wound under the collar and knotted in front. His heavy suede shoes had exaggerated square toes. He has small hands and feet and a very small short nose, which looks almost boneless. His left eye is larger and higher in his skull and has a mad mean look in it, like Peter the Great, while his right eye at the same moment may be twinkling and genial. He talks continually and loudly, with many gestures, and occasionally laughs with an unconvincing joviality, always at something he himself has said.

He gave us a copy of his latest book, *The Navy,* which Ward Ritchie printed beautifully for Longmans Green. We talked about that for a long time, while he drank three highballs. Then we had supper, which I really made just about as we would have had it (grilled steak, a salad of lettuce and shoestring potatoes, iced grapes, coffee), and listened to him tell about his trip this summer. He has unpleasant table manners, by the way, even though we did not sit at a table. He talked for about four hours and ate all the grapes and drank all the coffee. Now and then he would say, "Do you really want me to go on?" and before we could say yes, he would go on. Or he would say, "Shall I tell you about a most amazing and wonderful thing that happened on the road to Milwaukee? It will take perhaps ten minutes, and then if I tell you about that weekend it will take about thirty minutes more?" And on he would sweep. He was interesting, in a way he did not realize . . . so completely the pusillanimous snob, bragging about the riches of his friends and whimsically referring to his various hostesses as ghastly old bitches.

16. ix. 40

I started to work this morning . . . got all my notes in order for the book on eating. I don't want to write it particularly, but I want to write. It is like having the itch. Now that I have started to work again, I am easier, as if I put ointment on my mind.

17. ix. 40

Yesterday afternoon I wrote quite a lot about patriotism and gastronomy, none of it good enough. This morning, though, I have finished collecting everything for what should be a good section about oysters and eating them. I'll try to do at least part of it this afternoon.

It rained now and then all night, and at times the air was so heavy with the smell of sage and wild buckwheat and wet stones that it was like breathing a rich sweet Greek wine, so that it was almost better not to breathe consciously.

T. was in such pain that he did not even go to bed but sat up all night or wandered quietly about, fixing himself warm milk and looking at the wild moon-edged clouds of the storm. This morning, after a massage, he is working again. I don't know what to do for him. I wrote again to Hal, asking really for some further reassurance that the pain would diminish as he and the men at Rochester said. But he probably will write a note asking us to come up to Pasadena and hear some new records, in reply. It is not that he is callous . . . but I think he has nothing to say to help us.

This morning T. and I were sitting in the bar, eating some grilled steak for breakfast, and he looked out the window and said, "Butch must be terribly constipated. He has been trying to drop a turd for about five minutes." I looked, too, because I was surprised, and almost at once we realized that it was not a turd but that the poor little creature was in the grip of a really terrible erection. We went down at once to the kennel and found him immobile, unable to walk, with his back curved high and his penis as big as a large man's and dark purple. He did not seem to suffer but had a bewildered look on his face. It was terrible to see, because it looked so hopeless—his little body curved and stiff and that monstrous organ hanging from it. I ran to the phone and got Walkerdine, who said to put ice water on it. By the time I got the ice and a towel, Butch was much better and lay quietly while we put compresses on him. As the inflammation went down he began to jerk, so I thought to distract him by taking him for a little walk. But the poor little wretch could hardly make his hind end follow his front, so I put him alone into the kennel, and now he is all right, although quite exhausted.

Tawny is pregnant again, with an unknown mate this time, and is so crazy and disagreeable that we think we may take her into the Riverside animal shelter and have her killed. She has never been an agreeable or even friendly animal, and since her first heat, which was unsatisfied because of the astonishing lack of any Toms in that part of Moreno valley, she has been definitely disagreeable . . . snarling and dour, and really mean with the new little kitten Blackberry, who is one of the merriest animals in the world.

4. x. 40

It is so long since I have written that I almost dislike the thought of starting here again. Too much has happened.

Last night sometime Tawny had five more kittens in Tim's paint-rag bin and is cheerful now for the first time in weeks. I moved her into a box in the toilet, but she is still rather mussy, although this time was much cleaner than last. I can't help liking her again, so proud and purring, but I dread having to go through the business of disposing of the little things and feeding the rest and on and on. We now have ten animals!

Two weeks ago tomorrow, Rex and Dave were here for lunch on their way to Colorado. Rex was happy as a child at the thought of a week with Dave. But that night Mother collapsed with angina pectoris, and by Wednesday Rex was home again by plane, and the whole family had gone through one of those lightning changes so that all our positions are different and strange and even difficult, and we are bewildered for the time. Mother is still in the hospital, perhaps a little better as far as blood pressure goes but having attacks of pain irregularly, which must be helped by shots. At first she protested at being there, but now she is content to stay, frightened of having an attack at home when the nurse might be away.

We went up as soon as we could get the things in order here and stayed for about a week, with one night down here in the middle of it. At first the doctors thought Rex need not cut short his vacation, and they told me that Edith might come home in two or three days if we could get Shaun away and muzzle the cook. Edith, too, told me that she longed to come home but could not bear the thought of Grace's talking, and asked me to speak to her. Sis and Tim and Noni agreed that I should, so I had a fairly sensible talk with the woman, who parted from me at the end with tears of love. For three or four days she was much less chattery and worked quietly and well.

Rex came home . . . and the second morning he was there she pounced on him at seven o'clock and apparently told him that I had told her we did not want her anymore and that we had another woman to take her place. (This was probably the result of her constant listening via the kitchen door to everything we discussed in the front of the house, and once Tim and I had said to Noni that perhaps we could get Sweetie-pie to help if Grace had to leave, since she was having her change of life and had been too "poorly" even to do the washing when we arrived.) Father was much upset, naturally, at the thought of changing cooks along with everything else, and although he said nothing to me, I knew from his manner and from what Noni said that he was disgusted with me for precipitating all this with my meddlesome ways.

I was disappointed that Noni, who knew why I had spoken at all to Grace and knew that I had not told her either that we wanted her to go or that we had another woman engaged, should not tell Rex that I was less interfering than he thought me. But Noni was, for the first time, showing a side that I had never suspected before and that has been a shock to me. She almost openly resented my being at the Ranch, and grew cold if I even suggested helping her with the marketing, and said things like "Well, I'd *thought* that I had things pretty well in hand . . . but, of course, I'm delighted to have you step in and manage everything, Dote." It was difficult for me, because I am the oldest and the most used to assuming responsibility in a thousand crises at the Ranch, and I was really straining to give it all to her and at the same time help her without seeming to, because I knew that she was the nominal head of the house and that it would be unpleasant but good for her to have some responsibility. But things got less pleasant all the time, and we came down here as soon as we could. Now I telephone every night, and all Noni will say is that Mother is all right. Occasionally when I pump her with questions, she will admit that Mother has had another attack. But I know nothing, really, about how she is. It is very hard. Last night I tried for two hours to get the Ranch (Sis and I both asked Noni never to let the Ranch be left alone, even if it meant hiring someone to sit by the telephone at night now and then, because Mother might need some of us), and finally called the hospital, where someone told me with customary hospital vagueness that Mother was fairly well and had had two attacks that morning. I was terribly upset and angry with Noni, since I had told her that I was going to call last night and felt that if she had gone out with Rex or to see some people she could at least have called me first and told me how Edith was. It is wrong to be so ready to be upset and exasperated, I know . . . but I am down here simply because it was impossible to stay at the Ranch, where I want to be, near Mother, and I feel really depressed that the result of twenty-three years of my being Noni's older sister is finally, at this unfortunate moment, turning against me with her sudden cold resentment. I know, and none better, that too often I have felt obliged to step in, to boss, to direct, where perhaps it would have been better, and certainly easier, to let things go every which way rather than antagonize the younger ones of the family. I have always been given too much responsibility, because I usually took it well, and sometimes I have taken it unnecessarily. It is easy to see things like that as I grow older, and I regret the fact that I was so willing to lead and that so many people who should have known better were so more-than-eager to give me jobs that were really much too heavy and old for me to assume. Now, at a time when I could and would like to help at the Ranch, these sins of omission and commission, not alone mine, are putting out a fine crop of antagonism and misunderstanding between Noni and me.

Of course, the whole thing is difficult for her. She is too young to be stuck there and knows it. She is alarmingly anemic and listless and probably morbid. We urged her not to stay at the Ranch when she first got back from Honolulu, but with her characteristic torpor she said she thought she'd stay a few months and then maybe move on. But now that her freedom is threatened she is inwardly frightened and furious at the trick and told T. that she *would not* be caught, that she *must* escape. She must, of course, and we'll do all we can to help her . . . but at the moment she can no more escape from the dreary routine of running the Ranch than I can escape from my helplessness at being here instead of there where I feel I should be. Noni is egoistic with that bland egoism of a young person, and quite possibly feels that she is the only one who is caught. She is unwell and given to defeatist thoughts, I know.

Grace, after talking "confidentially" to every member of the family and apparently trying to turn each of us against the other for some strange unhealthy reason of her own, is now on a two weeks' vacation, and as far as I know, Noni is running the house and doing the cooking, with the cleaning and the laundry done by Goldie. I asked her please to get extra help now and then, and to take care of herself, and so on, when I telephoned the other night.

But she barely responded, and I felt like an unpleasantly boring old woman who was quite obviously poking my nose into what was none of my business.

Shaun is in a school that was picked out by Rex over Sis's head, so that, too, was unpleasant at home. Of course, Rex has all the financial responsibility of Shaun and feels fairly correctly that he should have the say in where the poor child goes, but Sis was upset and angry at his lordly disregard of her. And no one can be more lordly than Rex. He is difficult to live with unless he is constantly flattered and appeased.

So it is plain that for the moment, at least, the family is at odds—and at a time when by all the rules of sentiment we should be knit closely by our concern for Mother. It is a strange and disturbing thing to happen, and quite unexpected, by me at least.

6. x. 40

Night before last I called Noni, who said that Mother was much worse. I told her I would call again the next night.

In the morning a letter came from Hal, and I read it aloud without thinking that at last he would speak the truth in it, so that before I could stop myself I had read that there is nothing more to do for T., no way to help him. I was so sick that I turned very hot and tried not to realize what I had read. T. cried, but not much, and said that he wanted to wait a little longer, and then perhaps start taking what Analgeticum is left. I thought that probably I had never been so sad and went about work filled with a leaden bitter hopelessness.

At the same time, I had a pleasant day. I worked violently about the place, raking and cleaning the kennels, cleaning the patio, straightening the paint and nail shelves, on and on. The day was mildly hot, and part of me felt almost happy to be working that way.

Arnold Elliott came up, much discouraged that he was laid off work for two weeks with a bad back, so to cheer him, Tim and he went over to Soboba . . . or rather to the Soboban, where they drank rather a lot, and did not get back until about 3:30. I waited quite a while, mildly annoyed that Tim would not telephone me, and then had a nice reckless lunch of beer and celery and raw beef, with a nip of whiskey first, in the patio. I knew why Tim was staying away, and I wanted him to, much more than I could ever be cross. When they finally came back, they looked quite cheerful and rather mellow.

After Arnold left, Tim said he'd like to go over to swim and have a massage. The water was cold and fine. We were alone in the pool. The sunset in the air was the goldest I have ever seen, so that as we floated on the water the air seemed to shimmer and vibrate between us and the tall cottonwoods with their yellowing leaves. I had a drink in the bar and then sat in the Ramada while Tim was rubbed.

About 8:00 I called the Ranch, and Father answered. He is hard to talk to because of his deafness, but after the first noncommittal answer or two, he told me quite a lot . . . for him. The doctor wanted to see him in a few minutes. Mother was worse, especially in her mind. Father seemed for the first time to have admitted to himself that she was terribly ill. I asked him how Noni was getting along, and he said that she had got a fine dinner and was a good cook. He sounded affectionate and courageous.

In a few minutes Sis called, also from the Ranch. She was rather incoherent and upset—had been getting some furniture out of storage and then had spent almost an hour with Mother, who wept and talked hysterically of being useless and wanting to die. Then Sis came home, much disturbed to find Rex and Noni at a football game, while the phone was ringing with people like Aunt Mary frantic for news, and found the house full of dead flowers and dirty ashtrays and so on. Sis made drinks, thinking they were going out to supper, and when Rex and N. came home, was disgusted to see Noni open some canned corned beef and some canned beans. She told me this on her second call, from Los Angeles two hours later, since Noni was listening at the Ranch. Sis said that when Rex went up to Barmore, Noni announced that she was willing to stay and take care of the Ranch for one year exactly, and then she was leaving. Sis was furious at what she thought was Noni's cold-blooded selfishness and said that she was so busy dramatizing herself as the martyred spinster daughter that she could think of nothing else. This is partly true, but Sis did not like it when I said that it was hard for any twenty-three-year-old person not to dramatize herself. Sis was almost crying with annoyance and depression, and our two conversations were incoherent. She said that Barmore had told Rex that Mother was growing worse and that if she ever had another good day, she should be moved to the Ranch where she would be happier, but that it was doubtful that she ever could be moved. Apparently there is a progressive thickening of the walls of the heart.

Last night was wretched, and poor T., in spite of taking two of Hal's blue capsules instead of the one prescribed, was not able even to lie down until about 7:00 this morning, on the couch in the living room where he slept heavily until about 10:30.

I called Noni, who seemed genuinely glad to hear my voice. She said Rex was at the hospital and then was meeting Mrs. Kelly, who had arrived last night in Whittier and wanted "a good long talk" with Rex about Anne's impossible and vindictive actions with Ted about Shaun. Poor Father. He is very good with Mrs. K., and I think will be able to smooth things out.

I am going to call Noni now and if possible go over there this

afternoon. Tim should not make that 175-mile drive in the shape
he's in, but he wants to come, too. I feel that if I can, I must see
Mother. She has confidence in me, and it may help her to know
that I am there, even for a minute or two.

. . . Mother is much better, and neither Rex nor N. wanted
us to come, because of the long drive, but we want to, so we are
leaving soon. I'll see M. for a minute, and we'll have supper at the
Ranch and then drive home.

7. x. 40

We drove up to the Ranch and had a drink with Father and
Noni, who had just got home from seeing Shaun at his school.
They found him well and happy. Rex was worried because Shaun's
service uniforms, which cost $10 apiece, did not fit at all well,
and had told the captain to send them to the local tailor for taking in a
bit here and there.

Rex looked thinner and tired but was kind and gentle and
thoughtful. He came out into the kitchen later and stood leaning
against the sink, talking with a highball in his hand while Noni and
I got supper and Tim sat in the "nook." He is being patient and
good and is so sweet with Noni and so bewildered by the changes
that I could weep at him.

Noni looked very badly, thin and white, with no life in her at
all. I think I will try to take her to Hal or any other doctor she will
go to, sometime this week. She admits that she is anemic, and at
this time when she should be taking especially good care of herself,
she is sinking deeper and deeper into ill health and lassitude.

The house looked bleak, with no fire ready and one small vase
of dead zinnias that I took up from Bareacres two weeks ago. The
ashtrays were dirty, and we ran out of coffee and had to go up to

the corner market for some. I got supper, of ham in cream, baked noodles with mushrooms, a salad by Noni, and very bad coffee by Noni. But it was a pleasant meal, and we talked with rather too much liveliness about a great many completely dull things. Rex is wound up to a flow of conversation, doggedly trying to avoid any mention of present things. When they inevitably appear, he answers or remarks briefly and then swings again into an interminable monologue about the Indian weavers he saw in New Mexico or what Mike Robinson told him about trying to heat a big house in London many years ago.

We went up to see Mother about 5:30. The room was dark, and when we went in she was startled, mildly, and had a hard time coordinating her voice, which was high and small, like a sleepy child's, to her words, which were mumbled and drunken. She concentrated once or twice, and her eyes seemed to focus, but for the three or four minutes we were there, she was for the most part very muddled. I thought she had been doped again, but apparently she had not had a shot for many hours, and it was weakness and yesterday's pain that had addled her usually precise speech. We stood up to go once, and she cried out, Oh, don't go . . . the days are so long! So we sat down again, although we knew we should not . . . and then she almost went to sleep, as quick as a mouse. When we left, she said, Take some flowers . . . they are so lovely, and then she held out her arms to T. She had always loved to kiss him, over and over again, so that her subsequent kisses to me have seemed perfunctory and dutiful, and yesterday she held him close and kissed and kissed him with that weak ferocity of sick people. Then he stumbled away, and she put her arms softly about me and began to sob, in little quick sobs. I whispered to her of her soft sweet cheeks and left, ready for tears but filled instead with a dry pity that made me dizzy and aching as if I were ill with influenza. Take some flowers, she whispered, lying with her eyes shut and tears on her cheeks, almost asleep again with exhaustion. I pulled a bad red rose from a vase and went into the hall. T. stood leaning against the walls, weeping. We drove home and I rubbed him, and he cried more at the foulness of our own natures that we must make people live when they are through. So that now when Edith has an attack, we will give her restoratives to make her live for another one.

We drove back before midnight, against Rex's wishes. It was better, though, and T. slept well with only one capsule, for the first time in several nights. Today he is painting again, and I am fussing here and there, rearranging furniture to make places for the two ugly heaters that Mr. Ankum and his airy-fairy son are installing in their own lackadaisical way, and putting off getting to work.

We had a letter from Pat, written in his cellar during a raid. A great many English people are doing that, until I am almost sick of hearing about what gallantry it represents. God knows it does, but I get sick of being told so, every time I meet anyone who has had a letter from the Old Country. I must write to him, but I will put it off a little longer. He will be sad indeed to hear of Mother. She has always had something more than a maternal affection for him, and he has reciprocated with the kind of flattering love that lets him tell her every time he confides something in her that he would not in his own mother. Poor Alice Maud . . . I wonder if she is still doggedly living in her service apartment in London with her shell-shocked butler. The big American-style buildings in Madrid held out better under bombing than the old stone ones . . . perhaps she is wise to be as stubborn as she was when I last heard.

The air is full of smoke, not for the first time this autumn, and we are watching the horizon. It makes a good smell, and we know what to do if we see clouds pouring with the wind in our direction, but still it would be terrifying to watch the flames and the brown fumes racing toward our house in this capricious air.

Sis called the Ranch last night from a party. She sounded drunker than I have ever heard her, and breathless. She is to call me tonight, after a visit to the Ranch. I kept thinking, Thank God I am not at a party, all the way home. She was almost hysterical, in a restrained, dramatic way. She has read too many cheap novels about gallant young beautiful career women who drown their sorrows with complete sophistication. I can say that with sincerity, but I know, too, that she is unhappy. Different people have different ways of showing their sorrow and pain, and she is suffering, even if she does it at the top of her voice at a rowdy cocktail party, just as much as Z. or Y.

Material came from the government today about the oyster. I am working in my head and have sent off one chapter, which is a short story. T. suggested a good title today: *The Wild Life of the Oyster*. I think it is amusing and will use it for the chapter on vital statistics, probably.

Our car will not be here until Saturday, in spite of being promised for Thursday or before. It is annoying.

9. x. 40

We went up to the Ranch yesterday, and I saw Mother for a few minutes in the hospital. She was more coherent—they had cut down on the doses of phenobarbital—and can come home whenever she wants to. But she doesn't want to much. A nurse is engaged and a hospital bed is in place, but everyone hopes she'll stay longer at the Murphy Hospital, including Edith.

Noni looked better—thanks largely, I think, to Lera's self-assured and efficient presence. Lera will be there a few hours every day. She had baked a large chocolate cake—and I, thinking how bare was the larder, took up a large box of cookies and a cake by

Mrs. Purdy! Rex, too, looked better. He had won $3.35 at Pangingee—winning always cheers him. We had a drink with him and then a mediocre enchilada up along the road with Noni, and got back here by 11:00.

In the moonlight the house looked like some strange land crab, with two antennae feeling the sky. The two new heaters were in but with ridiculously long chimneys. The Ankums are cutting some ten feet off each one—poor dolts.

I have an uncomfortable thumb—am afraid it may be something disagreeable like a felon. I'll see a doctor this evening because it makes me awkward.

We drowned three kittens this morning. Much less messy than other ways—but it is true about the nine lives. After almost half an hour they were still kicking.

1. xi. 40

It is the first of the month, and perhaps I should make some promise to myself to write every day or to stop drinking or to do something. Instead I shall only admit that I have no idea where I last wrote nor when, and do not much care.

We went up to Pasadena, after a discussion that enough was enough, and stayed in a sterile, tidy "home" run by one of Hal's old women. We felt penned, even though we would go out during the day, and for one night I was as unhappy as I have ever been . . . more than that . . . thinking of what I had heard about T. and so on. But in the daytime we could go out, and during our stay there we had a decent time, driving in the new car about the towns and stopping once for beer and fried shrimps at a drive-in place, and so on. When Hal said we could leave, sooner than we thought, we fled like bats out of hell. I insisted on shaking hands with the

shriveled old woman who ran the "home," and she was embarrassed and held out a hand covered with soapsuds that felt like a
rubber glove filled with lukewarm consommé and old fish bones.
Her name was Mary Elderkin.

Two days ago we went to see Mother. She was in bed, with
the door closed. Timmy, who had had a bad fall helping me put
down the kennel top the night before, planned to lie down with a
massage and a pill, but we learned through Noni what surprise
Mother planned, so I stopped T. from disrobing in the guest house
and we came in to find Mother's door open and her in her Chinese
robe in the Irish chair. She looked very pretty—her skin was
younger and fresher than it had been for years, and I felt that she
smelled better, probably, in her intimate cracks—and she was
playing "The Pretty Tyrant" as she has not played it since she was
a bride, I wager. It has its boring side . . . mainly because her
twenty-five-year habit of talking anywhere in the house and expecting everyone anyplace else in the house to listen has become
exaggerated by her power, as an invalid, so that she talks in her
rather weak voice almost constantly and expects us to listen no
matter where we are. That may be one reason why Rex is such an
accomplished deaf person. Anyway, we are so relieved to have
Mother still alive that we submit with fatuous and unbreathed
gladness to her coquetry, and only occasionally do we admit to
boredom.

Noni is long overdue for leaving and has had a quarrel with
Anne. I heard about it from N. and then from Rex who drove out
unexpectedly for the weekend, and then from Sis who wrote a
furious letter just after the quarrel. It was about Noni's refusal to
come in and fetch Sis out to Whittier for the weekend. Sis blames
it entirely on Noni's smugness as Present-Savior-of-the-Situation,
but Rex and Edith both refused to let Noni drive through the
Saturday traffic in her present inexpert state, and Noni, to cap

things, got rid of a lot of rancor by telling Sis she didn't care if she *never* came out. Sis, on the other hand, feels ousted and hurt. She hung up. Mother had a bad day. They all stew mildly. It is to me but one more sign of the disintegration of my family as such.

Tomorrow we take Arnold Elliott into Riverside to see Dr. C., who fixed my slipped sacroiliac and can perhaps do something for the sprained back that has kept Arnold out of work for some seven weeks. It is all bootleg and may make trouble with the insurance doctors, but Arnold is willing to take the risk.

17. xi. 40

J ust now T. and I went out from the warm lighted study and the whuddering firelight of the living room to the porch and watched a half rainbow grow and die against the hills. Sunlight, long and yellow, flung itself against the middle distance of San Jacinto in an intense blot—San Jacinto hills, not the mountain, which was blue and far from us. The hills showed their folds and meadows like old elephant hide, and in front of them the valley and the little lizard of land blazed with arsenic, Paris gray, as violent as dying California leaves can be, yellow and hideously beautiful. The rainbow curved up, more and more intensely, never higher than the quarter-arm but plainly from Soboba, and then it faded. We felt cold and came into the reassurance of the house. The harsh yet measured beauty of the scene before us was disturbing.

The Powells were here and departed in a warm friendly mood, I think. Fay was older physically but more attractive—her beautiful feet and her slim beaky skull have always drawn me to her in spite of some less handsome features—and Larry was mellower. They were genuinely stirred by some of T.'s pictures, which pleased me.

It's long since I wrote here. There are days when I want to, but I am too content—and other days my spirit is too black. Today, after a weekend of company and, just now, a highball, I am verbose but uninspired—and today I choose to write. My mind is full of my own despair, muted fortunately. It is best to write of things like weather and furniture.

The weather toys with rain: to rain—not to rain. I long for rain, to help the plants and more especially the springs—which are still strong, thank God. There is an occasional spate of warm gray drops against the patio windows, and the fire feels good. I brought in several logs, just as the weather changed, and the incredibly fine brown powder from the wormholes made me sneeze.

I look at the cat who sits on the couch beyond my chair and see by the tawny patch beneath her chin that it is Suesky Jo, Tawny's first daughter, a cold neurotic virgin still, rather hateful usually and for no reason since we treat her well. Tawny has grown lovable since her second litter, and her one child from it is a pretty creature, striped white and gray, either male or female.

As to Bareacres: apparently we owe one-half of 1939's taxes but are tax free because of T.'s veteran exemption. The land is as we found it, except for a cleared firebreak around the house, and the road up to the flats has been smoothed out a bit by Old Man Gibbel. The springs are flowing sweetly. The tank springs leaks, and we go up now and then and whittle a plug or two of soft pine and fill the holes. In a year or so we'll have to build a reservoir, preferably of stone. The land around the house is much as we found it. I've cleared it off near the buildings, because of fire, and behind the house have cleared and nourished a little rocky knoll planted with tamaracks, which may someday be beautiful. It must have been planted there among the rocks by old Captain Hoffman. The little dwarfed trees respond almost pathetically to encouragement. As soon as this possibly rainy spell is past, I'll scratch the ground here and there and scatter the wildflower seeds that Arnold gave me.

The house is fairly well tightened against winds and rain now, and as I lie on the couch before this gentle fire and know that in another room is a good oil furnace, I feel coddled as an orchid and, in spite of myself, apologetic.

We have a handsome harrier, who leads Butch the little Pekingese far into the hills so that they both come home exhausted. We keep Butch to please ourselves, and we keep Wheeler to please him—but if Wheeler steals him from us, what is the use of keeping either? Butch just came in, completely fatigued. I hear Wheeler bugling in the hills, and so does he. But he's not built for chasing hares. He pleases and amuses and charms us more than Wheeler. Therefore, we should get rid of Wheeler. Perhaps. But Wheeler is so handsome—

Later

I have fed the cats and dogs, and now, with a Charles McCarthy program on the little portable radio and the fire chattering and a cigarette fuming in my holder, I look out past the blue Swiss chair, through the little hallway, into the kitchen. There, past the top of the smooth white icebox I see the rafters of the high wooden kitchen, satiny and brown and reassuring.

My heart is heavy, thinking of my friends in France and of England so hard pressed. I can hardly bear to think of anything at all these days, and dwell resolutely on the growth of a kitten or an acacia tree and the progression of clouds in a winter sky.

4. xii. 40
Globe, Arizona

The second day of our trip to Delaware has been one of the strangest of my life, because of the road we took. We went only about 115 miles, but it took us most of the day and left us tired in a good hollow way, and exalted. It was no more like ordinary motoring than childbirth is like ordinary pain, or *épinards en branches* at Foyots was ordinary spinach.

We started at 11:00 from the fake-posh Westward Ho in Phoenix, where we had a comfortable room and excellent service and good hotel food and yet hated everything for its standardized comfort and excellence and goodness. The doorman said, "Well, you folks going over the mountains? It's like riding on the pantry shelf all night!" We said no, but after a stop at the AAA for guidebooks we decided to try it—the Apache Trail, which is longer and more mountainous than the ordinary road through Superior to Globe. We drove a little through the Papago Saguaro Park near Phoenix—and laughed later to think we'd been awed by those first giant cactuses. (I know that's cacti but I don't like the word.) The red rocks there were handsome.

At Apache we did not stop at the zoo, which advertised animals of the country like Gilas and wild hogs but also had spider monkeys. We headed northeast into the Tonto country, on a fine dirt road, past a mountain that is the most beautiful mountain of my life. We knew there were Superstition Mountains near there, and I didn't want to know where they were because it seemed as if that one beautiful mountain should be the Superstition, even if it wasn't. But that was it, sure enough—on the map. It made me feel good. The mountain was red and like a Gothic dream, more or less.

Things got stranger and stranger. There were badly defaced

signs pointing to various landmarks, but they were unimportant. The colors of the rocks and mountains were red and pink and black, with a greenish moss now and then turning the surfaces sulfurous. The *palos verdes* and *ocatillas* were green, and different kinds of small cactuses grew everywhere, almost too prettily in the crannies, like a professional garden. Everywhere, even up to the tops of the fantastic mountains, were the saguaros, stately as a forest, without visible leaves. Some of them were taller than houses, fifty or sixty feet, with a dozen strong fingers or new sets of little light green balls beginning on their sides.

The road was excellent. There was no traffic, although near Canyon Lake we passed a car and an old woman and a girl eating lunch, and we all waved as people do in wild places. Twice we passed roadworkers, friendly thin men with brown faces. The road once made my knees weak, near the Walls of Bronze—it was the steepest mountain road I'd ever been on, and everywhere I looked was so beautiful that when we got to the bottom of the gorge I drank some whiskey. I felt quite exhausted.

We kept going up and down, and everywhere it was beautiful and terrible. I never had the feeling, though, that the country was sinister the way San Jacinto is, or the Bodwin moors in Cornwall. I wanted to lie flat on the red earth and close my eyes. Then we passed Roosevelt and the dam, which Timmy said was an ugly dam with the wrong curve to it (I think he disliked it partly because it had sucked the great fjords of the Salt River down into little scarred creeks), and I drove the easy half of the way over the smooth curving dirt road to Globe. I can never say, even to myself, what happened today between me and that country, driving as I was with T., beside him in the car in all that red wilderness.

We are stopping at an auto court, my first. It is clean and pleasant and decorated with so many red-yellow-blue-green Mexicans sitting under cactuses or riding burros, painted, embroidered, drawn, that I feel almost as if I were undressing in the middle of Tijuana or some such place. The beds are good. The man next door snores. There are many advantages to these courts, certainly, and one of them is price: $3.06 here with no tips, for a nicer room than we had last night for $7 and many tips. But, of course, we do all the bag toting, and it upsets T. not to be able to help me with that—and we must drive downtown for food—

We went, somewhat unwillingly, to one of the first restaurants we passed in this typical little mining town, down by the copper mine in the "rough" section. It was small, neat, blue—the Sobeston's Pic-a-Rib Café—and when we saw it was recommended by Duncan Hines's loathsome and unfortunately popular guidebook, *Adventures in Eating,* we said *no.* But the landlady said it was very good. We went, and so it was, and yet we came away feeling irritated at what we didn't know. The martinis in the hideous black-and-metal-painted bar were unusually good. The waitress had pretty legs and a tired pasty face and served deftly and intelligently. There were tea-roomy dripping candles on the tables in the small dining room, but the seats under the foolish curved awnings were soft and comfortable. The people were uninteresting—well-fed and smug. The proprietor actually made the salads himself and the drinks, and brought a big chalked blackboard for us to order from. We had good vegetable soup, at his command, and delicious grilled spareribs cooked with sherry, and a fine salad made with wine vinegar, and goodish French bread, especially in a town this size. And still we left feeling vaguely irritated. I don't know why. I'd certainly send other people there, and I'd like another plate of the spareribs, and yet I don't want to go back myself.

We drove westward after supper—busman's holiday—through Miami. It was all saloons, with the mines and smelters upon the hills all lit. We stopped at the one little grocery we saw in the whole town and bought some bananas and two little tins of sardines for tomorrow's lunch.

I told Edith when we left that I'd write to her instead of in my diary, but I'm not doing it. In some ways, it is a good idea—my letters home are thus more interesting, to me at least, and I kill two birds because I ask for them back later. But on the other hand, there are many things I can never say in my letters. I can never say, for instance, how wonderful, how nearly miraculous and fine it seems to me to be going *away* from them all, to be gone willy-nilly from any part of their involved lives. They would never understand, nor would I probably, if my child tried to say the same. But it is true. And I am happy now in a completer way than I have ever known, to be alone and unrecognized with my love. Now, to me, is always—more surely than I ever thought possible.

11. xii. 40
New Monteleone
New Orleans

Dearest Edie—

We were disappointed not to have any letters from you when we got in this afternoon, but maybe some will come tomorrow. I do hope all goes well at the Ranch.

I'll write a real letter tomorrow. This is merely to tell you a few vital statistics. The trip goes like cream, with perfect roads and weather so far. We're a little slower than we'd planned, since we find that Tim needs to "lay over" every two or three days. He's only had two really bad nights, though, and his morale is better than for some time. As for me, I'm in the pink of health—my only trouble is that I doubt very much that I'll drop that superfluous two pounds I'd planned to, since (believe it or not) we have struck such odd drinking water that I've been easily talked into taking beer instead— However—

The New Monteleone is a typical convention hotel, complete with hordes of supercilious clerks, fat drunks with cigars and buttons saying "Call me Joe—or Butch—or Gus," dirty bathtubs, and running ice water. I think Aunt Petie romanced a bit about looking out over the river, since it is several blocks away and well hidden by factories and warehouses. However, the room is fairly quiet—and I doubt if we could do better in "Nawlins," which after some six hours reminds me of a mixture of salesmen's convention, the American Quarter in Paris in 1929 (full of shoddy bars and whiskey-voiced blonde divorcées), and the brothel district of Colón.

We caused a minor revolution by refusing to go to Antoine's our first night here, and went instead to a fine place recommended by the cabby, which was so much like Lipp's in Paris that we felt like ghosts. We'll remedy our heresy by going to Antoine's tomorrow night. We may even order oysters Rockefeller—but I'll be damned if I'll have crêpes suzette, guidebooks or no guidebooks.

Much love to you all.

It's swell to hear the river steamers. They moo like divine cows, musically and with a kind of maternal lonesomeness.

12.xii.40
New Orleans

Dearest Edie—

It was good to get your letter this morning—and don't ever say it was dull. I was glad to read every word of it. As you know by now, I'm only writing from big towns. It's silly to send postcards from little ones, since they'd reach you long after you'd got letters from big ones—and at night sometimes our one idea is to take a bath and fold.

I've meant to tell you for the last week how wonderful the heater is. We've used it almost every day (not down here in the gray mugginess, though) and have blessed your bones a thousand times. It works beautifully and warms the car up in about a minute flat. I don't see how we could have got along without it.

New Orleans has got us down temporarily, and we're leaving in the morning, with the definite idea of coming back on our way home. The combination of low altitude and very gray wet weather has played hob with poor Tim, and we're going to leave as soon as we can. We plan to be in Claymont December 23 or perhaps earlier, if all goes well. It has been slower than we'd thought. We've had a lot of fun, though.

How nice of Aunt Gwen to send us a present!

And speaking of presents, we've been sending a few packages to the Ranch. Please don't think we're crazy to have sent such silly things to you and Rex—but we decided the house had enough brass candlesticks and snuffboxes and that you'd like something you could use—at least once!

I'm so glad you nabbed off my coffee cups from the bazaar! I've bought some New Orleans coffee for them—the best I've had in America—but don't know whether I can make it right in an electrical drip thing. It has a lot of chicory in it—I think you'll like it and will split my box with you.

We plan to do some sightseeing next time we're in town. In the meantime I can smell fine smells, even up here in the room.

We stopped in Lake Charles night before last. It's a pretty little town on a sort of bayou, and the hotel was adequate and agreeable, with nice Negroes and bad food. You'd love the little towns in southern Louisiana. There are big old wooden houses, painted white, and the most enormous oaks I've ever seen, all green-gray and mysterious with Spanish moss. There are lots of sugar refineries, and the Negroes still live around them in the old slave cabins, which are gray now and quite beautiful.

There seem to be two main types of people here, the Cajun-Creole type, long and dark, with small black eyes under thick brows, narrow-lipped mouths, big noses, small heads on stiff thin necks—very proud looking, rather of Rex's and Dave's type—and the carp-faced, soft, sly, shrewd type rather like Huey Long. The latter have bad manners, generally. The Negroes are slow and thin and the most primitive I've seen. They hardly speak so I can understand—it's rather like Stepin Fetchit in the movies, only worse.

We'll probably go to Mobile tomorrow, if Tim feels like it. I may write from there. In the meantime, don't expect too many letters from me, but for goodness' sake don't worry if you don't hear every day.

Our love to you all, and very much—

24. xii. 40
Claymont, Delaware

Dearest family—

This will probably be a note, because Tim and I are driving down to Wilmington in a few minutes to collect a bundle from his uncle's office, and I want to get off a word or two to you while I can. You know what being company means—you think you'll have long quiet hours to yourself, but somehow they all went into talk and delivering Christmas baskets and so on and so on.

We got out here for lunch yesterday and found Mrs. P. much better and livelier than she was two years ago. She is even tinier and is slightly deafer—but since she talks constantly herself, it isn't necessary for her to hear what others say. She's an extremely attractive and interesting conversationalist most of the time, fortunately, with a good sense of satire and drama.

Uncle Boney, home on the dot of 5:00 or something, at the table at 6:00 sharp, to bed at 9:55, looks less well and to everyone's amusement was almost garrulous. T. says tonight he'll be taciturn and by tomorrow will have lapsed into his usual monosyllabism— ordinary treatment of honored guests.

As far as I can figure, we decorate the tree tomorrow morning and have presents tomorrow night. There is no early communion at All Saints'—only midnight mass and a 10:30 A.M. service—so I'll probably go to the latter. Uncle Boney disapproves of the former because it's "high church" and because it's decadent.

It seems queer to be in coal-soot country again. The weather is cold and sunny—very beautiful, but I had wished childishly for a white Christmas.

Sunday's ride through Washington and Baltimore was tiring —typical Eastern traffic. We were glad to get to Wilmington and fall into tubs and broiled lobster in the Darling Hotel.

More later—

26. xii. 40
Flower Hill Farm
Claymont, Delaware

My darling Edie—

This is to tell you we're still alive and that I plan to write a decent letter, so help me, before the sun sets on me. Last night we had Christmas, which was one of the most exhausting of my varied experience, largely because of sheer dullness. We fell into bed at 9:30, and from exhaustion and the fact that we hadn't slept much for two nights, woke up at 9:00 this morning! (I got up twice for Tim, but hardly remember.)

Much much love—and thanks for telegram—

14. ii. 41
Bareacres

I have two queer ugly pains, one on the inside of my left knee and one between my second and third fingers near the second joints on my left hand. It—they—feel like bruises, throbbing and not constant and never together and not in my body really but about half an inch in the air. They are ugly, as I said, and might bear out the neurophysics of some such addlepated astrologist as Larry Powell's mother—or equally well support the invert philosophy of any typical hypochondriac.

Tonight small showers beat on the roof. Tim prepares himself for bed. Butch taps about busily—his nails should be cut. Tiny, back from a disastrous spaying at the vets, sniffles and stinks and twitches on a pillow, and I should be caring for her now, putting Vaseline and cotton on the ugly hole in her back that came from too many glucose injections and tucking her into her little red coat for the night while I do my best not to smell her incredibly foul breath. Pour little rat—I should have said kill her—and now a kind of vanity tells me that in the two days she is home there is a great change for the better. I don't know. I see she is chipper, and that her ugly wound—infection from a careless injection? I want to believe the new vet is good—is closing, and that she coughs less. Vanity. And yet I think of the hopelessness of seeing any creature weak and ill and ugly, and of my mother and of Tim and of my own self occasionally helpless with acid-ridden guts, and I know that if we had the power of yes and no for suffering, most of us would be dead. If I could say—for others—what they may have wished poignantly to say for me—I'd be dead long since and they, too, and probably, possibly, things would be better. Yes or no, I must go now and make myself swab sensibly at a hideous white-rimmed hole, bolstered by the proud certainty that Tiny, poor do-less bitch ex-bitched, may soon be better for my care.

12. iii. 41

I've been unable to write in this notebook lately (I am almost unable to now but because of Tawny, who, about to drop the third litter in sixty months, is unusually fond of me and even more than usually snarlish with the other animals). It has seemed foolish to write, partly because although I have never reread any of this journal, I remember it was shamefully personal and thoughtless. Of course, I can say to myself, Is it necessary to prove a capacity for profundity in every paragraph? Is it best to comment, when I watch a spayed bitch humping like an old bull as she plays on Butch's back, that Mussolini still plays with Latin bombast on the unconscious, scornful backside of die Führer? Or that life, etc., etc., etc.? I could probably dish out a certain amount of this philo-sophical (quasi) guff, and even sell it in condensed form to the *Reader's Digest* but I am a defeatist or a realist or a procrastinator (God help us all if that still lies before me!) and cannot as yet steel myself to such wholesale crap mongering. Instead I shall go on, my lap full of cat-cum-kittens, my ears filled with Tim's flattering sweet melodies as he plays our new piano, my thoughts resolutely non-thoughtful.

18. iii. 41

Tonight I wanted several times to write here. I knew that it was because my heart and my mind were too full and that I would relieve myself, like a purged man, of a lot of self-pity and self-praise. So I withheld this doubtful pleasure from myself—and later indulged it in becoming captious with poor Tim about how silly it would be to keep the dogs out of the kennels when doubtless the whole house was infested with Butch's attack of lice. I grew grim and almost peevish, and made things no easier for Tim, and suddenly realized that it was simply because I had too much within. Perhaps it would have been better to write here in the first place. But I should have said much more than now. And why say it? The fact that I am dismal is enough, or even too much. My hands smell of liniment. If I read this years from now, which I do not plan to do, I would remember why: that Tim's other leg had increased in pain, like a scalded thigh, like skin held under steam, so that at nights sometimes he howled like a dog. Well—why go into all this? I hate myself—I'm like some women who have to tell someone, anyone, even their hairdressers, how they had three lovers in one night—

30. iii. 41

I've had no great drive to write here, or in letters, or stories or books, for some time now. I finally made myself answer a few letters, one of them eight months old. Now I don't feel like writing at all—I brought out this book simply because it's a wet lazy day and I felt I should be "doing something." This is not it.

18. iv. 41

Tonight I have not much more inclination than usual to write anything in this spasmodically attentive journal, but I think it might be a good idea. The night is cold . . . we have a fire and even one of the oil stoves lit for the first time in days . . . and T. sits wheeling through the Haydn sonatas at our lovely little new piano, which perhaps I've not yet mentioned here. (It is small, with a good tone, and although we were fools to buy it at $10 monthly for some three years, we have not yet regretted it.) T. says this [typing] doesn't bother him, and perhaps he is right. I am in my room. I could fill my empty pen and write silently on my knee by the fire, where I'd rather be . . . but I am too do-less tonight, and such small jobs irk me even to think of.

Tomorrow probably I shall buckle myself up a bit and concentrate on several things that need such attention. For one, I shall stop drinking whiskey, partly because it is expensive and partly because I am definitely overweight: I weigh about 150, which is at least ten pounds too much for me at my age. Then I shall try to finish staining and waxing three wooden chairs already built for the porch and build, stain, and wax three more . . . this week, if possible. Then I shall gradually oil all the floors, while Mrs. Purdy is on a two-week vacation in El Paso. She has some definite skunner against using oil or even an oiled mop on the floors, and in this climate oil is the only possible way to treat them . . . so, while she's gone, I plan to do all the wood in the house and then issue one of my timid ultimatums when she returns. Mrs. Purdy, I hear myself say, I want you to use this mop only for oiling, and please have it freshly filled each time you use it. This broom, also, is to be used solely on rugs . . . and the toilet floors must be washed with oily water once a week. Instead, I'll probably wave my hand vaguely at the O-Cedar mop* and then look at the soapsuds all over the floors. She exasperates me, but she's a good soul in her way and better than we could hope for here, I suppose. At times her blurred outlines, her vapid sentimentality get dangerously on my nerves, but . . . in the meantime, I am truly enjoying her vacation!

We have done a lot to Bareacres this past six weeks, and today Arnold came and built a fine stone staircase from the patio around the big rock and up in a good curve toward the hills. We arranged with him to help him buy a truck, for which he will come on weekends and pave our patio . . . good enough, since everything is in shape except the ground, by now worn powdery and soft and untidy on all our feet through the house. Arnold is the man to do it, with a real feeling for stone and how it should be laid, and with his new truck he can haul it, too.

Timmy made us some nice shelves on brackets for pots of petunias along the patio walls, and with them and the four strips of red and green and blue awning, all we need now is Arnold's floor and my chairs to have a lovely shadowy place for the summer. And in the winter we'll be there a lot, too, if we ever get the floor . . . any day with sun is warm and lovely there.

I almost hurt Arnold's feelings by saying in a joking way that amongst us we'd turn Bareacres into a damned park, but it's true —we fix one thing and then see another. This last week Leonardo has cleaned off all the weeds and with his extraordinary neatness has made the ground so smooth that I hate to walk on it, with neat, tidy, almost perfect circles around each tree.

We've built an arbor along the west side of the house and spent more money than we meant to on four grapevines. We've

---

* The O'Cedar mop was one that could be filled from the top with oil for the floors. Elsa preferred soap.

tended them as we were instructed for two weeks now, and they are all growing. The most amazing is the Rose of Peru, at the south end . . . we snipped off forty-three fine bunches today and left four on. The other three vines were almost empty of bunches, but we left one or two on each to see what would happen. They will be beautiful if all goes well and will make the end of the house cool and green-shaded in the summers.

I finished a book, *Consider the Oyster,* a little while ago and sent it off to New York, with a slight fanfare thanks to Idwal Jones. The three chapters sent to Mme. Metzelthin of *Gourmet* did not please her, but she wanted me to cut down a thing I wrote about Swiss restaurants, which I did with partial success. She wants me to write a series of articles about gourmets of history, which I should be glad to do . . . but I'd want at least to make enough money to pay for a week's research in Los Angeles, and she is on a limited budget. Oh, well . . . it would be good for me to do something with a deadline, probably.

Yesterday T. started again to take injections of cobra venom, at Bob Freeman's suggestion and under James Long's care. It will take ten days or so before there is any reaction, except the slight numbness and dropping of temperature that follows each shot. I have a feeling they may help. Something has to . . . the supply of Analgeticum seems pretty well stopped at San Pedro, thanks to the war.

Almost every word I write makes me think of another, and almost every word makes me think of something that has happened or is happening about war. I think of the hysteria, controlled so far, of people like the E.'s, who practice shooting at the whites of "their" eyes each morning and discuss hoarding food and tear bombs with passably self-contained passion. And then I think of David so lax and bitter about having to go into the army, probably this fall, and then I remember that I should write to J.B., a hospital orderly and apparently happy at Camp Moffett. That makes me think of the letters I ground out to Pat Nuttall and the Beutlers, word by word about the weather and such when I was wondering what the air was filled with around them and whether they were alive or dead or sane or screaming mad. I must write some more, to Mlle. Vodo-do-og-do and so on. I wonder about Georges Connes, very much, and Matruchot, and even about Paul Musset —or was his name Moussey?—and the Simonots and Michel de Vautibault. My mind is full of pain and speculation, underneath all the ordinary chaos of our lives here in this temporary quiet zone. I am puzzled about all these people and about my mother and about Noni and even about myself. I am puzzled and disturbed about the slow growth within myself of a need for religious faith, which has no reed to lean upon. I am not puzzled by the life between T. and me, though, and in that I am indubitably blessed above most humans.

Last night Blackberry, our strange lovely cat, developed a hunched gait and a painful glassy way of sitting down and squeaked with his usual good manners when we touched him ever so lightly at the base of his tail. He is still infinitely cautious about moving. I think maybe he's been stung—Arnold found one salamander, one angry scorpion, and several spiders and centipedes in his rocks today, and I've seen many blue lizards about. I'll take Blackie to the vet tomorrow if he hasn't loosened up a bit.

Today I deliberately watched the mother-cat, Smokey Josephine, vomit. Always before I've shut my eyes and my ears, if possible. I knew she was going to do it, out on the front slope, and thought to myself, Well . . . I'm almost thirty-three and supposedly have experienced many things, so I'll make myself watch this. It was queer the way her very red tongue stuck out in a kind of slide and then out shot an almost-perfect pale-blue lizard. Smokey seemed quite pleased by it all, but in spite of my reasonableness I felt a little nauseated.

We are taking care of Mrs. Purdy's little bitch Tiny, and I don't like her at all. We owned her for a time and decided she was too much like Mrs. P. to have around. Which indeed she is. I don't see, occasionally, how I can stand her for another ten days. She is so damned fawning. There is nothing bad about her, except bad temper now and then with the cats . . . but she brings out all my latent exasperation at other things so that I have to be careful to be nice to her, instead of whacking at her because I have broken a dish or stubbed my toe or some such thing.

9. vi. 41

One reason I write this is that I am putting off getting to work on my notes for a series of articles for *Gourmet*(?), which one moment is ordered and the next not, and the other is that I have just finished a stupid dutiful note to Aunt Maggie and am thinking about her and myself in relation to her.

I say the note was dutiful, and that makes me think of many reactions I have in spite of myself.

I remember with pleasure the times she used to come out to Whittier when I was little, and I know now that even then Edith loved her, rather as we did but much more so, as freedom and romance and what would almost be called glamour now. Aunt Maggie always brought us presents . . . always until Grandmother learned that we looked forward to her coming for that reason and forgot that there were many others, and told Aunt Maggie never again to bring us anything. Aunt M., even at some seventy years, obeyed her. She used to bring us each a little Japanese parasol, or in the winter once a fuzzy bathrobe covered with little rabbits and bears, or a box of crayons for each. Grandmother, when she heard us wonder what Aunt M. would bring next, decided we wanted her to come only for her presents and forbade them. Perhaps she was fighting against her own shame at never giving us anything gay like that. She did not know that, presents or not, we loved to have Aunt Maggie come.

Aunt M. had a tic that made the whole front of her face lift in one movement toward the top of her head. It lifted up her whole scalp every few minutes. It had begun when she was married, and when we knew her was gradually lessening, so that now in her ninetieth year it almost never shows. It fascinated us then, as such things will when you're a child, and later I remembered the irascible snarling man she married and could well see that something bad had caused it, which she forgot gradually as the years passed and Uncle Doctor died and she forgot the tantrums and neuroses of her nine high-tempered children.

She was a little girl with flat hair, according to the stories, and when my grandmother, several years older, decided that she should have curly hair, twirled Aunt Maggie's hair untiringly around a stick, nobody was surprised either that it turned actively kinky or that several of Aunt M.'s children had hair almost like a Negro's.

She was a happy creature, with a long thin jaw and one eye— my wee eye, she has always called it—that was higher and smaller than the other. I forget which one it is.

She married an adventurous man who practiced medicine but was at heart and sometimes actually the kind who went to Chile for silver (and always smoked Chilean cheroots afterward), who had a terrible cruel choleric sense of humor so that he tormented his patients by telling them they had scabies when it was really only a scratch, who begot nine or so frightened, spirited, truculent children.

Aunt Maggie also took care of her strong willful mother for many years, so that now she says without much bitterness but with her own kind of strength that she never knew what it was to have a home of her own until she was too old to have one.

For the last several years she has lived with her strange, painful, attractive daughter Mary, whose own unfortunate life is a plain result of her parents' and who has been good and kind with that unmistakably martyred kindness of neurotic women. The two women have lived together in what many would call luxury, usually with two ill-trained and mismanaged servants, in a mournful and extremely banal California suburban villa. And Mary, really in spite of herself, has managed to tell everyone what agonies she suppresses every time Aunt Maggie twitches her brow or, more lately, sniffs. It seems she sniffs nervously and constantly. To add to it, Aunt Maggie was raised to turn all her social energies into the church and consequently has made it almost imperative for Mary to do the same. Mary has been both intelligent and generous about this and goes every Sunday to a class she leads, apparently forgetting forever the days when she was one of the toasts (in champagne) of such rich-bitch country clubs and sets as flitted about Sewickly and such Eastern hangouts.

Aunt Maggie now is very old. She is a small woman who is unruffled at receiving callers in bed, mainly because she is still truly and delightfully vain and knows how attractive she appears in a fine ruffled linen nightgown to people used to department-store pink chiffon. She has great calm, partly because she probably does not care much what we think of her and partly because she is old and partly because she is a real lady. She does not hesitate to scold, knowing that her manner is too winning to annoy for long.

She is vain and spends hours choosing a silk, always expensive, for her summer or winter or fall dress, which is always made about the same way and yet never looks out of date except that it is long always. She wears nice low pumps and usually a piece of rich but very conventional jewelry given her by her children for some fete . . . the children being both rich and conventional themselves.

I am fond of Aunt Maggie for many reasons. One is that she was generous and gay when I knew no other age than the stiff and disapproving one of my grandmother, her older sister. Another is that she is a nice old lady now, after a rather twisting and hard life, and in spite of her enslavement to her sister, her mother, her husband, is a quiet, strong personality by herself. I like her because she is clean and dainty, too. And I like her because she has always been good and generous and merry and sweet with my own mother.

That is probably one reason why I am sometimes rather stupid about her. Mother, as she grows older, sometimes becomes actively fatuous about Aunt Maggie, and I feel not jealous, as it would seem on the surface, but embarrassed and wishing Mother would be more intelligent . . . a case of hurt vanity, of course, as always when someone you love does not behave as you think she ought. I think, Oh, for God's sake, when Mother says or does some silly thing about Aunt Maggie, and then Mother feels sad and hurt, and I feel badly and know that I can never explain how warm and grateful I feel to Aunt Maggie, not only for myself but for Mother. But when I try to say so, it all turns into hurt and ridicule and misunderstanding.

That probably explains why I write this now. One of Aunt Maggie's sons, a man I consider without much provocation to be a cruel, willful autocrat, has suddenly developed an almost diseased sense of mother worship—he has portraits painted, etc., etc.—and has sent special sheets to each cousin and so on to be filled out for a great birthday book on Aunt Maggie's ninetieth or something year. Everyone, even Edith, agrees that she will be bored ... probably. But we must all do it.

For a long time we all laughed, Mother among the loudest ... but now that the time approaches we are practically forced to write "tributes" to this grand old lady of the family, the matriarch, etc., etc. There was a great deal of family discussion about it, mostly my fault because I would quibble and balk. Finally I wrote in the book. Now I regret it, because in an adolescent way I insisted on being truthful and said that A. M. was the nicest old lady I know, and now I feel that I should simply have handed out the usual family guff and skipped everything I really meant.

The whole thing has been, I suppose, a kind of protest against sentimentalizing a family character. It is inevitable—I should know it from Mother's predilection for such novels as *The Matriarch* and some of Galsworthy's and so on—but I hate it. So instead of keeping my mouth shut and letting Mother have her little literary orgasms of family pride and Aunt Maggie her hard-won tidbits of whipped-up family loyalty, I must be truculent and worry Mother and not write what I should in the Birthday Book.

The thing is that I like A. M. probably as much as most of the people who will write to her ... more I think, complacently, knowing my own strong secret gratitude to her for many things that I cannot even write about ... but something stupid and antagonistic to seeing such people as Edith make fatuous fools of themselves forces me to be difficult.

I love Edith and would like her to know that I love Aunt Maggie ... but I don't think I could show her how, behind my partly jealous, partly hurt reactions to her sappiness, I see her own respect and feel my own ... or know my shame at being stupid and truculent and all that myself.

I am in one of those spells of putting off getting to work, which I suppose hits every worker who can choose his own speed. They are destructive, in some ways, because they make working patchy and difficult, and they are purely a mental state, so that I feel ashamed of my own dilatory frame of mind and spend almost meaningless moments trying to talk myself out of it. Logically I succeed, but physically I do not, so that, as now, I wander about the house and lie down and get up and drink Coca-Cola and occasionally write a letter or read a recipe.

I finished a short book about oysters a few weeks ago, typed it quickly and for me fairly well, and sent if off. It was sold easily, to Duell, Sloan, and Pearce, thanks partly to the kindly interest of Idwal Jones, who still likes *Serve It Forth*. Then I got into a little spate of correspondence with Madame (self-titled) Pearl V. Metzelthin, who edits *Gourmet* in N. Y., and partly through her vagueness (Mrs. Pritchett says she sometimes suspects Mme. M.'s head is filled with maline) and partly through Pritchett's enthusiasm, I thought I was supposed to do a series of articles about famous hosts and hostesses and dashed to Los Angeles for five days, where I grubbed in the library through unpleasant memoirs of Boni de Castellane, and Harry Lehr, and such creatures. In a few days I found Mme. M. had been mistaken—that was an old idea abandoned over a year ago, etc. I wrote a testy letter to Pritchett, and at present she wants me to do one article about a gourmet as a kind of try-cake and sit tight. The result is that my secondary mind is filled with data about what I somewhat glibly term the "Gilt-edged Gluttons" that I gleaned in Los Angeles, and yet I am halted in my fine frenzy to write about them by the knowledge that nobody wants to read about them and further halted by knowing that I should be turning out an article about some damn silly old boy "as a gourmet"—Richelieu or somebody—already safe and well known. Meanwhile I stew mildly about the house.

My secondary mind is well occupied, but my primary mind is a pained and aching blank, filled with the hollowness of realizing that T. is not well. He took fourteen shots of cobra venom over some four weeks, and no good came of it. When we were in Los Angeles, I saw for the first time what I should have known weeks before, except that we don't move about much here in the house, that stairs and even straight walking are almost impossible for him anymore. He must stop and rest every few steps, and it humiliates him who even with one leg has hopped about like a cricket. He suffers mildly and constantly on his good leg . . . a kind of tired yawning, rather like the preamble to what took off the other but slower, and his little leg is terribly sensitive to touch. Then there are two or three places—where an injection made a little swelling, where Blackberry licked his skin—that seem dry and red and painful. Christ, I think with that impotent half-blasphemous calling out of helpless people, what can I do? I don't admit that T. has any tenuous thing like Buerger's disease. Then I see strange signs like his increasing weakness and these occasional tiny dry painful places on his beautiful firm clear skin, and my mind grinds out a slow word *Christ,* in several syllables, willy-nilly, a kind of impotent protest, a kind of acknowledgeable acknowledgment of something I do not know but must recognize. What goes on in T.'s mind I cannot think. He is for the most part quiet and, in a controlled way, happy. Now and then he cracks open, like a hard-boiled egg that is accidentally dropped, and what I see then in his eyes and hear in his voice frightens and horrifies me so that I want to lie on my bed and go into a faint, or become a believing nun, or anything to hide from it. But I know that I cannot hide, any more than he can, and I know, too, most of the time that what he is doing may not be worth it but is the only decent thing to do.

The reason perhaps for writing diaries, among people who seem to have to write, is that they learn a certain clearness and focus. This I do not seem to acquire as I grow older. In fact, this journal, although I have not read it, impresses me with its agglomeration of careless typing, weighty incoherent sentences, and undisciplined moods. I hope that I have sense enough and *soon* to destroy it unread. T. knows I write it and sometimes speaks of it, hoping I think to read it. I have said nothing in it I would not have him see, but I am sure I have said many things that it would be well if he did not. Why bother, why worry, why exasperate people?

We are godparents. Jane and Bill Evans's daughter Barrie is the cause, and in two weeks, if all goes well, we will christen her. I am bored but tolerant, and when I hold the little smelly peeing bodkin in my hands, if I do, I shall quite possibly cry, wishing it were my own. The sentimentality, the pomp of procreation, and the ceaseless mystery cannot but affect me, and my sincere thankfulness that I am sterile is often swept away by stirrings that are as raw and gnawing as any sexual orgasm. I shall wear a white linen dress and gulp a bit and help the Evanses dry the dishes after the usual noisy lusty supper in the old wooden house in Santa Monica.

Anne's book I have finished at last and told her, without saying I liked it, that it is beautiful, strange, painful, sincere. It is indeed. I did not like it, because I thought it was undisciplined, and I feel more and more that a writer must know and self-impose discipline, of the tongue, the mind, the spirit, more than anything else in the world. I think I know many of the fallacies and pitfalls of that argument. But I still believe it. And Anne's book, in spite of its sincerity, was muddled spiritually and was a terrible hodgepodge of words and images and research and prettiness and realism and mysticism (what T. calls misty-schism, viciously), so that in the end my feeling was one of fatigue at having read it and a kind of intellectual nausea. It needs discipline. Anne thinks she knows it. Perhaps she does. God knows the book was sincere and full of prayer and work and thought. But still it was clouded, and I do not know what is the answer for Anne herself. She is a fine creature, but I think she has been deluded into thinking of herself as an intellect when she is really a strongly natural body with too large a vocabulary for her own strength, so that what she and some of her friends think is brain is really a sensitive and highly articulate nervous system. She is a wonderful sensual writer, and I wish, probably vainly, that she could realize it and not try to be a sort of Hearstian Saint Thomas Aquinas.

20. vi. 41

It is a hot day, and outside . . . It is another hot day now, the next one, and yesterday I was probably going to say something obvious and startlingly dull about the noise of the cicadas or the sound of cottonwood leaves on the brick patio.

David and Norah left about two o'clock for Mexico. They forgot their only map and came back for it, but otherwise got off with unusual finesse, acting much calmer than I could have under the circumstances. All their plans seem dreamy, and our only touch with them for the next few weeks is Wells Fargo, Mexico City. It is a sign of the difference in our ages that I cannot help wondering what we'd do if Edith should die or some such thing, while they seem never to have thought of such emergencies. They plan to reach the city in about a week and stay in a pension for a while and then go to a less expensive place. Noni is taking her typewriter and will probably write about Hawaii, and David thinks he will do a lot of sketching. They looked well, in brownish cotton clothes, but physically they seem too finely drawn to me for their ages: thin, pallid, with slender controlled hands, David's with curved nails, and both of them with tense lines at the corners of their mouths and smudges under their eyes. Of course, David is almost completely bald. And Norah, often, looks older and more worn than I do. I pity them both, for they seem finished too soon. They need new blood in them.

Last night I told Tim what he was waiting for me to say, that I can too easily get into an easy routine of doing research and writing articles and books about gastronomy and that I'd do this one small series about Gilt-edged Gluttons, which *Gourmet* does not want but which I can probably sell elsewhere, and then sit myself down to writing a novel. I've always thought that novels should only be written if there is something in them that *must* be said, and now here I plan to write one simply because it will be good for me. But maybe I'll have something to say that I don't know now. It will be hard, and I feel lazy and yet gnawed, so I'd better get to work.

There was a little bird in the house today, not very nervous. We took the screen from the closet window, and I think it is gone now.

Twice lately I have dreamed about oversized lizardlike animals. Last night I looked down from a window and saw Blackberry holding against the bloody ground a long gray lizard, about three feet long, and I saw that the cat was exhausted and that as soon as the lizard rested a little it would whip away. I knew that I must go down and pick it up with a towel over my hands and I was wondering what to do next when I awoke. And the other night Tim and I were on a small ship as beautiful as the *Normandie,* and an enormous crocodile was caught and tied firmly alongside the ship like another smaller ship before we all realized that it was our undoing. One whip of its great tail almost capsized us, and we knew too late that if it were freed it would destroy us at once and if it were held captive it would destroy us more slowly but just as surely by gradually weakening all the seams of the little ship with its occasional terrible lashings. There was despair among us all, but I didn't feel any fear . . . just a resignation and a curiosity that made me look down at the half-submerged malicious eyes of the creature and speculate about its food and its life and its possible thoughts.

3. vii. 41

Today I can't remember any other birthday than this. I got up early and fussed quietly around the house, in a vague spate of getting ready for Father's and Mother's coming this afternoon. Finally I dressed in work clothes, ready to clean the patio later, and now I sit on the porch on my little tuffet eating potato chips and drinking beer. My mind runs with absolute distraction on food for this weekend, on the pets, on the hack articles I've been writing grimly in the last few weeks. But inside all of me, like the bone in the flesh, the stone in the fruit, is the hard core of thought about T.

For some time now—perhaps six weeks—his leg has grown more tired, with a gnawing sickening tiredness. Yesterday the doctor tested it and found it strong and apparently normal. But when he went to bed, Timmy and his leg collapsed. It was a dreadful time. It was full of fright and agony. Now I don't know whether he can get up this morning. In a little while we'll see. Will he ever get up? I know he is abysmally discouraged. His eyes look strangely at me, and even when he is asleep I feel them rolling under their lids, looking for help or me or anything but despair.

15. vii. 41

I pause on my way to a bath and bed to record, here on this hot and in some ways hopeless night, that today I slew a literary god —or demigod. I perceived at last that E. M. Forster, the first and almost the last writer I nearly wrote a letter to, is but an intellectual E. F. Benson. That is praise—but for what Forster once meant to me, it means damnation indeed.

18. vii. 41

I try to imagine in my mind, in the part that sees colors, and smells, and tastes, what it is like to be Noni and Dave in Oaxaca, sitting in the *zócalo* drinking beer and watching the stately sexual parade each night while the band plays. Or working in the hot thin air, hearing the life in the patio and writing or drawing of quite another one.

Sis is here. Now and then we go into the patio and play water from the hose on each other. It is fun, childlike, and yet in a peculiar way more enjoyable, since I think we share a pleasure in looking at each other, sparkling and glistening in the leafy shadows of the cottonwoods, with the water spraying out from us into the sunlight. Her body, in spite of the scars on her belly, is fine and slender, less full than mine, with sloping hips and small breasts with brown soft nipples.

3. ix. 41

The old adolescent days (or nights) of lying alone looking at moonlight on the eucalyptus leaves are gone. Now when I turn off the switch, I twitch. Now I am afraid of quiet and the dark, and my mind, riddled like an old oak chest with four thousand loathsome wormholes, creaks and crunches at itself and makes insufferable such earlier pleasures. I drink a too-hot, too-strong toddy in bed, and if my luck holds I go to sleep after some dutiful trash reading (*Mystery of the Police, Death Holds the Cup,* et al.), and then in a while (I have no watch) I wake cold and sober and my unwilling mind leaps like a starved dog at the poisonous meaty thoughts. Finally, stiff with resolve, I achieve another bout of sleep, terrible with dreams that at last, in a few minutes or hours or seconds, wake me sweaty with nightmare. I get up, as soon as I'm able to unhinge my joints from horror, and weave to the bathroom and bathe my face and sit on the toilet and drink some cold water. In a while, diligently, I sleep again, and either dream another nightmare or sleep lightly, fitfully, almost peevishly, until after dawn. Then, about one morning out of three or four, I sleep heavily until 8:00 or so, without hearing the shot. I try to live (even asleep?) with what dignity I can muster, but I wonder if there is much in this abject procedure. I write it down here partly because this is the first night I am really alone and partly to shame myself, like a whiplash. I can hear a night dove in the arroyo, and Freda van Benschoten's spaniel, whose voice has just changed, barks heavily across the flats. I shall live, I know in spite of myself, and where and how?

9. ix. 41

I discovered several years ago that in order to stay at the Ranch without becoming almost frantic with boredom I must, early in the visit, establish some kind of excuse for leaving Mother and going to my own room. That is why I am typing now. I hope she can hear me. I want her to think that I am working. I *must* be able to come up here to Rex's room, where I am sleeping while he's in Chapala, and pretend to be doing something so that I can't be interrupted. It is a stupid trick, and I'm ashamed of it, but it's necessary. Otherwise I would spend all day, every day, sitting in the living room or on the porch trying to read, and all the time listening to Mother and having to answer, and eating too much, and listening to the radio news, and going uptown to do the marketing. Of course, I'll do those things anyway, but not *all* day . . . just most of the day, because I am trying to be nice and make Mother feel that I am grateful to be here. She is being nice to me and coming out to Bareacres when she really would rather stay here, so I must be nice, too, about these few unavoidable days at the Ranch. It is four weeks and three days now, though, and I know even if the rest of the family does not that I must stop this ghastly life of compromise and get to work. It is bad for me, this drifting about and postponing the truth: I must live alone. That seems to horrify everyone. But to me it is plain: I *am* alone, completely and unalterably, and living with other people or having them live with me can never make me any less so, as long as I live. So I might as well get down to it. I can't stand much more of the hopeless stupid life I've been leading since T. died. I must get to work. I must practice being dignified all by myself, instead of always having an audience to make it easier.

Pretty soon now I'll write about T.'s death, because I think I should. Of course, I wrote at once to Anne and later to his mother in answer to her first hurt, bitter letter. But I haven't written to myself yet. I keep putting it off. There are too many things that I can't write yet. They're in words in my head, but I am afraid of writing them. It is as if they might make a little crack in me and let out some of all the howling, hideous, frightful grief. It is difficult to know, certainly, how to live at all.

I won't keep up this typing any longer without getting too near subjects that scare me. Perhaps it would be better to write about other less inward things. I like this typewriter, for one, and wish more than ever that I knew how to use one properly. My half-taught system is not bad for composition, but when I have to copy anything, it tires my eyes not to be able to type without looking at my fingers all the time. I could go to school again and learn. When I consider that, though, I always decide to get along as I have for so many years. T. made Anne learn to type properly when she turned into a writer, and her typing is perfect . . . easy, even, correct.

Butch is lying beside me on a cushion, just under the end of Rex's bed. His coat is about half grown out now, and if the autumn turns hot, I'll have him shaved again. I hope I do: I love to see him all naked because he has such a funny trim little body. He has been all right for the last three days, but until then I worried that he might die of grief, as I have read that sensitive dogs sometimes do. He ate without enthusiasm, and his coat grew dull, and he almost never played but instead walked heavily about the house all his waking hours, looking for T. Occasionally he would fall into a kind of frenzy and run frantically through the studio and the porch and my workroom, sniffing and whimpering at all the fading odors of T.'s crutches or hands or body on the chairs and the floor and the books and curtains. It was sad to see, and there seemed nothing that I could do. Butch was polite with me but quite unresponsive. Now and then he would seem to be interested in Sis or in Mrs. Purdy, but in a few minutes he would begin his search again. A few days ago he began to notice me again, and now he will not leave me if he can help it and seems almost to be trying to entertain me and accompany my spirit.

I left the little puppy at the vet's for the first time. He was very quiet in the car to Riverside, but the ride loosened his bowels and he made several messes, poor thing. He is a jolly little mongrel, and I love him. T. did, too, and asked that he be called Colonel Timothy instead of plain Colonel, and then I added Arrow Ass because of the little buff arrow under his stub of a tail, so he has quite an impressive name. I usually call him Colonel and refer to him as "the" Colonel. He is glossy black, with curly spaniel ears and what looks rather like a Doberman body, with buff feet . . . a thoroughly comical mixture. His eyes are black, and he rolls them so that the whites show, like a blackface actor. He is very quick and imitates everything Butch does, so I'm hoping he won't be too hard to train. He is stubborn, though. I am proud of how healthy he is. He is now three months and one week old.

Blackberry is in good shape. He seems to hunt all night, and I have to keep the cat doors closed or he brings his catch inside to eat. He sleeps most of the day on the red chair in the guest room. The strange pearl-gray tufts behind his ears are clearer than ever and more obviously made of fur unlike the rest of him. It is almost like cobweb. He is less impish now that he is older, but is very attractive. He still hasn't learned how to purr but has a large vocabulary of sounds, most of them tiny and theatrical.

Susie, now about three months old, I think, who was given to us the Sunday before T. died, is still very small. She is very funny and appealing and impudent, with a big-eyed pale face like a marmoset. She has a painful habit of walking up people's legs as if they were trees.

The other night when I took Butch and the Colonel down to their kennel, Butch ran into the thick weeds in the arroyo where Sis and I heard the two rattlesnakes a couple of weeks ago, and he refused to come when I called. That is unusual for him. He was silent, but I could hear him moving. I knew it was not a human he saw or he'd have growled, and I could not hear the snakes. I got a cane and the flashlight and rather unwillingly went after him, because there seemed no tone of voice or threat that would bring him up. He was leaning his front feet against the trunk of one of the big trees. Blackie was down there, too, watching. Their four eyes gleamed like lamps, and they were quite silent. I flashed my light all over the branches, and there in a high crotch I finally saw a tiny black and white creature, with a round innocent face like a teddy bear's. It peered down at me, blinking cautiously, and I peered up wonderingly at it. Maybe it was a chipmunk. I know it was not a baby skunk, in spite of its definite black and white markings. Finally I dragged Butch away and left it. I am sure Blackie could not reach it. It was a sweet little animal. I wonder how Butch knew that it was up there . . . it must have been two hundred feet from the house, but he went to that tree as unhesitatingly as if it were rehearsed beforehand and made not a single sound.

Mother is having her massage this morning. She seems fairly well, I think.

We are anxious to have a letter from Mexico.

14. x. 41

When you look at a man, it is easy to imagine what may have been his pleasures, given a certain destiny—that is, given a way you might place his present or future action. If he is a murderer, you can become completely involved in the things he saw and thought and dreamed and ate when a child, that he should thus evolve.

But if you look at a man who is nothing, a man like S., who at fifty-two looks eighty-two, who snarls and hawks and spits and inches thinly through his miserable days, what can you give his past as pleasure? Did he ever see straight? Did he ever smell right and clear the smell of a rose or a woman or a toasted bacon sandwich? Perhaps he went to a few pasty brothels, and probably he was seasick coming from England to Chicago as a lad, and certainly he got irascibly drunk quite often, in the inimitable way of tall thin men who are to die of stomach ulcers. But where was his pleasure?

My spirits heave at the thought of this human waste.

The other day his wife flushed and tittered at a sudden flurry of excitement among the animals, when Butch, upset by the smell on himself and the Colonel of a new flea soap we'd used in their bath, began to hump and move himself over the puppy. S.'s wife, wet as I was from the scrubbing we had given the two dogs, watched them sideways until I broke up the business, and then giggled, "I hope S. doesn't take a bath today!"

"Why?" I asked absentmindedly, and then laughed dutifully to realize that she was trying to be intimate, "just girls together." I was shocked at the connection of these innocent dog movements with human copulation, and then sickened to think any woman could feel thus about her chosen man's desires, and then I averted my mind from the hideous pictures of S.'s thin white bones thumping flaccidly up and down between her soft-fleshed thighs. And then my mind filled with those intolerable lines, "Christ, that my love were in my arms, and I my bed again." And I shut off words.

10
War Story

Almost all the books and stories now have touched war, vicariously or with true sweat and noise and fear. Of course, people, too, everywhere have touched it, even in the quiet dead-end valley where I live. I know that the iceman's daughter, soon to have a child, has lost her husband on some dry far island. I see the women in the unused store building bent over their piles of bandages, rolling and rolling, with their heads wrapped prettily in white and their hearts perhaps heavy with the pain they prepare for. And now and then a boy who graduated from high school a few months ago has his picture on the front page of the weekly paper. He is dead, or he wears a new medal maybe, or both.

Things like that go on, but when I read printed books, the war seems far from here. We have no stink of it, no frantic tortured eardrums, none of the strained gallantry of men and women who have touched it. I sit passively on my hill, reading about the stench, the roar, the high courage.

In letters from England, people I love say defensively each time they get a box of food from here, "We are really *quite* well off, you know . . . but the powdered lemon *did* avert a wretched chest cold."

And Emily Hahn in Hong Kong decides not to walk up to tea that day, because there is really too much going on, what with all the bloody bombs and then the ack-ack and the rioting. She has tea at home instead, with refugees and her baby and the cook saying Charles is wounded badly and she cannot get to him. . . . The tea is hot, what there is of it.

Or I get word from a man I've never heard of at an unknown Midwest college, saying that a friend of his has heard through the underground that Georges, dear gaunt fine-browed Georges, was safe a year ago somewhere outside of Dijon and sent word for none of us for God's sake to try to get in touch with him because of his kids who were still in Caen with their grandparents.

So I read all this—and even books by correspondents—and it seems sometimes as if I had already died, here on my quiet hill.

The other day, though, I knew I was still alive. J.B came to see me.

J.B. is the son of Spittin. They all lived at the turn of the road where it went into the main part of the valley, and I had to shift gears there after the curves and the tricky ruts, and I got so I stopped to wave and then to talk. I would have had to stop anyway, because of all the children under my wheels.

One time I asked Spittin, who was called that because he spat so much, how many he had. He was slow in answering but finally figured out, "Abaht nine livin', and fahve dade."

But his wife told me that more than that had died, and she seemed sad about it. She was pregnant then, and soon after our talk I heard long cries, like a lost calf, and finally I drove down the mile of road and found her writhing on the bed, with only three or four of the smallest to watch. There was almost nothing I could do by then, and I was very ignorant, but by late afternoon when the children started coming home and Spittin rolled in from whatever pub he'd been at, things were fairly much all right again, and he could think a while and say, "*Six* dade."

J.B. was the oldest of this clutch of hostages to fortune. He was about seventeen when I first knew him, and probably the dullest of the lot, a tall thick boy with pasty skin and eyes emptier than a dead man's. He was still in school, but his grades were so bad that they weren't even marked on his card, and he and his teachers longed for his next birthday when he could legally stop going to classes. He used to shamble up the hill to see my husband, and I'd hear him talking, slowly, painfully, in the studio. Gradually he began to pose, and some good pictures came out of it, although he did not seem to see them but only the Coke bottle he held permanently in his hand. After perhaps ten Cokes, he would talk more, and we began to think that the reason he was so slow was that he was never spoken to as a grown boy but always as if he were the same age as the current baby in the brood. This was partly because Spittin and his wife were not much older either— about seven or eight, at most. They didn't realize what they were doing to J.B., of course. But he was *lonely*. We'd say something about how cool weather was easier to work in, something simple like that, and J.B. would think for a minute, and then his clay face would lighten and he'd answer, with a kind of piteous delight, "That's right." What he needed, we thought, was to get away from all the babies.

Finally he was eighteen, and right away he left school and drifted to the nearest beer parlor. He was too clumsy to play pool and too poor to drink much, but a couple of times I picked him up on my way home from the village and he was mumbling drunk, for the other men would give him liquor so they could tease him better, with his baby speech.

Spittin was worried, and whenever he saw J.B. come into a bar, he'd leave by the back way. He talked to my husband. We suggested that J.B. enlist—this was just before the first draft. J.B. did, but the night before he was to report he ran away. That was bad; we felt to blame. Then he came home, and as soon as he could, he enlisted again. He was in.

It seemed queer at first not to see him when I stopped by Spittin's house, sitting on the doorstep with his heavy puffed face between his hands and two or three little siblings climbing over his thick legs. His mother stopped doing the daily washing in an old tub over a fire of chopped-up auto tires, too, and when I went in one day to see why, thinking I might find her bedded again, she beamed and showed me the rattletrap washing machine J.B. had made her buy with his first pay.

A few days later she walked up the hill to see us. She had on some kind of corset, and her hair was curled, and she looked ·almost my age, although I knew she was really younger. We sat formally in the living room. She thanked us for getting J.B. to go away. It seemed strange, because she never had mentioned anything personal, like the time I helped her when she made the long ugly noises. We drank Cokes in little polite sips, and then as she went away, she smiled shyly at me for the first time and said, "You see? I ain't got my bar' feet!" And I saw that she did indeed have shoes on, cheap high-heeled fancy shoes. She was really happy, and I never saw her again, although I have heard that she is working in the laundry of a training camp and has finally heeded the country nurse enough not to have any more babies. She left me a Christmas cactus, which still thrives.

I thought that was the last of them all, because they moved

away, and new people came to the little house and picked up all the empty hominy cans and raked the yard clean of empty Coke bottles and dung.

Then last week J.B. came back to see me. When I went to the door, I didn't know him, of course; he seemed taller, thinner, with a fairly clear and almost intelligent face. His uniform was immaculate, with the shirt buttons, the buckle, the fly all in line, and the creases just so down his arms and thighs and over his deep chest. He looked fine, for Spittin's son or anyone's.

I was busy, but I was glad to see him, too. We sat in the garden in the gentle sunlight. He fidgeted, but not as he'd used to. His hands were still clammy to the touch, I noticed when we met, and there was nervous sweat on his face, but as we talked, he looked straight at me instead of sideways and almost didn't stammer. He was in the medical corps. He wanted to learn about surgery, he said. He shook his head about the fliers at his base.

"They're crazy," he said firmly, kneading his hands together. "They crash, and they see their friends spread all over, and they go right up again. They're crazy. They don't have to pick up the pieces the way we do."

He shook his head, and his hands looked moist and frantic, but he had improved. He spoke coherently, if very simply. He knew my husband had died, and when he said it was too bad and asked if he could have something, I went into the house and got a necktie. He folded it carefully and put it in his breast pocket and then went on talking about the hospital and an operation he'd watched there on his own stomach. I was glad to see how he'd grown up, but I was busy, too, and wished he'd go.

Then he seemed almost to pull his hands from their arms and told me, with his eyes on the ground, about how he had a three-week furlough because of the operation and had only been home two days and couldn't stand it.

"Nothin' to say," he said miserably. "My folks don't talk much. My dad was in France last time, but he don't know nothin' about this one. There's too many kids. And I can't eat the food. It rises on me. We eat swell at the base. But I can't eat at home no more."

He was trembling. He was lost and terribly lonely for his prolonged childhood.

"I just can't stand it there no more," he said, so low I could hardly hear him.

"Let's have a Coke, J.B.," I said, and without waiting for an answer, I went into the kitchen from the garden, leaving him with his head low, as if he were wounded.

I felt awful. I felt that something was my fault: I had helped to pull up his roots, and now he was alone, nevermore to be a child with other children near him. Suddenly the hill seemed emptier than I could bear. I felt like running away. Alone, alone, my heart cried. *Seule, seule,* wept the dove imprisoned in the tapestry. I, and he, and all of us . . .

I left the Coke in the bottles, the way he used to like it, and when I got to the door into the garden, I stopped with a horror that seemed almost a natural part of my inchoate misery.

J.B. stood weaving and winding in the middle of the stone-flagged court, turning slowly round and round, with his hands hanging at his sides like an ape's. He has lost his mind, I thought at once. He has gone mad with all the blood and the pieces of fliers in baskets and not being able to talk to Spittin. I am here with him on the hill, and he is mad.

I stood for a minute with the two Coke bottles steady in my hands. Then I went out without banging the door and touched him on the shoulder.

He swung around until he faced me, and his dull little eyes were full of tears, and his face was lighter than I ever thought it could be, almost as if something had turned itself on inside his thick pasty head. He smiled at me, and a tear ran down into his wide mouth.

"Ain't nothin' changed," he said softly. He swung around once more, as if something had spun him from above, and his eyes touched the rocks, the hills, the far bending silvery eucalyptus trees, before he looked square at me again.

"Ain't nothin' changed, really."

He drained the bottle and handed it absently back and then very simply wiped his cheeks with the back of one clean pudgy hand. "I got to be gittin'. Gonna send myself a telegram to report for duty."

He looked seriously at me, with more intelligence in his face than I'd ever seen there. "We got ourselves to think of, you know."

We shook hands, and his was dry and firm, and then he swung off down the hill. He had escaped, and I, alone but no more lonely, felt that for a few minutes I had touched pain and death and strength very near me, instead of on the written page or even on the bed of childbirth or at the grave.

—*Bareacres, Hemet, California, 1940*

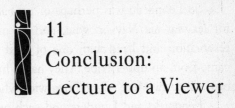

11
Conclusion:
Lecture to a Viewer

Yes, this painting is a very strange one. You will notice the shell and the involuted use of both live and dying flower, and it seems to go far beyond the shell and the flowers, the dahlias or whatever they were—yes, dahlias. There is the limitless horizon, which was there in the near-desert when the picture was painted.

The air and the brush were dry. The flowers were vivid but dying. The painter was dying, too.

We went often to the graveyard of the Pala Indians, farther south from our place. We knew a young man named Leonardo who was of the Palas and who for a time had moved up instead of down on their scale by marrying a Navaho. This did not last, and he moved away from his agrarian culture, northward toward a lower tribe, the Sobobas. (This word *lower* sounds very snobbish, and such it was: the Sobobas were not as skilled and perhaps as subtle as the Palas. They were far below the Navahos in that complex pecking order.)

So Leonardo was perhaps or probably ousted from his tribe for leaving his Navaho wife, and he moved up to the Soboba reservation and lived with one of their best women because he came from an upper tribe. They had a fine little son named Cowboy, about two feet tall and two wide when I knew him.

Leonardo and I understood each other, I think. We pruned tobacco bushes and walked past a couple of rattlesnakes without resentment.

One day he said that my husband and I should go down to Pala to stay in the cemetery for a few hours. It seemed to be a message, and we obeyed it.

It was not the first time we had been there. The quiet old mission was a haven. There was the chapel, of course, with its basically pagan symbols on the plastered walls covered thickly with whitewash. And there were the softly reverential garden and its burying ground, all one. At the western end, as I remember, was the bell tower in a separate clumsy adobe structure, which an old man climbed up and into to ring the bell.

On the dry mounded graves, out past the few small Anglo-style tombstones, there were shells that had come up from the Sea of Cortez. They were laid out in puny crosses or in opulent outlines of where the bodies lay below. They were broken, rarely whole, and they glowed like pearly gems on the dry rich soil. The people had carried them this far. We knew that nothing should be touched, but I would have liked to take one faraway shell to help me remember these days of return, of farewell.

Then, the last day, an aged man climbed down from the stubby crude bell tower. He walked toward us, with a shell in his hand, and he was smiling confidently. He came right toward us and put the shell from his hand into my husband's. They looked deeply at and into each other. Then he went back toward the mission.

My husband held the shell for a few minutes or seconds or years and then handed it to me, and we went on toward the car and home.

Once there, he painted the message, the shell. And I have the canvas, very reassuring and beautiful, and I have the shell, not as a fetish but perhaps as a kind of guarantee of peace or fulfillment.

—*Bareacres, Hemet, California, 1941*

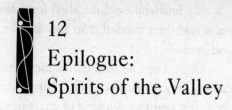

12
Epilogue:
Spirits of the Valley

Some people believe that it is a fortunate thing if a person can live in a real valley instead of on flat open land, and they may well be right. For some sixteen years, from 1940 on, I lived most of the time on ninety acres of worthless land southeast of the little town of Hemet in Southern California, and they were fine magical ones, important in the shaping of many people besides me, perhaps because Hemet Valley was a true one in every sense. At its far eastern end rose the high mountains that separated coastal land from desert, and our little town lay almost as near their base as Palm Springs did on their other side. Mount San Jacinto loomed on the north; to the south, high rocky hills rolled toward the Mexican border, and westward the valley opened gently, as any proper valley should, toward broad coastal flats and the far Pacific Ocean.

My husband, Dillwyn Parrish, and I bought our land for almost nothing: it was haunted, for one thing, and completely untillable. And we lived there intensely until he died three years later, according to medical schedule, of Buerger's disease. Then I stayed on, through another marriage and two little daughters, who spent their first years there with me after I divorced their father. When the oldest was going on six, we moved to my family ranch near Whittier to live with Father after Mother died. I worked half-time on his newspaper and ran the household, and as often as possible (weekends, vacations) we went back to Hemet to the little ranch house in the wild rocky hills.

It became clear that I could not raise two growing females there alone, where I had decided to remain. Now and then I found someone to repair storm damage and so on, but finally it seemed wise to sell the place. I felt thankful for everything I had learned there, and when I said it was no longer mine, I withdrew forever from it, even though ashes of my love and my mother may still blow from under some of its great rocks. I know the wind still sings over the Rim of the World and always will.

Tim (my husband was always called that by people who loved him, which meant everyone) named our ranch Bareacres, after a character in *Vanity Fair* who had several marriageable daughters and countless acres of barren land. He managed to sell the land, bought a string of pearls and a husband for each girl, and he and Lady Bareacres lived penniless but happy ever after, as I remember.

Certainly our land was bare! It rose in rough steep hills, with one deep canyon that split it down from the Rim of the World, its horizon, to the wide dead riverbed that was its northern boundary. A thin little road track went up from the valley floor, past our house and on up past the trickle of our only spring, to a deserted old ranch on the Rim of the World. There was a big sturdy redwood tank at the spring and a handful of stubby cottonwoods, and down nearer our house in the canyon, dry except for an occasional

mud puddle from the underground trickle, stood a few tall eucalyptus trees. The rest of the place was covered with great harsh
boulders, some of them bigger than a house. On the flat top of an
enormous rock above the spring, two oblong tubs had been
chipped out centuries ago, and we were told that sick Indians were
brought there to lie in the hot sun while soothing water was poured
over them, water that we found was heavy with lithium.

In front of the house, which stood about a thousand feet up
off the wide dry riverbed that separated us from Hemet Valley, the
land was steep but with fewer big rocks, almost like a meadow,
covered with sage and mesquite and low cactus. Across the riverbed, northward, between us and Mount San Jacinto, lay the flat
valley land, rich with apricot orchards. It was neatly laid out with
roads and little houses here and there, but we could see only a
general kind of lush carpet, flowery in spring, then green, and then
winter-silver. Hemet was westward, invisible.

Our narrow dirt road went straight across the riverbed and
up to the valley floor to meet Crest Drive, which curved the whole
length of the valley. Directly opposite us, a small grove of eucalyptus trees grew down the slope where Fredrika van Benschoten had
a little orange orchard along Crest, and in that grove the Squawman, who had left his land for us to find, had a correct Navaho
house built for his bride. It was of adobe, one room and a wide
closet and a corner hearth, and it was so heavily plastered that
there were no hard corners or lines but a softness to everything
under the thick whitewash, as if it were a robe to be worn, firm
and protecting but with no part of it to cut or hurt or rub against.
The floor was of dark crude tile. The beams across the low ceiling
were slender eucalyptus trunks. There was a kind of kitchen in the
closet whose wall came up only eye height, and Freda had piped
cold water to a small sink. There was no toilet, and since the

Squawman had not made an outhouse, I decided the grove was answer enough.

I spent much time in the squaw house, mostly after Tim died. I wrote a couple of books there. I never slept there, strange to say, but would go down from Bareacres in the mornings. I always took a thermos of broth or a cool drink, and about 11:00 I'd go out and look up across the riverbed and see my home there, sometimes with my two little girls waving from the west terrace, with a neighbor to watch them until I got back. The trees Tim and I had planted back of the house and down into the canyon were thriving: sycamores, eucalyptus, tough cottonwoods.

When Tim and I bought the place, with a veteran's bonus of $2,000 plus $225 we borrowed (we were dead broke after his illness made us leave Switzerland in 1938 when World War II got under way), it was flatly undesirable, even according to the realtor who showed it to us. It had been owned by a shady fellow said to be a degraded government Indian trader, an army officer, whose Navaho woman followed him to Hemet Valley. He bought what we called Bareacres twenty years later, but she, of course, did not live there, so her relatives unwillingly came from New Mexico and built her a decent house across the riverbed in Freda's grove.

Because of strict caste laws, the Navaho was not only called a lost member of her own tribe but could not have anything to do with the local Indians, the Sobobans, who were beneath her social level. It must have been very lonely for her. The Squawman, as he was always scornfully called, had a lot or some or a few valuable Indian artifacts, depending on who was talking about him to us, and most of them were gone when his body was found in the house and a clean bullet hole showed in the south window. Perhaps it was robbery? Navaho are good shots, we were told. The little house in Freda's grove was empty, with not even a blanket or cup left. Nobody knew "anything." Up on the hill across the dead riverbed the air blew through the unlocked door of the Squaw-man's house. Everything in it was stolen, gradually and without real harm . . . no vandalism, no ugly dirt, no mischievous fires. It was haunted, for sure.

It looked empty and welcoming when Tim and I first saw it in the kind January sunlight, and we stepped into it past the bullet hole as if it had been waiting. We rented an airy little house near Moreno, toward Riverside, and came every day over the Jack Rab-bit Trail around the base of the mountain with two old carpenters Tim found. We shifted a few walls around and screened the long front porch that was held up by six trunks of cedar trees that Indians had brought from Mexico, it was said, for the Squawman.

His rock foundations were good. The porch floors across the north and east sides of the little U-shaped house were of well-poured smooth cement, and there was a big fireplace of rough brownish stone in the living room. We made one room and its porch into a fine studio, and put in another little toilet and lavatory there, and slept on the porch outside, looking east. The kitchen spread out to the east, too, over the old cement porch. Down in the canyon we built a big doghouse, with a fenced yard to fool the coyotes and the occasional lynx. On the west side of the U was an entry and office for me and a bedroom and bath for anybody we liked enough. (Hemet had no motels then, but there was a small adobe hotel behind a half circle of fine palm trees in town.) And in the hollow of the U was the patio, the most delightful one I have ever known—indeed, the heart of the place. French doors opened onto it on all three sides. We paved it with flat stones from the canyon. Tim devised a series of strips of bright canvas on slanted wires that pulled across it at will, so the air and light would stay filtered. We pulled them back and forth according to wind, weather, the time of day.

There were low tables and chairs, all-weather stuff, and two chaise longues that could be beds. A wide Dutch door opened into the kitchen. The south side of the patio was a stone wall perhaps four feet high, and on the terrace above it were cottonwood trees and some sycamores, so that always there was the sound of leaves growing, blowing, falling. The Squawman had started the wall, and we carried it on past the house to make a fine terrace of sandy earth. Tim and I kept native succulents and cacti growing in the wall crevices, and when my girls were small, they played out there in the warm dry winter days, and now and then we put out a croquet set for the long hot summer twilights. And often we pulled the chairbeds out to the terrace in the brilliant August nights and lay naked in the silky air, watching the meteors shoot and tumble in the pure black sky.

Bareacres bordered the Ramona Bowl on the west, where the pageant based on Helen Hunt Jackson's book about Indians was given every year in a lovely little open-air theater. Tim helped rewrite some of the new script, and we maintained an aloof cordiality with the cast every year. The Indian hero was played by a skilled actor from Hollywood, much as summer theater on Long Island is now held together by stage stars who need fresh air and a nice piece of pocket money, and we knew a few visitors like Victor Jory who came to Hemet. Ramona the Beautiful Indian Maiden was always played by a local girl. And the finale of the long afternoon performance was when a posse of thirty or forty of the valley's best horsemen thundered through the amphitheater and up over the eastern horizon and down onto our land! We always had bottles of cold ale, open and ready, for the excited riders on their panting prancing horses. It was fun. . . . We waited to hear the guns sound to the west and then opened bottles as fast as we could. And they would come pouring over, a thunder of hooves, wild yahoo yells. We forgot that they were hunting the Indian Alessandro, poor devil, every afternoon at precisely 4:54 for three weekends. (He, or some reasonable facsimile, was safely panting in a hidden bunker up the theater hill.)

We stayed aloof from active life in Hemet while Tim was there, because we knew his time was short and he had a lot of painting to do. We made fine firm friends, though, and some of them still live. And later I made many more, when my little girls were starting there. Of course, they don't remember much about people, but they still know how to walk away smoothly and quickly when they meet a rattlesnake and how to listen to what the wild quail mothers say.

Freda stayed my dear friend until she died, a very old woman, the last of all her group of strange witty people who seemed to take Tim and me for granted as a part of their own very private lives. And there was Spittin Stringer, who lived in the cottage at our turn off Crest Drive down into the riverbed and on up homeward. Spittin was called that, of course, because he spat a lot. He was the only man we ever met who had gone to France in World War I and then back to Oklahoma without setting foot off dry land. He knew this was a fact because he had just gone with his buddies into a big dark room that had bumped along the road a long time and then they had gotten off and started fighting. There was no arguing about a fact like that. What's more, nobody in his whole family could rightly remember how many kids there were. He said around thirteen. His wife couldn't rightly recall either, and if she had ever counted she would not admit it in front of Spittin. But the oldest boy, J.B., said flatly it was fourteen.

J.B. used to pose for Tim, once he and his mother had walked up the hot hill together so that she could see if we were decent. When I met her at the door, she had on a store-bought dress and shoes, but she took off the killers when she saw I was barefoot and went back with them in her hand, satisfied that J.B. would be all right. Though I never saw her smile, the next time I passed she called out, "Hi ya! Still got mah bar' feet!" and stuck one big muddy toe out from behind the washtub by the door.

When J.B. enlisted, Spittin could not think of what the initials might be for. J.B. was simply his oldest boy's name. And on second thought, maybe his, too. So Tim suggested putting Joseph Benjamin on his papers to satisfy the army, and perhaps he is still alive to remember that J.B. might as well stand for that as anything else. Tim painted one unforgettable picture of him, a thick young boy sitting dully, vacantly, with one hand on his knee holding a green Coke bottle. Tim called it *Kola High*.

On the other side of our turnoff, up on a knoll in a grove of trees, was the Lee house. It was something of a palace, at least compared with Spittin's place or Bareacres or even Freda's prim little white house behind the orange trees on Crest Drive. The younger son of its owners lived there with his wife and a burgeoning family, and they raised turkeys and a few noisy beautiful peacocks and stayed pretty much to themselves, the way we did. Later, though, my girls and theirs were peers, and their mother Isabel became a quietly true-forever person in my life.

And over all of us rose proud San Jacinto Mountain, sacred to many Indians of its own and other tribes. The Jack Rabbit Trail snaked around its west side, between Hemet and Moreno, and it seemed to hold the raw steep slopes up almost like an invisible wall. The Indians called it a hot mountain, and steaming water burst out of it, more or less controlled for human bathing, in places like Gilman Springs and Soboba Springs and even downtown in the little town of San Jacinto just outside the Indian reservation. Once when I was about ten, relatives came from the Midwest to spend the winter at the Vosburg Inn so that an uncle could "take the baths," and I was embarrassed to have my aunt tell us how Mrs. Vosburg cut up her very fat husband's worn trousers to make clothes for all her small children. Years later one of the Vosburgs was a very beautiful Ramona in the pageant, and I helped with her makeup and never told her what I knew about her father's pants.

A man named Leonardo came often to help us. He was a Pala Indian from the agrarian tribe farther south, but had lost caste by taking up with a Soboban girl. He was cut off from his tribe, and gradually I watched him turn heavy and morose. He was always courteous to me but did not really see me, the way one does not see every leaf on a tree. He loved Tim but would not pose for him. Now and then he drove his girl and their little son Cowboy over to see us in his shabby truck. Cowboy was a dimpled brown nugget, but we only smiled at each other. The girl was silent, unsmiling but not hostile. Leonardo and Tim talked in his studio. Then they would go away, without any words to me but a quick wave and a smile between the two men.

After Tim died, Leonardo returned a few times and cut back some branches in the cottonwoods and made the little tool shed outside the kitchen very tidy. But he grew heavier, and I knew that he was drinking much of the time instead of only for the few religious retreats that the Sobobans were allowed to mix in with their Catholic celebrations at Saint Hyacinth's Chapel on the reservation. And, of course, every year it was almost as ritualistic to round up him and a few other gifted braves for fire fighting. They were sold or perhaps given spiked gallons of sweet muscatel wine, fixed with a half pint of straight alcohol to fill the drained tops. A friend who ran the local bar showed us how this was done.

The men got drunk very fast, and the one cop and the judge who was also the bartender knew when to move in. I felt as shocked as I ever have in my life, and as disgusted. But it was considered fair play there in those days, when good fire fighters were as much a need as water itself and the best ones could be had for a gallon of spiked wine and a couple of nights in jail to make their indenture legal. The awful thing was that every time it happened, it got easier for the men to *stay* drunk, of course, so that after several seasons Leonardo was half lit most of the time, with a fat body and a bitter dull face, no more the lithe man who ran up our road with a flashing smile when he saw Tim wave from the big studio window.

Another fine friend was Arnold. He was always thin, although I am sure he had drunk his fair share of rotgut all over the world. He had been a desert rat for many years, the kind of shadowy drifting loner who becomes almost dust colored—protective coloration, it is called in toads and mice and serpents, and the few real desert rats I have met were the same. By the time he came to be our friend and protector, he had married a little round brown girl named Lena and they had two little round brown daughters, but he still wore dust-colored cotton clothes, and his eyes were as hard and colorless as stone, except when they smiled at Tim and now and then toward me.

Arnold knew more about native desert plants than anyone I ever heard of, and while he was the caretaker up at the Ramona Bowl, it was a kind of secret paradise for botanists and crackpot gardeners who came to watch him plant the unplantables and whom he in turn watched like a hawk, because they almost always tried to steal some of his cuttings. It was a game they all played, and Arnold reported every sneaky trick, every artful dodge, of this unending tournament of trickery among the famous people who came to watch him. He turned weeds into jewels, for sure.

After Tim died, Arnold buried the little tin box of clinkers [Tim's ashes] under an enormous hanging rock. I said, "Let's go up to the Rim of the World and let the winds catch them," but he said, "Nope," and simply walked off. I knew it was all right, and went back to Bareacres and waited, and when he came back, we had a good nip of whiskey.

Arnold did a hitch with the Seabees, and I felt responsible for Lena and the little dumplings, for a time anyway. Then they met him someplace up north, and I never heard from him again, except that he is still clear and strong in my heart.

That is the way Bareacres is, of course. I am told that the fine pure air that first drew us there, half mountain and half desert, is now foul with smog and that the rich carpet of fruit trees we looked down on is solid with RVs and trailer parks. One block on Main Street is now in the *Guinness Book of World Records,* or maybe it is *Ripley's Believe It or Not:* something like 182 banks and savings-and-loan offices on that sleepy little stretch of sidewalk! And there are almost a hundred doctors, most of them connected with "convalescent homes" of varying status and opulence. And Crest Drive is lined with million-dollar villas, with the subdivision where Bareacres was (a "ninety-acre hell of red-hot rocks and rattlesnakes," as one New Yorker described it to us after a lost weekend there) the most snobbish and stylish area between Palm Springs and Los Angeles.

That is the way it is, I say, and I do not grieve or even care, any more than I did when Arnold went up the hill with the little box. I have taken and been given more than can ever be known that is heartwarming and fulfilling forever from that piece of wild haunted untillable land we named Bareacres for a time. No doubt roads have been cut into it and rocks have been blasted away, but I know that the contours cannot change much in a few hundred years in that country. And meanwhile the ghosts are there, even of the sick sad Indians who went to lie in the magic lithium waters of the spring, and even of the poor Squawman with a bullet in his heart, and of my own mother who loved the place . . . they are all there to cleanse and watch over it. They, and many more of us, keep an eye on things so that time itself can stay largely unheeded, as anyone will know who spends more than a few minutes in country like Bareacres.

There are many pockets of comfort and healing on this planet, and I have touched a few of them, but only once have I been able to stay as long and learn and be told as much as there on the southeast edge of Hemet Valley.

When I decided I could not stay there alone with my young girls and then had to decide further that I could not pretend to be an absentee owner, it did not hurt me at all to sell it. I felt serene about it then, and I do now. I had found what I needed there, and now other people will. I do not care how many millions of dollars Bareacres is now worth, nor how many days of smog alert there are each month in the little valley. I do not have any of that money, but I still breathe sweet fine air. My mind and my heart are bursting with unsuspected scents and notions and strange whiffs from other places, and I would like to write ten thousand times more than any human could about that one spot in my own tiny cosmos! All I dare hope, with perhaps some embarrassment for this unabashed gluttony, is that other people can open long-locked doors in their memories and enjoy some such rediscoveries of bliss and pain and beauty and foolishness and general enjoyment of our human condition.

—*Glen Ellen, California, 1984*

 Last

House

Reflections, Dreams, and Observations

1943–1991

Introduction

NORAH BARR, MARSHA MORAN,
PATRICK MORAN

Last House is M. F. K. Fisher's last book. It spans five decades and is her final word, in her own hand, in her own voice.

It is also the one book—out of more than twenty-five, written over her lifetime—that was literally the most difficult for her to write. *Last House* began in the early 1980s as Mary Frances's "secret project" and ended just prior to her death in June of 1992 as her final undertaking. Along the way, its form and content changed dramatically, and what started out as a collection of random thoughts, ideas, and digressions metamorphosed into a more serious and sometimes painful personal account of the aging process.

Mary Frances first envisioned *Last House* as an anthology of eclectic information that Fisher readers might at one time or another find useful, or at the very least interesting. She originally saw the book as a literary glory hole, brimming with promise, potential, and an occasional surprise or two. She thought then that the project might take the form of an alphabet, which could contain the observations of a writer who with age could strip away layers of pretense. She began work on the manuscript soon after she moved into Last House on the Bouverie Audubon Preserve in Glen Ellen, California.

From the outset Mary Frances was filled with ideas and enthusiasm. Indeed, her working folders are stuffed with small pieces of paper on which just a word or two serve as seeds for future germination and illumination. Unfortunately, however, she had neither the time nor the energy to expand on many of these thoughts, for soon after commencing work on *Last House,* Mary Frances began to be overwhelmed by a combination of physical limitations, and the struggle to put words to paper grew progressively more difficult. First came arthritis and then Parkinson's disease, both of which in their own cheerless ways deprived Mary Frances of the mechanical ability to transfer her thoughts directly to print. And although neither illness diminished her ability to formulate thoughts, what had once been a short sashay from imagination to page at nineteen—or thirty-two or even sixty-five—became at eighty a truly formidable crossing.

Arthritis made typing impossible. And the Parkinson's cramped her handwriting into tortured contours whose jagged outlines only one or two people were able to decipher. Yet despite these unwelcome twin sisters of old age, Mary Frances's work continued to flourish. For still there was her voice—breathy and thin and curiously adolescent—which matched a style that had always been natural, conversational, accessible; thus dictation was something that came easily to her, and some of the material in *Last House* was created in this manner. In the late 1980s, Mary Frances, hoping to embrace technology to her advantage, took a turn at using a tape recorder to compose her works, and a number of pieces were produced first on tape, transcribed, and then edited by her own hand.

Finally, the Parkinson's stole Mary Frances's voice, although it was apparent that the disease had done nothing to diminish her ability to think or her determination to tell others what was on her mind. When it became increasingly obvious that she would be unable to finish *Last House* as she had first conceived the book, Mary Frances decided to include a number of previously written, unpublished pieces. Yet even this was a painstaking process since she could no longer read and had to depend on others to be her eyes. The sorting of material appropriate to *Last House* required numerous readings of earlier works that had been accumulating in cartons at the far end of her bedroom. It took many months, and it was very near the time of her death when these pieces were finally added to the work that Mary Frances had previously done on *Last House*. By then, the writings that seemed to fit the book, and those that Mary Frances was drawn to, were quiet, sober, and often about aging, and even death and dying. The memory with which she chose to begin the book was written when Mary Frances was young, vigorous, and in love. It is a dreadful picture of the lives of young men in World War II drained through the Golden Gate. The book ends with a reminiscence about, and a longing for, a few beloved friends and pets that had died many years earlier.

Throughout the 1980s, Mary Frances recorded her long night thoughts, as she worked, became famous against her will, and was dealt the sharp blows of catastrophic illness that led to her death. She was honest and brave, and had to be honest, brave, and witty as well, for a much longer period of time than she would have wished. Everyone alive wonders how they will die, and how they will face death when it happens. Most of us are quite practiced at denial, but we welcome a book that gives us a few hints about how it can be done, by an honest writer, with superb grace.

For those fortunate enough to have witnessed or participated in Mary Frances's struggle to continue working during this period, there can be no greater source of inspiration, nor additional need of confirmation that the process of creation—for a writer or for anyone else—is as necessary as breathing, and critical in sustaining one's dignity and humanity. And although senescence forms the backdrop for many of the later pieces in *Last House,* this in not in the end the work of someone whose powers are in decline. Rather, it is an affirmation of the wisdom of taking on life—and death— as one's only real work.

Why Again

At first, in the immediate impact of grief,
The body lay criss-cross.
The arms were spread out, and the legs stretched.
Gradually the immediate impact of grief grew less.
The legs came up, and crossed at ankles.
Arms folded softly across the wracked chest cage,
And the abandoned heart softened and came alive again.
The body grew quiescent, receptive,
A chrysalis, not dead
But reviving, curling into a further acceptance of the same
        process, the same physical position.

Within, there was still protest.
Why again, asked the vigorous spirit.
This time is surely enough, to be stretched out and pinned,
Pickled in the brine of the spirit.

No, said the spirit.
But the legs straightened and then pulled up,
The wracked arms crossed with gentle resignation over the
    breasts,
And the life began to slow to the waiting throb in the ever-
    hollowed still soft bosom.

Everything was ready for more.

—*St. Helena, California, 1965*

1
War

She . . . is it I? Is it the woman I once knew? Is it a stranger walking in my shoes, accustoming herself to the unusual phases of this life? . . . she went down the stairs unwillingly. The house was new to her, and she had crept first up to the second story to snitch the flashlight from the table by Elsa's bed. It was late. Elsa breathed heavily, luxuriously. The woman . . . yes, it is, or was, I . . . breathed heavily too, from all the stairs that she had climbed to get inside the door of this San Francisco house she was renting for herself and her baby and Elsa, who shared the care of the child. She stood listening to the easy breathing, in, out, in, of Elsa. Then with the flashlight she went down to the first floor of the house, and on down into the strange mossy bowels, to where the furnace hummed and whuddered. It lay, strange to her eyes, in a little room of extra-fancy bricks, like a monster in a special cage. The bricks seemed to hum with it. The lights quaked. She touched the bricks, and then the button on the nearest light, and when for a minute it went out and she felt the hot brick under her hand, she was blown into a trillion inescapable atoms. Then she thought of the little child upstairs, and Elsa breathing with such trust into the foggy air. She withdrew, both from the brick and from the surcease of fantasia. The air about her shook, and she was downtown, downtown in an office, laughing into the sardonic laughter of a man who said bitterly, "There is nothing left. Why do we bother to dine anywhere?" "Do you mean we should stay here and drink sherry?" she asked with a kind of tentative irony, or at least so she thought. "No," he said, and looked sharply at her, and out of the window she looked at the side of the Wells Fargo Building and thought in one wordless rush of express coaches and prairies and Lola Montez and even of a bar at the Palace Hotel where pictures of Mark Twain and Lola and old photographs in fake gold frames hang tidily above a lot of drunken heads. She looked again, and the air was sharp, and simply because it was over the bay and she knew it was over the bay, she thought of it as sharp and cold. "No," she said, "I didn't mean that either. We should go to a bar." They went to several, and everywhere there were two kinds of men and one kind of woman. As the evening went on they became more conscious of this fact. They commented on it, and through the good honest California wine and the fairly honest California brandy, they commented on it. They commented on it at the Fair, which was a pub where the bartender was old and made them a Gibson with loving care. Then they commented on it at Ernie's, or at least that was probably the name of the place, where when the man asked for a plain Dutch gin for her and a Gibson for him, the bartender said violently, "Oh, for God's sake, let's mix it in one shaker! What difference does it make?" Then when the man said with a kind of muted, old-school astonishment, "But the lady wants a straight gin," the bartender got a crumpled look on his face and became embarrassingly humble and even cringed, and the lady could hardly swallow the straight gin. (I was the lady, at least there.) And then they commented again on the two kinds of men and the one kind of woman in the bar at the Palace where a mural of Mark Twain hangs over the bottles, and all around the room are quaintly framed prints of his period and people under them on sofas who should be framed and perhaps are. The bartender was young there. He knew the lingo of soldiers, although most of the men he served were lieutenant commanders and, once or twice each evening, an admiral. When the man and woman (yes, I! I!) came in, he made them a passable Gibson, and almost at once they began talking about how hard it was to grow old and have no place to go but alone or in company to such an upper-class bar, and how sad it was to be old without philosophy, and a very young officer of the navy said, "Will you please excuse me if I butt in?" He had a bourbon and water in one hand, and there were dark tan circles above his cheekbones, and his eyes were young. "Of course not at all certainly," the man and woman said. "I heard what you said. It is absolutely right. The attitude . . . What is there, after all . . . What right have people . . . I mean . . ." The young officer waved his glass, and his tired innocent eyes looked worriedly at the two people. They felt as old as all the hills of Israel. Pretty soon they got off their high seats and left him standing there, and although they had been more than nice and he had been equally discreet, they worried for some time about whether they should have invited him to dine with them. He had been drinking bourbon. They were going to drink a Château de Camensac, 1923. How could they? They felt guilty, foolish, stupid . . . and yet the bottle waited for them. It had been waiting since 1923, or at least such reasoning seemed logical. And there the bottle sat on the table, waiting to be violated, in the candlelight, in the soft music that flowed over all the medals and all the taut mouths and the thirsty eyes. And it was good wine. The food was less good. The maître d'hôtel came up and whispered sadistically that the chef had sacrificed his one free afternoon to drive into the country for the meat. There was no butter. The flavors were strained. But it was well served, all of it, and the wine, tired as an old man with blue veins on his hands, lifted them into a special paradise. They sat like humans full of opium, and watched the people float weakly, obliviously, past them. There was one strong-faced woman who ordered a horrible mess of precooked wartime food, and ate it heartily and then smoked a long thin cigarette without touching it, as if it were a rare cigar. And there were tables everywhere of soldiers and sailors, all of them hungry for their loves or for unknown loveliness, who ate doggedly at expensive nothings, or perhaps ordered steak-and-kidney pie and waited for it and then pushed it away. One man leaned heavily against the shoulder of a pinch-faced supercilious corporal and told him of his dead son, and the corporal, who had perhaps looked down on that son's grave, listened almost mockingly and, if he had not been a brave fairy, would have pushed the old man in the face. He hated the old man. He hated himself. And there were other things to hate too. There were the two kinds of men and the one kind of woman. After the winey meal, in a bar up the hill in the Italian part of the city, the man and woman felt it. The woman, because of her fairly clear-tracked past, dreaded to see two gently silly humans still called men come into a bar and lean gracefully against its edge, and then watch hackles rise on other humans in uniform. That happened, in and out, up and down, in the mirror in front of her, behind her. And women in fluffy fur coats rubbed themselves against the sailors to their left, rather than against the old heavy-lidded husbands to their right. And the soldiers and sailors brought in their friends. All the women seemed alike, so thirsty in this port, wanting to drink deep of the blood of life. And all the men were so desirous of being drunk, drunk up, made alive once before the great debauch of battle. The Golden Gate waited. It was a throat. It was a vein. Men flowed through it. It was a thirsty hole, and the bright blood of the world gushed in spurting convoys toward the East, every day, in the gray ugly ships fat with men. The men reasoned or they did not reason, but the women had but one course. And the woman who watched all that, the night of the bottle of Camensac 1923, thought that perhaps she had found the answer. Then she drank, after one or two brandies at La Tosca, an Americano, a sage biting mild drink. She looked down the bar at all the thirsty people. There were two soldiers getting ready either to beat up two dainty civilians next to them or go to sleep. There were a few pretty girls, from thirteen to sixty, and at the end of the bar, just beyond the espresso machine, was the star of a nearby floor show, complete with long eyelashes and cheaters and a boyfriend. In the air, over the sound of Nino Martini on the jukebox, she heard the foghorns blowing, and she thought of all the men waiting below-decks and of all the dog tags dangling on the warm-skinned ribs. Soon after that, at home, she went down into the strange cellar, full of the thoughts of love, and of the men everywhere who had no such warmth. She was full of pity. The furnace was humming. She opened the door, so staunchly lined with bricks. The round box glowed and with a startling suddenness roared and shivered. The dog tags came in a leisurely way into her mind, and then she thought of her child on the top floor of the tall wooden house, and then as all the whiteness wrapped around her, she saw the Golden Gate like an artery, a cut artery, with all the proud bitter men flowing out through it toward the East, in a rush, a gush, a stream, a hot flood that made her smile once more.

—*San Francisco, California, 1943*

2
Rex—I

There is a book I must write, and one I have long thought upon. Let me say that it will be about all good old people, of which I hope one day to be one; it is, perforce, about many I have known and lived with; it is about an oldster I would like one day to resemble. It is about Rex.

I shall draw upon my files I have kept for about twenty years, to put it safely, for long before then I was keenly conscious and even knowledgeable of the ways of old people. I thought, even so long back, that they must be even more important than I, and this, from a human being of fifteen or twenty years, is an almost monumental thought. Very soon after that I began to clip little sayings, quips, or bright quotations about the far from happy thoughts of people over sixty-five or seventy. (I do not rightly know when old age begins, but according to the welfare agencies and the insurance companies, two fairly respected authorities, it is at about such ages.)

I have kept my files going, to my intimates' amazement. I have countless clippings. I am glad. I can look, more or less at will, at what a baker's dozen of experts say about the physiological, emotional, glandular, gastronomical, gonadal-or-do-I-mean-glandular-again, psychological trends (if not traits) of those of us who are past fifty. It is a very reassuring picture.

I like old people.

I like to be old.

I'll write of Rex.

I have always known I would, but I've thought of it as past his coffin, over the hump of his disintegration, and in words tinged, imbued, weighted with the essences of my sorrow for a man lost to me.

Now I feel that I am strong enough, since he is, to write of him as an old man while he still is one.

Instead of waiting until he has died, and until my own harried emotions have settled into a kind of quiescent awe, I am, suddenly and unexpectedly, ready to write about him now, while he is alive, breathing, coughing, eating, defecating.

The best thing about this almost extrasensory decision is that I know it would meet with his approval if I cared to bother him about it. He acknowledges my small professional skills. He bows to my discretion. He would listen to my plan and smile with only slight apprehension, inevitable in a small-town editor, and then would read each chapter with a kind of patience impossible to anyone younger, fresher, less tolerant—anyone my age, for instance, forty-two instead of seventy-three.

That is why I think I should write the book about old age, about Rex, now, not later. It is the very fact that he does not much care, that he trusts me, that makes me want to put all these things into words—the things I have thought over a long time about old people and now *know* about such a fine, such an old, MAN.

I went in after he had turned his lights off and put the glasses beside his bed, and his face turned up to me like a child's when I leaned to kiss him. My heart turned over.

—*Whittier, California, 1950*

3

Rex—II

Hatred, hatred. What venom it distills. Tonight, filled with it, I give off poisonous exudations, I well know. Rubbing his feet, I could feel my hatred flow like bile through my fingertips into his strangely warm knobby venous toes ankles calves. Now, warm and alone in my bed, wrapped in a garnet shawl, sipping at an unwanted highball which I down almost as a punishment, I can smell the hated sourness on my hands, and can realize my puny foolishness to be so wretched, so voluptuously wretched.

My mind races volubly. Every word it says can lead in many a direction, and it is hard, as well as basically destructive, to force myself to follow one line of thought, or of suggestion.

God, but I have been angry tonight. By now I am coming into focus again. And even when I was most filled with the poison I knew my basic impotence, for I see no reason, really, for wounding Rex, no matter how slightly. He is old. He is tired. He is an astonishingly spoiled man: that is the crux of it, and I am too old and he is even too much older for me to try to show him how he could be easier to live with. Besides, I am not in love with him. Mother, and later Sis, tried hard to make him toe the lines they drew. They had rows. They wept. They stormed and sulked. As far as I can see he did not really ever hear them. But it was worth it, I suppose, because of the love. Me, I don't love him.

Now and then I loathe him, for the stupid waste, the basically timid arrogance in him. Mostly I accept him as a kind of foreshadow of myself, for we are much alike, glandularly and in the basic timidity and the arrogance. (But I think I am wiser, and therefore less impregnable.) There are times, like tonight, quite possibly dictated by the tides, when I am filled with a consummate revulsion. Most of the time I shed off things that other women squirm at openly or must turn away from: the dribbles of urine on the floor by the toilet, the long sensual belches at breakfast, the knowledge that he is restrained and charmingly gallant for any goddamned fluffy fool of a scheming small-town Bovary. But now and then I cannot, or do not, shed my deep and perhaps instinctive distaste for my intimacy with my father. All his odors repel me, and at his age and with his background of cautious midwestern plumbing, his odors are many. (I know about the difficulties of keeping clean in the aged. I know about earlier conditioning. I know . . . Still I hold my breath when I must step over the steamy underwear on the sitting room floor at night in order to reach the toilet; and I hold my breath again when after the fairly neutralizing oil I put on the alcohol and it pulls out from the blue-white feet a wave of bitter fumes; and I hold my breath now, an hour later, not to smell my hands, scrubbed, oiled, but still subtly stinking of those poor trusting rotten feet.)

Yes, the odors repel me, although I know they are largely involuntary. The sounds repel me, the long masturbatory belchings when he need not restrain himself—that is, when he is with the children and me. The equally long and voluptuous pickings at his nostrils, while he reads at night or even sits over his coffee: they repel me. And I am *agacée,* hurt, rebuffed, annoyed, everything like that, when he slams into his room, leaving all the doors open, and pees noisily. (Often when I rub his feet they are still damp with the urine he has dripped casually.)

Yes, many things about living with this old man exasperate me. Usually, given the situation and my increasing capacity for dispassion, I can sublimate my feelings fairly successfully. But now and then I cannot, and the thing I have the hardest time with *always,* no matter what the tides, is his spitting. I know he has to spit. I know what is wrong with him, I'm sure much better than he does himself. I know all that. But Jesus Christ in a handbasket, he need not be so thoughtless, so self-absorbed, so morbidly preoccupied. Or need he, given his seventy-four years of preoccupation and self-absorption? How can I ask, or blame?

All I know is that when I came home from getting the girls at school, and hurried into the kitchen to start organizing One More Meal, and saw a foamy blob of his spittle in the sink, I was as near physical revolt as I have been for several years. I thought I would vomit. And all the time I was thinking, This is a very *healthy* reaction, the best one yet—you are healthy now, much better. (I think I was right, too!) I had to go out, as soon as I had flushed the sink. I made myself a distastefully strong drink. I thought, This might even make you drunk. (But it did not.)

I was censorious and quietly horrid with the children, as my obviously easiest outlet. (They were patient with me, and now I think with a desperate resignation that I would to God I had the past hours back again, with those two budding beautiful little creatures.) I kept on sneering and blaspheming—no, that's not the right word—in my mind, and making chitchat and swallowing food and recognizing many of my familiar impulses toward escape.

I kept telling myself how much more "normal" my present revolt was—no remorse, no guilt, just a damned good physical reaction followed by reasonable and reasoning resentment. Now and then as I sat amicably chatting, I contemplated A Good Scene. But I'm no good at them, and anyway I do *not* think they are right for children.

So—I went upstairs, and drew some creature comfort from an enema, which did indeed expurgate some of my rage. I lay down with Anne. She caressed me forgivingly with her slender dirty hands and made me feel both foolish and happy. Mary snored calmly in the other bed, but I did not feel that in her heart she was either calm or dormant. Then I went grudgingly downstairs, where a good fire burned. I felt mean and hateful. Rex picked at his nose in his own corner. I lay down, got up, moved about listlessly. It's either a scene or get out, I said. I'm no good at scenes. So . . . I got out. He felt my hatred, I know.

He went early to bed. He opened his sitting room door and tapped the jamb twice, our signal, and I turned off the tropical fish and the lights and fixed the fire screen and went in. I held my breath, and rightly. I flushed the yellow water down the toilet, and pushed the rug over the splashes of urine on the floor. I saw the teeth in the glass bowl, with flecks of food rising slowing in the water. The radio blasted, and as always, that annoyed me, for Rex knows it hurts my ears and that he can turn it up after I've rubbed his feet, but he never does. Often two or three stations blare together—two tonight. I thought that he'd bathed yesterday, but already he smelled like Wednesday instead of only Monday. I felt his toenails, like pieces of savage carving. He must go soon to the podiatrist—I must call for an appointment, and see that he puts it in his book, and then remind him and remind him.

All the time I was trying not to breathe, and increasingly I thought about hatred, and the different ways it can be what it is, and I grew more certain that this revulsion of mine tonight was a very healthy normal one. I did not hit anyone, except my children, with what I hope was a glancing spiritual blow (I do not say that lightly). I did not kick or yell or weep, although I was for a time near the last. *I* felt like hell. I took an enema. Then I drank a highball by myself with an electric pad turned to Low on my belly, and a chilly east air blowing over me, and the children breathing, perhaps disappointed but with confidence, in the other room.

I feel sorry, yes. Tonight I could not really *look* at Rex, because I was so angry at him for spitting in the sink: I knew he would see my anger. Perhaps that would have been a good thing. But I do not love him that way, and am not able to have good rousing battles with him. So I hide my bile. I don't think it really hurts me at all—except that I am still clumsy enough to vent some of it on the two people I love best, my innocent children. I sometimes feel that they know more than I, and therefore are as forgiving as they seem to be. But through my pores, through my lips pressed desperately upon their chaste temples, am I teaching them hatred?

—Whittier, California, 1951

4

Tea with Agamemnon

One day in the spring in California, two women sit talking in a eucalyptus grove. There is a mountain behind them, snowy still, and under them sweet alyssum blooms with a wild heavy smell of honey in the sun. A dog lies watching, waiting for crumbs of love and cookies, as the humans drink tea with their own brands of easiness. Fredrika is the older, with long bare legs and a band of turquoise silk tied optimistically around her wisps of white hair; Mary Frances, the other, is remote and teasing. Both of them are shy, the way old friends can be without premeditation. Fredrika says, in her soft voice with the strange sweet crack in it, "They are all I remember about Greece, really. My mother got the recipe from her cook when we lived in Athens. I was about five, and Agamemnon and I . . ." Her voice fades vaguely, and she holds out a plate of little round flat cakes so dreamily that they almost slide off. The dog watches them, his tail wagging. Mary Frances takes the plate and puts it on her knees, and when she bites into one of the cakes, she sees the dog looking at her sadly, intently.

Mary Frances: They are good, delicious. Are they really honey cakes, the kind the gods ate?

Fredrika: Probably. Nothing changes in Greece—nothing basic, that is. Agamemnon lived next door to me and was about my age. His last name was Schliemann. His father unearthed Troy, you know, and his mother was Greek. I suppose she was beautiful —all Greek women are, in my mind at least, although I can't remember anything about them actually except that my nurse wore a black woolen dress that scratched my face when she carried me upstairs. My mother told me later how to make the honey cakes. Agamemnon and I would eat them in the afternoons on the long marble porch of his house, with goat's milk. That is, we did until my father discovered what the goats lived on in Athens.

Fredrika pauses and laughs in her shy way, bending over to put half a cookie between the dog's polite soft lips. Mary Frances drinks slowly at her cup of tea, watching her friend, smelling the honey in the air, and tasting it on her tongue.

Fredrika: Father couldn't understand why his children weren't thriving on goat's milk. It sounded so *Attic!* and therefore perfect. And then he saw that practically the only food the city goats had was the flour paste they licked off the huge paper funeral notices that were stuck up every day on the walls. He was horrified. He made himself taste a little of our milk, and sure enough it was pure paste, or so he swore later. So after that we didn't drink anything but lemonade, as far as I remember. (She adds firmly, as if reassuring herself:) I *don't* remember *much,* of course.

Mary Frances: Oh, yes you do. Tell more. Go on. Do these cakes really taste the same?

Fredrika: Not quite. Hymettos honey, from the hills around

Athens, is sweeter, because of all the thyme blossoms the bees have there.

Mary Frances: It goes with the sweet alyssum, today. What else do you remember?

Fredrika frowns, a little impatient at her stubborn friend. She speaks slowly at first: Well . . . nothing about food, really. There were dry gullies, like the ones here in this country, but often they were like torrents, like floods of purple and rose and lavender, with anemones. The flowers were higher than my knees. And then . . . then at Easter there were big hens' eggs, blown out and painted with Christ Crucified, in beautiful colors. You exchanged them with people, and they were as light as feathers, but they didn't seem to break. My mother still had one or two, when I was growing up in Connecticut. And of course there were the paschal lambs, roasting everywhere.

Mary Frances: Well?

Fredrika: Well, there wasn't much meat in Greece, I suppose. I don't think people ate it often. But at Easter almost everybody had a lamb. You'd see the boys and men carrying them home, hung over their necks, bleating. My father said they were always killed very tenderly . . . part of a sacrifice. Then all the insides, *everything*—(She interrupts herself:) Once Father went up to the monastery on Mount Athos, pulled up in a basket. He was a man. Women couldn't get *near* the place. And as the guest of honor he was served the roasted eyes of the lamb. He ate them, too . . . but it never left his mind again . . . They don't throw away anything at all, you know, and when the lamb is dead, they put all the parts except the carcass on a long fresh skewer of pinewood, highly seasoned, laced together with strings of the cleaned guts. That's called . . . (Fredrika hesitates and then looks at once pleased and confused.) Now, how on earth do I remember that? I haven't even *thought* the word for years! It's *kokoretzi*. It smokes and cooks beside the carcass of the lamb. That's on another long fresh spit. I think there must be handfuls of thyme inside it, because I can smell that mixed with the heavy smoke of the fresh pine boughs. At Easter you smell that everywhere in Greece. Or did. (She closes her mouth bitterly, as if ashamed of speaking of food once eaten in a land so sorely tried.)

Mary Frances, quickly, teasingly, to divert her: I thought you'd forgotten everything!

Fredrika, weighing two halves of a honey cake in her thin, weed-stained fingers and then giving the larger piece to the dog Pinto: Nonsense. It's as clear as yesterday. I stood looking from my window, and it was black-dark, so I was naughty to be awake. We lived near the great field where the soldiers had maneuvers. There was a circle three deep of evzones around the roasting pits, turning and basting. They laughed a lot, and they were the handsomest men in the world, with their stiff white skirts shining in the firelight, and their teeth flashing. There was music too, although I don't know know whether it was flutes or bagpipes or what. And the smell of the hot lamb meat and the burning pine boughs is something I'll never forget. Nonsense . . . it's as clear as yesterday. (Fredrika pushes back a lock of hair, and sits up very straight.)

Mary Frances: What went with it?

Fredrika: Oh, a pilaf, of course. My mother's recipe was for one cup of rice, washed well and dried, browned in four tablespoonfuls of butter or olive oil. Then one cup of tomato puree and three cups of good meat stock are brought to a boil and poured in, and the lid is put on tightly until the rice is tender and has absorbed all the juice. No stirring. Then the pilaf is shaken, and a dry cloth is put tightly over the top of the pan and the lid is put on again for about ten minutes.

Mary Frances: Like a risotto, practically. Simpler. Don't the Greeks use garlic or onions?

Fredrika: I don't remember . . . Yes, of course . . . but with the pilaf, I think, chopped fresh thyme or dittany, tossed in at the last.

Mary Frances: Dittany . . . it sounds like something from Ophelia's song.

Fredrika: It's a lovely herb. It grows wild on the hills, with tiny blue flowers. It used to be thought so powerful for healing that when stags were wounded they ate it and the arrows fell out of them. It was called *dictamnus* . . . or (and Fredrika coughs apologetically) so Father said. College professors' children keep strange things in their heads. But I do know a little dittany is wonderful in green salads. We should grow more of it in America.

Mary Frances: I read of a Greek pilaf of chicken in Escoffier, the other day. Mutton fat was used for browning the meat, which was cut up, and then . . . *here's* an onion! . . . an onion was browned, chicken consommé was added, and a chopped pimiento and a handful of currants. It was served in a ring of pilaf.

Fredrika: Yes. That would be Greek . . . and good.

Mary Frances: How about wine, though? I've heard people say they hated Greek wine.

Fredrika: I was a little young for it, even as a substitute for goat's milk. But of course it has a lot of resin taste to it. The Greeks like that. They still chew resin. It's a delicacy, and used to be reserved for the upper classes. It is supposed to sweeten the breath, cleanse the teeth, all that . . . And everywhere in Greece is that piney smell . . . even in the roasted meats. It's so clean . . .

Mary Frances: And did you and your Aristophanes—

Fredrika: *Agamemnon* . . . (She adds dreamily:) Agamemnon Schliemann . . .

Mary Frances: Did you have anything besides these wonderful, delicious, funny little honey cakes?

Fredrika: There were lots of cakes made of very thin layers of pastry called phyllo, with pounded dates and almonds and so on in between, but they were too rich for us children. Once in a while our nurses would give us a spoonful of rose-leaf jam. It was the sweetest, most perfumed thing I've ever eaten. I loved it then, but when I've tasted it since in Near East restaurants, I've almost hated it. Once I tried to make it, but I think maybe the roses weren't red enough, or my heart had grown up too much. (Fredrika coughs self-consciously, as always when she feels she has said something less restrained than she was brought up to feel was ladylike.) I took equal parts of clean dry rose leaves, the darkest red in the garden, and sugar. I moistened the sugar with equal parts of lemon juice and water until it was easy to stir the petals, and then let the whole thing lie in the sun until it was hot and well melted. Then I boiled it for about a half hour, stirring it all the time. And then I didn't really like it.

Mary Frances: Did you ever eat the jelly made from cactus apples that is served with grilled wild birds in northern Mexico? That is very sweet and perfumed, too.

Fredrika: No. But it couldn't be worse than the rose-leaf jam I used to think was so delicious. Of course I was young . . .

Mary Frances: And in love . . .

Fredrika, standing up abruptly and lifting the tea tray: Well, I *did* like having tea with Agamemnon!

—*Hemet, California, 1951*

5
Eaters

She sat facing me, one table ahead and to my right, in the noisy pleasant place. Deft men in red jackets skimmed between us, and short thicker busboys carried loaded trays of used silverware and dishes. The place was a popular crowded famous old fish house, and people who went there, inevitably to wait for a table, did so because they liked it very much.

I wondered about the old woman whose face I was not precisely forced to watch, but which came often into my gaze.

She did not look relaxed and hungry and gay, like the rest of the chattering chewing talking people. They all leaned across the plain uncovered tables and ate as they talked, eagerly. She sat stiffly upright. Her eyes were always on the man across from her, or sliding across to me as if for criticism or comment. She ate with precise good manners.

There was behind her well-bred front a feeling of dismay, perhaps of desperation. I did not like her face, for it was drained and stiff, with pale blue eyes, a thin unhappy mouth, and flat white cheeks under a coy blue hat set on her carefully curled, short snow-white hair. She wore fashionable junk jewelry in her ears and around her stringy old neck, and her blue dress matched her hat in a coquettish way. She was what Philip Wylie would call a "Mom."

She was perhaps seventy. The man facing her and with his back to me, I at first assumed to be her own age. He sat upright exactly as she did, with hair almost as white and close-cropped above his stiff neck. He was perhaps twenty years younger, though, and he was most probably her son.

He wore a white collar and a dark coat cut in such a clerical style that at first I thought him to be a priest. When he stood up at the end of the sterile prim meal, I saw that his slacks were gray. As far as I could see, he never said more than a monosyllable to the old woman sitting across the little table from him. Some of the remarks she made were sour or complaining ones, judging from her tight mouth and the way she looked almost shamefacedly toward me. As she stood up to leave, she smiled at him, but it was a polite grimace taught her long ago, a kind of female thanks for the food she had eaten. Then she awkwardly put on her own coat and followed the son out through the crowded noisy tables.

He had read all during the meal, and as she stood, he too got up, put his book in his pocket, and walked out confidently, knowing she was behind him.

I stared a little, trying to see the titles of the books (or rather the paperbacks) he was reading so insolently in the face of her attempts to look like the rest of the people. They were reviews, perhaps, printed in two columns on limp paper, and he tucked two of them in his jacket pocket at the end of the meal. I suspected that they were either religious or pedagogical.

It is interesting that while I was really observant of what different kinds of men and women were ordering and eating, all around my table, I never once looked at what had been on the savage plates, the cold venomous platters, set before these two. There was a feeling of such scorn and despising and fear between the woman and the younger man that the thought of their breaking bread together was beyond me.

As the man stood up and the old woman across from him struggled into her carefully matching blue coat and put on her gloves, and as he slid his flat books with an accustomed gesture into his pocket, I noticed the straight thin line of his body. He was almost gaunt, and very consciously and austerely well tailored. I forget about his hands. But when he turned with a kind of insolence away from the woman, who still smiled a little, very politely, I had to avert my eyes from his face. Instead of matching the good set of his grayed head upon his straight thin neck, it was small but heavy and brutal in a pinched way obviously inherited from his mother. He looked infinitely self-indulgent in a very attenuated way, a hermit on a cozy pillar or flagpole. Sensual disdain was in every cell of his face, and in a flash I recognized the deft white sensitive fingers that could torture other bodies and his own, the quick tongue behind the thin lips, the skill and detestation of his secret life. The books in his pocket and the cold intelligence of his spoken clipped monosyllables were his disguise.

The old woman had shaped him. He believed himself free, except for having to sit opposite her in a crowded restaurant filled with the vulgar. He thought his outward rebellion and arrogance were his escape, but really she was stronger than he.

—Berkeley, California, 1959

6

Death of a Mouse

Before I try to start work again after several weeks of illness and convalescence, I think I should make some sort of report on the surprising attempt of my soul to reappear. Perhaps I should call this report "Notes Found in an Empty Achromycin Bottle," although the actual encounter with my soul for the second time, as well as my sudden ability to recall the first one, happened before I began taking the pills.

I knew for some time that I did not feel well, but I had no idea that I would become so defined by pain and fever that I could be near such an experience as the one I had. Four days and nights of the white tablets emptied the little bottle, and I was pronounced ready to begin to recover.

The recovery has been interesting and lengthy, and while it still goes on I feel impatient of the waste of time and of myself, and yet almost voluptuously, I cling to the need for sleep and miss the cosmic mouse that squeaked to me in my left lung when I was alone and wandering.

Now I am nearly well again, and must begin to stay upright and make the correct moves in the right directions, and not wonder too much about when my soul will come again.

Physical illness is ugly and I shall speak of it as little as possible, and only in connection with the other thing.

Apparently I was really ill, and like most stubborn healthy people I was incredulous about it, so that I waited several days before I admitted that I could not get up and make breakfast for my family, and then spent five days in bed before I started to cry when I confessed that I needed a doctor's help, no matter how pill laden and generally unwelcome.

The night before I made this last feverish pain-stiff admission, I coughed steadily in a small dry exhausting way, perhaps a little more so than for the previous long time. It seemed by then a normal way of existing. The poor body was at once all-absorbing in the energy it demanded but at the same time almost despicably unimportant, thanks to long fasting. I listened to the cough, always on the same level of sound and effort, with a detached recognition. Brother Cough, I said philosophically, as to a longtime companion. Friend Squeak, I said affectionately, for it was the mouse living in my dark hot lung-cabin with the rigid roof beams and the walls so tinder dry that comforted me with thin songs and chatter.

Then that night the speed and sound of the cough changed, and the mouse multiplied into mad rats eating me. And up into my throat moved my soul.

I got out of bed, as if to meet it courteously.

Dreadful sounds were coming from me.

The soul, smooth and about the size of a small truffle or scallop or a large marble, rose firmly into my upper throat. It cut off my wind, but that did not matter for the time we both needed.

I knew what it looked like, for I had seen it long ago. I knew its color and its contours and its taste, for I had held it in my hand once and studied it and then chewed and swallowed it to wait within me. But this was not the time for its return.

"Go back," I cried out to it, in language it recognized through the wild coughing, and through the way the bloody rats scrabbled behind it to escape with all of me dragging from their teeth, with my lungs my liver my guts all waiting torn and ready to stream out like flags behind them, if my soul should flee first, leaving only bones and shell and the little mouse.

"Go back," I begged ferociously as it stayed there for years that night, turning slightly as breath pushed it and the rats waited. It was interesting to feel it turn, for I remembered its shape, pure and smooth in my red gullet.

There was very little left now, of the breath it had trapped behind it with the rats, and indeed of me the fighter. It seemed as if most of my solar plexus had been torn loose by the impatient invaders. If the soul left me then, I feared fastidiously that I would seem to be vomiting, but it would be *me,* not some extraneous thing like fried fish wolfed in a greasy restaurant. It would be unworthy.

"*NO.* No, *wait,*" I begged it, and I promised to accept the next visit it would pay me, and I reminded it of our long years together.

I told it, in a flash as long as the eon of time it takes for one molecule to wed another, of our first meeting, and of the mystery and respect and indeed affection I had battened on from that day.

I was about five, maybe four. It was a beautiful morning, maybe spring or winter but good, maybe a Saturday. I lay in my bed waiting for my little sister to awaken, studying the white painted iron of the bedsteads. Surely there were birds talking, and curtains stirring in the windows of the pleasant room, and sounds from downstairs, but all I remember is that in a ruthless slow way, but without any pain or fear for me, my young small soul rose up into my throat and then came out.

I did not choke. I did not spit it out. It simply rose from inside me, glided along the root and the rest of my tongue, and then lay in the palm of my hand, which must have been waiting for it in front of my mouth. I was dazzled and yet unastounded.

It was about as big as a little hazelnut or chickpea, of the subtlest creamy white, like ivory but deeper. It was delicately con-voluted, like the carvings on a human brain or a monkey's, but worn by thousands of years to its present silkiness without ever being in danger of turning into a ball or egg. It was perfection in form.

Nothing has ever been seen so clearly by my mind's eye, I think. I still know the simplicity and the yellowish shadows in the whorls of its surface, and my hand behind it with the skin infinitely crude and coarse and lined, the fresh palm of a child.

I held the thing carefully for what were probably only a few seconds. I recognized it fully, without any doubt or timidity, as my own soul. Then I put it gently into my mouth, bit into it, and chewed and swallowed it.

It had nothing to do with food or even nourishment, being without taste, and moist, but at the same time almost floury.

I made sure that none had stayed in my mouth and that all of it was well down my throat, for it was important that it reassemble itself and stay there inside me, to grow. I knew that I would see it again, just as I knew that something very important had happened to me, perhaps the first since being born. It was in a way like becoming a person instead of a creature, woman instead of baby, big instead of little. I was myself, *me,* and I had seen and touched the proof of it. I had been shown.

The good day unfolded like all other days before me, the happy child, but of course I was different, for I had a core now.

For many years, I occasionally remembered this, but without any questioning at all. I never wondered about its next visit, but I knew there would be one, just as I knew that people would tell me it was a little accident of bodily secretion or digestion, or a dream, if I talked of it.

But the night that it did come again was a mistake, except for the reassurance that it was still there.

It was as if I thought this occasion unworthy of it. I was befouled by fever; the different parts of me seemed to be sending off almost visible fumes and stinking gases, when I would choose to be silk and sweet oils for it. The rats were behind it, trailing their shreds of my tissue, my lining, my guts, and still ripping and gnawing at me with their filthy teeth as I coughed passionately in the middle of the black room by my bed. It was ugly, my state.

"Go back," I screamed, as my soul rose like a smooth nut in my throat.

It had grown since our first meeting. Some of the convolutions of its polished carving had worn even fainter since I'd seen it like a little quiet keepsake in my hand, pearly but not gleaming, wet but not slippery, ivory colored but not dull.

It sickened me that I must ask it to return to the bloody mob below, yet I knew with all my tattered force that it was not yet time to hold it in my hand again, and that I could not do so with dignity.

There was no clash of wills between us, certainly, but I learned something of eternity before it did withdraw.

I hate to think of it then in the red caves and the long flaming tunnels, for that was a bad night for it and me.

The next day I asked for help, being in a state of exhaustion that I could never try to explain to anyone. A professionally kind stranger came and left some advice and some fresh courage, and the Achromycin pills in a little bottle, to drive out the mouse in my left lung.

I felt sorry about that. But it was the mouse or me, the doctor said, and I am important because the next time my soul shows up, I must be in good shape to welcome it. I may be very old, with no teeth to chew it, no juice left to swallow it, but I shall catch it in the palm of my hand as I did when I was a child, and this time let it lead me.

—*St. Helena, California, 1965*

A Few of the Men

Any confession of love, especially a shameless one, is an open bid for speculation from the curious, the jealous, and even the malicious. There is some trace of all this in my own self, as I set forth in public, after long private consideration, what I think about a few of the men in my life.

How best to name them in cold print, and deliberately, is really a question of loyalty. It is a mean choosy business, to narrow to a handful the list of one's true loves. Half of the ones in my life, perhaps fortunately, have existed wholly or in part on paper and in ink. A few still do: in and on my reading conscience.

Jean-Anthelme Brillat-Savarin, for instance, lived in the flesh as surely as did Sam Ward. Sherlock Holmes and Inspector Maigret, on the contrary, are chemically compounded of wood pulp and printers' blood. My feelings for them are equally real. I know what they look and sound like, and how they think, and even what they like to eat and wear, as clearly as if I had lived alongside all of them.

Of course there is a small something of both awe and sisterliness in all such relationships as the ones I must have with my real loves. It has since the first been necessary for me to feel shy and basically inexperienced, pupil and not teacher, with the men in my life, whether of the mind or the body. How could I not feel awe, in my long close knowledge of Brillat-Savarin, nor a certain amount of warm tolerant sibling love for Inspector Maigret, whose drinking has sometimes worried me and whose wife often bores me a little, in a familial way?

Brillat-Savarin lived from April 1, 1755, to February 2, 1826 —long for those days—and his classic *Physiology of Taste* was published anonymously a few months before he died. It was his only literary offspring, and his only self-portrait in a mysteriously reticent lifetime as an obscure Parisian lawyer.

Samuel Ward was born in New York City on January 27, 1814, when Brillat-Savarin was getting along in years, at three in the afternoon. This was "the fashionable hour for dinner," it is noted by Lately Thomas, whose biography of Ward is new and definitive. "Promptness at mealtimes was to be a characteristic of the new arrival through a long and eventful life." My dear Sam died on May 19, 1884, leaving hundreds of letters and poems to reveal his warmth and brilliance, through a wild and often shady career as Washington lobbyist and charming rascal.

Sherlock Holmes was born, full-fledged of course, from the head of the Scottish Jupiter Dr. Arthur Conan Doyle, in 1887, in *A Study in Scarlet*. Then from 1891 until his *Return,* his astounding imperturbability developed into an international and probably indestructible legend, as he solved hideous as well as voluptuous crimes from his "bachelor flat" in Baker Street, London. He is undoubtedly one of the most *tangible* imaginary human beings of this present world.

As for Inspector Maigret, he was born as far as I am concerned in about 1930, although he was probably then in his early thirties himself. I began a long liaison with him that year, through Georges Simenon's almost uncountable series of books about his adventures with the French police. Maigret was somewhat younger then he is now, although not the decades that calendars would indicate, and he has been getting a little slower and heavier physically, being as human as anyone else. When last I met him in print, he was seriously considering retirement, an intolerable prospect from any point of view. Both his wife and I fret about this.

And here is an emotional hazard one runs with modern creators of men like Maigret. Simenon, for instance, is almost uncomfortably realistic, so that one must accept with resignation the thickening waistlines and the thinning hairs on the printed page, which one also faces in actuality. Dr. Doyle's Sherlock Holmes, in comparison, is unreal. His worshippers have done all they can to make him human, and the Baker Street Irregulars, both actual and wishful, have evolved desperate little familiarities with his personal habits. Nothing really makes him, however, anything but an arch-human, untouchable, just as he is/was an archmisogynist. It would be an impertinence, for instance, to think of him as bilious, or thirsty or sweaty, as I know Sam Ward and Maigret and even Brillat-Savarin must often have been.

There are many fine aspects about the long affairs I have carried on with all these men. One is that they can be managed synonymously, without travail or guilt, and can warm me in their own ways without any quarrel of the mind or heart. Another is that I can accept with equanimity the cold fact that probably not one of the lot would have given me a second look. Thus I can snoop into their affairs with detachment, immunity, appreciation . . . and no feeling of personal involvement.

Of course Mr. Holmes had Dr. Watson to watch over him: friend, buffer, stooge. And Maigret has Madame Maigret, a fine woman of whom I am fond. She is perfect for him: devoted, practical, patient, a good cook, and above all kind, although like Dr. Watson she is inclined to fuss about things like wearing an overcoat in bad weather.

It is different with Sam Ward, and I must confess to a more active personal curiosity about his two beautiful wives and what I know in my heart was a life filled with the skilled appreciation of witty sexy fascinating women everywhere. Perhaps (and a tentacle of my nature curls around this prospect), he might have found me worth at least one fleeting but pleased glance?

As for Brillat-Savarin, in many ways he affects me as Sam does: I accept the plain fact that his interest in me would be casual and possibly cool, except across the dining table, but still I feel a lively, personal, but unpossessive curiosity about the women he did know.

He was always attractive physically, even when old. "A man of great wit," his friend Dr. Richerand wrote, "a most agreeable dinner companion, and one endowed with measureless gaiety, he was the center of attraction in any gathering fortunate enough to have his company, for he gave himself up willingly to the seductions of worldly society, and only spurned them when he could delight in the more intimate pleasures of true friendship."

There's the man for me. I first met him when I was perhaps twenty. I was living with a family in Dijon, where my husband and I were going to the university. Madame Ollagnier was an almost pathologically stingy woman who still managed to set a good table, with the help of a series of terrified slaveys and the firm gastronomical demands of her architect husband. We ate well, twice a day, and occasionally with what Dr. George Saintsbury would call supernacular finesse.

Once, and I believe it was to celebrate the end of Lent in 1931, the dull wine carafe was not on the table at noon, nor was there any sign of the water that we were urged to use "for reasons of health" to dilute our subordinary Burgundy. Instead there were two dusty bottles: exciting, encouraging! And with ceremony a cobwebbed and indeed moldy casserole was produced reverently from the tiny kitchen, and Monsieur Ollagnier informed us with a flourish of trumpets in his voice that it was from Belley.

He was a tactful man. Undoubtedly he sensed our timid ignorance of why the origin of this odd blue-green-gray dish should ring bells, and he told us deftly that Belley was the birthplace of Jean-Anthelme Brillat-Savarin, one of the glories of France. Then with a dramatic shrug, implying that our own minds must take over from there, he plunged his two knives along the edge of the mildewed crust.

"This pâté has spent at least a year on the shelf in the cellar of a distant cousin of mine, who carries on the classical traditions of the region," he said. "It will have shaped itself into a miracle of flavor. Once correctly served, as is its due," and here he lifted off the whole crust with a surgical flourish and tossed it disdainfully onto a platter Madame held for him, in a shower of pure penicillin culture, "and after we have had a few sips of these slightly weary but still robust Arbois, served in honor of the sainted lawyer, gastronomer, raconteur par excellence, and amateur physiologist, we will sit here until we have eaten this whole damned pâté, for to expose it more than a few hours to the open air would be a sacrilege, an infamous desecration."

And this we did, for a luncheon lasting perhaps four hours, when even Madame stopped counting the wattage of the light that burned above us in the hideous little dank dark room. We protected the Belley masterpiece from ignominy, and did away with at least three long loaves of bread and two batches of salad, and of course the first two bottles of wine from Brillat-Savarin's general district and a couple more, and when I finally confessed that I had never heard any of the names before, Monsieur Ollagnier said scornfully that many Frenchmen never had either, which I find to be true to this day.

As we went on rescuing the pâté, and toasting almost everything that came to mind, he told me many things that I later found to be incorrect, but that gave a good picture of the somewhat shadowy old lawyer who startled all his friends by publishing, a few months before his death, *La Physiologie du goût*. Apparently I fell in love then, that day of the massive mildewed dish, but the affair really did not take shape until I was almost accidentally talked into making a new translation of his odd book.

I was composing an anthology of great feasts, and I found myself affronted by the awkward English versions of the *Physiology*. "I can do better," I protested, and I added that this and that should not have happened to such clear delightful prose. "Then why don't you?" I was asked coldly. So for about two years I lived, as closely as human beings can live with the printed word, in the mind, the life, the world of this wonderful old man.

As a matter of fact, there are conflicting reports on whether he *was* wonderful. Certainly his Paris set was amazed when he quietly produced a small classic. His admiring young friend Richerand wrote well of him, but other people did not; he was described disdainfully as an oaf, a hulking tall figure in the courts of law who often carried dead birds in his coattails to hasten their gaminess for a dinner dish.

It is a dubious thing about his being married, but I do not care. Certainly it is too bad that if he had a wife, he did not want to show her to his friends. He wrote of himself as a bachelor, perhaps wishfully, and it was not until more than fifty years after he died that Charles Monselet stated, upon talking with many people who still remembered him (How many are there now, who can remember a modest man dead that long?), "His widow lived long after him." I think she was a relative of one of his brothers, but a pleasant facet of the love life of the intellect is that this does not matter, least of all to me, the faithful one.

Brillat-Savarin enjoyed the company of his cousin Juliette Recamier, as did many other men of her time. I admire his taste here, without any cavil except about the rumor of her reluctant virginity: he, and she too, might have been happier otherwise.

It is also rumored that in America about 1795, when he was a dashing young refugee playing his violin and appreciating the virtues and accents of his female language students, he may possibly have fathered a child who became one of the ancestors of S. L. M. Barlow, trusted intimate of my friend Sam Ward! Descendants of Barlow regretfully deny that there is any branch of the family tree on which to perch a by-blow of the professor, but at least he and Barlow and Ward himself all shared knowledge of the good things in life.

My first meeting with Sam was when I read *Oscar Wilde Discovers America,* shortly after it was published in 1936. (There, I thought, is a man for me!) In 1882, when Ward introduced young Wilde with glitter and fanfare but withal respect to the voracity of American society, Sam was a ripe but seething sixty-eight, much beloved and despised and already something of a legend on both sides of the Atlantic . . . "delicious uncle," he was called, "the Universal Uncle" . . .

(I am interested to note that while I savor his avuncular reputation, and agree with its many merits, I cannot but feel that it overlaid, as it were, his true nature as a Complete Man, aware sexually in the right way always, whether he beamed upon a homesick grandchild in London or wrote a wittily effusive love lyric to Lillie Langtry in New York.)

My second meeting with this wonderful rogue, crook, con- noisseur, wit, linguist, bandit, counterspy, gastronomer, political reprobate, and all the other things he has deservedly been called by his exasperated and adoring relatives, friends, and enemies, was when I had the chance to correspond about him with Lately Thomas. Again there was instant recognition; plainly I am at- tracted, like many women, to the rascal saints . . .

Of course Sherlock Holmes will always remain beyond this dar- ing familiarity. He was born about thirty years before my own birth in 1908, and when I first met him, during a bout of measles at the age of eight, he shifted easily into a father image. Holmes was thin and tall like my sire Rex Kennedy, and as far as I can tell he wore the same tall thin nose. (Here the image confuses itself with Basil Rathbone, the consummate portrait of the other two men: Basil- Rex-Sherlock-Rathbone-Kennedy-Holmes.)

My father, of course, never sawed away at the violin in mo- ments of fleeting perplexity, as did Holmes, nor call out occasion- ally for a deft application of "the needle." There remains in me to this day, however, a feeling of daughterly devotion to them both, and one I could not shake off if I wanted to. This means, naturally, that there is a touch of awe in it, and that is right too: I can still flinch as any good child should before the slightly scornful impatience, the veiled sneer, in Basil-Sherlock-Rex's remote voice as he/they touched on some imbecility of mine.

Once past my first view, absorbed and naive, of the various shoddy volumes that now make up *The Complete Sherlock Holmes,* I felt at home. Reading steadily, in bed and with a fever, is an act that can make any tale burn into one's heart. I learned this for all my life when I was eight, and have often seized the chance since then, and when next I picked up the thread with serious intent, some thirty years later, I was at home again.

This was when I suddenly knew that my mind needed a purge. I had been working and living and even thinking too fast. As instinctively as a constipated cat seeks out tender grass stalks, I put *Sherlock Holmes* by my bed, and looked at nothing else ever printed until I had chewed my way amiably, contentedly, through *A Study in Scarlet, The Sign of Four, The Adventures of Sherlock Holmes, The Memoirs of Sherlock Holmes, The Return of Sherlock Holmes, The Hound of the Baskervilles, The Valley of Fear, His Last Bow,* and *The Case Book of Sherlock Holmes.* I arose resigned, as after a restorative and leisurely feast with rare friends.

I doubt that I picked up any mannerisms from this prolonged intimacy, as writers and lovers are in danger of doing, but I felt, and still feel, that I learned many ways *not* to do and be, much as a child who hears correct grammar does not split infinitives nor say "he don't." There is something exciting and cleansing about even a page or two of Arthur Conan Doyle's fast simple unadorned prose. Logic is there, far stronger than any ridiculous cliff-hanging, but the real medicine, especially for a person like me, inclined to involved and occasionally shaky syntax, is the complete plainness of the prose. There is no nonsense about it, and yet it is magically romantic, in the best sense.

As for my first meeting with Inspector Maigret, I owe it to my younger sister Norah, unwitting entrepreneur, who in 1931 was fourteen years old and living with me in France.

I had got her into a bit of trouble at the convent by encouraging her to read a copy of Colette's *L'Envers de music-hall* as an example of good tight French. The mother superior was horrified. I cast about for some substitute, and with almost the same felicity started my sister on Georges Simenon, this time more discreetly. His books were easy to buy in railroad stations, and were cheap, like Colette's. I worried a little because he encouraged Norah to use dots instead of more classical punctuation, but at least she knew what they stood for, and his past subjunctive was impeccable. Of course I read the dots, and verbs and what went along with all of them, and realized quite soon that I would be happy if I could spend the rest of my life with Monsieur Maigret, Simenon's fabulous creature. And I have done so.

Ours is a comfortable relationship. There is naturally a certain amount of sex in it, but this is no menace to any of us, including Madame. I feel at ease with them both, not daughterly surely but without any need to try to interrupt their fine marital pattern. Maigret has taught me a great deal, like all the others. In his case it is not so much a question of syntax and logic, as it is of being with other humans. His understanding of them, and his quiet wise tolerance, have been good for me. And through him I have of course been able to meet many people I most probably could never have known otherwise—just as Mr. Holmes introduced me long ago to "a gigantic hound," "a lady dressed in black and heavily veiled," and to the archdevil Professor Moriarty himself.

Oftener than not, the most interesting people in Maigret's adventures are corpses, but very soon I am led expertly to see why, which in turn makes many other things plainer to me in the outside world.

The people Sam Ward has introduced me to, on the other hand, (even Oscar Wilde!) tend to look pale beside Sam's own dapper and usually well-fed image. I am a little shy before them, bedazzled by their cleverness and their worldly glow. Sam is enough for me.

This fading of the background is not true of Brillat-Savarin. I warm to every person in his life, with and through him. With Sam I actually see only Sam, but with the old French lawyer I am in a world that is as much mine as his, because of the way he reveals it to me. I know Juliette Recamier, the teaser, and young Dr. Richerand who ate too fast, and the two old brothers Dubois who could never eat too much.

The brothers were seventy-eight and seventy-six, ancients in those days of early mortality: "freshly shaved, their hair carefully arranged and well-powdered, two little old men who were still spry and healthy." They invited themselves to breakfast one morning, sharply at ten, and began with two dozen oysters each, "and a gleaming golden lemon," washed down with plenty of sauternes. Then grilled skewered kidneys were served, a pâté of truffled foie gras *en croûte,* and finally the cheese fondue that the brothers had expressly asked for, a recipe their host had learned while he was a refugee in Switzerland. After the fondue came fresh fruits and sweetmeats, coffee, and "finally two kinds of liqueur, one sharp for refreshing the palate and the other oily for soothing it."

The three gentlemen then took a gentle constitutional around the apartment. It was discovered to be two o'clock, the correct dinner hour in those days, and without any real protest the brothers Dubois "seated themselves, pulled nearer to the table, spread out their napkins, and prepared for action."

After the unexpected but delectable meal that Brillat-Savarin and his cook managed to turn out (thanks to their own resources and some help from restaurants in the neighborhood), my friend introduced the newfangled idea of a cup of tea to the old fellows, and they enjoyed several rounds of it by the hearth. And then, without more than lip protest, they shared a bowl of hot rum punch and one plateful and then another of "beautifully thin, delicately buttered, and perfectly salted slices of toast" . . . and it was past eight o'clock and never one dull moment, thanks to the subtle and untiring attentions my dear professor paid to his two ancient and delighted guests. The next day they reported by note to him that "after the sweetest of sleeps [they] had arisen re-freshed, feeling both able and eager to begin anew."

This warms my heart: tact, interest, complete generosity. So, in much the same way, does Thomas's account of the time when Sam Ward was an old man in London and cheered a lonely suffering little granddaughter in Brown's Hotel by sending her a surprise bundle every few minutes (a beautiful ring, an elegant traveling case, baskets of ripe fruit) before she sailed to America to die— which perhaps because of his magic she did not do for many decades.

Sherlock Holmes did many small kind things too, generous and warm behind their sardonic restraint, and of course Inspector Maigret is the epitome of gruff kindliness, capable of true compassion. He, like all the other men, has the gift of making people *trust* him, even in his detested role of cop, judge and jury, and occasional executioner.

After the years and the lives I have shared with these four people, they are clearer to my mind's eye than many I saw this morning, and clearer than any picture could ever paint them. The nearest thing to a good portrait of Maigret is the blocklike silhouette of a slouched hat brim, a pipe between thick firm lips, a jutting nose that advertises most of the paperbacks about him. This does not bother me at all. I know better, just as I know old Sam Ward because and then in spite of every cartoon and photograph of him, bloated, corrupt, always dapper.

Sherlock Holmes is of course inextricably composed for me of my father's graceful lankiness and long nose, with Rathbone in there for the right curl to the lips.

As for Jean-Anthelme Brillat-Savarin, little need be thought about his personal appearance. He was variously described by some of his contemporaries, but I myself know that he was a tall healthy man, fastidious in spite of what might be warming in his coattails, with a tendency to corpulence, which he diagnosed and coped with, wearing his own scientifically designed corset when other efforts failed.

Perhaps the most rewarding thing about all these love affairs that I have kept up so enjoyably for so long is that, except for Maigret, I know and accept how the gentlemen died. Few women can say this with equanimity.

There are a few accounts of the last moments of good and even bad men that never fail to move me to actual tears, whether or not I loved either the writer or the person whose death made the words ring with the adequate poignancy. This is true, somewhat to my surprise, when I read of Sam Ward's dying: I am physically moved. I am there in the villa in Italy, in May of 1884. The old man is very ill, perhaps from a Carnaval feast of "succulent steamed mussels" in Naples with an old friend. Sam is awake, breathing heavily. He dictates a wryly jaunty letter. Then, fixing his always brilliant eyes upon us, he says clearly, "I think I am going to give up the ghost." (And here I must steel myself, as I have in my life before . . .) And with a long sigh he is gone. In the next room his niece Daisy weeps. Beneath his pillow is the dog-eared Horace, and on the bedspread beside him, Khayyám, open at Omar's envoi:

> And when like her, O Saki, you shall pass
> Among the Guests Star-scattered on the Grass,
> And in your joyous errand reach the spot
> Where I made One—turn down an empty Glass!

I weep here. Every time I must weep a little, and Sam would like that. But one cannot feed too often on such helpless tears, and I am glad Maigret has not yet brought me to them. He is getting on, but I do not fear for him in my own lifetime.

As for Sherlock Holmes, I suffered along with myriad others when he and Professor Moriarty died together in the Reichenbach Fall, and then I returned to a confident acceptance of his immortality long before he himself did a quick jump back into print. He *Return*ed. Naturally. I knew he would when I was eight years old, and I still do.

Perhaps it is odd that the proof of Brillat-Savarin's command of my love is that I can read of his death, and think upon it, with complete serenity. He taught me how.

He died fairly quickly of simple pneumonia, contracted after an obligatory attendance at a chilly mass for the repose of the soul of Louis XVI, for which and for whom he felt small reverence. His relative and godson Dr. Recamier attended him, and noted that he seemed to understand that his end was upon him. He waited for it without regret, for his writings proved that he had long looked upon death with the same philosophical detachment he felt toward life. One of his admirers wrote, "He left the world like a satisfied diner leaving the banquet-room . . ."

It interests me, and may even lead some to the speculation that this type of confession can, that at least two of the main men in my life are detectives. Jacques Barzun, in his introduction to *The Delights of Detection,* says that "the emotion called forth [by detective feats] is that of seeing order grow out of confusion." This is something, of course, that gives courage and reassurance to no matter what type of woman, and I feel especially sensitive to it because of my wishful dependence upon a better order than my own.

Dr. Barzun goes on to describe a detective as "a man of independent mind, an eccentric possibly, something of an artist even in his scientific work, and in any case a creature of will and scope superior to the crowd. He is, in short, the last of the heroes."

Yes, of course: that is it! Here is Everyman; here are all of them, sleuths or not, and it is plain that I have openly searched all my life, or at least since I was a measly eight, for a hero. How amazing, how undeservedly rewarding, to have found at least four to lean on forever!

From Mr. Holmes I have learned the virtues, if not the practice, of being succinct. From Inspector Maigret have come a deepened patience and compassion, and from Sam Ward, "delicious uncle," has flowed over me the meaning of human gaiety, for he was, in both the catholic and the Catholic sense, debonair. Longest and best of all my learning has come from Brillat-Savarin: delicate discretion, warmly conceived and practiced, always beyond my common grasp, never to be feared or disdained. I am rich to have known these gentlemen, and to remain faithful to them after my fashion.

—*St. Helena, California, 1965*

8

The Blue Gun

This may not be an extraordinary experience, but I think it is at least unusual, that a person can actually experience death in a dream. I did, nearly twice. This time I seemed reticent, or perhaps cautious, about the final bliss I had felt the first time.

I was almost asleep tonight, lying on my left side, waiting without impatience for my night life to begin. Suddenly I was recollecting, but without meaning to, a dream I had completely forgotten in my waking life, one I had had perhaps a week or a few nights ago. I knew that I was merely remembering and that I was not redreaming. I did not question, but I was conscious that this was a strange occurrence.

The second time, it was the actual dying that was important, much like the last chapter of a well-remembered novel. I felt the hole form around the bullet as it entered the base of my skull and proceeded firmly up toward the right eye socket. Then, deliberately but with no fear, I stopped the thing, wakened myself, and for a time was in full possession of the first dream, of which this was the rear end. Already it fades, but a wonder remains.

In the beginning I was a fictional woman, having an affair with a strong, vicious or at least ruthless man. We decided to kill his wife, and got a beautiful little gun. It was blue, I think, a little toy.

Then she was sitting at a table, her back to a low stone wall, and she became me, as behind her/me the man spoke over the wall, framed in dappled sunlight and leaves and flowers and as from a gladsome pergola. He said that he had decided to kill me instead.

I turned slowly and saw the gun. I knew it was my turn to die, and at once. I felt a flash of fear, but only a flash, and a question about how long it would hurt, but there was no time for protest.

I leaned a little forward on the table, which was the stone one I once sat at in a garden in Provence. "Look," I had said jokingly that day. "There is my typewriter and I am writing a book, a really beautiful one, a masterpiece!"

Behind me now I knew the little blue gun in the dappled light was aiming. I did not hear it fire, but as I dropped lazily onto the table, the hole at the base of my skull formed itself to welcome the bullet, which traveled in an almost leisurely way toward my right eye socket. I was somewhat surprised at the obvious path it took, and at the general lack of confusion. I had guessed there might be lightning or ugly noises, but the only positive thing was its irrevocability: it was an accomplished fact.

When the bullet was about halfway through my head, I began to fade, or rather there was a strong cloudiness that seemed to spread out from the bullet. I was almost dead. There was no fear or pain. In another inch, I was almost formless, a log, a great mist. It was a merging of my identity with nonidentity, and never had I been so real, so vast, so meaningless. I disappeared, and the bullet no doubt emerged through the right eye socket, but it did not matter to anything.

—*St. Helena, California, 1966*

The old man was reading a current magazine devoted, that month, to Paris. "This is supposed to be about Paris," he said. I asked him three times, "Does it make you want to go back, does it make you want to go *back,* DOES IT MAKE YOU—" "No," he said with dignity. Then he added cynically, "Love in Paris, this and that in Paris! Hah. One thing, dining and dancing—that does interest one a little—"

I thought of his obviously dogged efforts to down something, anything, at table. I thought of his belchings and hackings.

And then I thought of the last time I was in Paris with him. We were staying at a small old hotel beside the Continental, and could walk a few steps and dodge a few cabs and be in the Tuileries. We could go down some graceful steps, the kind architects would put in an opera house or a luxury liner for ladies to float down in fabulous gowns, and we would be on the hard-packed earth of the gardens, with flashing tiny sails visible to our left from the round pond and the haunting wails of the Punch-and-Judy shows to our right, and before us, topless towers, Paris, blue air, bliss.

One day we walked down the little dingy street. It was about three o'clock, I think. We had lunched in the back room of the Café de la Paix—lots of caviar and lots of iced vodka, and then, as I remember, artichokes and then Turkish coffee, a strange good meal. Edith (my mother and his wife) felt weary. She lay down on the elaborate brass bed. I pulled the cherry-colored satin puff over her, and she smiled in a gay knowing way at me and closed her eyes. We went down in the gilt-wire elevator, a shaky little cage, to the drab street that let so abruptly onto the almost intolerable gaiety of the Tuileries—yes, gay and tender with that ineffable and perhaps aphrodisiacal blue to it.

I don't remember anything except feeling free, with the caviar and vodka and pungent coffee in me and the warmth of my mother's smile, until we got to those steps, the ones that go down from the street. My father strode along in his monumental way. I think we talked about breakfasts, and about one he had vanquished that morning in the Anglican catacombs of the Continental, across the street from our hotel. I have a feeling of midafternoon noise, the honkings and clackings.

Then we were halfway down those wonderful steps. Light flashed on the sails on the pond far to our left. Taxis bleated behind us. The trees trembled like a sea, and up from their shade came the treble of a thousand children's voices. Space, space . . .

My father, a tall man dressed outlandishly and beautifully in white linen, with a wide Panama on his fine beaky head, waved his cane, which he used only outside the boundaries of the United States, and cried out, far over the Tuileries, the flowing river Seine, the Left Bank, perhaps even backward to the room where his wife lay dozing, a big triumphant shout, with the cane lifted and the beaky head back; *"God,* but I feel good."

It was possibly the best I have ever heard his voice. It was everything I wanted anyone I love to feel in Paris.

It would be impossible for me ever to recount the ways I have existed in that place. I have told a few. But one thing I can repeat, that when my youngest sister and my brother, she twenty and he eighteen I believe, came there and I met them, while I was living in Switzerland, I said to my husband, "Oh, I could weep for them —it is not the beautiful place it was when I first came to it in 1929. The quays have changed, trees are down, the taxis all have tops— oh, no!" He looked at me in a remote smiling way and said, "I once could have wept for you. Nineteen twenty-nine! What a crude year! You did not know Paris when it was Paris, in 1915, when I came back after seventeen days at the front and the janitor of the little Hôtel Foyot above the restaurant cut off my boots and bathed me and after I had slept for twenty hours brought me a bowl of wild strawberries. No, poor you. You never knew—and your brother and sister will pity their youngsters just as you and I . . ."

That is true. It has happened. By now I am pitying my chil- dren, and at the same time my heart is thick with envy, to be them, to be in Paris for the first time. I would once more be my father, so tall and complete, raising his cane against the pale sky and shouting out in the freest gesture of his life, "God, but I feel good." I would be my mother, under the satin coverlet, smiling so wisely. I would be that husband, arriving there wet and weary and finally fed by a gentle furnace man. I would be me, yes, in Paris, I would be me.

—St. Helena, California, 1969

10

The Green Talk

Two nights ago I worked for a long time, mostly in my subconscious, I suppose, on finding out about the Green Talk.

In my dream, the Green Talk was in the same class with ESP, and the ability to use it varied with people, so that June Eddy, for instance, could speak the Green Talk more easily and naturally than could I or Joe Abegg, or other people I was apparently concerned with that night.

If a person has any capacity for it at all—and most of us live and die unaware of it—it can be consciously developed, through exercise directed by someone who has the gift strongly. Apparently it is best to live very closely with such a person in order to attain any skill. For instance, married people often have the Green Talk.

In itself, the Green Talk is the ability to speak without sound —a kind of transference of speech from one spirit to another. When people use it well, questions can be asked and answered without any physical contact: expressions in the eyes or mouth, touch, or of course sound. What is best, and rarest, is that long and witty conversations can go on, between two or more people who have the gift for Green Talk and who have exercised it deliberately—*practiced,* that is.

I cannot remember from the dream whether it is used in prisons, but I rather think so, if the right people are confined together long enough (as in marriage?!)

In the dream (it has already lost its sharp edges, but the fact that I still think about parts of it makes it worth holding on to), I had enough of a gift for the Green Talk to work on it, and several friends helped me. As I became more at ease with it, through their gently patient help in communicating, I felt an increasing sense of pleasure. It was delightful to be in communication with other minds that attracted mine. Of course, this idea that there are two or three levels of speech that can go on in one person has often been written about—I think of a long play by Eugene O'Neill— but I don't remember ever hearing about the Green Talk. In that old play, which interested me very much when I saw and then read it, the third language existed solely within the person who spoke it. The Green Talk, in contrast, is strictly for communication between two or more people. It is not at all secret, and can be picked up by anyone who knows it—or rather, who is aware that it is being spoken and who can go along . . .

I am sure that at its best, it can be used by two skilled people at long distance, much as letters can be exchanged, or voice by telephone or wireless or satellite. In my dream, my own experiments were limited by my fumbling ignorance of the potential within me, and I had to be in the same room or garden or elevator in order to speak it, even with a person much more in control than I. There was no need for any physical contact, although apparently there had to be sympathy, even love—and of course familiarity.

Once this invisible contact was established, no matter how

clumsily, I had an almost exalted feeling of enjoyment, of success, of having grown a little farther past the terrible blind limitations of *matter*.

There is no doubt that this feeling of having opened one more tiny door is attained in true meditation, which of course takes great self-discipline and training. It is an inner triumph, and one that I know only indirectly, except for a few instants of realization that flashed upon me and then past me as if to show what *could* be done. But the Green Talk is not meant for anything but communication. In my dream, there was no fear that it would or could be abused, as the telephone can be. The Green Talk is not an instrument but a way . . . and it interested me, even as my subconscious explored it a little, that I could recognize my own limits of attainment. There was no false modesty about this, any more than there is when I know that my skills as a writer, by now developed about as far as they can be, are infinitely smaller than many people's. In the dream, June, for instance, was so much more at ease with the Green Talk than I could ever be that I felt a warm deep gratitude for her for even bothering to help me stumble along. It was rather like a dialogue between Gandhi and a first-year Methodist minister . . . between Einstein and a high school math teacher. But there was nothing but gentle patience toward me as a learner, and June and several other people helped me slowly to speak the Green Talk. My sister Anne was there for a while; several other people I have known, and many I have never consciously met before, began to communicate easily but in what I knew was a simplified way with me.

Always there was the feeling of joyfulness.

I don't know why this form of inaudible invisible conversation is called the Green Talk, but all the time I was dreaming, I kept reminding myself to hang on to the name, to remember it deliberately in the flash before consciousness, and to repeat it sternly because of its terrible importance. This I did, even while I tried to continue the dream explanation. (This process, often used by deliberate dreamers, is much like trying to prolong and hold on to a sexual orgasm, I think.)

Why "green"? Why "talk," even?

To answer that last question, the communication was clearly in words, phrases, sentences. It was not simply a wordless understanding, the kind often experienced even by dull people—the rush of love or compassion, the fleeting exchange of recognition that often flows between people in buses, on streets, in beds. The Green Talk was *talk,* but it was silent.

It went on, perhaps, in the same way that a skilled pianist will play on a silent keyboard while he travels in a plane or bus, or even will move his fingers in his sleep to the sounds his mind conjures. The Green Talk could be carried on at a large dinner party, in a quiet room where only two or three worked or sat or lay, or in a crowded public place. But it took two people. That is perhaps the crux of it—two or, sometimes in my dream, several. And it need not be an urgent communication. Indeed, it was simply a higher form of inter-talk than most of us are aware of.

And I was the novice, plainly touched by the gift but in a very simple and crude way. I stumbled along, and felt happy and excited. It was one more way to be sensate, *awake,* even if in a dream.

—*St. Helena, California, 1971*

11

Strip Search

The question on a talk show was about how and why and if women should be stripped and searched by the police. Men were mentioned too, of course, and a few called the station. One said he thought men enjoyed it, and another said that men are used to being naked on command, in locker rooms for athletics and in enlistment centers and things like that. One man said he found his one strip search traumatic and afterward felt as if he had been raped.

But all the breathless trembling women who called, no matter how skilled at being breathless etc., sounded violently outraged.

Most of them, and this was the problem of the show's hostess, too, had been submitted to the search unjustly, for ridiculous things like letting a dog out without a leash or for signing a small check knowing that it could not be paid at once.

Of course I think such invasion of privacy is outrageous, unless public safety is involved.

Some of the police and some of the male callers argued that lice and other social varmints were taken care of in such searches. This was done by means of an injected spray of chemicals, without the victim's permission, in "the public good."

Well, I listened and sympathized here and there, as is usually the case with such shows and especially with certain hosts I have come to recognize since I read less. (Progressive cataracts on both eyes, and I manage to listen at night while I prepare vegetables and so on for the next day's meals . . . it is an agreeable schedule.)

Yes, I said, when the voice asked in a hard way, "Has this ever happened to you?" Yes, it did once. But I know that I was a very fortunate person, because it did not hurt my amour-propre at all, and I felt there was no real outrage to my private self; my main feeling was one of great compassion for the policewoman who had to do it to me.

This reaction may sound very sanctimonious and holier than thou and a lot of other revolting things, but it is true. I still feel sorry for the officer who had to do it to me. I know that she was required to do it, and at the same time I know how it would be if it happened to me in another time and place, for instance, with male cops watching on closed-circuit TV in case the female examiners "needed help."

Well, I had nobody, either. But I did not need anything but my own self-control, as it turned out, and my firm wish not to yawn.

It was at Heathrow, an airport that has never been even amiable to me. It had started several days earlier, when I told a travel agent very firmly, down in Marseille, that I did not want to travel on a DC-10, either from Marseille to Paris or from Paris to London or, most especially, from London to Los Angeles. For one reason or another, though, I was on this abominable wide-bodied piece of airborne cardboard and chewing gum, and I sat back like a fatalistic Fury past anger, as we jiggled in and out of airports. It seemed always to be the same plane, but of course we had a new set of stewardesses now and then, so I knew to look for rest rooms in different places.

Finally, on the last leg, somewhere over the North Sea, the lights blinked out several times and a pale-lipped stewardess made a little joke about candlelight dinners as she tried to fit a plastic tray over my middle, and then dropped her flashlight as we went into real dark. Across from me a tiny dark man, who was buckled into his double-width seat with his legs crossed, was praying to Allah. He was the prime minister of some eastern kingdom, and behind him sat his empress, a tall Paris model, and back from her in the other "class" were about thirty of their servants and a couple of little princesses. Most of them praying too, I felt sure.

So we got back to Heathrow, after dumping almost all the fuel into the North Sea and being refused permission to land in Ireland. We went in sideways, to the middle of a field of brussels sprouts, with lights playing on us and ambulances winking. It was nice to see lights again. The trip had been bumpy, dark, and cold, since everything was off or out except the quiet voice of the prime minister, saying in an almost conversational chant, Allah . . . Allah . . . Allalalalah . . .

When the lights went on, once we were quiet in the little cabbages, I looked at him, almost dozing in his double seat, a tiny tired old man. Behind him the beautiful empress looked straight at me. We did not smile or nod, but there was an instant of complete communication.

In the airport we stood in a lengthy line, and I saw long rods being held out toward us as we shuffled past officers and guards. We were tired. We were taken to a shoddily bright and elegant hotel at the airport, and I remember taking a long shower in a shoddy elegant room. Then I lay on sheets starched to make them seem thicker, but clean ones, until in about two hours I was summoned to return to the airport for takeoff. I think we had breakfast first in a big restaurant that must look the same way all day and all night. There were big buses outside, and when I told a driver or somebody who was getting us into one that I had two bags and did not see them, he patted my shoulder and said, "Daountcha worry, luv," in such a soft nice way that I almost fell onto his shapely small shoulder with happy reassurance. I still feel warmed by his voice.

Once in the business part of Heathrow, though, things were cold and crisp, and there we all were again, like herded sheep, shuffling slowly toward a row of officers and desks and guards. I paid little heed. I felt fatalistic, victimized, invaded. There was no way to escape the lines, the eyes looking, the ghastly politeness. We shuffled toward the place where the desks were, and facing them to our left were the men with the cattle prods or whatever they were, darting and weaving them indirectly at our pockets and our minds and our even more private parts.

Two men ahead of me was a well-dressed youngish man whom I'd seen but not noticed as we boarded the night before. I remember thinking that he must have been back with the royal children and all their servants when the lights began to flicker. I noticed that he had not had a chance to shave, so that his beard was making his pale-dark skin blue.

Then all the cattle prods went off at once, and it was like a Mickey Mouse cartoon of twenty cops disappearing into one telephone pole in a flash of precise marching. Whoosh and the young man disappeared.

Nobody faltered or blinked, and we went on walking toward the desks on our right, and the man ahead of me was escorted courteously away and then I was pulled gently out and away and I am sure the people behind me were too, but I shall never know, and I do not care.

I was led to a small white room, and a short trim woman gave me a nice uncompromising neat smile and told me her name and said that here she was called a lady bobby, a policewoman. Then she apologized to me for what she had to do, and suddenly I was about six years old again and I had to undress as fast as I could so that it would not take long and everything would be all right and it was nothing but a bore and would soon be over. She called me "madam" without smiling.

The odd thing was that all the time I felt almost complacently young and obedient, I was really being the lady bobby too, and was feeling sorry and embarrassed and almost apologetic for her. She was about my age, probably, and much smaller. She kept murmuring, "Oh dear, oh dear me, how you must hate all this, madam. Oh, what a bore! Forgive me, will you? Oh Lord."

I had never been strip-searched before, but I felt helpless and docile, and I really liked this small neat woman. She was as sweet as lavender, as clean as a fine razor, and I did not feel affronted in any way at all as she pulled on rubber gloves quick as scat and stuck one little finger up my anus and then probed all and every orifice. It was her sweet steady little murmur that kept me from any affront: "Oh, poor dear! This is such a bore! Over soon now, soon, madam!"

She laughed shortly, like a puppy barking, and stood back, pulling off the gloves. "Out! I'll come with you. Out you go, love. Get into your things."

As she walked ahead of me, after she had helped me get back into my clothes, I felt I wanted to see her again, to talk with her and thank her for keeping me so dignified and for being such a mysteriously detached, kind person. I felt that I *must* see her again. I must thank her. But the line seemed the same, and finally I was back on the plane, and the next time I left it was in California.

And tonight I remembered that yes, I have been body-searched, stripped to the buff, with a gloved living probe pushed into my secret hollows. And suddenly I remembered that at one point I asked my lady bobby in a mild, almost dreamy way, "Couldn't they do this with the cattle prods, if they are looking for whatever they found on that man?" And she said, "No, madam," and went right on.

That is all there is to report, I think, about my own small experience with this kind of police interference or whatever it may be deemed. I was fortunate in many ways. For one thing, I knew that something was very wrong with the flight I was on, whether it was mechanical or purely a problem of international politics. I felt fatalistic about it, just as I had about being put on it when I had so firmly insisted on almost any other type of flying boat, *vache-qui-vole* . . . And then I also knew that the small trim impersonal policewoman who had to look into me for hidden weapons or whatever she was told to find was one of the nicest people I had ever known.

—*Glen Ellen, California, 1972*

12

M. F. K. F.

You can't accept people who fall for you. If they fall for you, you think there's something wrong with them.

When I was young, I liked to reduce my schoolmates (always female) to a state of abject devotion. Then I would despise them and behave with callous arrogance and a kind of tipsy power. Instead of hating me, they seemed to like my treatment and often became longtime friends.

Gradually I saw that I felt scornful of their devotion because I knew that I was not worth loving. This proved that they were fools. So I could treat them as such . . . or as clowns, or courtiers, or plain idiots. It was cruel of me, and both sadistic and masochistic.

Later in life I did the same thing to many men. I now feel ashamed of this, as I do of mistreating my young mesdemoiselles; it seems arrogant, but actually it may have sprung from deep humility, a feeling of unworthiness. I felt that I was cheating people by letting them think that I was bright or pretty or desirable. I felt like a humbug.

And so I hated them for not seeing through me, and in turn hating me.

I don't know about all the little girls, and the adolescents, but I like to think that some of the men did see through to this truth and did hate me. They would have hated me because I had let them believe in a lie.

And this is why I am very careful about letting people like me now, although I really do feel better when I do not sense active suspicion or envy or scorn in anyone. It surprises me that I even care. But the real enjoyment of another human being is a fairly facile and sociable and usually trivial élan that one can spread. I pay almost no attention to it in gatherings where I meet many new people, but I am very cautious about using it in small groups. I do not want to *mislead* anyone.

(This is complicated to discuss, I find.)

I never hoodwinked Dillwyn, and therefore I never felt ashamed with him because I had not been anything but trusting and naive. With my first husband, Al Fisher, I think it was a mutual game we played; I loved all his tricks until I began to know that we must part, and by then neither of us really cared, although it was a cruel thing that I could not even offer him my old tempting promises. Certainly I never treated him with anything but passionate gratitude for rescuing me from the Ranch. We were mutually generous, at least on that score.

As for my third and last husband, he hated me from the first, because really he feared and loathed all women, but with him I began to despise his "use" of me as a potentially profitable literary property. He mocked my provincial habits and manners, but at the same time he bowed to my ingrown and toplofty mannerisms, left over from the early days with my very young peers. He was impressed by my faked skill at commanding the full attention of a headwaiter in a famous restaurant (simply to reduce him to furious impotence), while at the same time he sneered at my small-town mind, and hated me for bringing off what he felt was a social coup and what I myself knew was just another *trick*.

And so that went.

And now all I feel is a kind of helpless remorse at how I've been such a hoax to so many loving people, when I disliked or hated them for liking or even loving me. It is a shame, a pity.

It was not their fault but mine.

Meanwhile, this late, I accept whatever they offered me, and by now I think I know the value of what I so scornfully pushed aside when I was less aware of meanings.

The cold fact remains that I did indeed feel that people who loved me were blind and stupid to do so, instead of seeing that I was not worth the effort. And yet they did love me, and now, so late, I am grateful.

—Glen Ellen, California, 1975

13
Stealing

Sometimes stealing, or thieving, is wrong. (This means that *I* do not think it is *right*.) For instance, I don't think that Elgin should have removed the marbles to England from where he found them. Of course, they would have died, probably, if he had not. But he should have said something like "Do you mind if I move these artifacts to a relatively dry safe place where they can be preserved for our future enjoyment?"

I was raised on Gayley's *Classic Myths* (which means that I know all of the ins and outs of gods and goddesses), and I think I know about many of the intricacies of those "Elgin marbles." They were a kind of comic strip, a Mickey Mouse or Spirou story, running across the page and full of promise and threat and portent. But their removal was, to any young and now old view, a theft.

And like many others, that theft was in some way justified. Sometimes stealing is fully right.

It is my basically puritanical or moral nature that frowns on stealing, yet still leaves me feeling as innocent as anything newborn about two or three real robberies I have committed. I think I was right, just as Elgin may have been, although I reaped lesser goods.

A few minutes ago I reached for the scissors on my desk, to cut off some extra tape on a package I was wrapping, and I almost purred with pleasure to pick up *those* scissors, and feel their sure small blades cut with such pure balanced exactitude across the gummed paper. I looked at them with a small smile. They are of a dull pewterish alloy, probably, not to be polished but graceful in the hand and light to hold. They cut with a quick sureness. I would hesitate to take them to a sharpener in this country; he might try to brighten the look of them, or put the slim blades under the electric sharpener.

I decided to steal them about three hours after I moved into a rented apartment in southern France. It was the bottom floor of a *mas* or farm, owned by an architect in Paris/London. I did not know her, and of course hope I never meet her because of my thievery, but she was a friend of a friend, and she let me stay there for several weeks. When I finally left for other pastures, I took the/ *my* scissors without a thought, because they had been mine since the minute I saw them in the top right-hand drawer under the kitchen sink. I moved them at once into the other room and put them on a table that would be my desk, and from then until this minute, many years later, I feel good when I see their almost dainty shape and their subtle color, and I feel thankful that I took them with me. (That is a euphemism: I *stole* them.)

I left three pairs of good metal, more modern of course, in their place; in the kitchen and on the desk and another in a closet. They cost plenty, but the pair I stole was, and I admitted it, *irreplaceable.*

I think—in fact, I feel sure—that the architect never knew

that my scissors were gone. I have never written to inquire. I could —but why?

Of course if I'd stolen a baby, or a fine painting, I'd write and say why I did so. I might even be jailed or hung, even if the stolen goods were not wanted or were never looked at.

But my scissors are wanted (coveted, desired), and I look at them several times a week with an inner delight at their delicate precision.

Of course I've stolen one or two other things in my life. I suppose that most people have, if they look back far enough to admit sin at all.

Once I did not steal, and I shall always be sorry, and repelled by my cowardice. I was staying with friends in a rented house in a canyon in Hollywood. There were a lot of ugly steps going up to the really ugly house at the top. My husband and I were tutoring the children of O. K., a refugee conductor from Berlin. He was renting the house from a film writer, so that there were a lot of books, mostly French, which I read while the scared kids learned to breathe again and in another language. And there was one book I decided to steal, at the end of that strange summer of *mittagessen* [midday meals] and famous Americans and having to sit in the conductor's box at the Hollywood Bowl.

It was a book I read, by an Englishman named Cyril Something, I think, that had about three pages of superb and unforgettable prose in it. It was about a baseball game. I had never been to one. It described a game played outdoors in crystal light, with tiny athletes, tiny watchers, darling tiny lights and colors and faces and figures and bodies in the clear light. He told all that about a *baseball game*. And I knew I had to take that book.

I did not want to embarrass the friends we were living with while we had the job with the conductor's children, but as the summer ended slowly (because I felt so sad for the children trying to be in a new world—the father seemed beyond human pity by then, and I never really saw the opera-singer mother except as a gracious bowing female at the Bowl), I began to plan ways to get the book.

It seems odd now (and suddenly I remember a name: Cyril Hume—I must investigate) that I did not talk or ask or tell that I wanted that one book because of that one beautiful description.

I had seen and felt the light the author described, a few years earlier—it was like being in a country fair by Brueghel. My father and I had gone up to Whittier College from the Ranch so that he could report on a town gathering: he was editor of the *News* in Whittier. We went out onto the football field, at near twilight, and there in a crystalline and impeccable beauty were townspeople, known but transmogrified, moving like angels on earth in a green delicate electric beauty. I remember it now as I write about it, and I feel breathless. It was a moment caught in time, like a fly in amber, maybe. The light went from the west and the Pacific over toward the eastern hills, and then from the flat grasslands to the mountains and the Salton Sea. It slanted all the shadows eastward. The familiar football field was packed with ambling happy people eating almost languidly from long tables, and talking, smiling, moving in the magic.

I have never seen that again, anywhere. But the book captured it, and I don't remember if it was at an American college or where. But it was the magical way of catching the light that was there in that cheap ignored book, which I felt I must steal.

I did not. We all left the house, a drab elegant sad place that one day later was sold. I asked vaguely, several months after, what had happened to the books and was told that someone had bought all of them by shelf, at five dollars a foot or something like that.

So there went that book I knew I should steal.

But whom would I have asked? The owner of the house was

not there. Our host was gone most of the time. So was my husband, who could not have told me to take the book anyway. And I was pusillanimous.

About a year later, I was going down Hollywood Boulevard and saw a tall white-haired heavily shaded man weaving, staggering in a nice well-behaved way, and it was, I was told, the once-famous or well-known English writer who had "come to Hollywood."

I felt badly, and I still do. I wish I had got out and gone over to the old lush—or perhaps he was not much older than I—and told him that he had written, in *My Sister My Birds,* one of my own dreams.

—Glen Ellen, California, 1976

14

Fossils

Out of the nowhere and into the here (Where did you come from, baby dear?) a cloud drifts swiftly through and over, and I wonder what I ate for breakfast or lunch, a few thousand light miles away in my inconsequence. What did I really do since I last came into consciousness at about 5:45 this morning? Did I pot a hybrid tomato? Was I really at the lunch table with two strangers passing through the Valley of the Moon? They had called two days before, and I had made a nice little meal for us, with some good wine . . .

But where was I? Am I asking this of Time, or Space?

The only reassurance I can give myself in this spinning world is to look at and even to think about older things than I, and to laugh at my ephemeral state. I have several such reminders of it. Of course, there are furniture, silver, pictures, all that, but they are almost as transitory as I. The best things are the fossils.

I saw one in a window a couple of years ago. In fact, I saw

two, and so did my younger sister, and neither of us could afford to buy them, but we kept looking in as we went through the Passage Agard in Aix, and thinking about them in our own ways. They were small exquisite imprints or skeletons, or whatever archaeologists call them, of little fish, about two inches long, and slanted sideways into aluminum cases designed by their finder in the southern French terrain. He was an engineer, we were told, who had forgotten everything but the pursuit of the tiny fish, thirty million years old, which he caught in his strange metallic showcases. We kept looking at them, and the day before we had to leave that fair country again I left my sister and went up the Passage and bought the two fish, so long imprisoned. She had one, and I had one, and we felt fine about it.

Once back in California, I showed mine to a friend who goes on erudite diggings and half starves and has diarrhea but feels renewed inwardly by finding that this planet was lived on long before we evolved. She found my tiny old fish pretty enough, but the next time she came she gave me a beautiful lump that was obviously a clam shell molded around solid lava or prehistoric clay, and it was not thirty million years old but one hundred and fifty million.

I held it gently, although I think I could have bounced it off the floor, and I agreed that she had topped my joke. And now I look at it and think of it, although I look oftener at the less clumpy and much younger fish that the ex-engineer found and shaved and mounted for me in the southern mountains of France.

There are many less ancient but equally matured things around me, and I find some reassurance in them, or at least amusement. Now and then I wonder why I like oldness. It is certainly not a question of my own age, since from my first conscious days I have known and sought out and wooed older men and women. The main trouble with this fixation or habit or whatever it may be called is that in the end one is left forsaken, since men usually die younger than women and even an eighty-year-old female will die sooner than one twenty years her junior. This is an emotional hazard that must be faced, and owning a fossilized tiny fish or a clunky old clam shell makes it seem more reasonable.

—*Glen Ellen, California, 1976*

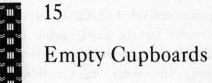

15

Empty Cupboards

Once I spent several weeks as a professional guest of a famous teacher of gastronomy from America. We were in the far south of France, in the house of another famous teacher of gastronomy from America. I got to the somewhat isolated country house about midmorning, under my own steam because my host and his wife had to be away. I was very hungry, indeed almost famished. But I felt secure in this epicurean stronghold, and once I had emptied a few things like hairpins and slippers into the sumptuous quarters obviously meant for me, I headed for the kitchen of the silent house. I felt a little desperate for food after the long train ride and a night in a hotel dedicated at that time of the year to overfed tourists from Luxembourg. I went first to the icebox in the good dim cool kitchen, which was Americanized but still real, with a scoured and generous table in the middle. I felt fine and at home in that kitchen. But the icebox was empty, except for one withered small tomato at the bottom. I doubt that I have ever seen such an empty icebox: there was no cheese in the pullout metal compartment labeled CHEESE, and there was nothing in EGGS, and except for the dead tomato there was nothing in RE-FRESHER. Certainly there was nothing in MEATS. And since this humming little machine was something of an astonishment in that neighborhood, there was no kind of freezer. It was enough to survive as a plain icebox in southern France!

I went impatiently to the shelves that lined the good room promisingly, but all I turned up was a strangely shaped tin mentioning duck packed in cabbage. I must admit, this far from the scene, that I seized on it and then looked vainly, in every one of the many drawers, for a way to open it. If I could have, I think I would have gnawed the whole little duck to its marrow. As it was, I felt like tearing into the tin with my teeth, except that I recognized their merits. There was nothing for me to do but contain myself and contemplate my navel, which I did.

This pecular introduction to a transplanted American kitchen cult gave me great pause to wonder, and I have thought long and often about it. There we were, my hosts and I, in a land almost audibly bursting with delicious vegetables springing from the soil. In the village up the hill were three or four places where farmers left their culls as they went to the markets in Cannes and Nice and Grasse: boxes and baskets filled with small ripe tomatoes, green beans as slender as knitting needles, dirty scraggly lettuces with hearts as sweet as milk, little tennis balls of zucchini, olives of every color, and now and then a few late but still tender almonds in their green coats. There were not many fruits then, except for melons and some cherries from the high meadows, but the wasps still came to taste in front of the main store, and inside there was a simple supply of cheese and, twice a week, some of the best plain bread I have ever eaten. I came to know all this because I stayed hungry all the time I lived with the famous teacher of gastronomy, for there was never anything more than I had first found in his icebox. He went out. I did too, when it seemed best for professional reasons. Otherwise I subsisted on little sneaky snacks. I even hired a taxi a few times and went to Grasse, where I headed for an open-front stand where a man or a girl made huge paper-thin pancakes on a stove on the sidewalk. I would eat one folded over with cheese. Then I would eat one made with ham. Then, to the astonishment of the man and the girl and perhaps the other customers, I would eat one made with sugar and lemon juice. And under my legs at the table (there were three small ones, behind the griddle) would be a few things I hoped we could perhaps eat in the beautiful kitchen, instead of going out to another two-star restaurant screaming with tourists from Luxembourg (the richer ones). We never did, and the few things I bought at first, like green almonds and small pungent olives and slices of peculiar sausages, gradually diminished; I knew that unless I ate all of them myself they would die. Finally, once, in an almost adolescent rage at this gastronomical impasse and deception, I bought a bar of chocolate. I put it on the nightstand in my lovely room, and a couple of days later I threw it, unwrapped, into a thicket of surging herbs and wildflowers under an olive tree.

—*Glen Ellen, California, 1977*

16

Thimble

There is a difference between owning and possessing.

I am thinking now of my thimble, strangely enough for me because I never much liked to sew, although at times I have done it well. Sewing has always served as a practical rather than an aesthetic means to an end. In contrast, my goddaughter Solveig is an unpaid designer and executer of beautiful patchwork. But I have never done more than darn stockings when I had to, patch pillow slips to save them, make dresses if I could not buy them.

This morning I was tidying my household sewing kit, and I found more than six thimbles. Among them was an oddly familiar one of darkish steel with a wide band of rather boring gold around it. It looked a little Pre-Raphaelite, and it must have been designed in perhaps 1900, because on one section of the tiny mixture, written up and down and romantic, there are my mother's initials—four, because she was married in 1904. I must send it to Solveig in Wiltshire, I thought.

And I thought about one time when I was between eight and eleven and I felt that my grandmother's thimble must sometime belong to me. I did not crave to own it. I am sure there was no overt lust. Neither did I want to *have* it. I simply assumed that it should and would be mine.

It was made of gold, and very finely, and because my grandmother was a Puritan who believed and practiced abstinence from all physical pleasures, it surprises me that she permitted herself to use this gaudy elegance. For it was set around the bottom with perhaps six glowing buttons of coral, softly orange-pink, and above them, before the little indentations to catch the needle tips, common to all thimbles, there was an exquisite engraving, all around the thimble, of a *village!* There was a church as the focal point, of course, and along one side of the main street stood tiny cottages and even a shop or two near the church. It was almost invisible except to a child's eye, complete there between the coral and the grainy golden tip of Grandmother's thimble, and I looked at it with what I now think was complacency but even then accepted as true pleasure. It would be in my care, I knew.

As I looked at it in the sewing basket or on my grandmother's finger, I loved knowing that my own eye had seen the church and the shops and the cottages strung out for perhaps half a mile above the smooth beads of pink stone and that Grandmother had let me use her name and later would lend me her thimble. She first taught me how to knit and then purl, so that in 1917 I made a little pale green pullover, big enough for a young baby perhaps, that was auctioned at the first public Red Cross meeting after "we" entered World War I, which my family had been quietly fighting since 1914 because of our connections in Europe. My contribution cost some patriot seven dollars, I was told somewhat deprecatingly the next day.

I felt at least seven inches taller, until Grandmother said coldly that perhaps I was now qualified to try knitting a stocking. Still, I felt more elated then deflated, because the little pullover, while only a step higher than the straight knit mufflers I had been knitting in hideous khaki-colored yarn for Our Boys in Britain, was still infinitely better than Mother's Washrag, as we all called it.

Edith, whose thimble reminded me of this when it turned up this morning in my spring cleaning, hated to sew, knit, clean, cook, in fact, do anything her mother expected her to do. That is doubtless why her thimble is still so fresh and dainty. She tried *not* to use it properly, so that all her seams pulled out and all her hems fell. And while all of us sat furiously knitting mufflers and mittens and scarves for Our Boys and turning out tiny masterpieces for the Red Cross, Mother worked with scant amusement, throughout the whole war, on a washrag of gradually graying wool that she kept laughing about as she deliberately dropped stitches and forgot whether to purl three or knit two. It was a small family joke, and only Grandmother, who did very much resemble Queen Victoria in her general grim small plumpness, was "not amused."

I, with one eye on my clumsy smiling mother and the other on my stern grandam, sat much of the day with the elder, who was always kind, if imposing, and I learned a lot about many ways to read the Bible and at the same time sew a strong seam. I agreed when Grandmother told me that a lady's hands are never idle. And all the time, as I learned almost unwittingly to sew and read and knit and stay silent until spoken to, I was watching Grandmother's beautiful thimble.

Of course she did not wear it except for sewing, but as I try to remember how she sat in a low chair in the sunroom with me leaning against her knees and the two of us keeping an eye on the new little sister lying on an afghan in the soft warm light, I think that the more I was learning to knit, the more she was sewing, mending all our tears and snags, making clothes for the next baby, doing cross-stitch samplers for me to try to copy.

Her daughter Edith best liked to keep her idle hands free to hold up a novel, any novel but mostly English, as she lay undoubtedly working out our procreative schedule. Perhaps this is why it never entered my young mind that I would ever use her thimble, the one with the late William Morris look in its gold band.

And it never occurred to me that the oddly luxurious and elegant thimble that Grandmother used daily, as if it were a cheap steel-tin job, would not one day be mine. After all, she and I had the same names—Mary Frances—and she had taught me to read, which I still do, although not with my mother's abandonment of several other pleasures.

But when I was about eleven, a plump dull cousin turned up for the summer, as many relatives did in those preplane days of more frequent and longer visits, and one day Grandmother said to her, "Here, this thimble is for you, my dear," and the cousin put it in her pocket and probably lost it on the long way home without even knowing she had what was really mine.

And that is why I know there is a difference between owning and possessing.

—Glen Ellen, California, 1978

17

Not Enough

Perhaps the main difference between Norah and me is that while we are friends (by now), she still thinks of me as her older sister, and I think of her mostly as a friend.

Or in other words, I ask for and accept many things from her that she has never asked from me. I have often called on her for help, and she has without hesitation changed all her complicated plans and come as fast as possible, and I have never doubted her love or her familial devotion. But she is a prouder person than I am, and as yet she has seldom admitted to purely human weaknesses, although lately she does creak audibly when the going is rough.

Once, though, when she asked me for immediate loving help, I stood her off. I think now and then of this strange happening, with self-disgust, or at least an uncomfortable kind of self-doubt.

One Sunday at the Ranch, in perhaps 1950, I asked Nan and Chuck Newton and their little boy Chas to come for lunch, mostly to perk up Rex a little but also because I enjoyed them very much and my girls loved Chas. Rex ambled out in his Sunday velvet house jacket, plainly old and grumpy and not well, and when Chuck came they went off in a corner and Nan came out to help me get lunch, and the children were on the side porch on the floor, playing something.

Norah telephoned from Los Angeles, I think, and she said that she was up there from Sunset Beach where she was living while she and John got a divorce, and that she had a badly infected thumb or finger and that John would drive her and the three children out to the Ranch instead of her going back down to the beach. I said OK, fine indeed. And sorry about the hand. And she said they'd be there in an hour.

So Nan and I held off lunch, and we told Rex that we were going to wait for Norah and the boys, and he suddenly became almost hysterical and was very bitter about John Barr: he'd never set foot on the Ranch again, by God, and so on. I was a treacherous female to let him weasel back in this way, etc., etc.

Chuck took care of him, and Nan and I half fed the three little kids and then we waited around, and finally the car drove in, and Rex got very upset again and Chuck calmed him again, and Nan and I went into the kitchen to welcome the poor lost roaming Barrs.

The two older boys, very small and quick, dashed in and at once settled themselves onto the floor with Chas and my girls, and I think John brought Matt to the door, the back porch door.

Norah came last, looking very gaunt and wan, with one heavily bandaged hand held up as she'd been told to do, after minor but nasty surgery to lance an infection. She was shot full of whatever one was given in those far days—penicillin? She sailed in, and Nan came out to get Matt, and I said to John that Rex was on a tear and would not let him come in.

It was a bad moment.

I think John trusted me as much as he could any of us in those hard days, and he unloaded some stuff from Norah's car so that she could stay overnight with the three boys instead of going down to the beach—the doctors had prescribed several days of rest, but how can a single woman with three small children tackle that?—and then he got into my car and we drove almost silently up to the bus station. We gave each other a good friendly hug, and I did not see him again for several years, which was all right.

When I got back, Norah was standing in the dining room, beautiful and disdainful. Behind her through the three wide-open French doors sat the five little children, aware of tensions and thunder but playing on the floor, something about cards and dice. Nan and Chuck sat having a drink with Rex in the dim living room.

Norah suddenly put both arms around me as if to hold me with passion, a most unfamiliar gesture in our overly decorous family. She was vibrating the way a good arrow vibrates or thrums or shivers after it has been shot out and has then plunged into its target.

But instead of bending to her need for aid and succor, I did what still haunts me (thank God, rarely), and I stiffened and gently undid her long loving needing arms from my shoulders.

She was whimpering. I looked down over her high shoulder and saw the worried eyes of five little children looking with pain and puzzlement up at our sadness, and I said, as I pulled off her beseeching arms, "The children are looking. Stop this!"

I do not know how I said this short cruel thing, but I believe that I was trying to protect them all, no matter how foolishly, from something I myself feared—our futures, maybe.

Norah stiffened and withdrew, and I knew that I had lost a moment of need and comfort that would never happen again. She looked down at the five little mice peering up at us and said with so strong a scorn that it was almost shocking, "To hell with them."

It was a flat statement. The children paled with shock, and then as I withdrew from Norah's desperate embrace, their faces calmed and they went on with whatever it was they were playing —cards, bones . . .

We went into the living room and behaved properly and then went back to the dining room and behaved properly, and after a long good winey lunch, Nan and I tended to the kitchen stuff and Norah, who was saggy-dizzy with past pain and present medical stress, sat on a tuffet while Chuck played old Fats Waller records in a dim corner of the living room. Rex sat at the other end, smoking.

Nobody seemed to know but me and perhaps Norah—who may by now have forgotten it, if she ever realized it—that I had rejected her that day. Why did I say "the children"? She was right, in the long run, to say, "To hell with them." She needed *me* then, and I was not ready to forget the demands of my current world and give her the true warm love I shall always feel for her.

—*Glen Ellen, California, 1978*

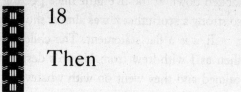

18

Then

By 9:59 P.M., the crescent moon and the satellite had set beyond the Jack London ridges to the west. A fine sight.

I sat in deep silence, and I was in Laguna—Arch Rock, Top of the World. The time was important. The place was chooseable there, depending on temperature and local whims. Here the place seems set. And time is even less out of control than when Aunt Gwen would say mildly in the morning that we'd watch the sun set from this or that rock, cliff, hill along the coast.

—*Glen Ellen, California, 1978*

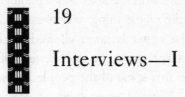

19

Interviews—I

I've often said that I'm proud of being a fifth-generation newspaper person, and indeed I am. I feel that real newspaper people, on any level of the pecking order, can be and more often than not *are* honest human beings of integrity and scruples.

Many of my friends love to tease me about the horrible lack of both scruples and honesty in many good journalists, who print gossip for political reasons, who deliberately misquote, who take things out of context, and all that business. This is true, I know. But in general I admire and like newspaper people.

However, I feel very strongly about one thing in modern journalism, and that is the use of long, close-knit, often photographed interviews, which are run exactly as is a one-inch squib at the bottom of page six. They are never read back to the subjects. More often than not it is the so-called editorial policy not to check in any way on fairly important but not essential-to-the-minute interviews with people like me, or with much more important people in every field. A feature writer, and usually a photographer or a sound man who tapes the whole thing, will spend a day or two on a story, and then the writer is never allowed to check back or even to read it by telephone to the interviewee. Of course, one common complaint is that some of the people interviewed want to rewrite the articles. I would never think of doing that, but I do think that the vital facts, for instance, should be checked, even double-checked.

In one year, I remember, I was born in Atlanta, Georgia, and Nome, Alaska, and I was said to be peaking sixty and well into my eighties (I was really about seventy, I think). So I feel, and very strongly, that editorially there is a difference between a feature story on a person and a straight news story.

One time I was asked to give a long interview to a young woman I know in San Francisco. She was trying to be a feature writer for a local newspaper, and she suggested that she do a story on my recent trip to Japan. She came here with three other people: a sound woman and maybe two photographers. She wanted to talk about a book I'd worked on with a Japanese friend.

I'd had a rather boring time with that book, because I was expected and even believed to be an erudite, rather sententious writer, very scholastic—in sum, *well educated*. Instead, I'd written a rather light, informal, almost flippant introduction to the very formal subject of classical Japanese cooking.

The newspaper people and I talked very seriously all morning and everything I said was recorded. Then, I remember, we all sat down to a nice long lunch. We chatted about personal things: the girl's absent husband, some mutual friends. I said once, "This is all off the air, isn't it?" She said, "Of course."

We talked on, informally, about how I was trying very hard to have the newspaper guild acknowledge that there is a difference between "in-depth" interviews and short squibs of local or newsworthy interest that are run immediately, so that there is no time to check anything. The girl said very firmly that she could not possibly go against the paper's policy of never checking back. We left it at that.

Then, about two hours after the story came out, which I suppose was within the next week, the Japanese consul general in San Francisco called me personally to ask me *why* or *if* I had said, for a local paper, that our walls and our car and our bathroom were bugged all the time I was in Japan with my sister.

I was horrified, and he was very cold, and I didn't blame him one bit. Indeed I had said just that, and it was true.

I felt quite sure then, and I do still feel sure, that we were bugged, but it was not particularly important. It did not bother us a bit. We didn't ever say anything that we shouldn't have said. "God, a drink would taste good! . . . Hurry up! . . . Should I wear the pants or the skirt?" And was it my sister's turn to go to the bathroom? What we said was of no political or social importance at all, but it was checked, and probably rightfully so, because we were being treated almost imperially by the Japanese government, as well as by our hosts. And I could not blame the consul general for being irate and upset at what sounded like a betrayal of national courtesy.

I was furious with the young reporter, because she had printed something that had nothing to do in any possible way with the story she got from me. It was a piece of non sequitur chitcat, dropped into her report without any reason at all. Furthermore, she heard me say it after we had sat down at the table and were talking informally and off the record. I thought this was a breach not only of manners and etiquette but of professional decency. I felt sick about it then, and I still do.

There was one other time when I felt rather sick about bad newspaper manners. A California magazine that was published in

San Francisco and Los Angeles called me in Sonoma. The editor was out of town, but his secretary asked me if I could give her a quick little thing that would run with items on a group of about ten writers who were being interviewed. Of course I agreed. It was an easy favor.

The question we were each asked was, What would you do with a very famous stranger if he came suddenly for one day? Where would you entertain him, and how? I asked if anything I said would be read back to me before the magazine went to press. The girl said, "Of course, of *course!*" Then she named Craig Claiborne as the man who would be thrust upon me for one day.

The funny thing was that right across from me at my lunch table sat Craig, who was an old friend and a good one. We grinned at each other, and I went on talking on the telephone. I felt hysterically amused by this situation, and I said solemnly among other things that Mr. Claiborne had to go out a lot. She said, "Where would you go to dinner? *How* would you take a famous man like that to dinner?" We were eating a very nice lunch at that moment, but he was going to stay for supper too, so I said, "Well, probably a man like Mr. Claiborne would be invited out so much to restaurants that I think it would be rather nice to ask him just to come to my house." Then I added, "After all, there are no really exciting places here in town to go to, anyway!"

Well, of course, I never would have said that last at all, if I had been writing it, or talking less hastily. And I assumed that I would have it read back to me, when I would have caught it at once, and deleted it. But I didn't think, and the girl didn't call me back, and I forgot the whole silly incident.

Then, about two weeks later, after the appearance of the little magazine, the telephone rang, and it was a local restaurateur, a friend of mine. He was almost crying. At first he sounded abjectly hurt, and he said among other things, "You've driven the last nail in my coffin," because he was having a rather hard time financially. Then he got quite abusive, and it was very unpleasant indeed.

I immediately wrote to the editor of the local paper and told him I was in a pickle. What should I do? What he did was to print my letter as a kind of a statement of my deep regret, and of why I had done such a thing, and of how I had fully expected my words to be deleted if I'd had the chance to hear the story before it went to press.

I also wrote a coolish letter to the magazine editor. I didn't want to get his secretary into trouble, but it was a very careless thing for her to do, I thought, not to call me, not even to tell him. He was upset, too. (She was not fired.)

I feel very badly about how this silly bit of journalistic carelessness has changed my whole feeling about going to my friend's restaurant. He has been hurt, and I hate that!

I think these are my two newspaper gaffes that I know about, but I am very sure I have said or done other things that have seemed rude or crude or indiscreet, in some way or other.

I remember one thing I did *not* say that caused a little pain. Many years ago I came home to Whittier after a long time away. I was making my living then as a freelance magazine writer, mostly about food, and I'd said something, laughingly, about how people in small-town tearooms (there were lots of tearooms in the thirties and forties) always brought around trays of relishes and little baskets of hot bread, buns, muffins. The patrons nibbled away, and the more generous and lavish the trays of homemade relishes and hot rolls were, the more they thought they were eating a generous lot of free food, which of course they weren't. I wrote something about that, not mocking or supercilious, but pleasantly teasing.

Then, when I got home, my mother was almost tearful about how hurtful I had been to the local tearoom people! She and

Father went there about twice a week, when it was the cook's night off. Often they took my sisters Norah or Anne. It was a very nice tearoom. It was in what had been the living room of a house. The waitresses were inept but nice young schoolgirls, friends of the granddaughter of the woman who ran it, etc. It was *nice*. There were creaky floors, I suppose, no rugs . . .

This was about the time when people put candles in bottles and let the wax run down, and felt rather bohemian. And they did indeed have these candles at this tearoom, which was called something like the Grape Arbor or the Rose Trellis. They did indeed have trays of relishes, and they did indeed serve the owner's famous hot muffins with raisins in them.

I'd never been there in my life, and of course I was not laughing at it, but Mother said that the people, all of them fellow church members, now hardly spoke to her, and that she didn't dare set her foot in there, because I had been so cruel about them. I felt awful . . . but it was funny too, in a way, and later everything was all right.

This was an inadvertent slip of my own journalistic manners, I suppose. But the other two were careless errors and really not my fault. It is hard to earn your living as a writer, or even as a freelance hack, and always think of how every word will look in print to every single person who reads it. I have never done that, and I never can—nor will I, nor should I. But it is dreadful to have a good man cry over the phone, and tell you that you've driven the last nail in his coffin. That's *bad*.

I think I am going to fight as long as I live, through authors' leagues and newspaper guilds and also by word of mouth and so on, to get the editorial people to separate plain news from interviews. There is no reason why any editor who has time and money enough to send out a feature writer and a photographer from New York cannot afford to have his writer pick up the phone and check on when and where I was born. This would be a courteous and face-saving thing to do, and it would strengthen my unfaltering if occasionally battered faith in the basic decency of the newspaper profession.

—Glen Ellen, California, 1979

20

Poor Food

I am thinking now of some of the best meals in my life, and almost without exception they have been so because of the superlative honesty of "poor food," rather than sophistication. I admire and often even *like* what is now called the classical cuisine —the intricate sauces of great chefs, and the complexities of their entremets and their pastries. But for strength, both of the body and of the spirit, I turn without hesitation to the simplest cooks.

I remember the best sauce I ever ate.

It was not at Foyot's, in the old days in Paris. It was in a cabin with tar-paper walls on a rain-swept hillside in southern California. The air was heavy with the scent of wet sage from outside and the fumes of a cheap kerosene stove within. Three or four children piped for more, more, from the big bowl of steaming gravy in the center of the heavy old round table crowded between the family's cots. We ate it from soup plates, the kind you used to get free with labels from cereal packages. It was made from a couple of young cottontails, and a few pulls of fresh herbs from the underbrush, and springwater and some Red Ink from the bottom of Uncle Johnnie's birthday jug—and a great deal of love. It was all we had, with cold flapjacks left from breakfast to scoop it up. It was *good,* and I knew that I was indeed fortunate, to have driven up the hill that night in the rain and to have friends who would share with me.

I remember the best stew I ever ate, too.

It was not a bouillabaisse at Isnard's in Marseille. It was made, further east on the Mediterranean at Cassis, by a very old small woman for a great lusty batch of relatives and other people she loved. Little grandnephews dove for equally young octopuses and delicate sea eggs, and older sons sent their rowboats silently up the dark *calanques* for rockfish lurking among the sunken German U-boats from the First War, and grizzling cousins brought in from the deep sea a fine catch of rays and other curious scaly monsters. Little girls and their mothers and great-aunts went up into the bone-dry hills for aromatic leaves and blossoms, and on the way home picked up a few bottles of herby wine from the tiny vineyards where they worked in the right seasons.

The very old small woman cooked and pounded and skinned and ruminated, and about noon, two days later, we met in her one-room house and spent some twenty more hours, as I remember, eating and eating . . . and talking and singing and then eating again, from seemingly bottomless pots of the most delicious stew in my whole life. It, again, had been made with love . . .

And out of a beautiful odorous collection of good breads in my life I still taste, in my memory, the *best.*

There have been others that smelled better, or looked better, or cut better, but this one, made by a desolately lonesome Spanish-Greek Jewess for me when I was about five, was the best. Perhaps it was the shape. It was baked in pans just like the big ones we used every Saturday, but tiny, perhaps one by three inches. And it rose just the way ours did, but tinily. (Many years later, when I read *Memoirs of a Midget* and suffered for the difficulties of such a small person's meals, I wished I could have taken to her, from time to time and wrapped in a doll's linen napkin, a fresh loaf from my friend's oven.)

Yes, that was and still is the best bread. It came from the kitchen of a very simple woman, who knew instinctively that she could solace her loneliness through the ritual of honest cooking. It taught me, although I did not understand it then, a prime lesson in survival. I must eat well. And in these days of spurious and distorted values, the best way to eat is simply, without affectation or adulteration. Given honest flour, pure water, and a good fire, there is really only one more thing needed to make the best bread in the world, fit for the greatest gourmet ever born: and that is honest love.

—*Glen Ellen, California, 1979*

21

Noëls Provençaux

The problem: should I try to carve a smoked trout for lunch tomorrow for a Ticinese patrician and her Philadelphia lover or write about what these strange piping songs have done? I resolve everything by ignoring the smoked trout.

I have been listening to a new recording of music played in Provence at Christmas. It is very neat and slick and well done, and it was made in the Abbey Saint Victor in Marseille, right below where I lived for some time. It is *echt* all right, and the acoustics in that familiar vault are right for it, but still it is not the way I hear inwardly that ancient Greek-Roman piping and drumming.

The first time it got into my blood and heart I was almost unaware of it, except as something in the dream of submissive ignorant bliss in which I lived with my first husband. We went blindly down from Dijon to the Côte d'Or in 1929; Cassis was an almost unknown fishing village then.

Germans took it over in 1940 and built a casino there for the officers, and later it was a convenient and beautiful place for both the French and foreigners, but when we went there, it was an ancient secret tiny port, dangerous to find on the Mediterranean coast between Marseille and Toulon, and with few trains that would stop up on the highlands for an occasional tourist. There were no taxis and, in winter, no restaurants. The few villagers who used the train walked up to the station and down, with a quick stop at the chapel on the way.

So the landlord of the little hotel on the quay, who had probably been tipped off about our naiveté by his old school pal and our landlord in Dijon, led us gently to the door of his inn at about 11:30 on Christmas Eve, and pointed our noses up the hill. We walked fast in the chilly air that seems right on Christmas Eve, even in Provence, and got there in time to find a place in the small redolent chapel. It was lit, as I now remember, by many tapers, and by torches outside the entrance. It was glowing and warm.

A choir sang in the little loft above our heads, with much shuffling and rustling of voices and starched vestments. Men marched in the church door blowing on wooden flutes and curved things and what I assume were oboes *(hautbois),* and there were several proud prancing young drummers beating their tambours with one hand and piping with the other. Then there was a procession of *people,* who took their places near the altar. I do not remember all I saw that night, but of course I know now that they were Joseph and Mary and that the shepherds came along and then Three Wise Men. All the time the piping and the tambours' beat and the high innocent crying of the woodwinds flickered with the candles in the little chapel, and it got into me without my knowing it.

We went out with the rest of the people, down to the little quay-side hotel, where we were given some wine and cake because we were strangers at the family feast.

That night a small furtive cargo ship docked under the windows of the hotel. I watched in silence. I put on my husband's overcoat, so that I could stand by the open window in the chill. The ship was plainly bringing in some kind of contraband, as a handful of men moved like silent rats from it into two or three dark open doors along the quay. Before dawn it slid away and out past the flickering harbor light.

It was a death ship, I knew, because I had read B. Traven's books and I recognized the horrible rattle in its doomed engines, just as I knew when and why the humans who scuttled across the quay were coughing their lives quietly into the blackness. But all the time I stood there looking down, my mind and my heart were uplifted by the sound of music I had not actually heard, so shy had I felt at being there in the glowing chapel, a stranger, and an innocent one.

By now I know a lot more about the music of Provence, if not its strange age-old traffickings. What slips in and out of small and large ports, by sea or air or even land, cannot hurt the sound of the music that still beats there in that rocky and gutty and haunted old country.

As I matured, slowly, I began to hear all the music in the pageant. I have returned there like a homing pigeon for countless years since that far-gone day—perhaps it is my "spiritual home." And the music is in my blood, from that first stupid open loving trial, in the little chapel in Cassis.

The underlying Near East sounds began gradually to hit my spirit, and by now I am astonished at how overt the acceptance is and perhaps always has been, in Provence, of this skirling whirling sensuous tantalizing rhythm from North Africa, from Algiers and Tunis and Morocco and westward.

It came easily to me to listen, once I was in Provence as an older person. And finally I lived on a street in Aix where the women left their radios turned high, all day, to broadcasts of Algerian disc jockeys. The wailing beat in, but it did not bother me, any more than the sound of pipes wailing in Provençal music can. I had heard it before, and was waiting . . .

So after that first ignorant Christmas in Cassis, with all that music in my inner heart, it took some time and space to get back to it, and even more to know what I had heard. By then the "Noëls de Provence" were becoming fashionable folklore. They were being televised. People reserved seats at high prices to fly down to Les Baux, for instance, where the helpless lamb or goat kid was still trundled in as the cameras whirred, and the society reporters caught names, and the innkeepers chilled the Dom Pérignon or other fashionable wines, and laid out fatuous dainties.

But the music was still good, even when stylish. The local people who could tootle their old cornets and oboes, and mostly the youngsters who wanted to go on playing pipes and drums, kept right on. This was heartening.

Once, not at Christmas but at Easter, a whole churchful of people in Aix waited because a young lamb being led down the street to enact the pageant was late for some reason. The music piped on, and people fidgeted, and two minor priests went out to the steps of the big doors to watch. Finally the lamb came, in the arms of his young shepherd who had missed a bus somewhere, and the mass began.

One time in Aix, my children and I bought tickets to watch the *Pastorale*, which is an enactment of the coming of Mary and Joseph to Provence. The story is that the village where they sought an inn was torn with hatred and strife. The miller could not work with the mayor. The priest was uppity. The old woman who sold fish quarreled daily with the miller. Then the Baby was born in a manger because none of these bitches and bastards had room for such a problem, and at once they all turned into sappy-happy saints. They loved one another. They lifted their hands to heaven, and rolled their eyes.

And all the time the pipers and drummers, with that strange undercurrent of Eastern enticement, played their songs. Sometimes the tunes were short and bouncy, and sometimes almost reverential and churchlike—because a short time ago, like 45 A.D., the south of France became somewhat Christianized when Mary Magdalene and some of her family and servants landed at a little port called Les Saintes Maries de la Mer.

She had been put adrift in a boat after the death of Jesus of Nazareth, who had told her she could baptize his people. She left with some relatives and hangers-on and a pot of magical chickpeas, which lasted all of them for days or weeks and became the symbol of nourishment for countless generations. She made her way to a good drippy grotto and after some thirty years died of bronchitis, and became a saint. But in spite of all that she is still a leading citizen of Provence (and especially Marseille, for various reasons connected perhaps with her early life of ease and promiscuity).

So the Oriental influence seems logical in Provençal music. It is there all the time, and in the new records I have been listening to, made in 1979 in Marseille, it is very good, if "contrived." (By that I mean that it seems cleaned up and even perfected, alongside the stuff I have listened to and lived into, in many places in Provence. It is "slick.")

I know that there is by now the whir of the sound machines in the ancient chapels, and the glare of lights and the musicians have been rehearsed and they wear makeup; and the audience will appear next week in fashionable West-World journals—but the music is still compelling, probably because it is so old/new.

Once my two daughters and I were living on the top floor of a little hotel in Aix, so that they could be near their schools. The hotel was owned by the elderly son of one of Frédéric Mistral's band, called the Félibriges. All those young men dedicated to reviving and prolonging the local language of the Languedoc met there, and the dining room of the little hotel was decorated with a delightful mural on three sides, painted on good canvas, of the old countryside between Arles and Aix, or Aix and Avignon. It was banal but irretrievably beautiful. The dining room was no longer used, but we liked to sit in there for home lessons: Latin, French history . . .

Next to our two-room palace on the fifth floor was a little cubbyhole for special favorites of our landlord, and one of these, a descendant of one of Mistral's intimates, was a boy about twenty who was a *folklorien*. He carried on the ancient art of playing his tambour with his left hand and his little pipe with his right. He did this for his own reasons, of course, but plainly he was a fine racy young man of upper birth in the Provençal pecking order, with long bones and a disdainful shy look. My girls seemed dizzy when they met him on the six flights of stairs, and when he started to practice his little pipe and make muffled taps on his tambour, they turned paler.

I felt very sorry for them. They were listening to sounds that had been wandering through the air in Greece, more than two thousand years ago, and then had gone on relentlessly in the country we were living in, through all the dark ages until our lighter years.

The lonely boy piped and drummed, of course not knowing what he was doing to all of us on the other side of the wall, and then he went away. But the rhythm of his music is still in my heart, and probably my girls', although I have never asked them.

—*Glen Ellen, California, 1979*

22

One Verse of a Song

It is too soon to write the real story of the house I lived in for a long time in northern California. The Judith Clancy drawing shows more of its western Victorian dignity than I can, and its strength and beauty, and the honesty of birds in trees and tolerant cats dozing beneath.

When my two young girls and I bought the house, in about 1954, it lay under a passing cloud of sadness and decay. I went into the long dim kitchen once, and at the end of a big table sat a skeleton of an old woman, staring remotely at trays and platters and plates of rotting food that neighbors had brought to her for countless unheeded days. Books of philosophy and early feminist writings were tumbled on shelves and piled in corners on the floor. Over the sorrow and the stench, I felt the vitality of her and of her house, and I was by nature unafraid of ghosts.

Before long she was snoozing off in a kind cousin's warm clean sheets, and my girls and I were scraping and painting and airing her fine old house.

Below the high first floor there was a half-underground basement that ran the full length of the building, as was the custom in
Napa Valley when many of its settlers were Italians who wanted to
store their wines and olive oils and grains in dark cool places. The
floor was partly paved, with little runnels in it for the rainy seasons,
and the thick foundations, about forty inches high, were of local
stone, often dry-laid by the Chinese laborers, a dime a dozen in St.
Helena in 1870 (or more correctly, about sixty cents for a twelve-
hour day). The workmen laid clumsy cement tops on their stubby
walls, which later made fine shelves for our plates and books.

After the house was aired and brightened according to our
tastes, and a few ghosts made their peace with us, we invited some
Boy Scouts and 4-H buddies to dig out the half of the basement
that had been left walled but unpaved. Vague legends were used
as bait: the old doctor who had built the place, a miserly eccentric,
was said to have buried treasures under trees and in heaps of
rubble . . .

The young people worked like stevedores, bolstered by
healthy snacks and swigs and dreams of hidden gold, and they did
dig up some artifacts that pleased me, no matter how disappointing
they may have been to the diggers. There was a Chinese paring
knife, with a teakwood handle inlaid in pewter and a strong pure
blade of steel. It sharpens well, and I use it almost daily. There was
also a crude but lovely rice bowl. And there was a tall six-sided
bottle of brown glass, with a tiny neck. The budding medicos and
farmers who uncovered it assured us, with discreet titillation, that
it had probably once held a specimen fetus, coming as it did from
the old doctor's leavings, and I never asked them how much more
than a cobweb could have passed through that opening. I still have
the jar, a handsome thing on a high shelf.

In the basement we installed several windows, short and wide,
of what was then called cathedral glass, almost the color of the
bottle. The rest of the dirt floor was paved, always with the artfully

graded little runnels for possible flooding in the rainy seasons, because we were below the gravity-flow level. We put in a half-bath. Part of the space turned into a kind of wine-cellar pub, and there were beds for four people, like couches, in other stony places. We put thick hemp mats on the floors, and hung a few translucent bamboo screens between some of the beams that held up the whole house, and there were books everywhere on the wonderful wide ledges.

The big stone base for the fireplace upstairs stood in the pub, a handsome wall of stonework more probably laid by an Italian mason than by the Chinese. And there was the hulk of the old gas furnace, with five ugly asbestos arms taking heat to the first floor. It was infallible, never-failing, ready to take over at the slightest drop in temperature and quiescent as a happy dog in the hot dry months, so that the basement itself stayed warm or cool as needed —a magic trick!

Much of our time, during the years we lived in St. Helena, was spent down there. It was fine for good bashes and dinner parties and meetings. It was easy to bring edibles down from the kitchen, and the wine was already there! And soon after we moved into the house I found myself working more and more in the basement, so that finally everything I was pondering on was down there, close beside the bed I grew to prefer to all others in the lighter rooms upstairs.

The main floor had two bedrooms for my children. Now and then, as they gradually left for schools and as we all gravitated into the basement for various reasons connected with peace and its components, the girls gave their rooms to the people who sometimes came to stay with us. Now and then I myself would sleep in one of them, for a change or if the runnels were gurgling after a storm. But up in the attic was my official bedroom, even after I sank permanently into the basement.

Like it, the attic ran the whole length and width of the house.

The roof sloped sharply to the eaves, of course, but there was plenty of fine stand-up room down the middle. The front part was partitioned with heavy chicken wire from the rest of the generous space, and people told us that this may have been to contain some relatives of the dotty old lady from whom we had bought the house. We knew better: her sons had once raised pigeons there, to fly in and out the tiny lamp window, and we had cleaned out a lot of feathery old dung, certainly not human.

At the other end of the attic, looking west, the handy sons had built a fine room over the back porch below, with a whole wall of windows and plenty of room for my big bed and many bookcases, and a few old trunks and cases set against the redwood walls. It was a good nest for my nightlife, until with the force of time and gravity I sank more and more into the dim quiet depths of the basement. I always went up there, though, to be alone when I needed to.

In between those two levels, on the first floor, the house was airy, filled with clear colors and the lacy flicker of light through bamboo leaves. The woodwork everywhere was flat white, and the floors were of large black and white tiles (vinyl, but more than adequate). The ceilings were all fifteen feet high. The walls in the front room were "museum gray," fine for pictures and long bookcases and old rugs, and there was an excellent, if rather ugly, brick fireplace at the far end as one entered from the little hallway. The front door, with a dark yellow glass panel in it, had a funny handbell built in, with a loud mean ring. It was really a *good* room.

The kitchen behind it was good too, and almost as big. The walls were dark green; the furniture was brown; everything else was white. It matched a copy of one of my favorite Braques above one of the two long bookcases, opposite the kitchen counter and across from the generous table, which often seated ten at a pinch, or preferably six or eight.

Off the two main rooms were the children's, with a bath and

a toilet where the plumbing was old-fashioned but adequate. And to the left of the front door was a small office (doubtless where the doctor had pulled teeth and set bones and so on), which after my short happy tenure there with my typewriter became the glory hole. Extra copies of books, wrapping supplies, Christmas decorations, picture frames too bulky to carry up the narrow stairs to the attic, boxes that might someday be useful—they all went into this family reservoir, which by some miracle kept its own chaotic tidiness.

Plainly, it is hard to know which room in the house was the best, the most pleasing, but perhaps it was the back porch, under my attic nest. It too had been build by the handy boys who'd kept pigeons, and the many windows and the seams in the flimsy walls jammed and leaked and bulged now and then, but we forgave everything for the bright welcome that seemed to spread out from it the minute anyone came up the narrow steep back stairs and inside, no matter for the first or the hundredth time. Its long row of windows looked out into a giant fig tree. The walls were a light clear yellow. The curtains were of a soft red plaid, and the linings of all the open supply shelves and china cupboards were of the same red. The floor was black and white, of course. There were two good old rocking chairs. We kept table linens in a big highboy. There were racks for fruits and vegetables. The place was reassuring.

People grew used to the fact that the outside house would look shaggy and shabby while we lived there, and they came to feel easy within it. Outside, it was a soft faded mustard color, half-hidden by carefully controlled masses of Peking bamboo. Inside, it was a charmed mixture of light and color, where the air was always sweet and the leaves made fine delicate curtains against the wavery old glass in the tall windows. The fire drew well on the hearth, in winter. In summer, the basement was a cool dim windless cavern.

Other people now take care of the Dear Old Lady, as a lot of us call her, and they have made her look tidier than we ever did, certainly. She will outlive us all. Of that I am sure. And as long as I can, I'll sing my own songs of love and thanksgiving for the lives she helped us lead.

—Glen Ellen, California, 1980

23
Bugs

The last two days have been odd, so when I turned down my bed I was not surprised to see a small black insect hide deftly in a fold of the sheet. I shook it out and it hid again, three times. Finally I brushed it roughly and listened to hear it hit the tile floor minutely, so that I knew it was not in the bed anymore.

Then I went into the bathroom, a warm dim elegant place, and on the edge of the washbowl there was something dark, like a postage stamp. I looked closely at it, and its large eyes looked back at me, asking for pity or at least some understanding. It was a small frog.

I stared down at him, perhaps six inches from his anxious little face. Sometimes a frog seems mostly face and hind legs, but this little one was like a puzzled child, proportionately. His throat pulsed silently, and my own heart went along with it.

I knew that neither of us wanted him to stay like a stain on the edge of the porcelain bowl, any more than we wanted him to smell of my skin when I touched his. I got a piece of thin paper tissue, the kind put in bathrooms nowadays, and picked him up softly. I kept my grasp light but firm, and looked down at him in the paper, with his little legs spread out helplessly, and his mouth half open. He was colored black on his back, and a pearly gray on his belly.

We seemed to go out to the big fern together. He did not move, but I knew from the vibrations in my hand that he was alive and optimistic. Once near the big sturdy plant in its box, he was ready to leave, and I dropped him almost nonchalantly into the tender new leaves at its heart. I heard him land.

This was a strange encounter, not the first in my bathroom but perhaps significant because the last two days had made me confront other visitors. Yesterday, for instance, I turned out a vigorous earwig and a sturdy spider from my bed, when I plumped the pillows in the morning. Then there were two earwigs copulating in the washbasin when I wanted to wash my face and hands.

"Go *on*," I said. "Get along. This is my house. Please get out."

Later on in the day I washed a lot of vegetables, and flushed the sink well, and everything was spotless, except that a couple of hours later I went back to the kitchen and a fairly large slug was wearily making its way up the porcelain side. I dislike slugs in a way that is perhaps atavistic, as well as possibly Freudian, but I found myself speaking to this poor bewildered thing as if he could know what I was saying. "I'm going to pick you up in a paper towel," I said, "and because you can't possibly survive in this climate and air, no matter where you came from, I'll put you into the trash can, and the men are coming tomorrow to empty it and you will be gone."

I did pick up this poor thing, trying not to feel how his long body tensed into a kind of rubber in my papered fingers.

This is the day for confronting the crawlers and nibblers, I said. What are they telling me? Perhaps tomorrow I'll know. But that day is now, today, and I am thinking of the desperate patience of that little frog or perhaps toad as he sat waiting for me to get him out of the bathroom. He did seem to know that I would come, much more clearly than I myself could guess. And when I arrived, meaning as I did to refresh myself, he told me clearly that I could help him get the hell out of walls-tiles-windows into a big potted fern and then his own eternity.

There was another hint, yesterday, about the need of insects and other creatures to communicate with human beings. I wear what are now called panty hose: filmy or stretched tights that pull up over the hips, making stockings on the legs of bipeds. I got into some as usual, in the morning, and went out of the bathroom. In a minute or two, though, I felt something nibble at my left hip. I hit it and perhaps scratched vaguely at it, thinking it was perhaps an arthritic twinge, and realized that there was something between the stocking and my skin. I ripped everything down, without ceremony since I was alone, and felt a wetness around what I pulled out: a tiny black limp creature, *not* a beetle or a tick.

I felt shocked, and did not examine the plainly dead critter, except to note that it was small, black, and had once had feelers or tentacles coming from one end of its body. Where had it come from? Why did it get into my panty hose? And how? Where had it been until it got there?

All this made me shake out my pillows last night, in an almost smiling way. I wondered mildly about spring, and moisture, and so on. I thought of a book or story read long ago, about ants and how organized they were. I thought more definitely about the volcanic ash that was sifting and falling and drifting from Mount St. Helens, and about the Pacific mountains that were shaking. I wondered and I still do about what signals we are getting that there may be a change in priorities.

At this point I can get rid of a slug in my kitchen sink, an earwig under my pillow, a small sad-eyed froglet in my bathroom washbowl—but I think they are telling us something that is very hard to hear. Is it a question of plumbing, or one of a more universal nature?

—*Glen Ellen, California, 1980*

24

Light Sleeper

Today is Sunday, and for a pleasant change in my schedule, there will be nobody here. At least no one is marked in the book. I could lie abed if I wanted to and for a long time I did. I think it was about ten o'clock when I got up. It did not matter, because the night had been long and easy and sweet: a few good dreams, and an unusually intense enjoyment about it, so that I lay mostly in a half-sleep or quietly awake, in order to enjoy it. And I wanted it to last, to keep my gentled sensations sliding me along toward what would be left of the horizontal day. Once on my feet again, I well knew, such passive sensuous pleasure would perforce change, no matter how positively.

The main thought, if such rambling snoozy contemplation can be called thinking, was that I am lucky to be a light sleeper, and not someone who through habit and other tricks of nature believes that anything but eight hours of complete unconsciousness means insomnia. One turn or toss, three minutes of alertness after a dog's bark, or the inward tweak of an outraged bowel muscle, and such a miserable creature honestly feels that wakefulness, the bane of honest healthy believers in Law and Order, has invaded him. Sleeplessness is an enemy. Anything except full dormancy is frightening. It means illness, or even guilt. A pill, a pill! Doctor, help me. I can't sleep—I turn and toss. I sweat.

All this is nonsense to me. I welcome dreams. I've never bowed to the word *insomnia,* and I often lie awake for many hours with real pleasure, knowing that some day or some night I will sleep again. I feel fortunate . . .

—*Glen Ellen, California, 1980*

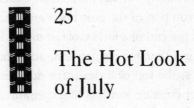

25

The Hot Look
of July

After the sun went down it grew cool and sweet, and across the little valley I watched, as I do almost every night, the darkening high ridge of desolate craggy mountains between me and the ocean, and then the nearer somewhat greener hills of a county park with easy trails for junior citizens and those in the "golden years," as our local brochures say to anyone who looks at them.

It felt fine to be in this world again, and not waiting for it to come around, as it seems essential to do for those two or three hours of near nirvana in the late afternoons. We lie naked and spread-eagled on our sheets, inertly waiting to come back.

Across the valley, an ugly bright hard light comes on after the sun sets, and I did not realize until tonight that it is set to ward off prowlers who might rightly surmise that the hillside property is largely vacant, owned by rich occasional tenants. I always try to block out this light as I watch indolently, peacefully, from my balcony chair. I look instead at a familiar, the big owl who sits for a long time on my one tall pole in the meadow and then suddenly is not the top part of the pole but a great silent dreadful swoop of wings and the end of a little mole or mouse in the sloping meadow below. It is a time for carelessness, and I may hear a small cry as the hawk at the top of a dead tree down in the meadow swoops for another creature and lifts him up in his lethal claws. But there is a general air of watchful surcease.

Tonight, though, there was too much activity along the highway that runs down on the other side of the meadows, under the first low range of hills that make the park. The park has two entrances, one into the grounds and one into a higher-up place that is occasionally lit at night with one big yard globe, as if somebody might come in later. The globe is further up and to the right of the ugly light.

Tonight, as the sky faded from a fine clear hot sunset into cool darkness, I saw that the ugly bright light had been set so that it went off at perhaps five-minute intervals, and that when it came on, after that lovely nonlight, it was at first a small bluish glow that turned within perhaps two minutes into the lean cruel white light I had come to avoid. It would go off, then glow into brightness again.

As I watched, a car came down the park road and slowly turned right, to the south as often happens, but this time I noticed that before it eased into the patchy weekend traffic, it blinked its lights twice.

Then a car that passed it coming south blinked its "far" lights, and after the first car got out onto the highway, the second car turned around and headed north.

At the mouth of the other driveway down from the ridge of low hills, a car that had come down without any lights, from the house that sometimes burned the ugly bright light all night, suddenly put on its high beam, so that its lights streamed across the highway and up into our meadow just as the car that had turned around passed it. That car blinked twice and went on. The car from up the hill kept its lights on as if it were waiting to come out carefully onto the highway. Finally it turned off its lights completely.

By now dark had almost come. I sat on the balcony feeling a little like the owl on the telephone pole, the hawk on the branch, waiting.

After perhaps two minutes, the darkened car flashed on its lights as if it had just come down the highway, and turned south and went on out of sight, but as it passed, the old light up on the hill that had been going off and on at planned intervals for at least an hour suddenly flashed out strongly three times: Eeee-Eeee-Eeee. The car blinked its headlights once, and disappeared.

I waited, but everything looked as it always did from my balcony on a hot July night. The new moon was almost down, and a jet plane lowered itself gently toward the city, coming perhaps from very far away. A few cars went up and down the old highway. I thought that maybe tomorrow I would hear on the early radio news that a big drug bust had been pulled off, or that child abuse rings were rampant again, or that maybe in twenty more minutes we would not have much more time because some current Strangelove was loose, pushing buttons.

A supper of cold salmon and blueberries with cream tasted fine, if you care about those things, and I'll sleep well, except that I wonder if heat has anything to do with people giving each other signals with their yard lights and car lights. I doubt that there will be any news tomorrow about this.

—*Glen Ellen, California, 1980*

It is difficult not to feel compulsive about this strange experience. I have been thinking about it for some twenty-two hours, trying to arrange and observe it.

A few days ago a young journalist came to interview me for her magazine, and then called me (I thought this was unusually courteous in the profession as it now exists) to ask if her photographer might telephone.

I agreed, of course. A day later Sandra L. called, and I invited her to come at 12:00 yesterday. She sounded young and pleased to break bread with me. It was agreed that she would come at noon.

The morning of our meeting, she called to ask if it would be all right for her to come at 11:30, since she had another engagement. It was not too convenient for me but I was agreeable, and hustled a bit to get the table set and the soup ready.

She did not come until 12:20, with no apology.

She was a very tall thin girl, in jeans of course, and wearing the kind of crimped-out dark blond hair that was stylish last year after *Annie* became a stage success: parted in the middle so that it went straight sideways and out, a real frizzzzzz. Her pretty face, which was almost masked, was like a child's, with resentful eyes and a bobbed nose and a mouth just beginning to learn.

Sandra unloaded a lot of tripods and other stuff.

She was an arrogant rude girl; I'm sure she has never been shown how to be anything else. She was very defensive, on the watch for "grown-up" slurs and put-downs. She affected a tiny mocking smile, which I caught now and then in the wild brush of frizzzzzz. I thought, Here is one of my godchildren. She had the tall lean insolence, the ashy light hair, the pale hating eyes.

She strolled in, moving like a beautiful giraffe with a very small head. I showed her the "two-room palazzo." This was to let her know that the house was hers to use for her camera, but she seemed to have no reaction. She asked me to change into something other than what I was wearing, which was neat and tidy and exactly what I wear all the time (except in bed).

I was so taken aback, to put it archaically, that I asked her what she wanted me to wear. The thought of changing into "costumes" shocked me so much that I decided to go along with it. She followed me into my clothes closet, and chose a djellaba that I've had for many years and seldom worn.

To my own amazement I stripped and got into a long black silk slip and the swimmy cotton thing, and put on flat silk shoes. After that I posed—*posed.*

The girl shot me in blinding light, on the west balcony, in ridiculous poses (or so they seemed to me).

She talked in a rather muttering insolent way as she fussed with her elegant equipment, and I learned that she was a Stanford grad and had majored in psychology and had a boyfriend.

But mostly she kept saying in a very quiet rude way that she had never worked with a subject who was so plainly hostile and quarrelsome. Such comments were mixed in with more casual talk. But I felt that she was deft at this game, and well practiced in taunting and trying to hurt the people she knew. There was also quite a lot of racial or ethnic resentment—her *name,* which she had first told me almost giggling with ethnic apology. And in a monotone along with her chatter, she asked if I really hated her. "I have never before worked with such a terrible subject," she said again.

I already knew that I should never have obeyed her demand to shoot me in another outfit, and I was cross with my weakness. She said, in the midst of her monologue, "I don't know why you are so antagonistic, so hateful."

I said once, "I am not. Let's get on with the job."

She went off into a speech about spoiled people, mostly female, who want only to look beautiful or intelligent. Finally I asked her what course she had taken in psychology. This really aggravated her, and she snapped at me. I felt somewhat alarmed, and excused myself and changed into a warmer djellaba. She took some more shots. Her small face behind all the kinked hair was sullen, and she made no response to my mild questions: Are you freelancing? Do you like the work? Would you like to live up here? Or down south? It was like being with a child who wants to punish you but does not know how. I imagined her keeping up this quiet sulky monotone while helpless parents and even doctors wrung their hands.

Once my cat Charlie came in, to sniff her, and she said, "I suppose you want some shots with him in your arms?" She implied that this was not only what all subjects like, but a last resort. I said, almost as casually but with no sneer, "No. I'm leading a crusade to forbid all aging writers from being photographed clutching their cats. We all are. Colette started it, perhaps, and it should end with her."

She asked blankly, staring out from her wall of hair, "Who's Colette?"

I was surprised by her interest, and almost caught her small blue eye, but lost it when I said that Colette was a writer at the turn of the century. She shrugged: what century and who cared?

She was very abrupt and bossy in her work, which she accomplished with a great deal of fuss about the tripods and light meters. "Turn this way. No. This won't be any good." She kept walking impatiently toward me with a meter and pressing it into my shoulder to see it tick. I felt like a piece of repugnant meat.

Later she drank two glasses of fruit juice, and when we finally sat down to what I thought was a good little lunch of Chinese-style vegetable soup, she drank about three spoonsful and ate half a slice of brown bread and refused the bowl of seeded black and white grapes that followed. She ate half a cookie. She was being true to some inner compulsion about her job, I said to myself.

A couple of times she peered out at me and said coolly, in a quiet trained voice, "I've never had such a venomous cruel assignment."

I said, "I honestly don't know what has gone wrong here." I hemmed and hawed a bit, because I could not tell her flat out that she was a rude spoiled brat. I refused to let her reduce me to a frustrated dither, which I felt that she must love doing to her parents and her friends.

After she left, she came back into the house, pushing past me. "I always leave something—I'll check again," she said, and went into the two rooms and onto the balconies, to see if she had left any of her luxurious equipment behind. It was a pathetic gesture. She did not like me because I represented a job, an obligation, a responsibility. I did not like her because she was arrogantly rude. And she was not yet mature, if ever she will permit herself to be. She could not be warm and trusting and overt because hostility had for a long time been her weapon against the world. (And "the world," to her, probably means parents and older people like me: *enemies*.)

I felt sorry about all this, after she had gotten all her gear into her sleek little car and had wheeled angrily away. I had never experienced such open disdain and anger in a professional meeting, and I wondered if I was growing crotchety. This is said to happen in one's later years, and certainly I feel remotely impatient of younger people's prejudices. But I had never met such an insolent young person. I wondered about her as I cleared the uneaten food from the table. (At least she was wise enough not to ingest food while angry! And she was indeed slim and quite lovely, except for her aura of disdain.)

I asked myself where I'd gone wrong, how I'd punched the bad button. I felt, early on, that she had made all her abrasive remarks before. But they were new in my experience with professional photographers. Did she resent my nonchalance and nonposing for her camera?

I'll probably never know, because I forget the magazine she was freelancing for, and doubt that a copy will be sent to me. I know that I am not photogenic now, as the pull of gravity forces my face downward. But I also know that I like to encourage younger people to take pictures, write reports, make themselves wanted if they are ambitious. Most of the ones who come here for pictures and so-called interviews are in their twenties and early thirties, and they enjoy the experience.

But this girl! I must ask a "head doctor" about her quiet monologue of ridicule and disdain. She was infinitely scornful and supercilious of everything in my house, and especially of me, and soon I understood that her quiet hatred was intended to make me afraid of her.

But why? Why use me as an object of scorn, in her insecurity?

As I now see it, she was trying to punish me, for being old and better known and perhaps more balanced than she. Through me, she was punishing her parents, her doctors, her employers. Most of all, probably, she was whipping herself, punishing her own ego, suffering.

At this point in my attempt to talk about this odd prickly meeting I feel very bored. Why do I bother to explain it? Perhaps it is because I have always assumed that when I permit a journalist or photographer to come here, and invite him or her or them to break bread with me, I am being welcoming and warm, and hope they will feel relieved and easier. But this poor soul was apparently so filled with distaste or scorn that she could not even swallow my good soup!

Ah, well, she may have forgotten the whole assignment by now. I have not, but I am no longer obsessed with it. I remember her tall lithe young body, her small pinched sneering face behind the mop of dyed tortured hair. I hear, but very faintly, her questions interspersed with the monologue on her camera work: Why are you so hostile to me? Are you scared of my camera? Do you mind if I show all your wrinkles? Do you hate being an unknown writer? Why do you feel such hatred for me?

Little could she know.

—*Glen Ellen, California, 1980*

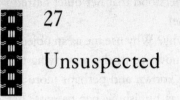

27
Unsuspected

On a trip to San Francisco in 1933, Rex and I stopped to visit Mrs. Fisher, my mother-in-law. She was like Edith, but she had continued to play the piano. Edith had not. As we were leaving, we turned back for a forgotten something—camera or briefcase or or or—and found that Mrs. Fisher had already gone into her tiny room filled with a grand piano and was playing a torrent of exquisite lush syllables of sound: Bach.

Rex was literally transfixed. We stood like statues out on the walk. I looked at him with a new and wonderful astonishment. For in that moment, he was not my father, but a man who loved his wife—my mother—and who felt lost because she no longer played the Schumann, Chopin, Brahms he had worshipped as a callow young editor.

And now another woman, much less fortunate in some ways —a minister's wife and not an editor's, but with much the same cultural upbringing—was playing beautiful music to soothe her own soul, alone in her small room with a weak boring old man as her husband, and the children behind her.

My father had his wife, my mother. She had four children too, but she no longer cared enough to touch the piano keys.

We stood outside the little house where my first father-in-law panted and prayed through his last pastoral assignment, and I found it hard to look at my father as he stood immobile on the path, listening to the wonderful waterfall of sound that fell on us.

Then we went to knock again at the door, and the tall full-bodied woman spoke courteously to us and found what we had left behind.

We left like awkward schoolchildren. A few times, many years later, my father asked me if I remembered the time we went back and she was playing. His face was full of light. I wished for both of us that Mother had not stopped.

—Glen Ellen, California, 1981

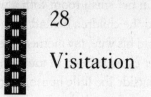

28
Visitation

Last night when the sun went down I sat for a long time on the west balcony. It was the end of the fifteenth day of heat over a hundred degrees in this valley, and I felt tired and hollow-headed. My cat Charlie lay on the cool tiles, after a late supper.

We both heard what sounded like a kitten, mewing weakly from down near Herger's Pit. Charlie was immediately alert, with his ears far forward. I stood up. We listened to two more periods of little cries, and when he became restless and worried I let him out into the courtyard. He sat on the wall, lashing his tail at first and then settling into a wary crouch.

There was no more crying, and I leaned back in my chair, to watch the slow flight of the present satellite toward what I think of as Jenner—north-northwest and right into the last sunset color.

There was no sound from Charlie, but suddenly there was a scrabbling and I saw a black cat hanging on the thin edge of the balcony, trying to get in through the thick Plexiglas shield. His eyes glared at me for a second, and then he fell back to the ground, which is at least ten feet below.

I went fast to check on what had happened. Charlie, when he was young, had dropped off the balcony a couple of times, but had never come up the bare straight wall to jump in.

On the ground, in dimming light, I saw a young cat, black as black. He looked up at me with eyes that seemed to fix mine into a clear focus, and yelled firmly. Charlie started a low warning sound from the courtyard wall.

I felt helpless: my cat would never permit this one to come into his domain, as I knew from past painful experience, so it would be wise to let them discuss it without interference. I went back to my chair, and a view of the sharpening horizon as the hills turned black.

Then the new cat leaped up onto the outer ledge of the balcony again, and hung there, crying frantically, before he dropped down onto the ground. I tried to shift the Plexiglas so that he could not possibly come through the space between it and the wall at the end, but I could not close the two-inch gap, and I went fast to telephone two neighbors to ask if they knew about a half-grown tar-black cat. Mr. King did not answer. Mr. Burns knew nothing about such an animal, and I told him I was sorry to have bothered him, for it was then about 9:30.

When I went back to the balcony, the cat had not only gotten through the gap but was in the kitchen, eating the crumbs of Charlie's supper. I said several loud *Nos,* and he scuttled out, and I made a new bowl of fresh food from the icebox as fast as I could, and we seemed to meet as if by arrangement on the balcony, where he ate furiously, growling without anger.

I closed the door into the house from the balcony, and very soon Charlie was crouched behind it—poor dumb fellow, so slow to figure out that if the interloper was not on the ground that he had been watching from the courtyard wall, then he must be inside!

The new cat was truly beautiful, pure black, probably a mixture of Siamese and Burmese, perhaps six months old, with good manners even though so plainly desperate for food. I sat silently in my chair, trying not to encourage his staying but wanting very much to. Charlie is a complete tyrant. It was impossible for the stranger to stay, but this fine creature had already insisted on coming and eating, and I believe firmly that when a cat chooses to do something, it will happen. I have proved this foolish theory more than once, and I tingled with wonder that it might happen again and that this time Charlie, who is now in his twelfth or thirteenth year, would accept a bold beautiful newcomer.

The black intruder finished his dinner slowly. Charlie fumed in the living room, crouched behind the glass door. Then the younger cat hissed directly at my friend; it was the loudest hiss I have ever heard, much like the sound of a rattlesnake. Charlie stopped growling and fuming and pretending to protect his territory, and I thought for a second that perhaps he would bow down to time and aging and and and . . .

The intruder hissed again, long and firm. There was silence. Then he leaped like a nonchalant flash of black lightning over the balcony railing. I saw his fine young body fly through the sky, and heard it land lightly far below.

I left his bowl until this morning, and then washed it so that my cat would not sniff another's presence in it when next I used it for him. I closed the door onto the balcony, so that Charlie would not fret about the other cat's having made it his own for a few minutes.

Today all seems tranquil, and the end of the unprecedented heat wave, historically both too early and too long, seems here, at least for two or three days. I feel less light-headed and much relieved. But the night visit was so strange, after such a long time of heat, that I thought I'd better get it onto paper before it went into legend and not a straight report.

I am eager for tonight's sunset on the balcony. Meanwhile Charlie is his usual demanding but unruffled self, and probably has the whole situation in hand. I think I want the young black stranger to come back. But he is plainly a con artist, taking what he gets (even by force) and then moving out. And now I wonder if, after the long heat, I was quite in focus about watching a half-grown cat leap up at least ten feet, three times, and cling to the balcony edge and finally come in and eat, and then cow Charlie.

Charlie was pretending to be asleep when I went out to the balcony. He jumped at once onto my knees, and I knew that he had made it clear that the stranger should move on.

I felt sorry—such a beautiful seeker for a place to stay awhile. But my cat told him that he was an arrogant and even detestable upstart, no matter how soft I might be about not turning him away. So I sighed and accepted, too lazy perhaps to urge the wanderer into what would probably be a miserable situation. He was wise to move on, and I feel certain that if he dodges road traffic he will find a more welcoming place. I feel equally sure that if the conditions are not to his taste, he will move on—not fat, but never too lean.

—Glen Ellen, California, 1981

29
Recovery

The process of growing well after being unwell is an odd one and has always interested me. For instance, tonight is the twenty-second day after I was given a complete new hip on my right side, at my request.

All has gone almost phenomenally well, probably because I had faint and few qualms about the minor side effects of hospitalization, and chose after some deliberation to try for even partial mobility rather than a few more years of painful frustrated "coping" from bed or chair. The thought of being attended to, and dependent upon, other more active people was literally untenable. Yes, everything went with unusual smoothness. For instance, the actual surgery took about two and a half hours rather than the expected five. Only three one-pint transfusions were needed instead of the five or six that had been readied. And so on.

I feel strong and firm, and except for small times of annoyance when I drop things, or occasional twinges of peculiarly horrible pain when I am careless about doing something that I know I must not do, I am cheerful and courteous, and I keep myself well combed and washed.

But tonight I would like to be changed into another being. It is almost dark, and the air is cooling after unusual heat, and very still. I sit in the big ugly Victorian armchair that has been brought in from the living room, with a hard pillow to keep me from bending the hip at a right angle, so that I am leaning back awkwardly. I am not too hot. I am not unclean—that is, I don't want to make the effort to shower and dry and so on. I feel all right in my skin.

But I wish I could be transported somehow to my bed at the other end of the room. Perhaps a perfume would make me lean back on the cruel old cushion, and I would smile a sweet docile stupid smile, one that would say, Yes . . . Now. And then I would be lying naked, flat, on the bed. At least three very old witches, almost as gray and thin as smoke, would pull off my canvas shoes and hold up my two bony long thin feet and say, "Ah, yes, ah, yes," and they would blow softly on them, so that they would smell as if they were made of exquisite wax and not hot cotton and foot sweat.

So as I lie cool and naked on the sheet, my feet, fresh and sweet, seem to finish me off down there, thousands of fathoms or miles down there. Then the two other smoke people—witches, fairies, angels—smooth my skin, and through my skin my nerves and muscles and then the bones and then the marrow and gristle and whatever else it is that holds us into one position or another, and there is not a sound, except outside the summer song of the wee toads in the few hidden mud packs under the rocks. There is an invisible singing.

The smoke-thin smoke-clear fingers smooth me, and I lie on the cool sheet smiling a little, like an animal or perhaps like smoke.

There are three of them, very see-through, like the angel Timmy painted who wept to see one green seed sprout from burnt-egg earth. It was Birth she wept at. I do not want to be born again, and the three smoke women do not wish it for me either, but there is nothing to do about it and they keep on silently rubbing my long tired body. By now it is thin, but I do not feel at all sorry, except for the deformed arthritic knobs on my inner knees, which I have always (seven years?) found an insult.

They came unexpectedly in Marseille, when Norah and I went up and down the old iron stairway at least once a day, on our way past the Vieux Port. (I forget now how many steps there were—perhaps 170. They clanged. During a bad mistral they swayed.) And one day I walked toward the mirror in my room and saw that on either side of my inner knees there was a soft meaningless bulge. I was astonished. I had always had straight legs. Later, in St. Helena again, I was told they were the natural result of my protective system giving my aging knees a bit of padding for taking that iron stair so often. I still have them, but since nobody sees my form now, I do not resent them. Tonight, as the three old smoke witches smooth me, one laughs or perhaps only smiles that it is all right. My good body has been kind to me, she says. I know.

And they keep on rubbing, in an almost intangible but completely knowing way, the way I sometimes press exactly the right nerves in the back of my cat when he has eaten a fresh kill and comes slowly to sit by my chair.

I hate him at first, and hold my breath, not wanting to breathe the fresh gut smells of the dead mole or gopher. Finally I lean a little, so that my arm touches the small of his back as he sits on the floor. Omnivore, carnivore, I curse him softly, and then I touch exactly the right nerves and muscles down toward the end of his spine, and know that I have communicated with him in a way neither of us had planned.

In the same way the smoky old old—well, are they witches? ghosts? nurses?—in the same way I am not here but I am on my cool bed, and they—they have touched or brushed or breathed upon or in some way made the tendons and even the flesh of my tattered body feel right again.

This is what recovery means, I suppose. I know that soon I'll be strong and firm. Tonight I like to know that even while the lights are still on and I talk and eat and awkwardly ready myself for a night that is not yet a good night, a rest that is not yet rest, there are the smoke ladies. I have not yet had to call upon them, and I hope I never do. But tonight might be a good time to try.

—*Glen Ellen, California, 1981*

30

Rewriting

Here is something about semantics and ethics, and it interests me enough to try to describe it.

I was trying to reread a story I wrote about thirty years ago for my two little girls, who were the protagonists along with a fine four-legged friend called Boss Dog. Several times I used the word *gay* to describe him, because that is exactly what he was, in my vocabulary and my children's and I assume his. He was merry, funny, giddy, happy, and in every sense of the word gay. And my father had been like that, and the children's father. They were very gay happy people.

But now I was having to change that word every time it came up in the story about Boss Dog and my children. I was by all current laws both written and spoken and even unspoken being forced to accept the fact that a gay person is now strictly a homosexual male living or professing a "lifestyle" frowned upon by born-again Christians and condoned with brotherly compassion by the self-styled broader-minded people of the western part of Earth.

So I was chugging along at this ridiculous bow to publishing ethics and so on, when the telephone rang and a loud passionate weeping flooded me, and I was no longer a white Anglo-Saxon something-or-other but a horrified female facing untrammeled Jewish grief.

Oh-oh-oh! A-hoo, a-hoo (e-heu, e-hue??). He's dead. Dead in my arms last night. Oh, a-hoo, a-hoo . . .

For many years I have lived with Orthodox and deeply religious Jews, although I am not one, and I heard what she said and I began to cry, not as openly as she did because I cannot, but in helpless (Anglo-Saxon?) silence. Then I asked questions and learned that my dear friend Rosie had indeed gasped, leaned onto her breast, smiled, and died.

Oh, Rosie, she cried out. A-hoo, a-hoo . . .

She was getting a little out of hand, my trained self told me while I tried to stop shaking and throbbing at the shock of Rosie's not *being* here in this part of the world anymore.

Oh, dear Anna, I said over her almost voluptuous and enjoyable wailing, he was such a wonderful gay person.

There was a complete hollow silence.

Then she said in a loud hard voice, *WHAT????*

I said that I meant that Rosie had been so happy, so merry, so . . .

Oh, she said, and then she went again into the a-hoo a-hoo, and I felt that everything was all right and I left her to her clustered relatives.

Of course I meant to finish the editing of the story about Boss Dog, but I have not felt like it. I keep wondering instead about fads in words and meanings. I would like to say that my father, or Rosie, or even Boss Dog, was a really gay fellow. But I cannot, because I have several close longtime friends who are "gay," not "gays," and I do not want ever to offend them. It did not enter my silly head that I could or would, until Rosie's widow suddenly stopped her genuine mourning wail: a-hoo, a-hoo . . .

—*Glen Ellen, California, 1982*

31

Gobbling

It is probably silly to form certain ideas or theories or even superstitions about anything at all, but since I seem to have reached a plateau of fairly tranquil recollection, for want of anything better to do, I'll note a few here.

One that occurred to me today, for a reason surely, but not one that seems worth tracing, is that I believe a great deal can be guessed about a person's ways of making love by his or her table manners—that is, by his way of eating.

My chances to observe this have not often been close or intimate, but I am fortunate that they have been good ones. And of course I observe much more than most people realize, so that often I feel quite willing to bet heavily after watching someone I'll almost certainly never meet or even see again, from across a restaurant for instance.

The connection between his table self and his bed self is largely one of speed. If he (and I use *he* because I am writing as a female)—if he eats slowly and with shy amazed looks at his companion, of either sex of course, he will be in bed as he was at table: shy, in a dream, almost an innocent.

If he eats slowly but with enjoyment, trying to share his pleasure in whatever the two consume, from fish and chips to beluga malossol caviar, and from ale in a stein to champagne, he will make love with the same sureness and delight and make sure that it is reciprocal.

On the other hand, and here I begin to prowl around the main action I have watched and been influenced by, if the lover gobbles, he will make love the same way, no matter what he is eating. He may not be gross or gluttonous, really, but later he will pounce upon his partner exactly as he has pounced upon his food. He will gobble like a hungry and usually happy dog, whether he is a registered thoroughbred or a mutt.

I am sure that one reason Charles Laughton was unforgettable when he played Henry VIII eating a roasted chicken is because Charles Laughton was that same man, and he knew it. He ate like a king who was a sated scavenger, who did not care if fat ran down his cheeks and glistened on his thick sensitive lips, who needed rich dainty flesh and coarse thick flesh and princesses and street sellers. Laughton was a real actor, which is why his king is still real. His personal pleasures were not those of King Henry, but I feel sure that in bed he could be as voracious and delicately vulgar as Henry was.

I am very glad that I never had to sleep with either of the two-in-ones. I did know a man for a long time whom I would have liked to be closer to than we ever were, but I found early in some forty years of good faithful friendship that he made love exactly as he ate, with excellent taste and style but so fast that it was almost as if it had not happened.

I cooked often for him, and it was much more fun than making love could have been, but I never knew how he could finish a dish or even a whole meal with such neat sensitive appreciative dispatch. Zipzipzip and the plates were clean, and not a crumb or spot anywhere! His manners were always excellent. His understanding was genuine, whether he tasted a fine sauce or a rare bottle of vintage wine.

But that was not right for making love and sleeping together, so I had to turn my back on such wishes because I wanted everything to last longer: I was not a truffle or a Romanée-Conti, but a nice slow voluptuous female. It was too bad, but what else was there to do but shrug fatalistically and vent my fleeting frustrations on the long slow preparation of a truffled hen, which I knew would disappear like magic in perhaps one-tenth of the time it had taken to roast it?

Of course plain gobbling is another matter, and one that does not interest me. I have never been attracted, sexually or otherwise, to people who eat grossly and without thought. In fact, most of the adult animals I have liked have eaten with what I like to think is appreciation and taste, no matter how noisily. Puppies, kittens, and two-legged people under eighteen or so are not yet appreciative of much more than the good feeling of a full stomach, but any young animal knows honest food from swill, and will not insult his budding taste if he is given any choice in the matter.

And I believe firmly that the way he eats will be the way he lives, whether it is as an unthinking hungry glutton or a fastidious libertine—or even a nice kindly small-town deacon. I have never known a man who fit into any of these three categories, but let me see him across the room and I'll know what he has been or is or will be in bed. His social class does not matter, any more than where he eats what he eats. I've shared meals with truck drivers and a couple of dukes, and although I have not slept with any of them, I honestly think that I know what it would have been like, because of the way they chewed and swallowed, and talked over and around and through what they put in their mouths.

Of course I cannot do anything to test this theory, given the realities of both time and space. In fact, as I expose it to possible view, I find it unworthy of speculation. I simply know it to be true! Perhaps somebody will think about it, and look across a room (crowded, of course) and see a stranger who picks up his fork and knife at exactly the right speed, and chews and swallows and then lets digestion take over at precisely the hoped-for rhythm. Then, as Brillat-Savarin would say, miracles may happen.

—*Glen Ellen, California, 1983*

32

Kicking Old Habits

I remember that I felt, when the doctors ordered that my father Rex should *absolutely* cease all use of salt in his diet, that I must evolve some substitutes. For why should a man at the end of his life live deprived and in fear? So I did my best with the food we ate, but since he was convinced that none of it would have any taste without salt, it took some time to return him to a fairly agreeable form of nourishment.

In the same way, both for him and for Dillwyn Parrish, I felt it sadistic to tell them to stop smoking. D. P. was so instructed about a year before his death, which had also been prognosticated. So why not let him continue? He did his best, with denicotinized cigarettes, but I think he would have been more self-assured, as he faced the inevitable death, if he had been able to lean on the crutch that had supported him for much of his life.

In the same way, Rex had lungs that were loaded with silt, and at the end of his life he breathed like a moth through blue lips, faintly, and sipped fastidiously at superlong cigarettes that had been studiously purified for him, and he continued to cough and to feel depleted.

This depletion of energy and interest was partly the fault of his age . . . maybe. But his lungs were clogged and perhaps fibroid, and why at seventy-six (or whatever he was) should a new regime be enforced? Why not let him go on coughing and wheezing?

My mother went through this too, but as a body confined mostly to bed for the last six years of her life, she had more energy and time to devote to the restrictions of her doctors.

They ordered NO SALT and prescribed for her a substitute that has since been proven dangerous and at times lethal. They said NO SMOKING, so after several decades of that nervous substitution for scratching or or or, she had nothing to do as she lay in bed, waiting for the next time she could take a drag at the oxygen machine or snap an ampoule of nitro.

And when, a few years ago, a friend stayed with me while her son and daughter-in-law and two adolescent grandchildren came from France, there were rare moments of complete accord when my friend smoked, voluptuously, one or two cigarettes, and sipped a weak brandy and water without ice. For the first time in perhaps forty years she was at ease, hidden, safe. (This is a supposition, of course.)

She came back last week, with her son. I noticed that he said triumphantly, when I remarked that she was not smoking, "CERTAINLY NOT! Cigarette smoke sickens me! She has absolutely forgone all that!" And she did not even sip a glass of wine at dinner, but in hopeless docility imitated her son when he loudly poured *water* into his glass. She stayed here with me, as before, but had bowed patiently to the dictates of the son. And now, without the relaxation of a cigarette, the pleasure of a little glass of wine, she goes back to France after her recent and unexpected widowhood, to live in a cottage near the son.

I don't advocate pandering drugs or alcohol to the aged, but I do think it is brutal to stop such calmatives toward the end of one's life, for reasons of health which should have been started fifty or seventy or eighty years earlier.

—*Glen Ellen, California, 1983*

33

Night Thoughts

A night thought does not happen often. When it does, it is of almost solemn importance, and should be heeded.

The trouble, though, is that its first clarity and simplicity become clouded and complicated almost as soon as it has happened, so that by the time it is set down, as I shall now try to do with my latest one, it is almost unrecognizable. Probably I should have got up into the cold November blackness before five—before dawn by several hours anyway—to write it straight from my subconscious or unconscious mind from whence it leaped into my sound sleep.

All night thoughts, in my own experience anyway, come as sharply and clearly as the sound of a silver bell or gong. They send me without warning into full consciousness, with no normal symptoms of interrupted sleep and blurred thoughts and blinking eyes. I am *awake,* perhaps with slightly hurried breathing or perhaps a fast pulse, but no sense of alarm or surprise. It is almost as if I had been shot through space, from one world to another, and words are simple and few in my mind, saying what I am waiting to hear.

Sometimes I can accept them as a solution to something that may or may not have been puzzling me but that I have had in my conscious mind. This was true, the last time, as I recalled a few hours after I first awoke. Earlier that night I had written to John Updike to thank him for a review he wrote in the *New Yorker* about my last book. I had put off writing to him, because I admire him very much, but I'd found when I finally read his review that he had looked at the book as if it were a personal or even autobiographical memoir, instead of the collection of old pieces about places that I'd meant it to be. Plainly this letter was working along in different levels of myself, hours after I had written it and signed it and recognized a sense of relief . . . a duty done. But before I dug up all this reasoning, the night thought was completely simple.

I was astonished. Everything I had been puzzled about in my reactions to the apparent "success" of the book was explained to me. By now I can't remember the thought exactly. I think it spoke to me as if I were a rather slow-witted and perhaps disobedient child. It said something like "You are disgusted and angry because you did not write what you should, for yourself, but you did what you were asked to do. Then you let it be changed into something else, and you did not protest. Then when critics praised it, you disdained their judgment, and when readers wrote to you, you felt disgusted by their acceptance of something you felt was a hoax, and you began to feel that they were stupid sheep to believe what they were told. You knew all along that the book was phony, not autobiography at all, not important. You are not a National Monument. You are not a stylist. You are not anything the readers want to believe you are. You are a docile fool."

Well, this is confused and wordy, not at all the clear firm

meaning that came ringing and singing so purely in the night thought. But its truth, even changed as it so quickly was, is there, and now I know why I cannot and do not and never will believe that *As They Were* is a good book.

I feel uncomfortable and impatiently amused that it is the first book that has ever had much other than critical attention paid to it. For the first time, I'll probably make some money beyond the initial advance. Reviews and fan mail continue to pour in, and it has been a best-seller now and then and here and there, and even good friends who should know me by now continue to disappoint me with their congratulations on my finding myself, at long last, in the limelight.

For years I have been sad and in a way embarrassed for my fellow writers who have had to write "idea books" for their editors and magazines. It has hurt me, as their peer, to know that when an editor has said, "Jane, or Bill, we need an article or a book on onions, or abortions, or or or . . . ," they have clicked their heels and in order to keep their jobs, or eat, or "get ahead," they have written an idea book or an idea piece. Ho hum.

But I have believed that I did not do that, did not have to do that, never would do that. And so when Judith suggested that I "put together" a book of short pieces about places, so that Knopf could print it and then, if it was any good at all, combine it with the two books on Aix and Marseille to make a three-book paperback about places in general, I agreed. I wanted the Aix and Marseille books to be reprinted, because a lot of people have asked how to get copies, and both are out of print.

I forgot how hard it is for me to look at old material, and almost at once I felt I could not possibly pull together any old stuff. But I was rather unwell, in a physical and mental slump, and I told myself that it would be good for me to prove that I could still function, somehow, if I did this job. But I was having a bad time of it, until I asked my sister Norah to help. And this was all right, because she needed to add some extra points or whatever it is to her Social Security standing, and I like any excuse to spend time with her. So she came almost every week, and patiently looked through a lot of piles of old printed and unpublished material about other places I'd made notes or written stories about. Gradually she pulled things together. I was of almost no help, because I felt a creeping distaste for the whole idea. I know now that this was because it was not *my* idea . . . I was doing it to order! This sounds egomaniacal, and I am not proud of it, but it is plainly so.

I thought the collection should be called *Places,* or perhaps *Other Places* or *More Places,* simply to make it clear that it consisted of short things not directly related to the subjects of the two other books. Then Judith said she did not like that. We fished around for another title. Perhaps it is my fault that the book took off in a new direction, because somewhat desperately I suggested *As They Were,* still thinking it would refer to *places,* and that was used.

But immediately I saw that it was no longer about places at all, but was being touted from the beginning as autobiographical memoirs and random personal chitchat. I was shocked-hurt-ashamed-resentful as the book took on real speed. I felt like a cheat and a charlatan with every fan letter, every sickening review. Judith was blissful. My agent purred. I was gently urged to give interviews, and be photographed, and I felt swamped by all the mail, all the eager earnest bright journalists and cameramen to feed and smile at and sparkle for and be nice to.

Well . . . it's boring to detail, of course. Probably the worst part was the fan mail, because a lot of really fine kind intelligent people kept telling me that I had changed their lives, saved their reason or health . . . I had been their solace during childbirth and divorce and even grave deadly illnesses. I had comforted them; I had inspired them to keep on living, etc., etc.

While Norah was pulling the book about places together, and I was writing feeble little introductions and explanations and so on, she (and I, a little) pulled out of the piles of material a book about aging,* and easily another book took shape, and I felt fine about it, because it was mine and I could simply offer it and say, Take it if you want it. So I/we did, and it will be published next spring, and it will probably not sell very well but it will be my view of some things about aging, just as I think even the "idea book" about places could have been just that—an honest little unimportant collection about one subject—if it had not suddenly become *not* about places at all but a random wandering attempt at "autobiographical memoirs."

MURDER.

Well, I finally read John Updike's review of *As They Were* and saw that he too considered it a kind of mishmash of such reminiscences. But since he reviewed it after it was obviously considered "important" by too many people to ignore, he read it rather grudgingly as autobiographical. This was in a way the *coup de grâce* for me, because I admire him as a writer and only somewhat less so as a critic of modern prose. It appalled me that he *had* to read this unimportant and rather shoddy collection. It hurt my pride.

But I could not tell him that. So I thanked him for his kind review, and sealed the polite note, and went untroubled into sleep. I did not expect or even want a night thought.

But there it was, the bell with one silver peal catapulting me into great clarity, for a few seconds or minutes, in the darkest part of the night. I lay listening to the words. They soon grew tumbled and thickened, and there were more and more of them, but I hung on to the first message: that the reason I had felt an increasing anger and sickness was that I had sold out. I had consented to an

Sister Age, Alfred A. Knopf, 1983.

idea book, and to a changed intent and title and aim, and to a new and big and fat audience. It was not that the reviewers and the fans and the interviewers and the photographers were stupid dolts and dupes. I was the dupe and the dolt.

So, as the first clarity clouded over, I hung on to all I could of the night thought, and felt strong and healthy and infinitely relieved. And I still do, in a way that is of course even more obfuscated by now.

I'll never let this happen again. I'll take whatever money that may come in and spread it as best I can where it will help the human condition. I'll help if I can with the book about aging, but I will not give any more interviews and I will not take any more jobs and I will not pose for any more photographers unless I want to—which is probably never, although many of them are interesting people. I plan to catch up with badly neglected personal letters, and write, when and what I want to write, and perhaps get rid of a lot of old notes and papers and so on.

I know fan mail will continue to come in for a time, and I'll answer it. It is a humbling experience, and never again will I feel scornful and disgusted because people have been led to believe something that is dishonest. If they have read some old pieces about other places than Aix and Marseille and believe that they have read autobiography, they are not perforce dupes. They read material I wrote honestly, and if anyone got fooled, it was I and not they, since it was fobbed off to them in false colors.

As for night thoughts as such, it is plain that they can be lifesavers! Certainly they must always be listened to, and if possible kept close to their first silver clarity. But even muffled and perhaps distorted, they can save us all. I'm sure I'm not the only poor soul who has willy-nilly been catapulted from a far world into this one in the black of the night, to listen to a true appraisal.

—Glen Ellen, California, 1983

34

Syndrome

The word *syndrome* is high style now, and of course is used carelessly by media and plain people.

In *Webster's Third International Dictionary* a syndrome is a group of signals or signs typical of a disease, condition, disturbance, or a set of concurrent things.

Not long ago, in perhaps October of 1982, several deaths happened in Chicago because people took Tylenol that had been poisoned with strychnine. After that, a wave of such poisonings, in everything from coughdrops to canned food, was reported all over the country, and in spite of the admission of mass hysteria, it was known as copycat murder and was often referred to as the Tylenol Syndrome.

I listened to many reports on the air, and threw down the toilet a bottle of extra-strength Tylenol-codeine pills that I had bought in 1978. I had taken four of them, with no effect at all on arthritic pain, but had kept them in my "guest cabinet" in the bathroom in case anyone wanted an aspirin-type medication but could not tolerate aspirin itself. So I was in a very small way influenced by the news on the radio, and I felt a little foolish as I disposed of the worn-out useless pills that should have been tossed long ago.

This morning my friend Richard called, to say that he and Gene had brought me a little box of chocolates from a dinner they went to last night in honor of Michel Guérard, the currently famous chef who was lecturing at the California Culinary Academy. Richard would come by this afternoon, with a visiting friend.

He brought them, then, with a bottle of some wine I have not known about, and we had a pleasant chat and I thought as I often do of how generous and nice he and Gene are. After he and the friend left, I ate a late lunch, very good, of some leftover frittata and a little roasted chicken, and then I opened the elegant little box (three ounces, it said in French and English on the bottom). It was the ultimate in modern design and packaging, in gold and deep brown, with a plastic inside that exactly fitted each of the eight or ten small bonbons, one wrapped in gold foil. They were small and delicately shaped by machine into a shell, a crescent, a leaf, a square. Even the milk chocolate was rich and of high quality. The fillings were fresh and quite liquid, with subtle but unmistakable tastes of vanilla or mocha or, in one, kirsch, and I decided to *eat them all,* instead of saving them for two or three niggardly desserts.

They were rather hard to dislodge from their precisely shaped plastic bed, and finally I had to take the plastic out of the little box and tip it up. The fourth one, though, rose a little higher from its bed, and as I pulled it out with my fingernail, I saw that a V-shaped piece of the dark chocolate had been cut out of it and then fitted neatly back into place. As I lifted it up, the tiny door fell out.

I picked it up and fitted it back. How curious, I thought.

Then the Tylenol Syndrome took over, and without excitement I tipped the little firm bonbon again, and the door fell out. Inside was a white and fairly firm but still soft fondant. None of it stuck to the door, which had edges as neat as fine cabinetwork.

I felt absolutely no panic, but only curiosity. I wondered almost carelessly about who had cut the neat little V-shaped door, and why, and if anything had been laid on the white filling, or perhaps stirred into it with a tiny wooden pick or needle.

Then I put the whole candy into my mouth, and let it melt slowly on my warm tongue, and go down my throat. We'll see, I thought, and ate another and another, and finished the whole exotic little collection in the next half hour, as I read the day's mail. I thought without really thinking that I had either been poisoned or I had not, and that I would know within a few minutes or at latest by six hours. It was then almost 5:00, so by 11:00 I would be either dead or alive, I thought nonchalantly.

I lay down for more than an hour, as I like to do now when I have seen a lot of people and worked hard and done a lot of telephoning. (Marsha was here from 9:00 to 12:00 for typing, and then the Sandmans came down from the Hexagon house until about 1:30 to have some wine and talk before they leave for three months in Holland, and I made some calls and puttered in the kitchen until Richard came with his friends, so it was pleasant to lie down and half listen to the radio.) I thought now and then about how strange it was to be part of the syndrome, yet to feel so disinterested in it. At the same time I felt that perhaps I should report it, in case I died or started vomiting or or or . . .

When I got up, I began to feel rather unsteady and almost dizzy, and I wondered if I was indeed part of the game or if the chicken had been spoiled or if I needed to have a bowel movement —things like that, but no sign of fear like a rapidly beating heart or shortness of breath. Especially I did not worry about why anyone would take the trouble to make such a skillful little cut in a box of expensive bonbons. It would have been easy, I thought; there was no plastic or cellophane wrapping to "seal" the little gift, and anybody could have taken out one candy and opened its side and poisoned it and who would know? There was only one that was wrapped in obviously untouched gold foil, the one with a tiny raspberry in kirsch for a center. The box was kept closed with a thin elastic tie of gold thread that anyone could slip on and off. Over the bonbons on their fancy plastic bed was a handsome kind of padding of gold paper backed with cellophane, and this lifted on and off. Yes, it would have been very easy to tamper with any but the one wrapped candy and the two flat leaves of plain unfilled dark chocolate. The little place for the fourth candy, the one with the neat door cut into it, was still obvious to me by its shape. I remembered it. But why? Ah, that was part of the syndrome!

Now and then my feeling of unsteadiness got worse. Finally I went to the toilet for an unexpected bowel movement—unexpected at that time of day, I mean. Afterward I felt all right, with no more light-headedness to take note of. And by now, at 11:15, I feel alert, myself, observant, detached. Of course that little door may have been cut in order to place a long-working poison, one that perhaps will not affect anything for months or years. But why waste it on me, an old woman? I ask coolly. Was it meant for Richard or Gene (who brought it innocently to me as a souvenir of their meeting with the famous chef) and because of their friendship for me? Or was it meant for just anyone at all, by the same kind of sick mind that killed nine people haphazardly in Chicago last year —killing to kill, to rid the earth, to get even with the world? And if there was no poison, then why bother to cut the tiny precise little door, which could not possibly have been an accident in that elegant package of cushioned plastic and gold foil and cellophane.

I fear that nobody will ever know the answers, here or in

Chicago. Or anyplace. But the Tylenol Syndrome will be coiled somewhere in minds and hearts for a long time, and will come out in the strangest ways, for its own mad unsuspected reasons.

I wish I did not know this.

—Glen Ellen, California, 1983

35

Les Vendangeuses

It is mid-September, 1983, and after ten at night, and I must stop everything to write about *les vendangeuses*, because I realize that they are very strong in my emotions right now, to my great surprise.

They are a small blue coarse kind of daisy that grows copiously in the ditches and neglected woods of Burgundy, the Savoy, the Vaud, every place I have lived where there are vineyards. And when the grapes are ready to pick, these wildflowers come suddenly into full bloom. They are the grape maidens, the blue-eyed faithful girls in even the brown-eyed countries like the Ticino.

And my house is full of them, and for the first time in my life I realize that to me they are Timmy. They have his strong blue strength.

When I met Patty De Joia, "La Ciuca," she brought me a bunch of them, and apologized for their being weeds but too beautiful not to pick. And I said, Oh, *les vendangeuses*, and I told her about them, and she said that she had brought them from a gully on the way home from her great-uncle's ranch where she and her husband Jim had been picking and then pressing the grapes since early morning.

Since then she plants them, I think only for me. When they are cultivated they make many more of the same blue flowers, with more small leaves and on stronger stalks. But they remain a kind of weed.

So now they are in jars and vases. And Patty and Jim are picking grapes, and everywhere the vineyards are bursting with promise, and I realize for the first time that *les vendangeuses* are Timmy.

Perhaps it is because I am quite old by now, into my seventy-sixth year, but I know that I am completely alive sexually for this man who died more than forty years ago. I have no need for anyone now, and probably physically I might prove to be narrow and withered in my sexual parts, although I have not cared or investigated for a long time. But I feel passionately aware of Timmy, more so than for a long time, and it is because of my new awareness of these strong little weeds, *les vendangeuses,* and the waning winy year.

I have had a few strong, not disturbing, fantasies lately about love with Timmy. There has been no orgasm, mostly because I do not want one. But I know that I love him with a continuing deep passion that has never been stronger than it is now. Occasionally I feel deep regret that I was not more knowing of the various arts of lovemaking, so that perhaps in his last dreadful frustrated years I could have solaced him, and probably myself too, with more physical pleasure than we dared permit ourselves. This will always be a sadness to me. But I did not know whom to ask, and Timmy was too proud. (Yes, I think that was it.)

So, now I am an old woman and I think passionately but with

a partly cautious deliberate detachment of the man I love. I'll never lie again with him, and feel him within me, but I'm thankful that I still have the memory so strongly always, and that the little sturdy flowers have brought it again to me. Dreams and half-conscious stirrings of strong sexual awareness do not bother me at all, and all I can hope is that other people may know some of them too, as happily as I do. I have no desire to bring them to any culmination, perhaps because they have already been fulfilled to my full capacity. I do feel deeply sad that perhaps Timmy could have known some physical passion openly, in his last days of enforced impotency, but at least we were good lovers while we knew how to be, and he never doubted my undying love, as these flowers now tell me, so long after he first showed them to me.

—Glen Ellen, California, 1983

36

Reasons Behind
the Reasons

The reason I am not in bed, or at least readying myself for it at 10:16 tonight, is that I have decided to stay up a little longer. I have just finished a bowl of rather overspicy but excellent smoked turkey in a kind of mishmash of scallions, green pepper, and mushrooms. (The turkey was left over from lunch with the Kellys here, a long pleasant meal after they brought me home from Norah's in Jenner. She gave me the meat.)

We had the turkey because when we went to Jenner from here, last week, we left hastily due to storm warnings. We expected gusty dangerous winds, probable power outages, no water, no heat. We took along my battery-operated radio and a portable battery lamp in case the electricity failed. We also took my chafing dish, and extra bedding. And along the way we picked up food that could be eaten raw, as well as the precooked smoked turkey.

The reason we were both going to Jenner, a few days before Christmas, was that on the eighteenth or thereabouts, I almost stopped, and I went down to Sonoma to the hospital, for the second time in a week, to ask to be started again if possible. I think I was almost done for. Everything slowed down. It did not much matter if I fell flat or stood upright, breathed or did not bother to breathe. The first time I went to the hospital, I was in prolonged and strong fibrillation. This time I was simply worn out, perhaps. Anyway, I went from emergency to a room, and after perhaps twelve hours I felt like recovering some sort of life, and the doctors decided to give me B-12 in the buttocks, and folic acid three times a day, and a digoxin too, every other day, for two weeks. Norah was here when I came home from the hospital, and we turned our backs on Christmas packages half-wrapped, and headed for Jenner, where she awaited many family people and friends. I felt pushed around—not by her—but I knew it was the best present I could give her, to go along so that she would not fret about me here alone, as I'd wanted (and had hoped and planned) to be.

So today the Kellys brought me over from Jenner, with the radio, the extra blankets, all the unnecessary unused stuff, and some of the enormous smoked turkey.

And the real reason, the reason behind the one about staying up after supper instead of going to bed as I'd have liked to do some time ago—the *real* one—is that my bed is still stripped bare and must be made before I can get into it. And I started a sinkful of laundry that must be finished and hung up. But before I can use the shower to hang it on, I want to wash *myself* there. In other words, I must completely make my bed, and then take a good shower, since I have not really bathed for almost a week, and then do my laundry and hang it to dry, before I can go to bed as I wish I had done, simply and easily and speedily, at least two hours ago.

The reason I feel as if I not only want but need a proper bath is that at Norah's the one bathroom is very cold. Also, it does not have anything but a long narrow old-fashioned tub in it, and I have not taken a tub bath for about eleven or twelve years. I am unwilling—really I am *afraid*—to, because I am very clumsy and stiff with arthritis, and I know that I would be a fool to try to get in and out of a tub without close and sturdy help, which of course I do not have. And I hate cold bathrooms, especially in winter. (*Two* reasons!)

It is now 11:18, and I feel overfed and too tired to move. But in order to Go-To-Bed I must do the other things, which I shall start *now,* in order to pretend to be reasonable.

B̲ut before I left for the bedroom I remembered that I must poach six fillets of fresh fish before morning, and cut three loaves of sourdough bread in half and wrap them for freezing. I did this, and as I turned out the lights on a warm and fairly tidy kitchen, I remembered something else that must be done before 8:15 tomorrow morning: I must count and list and put out in the entry the laundry that should have been off two days ago. I'd asked Patty to do it, but she forgot until too late, so she will take it to Santa Rosa early tomorrow.

So by now it is almost 12:00, and the reason I am not in bed is that I've remembered a lot of the reasons for not being there. Perhaps I should try to be like a cat, and sleep when I feel like it. But who will make my bed? I would simply wrap my fur around me and find a soft pillow to fit me—I am a reasonable creature.

—*Glen Ellen, California, 1983*

37

New Year's Day

I meant to sleep at will this morning. Last night I went quietly about the house, moving and putting things away here and there, lighting candles, watching the fireplace blaze—die—rebirth to blaze, until about 4:00. By then I felt tottery, and did not take as long a shower as I'd planned, the almost ritualistic cleaning before the New Year. I went straight to bed, to sleep at will and whenever I could and would. The predawn world was silent.

At about 7:30 or so, Maya Angelou and Guy called from Winston-Salem. They were warm and loud. I smiled, and went into a pleasant dream or two. Then at 9:30 S. K. called: he and P. would stop by *soon!* I asked for an hour's grace, and then almost went to sleep again, and finally forced myself into a very unreasonable facsimile of a coherent old woman. When they came at precisely 10:26 I was out in the garage putting an empty gin bottle into the trash can. I had drawn my eyebrows and put on a little pale lipstick, but my white-striped hair was brushed and still free, and I wore a nice Mexican shirt (presented lately from J. P., cotton, bright orange and purple), and dark black pajama bottoms and dark red velvet slippers. *C'est-à-dire que j'étais à moitié habillée, à moitié en robe de nuit*—and half-awake, too.

S. and P. are very nice warm boring people, and I feel that they love me a little grudgingly. S.'s mother is the same: she is careful with me, perhaps because she did not understand her husband and suspects me of enjoying his overt teasing pretenses at sexuality when he would *never* have wanted to be anything but a faithful lover to her. He talked and boasted, and dutifully she did too, of his wild amorous goings-on, and I laughed at them and also at him and also at her, but there was never anything but shared mockery and amusement there. And now that the husband is dead, the wife wonders a little: how innocent and funny was it really? I sense a wondering in S., too. But this does not dog me at all. And P. is latently attracted to me, as I am to her. She is a direct passionate woman, perhaps deliberately "free" with her long beautiful braids of black hair, and her Greek face. She weaves for a living, and runs miles every day, and takes courses in weight lifting and aerobic dancing. But she stays beautiful too, and today I enjoyed her warm unplanned embrace. S. did too—he is a subtler son of his two parents.

So they drove away, and I lied to them saying that other people were coming. They are not, but they are: I wanted to be by myself.

I wanted to be alone, by myself, selfish and alone, on Christmas too. I planned for it. I even knew what records I would play, all day, as I emptied old baskets and drawers—cleaned out shelves piled with unfilled boxes, put old unworn clothes carefully into a carton for worn-carelessly unknown people . . . instead, I went out to Norah's from the hospital.

If I'd stayed here alone, she'd have worried about me but

been almost helpless if she'd felt I needed her, for she expected David and Cory and Clancy and Hazel and Matthew and Sean and Anne and Kenyon and Brenton, and of course Lida had asked Niki. So I went to Jenner. (It was my intangible gift to my devoted and highly respected and loved sibling.)

(Here an interruption, telephone, from a friend who wants to "drop by." I don't like to have people drop by, *ever,* and this is a special day. So he will come in tomorrow at 2:00, while Norah is here! He is a bore, but she will help me with him.)

So for a week I stayed in Jenner. It was rigorous, but good. It made me think of the needs of others than myself and my wishes were unthought of. Now I push away selfish introspection.

Today is the second of delicious filtered sunshine, after too much odd rain. I can feel things stretching and smiling. (My handwriting grows worse. Ho hum. I am not used to watching over it. But today I want to stay away from the typewriter, the radio, the recorder. I want to listen and watch—light and dark and the shiftings thereof in this unfamiliar sunshine—and the sounds of fire ashes falling on the hearth—)

(Here I got up and put new fuel on the faltering fire. I am interested in how I am becoming clumsier lately. I fumble things and drop them. I am definitely slower in reacting to sudden stresses. Is it attention? Inattention? *Je-m'en-fichisme?* I suspect the last is very important in what is studied as old-age "deterioration": why *bother?*)

This morning, after the young people (P. and S. are perhaps in their late thirties and forties!) left, I did some cleaning in the bathroom, as a somewhat dogged proof that this is indeed New Year's Day. I got the storage cupboard for soaps, laxatives, hair-feet-body-bowels-eyes, etc., into ersatz order. It is ready for another year, perhaps. As always in such an operation, I found a few forgotten things like seven tubes of the Selgine toothpaste that

Norah and I got in Mouans-Sartout in about 1973. I tried some of the tubes and they are still soft, so I'll send half of them off to her.

Slowly I dressed for the day. It was almost noon. (I do everything very slowly now. This is part of the aging process, of course. I don't like being clumsy, but I don't much mind the slow getting out of chairs and all that. [Actually I *do*. I am bored by it. But what other way is there? If God himself blew a whistle, I would have to take my own slow time to rise to answer it.])

I've always wanted to try weaving my hair in a kind of controlled tousle on top of my head, the way it is left when I bend over and brush it toward the floor and then stand up. So today I am doing it. It feels good. The weight, if any, is on top, held up by seven gypsy combs—two red, two white, one blue, two yellow, in honor of La Unión in El Salvador. While I was pushing them in, I heard on the bathroom radio of increasing sorrows there. I can hear the bombs; I try not to think about the people.

I am wearing the Mexican shirt, so I put on purple pants and yellow-red canvas shoes. Then I put one long tinkly Chinese earring in my right ear, and in the other a shorter but still dangling one of cut steel, I think French Third Empire. It is fun, and I do not at all feel "in travesty" or pretending. I enjoy it. If anyone saw me this morning I would be sorry to have my privacy invaded but would not try to change my clothes.

As far as I can tell, the rest of today is clear. Now at 3:20 P.M., it is bright and mildly sunny outside. Part of me wants to go into my bedroom, lie down, perhaps sleep deeply for two to three hours. Part wants to stay here in the bright warm room to watch the fire for hours long, write to people about what they have given me so generously, sip some vermouth, and perhaps eat a piece of chocolate.

So at 3:33, I have tended the fire, eaten three pills and two chocolates, and decided to lie down. I hope nobody calls or comes—

And at 6:50, after a gentle snoozy afternoon, I feel rather "lost"—a little *dépaysée* perhaps: where am I and why, and what should I tackle next in this great pile of unopened packages and unanswered letters? I am aimless for a few more minutes. It was pleasant, in a stupid way, to lie passively under my pouf and ignore reality. Now I fight the return to it.

It is now 8:10, and I continue to feel rather listless and dull. I must do something, almost anything. The fire smolders slowly. I'll see what tomorrow holds—back here for M. V., I remember, a good omen of devotion to start another year. (I feel that I may not live this one out, at least as a whole person. I do not much care, except about how discreetly and without humiliation I can end it. In case I am meant to continue, I have several things to do. I'd like to do the library program on February 10, of course, and then perhaps go along with Andrew Hoyem's proposal to collaborate on a book with Helen Frankenthaler.)

Kennedy called. It was fine. Suddenly I feel almost alive again, and I'll go write a note or two. (Charlie wants some more supper.)

It is 10:25, and I have written to Jim Pollard and puttered here and there, opening presents, folding some of these back into their boxes to be given to others who may want or need them more than I do. (It is very hard to give "things" to people like me, I know. How would I know what to give to myself?) This morning: the beautiful afghan from P., and I don't want it. (That is, for *what?* I am already warm when I want to be, just as I can eat when I want or need to—there's an almost revolting *easiness* about caring for my current needs.)

I wonder how and when this first day of 1984 will end. I keep the fire alive, and plan almost subliminally tomorrow's lunch, tonight's supper, Charlie's breakfast, when to take two more rounds of pills. Gradually the house grows tidier, after too many abrupt changes in all my plans—two trips to the hospital and then the stay in Jenner, all in some eighteen days! I'll leave the Danish

Christmas bell on the front door until Twelfth Night, and the secretly amusing crèche in the far north window, but today I put away the two Christmas angels I always get out for beside the chimney, Anne Parrish's old colored lithographs that Tim liked. The house feels untidy but good.

Tomorrow P. S. is coming down from the Hexagon. She is bored and lonely, and suggests "helping" me with "something—anything." She has no conception of how I work, and of why I firmly said no when she told me she would write form letters, long or short, to all my fans! I'll be nice and so on. But she is impossible, except perhaps as a human being. (I mean that she is impossible as an assistant to me.)

M. V. will come before noon, I expect, as always. We'll eat, and I'll watch myself not to be teasing or exasperated by her. And at 2:00 R. N., who has met her, will come for a formal New Year call. Ah, yes. Ho hum. He and M. V. may have a little fine sparring. And I'll sit back and contemplate January 3—or 2, or 32—and meanwhile I wonder about the rest of 1. I still have almost one and a half hours of it.

And it is now well into tomorrow today—1:28 A.M., 2.i.84! Charlie is on my lap. I have done bits and pieces of tidying, and have eaten three pills and some toasted walnuts, and have read with enjoyment *Menu,* a New Orleans restaurant guide that I think I'll subscribe to. I'll pass this copy along to N. K. B.—it's well written, very "local." The fire is dying. I think I'll head for bed, after an artichoke and a shower. It's been an interesting up-and-down day. Why not? But first I'll look at a book I gave myself for Christmas, a collection of short stories by Colette. I expect to be envious, sad, bored, delighted in a detached way.

The next day, January 2: now I can finish yesterday in peace and well-being. The weather is brisk and bright, warm in the welcome sun. I feel fine and flush.

I went to bed somewhat after 2:00, and about 4:30 I took a pill "for pain" called Darvocet, I think, prescribed by Dr. Schantz. It did nothing to help the ugly gnawing around my new hip (metal does not feel pain, I am told), but it made me feel doped and soggy. I slept thickly until about 7:30 on my back, with my mouth open, unusual for me, and then rolled sluggishly onto my left side and reached for a mint to start my saliva again, and slept a good innocent sleep until the alarm rang at 8:00. And that's the end of the first day of 1984. It was good and bad. I shan't take another Darvocet. I'll not sleep often in the afternoon. I'll stay busy when I can, and sniff the breezes as long as there are any blowing my way—and try to understand what *really* happens in an hour, or a minute.

—*Glen Ellen, California, 1984*

38

Alarm Clock

A few months ago, or perhaps last year, I decided to buy an electric clock, so that when guests asked for an alarm in the morning, there would be one in the house—besides me, that is. I paid about fifteen dollars for a cheap but reputable Timex, a small white contraption made of plastic. It was guaranteed to be foolproof or drop-proof or something. I put it in its intricately designed Styrofoam box, and on a shelf in the hall cupboard.

Finally two young visitors, whom I'd lodged up at the Mammy Pleasant Ranch, asked if I had an alarm for them, and I felt almost jaunty when I reached easily for the clock. What a thoughtful hostess I was!

They returned it unused, the next morning: there had been one in their bedroom, but they were awake before it went off. So my little box stayed virginal until a couple of months ago, when for some reason I forget, I connected it to the outlet at the head of my bed, and set it on the shelf there. I think I had decided that it was foolish to spend several wakeful hours before an important hour when I *must* get up.

I use it often, by now, and I dislike it intensely. Its sound is artfully angry, full of exasperation and generally ugly abusive non-talk, like any sigh or whimper or sob or shriek, but purely *furious* without sadness or pain. It is a loud rapid rattle, snakelike but higher than an animate sound. It is man-made, like the voice of a computer I suppose, a mechanical imitation, so that even the shock it always evokes in me seems inhuman, nonanimal.

I have actually come to fear it. It hurts me. I would rather hear a real rattlesnake, even at the head of my bed. I plan ways to avoid it. I have foiled it, and on a morning when it does not sound I awake with a small feeling of triumph that once more I have got out of depending on it. I push in the little knob on its back a few seconds before it will buzz, and I am free again.

This sounds pretty silly, I know. Why don't I give it away, or put it back in the hall cupboard for an occasional visitor? (I think there have been only three or four people in my whole life who have asked if I had an alarm clock . . .) I leave it at the head of my bed, on my bookshelf, and perhaps twice a week now I tell myself that tomorrow morning I must get up by 6:30, and I remember at night to pull out the little knob.

At first I was clumsy about reaching for the clock, once the horrible rattle started, to turn it off, before finding the light button and sitting up in bed and so on. Soon I realized that this was foolish, since it was too easy to lie back, once I had stopped the sound, and let my ears rest themselves from its shock—and almost surely drift back into sleep. Instead, I soon found that the only way to take advantage of its nastiness was to leap out of bed and *then* reach for the knob, so that the warm spell was broken and any return to it was impossible, until perhaps the next morning.

Unfortunately I found a new trick, lately, that I knew at once

I must try never to play again. If by accident I push the little clock onto its back, the knob is pressed in, and the sound stops at once, and only my clumsy arm is out of the warmth, so that I have barely moved from my comfortable position in bed! No, I said firmly. If I am going to give this goddamned piece of machinery a decent chance, I must be fair to it. No more tricks, I said. If you are such a coward about that sound, either don't pull out the little knob at night and trust to luck, or be strong and wait for it to be there when you have chosen to use it. But stop cheating, I said.

And that is the way things are, today. I never turn it on at night unless I am ready either to awaken before it sounds, and get up and turn it off while I am upright on my two feet, *or* to lie in bed and turn it off as quickly as I can find it in the dark and then throw back the covers at once and be forced to hurry toward the warm bathroom. I think that I have compromised with its really brutal usefulness, and that I can let myself take exactly what I want from it and not let it disturb me enough to reject it completely.

—*Glen Ellen, California, 1984*

It may well be that spite and anger and even vituperation keep people alive longer than they should live.

Just now I looked at myself in the mirror for a fleeting halfway glance as I moved from one part of the bathroom to another, and I saw that my face looked hollow-eyed, with new little sags in the cheeks and deeper pouches and wattles, and a grayish tone, all over, and I realized that I might live a long time yet behind that changing mask.

I felt a new surge of the small and large annoyances and pettish furies that have passed through me lately, each leaving its slimy residue of plain *peevishness,* and I wondered if this was to be my bread and butter for the next weeks or years. God, I said, I hope not. I hate being angry and cross and peeved, and perhaps most I hate the egocentricity of feeling hurt and misunderstood.

It is all a form of self-pity, I said.

I thought of a famous old writer I admire. She has always

been angry, but she is not being so the way I want her to. She bickers and makes public quarrels in letters to the editor of big papers, and in general is an old bore and a figure of mockery, and I hate that and wish she would die so that she could stop it. But for a time now she will gain new life from every picayune quarrel she picks with critics or writers. She will turn uglier, and make more of a fool of herself. And yet she has such a brilliantly ferocious mind, inside that tottering old carcass, that she cannot be ignored. She is caught.

I am somewhat younger, on the calendar, but we both look like very worn old people, and we are both caught—in physical pains and demands that irk and nag at us—so that I know why she hates where she is. As I did, certainly, when I saw myself *her*. There I was, a harried tired old woman finding myself angry when instead I should be sweet-browed and tranquil!

Lately, after much thought and inner searching, I have written a letter chiding a good friend for abusing her right to use my name on a couple of recipes that were plainly adapted from mine and called mine, but *not* mine. And I have been less kind, but still thoughtful, to an interviewer who overstepped his position here as my guest at a meal, after his formal work was over, and printed conversation that had nothing to do with his professional reasons for coming here.

Peevish nothings like that I do not like. Neither do I like my increasing annoyance at the U.S. Postal Service for failing to deliver mail (most of it sent book postage and not first class). I am irked. I am frustrated. I do not know where to start any possible reforms, and meanwhile I learn from many letters that my packages and bundles do not ever arrive. This adds to my revivifying relentless *zap* of adrenaline, I suppose.

Certainly I do not want to end my days as a sweet-faced old Mom voted Dearest Citizen of the Year in her Hometown. But I can't stand the prospect of surviving on pure venom, into a haggard infamous death mentioned in all the obits with a sigh of earned relief.

I know just enough about glands to understand that we survive because of them, through what our genes gave us and what our lives have done to these gifts. In my own case I find it increasingly hard to believe that my dubiously good life must now be prolonged by my bile, my weltschmerz. The weary sad mask I saw tonight as it flashed past me in the dim bathroom was a message to me: *Beware.*

I would like to stop being frustrated by the loss of packages, and I wish people who are trying to write honestly would respect the common laws of journalistic discretion. I also wish that the plumber, who said he would come by the twentieth when I called him on the third, would perhaps come by the thirtieth.

But the main thing that makes me wish my face looked *nicer* . . . softer, calmer, gentler . . . is the vain and useless realization that it never can. My present small angers at the postal service and the local plumber and even my fellow toilers in the so-called media cannot alter the gradual settling of my nerves and tissues. My only recourse is to ignore anger as a poison, to reject it.

I decided to do that about ten minutes ago, knowing that it need have nothing to do with prolonging my own life, much less shaping my inner face and the time left to live behind it. Of course I don't expect anything to change visually, although it is possible that my life may be shortened by this decision if what I suspect about glands is correct—that I could live a lot longer if I stayed mad-as-hell about anything at all.

Lately I have been wasting a lot of time, waking harshly into pained awareness of where the moon is in the sky, with phrases and even paragraphs ringing in my dream-brain-mind-machine, complete with commas and periods, because I am a careful writer, even asleep. And the sentences were good. They were well and perhaps truly spoken, but they were also cruel, cutting, potent, death-possible. My mind was racing, my body warm, my breathing short and deep. It was a glandular and probably sensual gratification, no matter how unrecognized.

Perhaps this helped make my face harder and thinner. I cannot know, but now I have finished with this side of it. I am sure that my conversion, my being "born again," will have no effect on anything but perhaps my longevity. Indeed, my new state of blessed relief, this decision to stop being *peeved,* will almost surely pass unnoticed, since I have no familiars and do not care to mention it to anyone. It may even be thought that I have become a little dotty! Where is my old cynicism, sarcasm, bite? Where is my writer's heart?

I know that the mask of a tired old woman will not grow nicer. But I think that I may sleep better until I die, because tonight I stopped feeling peevish at fate, or whatever it is.

—*Glen Ellen, California, 1984*

40

Winding Down

It used to be called Aging, or the Aging Process if one was more discreet in speech and wording. It meant *getting old,* or *growing older.*

What it amounts to, in my mind at least and about midway in my seventy-seventh year (I was born July 3, 1908, and this is January 23, 1984, for computer's sake), is that I seem almost unconsciously, or perhaps only will-nilly, to be winding down. It is like being a wound clock: I have the original mechanism, but the ticking is slower, and some of the intricate tiny artful gears have worn down with long usage, so that·now and then the ticking may falter. (This is known in some circles as *attrition.*)

I notice, and have done so for some time, a slowing and faultier rhythm in my walk, my speech now and then, and lately my daily routine. For instance, today I meant to have the bimonthly laundry ready. I got up early, stripped the bed and pillows, brought fresh linen, got out the old laundry in its basket and added to it from bathroom and kitchen. I put the lapboard with its usual folded paper on top of the used linens, and got a pin out so that I could attach it as usual to the bag. I planned to do this at noon, after my typist left—which she did at precisely 11:55.

It was then that the bookkeeper called: she would be here at 1:00 instead of 4:00, because her new baby was awake then.

So, at 3:44 P.M. the laundry man has come, leaving his bundle of clean linens but taking none away, so that I'll have to try to reach his outlet office about the next pickup. My bookkeeper has come and gone. I have not yet eaten the salad I meant to eat before she came. (It smells good.) I have fed Charlie, and am ready to eat, but the telephone has rung often and I have made two appointments for next month, and the fire is not yet laid and I have not given an extra-food watering to the plants on the two balconies and inside, as I meant to do yesterday. I have not located a check for $1,000 that I must send my agent, to whom it should have been sent in the first place. I have not written to dear neglected generous friends. I must send off some checks and cash others, and perhaps thank my stars that I can pay the bills. I must rest a little, this late afternoon, after some wilted lunch.

But I know that this compulsive attempt to stay upright, as Rudyard Kipling might have put it, is futile. I am winding down. I don't protest the process, because it is inevitable. I regret it because I wish I had more time to observe its progress and perhaps comment on it. That is plainly not meant to be.

So I'll eat some tired salad and take a little nap, and wind down some more. Perhaps the laundry man will call, to remind me of the neglected rendezvous with dirty linens—

But how long can this last?

—*Glen Ellen, California, 1984*

41
Journeys

Why is it that some people refuse, or are unwilling, to go back to a place where once they have been happy? If you ask them, they will say that they do not want to spoil a beautiful memory, or that nothing can ever be the same. (A wonderful thing can only happen once!)

Perhaps they believe that they are being kind and complimentary, thus to imply a perfection that must remain unflawed. Actually I think they may feel afraid that they will be disillusioned, if indeed they have had to convince themselves that a privately dull or ugly event was indeed a glamorous one. Or they may suspect that they are less attractive than they wanted to be, or that the other people are.

This has puzzled me since I was twenty-one years old and first married.

My husband and I went from Dijon in Burgundy, where we were students, down to the fishing village of Cassis for Christmas.

I lived in a mist of clumsy passion and ignorant naive wonderment, and although I cannot remember a single word we spoke, almost everything else rings like crystal in my memory: midnight mass, with fishermen playing wild sad songs on oddly shaped *hautbois* and windy flutes, over the bleating of two sheep by the altar glittering with candles; a new human baby wailing in its modern cradle trimmed with blue satin bows, and filled with Christmas straw; all the short square women dressed in black, with shawls over their heads. We felt shy and bedazzled, later in the bright hall of the Hôtel Lieutard, when the villagers gave us thick glasses of a sweet brownish *vin cuit* and everyone talked a very fast dialect as if we understood it well, and finally kissed us and cheered as we went up to bed. And ten thousand other happenings that are yesterday and tomorrow for me.

Of course I never thought of anything but a long full life with my love, but a heavy foreboding hit me about two years into this planned bliss, when he said firmly that we must never go back to the fishing village where we had spent our first Christmas. And a cruel mixture of disbelief and sadness filled me as I came to understand how thoroughly and firmly he stood by his conviction, that if people know real happiness anywhere, they must never expect to find it there again.

I did not like to argue, then or ever, but I did want to find out why, and his basic answer was that it was foolish to try to recapture happiness. When I told him that I honestly did not have the faintest wish to be the ninny of two Christmases ago, to "recapture" anything, he was deeply hurt, feeling that I had considered him a fitting partner in our ingenuous love, a fellow fool. Plainly I was out of my depth; I fumbled along about how beautiful the wild hills were, back of Cassis, and how good the wine was, and how much I had learned since then. It would be wonderful to see it with older eyes, I said. Impossible, he said in a pitying way, as if I could never understand the pain of being a truly sensitive poet driven forever from his former paradises by crass realism.

So that year we went to Nuremberg, and the next year Strasbourg, but we never returned to any place we had been before, because once, according to his private calendar, we had been there. And in a few more years we parted. You might say that we ran out of places . . .

I remain astonished, and very puzzled. It was obviously impossible to find out why he felt as he did, or to understand it, because I did not, and I still don't. When I tried to tell him that I did not want to "go back," it hurt him that I had not recognized the bliss he had tried to give me. And when I said that of course we were not the same as we had been, he thought I was telling him that he was older, which indeed we both were, and that I was unhappy that we were, which I certainly was not. And so on. Yes, impossible!

Fear may be a reason for refusing to admit change. And why would anyone be afraid of that? It is as inevitable as death, or "the ever-returning roses of the dawn," or curdled milk. And what reasonable human being would want to see always with the eyes of a bewildered lovesick timid child, which I was in 1929?

Many years after I was told by my young lover that we must never go back, my sister Norah and her three young boys and my two little girls and I walked over the high white-stone hills above the little fishing port of Cassis, and I cried out, "There it is, exactly as it was! Nothing has changed!" And we ran down toward its quays feeling delighted and happy.

True enough, wisteria hung richly from the trellises above the fishermen's doorways, and newly washed jerseys hung bright against the blue and green and white walls. Tough bleached old boats moved up and down gently on the flat indigo water, and down the quay there was the sound of a pianola I remembered from some thirty years before. My heart pounded with delight, and I grabbed the hands of Johnnie and Anne. "It's all the same! It's exactly as I knew it would be," I babbled, and I gave a big happy whack to one of the old familiar rusted bollards that still stood like sturdy mushrooms along the quay.

And it was made of *papier mâché!* It tipped over like a matchbox and rolled off into the dirty bay, and my sister and the children watched while (as I was told often and gleefully for several more decades) my jaw dropped like a startled puppy's and I seemed to *stop*—stop breathing, stop being. And then we all began to laugh, which we still do whenever we think of that wonderful return to the real-fake-phony-true place.

Maurice Chevalier was remaking one of Pagnol's movies there, maybe *Fanny,* and the whole village was a set, as much like Marseille of many years before as it could be made, and everyone was in a high giddy fever of participation, with the mayor and the priest talking together in the striped sunlight of the main café terrace, with some of the stars and grips and other people laughing as much as we were, if for different reasons.

My sister knew about my lasting puzzlement at my first love's firm refusal to go anywhere that had been happy for him, and we talked about it as we watched our five kids melt into the little gangs of actors' and fishermen's children. We sat under the paper wisteria in front of a fake café at the edge of the main set, and watched Maurice or Marius or somebody get out of a very ancient limousine countless times, for the cameras. Every take looked perfect to us, and every time the old actor creaked pompously from the backseat and stepped out, we smiled at his skill and then waited for him to do it again.

And I doubt that either of us had ever felt much more contented, serene, reassured. Quite aside from being well and with our children and filled with various kinds of love, we were in Cassis, exactly as we should be at that moment in history and time. And Cassis was there as it had been for more than two thousand years, and as it would be as long as there was a fjord-filled coastline between Marseille and Toulon on the north shore of the Mediterranean.

I think I was the first of our family to be there, between the two World Wars, when my love and I went there in 1929. A young fisherman rowed us far into some of the *calanques* to show us where the homesick German sailors from the submarines lurking there had climbed up the stony sides and painted their sweethearts' names on the highest rocks: "HANS + ANNA," "Ich liebe Huldi," "K. V. G." We ate the yolklike meat of sea urchins that he reached down for in the still dark waters. It was so still that we could hear a fish jump. We did not talk much, but the three of us liked each other, and for several more days we could call and wave and smile, along the three short quays of the village.

He might have been any of the older fishermen who stood about now for the cameras so long later. They wore their grandfathers' baggy pants and stocking caps instead of Levis and beat-up visored baseball gear, and the children of Cassis were blissfully arrogant as they strutted among the real movie kids and our envious five, in some designer's idea of how Marseille street brats dressed when Panisse ran his pub. One or two little boys had tried some makeup in their adventure as potential stars, and marked freckles over the bridges of their noses, like some blond blue-eyed urchin they had once seen in a Hollywood movie. They looked touchingly improbable: dark-eyed descendants of the Greeks and Saracens *never* freckle.

But they were part of our private return. They had been there forever. And so had I. And I realized that the dear man who had first gone there with me had never really been there at all.

Where had he been, then? We'd eaten and drunk and made love, listened to the wild sad rejoicings of the Christmas midnight mass together. Why did he fear to do it again with me?

Norah and I moved on down past the cameras and the serious village extras and the old actor getting in and out of his ancient car, and sat under the bamboo slats at the big café, and wondered. Lots of children came and went, and Mr. Chevalier came in alone and smiled tentatively at us, wondering why I looked almost like somebody from the Paramount lot in Hollywood a long time before. The white wine was cool and like delicate flint, as it had been even further years back. (Why had my love not wanted to taste it ever again, at least there and with me?)

Norah and I decided without words to stay by ourselves, and not smile back at the charming old actor, who looked suddenly lonely and wandered away. The children came along the quay with two American kids traveling with their movie parents, and several locals, still exhilarated by their professional debuts as extras. They were incredibly rich, at three dollars a day, even if their pay would go directly to their parents, but temporarily they were as broke as any proper thespians and consented graciously to drink a lemonade or two with us. The whole gaggle sat at the far end of the striped shade, like a scene from a child's version of *La Dolce Vita*. Norah and I looked remotely at them, and out into the afternoon shadows along the broad quays and the darkening water, and wondered how we could be anywhere but *there, then.*

I still think that first fine young man was mistaken. Perhaps his stubbornness was admirable, but his refusal to change his idée fixe was plain stupid, to my older wiser mind. Who wants always to look at a café or an altar or an oak tree with the first innocence and the limited understanding of a naive lovesick girl, or a homesick born-again Byron?

Five minutes or five centuries from now, we will see changeless realities with new eyes, and the sounds of sheep bleating and a new child's wail will be the same but heard through new ears. How can we pretend to be changeless, then? Why be afraid to recognize the baby in the straw, just because it is not as it once was, innocent, but is now tied about with nylon ribbon? Is it wrong to see the phony painted mushroom-bollard on the quay and accept it, as part of the whole strong song that keeps on singing there, in spite of wars and movies and the turtling on of time?

—*Glen Ellen, California, 1984*

42

Being Kind
to Oneself

This is December 26, 1984.

It is dark and rainy and without interruptions of people or telephones or anything more insistent than hunger and cleanliness and sleep. It is one of those special days, partly deliberate but still directed by unknown and probably beneficent powers.

Yesterday was a day of even more deliberate nonlaziness and no dawdling. I told all my strengths to be up and functioning by an early set hour, and they were. Of course this gave me extra confidence and/or self-satisfaction. And then I chugged along all day, until about 3:30, clearing off cluttered surfaces and in general preparing for an invited influx of assorted people.

The people came, in little waves, and by 10:00 I was gently puttering and putting glasses into the washer and folding the good old red-checked cloths from a couple of tables. I was thinking about some of the people. I felt fine. I went to bed by about 1:00, and instead of telling myself to be up-and-at-'em, I made sure that the alarm clock was not set.

Today I awoke with deliberate but very enjoyable slow ease, drifting into several little dozes after asking my other minds unimportant questions like how to use the word *it* or *go*. We played amusingly. I felt at ease with the Sub and the Un, which except on this annual day I treat with much more respect and circumspection.

Well, today, Lazy Day, it is now past 1:00 in the dark drippy fine afternoon and deliberately I have not gone anywhere but this room and the bathroom, where I have done two sets of laundry from yesterday. This seems rather significant, in a very minor way —the cleansing of the vessels and so on.

Charlie has told me gently, a few times, that he would like something to eat. I myself would like something, but right now I want to write about the possible skills and the general therapeutic effects of being *lazy*.

(My typing is not an indication of any values at all. Rather it is proof that I am less adept than I was even a few weeks ago. Not only do I reverse words, but the actual spelling depends largely on what keys I may hit. I feel sorry about this, because for many years the typewriter has helped me put on paper what I am trying to say, and lately I have almost given up using it because of my increasing clumsiness. I think that it is a combination of clumsiness and *je-m'en-fichisme*. As one gets toward the end of this current life, some things like remembering names and hitting keys seem much less important than they used to. This accounts for much of what is called loss of memory and so on in the Aging Process. It is really a kind of sorting out of what is IMPORTANT. The fumbling and forgetfulness and lack of interests are partly, at least, because of a what-the-hell attitude.)

So . . . on with my praise of being lazy!

But before that I think I should finally breach the gap, or whatever it may be, between the Other Room and food and drink for Charlie and me. First I'll check on his fresh water and food, and then I'll look twice at the icebox as I get out his salmon, and then I'll build a fire and then I'll probably eat something slowly and maybe look at a couple of unopened presents, and then I'll lie down for a quiet lazy listening to whatever is on KGO by my bed. It sounds delightful.

The telephone has not rung once today. How fine! Yesterday it rang perhaps thirty times, and then the doorbell rang a dozen or so times, and the whole day was a series of too-small crystals. I think there was a string to them all. Today I am not enclosed so far in any such lovely web or trap.

—*Glen Ellen, California, 1984*

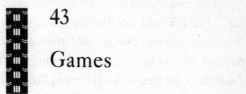

43

Games

I am now, as of about 2:00 on Sunday, January 13, 1985, going into a game with myself and also with Time, Space, and my friends and even people I dearly love. I feel both jaunty and scared foolish about doing it . . .

I've been talking for too long, several months, about finishing a somewhat amorphous but nagging "book."*

I went out to Norah's in July, and announced to my agent and a few relatives and friends that it would be done by Christmas. But in October I went out there again, to her welcoming and simpatico place, and I knew that the project would not be ready by the holidays. So of course I fudged along, because I honestly do not know if this hodgepodge of personal and arbitrarily organized stuff is any good. (That does not matter. What seems now to be important is that I do it, that I tie it up neatly, for myself anyway.)

* Her "secret project," this book.

I invited myself to go to Norah's tomorrow, and I told "people" that I would not be here until early in February, perhaps February 5. Then Norah said that the bottom floor was being painted and Lida would be sleeping in "my" room, the Think Tank. So I decided to keep to the plans and simply not tell anyone that I would indeed be here for a few more days. The thought of regearing my mind for cooking and being with both familiar and unknown people coming for lunch and supper, of marketing again and heating up the cold furnaces of my heart and mind—I decided *no*.

So I wrote to N. that instead of coming out after the paint smoke had settled, I would like to stay here, *secretly*. Everybody would think I was gone. A very few here would be in cahoots: Marsha, Norah herself, Kennedy, and of course the foreman at the ranch.

I have not heard yet from Norah. She may get my letter tomorrow. In it I asked her to call me: let the phone ring twice, hang up, and then ring again. Marsha tried this successfully.

It all seems odd to me. But the main thing is that I must try to establish, or reestablish, a different pattern of survival from the one I've let myself fall into. I believe and even fear that I feed upon the many people who come here. They not only give me an excuse for not facing my own work, but they give me a mental and moral challenge that is easier to me: I can be charming, thoughtful, attentive, the nice old writer belonging to her admirers. It is easier than putting myself and even my increasingly mussy and cluttered belongings into better order. I heap a few coals, here and there.

So at 9:00 tomorrow morning instead of fitting comfortably back into my old pattern of "Oh, do come to dinner, yes, yes, please do," I am going to pretend that I am on the way out to Jenner.

The road is familiar. I'll arrive, and after a good little drink, we'll have a delicious lunch, probably a pâté or some cracked crab and a salad. Then I'll unpack, lie down, snooze, pretend that I am really getting into a new skin, go out for a look at *M.A.S.H.* or something about 7:00 on the unaccustomed TV, eat a nice little supper, slouch off to bed . . . and the next morning I'll get up early and *start work*.

I do work well there. So why not here? It is a question of my own need to and my wish to, and I think they are both genuine. So . . .

I am indeed playing a game.

Today I am readying myself, so that instead of spending tomorrow getting into it, as I would at Jenner, I plan to start work at 9:00.

And instead of going out there at the end of the week, I'll be here. And instead of answering every ring of the telephone, I will wait for the code ring. This may be the hardest part for me, because when there is a telephone I listen. (In France I never heard one ring, in perhaps fifteen or so of the many years I lived there. But here I wonder if a child has fallen off a swing, or if Mother has had another heart attack, or if Father needs me at the office.)

And nobody will come for lunch or for anything. Everybody will think I am not here. I may feel very empty—never alone and probably not even lonely, but *away*. On Thursday Charmoon will come to go out for whatever I need to eat, and meanwhile I hope he will be able to hook up a new recorder-radio I've perhaps foolishly bought. And every day or so Marsha will come to get the mail and take it home for inspection—urgent, business, all that. She will call me using the code, as if I were at Norah's.

In other words, we are all playing a little silly game, because I want to try to order in my mind a book that may or may not please me. And if I don't like it, I'll scrap it. And if I do, I'll send it along to Bob Lescher and to Judith and to the *New Yorker*.

So now it's my turn. I've decided to play, and I am ready to —or so I like to think.

Actually I am very hungry, because I was about to eat lunch when the Freibergs came with oranges and so on, and then I felt that I must put this down before I stupefied myself with the good food that my innards want, even though I would much rather work here, right now, than eat. This will be another thing to cope with, during the next days. I often do not want to interrupt myself, but Norah and Lida have three meals a day, and I always join them for these. So for tomorrow I'll eat perforce about 1:00 and 7:30. All right.

It's my play.

—Glen Ellen, California, 1985

44

The Difference Between Dawdling and Waiting

Right now I think, or I thought so until a few minutes ago, that I am dawdling. I think (or thought) that this was because I am trying to cope with the odd chill fact that I can no longer write clearly in what we were taught to call "longhand" (pen or pencil in one's trained or undisciplined *hand*). It is not only difficult but tiring to try to keep even my signature legible. And what may be even harder to accept in both present and future is that my typing is even worse than my script.

I reverse letters (*nda* for "and"), which I've often done in the past. But now I not only write *tifleau* for "beautiful," but I am at times *unable* to write all the letters. It is as if I were rushing, too fast and busy.

This is clearly an advance in what is amiably called PD— Parkinson's disease. I am finding it almost too difficult (boring?), now and then, to accept. So I *dawdle*. I put off looking at the mail. I get out a recipe, but I wait until later to make it. (I even get out all the ingredients and put the recipe near them, and then I lie on my bed, under my warm soft pouf.)

This morning I asked myself when in the rest of my unnatural life I had dawdled. Perhaps when I was about fourteen, when I was a miserable human brat. Or perhaps when I was drifting arrogantly from one college to another, I coasted. I slept, or I cleaned all night, or I played tennis. But perhaps I was *not* dawdling (wasteful human lazy behavior). Perhaps I was *waiting*.

I was waiting to escape from being *entre deux âges* when I was fourteen. Later I was waiting to escape from my young life, which then meant losing my virginity and marrying into another physical and even mental world.

So now I understand that I am *not* dawdling. I am waiting. I am waiting to move on, which at my age means dying. I wonder about how best to do it, most neatly. I must now wait, to learn more.

—*Glen Ellen, California, 1985*

45

Leftovers

One reason that they are disdained is that usually they can never happen again. They can never taste the same, and good eaters do not wish to form any addictions that are hopeless from the start.

Another trouble with them is that their recipes are almost impossible to write. There is no way to capture again the taste of a cupful of yesterday's sautéed mushrooms put at the last minute into a spinach soup because two more people turned up for supper.

—*Glen Ellen, California, 1985*

46

Furniture

Looking across this room, I see a small rolltop, stand-up, veneered "secretary." I like it. It is lovingly restored, satiny with nutritive oils and waxes, a nice thing to feel friendly with. If I roll up the top, there are tiny nooks for inkwells, tiny drawers for pins or secret papers. There is a drawer underneath, copious enough. Below, two doors open on a place where the clerk may once have put his legs.

In other words, I like this artifact, and it is mine. It is in my current possession, partly because it belonged to my maternal grandfather, whom I met when I was an infant but do not remember. He asked my mother to give it to me, which I think was good of him. It was neglected for a long time, used to hold nails and screws in the tool room in the barn. Then Mother, who had a feeling for fine cabinetry as well as family, rescued it and had it restored, more or less, for my eighteenth birthday. I was not as impressed then as I was later.

By now I feel that I not only possess but love this tidy little piece of furniture. I am responsible for it. Where will it, where should it, find another home?

—*Glen Ellen, California, 1985*

47

Jumping from Bridges

Now I am thinking about jumping from the Golden Gate Bridge, and about other places where people have jumped to their deaths for many years. I think I should find out more about this, for I have an idea that there is some sort of collection of spirit strength or power or love in them that says *no,* or *yes,* or *now.*

I feel very strongly that this is true about the Golden Gate Bridge. Today, I heard that people are trying once more to build a kind of suicide-prevention railing along its side, which would keep us from seeing the bay and the beautiful view of the city. I haven't read much about suicide lately, but I believe that almost 98 percent of such deaths leave more evil than good after them. Even my husband Dillwyn's death, which I still feel was justified, left many of us with some bad things. And when my brother died, about a year after Timmy did, my mother asked me very seriously if I felt that Timmy's death had influenced David to commit his own suicide, which to me remains a selfish one, compared to the first. I said, "Of course, yes! I do think so, Mother." And I *did* think then that Timmy's doing away with himself helped my young brother David to kill himself, a year later. But there was *really* no connection; we don't know what the limit of tolerance is in any human being.

I do think, though, that there *has* to be a place where one can jump to one's death. There have always been such places. There is one in Japan that is quite famous. I believe it has something to do with beautiful Mount Fujiyama, which I saw in a strange breathtaking view from far away one day when Norah and I were in Japan in 1978. We had gone out with our chauffeur to meet some people for lunch, and suddenly the driver stopped the car abruptly. He said in an odd voice, "Look! Look!" And there, rising above a most dramatic Japanese-carved bank of mist and dark and light and lavender and white, was Fujiyama.

Even from a distance I could feel some of its enormous magic, and my hair prickled on my head. It was so beautiful! It was exactly like all the bad pictures I had seen on calendars and cans of beer. But it was *there,* and it was beautiful beyond the face of any god. It was all-powerful, and I felt like dying.

I have always known there are some people who must jump, but I never really knew about it myself until I was almost overcome once by a need to go off the Golden Gate Bridge. I feel quite impersonal about it now, just as I did the day Arnold Gingrich came out and dedicated one whole day to me.

He said, "Please, let's make a list of everything you like to plan but never really do." It was all very touristy: we went to the Cliff House first, and then we drove to the San Francisco end of the Golden Gate Bridge where I thought we would walk halfway across and then walk back. I never did tell Arnold about what happened, but about a quarter of a mile onto the bridge I realized that the whizzing cars on one side, and the peaceful bay on the other, were splitting me in two. The stronger half looked toward the city, the beautiful tranquil city, and I was almost overcome with the terrible need to jump off and be more peaceful.

I know it wasn't the sound of the traffic. It was a kind of force that was almost as strong as I, and I felt sick at the effort to resist it. I remember I took Arnold's arm and said, very coolly, "Let's go back now. Let's not go any further." And without any question we turned around, and I stayed on the inside track, near the bridge rail, and as long as I kept my hand firmly on Arnold's arm, I knew I would not do anything foolish. But I know too that I have never had such a strong feeling of forces outside myself, except once in Stonehenge—

No, now that is not exactly true; there *were* two or three other times. One, I remember, was on the steps of the cathedral in Dôle, a miserable little dim rainy city on the edge of Burgundy. I was standing on the steps of the cathedral when suddenly I was overcome by a feeling of evil. And instead of running into the church for holy reassurance, I ran away. I had to get away from the church, not into it. Maybe I could trace this back somehow to Carmina Burana and those secular plays that were given on the steps of the old cathedrals, like Dôle's. I don't know, but for a minute I was almost overcome by older spirits than mine.

And one time I felt a wave of horror, when Al and I were living in a room in Dijon above a pastry shop on the Rue Monge. I didn't know it then, but the little square where I went to get water in big pitchers for our cooking and washing and so on had been an execution spot during the French Revolution. The guillotine had been set up in that little *place,* and many fine Burgundians had had their heads roll there.

I remember our apartment was charming—one large room with three windows looking down onto the old *place.* It was big and airy with a red tiled floor and a little old fireplace; it had been a parlor, I'm sure, in a modest townhouse. There was an alcove with a bed in it, and Al slept on the outside of the bed and I was on the inside, and one night I jumped right over him and stood in the middle of the room, overcome by a sense of horror and fear. I felt filthy. Al woke up and asked me what was wrong. I said, "Nothing! Nothing!" But I felt absolutely clammy and horror-stricken by something I did not understand.

Such times have made me believe that there are congregations of evil and that they are stronger than any of us. This is why people who are perhaps weak to begin with jump to their deaths at times. Perhaps many of them, like me, do not want to jump off into the deep water far, far below, but something says: Get out! Jump!

This is why I have often said, in a rather casual way, that I don't think there should be a fence on the Golden Gate Bridge. Some people are going to jump. And if they can't join the waters deep below, and be swept out to sea—or, very rarely, picked up and made to survive the ordeal of hitting that surface so far below —I think there should be someplace else for them. But that place, and others like it, have always been chosen not by the citizens of San Francisco or elsewhere, and not by the people who built the bridge, but by something much stronger than we know about.

Perhaps there is something about water, or anything bridging a body of water, that seems to attract people to jump off out down into it. Very few people jump down into a pit of manure, except by accident, but there is something about a bridge over clear water, no matter how far down (perhaps the farther the better), that does pull people down into it, toward it. I know this pull well, and I have no feeling of impatience or anything but tolerance for the people who jump. There *must* be those places. There are those places.

I have not said that the Golden Gate itself had a feeling of evil when I almost jumped off it. Rather, I felt an urging toward oblivion, I suppose, toward peace. I do not believe it was bad. I do feel the Golden Gate Bridge is a place of great beauty, where many people merge with that beauty into a kind of serenity, a compulsion to get out of this world and into a better one. And that is not evil at all. But I do know that there are many evil things that lurk in the minds of the people who are left after the suicide of somebody they love.

—*Glen Ellen, California, 1986*

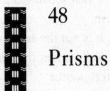

48
Prisms

When I went to school for the first time, at about seven years of age, my goddess had hung a prism in the eastern window of her room at the Penn Street School in Whittier, California.

Her name was Miss Newby, and the piece of simply cut glass cast mysterious colors here and there as the air currents and the seasons changed. It seemed a natural part of the new dimensions in my life. I watched the colors and wondered.

My little sister, two years younger, went to the first "kinder-garten" (an odd Teutonic word when we were not even allowed to call the "liberty measles" German!), which was built in the base-ment at Penn Street School. This was fine—for me, anyway. I was told to hold Anne's hand the whole way from our house to school, about three blocks, with only one street (Philadelphia) to cross. I was to bring her home for lunch in the same tame-bear-with-clown position. I did so, aware always that she was in love with Andy on the boys' side of the fence that separated us then. I never told her about Miss Newby's prism.

By now I have one. It is not the same, of course. Hers flashed and danced all over the walls, when the sunlight was sloping into her big room in the winter months.

—*Glen Ellen, California, 1986*

49

White Wine Trips

I have no idea how or when my family started to take white wine trips, just as I don't know where our family jokes and teasings and names came from. Perhaps it was my mother and father who started them. I don't remember. I don't think we took them, calling them white wine trips, until perhaps we all drank wine. But we have certainly always had them since we grew up.

Father would say, "Is there any more wine?" or "Is there any more of this *white* wine?" It was *always* white wine, for some reason. And Mother, if she sensed a little argument in the air, or even if she didn't, would say, "I loathe arguments." "No, it is only a little discussion, Edith," we would say. But she would go into her room, which adjoined the dining room, always keeping the door open so that she heard everything we said, and sometimes we would hear her chuckling. In other words, she withdrew but kept an ear on everything, and we ignored her, but were all aware of her.

Father would say, "How about another bottle, Dote?"—or Sis, or whoever was nearest the kitchen. And then I or somebody would go out and get another bottle of very nice wine, and we would sit back for the trip.

It was always fun to seek ways and means of getting out of where we were into another world, or perhaps another language. I remember once when it was about midnight, Father said to me very sternly, "Dote, you go to the telephone and call the Mexican consul." I said, "Rex, I think he is probably in bed now." But he said, "Call the Mexican consul," as if I had not spoken. "Call the consul and tell him we want to have passage, and a house in Guadalajara ready by tomorrow morning. Tell him we want to engage a Mexican plane to take us straight to Guadalajara. We will go from there to Chapala or Ajijic. You call him." So of course I did.

I think Chuck and Nan Newton, my dear cousins, were there at the table. Sis was there, I'm sure, and Mother was in the next room. She knew we wouldn't go to Guadalajara. We all knew we would never go. Rex knew that the consul would not be there. I knew when I made the call that nobody would answer. But we all waited and I did make the call and nobody answered. I went back and said, "Rex, nobody answered." He said, "Well, goddamn! Well, let's go on. Let's plan anyway." So we all went to Mexico for the next two hours and had a marvelous time.

One time Father figured that if Al Fisher and I could come over on a twelve-passenger freighter from Marseille, then he could do the same. There had been no doctor on board, of course, and Rex would have needed one by then, but he said, "We'll take this cargo/passenger freighter and go through the canal, and go to France, and we'll live there for a year. We'll get off in Marseille, and go on up the Rhône awhile." We all had different ideas about where we would go. I remembered one Christmas that Al and I had spent in Cassis, and I said, "How about staying down on the

Côte?" And Rex said, "No, too many movie stars, too glamorous. We want to get *away*. We want to live like French people." I said, or somebody said (Nan, or maybe Chuck, or Sis, or whoever was there). "What if we don't speak by the end of the boat trip? What if we all hate each other?" And Rex said, "Absolutely not. That is impossible, because there is no place to go on a ship, and we have to take care of each other. The captain will be the doctor. He always is anyway, and the first mate and I will be friends and anyone who wants to can play bridge. And the crew . . ."

But we knew, as Rex did not know, that there are crews and there are crews. He thought that people took care of each other, and he was never much disabused of that idea—certainly not by us on a white wine trip.

I remember one time Rex and Norah and my two little girls and I were sitting at the table having a rather quiet white wine trip because Mother had died. I had decided to move to the Ranch from Bareacres because I knew I could not raise the two girls alone, and Rex needed me, and I needed Rex, and the girls needed Rex. We were sitting quietly talking at about ten o'clock, having a second bottle of good Chablis, and the dining room door swung open. There in the doorway stood my young number one nephew, the only one I had at that time, Sean Kelly, who was then about sixteen. He was going to a school in Palos Verdes and his room-mate was Ricky Bercovici, who has since become Erik, a good producer-director, and who is still, I think, Sean's best friend.

Ricky was quite a bit shorter than Sean, who was then about six-foot-four. These two boys of sixteen were dressed in long black heavy coats down to the floor, and their faces were pale and their eyes were a little bit too bright. They both had on black felt hats, and their hands were deep in their pockets. Rex said, "Good evening, gentlemen, do come in. We're having a little trip here. We're having a white wine trip."

Ricky and Sean didn't smile. They came into the room, went

to the end in back of Rex, and stopped at the sideboard. Rex swung his chair around, as we all did, but neither of the boys smiled or spoke or even acknowledged us; they just looked intensely aloof. Father sat without a word, and we all sipped our wine and watched as Ricky took out oranges from every pocket in his long black overcoat, until there were twelve of them. And then he started juggling!

Our jaws dropped. Ricky was a wonderful juggler; I learned later that his worried mother had been told that he should juggle to keep his mind off his other jugglings, both mental and physical. He juggled at least twelve oranges in the air, and when he was finished they all fell back into the right pockets, which Sean had opened. The two of them then turned and walked out of the room and out the kitchen door. They never spoke a word. But they didn't seem rude; it was as though they were apparitions.

When they were gone, Father swung his chair around and we all took a big sip of white wine. "Now *that* was a white wine trip!" he said, and indeed it was.

—*Glen Ellen, California, 1986*

50
Sleep

I know that sleep is a gentle thing. It falls like dew and all that, but I have often wondered why it is so important to people to feel that they can sleep eight hours without turning over, or eight hours the minute their heads hit the pillow, or eight hours without a dream. All this has always been silly to me.

What is even worse, people often automatically take pills to help them get into this deep forgetfulness—forgetfulness of the day before, of what lies ahead . . . to my mind, it's a form of small suicide. Instead, I have tried always to keep dreaming, and apparently I do.

I'm thinking now of a favorite nondream: when I was a child, Mother always laughed and teased Aunt Petey, who traveled back and forth to Michigan a lot with her husband Moe. Each night of her life, Petey took one sleeping pill, and she always slept heavily, or well, or at least fully. One time, in about 1938, they decided to be really giddy and take a newfangled night flight from Los Angeles to Chicago, which then took about eight hours (a nonstop night flight with beds for first class, of course, and a stateroom). While they waited for takeoff, with Uncle Moe in the bar lounge, Aunt Petey did her hair as usual in their elegant quarters.

She always had it almost lacquered before she left for Chicago, so that she wouldn't have to comb it until she got there. She put a net over her stiffened coiffure and got into her negligee in case there was a wreck and she had to bail out. And then she swallowed her usual sleeping pill and got into her little bed and went soundly to sleep, as she had done for perhaps forty years. Eight hours later she woke up to find that the plane had never left the ground because there was something wrong with the engine. So it was the next morning, and there was Aunt Petey still in Burbank. And that was a favorite family legend.

My sister Anne, who took a lot of pills all her life, urged me once just after Timmy died to use one. She said, "Dote, you *must* get some sleep." I don't know why she assumed I had not. Perhaps she had not been sleeping well herself and thought that most other people were not either. Her remedy was a pill, always. I did not need or want one, but I took a Seconal, or two perhaps, because she insisted. She got rather hysterical, as I remember, about helping me in my grief, and I shrugged and tried to help her. (Sisters!)

I had a ghastly, horrible dream. In it I was aware of everything going on around me, but I could not get up because I was tied tightly by invisible cords to a log or a hard bed. I fought this. I think I fought it most of the night—a long, long time, anyway. And when finally daylight came, I felt that I had not really closed my eyes. I knew by then that I was not lashed to a straight surface, but that I was indeed lying on my couch on the porch at Bareacres.

I never told Anne about the bad time, but that was the first sleeping pill I ever took, and I wish it had been the last.

Then, in 1942, about a year or so after Timmy died, I went to the hospital to get rid of some little growths on an ovary. The anesthesiologist came to my room the night before the operation to talk to me about what she was going to give me. My one fear, I told her truthfully, was that I would feel, during the operation, the same panicky inability to escape from being strapped to something, held down, not able to get free, and to know all along that I was dreaming and yet suffering badly. She assured me that I would not —and indeed I did not. She did not let me!

The nearest I ever felt to that strange nightmarish thing after Anne's pill was much later, when I was in the Sonoma Hospital recovery room for several days after I'd had an emergency abdominal operation to let escape a tiny animal that had been biting hungrily at my innards. People thought I was dying of sudden cancer. But no. A little love knot had tied itself in my small gut, around the incision made when I had been in the hospital long before and had had my conversation with the anesthesiologist. This time it was 1978, and I was completely helpless. Tubes came out of me in every direction. I was pinned and tied to the bed, and all around me in the recovery section was the nightmare: everybody there was evil, basically *evil*. I was convinced of that.

Good people would come to the desk near my glass-walled cell to talk: paramedics, doctors, and one rather fat nurse who was pregnant. I had seen her before when I was conscious and not filled with Demerol and all the anesthetics. She was *very* pregnant, and she had lumbered to the desk just outside my door to tell the nurses on duty that she was saying good-bye for a while. They had laughed and made a lot of slightly crude jokes about motherhood, and she'd said, "Oh, hell, it's the fourth one and I said to him the *last*," and so on. It was all nice, in a chatty friendly way. But gradually, as my recovery went on and things became more and more nightmarish, I could see that what was really going on in that hospital was quite different from what everybody around us, all the stupid doctors and nurses, thought and accepted. They *did not know!* They could not know what I knew and saw and heard.

My fantasies were truly horrible. I cannot understand where they came from, because never in my life, as far as I know, had I ever seen or thought or heard some of the things I honestly believed I heard and saw and smelled, there and then. The pregnant nurse was not at home, for instance: she lay dead in a room around the corner from the big desk, her fetus lay between her legs!

As for me, I have been told by my sister Norah and my daughter Kennedy, who came several times to peek at me through the glass window, that my eyes were alive and peaceful all during this time. But I do not remember that at all.

Then one old-old nurse came in to braid my hair, and I thought, Next they'll wash my feet! Then they're going to carry me out. But before they do, I *must* tell *somebody* what is going on here, because it was becoming increasingly obvious to me that there was a terrible plot: first, to blow up the hospital, then to blow up Sonoma. And my duty, the only thing I could do in the world, was to warn somebody, to get everybody out of the building in time. I must escape from all my tubes, or perhaps I could simply drag them and all their squirting bottles down the hall and *out*.

Most of the plotters were the other patients in the dark cubicles around me, most of whom were dying. I know that several of them did die in the days I was there, and I thought, Well, they're just pretending. They want to lie here until they're sure everybody else in the hospital is really dead, and then they will come out and take over the world!

All this I knew was mad, yet I was in a panic to move, to run, to escape so that I could warn people to get the hell out of the hospital. But I was pinned to the bed, one hard plank, with the tubes thrust every which way into me.

Finally, I was taken to a private room, and I thought for two days that I was in the sanatorium at Angwin, where I had been before. So I asked a nurse where she had put all the religious books, because at the "San" there is a little shelf of them in every room—all the works of the founders of the sect of Seventh-Day Adventists, badly written tracts about how to die a true Christian, about how to live to be a true Christian. (Christians are Seventh-Day Adventists, of course, not Gentiles like the rest of us.)

The Gentile nurse in Sonoma looked at me oddly and said in a too-calm voice, "We took the books out." And I realized I was in another hospital where I had never been before.

When I first came to real consciousness, the head nurse came in and told me where all the buttons and things were, as if I were almost human. She said in a cold jolly way, "Now, we're going to keep an eye on you!" She showed me a little thing to press that rang a buzzer down at the main desk where she was. Then a voice was supposed to come on and ask, "What do you want, Mrs. Fisher?" And I would say what I wanted—"Pain!" or "Bedpan!" or something equally abrupt—and help would come. Then the nurse told me again she would keep an eye on all of us.

I pressed another button, as she told me to, and up in the corner of the room toward the ceiling a little crooked picture came on. She said, "We're keeping an eye on you, you see? So don't worry!"

I believed for several days that the picture really was an eye hidden somewhere behind the silly high screen that was keeping itself on me, as well as keeping its ears open. When I finally realized that I was looking at a small TV, I was simply back in the dream I had been having down in the recovery room. For Jonestown had just happened, and hundreds of people drank some sort of bottled pop at the command of their leader, a man named Jones, and died very quietly in an orderly mass, faces down. They did not die in pain; they just fell over dead. And here on the little screen were rows and rows of rather swollen bodies, all lying in the tent where they had passively, or with real resignation or fatality, watched their leader take his drink and die before them, and then they had died too, without question. (I believe a few knew of the plot and they escaped, or so I heard later. Anyway, it was a horrible nightmare then, and still is.)

So, there I was, pinned to the hospital bed, tubes coming out of every orifice in my body, and if there weren't an opening conveniently to hand, the doctors seemed to make another and another. And I was believing that I must keep the picture going day and night because my life depended on its keeping its TV eye on me.

All the news shots were of Jonestown, and the bodies, and of the leader as he died, or of the leader before he died. These tied in so clearly with my life of the past few days down in the recovery room that after a while I asked myself where I was—*there, again?*

Gradually I grew stronger, I suppose, and about the fourth day "upstairs" I told Norah, who had already heard me say some strange things, about the eye that was looking at me through the TV. She said that the eye really was an ear and that any time I buzzed, a voice would ask from the wall above my head, "Yes, Mrs. Fisher?"

We slowly got that straightened out. Then I said, "Noni, would you please tell the doctors that I'm hallucinating? I'm having terrible half-dreams, half-nightmares. I'm partly awake but not quite. They've got to change whatever they're giving me for pain."

Now, when people ask, "Are you allergic to anything?" I say, "Yes, Demerol." But they keep right on giving it if there is a need, which has only been once or twice since then.

But those terrorist dreams in Sonoma Hospital are the nearest I have ever come to feeling a hopeless inability to help people. They were the nearest thing to the feeling I'd had with that one sleeping pill I had taken from Sis. But this time it was *worse,* because the whole world was involved!

I finally did take another sleeping pill—to my amazement. I did not ask for it, and I did not want it, and I did not know I had taken it until it was too late to spit it out. This was just lately, the fourth night I was in the hospital with a dislocated hip. For three nights I had not slept because I was lying so immobilized that I didn't need to eat or sleep much. I suppose the anesthesia may have made me weak, but I never fretted about not sleeping because I'm made so that I do not twist around but can simply lie very still and breathe quietly and think about a lot of things and not let ordinary puzzlements bother me. I have many white nights—I suppose about one a week—and they never faze me at all, because since I was very young I have slept lightly. I have always liked to believe that someone might need me during the night.

But with the new hip, I had stayed awake three nights in a row, and unfortunately the nurses had peeked in on me every hour or so. They were appalled to find that all three nights I watched old movies; the late, late shows, the late, late, late shows—corny old movies, most of it terrible stuff. I kept the familiar old "eye" going because I did not want to listen to the people moaning, snoring, whining, coughing, dying. It is best not to *listen* in hospitals, anyway.

On the fourth and last night the nurses asked me if I wanted a sleeping pill, as they did every night. Or a pain pill. I said, "Oh, no." Then I thought, Well, why not? Tomorrow I escape, *this* time. And I said, "Perhaps one for pain."

But they gave me both before I could react, neither of which I needed or wanted, and I zonked off. I slept heavily. Hard. Without many dreams, I'm afraid, and for about six hours! I had not done that for a long time. I hated it. I really *hated* it! When I woke, I believed, although I knew it was wrong, that I had had my leg amputated. I suppose this went back to the fact that Timmy knew his leg had been amputated but believed, or *felt,* that he had a theoretical leg and foot. That leg almost killed him with pain, although it did not exist.

I was not in any pain, but I thought that there was no right leg there. How silly! I said, it should be the left leg, because Timmy's left leg was gone. And I thought, Well, we will match better! I do not know what I felt physically, but I was sure in my head that my leg was gone. I knew I was crazy, but still I told the young nurse who came in when I rang about my leg, "I do think that I should have been told! Somebody should have warned me about this—*discussed* it with me!"

I cannot remember what she said or did, except to hurry away. Another nurse came in and said, "You know what you need is a good piece of toast!" I thought of the limp horrible stuff they had been bringing up on the trays, and I said, "No, thank you very much," because I knew I was going home at one o'clock that day. I knew I had to get out of there while I was still able to. I also knew there was something wrong about my fantasies, because I saw as soon as I switched on the light above my bed that I did indeed have two legs! I could feel them both, and I moved my fingers up and down them lovingly.

(Of course, Timmy had always felt down his legs with his hands; he traced their outlines, because he knew anatomy so well. But after the amputation he did not seem to know that there was only one and kept on rubbing them both.)

The nurse came back with two slices of really good decent toast that had just been made in a toaster at the station a few doors down the hall, with sweet butter. She said, "I brought you some extra jam. Maybe sugar will help."

She obviously knew what was happening to me. And I ate every crumb. I think it was the first thing I had eaten since I had gotten there, and, of course, the sugar and the starch went to work and cleared my mind. But it was a truly scary experience, and I think, I pray, I hope I am going to make sure that this was the *last* time I will *ever* take a sleeping pill.

All I could think of as the nurse who had given me the toast wheeled me down the hall was Aunt Petey, all dressed and beautiful and her hair lacquered in place, waking up to find she was still on the ground in Burbank.

—*Glen Ellen, California, 1986*

51
Vomiting

People don't like to talk about it, the act itself, and I am not going to look up any definition of it, because everybody knows what it means. Most of us don't say the word. We say throw up, or upchuck, or or or ... Once I knew two little children on a mostly empty transatlantic ship in January who told me solemnly that their mother was "doing wom-up all the time." And of course there are current phrases in all levels of education and culture and snobbism for this act of getting rid, through the throat, of a noxious something below it, in the esophagus or the stomach.

The stomach is of course the main thing, the real target and harbinger and recipient of no matter what we swallow. Probably the commonest poison we put into it is alcohol in liquid form. And when the stomach has had enough, it rejects its load and we throw up.

How we do it is a personal thing. I know people who can vomit as easily as they breathe. I have known others who can rid themselves of this course or that of a banquet at will, so that in the nearest ladies' lounge or facsimile they will get rid of this layer or that of soup, fish, entrée, or dessert. (I was first aware of this basically anorexic trick with an aunt who had a beautiful figure until the day she died, like a dog, of cancer of the pancreas.)

Most so-called normal people are sick when they have abused their bodies' tolerance. They get punished; slowly or suddenly they feel awful, which means that they are dizzy, bewildered, with pale sweaty skin and haggard eyes. Then they are helplessly caught in a wave of nausea.

I don't feel like looking up that definition either, but it means utter submission to an enveloping whirl of green-brown urging and then helpless retching, and an enormous flood through the throat, or in extreme punishment a thin bitter thread, from the outraged stomach, where we seem to live and in this case to be dying.

Throwing up is an act that most of us know. I myself have seldom done it. I honestly believe that I could count on perhaps one hand but certainly less than two the times it has caught me. But real vomiting, at least in my vocabulary, catches and indeed makes helpless the people it has caught.

I never did like to look at it or think about it, which might be of some interest to a Freudian but was a plain pain in the neck to me when I was trying to grow up. I remember that once, in the back of the car my father was driving up from Laguna on a late Sunday afternoon, somewhere near Orange, on the road to Whittier, he slowed down and ahead of us another car pulled over to the side of the road. Then a girl about my age leaned out of the backseat of that car, and a spout of whitish liquid shot out of her mouth like the water from a gargoyle on Nôtre-Dame, and I felt sickish and horrid for years afterwards, when I remembered it.

But it was a waste of time to feel sick about it, and I am sorry I did not tell myself so, or ask to be told so, sooner. People *have* to throw up, to wom-up, to vomit. I would be better off, perhaps, if I did not have a prejudice against it.

One of my daughters can vomit easily, and indeed be almost unaware of the act. The first time she ever did this she was about two or so, already talking and of course walking, a beautiful dainty creature. I'd given her a little meal of half-frozen fresh applesauce with an egg stirred into it, because we lived in a hot part of the world and I had certain ideas about eating. She came into the kitchen in a few minutes and said in her precise way, which I did not then know was precocious, "Very interesting, what I have done. Please come and see. *Interesting,* Dotey."

So I followed this tiny creature, and she showed me proudly a very neat puddle of applesauce and egg, in a doorway. It was indeed interesting; she had needed to get rid of it quickly, and had done so and then reported it. And for probably the first time in my life I was able to clean up vomit without steeling myself to do it without adding to the mess—because I was laughing gently the whole time.

Many years later, I stuffed a big Christmas turkey with several dozen oysters, because I wanted to please the recently widowed husband of my sister Anne. I also wanted to please a friend, the new widow of my last and her last husband. (I was his fifth wife, and she was his sixth and last and best.) She too said she would like a big turkey filled with oysters, and my younger girl, the only child of this woman's sixth husband and me, thought a turkey stuffed with oysters would be nice. And his stepdaughter, my older girl, thought a fat stuffed turkey would be fine too.

I was in a stupor of housewifely motherly ex-wifely sisterly dedication, and not until later did I ask myself why nobody including me ever thought about the cold fact that I had lost *my* sister and *my* husband. So, late at night I stuffed the turkey with dozens of carefully seasoned and otherwise prepared oysters, and I put it out on the very cold back porch. (In hindsight, I knew better than to stuff a fowl before roasting it, but that night I wanted to have as much done as possible before the next day's duties called and so on.)

And during the night there was an abrupt weather change, and the temperature rose about thirty-nine degrees on the bird that should never have been stuffed anyway, and certainly not with oysters.

It smelled better than any bird ever smelled, and it looked handsome. The truth was that it was rotting. And everybody ate well of it, at an unaccustomed afternoon dinner. And then we sat by the fire, and then we walked about the town a little. And early in the night, as we all went rather soggy-happy to our beds, people began to feel sick. Not ill. *Sick,* in the English sense, which means "to vomit."

First my sister-in-law, my former husband's widow, asked our younger girl if there were any Tums in the house. I've always been stupidly prejudiced against Tums. I think they are for people who eat too much and then burp and swallow a Tums—people who are, that is, *stupid* about eating. So I was supercilious and unhelpful and rather bitchy about telling my girl that no, I'd never had Tums in the house and did not feel that my cooking needed them—that sort of thing. Hoity-toity.

I went to bed, up in the attic of the house in St. Helena. My younger girl would sleep up there with me. At the bottom of the stairway to the floor below, there was a little toilet-lavatory between my sister-in-law's temporary bedroom and my older girl's, where she slept with her young son next to the only real bathroom in the house. And in the basement below, where my brother-in-law was sleeping, was the toilet-shower.

And all night long the toilets kept flushing, and the people kept throwing up and purging their guts and then throwing up again—except for my daughter in the bedroom below (the one who could do it so easily). She simply leaned over in her otherwise untroubled sleep and heaved everything she had eaten onto a Chinese rug, which the next day her younger sister folded and took out into the side yard and hosed down.

The little grandson and I, who were either too young or too exhausted to eat the poisoned turkey, were not sick. My younger girl, the one who was in the attic with me, was too busy to be sick until late the next morning, because she was Miss Nightingale most of the time, alert before I was to the needs of our pale survivors.

In the morning I was aware that at least some of us had been very sick people. I kept samples of the vomit and the excrement in case the enfeebled wan victims died, and I was in my own hell of remorse and plain guilt when I called Dr. Neil about seven on Christmas, before sunrise.

I told him I thought that I had almost killed my family and gave him the immediate story and a brief report on the present condition of the three main patients. They were lax, chilly, weak, alive but only so-so. As I remember, he laughed, quite heartily, which annoyed the hell out of me in my state of fatigue and worry, and said to throw away all the samples I'd collected for the toxicologist, and to give the people weak tea and unbuttered toast when they asked for it.

Anticlimax. They did emerge from their vomitous states. They began to show some color in their gaunt faces. They nibbled at dry toast. My younger girl and I cleaned toilets, and kept the kettle boiling.

This is the end of the story about the Big Throw-up, except that my sister-in-law adjured me never to mention it, since it would look very strange to have international headlines about how a famous gastronomer almost killed off her family.

Why do I mention it? It is not a pretty act, nor a pleasant one as far as I myself know. I really hate to do it. Now and then I have wished I felt easier about it, or at least that it might be easier to do, but for me it is a major operation, a painful outrage. I think the only time I ever did it fairly neatly was before my older girl was born.

I was supposed to leave the house where I was hiding, by a certain date, but my child did not appear as scheduled, so Hal finally induced labor with a Japanese tea of savory. I had a biddy there to help me, one of his chosen retired nurses, and she was brushing my hair in front of the mirror, about an hour after he had broken the water sack in me, when I said with some embarrassment, "I think I am going to be sick."

She got a towel onto the dressing table and I neatly threw up onto it, without any feeling of nausea, and no ugly retching. It was rather like having a neat bowel movement, with no effort at all. The nurse took away the towel with its tidy little pile of vomit, and I did not even have to wipe my lips as she resumed her brushing.

The next time I had a child, everything was very different, because she came on Wednesday. But I do not remember throwing up. I hear that it is a normal way of easing the other functions of the body when everything is concentrated on the birthing.

I remember that before my mother was in a death struggle, she had to throw up, and now I am remembering too that one night when Father was trying to die he had to vomit, and managed to ask for a basin, and I got one. When he had heaved into it I showed it fleetingly to the doctor, and asked if I should throw it out, and he said yes. It had the black rotting lung of the man in it. It was horrible and part of my father, but I held it and then flushed it down the toilet with a deliberate coldness. Survival.

Vomiting is a good thing to do, many people tell me. By now I can contemplate it with deliberate impersonality, just as I can listen to a man with emphysema cough and spit out what is drowning him and not have my stomach turn over. I suppose it's a question of schooling.

But it still makes me feel like throwing up, if I could, to think about it without all the walls of self-protective reasoning. I hate the whole idea. I hate the muscular cramp that I have felt, the few times I have needed it, which forces the contents of my outraged stomach up through my throat and into the world. It is one thing to ready the body for birth, as I did, or for death as my parents had to. But the need to get rid of poisons, like rotting food or alcohol or something like heroin: that is another and uglier fact, and I accept it with an unconquerable aversion.

—*Glen Ellen, California, 1987*

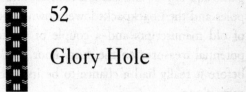

52
Glory Hole

There is one word that I love, and that I use sometimes when I think of this book as I hope it will turn out to be, and that is glory hole.

It is, as far as I know, completely American, and I feel that I am one and that I write and talk as one.

When I was little, my mother often used the word (although she was basically an anglophile and spoke *English*). To all of us it meant a closet or cupboard where we put all kinds of cast-off and unused clothes, tools, pots, canning jars, rubber boots, aprons with one tie string missing, paper bags full of odd stockings, broken lamp shades . . .

Mother said that every house *must* have a glory hole. Now and then she would say, when we asked where last spring's roller skates were, "Go look in the glory hole, but don't knock down that sack of dried mushrooms!" Something like that.

And I've always had a glory hole, wherever I've lived since I grew up. In Switzerland it was a low attic, with woven strings of garlic and onions and shallots hanging under the roof tree, and ski poles and then backpacks lower down under the eaves, and cases of old manuscripts and a couple of broken cameras and other potential treasures on the dusty floor. But I had to leave all that before it really had a chance to be itself, because World War II came along.

Later, I lived in a little town north of San Francisco Bay for several decades, and the glory hole there was a small room, right off the front hall, that had once been the office of the doctor who had built our house in 1870. He had set legs and pulled teeth and delivered babies from there. It was a good little room, but gradually it became our glory hole, and a fine one too.

We had a big attic and a bigger basement in that house, but it was the doctor's office that seemed to pull all our lives and their leavings into focus: dolls to mend someday, and a broken Singer sewing machine, and parts of several projects my girls started and did not finish in grammar school—and a couple of unfinished novels.

One mysterious thing about a real glory hole is that there is always the knowledge, the belief, the feeling that sometime whatever is in it will turn up, and be infinitely useful and valuable.

Perhaps this is why I was interested to learn, only a few years ago, that a real glory hole is a place where miners in early California days kept ore that they suspected might be of great value. They would hide it in a glory hole, sure that someday they could come back and reap their just rewards from it.

Any good glory hole may hide an unsuspected bonus for somebody, sometime! And no doubt some such childlike faith in me, or some egocentric hope, wants this collection to turn up an unsuspected gem of perception or wit or down-to-earth amusement, under the dust and neglect that must collect in any such mental storage place.

—*Glen Ellen, California, 1988*

53

Potato Chips

Most of our vices are relatively harmless to other people, two- or four-legged—that is, I doubt that I taint more than my own liver when I happily, indeed voluptuously, tweak open a cellophane packet of salt-encrusted, preservatives-loaded, additives-flavored, crispy-crunchy, and machine-made potato chips. (They used to be called Saratoga chips, I think.)

It seems logical, or at least convenient in a somewhat jesuitical way, that I have earned this latter-day respite from my early dedication to the pursuit of The Perfect. I have tasted the best, I argue, and therefore am justified in solacing my last years with no matter how unreasonable facsimiles, since the best is unattainable.

It is unattainable here and now, anyway.

Occasionally, and always alone, I put some substitute for the Perfect Potato Chip in a little wooden bowl (this is all somewhat dubious and fetishistic from a Freudian or perhaps Jungian or even est-ian point of view) and eat it before lunch. (Never dinner or supper.)

The ersatz potato chips are not good.

—Glen Ellen, California, 1988

54

Quotations

One of the easiest ways to start a novel or an essay or even a conversation, if one is not quite sure how to, is to quote somebody else. Current politicians or movie stars or even authors can help, especially if they are notorious. And a copy of *Bartlett's Quotations* is always close by, or should be!

Once when I was both younger and more foolish than I now appear to be, I ran out of apt springboards in the middle of a book, and blandly invented not only a personage of some wit but even what he might have said to prove the main point of my next chapter. For several years after the book was published, to some critical success and only a minor financial deficit, I went on ignorantly believing that I had fooled all the people all that time. Of course I was caught out, by a cruel Italian psychiatrist and amateur gastronome whom I admired highly, and his mocking dismissal of my feeble trick still haunts me. He was very right, of course, to make my childish self-service ridiculous; I'd ascribed to some invented wit like Johann Sebastian Appelmuss a foolish remark I needed so that I could then say what I wanted to, protected by his infinitely more important mind! It was a farce, and justly laughed at, and I never did it again. (The Freudian Machiavelli forgave me.)

And by now I find that on some subjects there is so much I can say that even Bartlett is easy to ignore! My trouble now is not where to go for help but how to sort out one single facet to concentrate on.

—Glen Ellen, California, 1988

55

Frustration—I

I am in an unfamiliar but not frightening state of mind and body, and this note about it may be of some use or interest. (My typing is increasingly bad and quite boring to attempt as well as to correct.)

I feel rather detached and cheerful, mentally. My mind is clear, but not sparkling or witty. My mood is rather who-cares-ish, *je-m'en-fichiste*. Physically I am very slow. I walk slowly, and like to touch walls and furniture lightly all the time as I go from bed to toilet to kitchen. I do not like to build a fire, or get dressed, or even read. It is especially boring to cook and to eat, and if I were not aware that I'd be a fool to try it, I'd like never to eat again, just as I would prefer never to bother to pee or defecate. I'd like to lie on my bed under the covers in one unchanging place forever.

I think of Miss Eleanor, and how she gradually got into a fetal curve and simply dried up there, like a leaf. She was almost 102, and the day before she died, her daughter bought a water mattress that might keep the woman's old bones from poking through her flesh and making sores. It was never used. I'd like to remain like her, but the thought of waiting almost twenty more years appalls me.

I think that I have tapered off in perhaps the last three months, moving less certainly, especially in unfamiliar places like streets and stores. I feel unsteady, insecure, and prefer moving about in this small familiar house. This is partly because of the slow natural progress of both the arthritis and the Parkinson's. But the decline happened suddenly for me anyway, and there is no use either denying it or trying to tell anyone about it. Why bother?

A week and five days ago I fell, here, and I am still not well— a really shocking experience, although it actually did not bother or scare me. It could have happened at any time in my long life. I have always taken for granted that I was deft and that I moved lightly and easily and with good balance, and I forgot for one second that I am not as I've so long been, and I lost my balance in a very small space and had to fall against a sharp bookshelf corner instead of down onto the floor, as would have been wiser. I was counting laundry from the basket into the bag, sitting on the edge of my bed, and in one habitual and unconsidered motion I stood up with the empty basket in one hand and tried to push back the door to put the basket into its usual place behind it. But the door, for the first time I know of, stuck on the edge of the little rug I was standing on, and I was off balance and started to fall as I twisted around between the stuck door and my bed.

Of course the fall seemed to last a long time, and I knew that there was no space for straightening out. I went limp and limber, as I'd learned to do in gym at Occidental in 1927, and knew with real resignation that I had to hit the edge of the bookcase. I did so, and then lay for a minute or two, with the empty basket on top of me, waiting to breathe naturally. I felt no trouble at all, and moved to check out my bones and reflexes. I think I said something aloud, like "Quite a fall" or "Great one!" or something like that.

By the time I started to get up, which by now is something I arrange almost never to do, since I am stiff and creaky, I knew it had been more of a tumble than it had seemed to be. My breathing was heavy and slow.

I walked slowly toward the sink in the bathroom, perhaps six paces. I meant to stop there and look at myself for a minute and then go about eight or ten more steps to the toilet. Instead I lost control of my bowels, and to my astonishment, for this had never happened before to me, I felt my panties fill with a rush of soft warm excrement. I simply stood there, and looked at my astonished face in the mirror. Then I said, but silently, "This is something serious."

I pulled off my shoes, stockings, pants, panties onto a towel that I'd dropped under me when the inevitable thing started, and reached for another towel and wiped myself off, and folded everything into a neat little pile. I was breathing heavily. I went about five steps to the shelf for some toilet water and back to the sink, but I felt increasingly light-headed and knew that it had been a real fall indeed. I splashed the bath scent all over, and felt clean, and then went with great care to my bed. I knew I was in trouble. I pulled a shawl over my bareness from the waist down, and dialed the ranch foreman, and tried to remember other numbers. But Paul was there, miraculously.

I said, "This is Mary Frances. I think I've had a bad fall. Will you come down?"

Of course he came at once, and the room was full of four young Glen Ellen firemen in yellow rubber uniforms and then two paramedics and I was feeling worse all the time. Dr. Schantz was soon in emergency in Sonoma. There were a lot of very painful X-rays. I had a couple of bad chills, and the pain increased, but I knew that there would be no broken bones. And in three hours I was home. Norah was here for the night, and I got used to being a badly bruised old body.

The verdict was "significant bruises on right rear rib cage." There were other lesser and more visible bruises of course. They disappeared in a week. By now, almost two weeks past the horrid event, I can turn in bed and walk slowly, and in general move (with care) in a fairly normal way. For the first four days I took the maximum dosage of eight capsules of painkiller every twenty-four hours. I also took half a Valium for two nights. Then I took the capsules (a Tylenol-codeine prescription) only at night for about five nights. Last night I took only half a Valium.

Aside from steady discomfort in breathing and even ordinary moving, my main problem has been severe and rather peculiar constipation, a natural result of the medication and lack of motion, and also a lack of my average eating. (I have no interest at all in food, which was convenient when there was nobody around to bring it to me, but which is now my problem, and my embarrassment.) I seem to have it more or less under control, with a complicated routine of Effersyllium, milk of magnesia, and Surfak and even bowls of Raisin Bran flakes! It is repellent even to write about, and at the moment my bowels are somewhat too "loose." It was fine for about the first six days; I had absolutely no muscular obedience down there, so that I could not even fart! Fortunately, I suppose, my kidneys kept on working, but very little, so that I did not need to go often to the toilet.

Well—tonight I feel like an automaton, sitting here trying to hit this out for possible use by a friend or a doctor or or or . . . I really am very ready to stop going through the increasingly difficult motions of being an upright human person. I would like to lie down and not move again. I do not want to eat, or drink, ever again. I hate the thought that soon I must stand up carefully, turn slowly so that I do not stagger or trip, and walk into the other room and eat something and listen to the radio and then turn out the lights and come carefully and slowly in to undress and get into bed. What I want to do is go straight to my bed, and lie cautiously down between two small pillows I have fixed so that my ribs do not hurt, and pull up my cover and lie in the dark. I am not sleepy. But I am tired. I think it may be time for me to die. Why not?

But as long as I can, it seems, I'll go on undressing slowly and brushing my teeth and seeing that Charlie has fresh water and and and, before I lie down. As long as I can I'll try to walk to the toilet when I need to, without falling down or dribbling. And I'll eat something so that tomorrow my bowels may move and so that I can take pills as if I really cared whether or not there would be bad consequences if I didn't. In other words, I am conditioned to living as decently as possible while I have to. By now, it is a chore.

Charlie, the cat who lives here, wants something more, something different, some Oriental tidbit I have never given him. I go slowly toward the kitchen. Soon I'll go to bed, and it is more than likely that tomorrow I'll get up again.

—Glen Ellen, California, 1988

56
Travel

It is seldom that anyone gets anything free that is very good, but the idea for this short statement was offered to me without any question of payment, so that all I can do is hope that what I say will be readable, which of course in my lexicon means *good*.

My friend said that "at eighty, the last thing you feel like doing is planning a journey." This of course is a complete refutation of that heinous conclusion.

It is true that I am in my eightieth year, which means that I will indeed be eighty. (I find that many people prefer to add or subtract a year or two in this silly way.) And the truth is that what my friend states is the *last* thing I should feel like doing is increasingly the *first* thing, as I add a little chronologically every day to my fairly full span of life.

In fact, I plan several journeys a day, and even more than that at night. This morning I went to a Mexican village I first lived in some fifty years ago. This was easily accomplished, of course, since

I was lying here in bed during the whole two years I spent there in Chapala!

Then, of course, I planned my second trip of the day, which took much more effort: I arose with extreme caution, reached for my cane, and with carefully measured steps went very slowly into the bathroom. There I performed my usual snaillike but always meticulous morning duties, and almost an hour later I was neat and tidy and feeling rather tired from this second long trip. And from then on it has been one journey after another.

A friend plans to buy a "perfect place" in Tuscany, of course on top of a hill and, of course, rather near Siena. So I went there with her, but not for much longer than to assure her that she must sign *nothing* without a local lawyer alongside. Then, I went quickly to Paris for about three days with another friend who has just come back from there. On the way home, we stopped in New York, since I would rather die than have to go through customs in Los Angeles ever again, as we would have had to do to get back to San Francisco. We went up to the Rainbow Room for a quick look at the new-old decor. It was fine, and the floor still revolved exactly as it had when I went there in 1937 to tea-dance to Paul Whiteman's orchestra. Then the phone rang, and while I was discussing going to a country club in Napa Valley in a few days, I was really in a small Swiss-Italian village with Romilda, who has just published a book in Napa about growing up in her native Ticinese (Swiss) village.

And I want to go over the hill from the Valley of the Moon to the Napa Country Club again, *not* to sign that silly book, much as I love it, but because I want to be once more in that little village.

Or perhaps on the way over the hill I may take another full-time journey and find myself in Athens. I have never been in Athens. Two of my friends are there this minute, though, and I don't see why I should not drop in on them. I might stay on, and learn enough modern Greek to read the newspaper every morning, and then go to a village on Crete and study the older tongue. I've always wanted to read Aristotle in the original language.

And all this is why I think it is incorrect that the last thing I want to do is plan another trip, simply because I'm not in my first foolish flush of youth.

Avanti!

—*Glen Ellen, California, 1988*

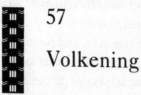

57

Volkening

One of the many reasons for my firm conviction that I am blessed, not only amongst women but just plain people of any sex at all, is that for some thirty-eight years Henry Volkening was what is too casually called my literary agent.

I met him because I'd just married Donald Friede, who unbeknownst to me had married me because he felt that he alone could change me from an unknown writer into a best-selling author. First in his scheme was to have me sever my pleasant relationship with Mary Leonard Pritchett, my genteel but successful agent. I was sad about this severance, which was done with more than the usual amount of misunderstanding and hurt and ill feeling and all that. Ho hum, indeed—and fortunately I could say this to Mary herself, many years after. She agreed thoroughly with me, so that we ended *her* days at least with a real and trusting friendship.

I was introduced to Henry Volkening early the first summer of my marriage to Donald, and by him of course. It was at a party given by Edita and Ira Morris from Mexico and Paris, both of whom I'd known better than Donald did. Henry was a small man, I remember, and a real gent, and he said a couple of nice things to me in an impersonal and somewhat bored way, and then I spent most of the evening talking to an old Swedish lady who sat cozily behind a pile of little cakes. I was shy, and liked the fact that she was nibbling and wanted me to sit with her and nibble too. Donald kept trying to make me stand up, and I realized that I was being gauche, and I don't think that I saw Henry again before we left.

He was definitely my agent, though, chosen and appointed by Donald, and by now this seems strange, because Henry was determined that I would never write a best-seller in my life. Of course, this was a great disappointment to Donald, but I don't think he really questioned the other man's motives or even his tactics, recognizing as only he would and could that Henry was a much better agent than he could ever be. That was one very fine thing about my third husband: he accepted and greatly respected people who knew more than he did about anything—about painting and writing, anyway. (In politics and other such Machiavellian pursuits, he knew without argument that he was tops.) He and Henry probably liked each other very much. Really, I *know* they did.

Myself, I don't remember anything at all about that first summer of my long good life with Henry. I was working hard on a kind of anthology that he no doubt handled for me, but I was apparently unaware of any directions he may have been giving me. Actually, I doubt that he did. Later on, he would chide me a bit, but rarely. I don't remember his ever saying anything in praise, although I'm sure that he would not have wasted his time on me if he had not thought me worth the occasional bother I'm sure I was to him.

Over the next thirty-eight years, he wrote many letters to me.

For a thousand reasons I regret bitterly that he never made a single copy of anything, nor did I keep one of his small closely typed pages. This casual way of running his own and his clients' lives made things difficult indeed when he died. In fact, they were a real mess, both after and before that sad day. His secretary Connie had no idea of exactly what he had written to anyone at all, and his partner Russell was in a permanent and furious fog about what and why and how Henry did his share of their business. Now and then Henry would write to me about somebody like Hannah Arendt, or Carson McCullers, as if I knew them closely, and probably he assumed that I did. He was pleased that I did know Jessamyn West, and I feel sure that he was disappointed that we were not closer friends. As for Eudora Welty, he seemed certain that I understood completely the hows and whys of his treatment of her, mainly because it was almost like his of me. He assured me once that she was both awkward and ugly as a girl and a middle-aged spinster, but that she would be a fine old lady as well as a great writer. I think he thought that although I was not quite as unattractive as she in my early years, I had less promise than she.

Still, Henry did his best to keep me from becoming the popular author that Donald had hoped I would be. And he hated my working for "women's magazines," especially doing easy monthly essays about potato salad and somesuch. Once he asked me why I continued to subject him to the female editors that seemed to be a part of any sheet I worked for, and I know that he was very happy indeed when I stopped supporting myself and the children by their monthly demands and wrote more often for magazines like the *New Yorker*.

Henry was cool about my earning anything at all, really. One year, I made $37.50. This pleased him enormously, and as he meticulously took out his own 10 percent and pocketed it before sending the rest on to me, he announced that we had finally got down to real business with the Martini Fund. This fund I kept fairly fat, since it was an unwritten rule that for anything under $50.00, the regular agent's fee would automatically go into the fund. Of course, I soon caught on that I too was contributing 10 percent. The Martini Fund grew for the first few years, and we kept up its somewhat flexible level even when we both knew that we'd long since exhausted it on my annual trips to New York.

We drank amiably over many more years, with Henry averaging six Old Grandads to my one New York–style martini, either in his Fifth Avenue apartment or in his chosen somewhat-grubby watering holes, most of them reformed speakeasies, where I assumed that he was pretending vaguely that I was one of the girls of that period, rather than a middle-aged to elderly matron. He always stayed gentlemanly and apparently sober, although I cannot believe that he was anything but a good stiff drunk for the last forty-odd years of his life.

Henry's wife Natalie was a once-pretty woman indeed. I don't remember that she ever drank or smoked or did much but refuse categorically to travel in airplanes, or even automobiles at more than about thirty miles an hour. This restricted their wanderings, of course, and once in New York I could not but wince when she nerved herself to take a cab with me, and about ten feet from her door she started talking to the driver in a completely artificial five-year-old whine: "Mr. Driver-man, now don't you go too fast for little me," etc., etc. I almost threw up with embarrassment, and I understood something of Henry's constant leaning on his Old Grandad. As a matter of fact, though, I felt sorry for him and Natalie equally. And aside from his obvious attraction as one of the wittiest and most erudite men I ever met, I did not *like* either one of them very much. I was saddened by her death, which was quick and hard, of lung cancer from Henry's constant smoking of Gauloises Bleues. He felt a horrible guilt about this, and died in the same way but much slower and more painfully, less than a year after she had literally been killed by him. (And it was not coincidental that less than a year later his partner died too, of lung cancer caused by those same damned cigarettes. The tiny offices literally stank of their ineffable blue smoke.)

After Natalie's death and before Henry himself died, he got rather passionate about a woman somewhere in the South. I urged him to pursue this, the last time we met in New York, but he knew he was dying and did not want to entangle her. *Toujours le gentleman!* He surprised me that time by asking if he might kiss me, and I remember that we walked stiffly down into the gardens of his apartment house. He put his arms around me and gave me one long kiss right on the mouth, and his lips were very hot and dry and unpleasant, and of course I did not want to let him know how repelled I was by the thought of the cancer and so on that he stank of, especially since I was sure that he already knew it. That day, after the kiss, we walked without talking to a cab, and held hands feverishly for about half a minute, and then he directed the driver to take us to one of his favorite old pubs, and we killed any possible infection in a flood of booze. We talked a little bit about Natalie and his current southern love, and about who would succeed him as my literary agent, and I never saw him again. By now I don't remember his dried feverish hands and lips at all. They had nothing to do with the gentleman I knew and loved (and still do), and I'll never drink another martini without thinking of the fund. It still stands at the magic sum of $37.50, Henry's first and final proof that I would *never* be a best-seller.

—Glen Ellen, California, 1988

58

Ho-Hum Stuff

And now I'm trying to say something very clearly that I do not wish to say at all. As I talk, I feel wrong. This feeling is quite familiar to me, by now, and at times I do not think that it is worth putting down, but I shall *anyway!*

The true fact is that I think I may be starving to death. I really don't wish to, and I hope that nobody else wants it either, but one truth is that I am not hungry, and two others are that I really do not want to eat much and that I really don't care.

This is not at all what I meant to say, but I feel that there is a plot and, what is worse, I know this is silly and so am I. The whole idea is foolish and trite, but it is happening. It also concerns fears in other people of such things as alcoholism. Alcoholism I have never feared. I love to drink, but I've gone for months and years without doing so *because* I've not liked the people I had to drink with. For instance, when I was working in Hollywood, I almost never touched anything alcoholic, because I always went to cocktail parties and *appeared*—and Mike Romanoff's men protected me. One of them, a fat man I called Bacchus, would say very quietly to me, "Are you drinking white tonight?" And when I would say or nod a yes, he and his henchmen would serve me throughout the evening tall, stemmed, beautifully iced martini glasses filled with water, always with an olive or a little piece of lemon on a stick.

But now I seem to be cast in the role of a Heavy Drinker, although I've not touched anything alcoholic for more than forty-eight hours at least. I do keep the "three-bottle array" of gin, Campari, and vermouth on my little bureau in the passageway to the bathroom, and that same array is in the kitchen. It is used, and the replacements are noisily and often made, and nobody ever sees what I pour down the sink.

Today at noon while I lay on the bed listening to a new tape of John Updike stories, a mug of the mixture that is called "*my* one-two-three" was put down by my feet at the end of the bed, with a plate of nibbles. I had asked for these. They were made up of a dab of chopped liver paste, which I made several days ago using Doro's recipe, and some cream cheese, and some spinach paste that I had invented and am rather proud of (reduce in olive oil one package of spinach, one chopped onion, and three cloves of garlic; put on stove to simmer until it is a paste), and some crackers or something crisp and fairly good. These and the almost ritualistic one-two-three were on a little table at the foot of the bed.

I was lying there, waiting for Marsha and unable to move, really, listening to John Updike and wondering again *why* Judith insists upon having him read his own stuff, and I gave a little kick to the table and it went clear across the room, and the mug of one-two-three broke, and the plate broke, and in general it was a mess. I was horrified.

Everything was made right, of course, but I was made to feel like an old drunk, and now there is another little plate of the remains on the same little table (now at the side of my bed instead of at the foot), and I have a cup of water there with a straw in it, and Marsha sits on the other side.

And for some reason the whole focus of this piece has changed as we sit together. And what I started to say about John Updike, and then about being hungry, or thinking I should be hungry, has shifted again. I honestly do think that very slowly and surely and neatly I am being put away, changed into a kind of clumsy oaf with no real thought or sensitivity.

I know full well that this is a common fallacy of elderly or aging people. I am one of these, of course, and I am astonished to find myself actually believing such nonsense. I *don't* believe it, and yet I do. I've written a lot about aging for fifty years myself, and I've read most of the plays and stories and so on about it, in both English and American, and I have smiled and suffered through them too. It seems important that I'm now thinking this—and I still do think I'm partly right!

There was a pause here, a kind of regrouping of thoughts. Marsha went down (or did not go down?) to the highway for the mail. I called David to tell him so. Or did he already know? Barbara came in or went out; she was peevish about something or other, possibly because she thought she had delivered the mail, yet Marsha had gone down for it, and so on. She may or may not be back tonight for supper. She said as she went out that I could have some chopped liver, cream cheese, spinach paste, if I wished.

I do not think I wish to, because I just ate a mouthful of the stuff on the second plate that was left here, and had crunched my way doggedly through a shard of pottery or glass from the remains of the first batch that had been scraped up some time ago, after I kicked it heedlessly across the floor.

So I think that I am probably still hungry. I do not feel so. I may or may not eat more, but at this minute I'm rolling between my fingers a piece of green pottery from that first inadvertent tossing of the stuff across the room.

All this seems really ridiculous as I say it, but I would and do agree with many of my mentors that it may clear some inner airs—not to mention graces!—to speak of it. (This business of spitting out pieces of china bores me.) Now I must think of what to do. Instinctively, I think I should let things slide on, and not protest in any way the inevitable reliving of an old old story. In my case, as in countless others that I know about, it is almost too banal to bother with, and I would really rather not. However . . . (And here I don't know quite how to finish. But I do not like this whole business. It seems clear to me in my head, yet by the time I ask Marsha to copy it down as I say it, it sounds almost too dull to put on paper. I'll try to sum it up now, and then Marsha and I will dictate some beautiful fan mail.) However, I do honestly believe that I am the victim of my own body, as well as of the designs of several others. I am being starved . . . and this is partly because I am not interested in the food. Yet I *can* eat, so that I can blame possible starvation on other people rather than on my own intellectual and physical deeds.

I do not look forward to supper. I'm going to make another railroad sandwich of local disrepute and renown (and by local, I mean familial, because my family has always been highly amused by them), but when Barbara said she was going away for the night again and I told her that I wished she would stay because I wanted and needed her to be here, she said in a laughing way that is peculiarly hers that she could not stomach the thought of another railroad sandwich, and that she hoped she would never see or hear of one ever again. I said that people were amused by them, and she said that she was not, and then she left. Then Marsha came back from doing the silly errand for David (and here I do not really mean silly!), and I pulled that piece of green porcelain out from between two teeth, and now we're going to work.

I hope that this will be some indication of my puzzlements. I honestly feel that I am dying of starvation, perhaps helped unwittingly by outside forces. On the other hand, I'm actually glad to do this (do I mean *die now?*), and I do not wish to implicate any human being in any way at all. If someone does want me to die, I do not feel that there is a reason for it except that I may be taking up necessary breathing space on the planet. (Perhaps I do not like to be reminded of this?) There cannot be any pecuniary interest here, as there was in some of the old stories I used to know about elderly duchesses and so on who were artfully done in by their butlers. So if there is indeed any malice in this plot, it is probably based on physical envy: I am taller, or older, or better known socially or in a worldly way—things like that. Yes, if it indeed exists, it is probably based on some kind of envy.

I recognize this and I feel very sad about it, and I think that is my story for now.

—Glen Ellen, California, 1988

59

Anon.

I know, I *feel*, something about the anonymity of being a bag lady. I want it. But my training is against this escape from responsibility, the escape into what this lack of responsibility might mean. I don't want to run away, to shuck off the natural "burdens." But I want to be *anonymous*. And how can one ever be, except by escaping, running away, hiding? No, I'll probably stay . . .

—*Glen Ellen, California, 1989*

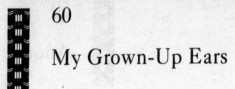

60

My Grown-Up Ears

One of the best parts about growing older for me is that I am increasingly able to watch myself do so.

Even a few years ago, a new step toward my maturity would happen without any obvious warning, so that I'd find myself, some soft gray day, doing or thinking or speaking in a way that would have been impossible the sunny day before. But now, I am more conscious of my own peculiar speeds.

I know that I am fairly slow. I acknowledge, without too much impatience, that it may take me several years to reach this or that stage of adult behavior, in spite of graying hairs and such, and I feel a kind of smug relief that I have developed so neatly, if at all, this far.

I was sure for at least ten years before it finally happened that someday I would be able to hear chamber music for more than half an hour at a time without strain. I knew too that there was no use worrying about my backwardness; it would change gradually and surely. And it did, so that at this point the intricate orderly notes of four stringed instruments playing together are almost the only kind I can actually listen to, and I am exasperated by classical "symphonies," which even a few months ago touched the quick. I admit without perturbation the possibility that if I live long enough, my spiritual ear may reshape itself to such a point that it will tolerate only the sound of a flute, or a Chinese whistle tied to a pigeon's wing.

It was much the same about reading the Bible. For a long time it did not matter whether I would ever like it, and then when I matured enough to know that it would eventually be important to me, I was able to wait patiently. I had no idea of when it would happen, just as I had had none about the place and time that would suddenly find me listening with my inside ears, my grown-up ears, to a Beethoven quartet. That is why I am thankful that the time did come: it is over with, so that I need no longer wait.

It was in August 1945, and I was sitting in the North Reading Room of the New York Public Library. There was heavy dark rain falling, and the enormous hall was full of the scratchy rustlings and the smell of unaired clothes inevitable when many research workers congregate. I was grubbing in a concordance, looking up some such word as *gluttony* and thumbing here and there in a very neat practical copy of the King James Version.

And then I was reading:

"In the beginning . . ."

The words came out clear and strong and in a most beautiful order. They were the most straightforward words I had ever read, and although they were familiar to me from my youngest day, I knew that I had never really heard them before. I read for many hours without any knowledge of time or weariness, and when I finally went out into the wet street, I felt a sense of great relief that the time had come, that the waiting was over, that I had grown up that much more. It was probably a little the way a woman who has long wanted a child feels when she knows that at last she has conceived. The thing had finally happened, and it was rich with promise.

My mother's mother, when I was a little child, lived with us. She was what was known then as "religious." There were many like her, strange products of the Victorian era: women who remained unsatisfied by constant childbearing and the portly bearded courtesies extended to them by their husbands, and who fed all their secret hungers through a fanatical and at times almost orgiastic devotion to one of the many austere Protestant sects that flourished for them and because of them.

Grandmother was a Campbellite or, as she preferred to call herself and her fellow church members, a "Christian." She was of course the dominating figure in her church, as everywhere, and as she grew older she increased her importance by giving almost all of her money to the various ministers, organ funds, and missionaries (all starving, vicariously or in actuality) that touched her golden circle. People bowed to her, and flattered her, and cadged shamelessly from her in spite of their real respect, and she flourished, and was happier than she had ever been in the ample bosom of her philoprogenitive family.

It is probably fortunate that she died before my generation reached an articulate state, but between my third and sixth year, she did what she could to prepare me to be a "Christian."

I went to Sunday school and church every week with her, and enjoyed it very much. Everybody paid the two of us extravagant compliments: "What a lovely picture they make—old lady, with her sweet little granddaughter, and perhaps today is the day to mention the ministerial pension fund again to that wonderful old dowager . . . " And even Grandmother was not optimistic enough to trust my interest in God's word, thundered or squeaked from the pulpit, without bolstering it with an occasional snippet of butterscotch or barley sugar slipped to me from her crocheted handbag.

After Sunday dinner, which consisted mainly of bland pale boiled things like old hens and dumplings, and flaccid puddings because of Grandmother's Nervous Stomach (a condition that almost always accompanied the more virtuous attributes of such female Victorian churchgoers, for reasons obvious to any amateur Freudian), she napped and I raced through the funny papers with my little sister—*The Katzenjammer Kids* and *Mutt and Jeff.* By the time she awoke and straightened the intricate cheaters that lay within her famous silver pompadour, we were lying decorously on the floor, deep in one of the many books about Christianity that she bought from deserving young divinity students and gave to us every Christmas and birthday.

Our interest was genuine: they were ingenious books, at least, and we liked the games they made of knowing the names of the Twelve Apostles and such. There was one, our favorite, that told most of the Old Testament stories in a kind of sign language: God was a mysterious symbol, perhaps the Jewish capital letter for Jehovah with a little piece of fire around it, and Adam was a little man behind a very large fig leaf, and all the birds and beasts of the story of creation were reasonable facsimiles of themselves, strung together with a few monosyllables to make the Holy Bible "fun for tiny tots."

Perhaps that is a good idea, but I do not think so. It was, as I reflect upon it, a complete vulgarization, done without sensibility, presented in a crude manner that could appeal only fleetingly even to five-year-old minds. It partially succeeded in reducing the Scriptures to the level of *Mutt and Jeff* and *The Katzenjammer Kids,* but I do not think it did anything at all to interest us in either the temporal or spiritual meanings of the stories it told. We might better, to my mind, have been reading or listening to less significant tales.

Sunday school did nothing but bore me. It turned all the excitement and clash and turmoil of the Old Testament to dust, and reduced the mystery of Jesus' life and death to a self-consciously painful confusion. After my confirmation, which seemed to reassure my parents about something or other but crystallized my own feelings into a quiet but firm rebellion, I became an agnostic.

When I went away to a church preparatory school, I got high grades for several years in the required Bible course, and knew Hebrew dates backwards and forwards, and five minutes after summer vacation started could not remember one word of what I had learned.

It was the same in college, except that there I was trying to convince myself, with the other self-styled intellectuals, that the Bible, "if considered solely as a fascinating collection of myths and legends" and so on and so on, was Great Literature. I was stirred as any young human must be by the passion and sensuality of some of the songs I read in it, and I admitted glibly that it would be wonderful to be able to "believe" in it.

Almost before I had finished talking that way, I began to laugh at other people who did, and for several years dismissed the whole thing from my life, except for a feeling of scornful impatience now and then when I heard of older people who read the Bible from cover to cover once a year, or did some other such narcotic trick.

Once, many years ago, I tried to read it in a time of deep sadness, but it was dead to me. I would have been grateful for any comfort then, and I wondered why I could find none in what had plainly stayed many another like me.

Then, as I began to recognize the pace of my gradual development, and saw myself waiting patiently for the moments when I would really taste lentil soup or hear every note in a trio or know what the bird said in a Chinese wall painting, I realized that at some time I would be able to read the Bible. And now I am.

It is not the fault of my grandmother or boredom or my own stupidity that it took so long. I was simply incapable of it, until the summer of 1945. Since then, oh rich fortunate me, I can go almost anywhere in it. The violence and the plottings and the blood and tenderness are more exciting than in any book I have ever read, I think, and they are told in a better simpler style. And the mystery of man and his faith, if no clearer to me, shows itself like a thread of water, forever flowing round and round the world.

For when Israel sang a little song to the well—"Spring up, O well; sing ye unto it"—and the well did spring up to slake his people's thirst, and when I remember that wandering Arabian tribes still sing thus to their wells, I know more about faith than I ever thought I would, and I am glad of it.

—*Glen Ellen, California, 1989*

61

The Best Meal
I Ever Ate

One of the most universal questions and therefore the one left most unanswered is "What is the best meal you ever ate?" It is almost impossible to answer, honestly anyway, so I can only reply that I don't know! I am as incapable of deciding this as I am of saying that such-and-such is the best novel I ever read, or so-and-so is the best painting I ever saw.

What I can do, however, and with very little hesitation, is to name the *most important* meal I ever ate, the one that for both known and unknown reasons came to have the greatest significance in the pattern of my life. (The gastronomical quality of the food in that meal, of course, had very little to do with its importance.)

I can say almost to the minute when I ate it, and although I cannot recall exactly what it was made up of, I must confess that it was a comparatively mediocre noonday dinner, as such feasts go on the overcrowded stuffy boat trains running between Cherbourg and Paris.

I remember that the train was wide open to the hot September air, so that cinders swirled everywhere in the cluttered second-class compartments. People pushed—harried traveling men, timid students and tourists, overworked waiters winging deftly along the aisles with their great trays of steaming scalloped veal and white beans and suchlike.

But I was eating the most important meal of my life, I believe. In truth I was absorbing it through every pore of my spiritual skin. I was breathing it, cinders and all, into the depths of my heart. As I looked out over the stained cloth, past the half-empty wine bottles and the flushed concentration of the strangers I dined with, I knew that I was, from that moment on, a thinking human being instead of a healthy young animal.

Everything that had happened in my life seemed, there in the rackety train with the tiny green meadows wheeling past me and the little sleek brown cows and the apple trees, part of the preparation for this Right Moment. I felt, and possibly it was so, that I had never been as conscious. Suddenly I recognized my own possibilities as a *person,* and I was almost stunned by the knowledge that never again would I eat or drink as I had done for my first twenty years, sanely and well but unthinkingly.

The first taste of bread, that day: it came in chunks, chopped from loaves four feet long stacked at the end of the dining car like skis, and it was the best bread I had ever eaten and I knew that forever, as of that noontime, I would be intolerant of the packaged puffy stuff called bread at home.

The salad, mixed roughly in a great bowl and shoved from one untidy table to the next along the car: it was made of very ordinary oil and vinegar, cinders and a few small bugs and beetles, and piles of the most wonderful garden lettuces I had ever tasted, long, short, dark green and light, bitter in this leaf and almost sweet in that. Never again, I knew fatalistically, would I more than tolerate the neat, bug-free, and almost completely tasteless salad stuff sold in stores at home.

And the little rolls of cream cheese called *petits-suisses,* and the trays of tiny gnarled apples, and the bitter coffee, and the crude good wine poured from a common bottle on each table: it sounds almost disrespectful to say it, but even the astonishing events of the past several weeks or so seemed but a logical preparation for this moment! Falling in love for the first time since I was nine, being married for the first time at all, crossing the Atlantic for the first time ("student third," but on the *Berengaria!*)—they all led irrevocably to 1:43 P.M., September 25, 1929, when I picked up a last delicious crust crumb from the table, smiled dazedly at my love, peered incredulously at a great cathedral on the horizon, and recognized myself as a newborn sentient human being, ready at last to *live.*

Healthy digestion took command of me, both physically and in my soul, for I had just eaten, not the best meal of my life, but the most important one—and at the Right Moment.

—*Glen Ellen, California, 1989*

62

Reading Aloud

I am fortunate indeed that everyone I know likes to read aloud. They usually do it quite well too, and I do not mention that I could do much better myself, since I have been reading aloud since I was about five years old. I started then with the only thing I knew, which was the Old Testament of the King James Version, as I read it syllable by syllable in my highest voice to my Grandmother Holbrook. I would go from her knees, where I leaned my head while I sat on a very little stool at her feet, directly to the cook's toilet on the back porch where I would crouch at the feet of my little sister Anne. And I would read in the same high voice to her what I had just learned from Grandmother, while Anne did her job on the toilet.

This was a lengthy process, and it was easy for me to repeat several earlier lessons, for our mutual enjoyment, before her job was done. I went from the Old Testament directly to the *Five Little Peppers* series, every volume from the first clear through to the end, or at least until the older Pepper boy got to the kissing age. Anne and I thought this was very silly, and I always stopped at the first kiss. Fortunately the children's series were almost endless, and in some few there was no kissing at all. *The Motor Girls* was one, and as I remember there was no kissing at all in *The Motor Boys* nor in any of the continued stories in *The Youth's Companion, Chatter Box,* and *John Martin's Magazine for Children.* These three weeklies, or perhaps monthlies, were more trustworthy than almost any serials, and they did much for good daily habits and evacuation as well.

The *Little Colonel* series was honest and decent and upstanding and all that Christian rubbish until the last volume, as I remember. It was called *The Little Colonel's Knight Comes Riding,* and we knew from the very beginning that we would never finish it. I read bravely through the first flutterings of her girlish heart, but soon after the third chapter Anne began to make disgusting noises above my head, and I tried to titter, but soon felt like throwing up, and that was the end of the Little Colonel for us both forever. (Much later I heard that the Little Colonel was very racist, but the black-white angle was completely ignored by us there on the porch toilet; it was love love love that induced our puking rejections.)

We read several more series of nonromantic quasi fiction, both in the toilet and up in our own bedroom where we hid in the closet and read by the thin light of one bulb high in the ceiling, which I pulled on and off by a long piece of string, so that I must have been at least eight by then. Of course we could have read in bed, at least until the lights were turned out at the door by my mother at 7:30, but we were used to enjoying fiction in a crouching position, and for two or three more years the dimly lit and probably rather smelly little closet was our chosen spot for the hidden pleasure of my reading aloud and Anne's listening. I wonder now if that explains any of my well-hidden aversion to being read to by anyone. Somehow I cannot quite imagine pretending to be my little sister sitting on a toilet, listening avidly to my dignified friends reading to me in a crouching position at my feet.

I think we hit bottom, if I may say so, in this latrine routine with *The Water-Babies,* written by Charles Kingsley. Here I am haunted still by that atmosphere so that I titter and think of water closets and privies and such things when I mention that small classic, and I can't remember just how or why the hero grows up enough to kiss a girl. We stopped abruptly and went into almost-preadolescent titters, loud noises of assumed pure disgust, because suddenly we realized that we too were interested in his wanting to kiss somebody. Our innocence was gone, and as a matter of fact, I don't think I read aloud again to my sister Anne, and neither one of us ever finished *The Water-Babies,* even silently. So to this day some seventy years later, I don't know how it ends, and Anne surely did not bother to find out before she died when she was fifty-five a long time ago.

By now I guard my ability to read almost ferociously. I know that I can read anything in this world if I must, and I may have to someday. Meanwhile I do not even read the address on envelopes; I hand them to L. or to Marsha to open and read them to me. L. read a short thing to me recently, and we have devised a cruelly efficient way of disposing of other people's manuscripts. It consists of three moves, and I think is fair enough, although perhaps it is silly of me to boast of it, in case . . . so I'll stop. But I can state honestly that it is fair and entails some real work on the part of both the reader and me.

Reading in itself is such a privilege, even secondhand, that it seems impossible to think of it in such terms as mine. It is true, however, that my sister and I learned from the Old Testament more than we could ever know any other way about the beauty of the language. By now I thank God that it was the King James

Version that we learned from. It is almost purification of the body as well as of the soul, and I can claim this now, in a room with black tile floors with fresh air coming in the window, just as clearly as I could in the toilet on the back porch, or upstairs in our equally smelly little closet.

There was something wonderful about the privacy of those first readings, and perhaps this explains why I do not like to go to public readings by a famous actor or writer.

There is also something about being read to that is completely different from reading. But both are honorable pursuits and greatly to be desired. When I was taught to read by my Grandmother Holbrook, I read in a loud, rather piping voice and without any expression at all, but correctly, straight through the Old Testament. I can remember the click of my grandmother's knitting needles above my head and how I became aware gradually that I was outgrowing the little stool on which I sat. I had settled down on her feet before we finished the Old Testament and I graduated to the New Testament—much less interesting and never to be finished, at least not while my head was against those knees.

I have always known that I was fortunate indeed to have a grandmother who insisted that the King James Version was the most wonderful way in the world to learn the value and beauty of the printed word.

A long time after these first lessons, but still years ago by now, I understood completely why Joseph Conrad's prose is as clear and simple as it is: he said that when he was a Polish sailor and stood watch at night, he would read one page from his pocket version of the King James Bible and tear it out and light his pipe with it and think about what he had read for the rest of the night. Of course I was never a Polish sailor, but I do feel that King James's language helped me learn to speak English with some of the same respect and simplicity that Conrad put into his writing.

I no longer use a crouching position when I read aloud, now that I have grown up a little more. But these early experiences may explain why I prefer to read to myself rather than be read to, even by another trusted and loved person. And the idea of going to a theater and being part of an audience and listening to a single voice reading something classical from the stage is almost nauseating to me.

My own voice is no longer piping and young, but it has been used often and well to read to people who loved me: my sister Anne and later my first husband Al Fisher, to whom I read everything ever translated from Russian into English by Constance Garnett. I think I read *War and Peace* twice or three times aloud. This seems impossible now, when I can't stand the thought of reading it even to myself.

—Glen Ellen, California, 1989

63

Frustration—II
(Final Scream)

6,9.23456789 89—which is to say, December 6, 1989 . . . And there is little point in my trying to type further. The performance will not be a good one.

I feel that I must try somehow to make a real change, though I am in a very angry mood, which I . . . This is an almost violent change, from the occasional frustration that has been eating into my bones for too long now.

Perhaps it has peaked. Or perhaps it is very bad, and is already a very present evil, a true danger to my reason.

The anger is a relief. I hope that I can hold on to it long enough to recognize it. I need it as a kind of ally.

The frustration is poisonous. I recognize its real strength and I fear it. Of course, I know the evil of anger too. But it makes a welcome change.

This may not really be legible. That is a chance I must take. Marsha must just try to figure out this typing.

My state of dangerous frustration is justified. And I think that the gradual changeover to real anger will be healthy. I pray so. I am angry because I think it is unfair that at this stage of my life when I should be in real control of the natural talent I have been developing for so many years, which is probably at its peak—yes, it seems unfair that I now find myself too blind to read, or even to type, and I cannot write legibly. And by now my voice has grown too uncertain to be used for dictating.

Here I was interrupted, so I cannot remember how many things I listed to make for such a long messy collection of frustrations. I know that I did name my increasing loss of sight. This is very bad, and I feel that there is little hope of any improvement. Sometimes I feel that I should make some pact, in any form—sell my soul— to give me the feeling for even a few hours, of being able to work once more with my own eyes, on notes that I know are everywhere waiting for my eyes alone—notes I have waiting in boxes at the end of the room.

7. xii. 89

What I typed last night may well be useless. This new attempt will perhaps be equally so—before it is stopped by Nina, who tries to protect me against my selfish wishes. She made me stop typing last night, so tonight I have started before Marsha leaves. I am sure that very soon now Nina will come in and try to convince me that I am too tired to work. But I am determined to go on until 6:00 P.M., when I am supposed to eat supper while I watch *Cheers* on TV. Perhaps I will at least have time to report that I am still very angry. I hope that something good will come of it. The mountain of frustration, which I *surely* mentioned last night, has changed in the past twenty-four hours into plain anger, which I'm surprised to find almost enjoyable. I am not yet sure why; basically I despise anger as such. I think it is a destructive and dangerous and poisonous emotion especially when it appears to be so welcome. I pray that it will soon change into something positive.

Productive is the word.

I must escape from this present *meaningless* state. It is essential, and it is just as well that I cannot understand why I am speaking now with heartily emphasized words: ESSENTIAL. ANGER. DANGER. PRODUCE. CHANGE.

Of course I shall always think it very unfair that I of all people should find myself unable to read or write or even speak—speak even clearly enough to use cassettes during the evening hours when I feel very alert, almost all of every night. But I refuse to stop. This sounds like pathetic bravado at best. I know it may well be all of that. But I do feel that an answer to some of the physical problems will evolve. It must. It has to and it will, and meanwhile I will try to do something more coherent, and soon, about putting some order into my papers. This may mean some sort of showdown, or even some kind of break with L. P. and even with N. K. B. I pray not, in either case, but of course mostly with Norah. No, that will not come about. Impossible.

A break with L. P. is more possible, although I don't want that either. At present, she does me no real good, but that too will change, if I can maintain my present air of subtle independence from her, and hide my real exasperation at her clumsy confusing chaotic attempts to put the many boxes of papers that she seems to have accumulated at the end of this room into some semblance of order. She comes two mornings a week, and if I am actively unpleasant with her, as I have been for the last two times, she will work for about an hour each day. I suspect that she *feels* that she works much longer and harder than that. I am also sure that she expects me to pay her according to her own scale. This I shall, but not until after the new year.

L. P. has no idea of sustained work. I taught her nothing, much as I wanted to, while we played with the book. I was a real failure there—except that I brought off a really dirty bit of play, and without any denying from her, I got her to sign what she herself called a book. When we started work, I soon realized that she had no qualms at all about changing any of my own prose as she transcribed the tapes. Initially, this annoyed me, mainly because my way of saying things was demonstrably different from hers. But when I realized that she did not see the differences at all, and felt that she was actually improving what I had added, I gave up. Before the end of our work, she was perhaps a little sheepish about this, and sent her final transcription off unread by me to her agent.

Ho hum. But I thought no real harm had been done to either of us. I encourage her almost daily to write, to finish some of the four or five things she has started since she first came into my picture. I continue to feel that she has enormous potential and, above all, creative energy. But it must be directed by someone stronger and more disciplined than she, and I am not strong enough. Nor am I willing to develop and in other ways carry her, especially now when I find myself almost powerless to do anything for my own self. Fortunately I don't think L. P. will ever find this out. Nor will she know that I really despair and feel somewhat ashamed of myself that I cannot do more.

It is the next day. I am appalled, in a mild way that is very offensive really, to realize that my anger, which I welcomed as a change from my frantic sense of frustration, may well become a kind of apathetic near peace. By now I don't even feel anger, the painful absorbing kind. I feel apathetic.

One proof of this latest change is that since the morning, only four hours ago, I think, I realize that I am no longer snarling and biting at myself as any frustrated animal does. I have escaped the trap, which is what I was trying to do, of course. I knew immediately that the frustration had changed during the night, because for the first time in longer than I can remember I slept for almost eight hours, and I shifted at least once during the night without any real planning. This planning has been necessary for a long time. Moving is often very painful, and every shift of my body is carefully rehearsed before I move one knee, for instance.

Well, it was 4:00 in the morning when I realized that I had slept without even thinking of shifting my body, and I knew that great changes had either happened or would soon come about.

And when I saw that I was no longer a helpless mess, a subhuman sick thing, but that I was instead an angry woman, that I was in a contained and tightly controlled rage, then I felt released, actually happy. It meant that I was still capable of change. But always there was the lurking sense of resignation. When I wrote Georges Connes that I felt quite philosophical about living at the Ranch with Father and raising the two children after I got the divorce from Donald Friede, Georges wrote back something like "You are not feeling philosophical, you are simply resigned."

And he was right, of course.

But this time I hope that this present almost cozy state, this comfortable condition, complete with several hours of untroubled sleep, does not mean that I have indeed GIVEN UP.

I honestly do not want to be comfortable and free from the mental frettings and much of the actual pain and discomfort that have for some time kept me as I still am—an aged female, almost bedridden, fighting an almost devastating weariness. There are times when I must steel myself to get to my feet, or even move one hand a few inches—

And here I could scream in silent impotent rage at the cruel fact that I cannot read what I have just written, so that I cannot in turn even finish this sentence. That is *very disquieting,* to put it mildly. I hate long involuted sentences. I realize that several times in these last few days of trying to write, I have gotten completely out of hand. It is worth apologizing to Marsha and Pat, if I decide to let them see this final scream or whatever it might be called. If it makes any sense at all, it may serve as a summing up of my long life of writing. I don't know now if anyone will bother to look at my journals, but when I could still see enough to look at two or three of them I was struck by my preoccupation with writing.

It is true that I always knew that I could write better than most people, but it is also true that I never thought myself of any importance at all in this field. That is why I always denied the often mocking remark that anyone who keeps a journal does so only to have it read. I did keep a journal but I never thought it would be read. I can't remember now, but perhaps I have left notes about my ideas about writing that may be of some value, after I have died, to people who are interested in the very slow process, if any, of me, M.F.K.F., mainly because I am not a writer at all. I was born with a somewhat keener way of using words than average people have. I also enjoy using words simply and honestly.

But the present flurry of interest in Fisher is not because I write better than most, but simply because I write now much as I did more than fifty years ago. In other words, I have stayed simple, and I am basically a simple person.

And right now I regret, more than I can say, that I must stop writing this. I am physically very tired. It is time to call for some lunch to be brought to me. I'll eat it on my bed, and wait for

Norah to come for the night. I hope I will have some voice for her; I want very much to work with her. I must get the work on the Dijon book under way. This is an urgent matter, more urgent than any other.

Of course, she could do it alone, perhaps having to carry on if I should die before it is done.

—Glen Ellen, California, 1989

64
Style

Now and then critics have referred to my writing "style," or called me a "stylist." This always astonishes me, and makes me feel embarrassed.

I have thought of people like Henry James as a "stylist," in our Anglo-American language, and perhaps somebody like George Santayana, but the so-called style of such writers bores me, turns me off, makes me feel tricked. Joseph Conrad was more frankly a seeker of a "manner of writing," as the *Oxford English Dictionary* calls style, but it does not matter if he ever occupied himself with it. Vladimir Nabokov, another example of this preoccupation with the rhythmic use of words, shines with the same strange luster of an acquired tongue, always shaping phrases and using them through and back to his native sounds—Poland, Russia.

Perhaps this happens in all of us, if we have the right chemistry. I was never born to be a real stylist, because I am limited compared to anyone I may mention in the writing game. But how can I know how far back I may have gone in the womb, listening to the way words can be used?

Meanwhile it continues to amaze me that anyone might think that what I have written has "style." I have never thought about this until lately, when the word has come up.

It has always seemed to me that the American language, which is what I have spoken from birth, is perhaps more alive and better suited than any other in the world to life as we live it. The French way of speaking pleases me, and I have been greatly helped in the use of my own tongue by my petty but intense study of the grammar and syntax I learned in Dijon long ago. By now my accent and my control are faltering, but I still dream and converse silently in fairly passable French, and what I have learned from it has made my use of American much clearer and firmer.

When I was about twelve, my father wanted all of his children to learn Spanish, and he was right: we should have, because we lived in the recently Americanized country of southern California. The man who came to teach us was Señor Cobos, the Quaker minister out in Jimtown, and a protégé of my father, but it was impossible to learn correct grammar from him when I already knew gutter Mex from my best friends in school. Later I studied proper Spanish in high school and breezed through it without any real interest.

Latin was different. I flunked the first year. My teacher burst into violent tears, and was sent off to a mountain rest home for two weeks, when I did my first essay on Caesar's cold-blooded invasions of Gaul. It was all in Latin, or so I thought. I tried again, the next semester, and passed, without the slightest idea that I was learning a lot that I still know about my own use of words and sentences and phrases. (My teacher felt all right the second time—resigned, anyway.)

I now wish that children could be taught basic grammar, in

Latin preferably, when they start in the first grade. Except for my one searing humiliation with Caesar, I never learned any grammar at all when I was going to school. This was because I came from an articulate family that did not split infinitives and so on, so that it was assumed that I knew a noun from an adjective.

I did not, until I went to France. It was there that I learned humility as well as what could be done with nouns and adjectives and their capacity for the finest honing. For the first time in my life I worked and I understood. It was like electricity. Nothing was easy. There, nobody cared if my father was the editor of the newspaper and my mother had studied in Dresden, and I was pitcher on the girls' baseball team and teacher's pet.

—Glen Ellen, California, 1989

65

Zapping

Dear K.:

Today is a wonderful day, really the first one of spring for me for some reason. I feel like dancing, whirling around any old way. It is astonishing and above all frightening, though, to realize that even before I am thinking this, I know that it is not possible. I couldn't dance if I had to. Actually I feel stiff and full of aches and pains, and why not? I am past eighty years old, and more than full of the usual woes—but I look out the window and it's so damned beautiful that really I am dancing. In other words, I feel quite silly today. What is even worse is that I would be willing to bet you ten cents or ten thousand cold ducats or whatever that you'd dance too. We'd go whirling off together.

Of course I got your letter, and you do indeed sound woeful. In fact, the letter is so damned miserable that it is very funny to me, and I don't mind telling you so right now along with all this dancing, which I am really doing. I am also laughing very hard. And all this goes on invisibly and inaudibly.

Of course, dear K., I've had a cataract operation. It was quite a while ago, and it went off very well indeed. I never felt as if I had two eyes in one socket, though. I am sorry you do, although really wouldn't two eyes be better than one, especially if they both work? As for the laser operation, I doubt that you will feel anything, except of course the boredom of having to go to the doctor's office and sit still for even a second or two.

Does your doctor say "zap"? The last time I saw mine, in Santa Rosa, he told me that of course he could zap me whenever I said to, but that he saw no point at all in zapping anybody who was as unzappable as I. Why bother? he asked. Quite possibly he would have to do it over and over. Why spend the money on it? I can make it with the help of other people, he said in a companionable, warm affectionate way. So I agreed, feeling properly warm and affectionate myself. But it's nice to know that I can be zapped whenever I feel like it *and* that he would do it. And I really do like him for talking to me that way. Maybe you have his twin zapping away at you.

I do agree with you that "something peculiar happens every minute" to make old age so "fascinating." Fascinating should be in quotes too because you said it when I would not. I do think, though, that aging is a very busy time. It can also be horribly expensive, "usually in a doctor's office," as you say. I am appalled to find or think of how much it costs to stay alive as one ages, and especially if kindly doctors are breathing down your neck every time some new symptom pops up. Symptom of what, though? I suppose deterioration implies that there is a constant process of disintegration or spoiling, but I don't see why these many aspects are called symptoms. The trouble with this steady fading away is that every aspect of it is viewed with alarm and is generally found unacceptable, when really it is the natural thing and is symptomatic of nothing at all. Doctors grow rich on it of course, and I often wonder why and how we are kept so ignorant of what is really a natural process. So one eye grows dimmer, and to protect its dimness a film forms over it. Help help help, and doctors are called in and operations are proposed and then performed as if each time it happened it was actually an unheard-of new development instead of something to be expected and prepared for.

So you had a cataract removed. It was the first time, plainly, and you wrote to me, "Ever had a cataract operation?" etc., etc., and I was amused and now I feel rather testy about it. "Of course," I said, and then I got even testier. The word *laser* made me angry too, after my first feeling of amusement and general danciness about it being spring today, with the new leaves looking very twinkly in the bright still pool of sunshine of midmorning. By now the words *cataract* and *laser* make me feel almost *angry*—not even testy but peevish, really peevish. Hell, I say, why does K. think he's the only man in the world who's ever had a bum eye? But is it really bum, or is it merely a signal that he is getting older, and does that mean that K., of all people, is caught in this silly syndrome of believing that he alone is fearing and hating aging? Hell and damnation, I say. This can't happen to K. Surely he more than most people has long since faced the fact that if he grows to be past fifty, chronologically anyway, he must perforce accept certain changes in his body. Yes, a little film will form over one eye, and then over the other perhaps, and he will feel astonished and finally he'll tell somebody about it. And then the doctors will move in, not because they are cruel or mean, but because they too must eat. And the jig's up. They will trot out little lasers that cost millions of dollars to operate, and they will make little tiny slits and marks on his most precious eyes, and he will shake and tremble and many people like me will laugh because they too shook and trembled. And we will all pay and pay, and the doctors finally will get little films over their eyes and they too will shake and tremble a little,

and we all will be pouring out money and grumbling and fuming
—and even dancing in the springtime.

In other words, K., I am as appalled as I always am at how
completely unprepared we are for this inevitable game. What is
most surprising probably is that I don't want anyone to be surprised (and by "anyone" here, I mean anyone that I love). I seem
to think that if I love a person, he or she will perforce be above
such common continuing universal things like fear and astonishment and anger and pain. I want people like you to know from the
minute you are born that if you live long enough, you will of course
find your eyes growing filmy, etc., etc. You will grow older. You
will deteriorate. I do and you do, because we are both human
beings and we are exactly like every other human being, except
perhaps we are more fortunate because we admit it. And admitting
that you are human makes it inevitable that you must admit to
growing older, if indeed you are fortunate enough to grow old,
and even to deteriorate, disintegrate, fall apart, and finally die. I
am very fussy about words, as you know, and here I use the word
fortunate with great care. I honestly do feel that anyone who can
live decently, or even with some difficulty into and past middle
age, and then attain old age is lucky. He is *fortunate*.

This does sound rather Pollyannaish, at least superficially. But
it is a statement that I don't make lightly and, I am quite sure, not
foolishly either. This is because I am old myself, and I know I have
experienced many of the less pleasant aspects of deterioration.
Actual years do not count, though. Often the symptoms that I
am now feeling (and here I could say enduring or surviving or
experiencing) have been felt by people much younger, men or
women perhaps in their sixties or seventies. Of course I have heard
of people almost 100 who swear they are not crickety and have all
their own teeth, etc., etc. They are, to put it clinically or coldly,
plain freaks. (Or liars!) You and I are absolutely normal just like

countless millions of others in our same sorry, lamentable, miserable condition. So we sigh and moan, and call the doctor for some help, and everybody feels much better to have passed along his misery from himself to another human being.

And yet I am telling you how nice it is to feel dancy. Really, it is laughable, this part of the whole aging business, for me anyway. This constant contradiction in terms. I should be commiserating with you, which means with myself. Instead I am teasing you and therefore myself. Poor K.! You just had a cataract operation and on March 31 you are going to have a laser deal, and then you say, "Keep as well as may be" to me. And I can hear your sadness and your feeling of dismay and astonishment that this has happened to you. And all I can feel is real annoyance with you. *Of course* you are sad, miserable, and so on. And you know damned well that I am sad and miserable for you. But, and here I do mean a great big fat *BUT,* surely you must in some way have been prepared for this dreadful condition. You must have known somewhere along the line that you were bound to feel sadder and more miserable than you had in your whole life—you must have *known,* K., that if you lived past seventy you would ache and hurt and things would grow misty and so on and that you would endure them all.

I do think that women have it over men here. They are more accepting. And perhaps they are less hurt by actual pain and sorrow than are men. I do not mean that it is their lot to accept suffering and grief. I do think, though, that they make less fuss about some things, basic things, like hurting and dying and so on than men seem to do.

If this is the case, I am luckier than you. I am not sure, though. I know that I feel awful today, for instance, but that it would not occur to me to say so. I tell myself that I feel this way or that way, but I am very matter-of-fact about it. If I were a man, there would be more surprise and astonishment, as well as futile anger, in any such admission.

In your letter you betray, to me at least, your real fear and petulance and fury too. I am truly sorry about all this. I don't sound as if I am, but it is true, and the main trouble, I think, is that you were unprepared for what is happening to you. All your life you have seen other people spoil, deteriorate, fade away, and yet you have never really accepted the fact that it would happen to you too. I suppose this is the difference between empathy and sympathy. It would be very easy to remain pedantic and distant and keep it all a question of words, period, with or without any wisdom behind them. That, though, would be too easy. I think that faculty and experience should be put together, and that I have both of them and should be using them this minute to write an article for K., the famous compiler of philosophical mouthings and professorial snacks of wisdom and snippets of advice and so on, and here I sit trying to tell K. how miserable I really am because I am old and rapidly spoiling (i.e., rotting away in a puddle of blood and tears—"no sweat," as you might say), but instead my eyes keep going out the window to watch the sun on the dancing leaves. My poor old body is out there too. The grass looks beautiful, a sudden tender green after last night's little rain, and the red lava stones look redder than usual, and the vines have a new fuzz of green on them. In other words I feel like spring.

You say that in what I wrote about Henry Volkening there was no war between telling the truth and expressing affection. Of course there was not. Why should there be? I feel the same way about you. I think right now that you are peevish and grumpy about being old, and I don't want you to be because I love you. But the truth is that you *are* grumpy this minute. Of course you have a right to be, very simply because your age gives you that privilege. I honestly feel, though, that you are grumpy because you are frightened, and I am very impatient about that because by now you should know better. You've had a whole lifetime to face the fact that you too will be old and sad and aching, and now that you are old you are suddenly angry at being so.

Unfortunately, most people who have the rare experience of being your age and mine are exactly the same as you. They deliberately choose to close their eyes until it happens, and then they are peeved as hell that it has happened. It may be because they are just plain stupid, either deliberately or by nature. I would not call you stupid by nature certainly, but I think you are dumb (i.e., stupid) to feel so astonished that you, *too,* actually must go through the indignity of having a cataract removed from *your* eye. It's the first cataract removed ever from any eye, of course (empathy?), and you have the gall to ask me if I've ever had an eye or cataract operation. Hell, man, I've had two! And the only reason I'm not having it done at least once more is that I see no reason at all to risk bothering.

You say, "Old age is fascinating"—and I see your curled lip and the fake jauntiness and the hidden mockery cum bravery etc., etc., and I refuse to reply. You go on that something peculiar happens every minute, and I agree completely with you. It sure as hell does happen every minute, and I look out the window and the leaves are getting dancier than ever and suddenly I feel like shooting my wheelchair across the tiles, and then your letter floats onto the tile floor and I can't even pick it up and I start to titter and so does my helpless friend who is typing for me, and altogether I feel quite silly and giddy and happy, and I am not at all peeved at you, poor man.

—Glen Ellen, California, 1989

66

Query

Perhaps the best thing about finding oneself old is trying not to be as dull and boring as all one's peers. Taking a look around can be depressing, but learning from what one sees is often very helpful in holding off the suppressed yawns that accompany almost any public appearance of an old person among potential grandchildren.

It's painful—devastating—to catch a badly suppressed look of complete resigned ennui on a young face, over a glass or teacup. It may be even worse to notice, suddenly, that one's amusing anecdote about Great-Aunt Mary's clumsy curtsy to Queen Victoria has already been told several times to the same dutiful young descendant.

Why is it that most people over fifty forget that they once hated their parents, and that they too tried to put a cow in the campanile or pin huge butterflies to the hands of the town clock? Why do people kicking sixty or seventy in the ass forget to watch for the glazed grin, that nodding courtesy, that they once showed to their own almost unbearably boring grandparents?

Have the scales grown willy-nilly over our spiritual eyes, the money become cotton in our ears? Or do we old people *want* to feel ignored, neglected, scorned, sad?

—*Glen Ellen, California, mid-1980s*

67

Medication

This is very difficult for me but it is something I am thinking about a great deal. I'll try to say it while I can.

It seems very ironic to me that at this point in my life, which I have spent consciously and unconsciously in talking to myself, I find it very hard to express my thoughts. I have always boasted, or at least I have said what seemed very true to me, that I am not a writer. I have written nothing but what I was speaking or saying to myself, and over the years I have developed a certain skill at this trick. I think always in phrases and sentences and paragraphs and even chapters. They are all a conversation with myself, in the true sense of the word *conversation*.

I am sometimes very dull, but I go right on talking, and at times I'm very witty or even funny, so that I find it hard not to laugh aloud, and still my mind goes on. But now after almost eighty years, during which I've practiced this strange art of private conversation and put it down in stories and essays and suchlike, I am increasingly incapable of conversing in any form. I can no longer write by hand, nor by machine, and mostly I am without a voice. In the morning I am better and can even say a few words that can be heard by a few other people, but they are without real meaning. Lately, I find that I tend to listen more to radio than I usually do to television. With the latter, I close my eyes mostly. They seem to tire easily and I never read a word anymore. Sometimes late at night from about three in the morning they are bright, and I watch whatever is on TV. I find that my powers are diminishing fast, partly because I'm not using them, but mostly because I tire easily. And lately, I must make this effort to speak clearly . . .

I feel I should continue to write this but will put it off until Marsha comes again, and then I will start it fresh and perhaps I will speak more clearly about this strange condition. I think of it a lot and I want to leave some record for Norah and Marsha and Pat. My medication makes my mouth very dry, which complicates the problem.

That's all for now.

—*Glen Ellen, California, 1991*

68

Notes on the Craft, Skill, Science, or Art of Missing

There is a commercial on, about a car called the Charger. A light-voiced man mimics an old-time vaudevillian. His timing is perfect, his mimicry impeccable. I prepare a salad or wash pantyhose or something on that level, the sound going on, and suddenly at a certain combination of rhythm–timing–voice play I am engulfed by a wrenching sense of missing June.

She and I never listened to this sort of music. There was always some going on, but she liked a schmaltzier beat than I did. When I stayed at her house I listened to it and enjoyed it. She liked big orchestras and a certain amount of uncluttered lilt.

When I lived for several years at my growing-up place, to help my widowed father a little and give my two small girls a good dignified man to know, June came as often as she could to stay for a couple of days with us. She and Father hit it off. We all did, and it was always fine.

He was deaf, though, and early in the mornings (he had breakfast and an hour of dictation before he got to his office at nine) we would be in the old kitchen. June would sit on a high stool, and I would be organizing his tray, coffee and all that, and a good meal for the kids and on weekdays their lunches, and we would listen to Fats Waller and Jelly Roll Morton.

I had the run Jelly Roll did with Lomax for the Library of Congress or wherever it was. (I still have it, but seldom listen to it now. I've heard it, thank God.) June would start out with a small cup of fresh coffee and then have a small glass of half water and half bourbon, while I moved around, my back mostly to her, and readied the other morning niceties, and changed records on the "box" I kept in the kitchen, as essential to me as the stove-freezer-refrigerator-toaster-ice crusher—all at the command of a person who hates gadgets.

Behind me I would know that June sat cross-legged on top of the stool, glass nearby, her eyes now and then filled with glad tears at a special word or sound from the old records. She was far from that kitchen, in a world nobody but she could ever fathom, and the trip there had some pain in it but she was willing to share it with her other selves and with me in those mornings when Rex, my father and our mutual friend, could snooze a bit later . . .

Now and then I would prance around a bit, at the stove or icebox, and she would chuckle, because we were both high on the music that pounded out. Long before in our separate lives we had heard it in different places, but those weekend mornings with light coming through the walnut tree by the kitchen windows at the Ranch, a good hour before my father and the little girls woke up, were a shared experience that is valuable enough to miss, in the highest sense of that word.

Tonight when I listen to that high affected voice, reminiscent of the old Orpheum circuit rather than what June and I listened to on early Sundays, the timing is part of other better jazzmen, and abruptly I am wracked by a sense of missing. I miss June. I miss being able to listen to the same music. Why did she dodge the trap before I did?

I feel puzzled about all of this. Why do I not miss my sister Anne at all? Now and then I have poignant regrets about how I failed her sometimes in her life, and how confused she was (to my mind), and how I tried with fairly complete nonsuccess to help her through financial-legal-emotional fiascoes. But I do not miss her. I am glad she has solved her own secret problems, although to do it she had to die a dog's death.

She introduced me to June, whom I miss more strongly.

I also miss one dog and one cat. The dog was registered as P'ing Cho Fung, but in the days when Butch did not necessarily mean a dyke haircut, I named him that defiantly, against his titles, and that he was. He was a highly dignified Pekingese dog. Now and then his spirit approaches my subconscious, and I feel that he is beside me, perhaps touching my hand subtly with his nose like a cool rose petal. And the cat, Blackberry, was ruler of the current roost, and by now is part of a hierarchy of the three great cats I have been privileged to harbor among countless lesser pensioners. He was a formidable friend.

There are other animals I miss almost physically, at times, as much as the two-legged ones like June. But here I must pull myself up, as I would a young pony, to ask what I mean by the word *miss*.

I can try to say that Missing is partly physical. There is a strong pull back to the warm kitchen with Jelly Roll and the friend cross-legged on the high stool, the friend gone now; to the princely little dog, also gone now. It is a wrench that is almost orgiastic, if one permits it to be, and it is always ready to pounce at unexpected moments, as when a canny-silly commercial comes over the radio.

Missing is also a more inward condition. It is something that must be accepted as part of any thinking existence, and made use

of. It is a force. The special flavor of true Missing should be chan-
neled. It is very strong. And I like to hope that the stronger the
person is who misses something or someone, the stronger the force
will be.

It continues to puzzle me that I miss June more than I miss
my sister. It comes down to the fact, perhaps, that I am glad one
died and sorry the other did. But I am not glad that Butch died. I
am not glad that Blackberry did, either.

What is left is a vulnerable spot in my acceptance of vulnera-
bility. These and many other people, like lovers and husbands and
even friends, have slid off the scales. They seem, now and then for
unknown reasons, to stand there stark and grabbing, in front of
us. They want us. We say, No, not now. But the statement is a
painful one.

That is why it hurts me when that silly commercial comes on,
about some car named Charger that is selling for less than cost.
The rhythm and timing—exquisite. The inexplicable anguish,
fleeting but poignant to the point of true pain, of missing June, the
little dog, perhaps a dozen other true beings, brought out by that
shoddy takeoff: why should I submit to it? And why should it
make me wonder why I loved them and not some other people?

—Glen Ellen, California, mid-1980s

About the Author

M.F.K. Fisher was born in Albion, Michigan, in 1908 and spent most of her childhood in Whittier, California. During ensuing years she lived in Dijon, Vevey, Aix-en-Provence, and southern California before moving to the northern California wine country in 1954. She authored more than sixteen volumes of essays and reminiscences, including *The Art of Eating, Two Towns in Provence, Among Friends*, and a widely admired translation of Brillat-Savarin's *The Physiology of Taste*. For the last twenty years of her life she lived in a house built for her in Glen Ellen, California. She died at Last House on June 22, 1992.